Dariusz Szostek | Mariusz Załucki (eds.)

Internet and New Technologies Law

Perspectives and Challenges

EUROPEAN LAW INSTITUTE

POLISH HUB

Nomos

The book was financed by AFM Kraków University (Poland) with funds from a scientific project commissioned by the Chancellery of the Prime Minister of the Republic of Poland.

Scientific review: Prof. Laura Miraut Martin, ULPGC (Spain).

The Deutsche Nationalbibliothek lists this publication in the Deutsche Nationalbibliografie; detailed bibliographic data are available on the Internet at http://dnb.d-nb.de

ISBN 978-3-8487-8307-6 (Print)
978-3-7489-2697-9 (ePDF)

British Library Cataloguing-in-Publication Data
A catalogue record for this book is available from the British Library.

ISBN 978-3-8487-8307-6 (Print)
978-3-7489-2697-9 (ePDF)

Library of Congress Cataloging-in-Publication Data
Szostek, Dariusz; Załucki, Mariusz
Internet and New Technologies Law
Perspectives and Challenges
Dariusz Szostek | Mariusz Załucki (eds.)
479 pp.
Includes bibliographic references.

ISBN 978-3-8487-8307-6 (Print)
978-3-7489-2697-9 (ePDF)

1st Edition 2021

Published by
Nomos Verlagsgesellschaft mbH & Co. KG
Waldseestraße 3–5 | 76530 Baden-Baden
www.nomos.de

Production of the printed version:
Nomos Verlagsgesellschaft mbH & Co. KG
Waldseestraße 3–5 | 76530 Baden-Baden

ISBN 978-3-8487-8307-6 (Print)
ISBN 978-3-7489-2697-9 (ePDF)
DOI https://doi.org/10.5771/9783748926979

Onlineversion
Nomos eLibrary

Introduction

Since the first UN IGF Summit held in Athens in 2006, the IGF Summit has functioned as a discussion platform allowing different individuals and groups of stakeholders to participate in the exchange of information, sharing of good policies or practices around the surrounding technology, Internet and related services. Since then the Summit has become a place of inspiration for people (politicians, scientists, entrepreneurs, social organisations) who make decisions (including legal and political ones) on the use of new technologies. It is also a place of exchange of knowledge and information, including the directions of changes of the Internet and the increasingly serious threats related to it, not only in terms of cyber security, but importantly also in terms of fiscal, social, cultural and digital exclusion aspects.

The digital world operates on different levels. From a very advanced level, using Artificial Intelligence (AI), through states, organisations at a medium and low level of digitisation and digital competence, to the level of the completely excluded. The disparities between actors are very large and the consequences of this inequality for global governance and security very serious. The IGF is a place where actors (researchers, non-profit organisations, politicians, ordinary citizens, the wider Internet community, entrepreneurs and, from 2020, young people) from all over the world work together. Different perspectives (technological on the one hand, but also social or cultural on the other) contribute to a more sustainable development of the Internet, or at least an attempt at regulations favouring a democratised Internet governance. It is important to involve representatives of various countries, from those highly digitised, with full access to Internet resources, to those with lower levels of opportunities or practice, i.e. to countries where "ordinary" citizens cannot use the benefits of the Internet (e.g. due to lack of infrastructure and access to the network, or due to content censorship). Discussions, panels, meetings, etc. allow for the involvement of all parties, be they developed countries, developing countries, social organisations or churches, to civil society and the network society.

The IGF does not adopt resolutions or create any binding treaties. Its importance lies in its unique ability to facilitate discussions between governments, intergovernmental organisations, private companies, the technical community and civil society organisations that are concerned or interested in public policy issues related to Internet governance. The IGF serves as a laboratory, a neutral space where all participants can present an issue for informed discussion among stakeholders. However, the IGF is not just about technologies and how they are framed in the context of the sciences. The IGF is also, and perhaps primarily, about the social sciences. In fact, from the very beginning it has been a platform for the exchange of views in this area. It is also of particular importance for legal studies, which, as a science following the summit, looks at, analyses and develops some of the concepts that appear there. There is no doubt that technological space cannot exist without legal space, or in isolation from it. Various social behaviours, including those "rooted" in the world of new technologies, form the basis for the functioning of the legal system, which in turn must determine, among others, the admissibility of certain actions, or the responsibility associated with them. This is the reason why law and technology, the Internet and law, cannot exist without each other.

There is no doubt that the study of law in many important branches has made a considerable contribution. The core disciplines of legal studies, which are primarily concerned with the development of the law in force, touch on important issues in a number of serious treatises and discussions, which after a while become the order of the day for scientific discourse. Although the main legal disciplines generally function well in analysing positive law, in the context of the technological changes taking place in society, there are often areas where scientific analysis has not yet reached, or has reached only to a small extent. However, this type of analysis is essential and sometimes of paramount importance. The explanation of the technological phenomena taking place and the consideration of the legal framework of the application of the benefits of new technologies is nowadays an indispensable element of legal science. Civil law, administrative law or criminal law, as well as individual procedures, need to be looked at from the point of view of the needs of society, which are often deeply rooted in various technological solutions. In this respect, however, scientific analysis is not yet far advanced, nor can it stop developing, just as new technologies are constantly developing and emerging. There is therefore a further need to develop the science of law, to pave the way for the technological solutions that emerge in everyday life, which can and do have an increasing impact on everyday life. It is therefore necessary to constantly explore the area of new technologies, to make generalisations about the social operation of law in this area, to show as far as possible that the need for research can and does also develop technology.

Thinking about the above, there is no doubt that the IGF Summit brings new challenges, also for legal studies. In December 2021 Poland is hosting the UN IGF Summit 2021. The theme of the summit - Internet United - is the Internet connecting all its users into one community responsible for its shape and functioning. During the COVID-19 crisis, for example, the Internet proved to be helpful in organising human life to a degree that had not yet been anticipated at the previous IGF Summits. This confirmed its immense value for all. Society operates in a digital world and needs both freedom and openness and security within it. These, in turn, are new problems for legal studies and scientific analysis is needed in this area. Hence this book, in which scholars from around the world address the challenges involved.

It is the result of a scientific research project "*The Future of the Law of Internet and New Technologies*", funded by the Polish government, which we have the honour to lead. The aim of the project is primarily joint international research indicating the latest trends of necessary legal changes in the field of Internet governance (primarily from the perspective of legal sciences) and discussion in various circles on the desired shape of the legal framework for the Internet and new technologies. We realise that it is impossible to address all the important issues of the Internet and new technologies in a single publication. Moreover, we realise that we can only address selected issues. This is precisely the case with this publication, where the authors primarily address four areas that link the Internet and new technologies. These areas are: society, justice system, sustainable development and privacy. In our opinion, there is no doubt that there are many more research issues surrounding the law and the Internet and emerging technology. However, these four outlined areas are only the basic issues that the authors have addressed in their research. This was done in an international dimension, where authors from many countries and five continents were primarily tasked with raising questions and starting a discussion that could perhaps form the basis for broader discussions during the UN IGF Summit.

We would like to add that the research carried out falls within the core objectives of the IGF:- to facilitate understanding and agreement on international public internet policies and their impacts; - better understanding and agreement on Internet governance and new technologies; - to strengthen cooperation and collaboration between key organisations and stakeholders working on various issues related to Internet governance and technologies; - enhanced capacity to support the sustainability, robustness, security, stability and growth of the Internet; - strengthened capacity of all countries, especially developing countries and their stakeholders, to participate effectively in Internet governance arrangements; - enhanced multilingualism and multiculturalism on the Internet; - mapping of multilateral and plurilateral public policy efforts related to the Internet.

The need for discussion in the areas discussed is, in our view, welcome. Drawing attention to issues that we believe are of significant practical importance, where solutions have not yet been developed to the satisfaction of all, where a number of controversies arise, is excellent material for scientific analysis, especially in the direction outlined by the social sciences. As we know, the essence of social sciences is the study of the structure and function of society, its culture, laws and regularities of development. The scope of research of social sciences includes, among others, the observation and analysis of the influence of such factors as the system of legal norms, political power or technology on the way society functions. From this perspective, and especially in view of the needs noted by legal studies, a broader approach to the areas indicated may have important implications for the further functioning of the Internet society and issues related to its governance. We therefore invite you to join the discussion.

UN activities as well as the Internet are global in nature. That is why researchers from many continents, many countries and academic centres were invited to the "*The Future of the Law of Internet and New Technologies*" project. Representing various legal systems together we want to point to the problems of legal and social space in terms of the future of the Internet. Interestingly, despite the differences in systems and views, scientists from all over the world pointed quite consistently to the problems of the Internet, providing interesting material for further not only scientific discussions and contributions to the work of the UN.

We would also like to point out that our work, although carried out as part of a single academic project, contains the views of many authors who do not always agree with each other. However, we consider the fact that there is pluralism in our team as well an additional value of the publication, although we must state that each author is responsible for his/her own views.

Kraków, Katowice, 06.12.2021

Prof. Dariusz Szostek
Prof. Mariusz Załucki

Table of Contents

Section Two. Internet, New Technologies and the Justice System

Section Three. Internet, New Technologies and Sustainable Development

The Future is Digital

Krzysztof Szubert[1]
WARSZAWA, Poland

1. The IGF and its role in the global digital diplomacy

The Internet Governance Forum (IGF) is a global venue for dialogue on a wide variety of issues related to digital space and its actors. Organised annually under the auspices of the United Nations Secretary-General, it brings together various stakeholders on an equal footing to exchange information and share good practices in order to foster the sustainability, security, and development of the Internet. Its participants are governments, intergovernmental organisations, as well as broadly defined communities: businesses, industry organisations, academia, and civil society.

Over the years, the IGF has identified a wide range of issues to be addressed by the international community. Through its annual meetings and intersessional activities, the IGF promotes the debate on regulatory frameworks, potential risks, and global trends, identifying practices or schemes that need to be adopted, modified or abandoned.

The Internet Governance Forum does not adopt resolutions or create any binding treaties. Its strength lies in facilitating discourse and forging common ground among all the agents involved or interested in Internet governance issues. As French President Emmanuel Macron once put it, 'The wide range of issues covered by digital transformation requires a coordinated and coherent representation between state actors and non-state stakeholders at global and regional levels, as well as strong coordination on the national level1.'[2] Despite not having a decision-making power, the IGF informs and inspires those who do. In fact, its mission is to share policy expertise, discuss emerging technology issues, reach agreement as far as possible, and escalate these ideas to executive bodies.

The IGF traces its origins back to the 1st World Summit of the Information Society, which was held in Geneva in 2003. Internet governance was

---

1 Co-written by: Grażyna Śleszyńska.

2 Excerpt from the speech by Emmanuel Macron at the Internet Governance Forum 2018 in Paris

one of the pivotal issues raised. It was found instrumental in achieving the development goals of the Geneva Plan of Action, but defining Internet governance and the responsibilities of the stakeholders proved to be complicated. The UN Secretary-General set up a Working Group on Internet Governance (WGIG) to look into these issues. The resulting report fed into the 2nd World Summit on the Information Society (WSIS-II), which took place in Tunis in 2005.

The signatories of the Tunis Agenda hammered out the following definition: Internet governance is the development and application by governments, the private sector and civil society, in their respective roles, of shared principles, norms, rules, decision-making procedures, and programmes that shape the evolution and use of the Internet. To keep up the momentum, they called on the UN Secretary-General to establish a multilateral, multi-stakeholder, democratic and transparent platform for discussions on Internet governance issues. That is how the IGF was born.

I am proud that the next edition will be held in my native Poland (Katowice, 6-10 December 2021). My country was one of the first to fully adapt the national legal framework to the provisions of the EU General data protection regulation (GDPR) of 2016. Poland was also a fervent supporter of the EU Regulation on the free flow of non-personal data of 2019, in a quest to remove controls on cross-border data transfers and government restrictions requiring that a country's data be stored and processed on national territory. It is from Poland that came the idea of organising, in cooperation with Estonia, the Tallinn Digital Summit in 2017 that gathered heads of state and government from across Europe. The same year, Poland took part, for the first time in history, in the G20 Digital Ministers Meeting, hosted by Germany in Düsseldorf. Such practices make it impossible to fully tap the potential of the data-driven economy, thus frustrating economic growth. Entrusting Poland with a mission to organise this year's IGF plenary meeting underpins our commitment to the cause of open and universally accessible Internet.

2. *The IGF 2021 priorities as stated by the MAG*

The IGF is much more than a once-a-year event: it represents a whole-year-long process including annual meetings and intersessional activities. The IGF process is coordinated by the Multistakeholder Advisory Group (MAG), which sets forth the guidelines for main sessions and where I had spent two terms of office as a member before taking the honour to cochair it this year. The community contributes by proposing and organising workshops.

A call for issues, launched in the run-up for the IGF 2021 summit in Katowice, Poland, resulted in over 230 responses. These were examined and prioritised by the MAG, which eventually fell into two issue baskets, each containing separate issue areas:

Basket 1: Main Focus Areas (outcome-focused):

- Economic and social inclusion and human rights
- Universal access and meaningful connectivity

Basket 2: Emerging and Cross-cutting Issues (discussion-driven):

- Emerging regulation: market structure, content, data and consumer/users rights regulation
- Environmental sustainability and climate change
- Inclusive IG ecosystems and digital cooperation
- Trust, security, stability

To maximise the impact, we chose to stick with fewer policy issues and deal with them in depth, making sure that all stakeholders have their say, and that the conclusions are communicated effectively and strategically. By taking on the issue-driven approach, we aim to deliver more focused and structured outcomes, while keeping the IGF open for new and emerging issues. A rough allocation of time has been proposed for each basket: 60 per cent for the main focus areas and 40 per cent for the emerging and cross-cutting issues. Of course, this ratio is flexible, depending on the quality and nature of the topics discussed.

2.1. Main Focus Areas – overview

2.1.1. Economic and social inclusion and human rights

Despite all the civilisational progress, social and economic inequalities are actually on the increase around the globe. While the most urgent are those existential and life-threatening – such as hunger, extreme poverty, or compromised access to healthcare and education – we must not neglect disruptive technologies, as these carry an enormous potential for positive change. Indeed, they can go a long way towards promoting resilience, sustainability, and inclusion, and thus towards achieving the full-fledged, indiscriminate participation in all walks of life. But this sword cuts both ways: while digital inclusion is a great amplifier of social and economic improvement, digital exclusion is a surefire way to deepening and entrenching all sorts of inequalities.

The paramount question is therefore how to leverage digital technologies to ensure that their benefits reach everyone. It goes without saying that promoting digital literacy and equity across age, gender, and geographies remains a priority. The gender gap in global Internet connectivity is in fact a stark example of digital divide – in two out of every three countries, more men use the Internet than women.[3] Similar challenges affect migrants, refugees, internally displaced persons, older persons, young people, children, persons with disabilities, rural populations, and indigenous peoples. These problems can only be addressed through a multistakeholder coordinated effort.

Digital technologies are crucial in providing online education or health services. But no less vital is their role in shaping policies in the fields of protection of privacy, freedom of expression, and freedom of assembly in the digital space. Digital technologies provide new means of exercising human rights, but do not shield them from violation. As Melvin Kranzberg, an American historian of science and technology, pointed out, 'Although technology might be a prime element in many public issues, nontechnical factors take precedence in technology-policy decisions.'[4] Put simply, it is a person and his/her human rights that should always be in the centre of digital decision-making.

The idea of freedom has been around for a long time in the context of debates about the Internet. Freedom, however, is not tantamount to chaos. We need rules that will organise the online bahaviours of companies, governments, and individual users. The existing regulatory frameworks have largely fallen behind the speeding digital train and need to be recalibrated to reaffirm its authority. Data protection, digital identity, surveillance techniques, online harassment, and content governance are of particular concern. Social networking sites, sharing economy companies, e-commerce outlets, fintechs need to be more accountable for their practices, and users need to become more aware of how to enforce their rights. But perhaps the most challenging issue is counteracting digital authoritarianism by

3 Report of the Secretary-General Roadmap for Digital Cooperation, June 2020
4 Melvin Kranzberg, Technology and History: Kranzberg's Laws, Technology and Culture, (1986) 27 3 Technology and Culture 544–560.

governments who claim to be exercising their legitimate powers. Sadly, it is often doomed to failure for lack of coercive measures within the UN system, let alone the IGF community.

2.1.2. Universal access and meaningful connectivity

The COVID-19 pandemic demonstrated that ensuring sustainable access to the Internet is a priority, indispensable for full participation in society, democracy, and economy. In keeping with the Sustainable Development Goals (SDGs), by 2030 every person should have a safe and affordable Internet connectivity, including the use of digitally enabled services. As of today, the brutal truth is that digital technologies are not there for everyone. Many countries and citizens are deprived of capacities and skills, which makes them illiterate in the digital era we live in. In fact, 40 per cent of the world's population currently does not have access to the Internet (as of January 2021, the global Internet penetration rate is 59.5 per cent, with 4.66 billion active Internet users worldwide[5]). In 2019, close to 87 per cent of individuals in developed countries used the Internet, compared with only 19 per cent in the least developed countries.[6]

The prerequisite for achieving social welfare headway is universal connectivity. Yet, the evidence is clear that access to the Internet is not sufficient on its own. A more human-centric and holistic approach to digital equity is needed. This means going beyond technical parameters and articulating a definition of digital inclusion that combines:

- affordable, robust broadband service,
- Internet-enabled devices,
- digital skills,
- applications and content designed to enable and encourage self-sufficiency, participation and collaboration (e.g. education, healthcare, economic development, health, agriculture),
- digital equity, meaning that all these services should be available for all, regardless of race, language, disability, or geographic location .

5 *Digital 2021. Global Overview Report.*

6 International Telecommunications Union (ITU), *Measuring Digital Development. Facts and figures* (ITU 2019).

Only once all these aspects are present, connectivity will bring us closer to achieving the UN Sustainable Development Goals and improving people's lives.

2.2. Emerging and Cross-cutting Issues – overview

2.2.1. Emerging regulations: market structure, content, data and consumer/users rights regulation

The concept of Internet governance covers two major layers: technology (carriers) and substance (content). Regulatory efforts should range from national and international initiatives by governments and NGOs, through private sector self-regulation, to co-regulation, with a special focus on:

- Addressing anticompetitive practices and monopolistic behaviours by large technology companies and ensuring the level-playing field on the market to encourage innovation and market-entry from small players.
- Enacting new regulations clarifying the responsibility of Internet intermediaries for the content they host, as well as their role in tackling issues such as online misinformation/disinformation and the spread of violent content and hate speech. This begs the question of whether, and to what extent, Internet platforms should be allowed to censor freedom of expression online through their content moderation policies.
- Leveraging data governance frameworks to enable the responsible and trustworthy use of personal and non-personal data. The issue of cross-border data flows remains high on the international agenda, as countries have different approaches towards the extent and the conditions under which they enable data transfers. Is developing unified data governance frameworks possible at the international level?
- Protecting consumer rights in the digital space (sales, advertising, etc.). Is more regulation needed to strengthen the enforcement of consumer rights and ensure that Internet companies do not engage in unfair and deceptive practices? What can be done (and by whom) to build consumer awareness (for instance, around practices such as cookies, tracking, and targeted advertising)? Is there a role for AI in achieving better consumer protection?

2.2.2. Environmental sustainability and climate change

Mitigating the climate change and ensuring the environmental sustainability are among the most pressing global issues. Here, again, the Internet and other digital technologies can play a positive or a negative role: cause harm to the environment (for instance, through e-waste and energy consumption), or help advance environmental sustainability.

Targeted policies and actions are therefore needed to green the Internet and foster the use of technologies such as AI and Big Data to address environmental challenges. Examples include improving the circular economy around digital devices, extending the lifetime of software and devices, and promoting technologies that help reduce carbon emissions and energy consumption.

Equally important is developing and putting in practice adequate governance frameworks that enable the sharing and re-use of environmental data. At the same time, more attention should be devoted to promoting environmental education and building awareness on environmental sustainability within the digital space.

2.2.3. Inclusive IG ecosystems and digital cooperation

The Internet serves as the primary tool both for mass and point-to-point communication, and as such provides the global infrastructure of the information society. It appeals to people because of its distributed and interoperable design. Innovations based on information and communication technologies (ICTs), such as social media and the mobile Internet, are empowering individuals and institutions by putting megabytes of knowledge right at their fingertips, wherever they live, work or operate.

There is also a wide-ranging consensus on the need to promote open information resources, such as for education and learning, the respect for personal privacy, the protection from surveillance, and the freedom of expression in an increasingly digital world. Over time, however, the percentage of the Internet that is open source and public has significantly decreased. Access to digital solutions is often limited by copyright regimes and proprietary systems. Moreover, digital public goods are unevenly distributed in terms of language, content and infrastructure required to access them.

It is symptomatic that we talk about Internet 'governance' rather than 'government'. The reason seems obvious but let us state it: what constitutes the cyberspace and what happens there cannot be handled by traditional national institutions. 'Governance' implies a polycentric order, reflecting the fact that the Internet is not a product of any institutional hierarchy, but requires transnational cooperation to represent the global population's common interest.

The Internet spread around the globe without direction from the states or intergovernmental bodies. It was a spontaneous and impetuous process, generating no new rules of international law. By virtue of relying on a combination of public and private components, the Internet has no single owner. Also, as it crosses boarders, no single government has the sole authority over it. However, governments, businesses and individuals can materially impact, locally and internationally, the availability and functionality of the network from a user's perspective. Internet governance is therefore a multistakeholder process. Its multifunctional and decentralised nature means that an array of actors hold a stake in it and thus should be involved in its development and enforcement. One of the challenges ahead is reconciliating the inputs by governments, companies, civil society and academia to effectively and fairly govern the Internet.

Digital sovereignty has become a hot topic in a wide variety of contexts. In fact, some countries have pushed to expand the influence of national governments at the expense of businesses and the civil society. They claim digital sovereignty to justify nationalistic policy frameworks regarding digital industrial policies, forced data localisation, and security measures, while reducing international interdependencies and reasserting their autonomy and control. Some actors back up this attitude as a necessary corrective to Internet-based globalisation, whereas others fear that values such as Internet freedom and openness, cross-border e-commerce may be jeopardised. To bring Internet governance under governmental and intergovernmental control, they argue, will produce dire consequences for innovation, commerce, development, democracy, and human rights, especially regarding censorship.

It is common knowledge that authoritarian governments censor political and social content much as they do in the traditional media. Mechanisms of online censorship include technical blocking of websites, search result removal, legal take-downs, and induced self-censorship. Against this background, the IGF defends democratic values that draw upon liberty. Never has an organised and inclusive global debate been more needed than it is now, and there is no better venue than the IGF to foster a meaningful dialogue.

2.2.4. Trust, security, stability

We all want a secure and stable Internet that will inspire trust and confidence among users. The borderless nature of the Internet, the new economy, the IoT-driven cyber-physical asymmetric interdependency, the impact of the Internet on democracy and elections, finally its role in global crises – all this makes for a complex policy, legal and operational context for cybersecurity.

Almost all sectors use ICTs and rely on the Internet for everything from the simplest to the most strategic tasks. Global supply chains are increasingly interconnected, with their ICT systems and devices exposed to various cyber risks, such as online gender-based violence, cyberbullying, and misinformation. Neither the public nor the private sector can combat these borderless threats on their own. The technical community and civil society are key partners. As stakeholders seek to find ways to address cybersecurity concerns, collaboration is required in order to build awareness of vulnerabilities and incidents and to increase resilience against these complex, borderless cyber threats. To be sure, we will work towards a broad and overarching statement, expressing a common understanding of digital trust and security in the cyber sphere.

3. Challenges for the global digital dialogue

While the very notions of 'digital foreign policy' and 'Internet governance' have been around for a while, a lot remains to be done. To begin with, digital diplomacy falls behind the speeding technological revolution. It is challenging because it requires a greater coordination effort, which is difficult to obtain in a multistakeholder environment, but otherwise, it is a natural course of things and not a reason to worry. Instead, what really bothers me is that digital issues do not seem to be receiving as much attention as they deserve at a country level.

The impact of technologies is indisputable. Every country should have a clearly defined digital roadmap and an established advocacy scheme to pursue its digital priorities and influence global tendencies. Yet, the issue features surprisingly low on countries' diplomatic agendas, and that despite a growing consciousness of its importance. Digital issues are dealt with superficially or downright missing from the strategic diplomatic documents. Likewise, digital sherpas are conspicuous by their absence in diplomatic service. It is my firm belief that it must change. Digital diplomacy should be brought into focus, become mainstreamed and relevant at the highest political level. It is indispensable if we want to have a meaningful and consequential dialogue that translates into concrete actions rather than bog down in rhetoric.

3.1. What and how to regulate in the world of technology?

First of all, we need to discuss regulatory issues relating to financing, partnerships and digital market business models. This involves:

- Developing the capacity of regulators and service providers to build universal Internet access;
- Ensuring affordable Internet access while incentivising the existence and extent of local language content and locally relevant content;
- Creating a friendly environment for smaller-scale providers, including broadband cooperatives, municipal networks and local businesses by putting in place practices such as facilitating licence exemption and tax incentive schemes;
- Leveraging universal service and access funds (USAFs), which are financed primarily through contributions made by mobile network operators, to expand communications services to underserved areas and populations;
- Setting universal affordability targets with respect to digital connectivity: it would be far easier to develop a financing platform to close the global connectivity gap, including vulnerable and marginalised groups, had affordability been defined as, for example, 1 GB of mobile broadband data costing a certain tiny percentage (1,2,3…) of an average monthly household income.

Another major challenge is settling the rules governing the circulation of Big Data, a precondition for unlocking its vast economic potential. Why is it so important?

The Internet-driven solutions are generating vast amounts of non-personal data, raising questions of who owns it and how it should be used. Governments need to strike the right balance, i.e. to address privacy concerns without stifling beneficial innovations. This is all the more important that, in a digital age we live in, data has earned the status of commodity, underlying the creation of value and the satisfaction of human needs. It is derived from human activity, from observation of the natural environment phenomena (e.g. geodetic, meteorological data) and industrial processes (e.g. production line sensors). Data can be seen as a factor of production, along with capital and labour, an essential substrate of social and economic undertakings. Scientific research suggests that data-based activities have a paramount effect on growth nurturing compared to other factors. Investing in the data-driven economy is perhaps the most promising growth scenario for the post-pandemic era.

Raw non-personal data should circulate in the economy, leading to welfare proliferation. This requires the resolve and effort pooling from governments to facilitate the forming of robust and liquid data markets. Currently, the landscape is dominated by isolated data collection systems dominate that create inaccessible silos. For data potential to be fully tapped, standards must be set for its circulation. Otherwise, businesses will remain reluctant to share, exchange or sell it.

Likewise, the time has come for the provisions on the free flow of raw non-personal data to be included in international free trade agreements. For this to happen, we need to work together within the UN, OECD, and WTO to overcome regulatory hurdles and reach a viable and operational consensus.

Inevitably, where there is data, there are data breaches, since with more people being brought online, vulnerabilities arise. The cost of data breaches is expected to grow annually at 11 per cent, from $3 trillion in 2019 to over $5 trillion in 2024.[7] As the nature of cyber-attacks evolve, cybersecurity needs to adapt accordingly. System developers must invent safer devices. Operators must leverage AI to develop new security techniques to protect networks and platforms against scammers and attackers. Services must be designed to run with the minimum of user information. And governments must work in concert towards commonly accepted measures – ones that will protect the cyber sphere without disrupting it.

Should the Internet become overregulated, it will lose its innate appeal. It is obvious that governments should protect their citizens, but this must be done in a collaborative way, with all stakeholders involved. If controls are imposed too tightly or/and in an erratic manner, they will do more harm than good. The Internet is a dynamic organism that functions like a system of interconnected vessels. No single actor can make a positive difference to its workings alone. Unilateral moves, attempting to draw sovereign lines and rules are ineffective, counterproductive and ultimately doomed to failure.

---

7 *The Future of Cybercrime & Security: Threat Analysis, Impact Assessment & Mitigation Strategies 2019-2024* (Jupiter Research, August 2019).

3.2. What and how to finance in the world of technologies?

Securing sustainable Internet connectivity requires substantial spending. The task is twice as challenging in developing countries. For instance, the ITU/UNESCO Broadband Commission for Sustainable Development estimates that achieving universal, affordable and quality Internet access by 2030 across Africa may cost as much as $100 billion.[8]

The characteristic feature of the ICT infrastructure is that most of its financing has traditionally come from private-sector companies who make substantial outlays seeking commercial return. Governments, sovereign funds and multilateral players, such as development banks, have played a relatively minor role, especially compared to the scale of their investment in other infrastructure sectors. The reason for this is a tendency to view Internet provision as a strictly private-sector activity rather than a public right. In the United States, for example, the public sector's share of ICT infrastructure investments is nearly zero, while the share of public investment in transportation and water and sewage infrastructure is about 90 per cent.[9] Moreover, procurement requirements of public institutions, which can add months or even years to project timelines, are at odds with the rapid speed of progress among ICT technologies and, therefore, undermine the suitability of public investment processes for ICT infrastructure projects.

Interestingly, equity markets, which eagerly get involved in various infrastructure projects, are absent from the ICT sector, dominated by industry players (network operators, ISPs, tower builders, satellite companies). Many private-sector investors exclude ICT infrastructure assets from their portfolios altogether, considering them too complex and largely the domain of network operators and ISPs. And those who do make infrastructure investments avoid going beyond core population centres. Indeed, the cost of extending infrastructure to remote or sparsely populated areas is unprofitable to mobile network operators unless they receive significant support from public-sector or international funds.

Meeting the global need for advanced network infrastructure requires the development of financing models that account for returns on investment beyond simple business cases. In most developed and emerging markets, the public sector must improve the attractiveness of ICT investments.

---

8 *Connecting Africa Through Broadband: A Strategy for Doubling Connectivity by 2021 and Reaching Universal Access by 2030* (Broadband Commission for Sustainable Development, ITU and UNESCO, Geneva, 2019).

9 *Bridging Global Infrastructure Gaps* (McKinsey Global Institute, June 2016).

This can be done through blended financing and risk-sharing arrangements: government subsidies and operator fees would be pooled over time to pay for infrastructure expansion in areas that are sparsely populated, topologically challenging or difficult to serve. These arrangements help investors overcome many barriers, such as low returns relative to risk or inefficient local markets. Universal service and access funds (USAFs), set up by governments to address gaps in coverage that cannot be served by the private sector alone, have a prominent role to play here.

Infrastructure projects can be bundled into dedicated investment vehicles or funds that reduce exposure to individual risks of geography or technology and enable smaller projects to attract capital from larger investors. However, their use in ICT is limited. For example, only 3 per cent of all deals undertaken by infrastructure funds in Asia from 2010 through 2015 involved telecommunications, compared with 44 per cent involving energy, 22 per cent utilities and 16 per cent transportation.[10] Another option allowing for risk mitigation is bond issue by international finance institutions who then invest in eligible projects through financial intermediaries.

3.3. Technologies and sustainable development

On one hand, technological progress inevitably with pollution (from infrastructure exploitation and manufacturing/disposal of electronic devices) and power consumption. ICT operations are estimated to represent up to 20 per cent of global electricity demand, with one third stemming from data centres alone.[11] On the other hand, the Internet-driven Fourth Industrial Revolution has largely succeeded in decoupling economic growth and environmental damage. ICTs have steered the economy away from energy and material-intensive activities, ushering in three major phenomena: dematerialisation (less resource input), virtualisation (substitution of tangible goods), and demobilisation (substitution of travel).

Not only less harm is caused to the planet, but actually a lot of good is done to protect it (electronic monitoring, remote sensing etc.). The environmental SDGs cannot be met without frontier technologies and inte-

---

10 Georg Inderst, *Infrastructure Investment, Private Finance, and Institutional Investors: Asia from a Global Perspective* (2016) 555 Asian Development Bank Institute, Working Paper Series.

11 Nicola Jones, 'How to stop data centers from gobbling up the world's electricity' (2018) 561 7722.

grated data. A combination of satellites, drones, mobile phones, sensors, financial technologies and IoT devices collect real-time data, something that is able to transform the management of natural resources and ecosystems. This potential can be harnessed to combat climate change and advance global sustainability, environmental stewardship and human well-being.

4. *The new skills needed*

The future of work presents unparalleled opportunities, but also significant challenges. The digital transformation is upending everything: it is redefining economies, changing the way companies operate, introducing new business models, changing the way countries are managed and the way people communicate with each other. The International Labour Organisation estimates that 24 million new jobs could be created globally by 2030 on account of the adoption of sustainable practices in the energy sector, the use of electric vehicles and increasing energy efficiency in existing and future buildings. Meanwhile, a report by McKinsey Institute[12] suggests that up to 800 million people could lose their jobs to automation by the end of this decade. Polls reveal that employees worry that they do not have the necessary training or skills to get a well-paid job.

These fears are legitimate, as the future of work will see a shift in demand away from office support positions, machine operators, and other low-skill occupations towards ICT professionals. Acquiring and maintaining appropriate staff is therefore strategically important for the development of modern economies, especially looking globally through the prism of potentially high unemployment and at the lack of a qualified workforce.

It is crucial that policies help workers, employers (SMEs) and society at large to manage the transition with the least possible disruption, while maximising the potential benefits. This requires changes in our approach to education, for instance, by placing more emphasis on science, technology, engineering, and mathematics; by teaching soft skills, and resilience; and by ensuring that people can re-skill and up-skill throughout their lifetimes.

---

12 *Jobs lost, jobs gained: Workforce transitions in a time of automation* (McKinsey Global Institute, November 2017).

5. *Digitalising our way into a post-pandemic recovery*

The calamitous fallout from the COVID-19 pandemic brought to the forefront the imperative to take a concerted action to revive the stifled economy and unlock growth factors. The global economic growth was weak even pre-pandemic and now it is outright depressed, with thousands of people having lost their jobs and being forced to shut up shop.

However, as vaccination rolls out and long-lasting recovery instruments take effect, the world is – hopefully – on its way to emerge from devastating lockdowns into a new normal. Against this background, it is time to revisit the established patterns of growth and reshuffle the existing toolbox to move forward with digitalisation and have it implemented across the board. Whether we will come out stronger from this unprecedented crisis depends on how effectively and comprehensively we will address the digital challenge.

As trivial as it sounds, the fact remains that today's world is defined by speed. The economic environment is as dynamic and as competitive as ever. The digital footprint is overarching in business, production, communication, transport, energy, and health care. And it is bound to grow ever stronger in the future, with digital technologies moving on to permeate whatever sector of the economy. Notably, the recent study by the International Data Corporation (IDC) suggests that 65 per cent of global GDP will be digitalised by 2022.[13]

It is impossible to gain and maintain a competitive edge without investing in ICT technologies, including: AI, machine learning, autonomous and assisted vehicles, edge computing, quantum computing, blockchain, Big Data analytics, additive manufacturing, robotics, and 5G telecommunications. Characterised by strong interdependencies, they make for a connected and augmented world in which multiple devices talk and learn from each other in real time.

Interestingly, a phenomenon that started as 'platformisation' in B2C is now making its way into B2B, with smart devices being poised to result in a disruptive industry shift. The Internet of Things is in fact a potent enabler of growth in businesses across the market. Data gathered from the IoT sensors help retailers and service providers attract and get know their customers, just as they help manufacturers to streamline their production lines and R&D activities.

---

13 *Worldwide Digital Transformation Predictions 2021* (International Data Corporation).

This brings us to the issue of a data-driven economy where insights are drawn upon Big Data analytics. It is no accident that data is called 'the oil of the 21st century', as it can be seen as a factor of production, along with land, capital and labour. As such, data will be the engine of growth in the future – growth that has been hugely disappointing everywhere except in China over the past decade. The economy needs it just as lungs need air. Consequently, an absolute priority should be given to collection, analysis and processing of data. This involves encouraging digitalisation across industries to have data generated in the first place, in addition to building analytical skills based on artificial intelligence.

Digital transformation is something that especially developing and emerging countries should set their eyes on not to miss out on a genuine chance. For them, it is a double bet: making up for the pandemic-inflicted economic loss and catching up with the prosperity leaders. ICTs are offering even less developed countries a window of opportunities to leapfrog the industrialisation stage and shift towards high value-added information economies that can compete with global leaders. Take the example of my native Poland. We have been extremely successful, we have managed to achieve impressive progress over the past three decades, we have made up for huge arrears left by the communist rule. And yet, we still have a long way to go before attaining the standard of living enjoyed by Western Europe.

Digital transformation, along with energy transformation that is itself driven by technology, represent two megatrends critical for recovery and resilience building. Digitalisation does indeed hold tremendous potential for value creation and is able to propel the economies and industries that suffered as a result of the pandemic back onto a growth trajectory. What we call 'disruptive technologies' will be instrumental in boosting basic growth factors: innovation, productivity and competitiveness.

To keep up the pace, businesses must think forward and innovate. With this in mind, governments should create the conditions for SMEs to embrace digital improvements. Depending on the country, SMEs contribute between 50 and 70 per cent of GDP, and are crucial to the future of work, being more likely to hire people with lower chances of finding employment, such as the 50+ and less-skilled workers. However, they cannot invest in training and equipment as much as large companies do, to increase their productivity, pay higher wages and offer better working conditions.

The role of the public sector in stimulating digital transformation is often stressed by Ursula von der Leyen who wants the European Commission to 'lead by example.' The benefits are plentiful: cost reduction, more adequate due diligence, enhanced risk management, efficient and resilient supply chains, greater connectivity throughout the market, upgraded operational and financial performance, increased market penetration, and venturing into new markets. Last but not least, digital investments can drive innovation forward at many otherwise struggling or undervalued companies. Ultimately, businesses are able to boost sales and revenues, which feeds into greater investment and employment. The whole economy – and society – benefits.

Special consideration should also be given to start-ups since they are playing an extremely important role in digital transformation. Despite the high-tech potential they carry, start-ups find it difficult to raise scale-up capital to fully capture the growing demand for their products and services after the first commercial launch. Here comes venture capital whose role in nurturing innovations cannot be overstated.

No one could have predicted the level of disruption and uncertainty that we have been up against for months now. To weather the storm and prepare for recovery, we have to prove more agile to anticipate things, and act faster, and more decisively. Most sectors have now passed the stage where being digitally advanced was simply a competitive advantage and it is now very often a matter of survival. We cannot afford to lose time. If there was ever a time to be responsive and actionable, then it is now. The lesson of past recessions is that fortune favours the bold who dare to turn a crisis into an opportunity to consolidate their market standing or even challenge the status quo.

6. *How the IGF's current format aligns with the challenges ahead*

The IGF has evolved since it was first held in 2006. Over the years, it succeeded in becoming more open, bottom up, inclusive and collaborative. It has broadened stakeholder participation, with a view to empowering its participants to create informed and tangible solutions that benefit everyone. It has namely developed a supporting infrastructure of IGF's National and Regional Initiatives (NRIs) that add value both globally and in their own locations. Finally, it has launched intersessional activities that keep the dialogue going all year round and thus help achieve more substantive outcomes. The IGF is now better placed to constructively work with the ISOC-Internet Society (ensures that Internet remains open, accessible, trusted, and secure), the IANA-Internet Assigned Numbers Authority (responsible for the global coordination of the Domain Name System-DNS), and the ICANN-Internet Corporation for Assigned Names and Numbers (coordinates the system of unique names and numbers for an Internet secure, stable, and interoperable).

As the IGF evolved, a host of alternative and complementary forms of participation have emerged, surrounding the Main Focus Sessions. For example, Dynamic Coalitions are groups consisting of stakeholders involved in a particular issue but are not necessarily like-minded or have convergent interests. This format allows to take a thorough look into specific topical segments, such as Accessibility and Disability, Child Online Safety, or Freedom of the Media on the Internet. The Best Practices Fora are meant to build consensus around best practices that contribute to capacity building and can serve as guidance for future occurrences.

Dynamic Coalitions and Best Practices Fora work between annual sessions. So do the National and Regional IGF Initiatives, organic and independent formations established in around half of the countries of the world. There are currently more than 135 NRIs located in all five UN regions, in addition to several new ones, now forming and working to hold their first annual event in 2021/2022. To support the recommendations of the NRIs, the IGF hosts regular (bi)monthly virtual meetings where the NRI Coordinators share updates.

I often hear people from various milieus say 'talking shop makes sense'. And there is so much truth about it. Formal conventions do not work for multistakeholder gatherings. Therefore, in addition to official discussions, a portion of time must be allocated for meetings within the working groups and on the sidelines. Too much of formalism stifles real debate (and progress!) in such fora. That was the idea behind Flash Sessions and Lighting Sessions, both of which are less formal versions of full-length workshops.

What I find extremely useful in terms of ensuring continuity and coherence of our debate is a custom, practiced since 2017, of issuing the consensus-driven IGF Messages at the end of the meeting. These provide an overview of the talks and highlight the crucial points raised, in particular with regard to actions and steps needed to be undertaken. Finally, the IGF agenda has also been extended to include high-level sessions, a parliamentary track, and last but not least, a youth track. All these changes are meant to make the IGF more diverse and more inclusive alike.

The parliamentary track was initiated during the IGF 2019 in Berlin and will be continued in Katowice. We want the debate with parliamentarians to be user-oriented. Preparatory talks are under away with the United Nations and the Interparliamentary Union, and the Sejm of the Republic of Poland whose Speaker was invited to chair the meeting.

As the host country, Poland is vocal about engaging the youth in the Internet governance dialogue. In the run-up to the IGF meeting in Katowice, they could participate in monthly (April-October) webinars devoted to specific issue areas. Also, an international competition called 'My Internet of the Future' was played out among 18-28-year olds. Entrants were supposed to express their visions of the Internet through creative works (categories: graphic work, short film, written story). The winning ones will be presented in Katowice. The summit will also feature, traditionally, the Youth IGF Summit will be held during the IGF 2021, along with many accompanying events.

7. *Looking forward*

The IGF pays attention not to leave any country or any stakeholder group outside the process. That said, it remains a project dominated by the like-minded and the Internet insiders, with those of different views and from outside the digital sphere underrepresented. Suffice it to take a glance at private sector participants: they come overwhelmingly from major global corporations and the supply side (Internet service providers), not from demand-side businesses that make use of it (whether big businesses or SMEs).

Developing countries are also underrepresented, both at the level of stakeholder communities and governments. A special effort should be made to get them engaged in the debate on Internet governance and help them build adequate capacities. In theory, this is already happening. Still, an organised framework (including financial assistance) should be put in place to nurture new skills with which developing countries could fully participate in existing and future Internet governance institutions and arrangements. Ultimately, the involvement of all stakeholders, from developed as well as developing countries, is necessary for advancing dynamic public policies in Internet governance.

Not only should the IGF be reaching out to new communities but, above all, we ought to find ways to engage them. It is one thing is to obtain a coherent output, it is another thing is to make a meaningful use of this output rather than simply archiving it. The same goes to NRIs (regional IGFs as mentioned above) whose voice is not heard enough globally. The intersessional framework should be enhanced to translate into specific results. Otherwise, participants risk losing vigour and motivation.

As the IGF 2021 host country, Poland hopes to inaugurate in Katowice the Multistakeholder High-Level Body (MHLB), proposed in the UN

Secretary-General's Roadmap for Digital Cooperation. It would create a link between the decision world and the discussion world to leverage knowledge and networks of high-profile participants who are not always directly engaged in operational and technical discussions. To this end, we would welcome a greater involvement of individuals representing the past, present and future IGF host countries. This would be an added value as these countries have broad contacts and experience in gathering the IGF communities as well as other entities. Building on their expertise, an informal presidency of the MHLB could be set up in the troika format, with a special place reserved for the UN Tech Envoy. Moreover, the MHLB would have an overall supervision of the UN SG. The MHLB would be a permanent advisory panel composed of those who could play a prominent role in the IGF ecosystem but have not been part of it so far. Its scope should encompass governments, academia, private sector, NGOs, national regulatory authorities, heads of UN entities that deal with digitalisation, e.g. the International Telecommunication Union.

The IGF is one of the many Internet and digital venues. A pronounced promotion strategy is needed to make it a globally recognised brand and have its impact multiplied. But the fundamental question is whether the multistakeholder model proves sustainable in the long run. A purely deliberative format is IGF's strength as much as its weakness. Given that global problems are most effectively solved with binding rules, does it make sense, and is it even feasible, to transform it into a decision-making body? And if not, how should it align with the evolving digital executive ecosystem to avoid undermining its openness and freestyle? That is the question of the day.

***

In an opening address of the 75th session of the UN General Assembly in September 2020, UN Secretary General António Guterres warned of a 'great fracture', with the world's two largest global economies creating two separate and competing worlds, each with its own dominant currency, trade and financial rules, their own Internet, AI capacities, and its own zero-sum geopolitical and military strategies. He urged to pull all the stops to prevent the world from splitting in two and to maintain a universal system, governed by respect for international law and strong multilateral institutions.

It is our responsibility not to let these mounting particularisms erect a digital Iron Curtain.

Section One.
Internet, New Technologies and the Society

Connecting Law to New Technologies: Perspectives and Challenges

Alexandre Cavalcanti Andrade de Araújo
<alexandrecavalcanti.adv@hotmail.com>
BUENOS AIRES, Argentina

Abstract
Currently, countries all over the world have undergone an expressive technological transformation called digital age, in which a large part of human relations is determined by algorithms and / or artificial intelligence. The fugacity of the information age poses new challenges for the Social Sciences as a whole. Thus, Law, as a result of human rationality, will need to undergo significant transformations in order to adapt to the new social categories in metamorphosis. This article aims to discuss challenges and impacts of the postmodern technological revolution and reflect on the paradigm shifts for Law and its new directions in the digital age. It will be carried out a theoretical-critical-documentary analysis, through national and international bibliographic review, involving books, specialized periodicals, legislation and electronic sites, in order to understand the main changes in the various branches of Law. Regarding to the researched references, many speculations pointed to a situation where technology exacerbated individualism, particularism, psychological diseases, human and environmental conflicts, political division and influenced electoral processes. However, it facilitated access to information, reconfigured the relationships of time and space, optimized production processes and developed new forms of communication.

Keywords:
Digital Age; Law; Transformations; Challenges

1. *Introduction*

There is no stable product in the fluency of law. Apparently, however long-lasting a legal order is given, its evolutionary march, its perishing and its exhaustion is simply inevitable. With this, there is an irrepressible wave of constant transformation of society, under the tutelage of a Law that is at the same time product and process of that space, as said by the Brasilian teacher Flóscolo da Nóbrega[1].

The objective that, at a certain point in human life, was merely controlling, constantly subverts its profile, in function of the social landscape, reducing the duration of human knowledge in this area to the specific conditioning of the social fact. This point of view even brings to the precise concept of Rudolph Ihering[2], which sums up the question: "Law is not a pure theory, but a living force".

Up to irrefutable findings, it achieves uneasiness caused by the great Polish sociologist Zygmunt Bauman[3], in his theory of liquid modernity, characterized by "a society full of confused signals, prone to change quickly and in an unpredictable way, where nothing is done to last".

Describing the dichotomous and metaphorical transition between traditional / solid society and fluid modernity, the celebrated Polish philosopher teaches:

"What all these characteristics of fluids show, in simple language, is that liquids, unlike solids, do not maintain their shape easily. Fluids, so, do not fix space or arrest time. Solids have clear spatial dimensions and neutralize impact and, therefore, reduce the significance of time (effectively resist its flow or make it irrelevant), fluids don't stick to any shape and are constantly ready (and prone) to change it; thus, for them, what counts is time more than the space that they have to occupy; space that, after all, only fill "for a moment". In a sense, solids suppress time; liquids, on the contrary, time is what matters. In describing solids, we can ignore time entirely; when describing fluids, leaving time out would be a serious mistake."[3]

In this perspective, Law, as a social science, is frontally provoked to reissue its main foundations, given the impact of new technologies and the fugacity of the information age, receiving a great message of modification of the natural existential way of humanity.

---

1 Jose Flósculo da Nóbrega, *Introdução ao Direito. 7ª. ed. Paraíba* (Sugestões Literárias 1987).

2 Lucas Bicudo, 'Robôs inteligentes podem acabar com o emprego de 40 % dos advogados' (startse.com, 20 February 2017): <https://www.startse.com/noticia/mercado/inteligencia-artificial-automatizar-direito> accessed 12 February 2020.

3 Zygmunt Bauman, Modernidade Líquida (Zahar 2001).

2. *New Technologies - The Future of Law*

Adopting a skeptical and objective view, the information age will bring several paradigm changes, presenting benefits and harms for traditional Law. On one hand, the use of artificial intelligence (AI), robots, lawtechs / legaltechs, will come to assist Law on numerous relevant issues. However, on the other hand, totally new and unknown problems will arise, thus challenging the human / technical / professional Law capacity.

Within this perspective of uncertainty about the future of Law, a Deloitte Insight report, released in 2016, says that major reforms will take place in the legal sector over the next decade, estimating that almost 40 % of jobs may end up being automated in the long term.[4]

Still in this panorama of paradigm changes, it is estimated that 85 % of the jobs that will exist in 2030 will be new and have not yet been created, as shown by the project Designing 2030: a divided vision of the future, commissioned by Dell Technologies from the Institute For The Future (IFT)[5].

Data are clear, future has already arrived. How should Law professional behave? In recent survey, Getúlio Vargas Foundation (GVF)[6] concluded that Law professionals will undergo a readjustment in their activities, reflecting simultaneously: (1) in the emergence of new functions that require new skills, generating completely new positions (hybrid professionals, who dominate legal specialization and familiarity with notions of programming), (2) new skills required from old roles (the requirement that lawyers start to master elementary technological vocabularies) and (3) in the new emphasis on skills and specializations that were already required to some extent and that, from the processes of technological change, acquire greater importance (the ability to work in groups and to face complex cases from interdisciplinary perspectives).

Taking into account the new skills required for Law professionals, they must also understand what challenges will be proposed for the main areas

---

4 Lucas Bicudo, 'Robôs inteligentes podem acabar com o emprego de 40 % dos advogados' (startse.com, 20 February 2017): <https://www.startse.com/noticia/mercado/inteligencia-artificial-automatizar-direito> accessed 12 February 2020.

5 Rafaela Carvalho, '85 % das profissões que existirão em 2030 ainda não foram criadas' (Projetodraft.com, 8 January 2019) <https://www.projetodraft.com/85-das-profissoes-que-existirao-2030-ainda-nao-foram-criadas> accessed 12 February 2020.

6 Fundação Getúlio Vargas, 'Futuro das profissões jurídicas – Você está preparado?' (FGV, 3 December 2018) <https://direitosp.fgv.br/sites/direitosp.fgv.br/files/arquivos/cepi_futuro_profissoes_juridicas_quali_v5.pdf> accessed 11 February 2020.

of Law with the implementation of the digital age. Thus, through a brief example, people can have an approximate idea of the new paradigms that Law will face:

Law Specialties	Paradigms related to a new technology
Administrative Law	Public service and police power, besides other similar state activities (such as regulation, promotion, economy intervention), are directly influenced by new technologies. As these administrative activities (helpful or restrictive from citizen's point of view) are dependent on acts, contracts, procedures and plans, all forms of inclusion of new technologies that reach these legal institutions automatically generate consequences for classic administrative activities that develop between public administration and citizen. The growing adoption, by the public authorities, of automated and digital acts, electronic contracts, performance of procedures over the internet (for example, in bidding), digital processes and many other phenomena evidences this statement.[7]
Environmental Law	Progress, stemming from technological innovations linked to biological sciences, has contributed to the discovery of many species of living beings, which had not been discovered yet. As well as new elements derived from fauna and flora that can provide higher expectations and longevity for human being. However, linked to this progress, other concerns related to human life arises. And the most important of all are: the right to life and the environmental preservation. Through this logic, the controversial discussion about the existence of effective protection, as well as the sustainable use of natural resources arises.[8]
Banking Law	The topics related to blockchain, cryptocurrencies and smart contracts cause many questions, doubts and, of course, a lot of curiosity in the legal environment. So, there are some main challenges: **Difficulty in reaching the concept** - The theme is complex and involves a series of new concepts and practices, so keeping yourself well-informed is important, above all, to follow the details of this subject. **Immunity to censorship** - Regulate and limitate bitcoin mining, for example, are requirements that may not be effective in today's reality. **Poor flow control across borders – It is being even more difficult to have a sistematic control due to the fact that the resources circulate without state control.**[9]

7 Thiago Marrara, 'Direito Administrativo e Novas Tecnologias' (Genjurídico.com, 19 December 2017) <http://genjuridico.com.br/2017/12/19/direito-administrativo-novas-tecnologias> accessed 18 February 2020.

8 David Silva de Souza and and Daiane Acosta Amaral, 'Meio ambiente, sociedade e tecnologia' (Ambitojuridicio.com, 1 July 2014) <https://ambitojuridico.com.br/cadernos/direito-ambiental/meio-ambiente-sociedade-e-tecnologia> accessed18 February, 2020.

9 Rosine Kadamani, 'Blockchain e os efeitos das novas tecnologias no Direito' (blockchainacademy.com.br, 21 November 2018) <https://blockchainacademy.com.br/blockchain-e-os-efeitos-das-novas-tecnologias-no-direito-especial-aurumsummit2018> accessed 29 May 2020.

Law Specialties	Paradigms related to a new technology
Consumer Law	Companies are everywhere (in your home and in your neighborhood, your state, city, country), through the internet (social and commercial sites, such as facebook, twitter, instagram, virtual stores, submarine, free market, among others), causing direct and indirect autonomy control, when related to their freedom of choice. Due to the presence of these organizations is detected a high degree of competition, sending their products everywhere, without barriers, adopting universal strategies that meet the consumers interests. The State Power is silent in relation to this invasion, due to the fact that it benefits yourself with your own omission.[10]
Contract Law	The use of new technologies and the emergence of the 'stuff internet', made inter-system contractual relations grow, where machines manifests the ability to employ above others causing obligations between them and telematic contracts have evolved into a new concept, called digital contracts. The evolution of form was also accompanied by the transformation of the willingness manifestation. Even as the hirer and the hired will be represented by machines, the registration of this hiring, even if it is made by a human act, it will also be done by a machine, with the advantage of increase the legal security of the relationship through greater proof of authenticity (proof of authorship). In other words, what long clauses provide for indemnity, responsibilities, declarations, guarantees, escrow account, are used for?[11]
Philosophy of Law	It offers knowledge of logic, philosophy of mathematics, theory of knowledge, anthropology, rhetoric, argumentation, writing, as well as the ability to face problems and complex texts. It favors the abstract reasoning that allows to analyze the complex information that is received in a speech and, at the same time, integrate a lot of data in fragmented ways, from different sources of knowledge branches. It fosters a critical spirit and the habit of thinking by your ownself deeply, characterized by the ability to ask the right questions in face of new situations. Educates aiming to the hability to dialogue, which implies create an awareness that it is just a point of view. In this way, it is possible to achieve openness to news and your personal examination. It generates a special ethical sensitivity, gained through knowledge and reflection of the various ethical proposals that philosophers have offered throughout history.

10 Jeane Nascimento, 'As relações de consumo frente os avanços tecnológicos versus a globalização e manipulação no direito de escolha do consumidor' (Jusbrasil, 2015) <https://jeanecnascimento.jusbrasil.com.br/artigos/195135894/as-relacoes-de-consumo-frente-os-avancos-tecnologicos-versus-a-globalizacao-e-manipulacao-no-direito-de-escolha-do-consumidor> accessed 29 May 2020.

11 Por Patricia Peck Pinheiro, 'Contratos digitais: apenas um meio ou nova modalidade contratual?' (Conjur.com.br, 29 July 2016) <https://www.conjur.com.br/2016-jul-29/patricia-peck-contratos-digitais-sao-modalidade-contratual> accessed 4 March 2020.

Law Specialties	Paradigms related to a new technology
Philosophy of Law	Philosophers have the role of making a slowly, rigorous and integrating reflection on the consequences for the human life of the scientific and technological changes that we are experiencing.[12]
International Law	Modernization implied an increase in risk, for the individual and for the state. If at the beginning of industrialization the risk was personal or local, it is now impersonal and global. At the same time that modern society has a great technical and scientific knowledge, it is not free from the impact of multiple risks, as social, political and environmental (like the urban riots in Paris in 2005, that quickly spread to neighboring countries; like the contamination of water in international rivers; as the war between states and refugee immigrants, acid rain, the import of transgenic food, etc.). These are risks that know neither the borders nor the limits of the state legal systems.[13]
Criminal Law	With the increase in illicit practices through new information and communication technologies, social peace is undermined, with such illegal conduct being linked to financial fraud, apology to crime, violation of privacy, child pornography, among others. And Criminal Law, in face of new behaviors practiced on web or through these new technologies, cannot ignore and need to face the issue proposed. There is an influence on criminal and procedural rules showing that they are outdated, fragile or ineffective in face of new conduct that violates web rights, requiring updates.[14]
Civil Procedural Law	Online dispute resolution platforms; jurimetrics that is the application of quantitative methods, usually statistics, to law, using a quantitative approach to analyze judicial decisions; the use of robots, decisions by algorithm, virtual plenary, online arbitration. In summarize, there are many thought-provoking questions that challenge legal operators, notably proceduralists.[15]
Civil Responsability	Control technological development and its social and economic reflexes is certainly one of the most challenging missions attributed to Law. One of the main aspects of this challenge is to approach the development risks. These risks are imprecise and uncertain and they can be explained into a simple question: if the product or service had a problem that was undetectable by the scientific and technical knowledge at that time, the supplier must answer for damages resulting from something that did not exist at that time?[16]

12 Universia Brasil, 'Por que é importante a Filosofia na Era Digital?' (Universia.net/br, 19 Decemebr 2018) <https://noticias.universia.com.br/destaque/noticia/2018/12/26/1163322/importante-filosofia-digital.htm> accessed 9 March 2020.

13 Nuno Vieira de Carvalho, 'O direito internacional na era da globalização e do risco' (www.criticanarede.com, 2 April 2006) <https://www.mpam.mp.br/centros-de-apoio-sp-947110907/combate-ao-crime-organizado/doutrina/492-o-direito-internacional-na-era-da-globalizacao-e-do-risco> accessed 27 May 2020.

14 Dayane Fanti Tangerino, 'Direito penal e novas tecnologias'(Jusbrasil, 2015) <https://canalcienciascriminais.jusbrasil.com.br/artigos/293902178/direito-penal-e-novas-tecnologias> accessed 28 May 2020.

15 Darci G. Ribeiro, 'Processo e novas tecnologias: desafios e perspectivas' (www.migalhas.com.br, 6 December 2019) <https://www.migalhas.com.br/depeso/316523/processo-e-novas-tecnologias-desafios-e-perspectiva> accessed 28 May 2020.

16 Guilhereme Henriquie Lima Reinig And Daniel A. Carnaúba,, 'Responsabilidade civil e novas tecnologias: riscos do desenvolvimento retornam à pauta' (www.conj

Law Specialties	Paradigms related to a new technology
Labor Law	There was a change of paradigms in the ways of work relationship, and with automated and restructured production, another kind of worker came into existence. A tough battle is going on, with globalization being placed as an affront to Labor Law by eliminating employment through automation and the divisiõn of labor process around the world. There is a great demand on searching for qualified labor to adjust to the new flexibility requirement. In addition, sophistication in service is sought, the existence of an infrastructure in services to support the maintenance process of companies and globalization.[17]
Tributary Law	The digital economy implies challenges and perplexities that have not been articulated yet. It changes the way we communicate, consume and work. New businesses and types of commerce appears. Increases capital flow. Intangible assets are growing in importance. The tributary system must also change: adapt to challenges imposed by the digital revolution. There is growing evidence that many of the current taxes will soon become obsolete, given the dynamism of electronic commerce and new economy. Income, consumption and employment were deeply affected by new values, current forms of business and work. The three pillars of 20th century assessment had been shaken by the ongoing digital revolution. Although there is much literature and discussion on how structural changes will affect each macroeconomic variables and even how to modernize tributary collection, the discussion about the necessary changes in tributary systems remains incipient. It will not be necessary to change just practices. It is also important to rethinking about fiscal policy and, above all, the current configuration of tributary powers.[18]

As it turns out, the legal sciences are directly challenged to reflect and rethink their main fundamentals, since they are impacted by new technologies, without leaving apart the great role of Law to prescribe, at the same time, parameters and rules, limiting the unrestrained cyber character and giving protection and pacific cohexistance by the subjects.

On this situation, the teacher Maria Helena Diniz[19] in her Introduction to the Science of Law Compendium, exposes a feature of the systemicity of Law:

ur.com.br, 25 November 2019) <https://www.conjur.com.br/2019-nov-25/direito-civil-atual-riscos-novas-tecnologias-retornam-pauta#author> accessed 29 May 2020.

17 Lourival J. de Oliveira, 'Os princípios do direito do trabalho frente ao avanço tecnológico' (www.ambitojuridico.com.br, 20 April 2008) <https://ambitojuridico.com.br/edicoes/revista-52/os-principios-do-direito-do-trabalho-frente-ao-avanco-tecnologico> accessed 30 April 2020.

18 Celso B. C. Neto, José R. R. Alfonso and Luciano F. Fuck 'A tributação na era digital e os desafios do sistema tributário no Brasil' (2019) Revista 15, 1 Brasileira de Direito <https://seer.imed.edu.br/index.php/revistadedireito/article/view/3356/2344> accessed 19 February1 2020.

19 Maria H. Dinz, *Compêndio de introdução à ciência do direito* (Editora Saraiva 2012).

"Scientific knowledge - says the author - is not knowledge that is ready and finished. It is, rather, knowledge obtained and elaborated deliberately, with an awareness of the purposes proposed by the means to carry it out, aiming at its justification as true and certain knowledge."[19]

Thus, the previously reflexive attitude about the impacts of changes in the paradigms in Law, imposes a deep concern on how to achieve to merge or systematize the information age and the new directions of the Legal Sciences, taking into account the re-significance of the human condition and the new forms of transhuman sociability.

3. Conclusion

Given the situation presented, many speculations point to a scenario where technology exacerbated individualism, particularism, psychological diseases, human and environmental conflicts, political division and influenced electoral processes. However, it facilitated access to information, reconfigured the relationships of time and space, optimized production processes and developed new forms of communication.

In this perspective, the operator of postmodern Law will need a proficient qualification, because new technological skills will be demanded. However, as Giorgio Del Vecchio[20] points out: "a simple temporal association made to achieve some particular objective, but also a necessary communion, directed towards the perfection of life".

What is needed today, are not law operators who know the laws, or write a good contract, or know the jurisprudence. This, machines are already doing and will do even better! What is needed is lawyers who understand technology, operate their machines and, mainly, do what machines do not know how to do: understand the human being and relate better to each other.

---

20 Giorgio del Vecchio, *Filosofia Del Derecho* (Bosh Casa Editorial S.A. 1929).

The Changing Nature of the Consumer in the Digital Reality

Monika Jagielska[1] *<monika.jagielska@us.edu.pl>*
KATOWICE, Poland

Monika Namysłowska[2] *<mnamyslowska@wpia.uni.lodz.pl>*
ŁÓDŹ, Poland

Aneta Wiewiórowska-Domagalska <aneta.wiewiorowska@uni-osnabrueck.de>
OSNABRÜCK, Germany

1. *Introduction*

While it is only natural that the market, business models and commercial practices change constantly, the creation of the digital reality has had an impact on the pace and depth of the ongoing changes. The digital reality itself is also not constant – it undergoes profound and rapid transformations. Unsurprisingly, these changes exert an impact on the market actors, including on the perception of who an (average) consumer is. As the complexity of today's digital world is ever-growing, the challenges it brings about from the consumers' point of view are not static. What was incomprehensible to consumers at the dawn of the e-commerce era, and as such posed a threat to their interests, does not have to pose a similar danger now.

It is therefore clear that the market reality reshapes the notion of a consumer, as well as the model of a consumer, because they both are constructed to reflect the perils that the current market poses for consumers. To examine the transformation of the notion and model of a consumer, this article focuses on the reasons that triggered the changes in the concept of consumer, and the menaces that are decisive for distinguishing contemporary consumers in the digital world from other market players. It focuses on the process, fuelled by the digital revolution that has triggered

---

1 The research of Monika Jagielska leading to this paper was prepared in frame of the NCN Project 2015/17/B/HS/01416 "Protection of a weaker party to the contract".

2 The research of Monika Namysłowska leading to this paper was financed by the National Science Centre (*Narodowe Centrum Nauki*) in Poland on the basis of decision DEC-2018/31/B/HS5/01169.

and/or accelerated this transformation. It transforms customers, who cease being consumers of goods and become users of goods. Consequently, consumer protection measures based on the traditional design of a sales contract are no longer sufficient to ensure the parties have an equivalent position on the market. Next, it focuses on the new types of vulnerability created by the digital environment. Further, it presents arguments to prove that the traditional legal designs, originating in sales law set in an off-line environment, require a critical analysis and, most likely, a significant reconceptualization. Finally, the analysis focuses on the consumer model and the adjustments that would be required in order to apply the EU model of an average consumer for consumers who function in the contemporary digital reality.

2. *The triggers of the change*

2.1 *Departing from sales contract*

In the second half of the 20th century, when consumer protection became a well-grounded element of legal orders, the structure of the business chains was still rather simple, and the roles of the market players were clearly defined. Each actor in the chain was either responsible for creation or for consumption[3] – it was for the businesses to produce and for the final buyers to consume. Mass production, sales of finished products and the acquisition of goods for final consumption characterised the economic turnover of those times. A traditionally perceived sales contract played the role of the principal contract in legal systems that provided the basic structure for regulating this nominate contract.[4] Hence, until the end of the 20th century, the orientation of law was to protect the consumer as the final purchaser of goods.[5] Logically, the legal means of consumer protection were adapted to the market challenges arising in sales-related situations. Therefore, consumer law focused on ensuring the safety and the

3 <https://www.brandingstrategyinsider.com/2017/01/unveiling-marketings-new-definition-of-consumers.html#.XWuTgy3US00> accessed 17 June 2021.

4 Reinhard Zimmermann, 'Roman Law and European Culture' (2007) 2 New Zealand Law Review.

5 John Anthony Jolowicz, 'The Protection of the Consumer and Purchaser of Goods under English Law' (1969) 32, 1 Modern Law Review.

quality of goods on the market. Concepts such as strict product liability,[6] warranty and guarantees for consumer goods[7] and the right to withdraw from a contract[8] were the instruments that allowed market balance to be restored in trade involving consumers.

The market, however, has changed profoundly over the last few years, along with the development of new technologies[9] that have initiated a digital revolution.[10] First, the role of digital content on the market has significantly increased,[11] which only intensified the shift from sales to service contracts. Second, the sharing economy,[12] implemented mainly via online platforms,[13] started to gain increasing importance. Third, consumers, whose role was initially restricted to merely consuming goods, now gained the possibility to become producers themselves, fortifying the switch from

6 William Prosser, 'The Assault Upon the Citadel (Strict Liability to the Consumer)' (1960) 69 Yale Law Journal 1099-1134; Thomas Cowan, 'Some Policy Basis of Products Liability' (1965) 17 Stanford Law Review; Spiros Simitis, *Grundfragen der Produzentenhaftung* (Tübingen 1965); Friedrich Kessler, 'Product Liability' (1967) 76 Yale Law Journal; Marshall Shapo, *Product Liability, Cases and Materials* (Mineola 1980); John Wade, 'On the Nature of Strict Tort Liability for Products' (1973) 44 Mississippi Law Journal; John. Montgomery and David Owen, 'Reflections on the Theory and Administration of Strict Tort Liability for Defective Products' (1976) 27 Santa Clara Law Review 1; Vernon Palmer, 'A General Theory of the Inner Structure of Strict Liability: Common Law, Civil Law and Comparative Law' (1989) 12 JPTL ; John Fleming, 'Mass Torts' (1994) 42 AJCL 1994.

7 Friedrich Kessler, 'The Protection of the Consumer under the Modern Sales Law' (1964) 74 Yale Law Journal; 'Disclaimer of Warranty in Consumer Sales' (1963) 77 Harv. L. R. 1963.; Addison Mueller, 'Contract of Frustration' (1969) 78 Yale Law Journal 1969; Edward Murphy, 'Another Assault upon the Citadel: Limiting the Use of Negotiable Notes and Waiver-of-Defense Clauses in Consumer Sales. Consumer Protection Symposium' (1968) 29 Ohio State Law Journal.

8 Omri Ben-Shahar and Eric A. Posner, 'The right to withdraw in contract law' (2011) 40 Journal of Legal Studies 2011.

9 Georgios Doukidis, Nikolaos Mylonopoulos and Nancy Pouloudi (eds) *Social and Economic Transformation in the Digital Era* (Idea Group Publishing 2004).

10 Reiner Schulze and Dirk Staudenmayer (eds) Digital Revolution: Challenges for Contract Law in Practice (Nomos 2016).

11 John B. Meisel, 'Entry into the Market for Online Distribution of Digital Content: Economic and Legal Ramifications' (2008) 5, 1 SCRIPTed: A Journal of Law, Technology and Society .

12 Daniela Selloni, *New Forms of Economies: Sharing Economy, Collaborative Consumption, Peer-to-Peer Economy* (Springer 2017).

13 Kateryna Stanoevska-Slabeva, Vera Lenz-Kesekamp and Viktor Suter, 'Platforms and the Sharing Economy: An Analysis' (Report from the EU H2020 Research Project Ps2Sahre) <https://www.bi.edu/globalassets/forskning/h2020/ps2share_platform-analysis-paper_final.pdf> accessed 20 August 2021.

consumer to prosumer. The increasing popularity of 3D printing technology and the solar panel electricity production placed consumers in the position of a party that not only consumes, but also produces the goods they are interested in acquiring.

While the sharing economy was initially fuelled by the concept of creating an alternative business model, where social aspects of the business model were on an equal footing with profit making, in time it leapt back towards the traditional business concept. The increased access to goods, on a basis other than ownership, reflected (but also facilitated) the trend of slowly rejecting the concept of ownership as the leading market concept. This process lead to questions being asked about the position of the sales contract (that transfers the ownership) as the conceptual foundation for regulating contracts.

Modern consumers (known as 3.0 consumers),[14] especially the younger generation, do not show a far-reaching need to own goods.[15] Such consumers prefer to have an access[16] to the goods for a specific period that corresponds to their needs (taking the simplest examples of Uber[17] or Airbnb[18]), over the ownership of the goods. The market is witnessing a constant departure from traditionally understood consumption and ownership towards the temporary use of goods. The customer ceases to be a person who consumes the purchased products and becomes a user, one who needs access,[19] but who is not necessarily the "final link" in the chain of the economic process. Consumer interest in the temporary use or access to goods is even more pronounced in relation to digital content (for

14 Petr Houdek, 'A Perspective on Consumers 3.0: They Are Not Better Decision-Makers than Previous Generations' (Frontiers in Psychology 2016), <https://www.ncbi.nlm.nih.gov/pmc/articles/PMC4891336> accessed 20 August 2021.

15 See: Inara Scott and Elizabeth Brown, 'Redefining and Regulating the New Sharing Economy' (2017) 19, 3 University of Pennsylvania Journal of Business Law .

16 Antonis Kalogeropoulous, 'How Younger Generations Consume News DIfeerently' (Reuters Institute, September 2019) <http://www.digitalnewsreport.org/survey/2019/how-younger-generations-consume-news-differently> accessed 20 August 2021.

17 Elena Mazareanu, 'Uber Technologies – statistics & facts' (Statista, 6 November 2020) <https://www.statista.com/topics/4826/uber-technologies> accessed 20 August 2021.

18 Jaleesa Bustamante, 'Airbnb Statistics' (Iproperty Management, 2020) <https://ipropertymanagement.com/airbnb-statistics> accessed 20 August 2021.

19 Bronwen Morgan and Declan Kuch, 'Radical Transactionalism: Legal Consciousness, Diverse Economies, and the Sharing Economy' (2015) 42, 4 Journal of Law and Society 2015.

example, Spotify[20] or Netflix[21]). It should be assumed that this tendency will deepen[22] as the sharing economy also goes along with the growing public awareness of the need for action to protect the natural environment and recourses, in which the ides of permanent usage fit very well.[23] Hence, it has become necessary to reorient consumer law, still focused on protecting the final purchaser of consumer goods, into a system that protects the user, usually a long-term user, of various types of goods and services.

2.2 *Departing from the off-line world*

Although the consumer concept and the consumer model have always been built based on the consumer-trader juxtaposition,[24] the digital revolution has brought about a new type of imbalance of power. For a certain moment it seemed that the digitalisation would strengthen the consumer's position against traders, as it provided consumers with instruments that addressed the very reasons that decided about qualifying them as the weaker party to a contract. First, search machines and collections of data available online gave consumers instruments to combat the informational imbalance that distinguished them from traders. Collecting and analysing data became inexpensive in terms of time and money, which levelled

---

20 John Porter, 'Spotify is first to 100 million paid subscribers' (The Verge, 29 April 2019) <https://www.theverge.com/2019/4/29/18522297/spotify-100-million-users-apple-music-podcasting-free-users-advertising-voice-speakers> accessed 20 August 2021.

21 Seth Fiegerman, 'Netflix adds 9 million paying subsribers, but stock falls' (CNN Business 18 January 2019) <https://edition.cnn.com/2019/01/17/media/netflix-earnings-q4/index.html> accessed 20 August 2021.

22 Julie Beck, 'The Decline of the Driver's License' (The Atlantic, 22 January 2016), https://www.theatlantic.com/technology/archive/2016/01/the-decline-of-the-drivers-license/425169 <http://www.umich.edu/~umtriswt/PDF/UMTRI-2016-4_Abstract_English.pdf> accessed 20 August 2021.

23 Vanessa Mak and Enna Lujinovic 'Towards a Circular Economy in EU Consumer Markets – Legal Possibilities and Legal Challenges and the Dutch Example'(2019) 4 EuCML 2019; Bronwen Morgan and Declan Kuch, 'Radical Transactionalism: Legal Consciousness, Diverse Economies, and the Sharing Economy'(2015) 42, 4 Journal of Law and Society.

24 See e.g. Natali Helberger, and others 'Analysis of the applicable legal frameworks and suggestions for the contours of a model system of consumer protection in relation to digital content contracts. Final report: Comparative analysis, law & economics analysis, assessment and development of recommendations for possible future rules on digital content contracts' (University of Amsterdam, 2011) 17 <https://hdl.handle.net/11245/1.345662> accessed 5 May 2021.

out the informational imbalance between consumers and traders. Soon, however, it turned out that the instruments that were supposed to provide objective information to consumers, actually offered them biased data. The simple search machines and comparison websites were accused of presenting results with a certain degree of bias.[25] When it comes to reputational systems – the building block of the sharing economy concept based on platforms – they proved to suffer from manipulation. A report prepared for the UK's Competition and Market Authority in 2015 proved that, while consumers rely on online reviews and find them valuable, businesses write or commission fake positive reviews about themselves, businesses or individuals write or commission fake negative reviews about others, review sites "cherry-pick" positive reviews, or suppress negative reviews, which they collect or display without making it clear to readers that they are presenting a selection of reviews only.[26]

The ease at which news is spread also (at least temporarily) strengthened the negotiation position of the consumer (the threat of going viral). However, it soon became clear that digitalisation creates new types of imbalances that are driven by the technological advantages that the traders structurally enjoy over consumers.

Consumers have become more and more vulnerable, as traders collect increasing amounts of data about them and their preferences, which is subsequently used in sophisticated trade techniques and business models based on the AI systems. As Pasquale put it,[27] "tracked even more closely by firms and governments, we have no idea of just how much of this information can travel, how it is used, or its consequences." The manipulative potential of such tools grows steadily and they become nearly impossible

25 Dirk Lewandowski, 'Living in the world of biased search engines' (2015) Online Information Review <https://www.researchgate.net/publication/279240937_Living_in_a_world_of_biased_search_engines>accessed 14 May 2021.

26 See: Competition & Markets Authority, 'Online reviews and endorsements, Report on the CMA's call for information' (CMA, 19 June 2015) <https://assets.publishing.service.gov.uk/government/uploads/system/uploads/attachment_data/file/436238/Online_reviews_and_endorsements.pdf>, accessed 14 June 2021, see also: Christoph Busch, 'Crowdsourcing Consumer Confidence, How to regulate online rating and review systems in the collaborative economy' in de Franceschi (ed) European Contract Law and the Digital Single Market: the Implications of the Digital Revolution, Intersentia, (Cambridge 2016).

27 David Anthony Whitaker, 'How a Career Con Man Led a Federal Sting that Cost Google $500 Million' (Wired, 1 May 2013), as referred to in Frank Pasquale, 'The Black Box Society: The Secret Algorithms that Control Money and Information' (2015) Harvard University Press7.

to understand. Consumers are confronted with new types of risks, which they often do not even recognise as risks. Consumer behaviour becomes increasingly easy to affect, with traders obtaining tools that allows them to effectively control the group of consumers that they want to offer their services to (for example: medical data being used to evaluate the creditworthiness of consumers).

The frequency of use of these algorithm-based data-driven practices by the market players is also growing steadily, which is particularly endangering in the case of the large, global companies that accumulate vast amounts of data on their users. These two types of practices, combined with the size of the traders involved, leads to the creation of a unique asymmetry, known as digital asymmetry. This is understood as a structural phenomenon that affects all consumers and that cannot be overcome by the traditional means used as consumer protection measures, i.e. by providing more information.[28]

Another aspect of the new market reality is digital vulnerability. This concept assumes that in digital marketplaces most, if not all, consumers are potentially vulnerable.[29] Digital vulnerability is defined as "*a universal state of defencelessness and susceptibility to (the exploitation of) power imbalances that are the result of increasing automation of commerce, datafied consumer-seller relations and the very architecture of digital marketplaces.*"[30] Not only does digital vulnerability as a concept seems to be in opposition to the average consumer model, but it also refines the notion of a vulnerable consumer. EU consumer law does not foresee such a standard, which is why proposals are being made to amend the law accordingly.[31]

3. *Changes in the notion of a consumer*

Considering the depth of the current market changes, the need to reorient consumer law from being focused on protecting the final purchaser of goods into a system that protects users of various types of goods and services, usually in a long-term relation, became evident. Over the past 50 years, not only in the European Union,[32] legal mechanisms have been

28 Helberger (n 14) 51.
29 ibid 5.
30 ibid 5.
31 ibid 79.
32 Since 1985, the EU has developed a wide range of consumer protection instruments, mainly via consumer law directives; for more, see Stephen Weatherill,

developed to protect traditional consumers.[33] The fundamental question, therefore, is whether these traditional means of protection require merely an adjustment, or whether a complete change of concept is required, because the existing structure is completely inappropriate to address the challenges of the modern market.

It seems as if the most efficient choice is to focus on ensuring adequate protection for a new category of entity – users of goods (as opposed to the final consumers of goods). In situations where the sales contract is replaced by a contract for the use of goods, usually concluded for an extended period, the mechanisms of controlling the content of the contract begin to play a very important role. Contracts for the sale of consumer goods are usually concluded without complying with any formal requirements (save for situations when the law requires the observance of a certain form). In the contracts of everyday life, the parties usually reach a consensus on the basic issues, such as the price and main characteristics of the goods. Contracts for the use of goods, on the other hand, are usually more formal and are typically concluded based on standard contract terms, which is rather rare in trivial sales contracts. When such a long-lasting legal relation is created between the parties, provisions relating to the possibility of unilaterally shaping the content of a contract, and the mutual obligations of the parties,[34] including liability, as well as the termination of the legal relationship, gain particular importance.

An analysis of the contractual patterns used in this type of contract indicates that they contain provisions that may be considered unfair.[35] European law provides protection against such clauses in relation to all types

---

EU Consumer Law and Policy (Edward Elgar Publishing 2014); Geraint Howells, Christian Twigg-Flesner and Thomas Wilhelmsson, *Rethinking EU Consumer Law* (Routledge 2019); Hans-wolfgang Micklitz and NorbertReich, *EU Consumer Law*(Intersentia 2014); Hans Schulte-Noelke, Christian Twigg-Flesner and Martin Ebers (eds) *EC Consumer Law Compendium. The Consumer Acquis and its transposition in the Member States* (Sellier European Law Publisher 2008); Hans W. Micklitz, Jules Stuyck and Eevlyne Terryn (eds) *Cases, Materials and Text on Consumer Law*, (Oxford 2010).

33 Iain Ramsay, Consumer Law and Policy (Hart Publishing 1974); Geraint Howells and Stephen Weatherill, Consumer Protection Law (Routledge 2017); Geraint Howells, Iain Ramsay and Thomas Wilhelmsson, Handbook of Research on International Consumer Law (Elgar 2010).

34 Joanna Luzak, 'Digital age: time to say goodbye to traditional concepts' (2018) 17 EuCML.

35 Evelyne Terryn, 'The sharing economy in Belgium – a case for regulation?' (2016) 45 EuCML.

of contracts concluded with consumers,[36] though it may be worth considering which abusive clauses are characteristic for temporary use contracts, how they violate the contractual balance and then introduce such clauses to the catalogue of unfair contract terms. From a similar perspective, it would also be necessary to analyse the information obligations posed on the business, as well as the regulation of the unfair market practices.

4. *Changes in consumer model*

The changing nature of the consumer in the digital reality leads directly to questions about the parallel change of the consumer model, which is one of the fundamental concepts of EU consumer law. The consumer model is the reference point for determining whether a trader's conduct towards consumers is lawful or not. In other words, the accepted image of a consumer defines who is protected, and under what conditions. Although many consumer images exist, the basic consumer model is that of the average consumer. This roughly means that the standard of consumer protection is set by the expectations, perception capabilities and circumspection of the average consumer.

When discussing the digital reality, it is important to note that the currently applied model of the average consumer dates from pre-digital times and originates from the case-law of the Court of Justice on the proportionality of national restrictions under the free movement law.[37] The origin of the average consumer model implies that its development was not based on any idea of consumer protection. The aim of the Court of Justice was to promote cross-border free trade,[38] so the average consumer standard considers the interests of traders. However, it must also guarantee a high level of consumer protection, as required by Articles 114 and 169 TFEU. This is particularly important, as the consumer model has been gradually transferred to the acts harmonising the national consumer laws.

---

36 Council Directive 93/13/EEC of 5 April 1993 on unfair terms in consumer contracts [1993] OJ L 95/29–34.

37 C-210/96 *Gut Springenheide and Tusky v Oberkreisdirektor des Kreises Steinfurt* [1998], paras 30, 31. See also: Mateja Durovic, 'The Subtle Europeanization of Contract Law: The Case of Directive 2005/29/EC on Unfair Commercial Practices' (2015) 5 European Review of Private Law 715, 719.

38 Peter Rott, 'Der „Durchschnittsverbraucher" – ein Auslaufmodell angesichts personalisierten Marketings?', (2015) 5 Verbraucher und Recht 163.

The consumer model plays a pivotal role in Directive 2005/29/EC on unfair commercial practices (hereinafter: UCPD) which is the most powerful instrument for consumer protection, even in the new digital reality.[39] It is the average consumer model that serves as a general vantage point for establishing the unfairness of a commercial practice.[40] Since the Kásler case,[41] the average consumer model is used as a yardstick in the assessment of transparency of the contract terms. The average consumer model applies to food legislation,[42] the conformity of goods,[43] pre-contractual information disclosure[44] etc. It is also visible outside the core acts of consumer law, such as intellectual property law.[45]

It is worth noting that the omnipresent 'average consumer' is not defined in any legal acts. It is the Court of Justice that sets out a definition of the average consumer as a consumer who is reasonably well-informed and reasonably observant and circumspect.[46] Certain characteristics are therefore required from the consumer and the standard of protection is established to reflect them. The main reason for criticism is the assumption that the average consumer model refers to a kind of person that does not exist in real life.[47] However, when seen as a normative standard, this

---

39 Stefan Scheuerer, 'Artificial Intelligence and Unfair Competition – Unveiling an Underestimated Building Block of the AI Regulation Landscape' (2021) GRUR International, 4, <https://academic.oup.com/grurint/advance-article/doi/10.1093/grurint/ikab021/6178541> accessed 31 May 2021.

40 Articles 5–8 of the UCPD.

41 C-26/13 *Kásler and Káslerné Rábai* [2014] paras 74.

42 Article 5(2) of the Regulation (EC) No 1924/2006 of the European Parliament and of the Council of 20 December 2006 on nutrition and health claims made on foods [2006] OJ L404/9–25.

43 C-52/18 *Fülla* [2019] paras 40.

44 C-430/17 *Walbusch Walter Busch* [2019] paras 39.

45 C-456/19 *Aktiebolaget Östgötatrafiken* [2020] para. 40.

46 Recital 18 of the UCPD.

47 Vanessa Mak, The 'Average Consumer' of EU Law (in:) Dorota Leczykiewicz, Stephen Weatherill (eds.), *The Involvement of EU Law in Private Law Relationships* (Hart Publishing 2013) 335; Peter Rott, 'Der „Durchschnittsverbraucher"– ein Auslaufmodell angesichts personalisierten Marketings?' (2015) 5 Verbraucher und Recht 163–164; Rossella Incardona and Cristina Poncibò, 'The average consumer, the unfair commercial practices directive, and the Cognitive Revolution' (2007) 30, 1 Journal of Consumer Policy28.

concept allows questions to be raised about the presumed expectations of an average consumer in a given situation,[48] without empirical evidence.[49]

Under the UCPD, the basic model may be modified to the average member of a group of consumers when a practice is targeted at a particular group of consumers.[50] These specific average consumers are then the yardstick to be used when assessing the unfairness of a commercial practice.

The predominance of the average consumer model does not leave vulnerable consumers unprotected. The UCPD introduces an alternative standard – the vulnerable consumer model – for consumers whose characteristics make them particularly vulnerable to an unfair commercial practice[51] or the underlying product because of their mental or physical infirmity, age or credulity.[52] This definition was criticised as being too narrow,[53] arbitrary,[54] paternalistic and superfluous.[55] The Court of Justice does not delve into the vulnerable consumer model.[56] The European Commission claims, however, that, despite the wording of Article 5(3), the UCPD provides a non-exhaustive list of characteristics that make a consumer 'particularly susceptible'.[57] This is followed by the 'New Consumer Agenda': "*The vulnerability of consumers can be driven by social circumstances or because of particular characteristics of individual consumers or groups of consumers, such as their age, gender, health, digital literacy, numeracy or financial*

48 Vanessa Mak, 'The 'Average Consumer' of EU Law' in: Dorota Leczykiewicz, Stephen Weatherill (eds) *The Involvement of EU Law in Private Law Relationships* (Hart Publishing 2016) 335.

49 ibid 386.

50 Article 5(2)(b) of the UCPD.

51 Recital 18 of the UCPD.

52 Article 5(3) of the UCPD. See more Eleni Kaprou, 'The legal definition of 'vulnerable' consumers in the UCPD: Benefits and limitations of a focus on personal attributes' in: Christine Riefa and Séverine Saintier (eds) *Vulnerable Consumers and the Law: Consumer Protection and Access to Justice* (Routledge 2021) 56–63.

53 Bram Duivenvoorde, 'The Protection of Vulnerable Consumers under the Unfair Commercial Practices Directive' (2013) 2 euvr 201371.

54 Jules Stuyck, Evelyne Terryn and Tom Van Dyck, 'Confidence through Fairness? The New Directive on Unfair Business-To-Business Commercial Practices in the Internal Market' (2006) 43, Common Market Law Review 107, 122–123.

55 Rossella Incardona and Cristina Poncibò, 'The average consumer, the unfair commercial practices directive, and the Cognitive Revolution' (2007) 30, 1 Journal of Consumer Policy 29.

56 C-853/19, *STING Reality* [2020] paras 48, 49.

57 Guidance on the Implementation/Application of Directive 2005/29/EC on Unfair Commercial Practices, SWD(2016) 163 final, section 2.6.

situation."[58] The shift from internal factors such as age or physical infirmity to external and situational ones is clearly visible.[59]

Against this background, the question arises as to the consumer model that should be applied in the digital reality. Is it still justified to rely on an average consumer model that was defined long before the digital transformation, or has the time come to change the yardstick of consumer law to provide a high level of protection against the new challenges that consumers are facing?

It goes without saying that the digital vulnerability concept is based on valuable assumptions. Nevertheless, the new reality must not immediately lead to legal changes, especially as the process can take a long time and the outcomes do not unveil immediately. It is therefore worth considering whether an appropriate interpretation of the existing concepts, such as the average consumer model, is currently sufficient to maintain a high level of consumer protection.

The possibility of an interpretation suitable for the digital world results from the fact that the average consumer model is not static. No single average "Euro-consumer" exists.[60] Recital 18 of the UCPD emphasises that the average consumer should be defined by "taking into account social, cultural and linguistic factors," and that national courts and authorities have to rely on their own faculty of judgement to determine the typical reaction of the average consumer in a given case. The relativisation of the average consumer is thus required.[61]

It is therefore necessary to specify how the average consumer behaves in the digital reality. Several factors should be considered, e.g. the type of new technology (e-commerce, digital content, smart contracts, AI systems

---

58 Communication from the Commission to the European Parliament and the Council, New Consumer Agenda. Strengthening consumer resilience for sustainable recovery, COM(2020) 696 final, section 3.4.

59 Natali Helberger, Hans-W. Micklitz, Marijn Sax and Joanna Strycharz, Surveillance, Consent and the Vulnerable Consumer. Regaining Citizen Agency in the Information Economy (in) Natali Helberger, Orla Lynskey, Hans-W. Micklitz, Marijn Sax and Joanna Strycharz, *Consumer protection 2.0. Structural asymmetries in digital consumer markets* (2021), 15 <www.beuc.eu/publications/beuc-x-2021-018_eu_consumer_protection.0_0.pdf>> accessed 31 May 2021.

60 This notion applied in: Sybe De Vries, '*Consumer* protection and the EU Single Market rules – The search for the 'paradigm consumer' (2012) 4 Journal of Consumer and Market Law 228.

61 Thomas Wilhelmsson, 'Misleading Practices' in: Geraint Howells, Hans-W. Micklitz and Thomas Wilhelmsson, *European Fair Trading Law. The Unfair Commercial Practices Directive* (Ashgate 2006) 134.

etc.), the category of the practice and product.[62] Further, whether the consumer's attention is adequate to the situation,[63] along with their knowledge.[64] The average consumer may be not very observant or circumspect[65] and their ability to act rationally should not be over-estimated.[66]

The average consumer test does not need empirical or mathematical in content,[67] yet it allows empirical studies to be considered. For example, the assessment of the average consumer's expectations towards the application of AI systems may be influenced by a September 2020 study. This report revealed that 22 % of consumers think AI is very little or not at all present, while 21 % of consumers have never heard of AI or have no idea about its presence.[68] On the other hand, this perception of AI-driven goods and services will certainly change, at least partly, in the future. The dynamic reading of averageness allows, however, socio-economic changes and developments in consumer behaviour[69] to be captured and thereby to adapt the average consumer model to the changing reality.

For new technology practices, which are often based on personalisation, it is important that the average consumer model can also be personalised[70] by referring to the concept of an average member of a group at whom a practice is targeted.

---

62 See Peter Reuss, '§ 5 UWG' in: Peter W. Heermann and Jochen Schlingloff (eds) *Münchener Kommentar zum Lauterkeitsrecht* (C.H.Beck 2020) 98–103.

63 Hans-W. Micklitz and Monika Namysłowska, '§ 5 UWG' in: Gerald Spindler and Fabian Schuster (eds) *Recht der elektronischen Medien. Kommentar* (C.H.Beck 2019) 128.

64 C-673/17 *Planet49* [2019] ECLI:EU:C:2019:246, Opinion of Advocate General Szupnar, 114.

65 Wilhelmsson (n 61) 132.

66 Stephen Weatherill, 'Who is the "Average Consumer"?' in: Stephen Weatherill and Ulf Bernitz (eds) *The Regulation of Unfair Commercial Practices under EC Directive 2005/29. New Rules and New Techniques* (Hart Publishing 2007) 133.

67 Wilhelmsson (n 61) 132.

68 The European Consumer Organisation, 'Artificial Intelligence: What consumer say. Findings and policy recommendations of a multi-country survey on AI', (2020) 6 <https://www.beuc.eu/publications/beuc-x-2020-078_artificial_intelligence_what_consumers_say_report.pdf> accessed 5 May 2021.

69 Stefan Scheuerer, 'Artificial Intelligence and Unfair Competition – Unveiling an Underestimated Building Block of the AI Regulation Landscape' (2021) 1 GRUR International 4.

70 Philipp Hacker, 'Manipulation by Algorithms. Exploring the Triangle of Unfair Commercial Practice, Data Protection, and Privacy Law' (2021) European Law Journal (forthcoming).

Similarly, the notion of a vulnerable consumer can be applied if a practice/business model is geared towards the exploitation of particular vulnerabilities, understood as characteristics beyond the consumer's control.[71] These consumers need a higher level of protection than others, which may still be granted.

To conclude, all three types of consumer yardstick: the average consumer, the target group and vulnerable consumer benchmark may be applied in a digital reality. The condition is that they are used reasonably, striking a balance between the expectations towards consumers' abilities and those abilities in reality. If this is the case, they provide a comparably high bar for consumer protection as the recently proposed concept of digital vulnerability.

5. Conclusions

The main objective of consumer law, which is to ensure a high level of protection to counterbalance the structural inequalities between consumers and traders, remains unchanged. What has changed, however, is the subject of protection – the user who needs to be protected, the reasons why they need protection and the means of that protection. On the one hand, at a conceptual level, the situation is less complicated than those times when consumer law was being created in the second half of the twentieth century. The idea of protecting the weaker party and its justification is generally approved, appropriate protective measures have been developed and traders have grown accustomed to the idea of providing adequate protection to both parties to the transaction. At the same time, however, the technological advancements, and the increasing use of AI-based, automated systems require an appropriate reaction, not only at a legislative level, but it also requires the adjustment of the enforcement tools and mechanisms (a similar intensity of technology utilisation). In addition, it should be emphasised that the existing rules, such as the rules on monitoring unfair contract terms and unfair market practices, would be able to provide users with an adequate legislative protection scheme. What is important is that the protection measures available to consumers should work effectively (i.e. also without needing a lawyer's assistance for "normal" cases) in a digital environment. In other words, as the market

71 Mateja Durovic, *European Law on Unfair Commercial Practices and Contract Law* (Hart Publishing 2016) 43.

transforms itself into functioning in the digital reality, so should the system of consumer protection.

What is definitely needed is the reconsideration of the consumer concept (due to the changed market structure) and the consumer model (due to the new, specific nature and high complexity of today's digital reality). The existence of digital asymmetry and of new power imbalances cannot be denied and should be addressed by legislation (self-regulation advanced by many market sectors hardly seems an adequate response). The emergence of technology-driven challenges justifies the re-examination of the existing principles of consumer law, including the consumer model.

Ensuring a high level of consumer protection can also be achieved through an appropriate, dynamic interpretation of the 'average consumer', which protects against excessive protectionism and stigmatisation.[72] This standard enables a variation in the expectations placed on the consumer[73] and is future-proof because the changing nature of the consumer resulting from the changing reality can be considered. As consumers acquire a certain standard of legal and technical knowledge, the average consumer model will have to adapt. A proper benchmark of the average consumer in a digital reality may also result in consumer empowerment.

Nevertheless, as the notion of consumer and the model of the average consumer are only one element of the consumer protection system, a separate analysis should be carried out of whether the entire regulatory framework ensures an adequate protection of consumers/users in today's digital reality.[74]

---

72 See more on the stigmatisation of vulnerable consumers in Alyson Cole, All of Us Are Vulnerable, But Some Are More Vulnerable than Others: The Political Ambiguity of Vulnerability Studies, An Ambivalent Critique, Critical Horizons, Vol. 17, No 2 2016, 261–262; Gianclaudio Malgieri, Jędrzej Niklas, 'Vulnerable data subjects', Computer Law & Security Review 37 (2020), 3.

73 Paolo Siciliani, Christine Riefa andHarriet Gamper, *Consumer Theories of Harm* (Hart Publishing 2019), 36.

74 See Monika Namysłowska and Agnieszka Jabłonowska, 'Artificial Intelligence and Platform Services: EU Consumer (Contract) Law and New Regulatory Developments' in: Martin Ebers, Cristina Poncibò and Mimi Zou (eds) *Contracting and Contract Law in the Age of Artificial Intelligence* (Hart Publishing 2021, forthcoming).

Risky Business: Legal Implications of Emerging Technologies Affecting Consumers of Financial Services

Zofia Bednarz <z.bednarz@unsw.edu.au>

Kayleen Manwaring <kayleen.manwaring@unsw.edu.au>
SYDNEY, Australia

Abstract

Artificial Intelligence- (AI) driven Big Data analytics are becoming a core capability for financial institutions, giving rise to promises of profits and increased efficiency both for new FinTech firms and incumbent institutions. This, however, may come at a cost to consumers. This chapter analyses the challenges to legal and regulatory framework applicable to provision of financial services to consumers brought about by the use of AI and Big Data tools by financial services firms. We discuss harms to consumers potentially arising in terms of discrimination, privacy breaches, digital manipulation and financial exclusion, and argue policymakers and regulators must deliver a fit-for-purpose legal and regulatory framework, allowing both financial firms and consumers to reap benefits of the technological revolution.

Keywords:
Artificial Intelligence, Big Data, Financial Services, Consumer Protection, Consumer Harms

1. Introduction

Artificial Intelligence (AI)- and Big Data-related technologies have been recently causing major disruptions to the financial services industry. These technologies create important new opportunities for financial services providers, in terms of costs reduction and increased efficiency.[1] The naturally data-rich industry is a perfect environment for AI and Big Data tools, which are leveraged to create value, offer innovative products and introduce new processes through AI-enabled analytics, risk management, customer acquisition, customer service, as well as automation and process re-engineering.[2] AI and Big Data analytics are becoming a core capability for financial institutions, with the technology playing 'an increasingly central role in creating value for banks',[3] insurers[4] and financial investment firms,[5] as well as their customers. The focus of this chapter is the use of AI and Big Data tools for automated decision-making in relation to offering of financial services to consumers and challenges it poses for legal and regulatory frameworks protecting consumers of financial services.

Recent studies are consistently showing increasing adoption of AI technology by financial services firms, indicating 85 % of firms are already using the technology,[6] and in particular, machine learning (ML) models.[7] The industry is making significant investments in AI technologies,[8] expecting consequent important benefits for firms. FinTech organisations are leading technological transformation of the industry.[9]

These promises of improvements may, however, come at a cost to consumers. Many customers will likely benefit from more accessible, cheaper and personalised services. Nevertheless, the technologies' use and automated decision-making may affect some consumers negatively, leading to harms related to discrimination, exclusion, invasions of privacy, unfair prices and digital consumer manipulation. Some of these issues are known, 'old' problems, which may become exacerbated through the tech-

1 Tom CW Lin, 'Artificial Intelligence, Finance, and the Law' (2019) 88 Fordham Law Review 531, 532–33.

2 Cambridge Centre for Alternative Finance and World Economic Forum (CCAF), 'Transforming Paradigms: A Global AI in Financial Services Survey' (January 2020) 30–33.

3 Sven Blumberg and others, 'Beyond Digital Transformations: Modernizing Core Technology for the AI Bank of The Future' (McKinsey & Company Financial Services, 28 April 2021).

4 Ramnath Balasubramanian, Ari Libarikian and Doug McElhaney, 'Insurance 2030: The Impact of AI on the Future of Insurance' (McKinsey & Company Insurance Practice, March 2021).

5 Deloitte, 'Client-facing technologies for investment banks' (December 2020).

6 CCAF (n 2) 25.

7 Deloitte Centre for Financial Services, 'AI leaders in financial services' (Deloitte Insights, 13 August 2019).

8 CCAF (n 2) 18.

9 ibid 26.

nology; some are new, arising directly out of this sociotechnical transformation. The use of AI and Big Data analytics may thus present a number of important challenges for law and regulation of retail financial services provided to consumers.

The issue is time sensitive. This sociotechnical change is already occurring, and it is crucial to analyse how existing legal rules govern this new reality, and if law reform is needed. The rules need to achieve a balance between protecting the market, as well as consumers, from harms, while at the same time creating a space in which innovation thrives. Timely examination of the problem against these criteria will allow us to assess whether the current legal and regulatory framework is fit for purpose, in order to both incentivise beneficial innovation and discourage harmful business models, that may otherwise become too entrenched to be easily dislodged later.[10]

This chapter proceeds as follows. Section 2 starts with a brief overview of AI and Big Data technologies, analyses how they are currently used in financial services, and outlines their potentially concerning characteristics. Section 3 focusses on challenges posed by these sociotechnical developments to legal and regulatory frameworks, including possible harms to consumers arising out of algorithmic bias, excessive data collection, digital manipulation and personalisation of financial services. Section 4 concludes.

2. *The Technologies: Characteristics and Use in Financial Services*

2.1. *Emerging Technologies Used by Financial Services Firms*

The sociotechnical change brought about by AI and Big Data technologies in the financial services industry is nothing short of revolutionary.[11] To

---

10 This conundrum or incentive for timely analysis of regulatory regimes in the face of sociotechnical change is also known as the 'Collingridge dilemma'. For a detailed discussion of the effects of the Collingridge dilemma, see Lyria Bennett Moses, 'How to Think about Law, Regulation and Technology: Problems with "Technology" as a Regulatory Target', (2013) 5 *Law, Innovation and Technology* 1, 8 and Kayleen Manwaring 'Kickstarting Reconnection: An Approach to Legal Problems Arising from Emerging Technologies' (2017) 22 *Deakin Law Review* 51, 58. Collingridge himself described it as the 'dilemma of social control': David Collingridge, *The Social Control of Technology* (Pinter, 1980) 11.

11 See eg CCAF (n 2) 11; OECD, 'The Impact of Big Data and Artificial Intelligence (AI) in the Insurance Sector' (Report, 2020) 6–7; Linklaters, 'Artificial Intelligence

properly understand the legal and social consequences, we need to understand what these technologies are and what makes them so disruptive.[12]

Artificial Intelligence and Machine Learning

The term 'artificial intelligence', coined in the mid-1950s,[13] can be defined in a number of ways, both as a sociotechnical concept[14] and as a technology. As a technology, AI encompasses a range of tools and techniques.[15] One of the most common forms of AI of particular interest in the context of financial services is machine learning (ML).[16] ML models can be used in decision-making processes. These models improve their outcomes through learning, ie 'modify[ing] or adapt[ing] their actions',[17] eg using methods which detect patterns in data, which can be used to predict future data, or in probabilistic decision-making.[18] ML models tend to be empirically constructed, so their outcomes are based on the identification and application of correlations in the data, rather than causal reasoning.[19]

in Financial Services: Managing Machines in an Evolving Legal Landscape' (Report, September 2019) 4–6.

12 Chris Reed, 'Taking Sides on Technology Neutrality' (Pt 2007) (2007) 4(3) *SCRIPTed* 263, 282; Bert-Jaap Koops, 'Ten Dimensions of Technology Regulation: Finding Your Bearings in the Research Space of an Emerging Discipline' in Morag Goodwin, Bert-Jaap Koops and Ronald Leenes (eds), *Dimensions of Technology Regulation* (Wolf Legal Publishing 2010) 312.

13 Gil Press, 'A Very Short History Of Artificial Intelligence (AI)' *Forbes* (30 December 2016) <https://www.forbes.com/sites/gilpress/2016/12/30/a-very-short-history-of-artificial-intelligence-ai/?sh=45bbb6e96fba> accessed 26 May 2021.

14 Michael Guihot and Lyria Bennett Moses, *Artificial Intelligence, Robots and the Law* (LexisNexis, 2020) Ch 1; Toby Walsh, *It's Alive! Artificial Intelligence from the Logic Piano to Killer Robots* (La Trobe UP, 2017) 17; House of Lords Select Committee on Artificial Intelligence, *AI in the UK: Ready, Willing and Able?* (Report of Session 2017–19, HL Paper 100, 16 April 2018) 13–14. Also See eg High-Level Expert Group on Artificial Intelligence, 'A Definition of AI: Main Capabilities and Disciplines' (European Commission, 8 April 2019) 1.

15 Toby Walsh and others, 'The Effective and Ethical Development of Artificial Intelligence: An Opportunity to Improve Our Wellbeing' (Report for the Australian Council of Learned Academies, July 2019).

16 CCAF (n 2) 16 –17.

17 Guihot and Bennett Moses (n 14) 23.

18 Kevin P Murphy, *Machine Learning: A Probabilistic Perspective* (MIT Press, 2012) 1.

19 Clarke, Roger, 'Why the world wants controls over Artificial Intelligence' (2019) 35 *Computer Law and Security Review* 423, 428 and Table 2. See also Kalev Leetaru, 'A Reminder that Machine Learning is About Correlations not Causation' *Forbes* (15 January 2019) <https://www.forbes.com/sites/kalevleetaru/2019/01/15/a

The advancements in AI technology bring about a paradigm shift. ML offers tools allowing for data analysis which are unprecedented in terms of their potential for managing large quantities of data and uncovering new correlations and trends difficult or impossible for humans to discover. Furthermore, the models now, as opposed to traditional, statistical ML, work with unstructured data, having capability to process high volumes and variety of data to produce a wide range of inferences, in particular about individuals.

Big Data

The AI models described are able to process 'data with high volume, velocity and/or variety', ie Big Data.[20] The volume of Big Data is significant, usually in excess of terabytes, and is continuously expanding.[21] 'Velocity' describes dynamic data generation, creation and modification requiring high processing speeds.[22] 'Variety' of data 'refers to the fact that data will not all lie within a single database architecture'[23] and includes 'large volumes of structured and unstructured data [held] in different formats from which insights may be drawn'.[24] For example, it is possible to link different forms of data such as images, text, audio and video files, and numbers.[25]

2.2. *Use of AI and Big Data in Retail Financial Services*

The properties of the technologies described promise important beneficial capabilities for the industry. The technology uptake within the industry is growing, with new FinTech market entrants quite literally enabled by the

---

-reminder-that-machine-learning-is-about-correlations-not-causation/?sh=5f2b93d66161> accessed 26 May 2021.

20 Guihot and Bennett Moses (n 14) 9, citing Rob Kitchin, *The Data Revolution: Big Data, Open Data, Data Infrastructures and Their Consequences* (Sage Publication Ltd, 2014) 68.

21 Terabyte is 2^{40} bytes, see OECD (n 11) 10; Rob Kitchin and Gavin McArdle, 'What makes Big Data, Big Data? Exploring the ontological characteristics of 26 datasets' (2010) Jan-Jun *Big Data and Society* 1, 6.

22 Guihot and Bennett Moses (n 14) 76.

23 ibid 9.

24 ibid.

25 Kitchin (n 20) 77.

technological advancements, and more traditional incumbents, including banks and insurers, quickly catching up.[26]

Due to 'entrenched corporate secrecy practices and a consequential lack of transparency',[27] some of the data practices and harms mentioned in this chapter are as yet unconfirmed in a financial services context. Also, some of the examples are likely to be much less complex than the reality. The corporate secrecy around AI models and data used by financial firms makes it even more challenging for policymakers and regulators to adequately address emerging issues, including potential consumer harms.

Surveys indicate the great majority (85 %) of financial services firms, including banks, investment firms and insurers, use some forms of AI.[28] Financial services, as a data-rich industry, benefit from a wide variety of applications of the technology. Our focus in this chapter is the automated decision-making affecting consumers. It is already considered a standard practice to use Big Data analytics for consumer credit scoring and lending.[29] Emerging evidence also suggests insurers are increasingly engaging in using ML models for underwriting of contracts.[30]

2.3. (Concerning) Characteristics of the Technologies

AI (in particular ML tools) used in Big Data analytics often presents certain characteristics that can be concerning, especially in the context of decision-making processes affecting consumers of financial services. The most relevant issues for our discussion are the opacity of ML models and the potentially inaccurate inferences they produce.

Opacity

The *opacity* (or lack of *transparency*) of many AI and Big Data processes has attracted significant attention. This attention arises particularly in contexts

26 CCAF (n 2) 11.

27 Kayleen Manwaring, 'Will emerging information technologies outpace consumer protection law? The case of digital consumer manipulation' (2018) 26 *Competition and Consumer Law Journal* 141, 180.

28 CCAF (n 2) 25.

29 Blumberg and others (n 3).

30 European Insurance and Occupational Pensions Authority (EIOPA), 'Big Data Analytics in Motor and Health Insurance: A Thematic Review' (Report, 2019) 29–41.

where those processes are used to make decisions resulting in social consequences, such as a decision to grant a loan or insurance. Three types of opacity seen in AI models can be distinguished:[31]

1. an opacity resulting from deliberate corporate secrecy, for reasons such as protecting trade secrets, limiting 'gaming', and avoiding scrutiny and/or regulation of dubious activities;[32]
2. 'technical illiteracy', as most people lack specialist skills required to understand algorithmic design; and
3. opacity due to complexity arising out of:
   (a) multi-component systems; and
   (b) interplay between large datasets and the way the model processes data: complex ML models are notable for the difficulty or even impossibility to understand why a decision was made, or outcome arrived at, even by the original programmer.[33]

(In)accuracy of Inferred Information

ML models have been shown to be capable of inferring things such as a person's sexual orientation from their face photos,[34] or a person's suicidal tendencies from their posts on Twitter.[35] However, a question arises as to accuracy of such predictions. Models operate on correlations between input data and target variables, rather than confirming a causal relationship between them.[36] Consequently, where certain features of a person or their behaviour *correlate* statistically with a ML model's desired outcome, this

31 Jenna Burrell, 'How the Machine "Thinks": Understanding Opacity in Machine Learning Algorithms' (2016) 3 *Big Data & Society* 1, 3–5.

32 See Frank Pasquale, *The Black Box Society: The Secret Algorithms That Control Money and Information* (Harvard University Press, 2015).

33 Eg the Deep Patient ML system was able to come to accurate predictions of schizophrenia in patients, but the developers have admitted they do not understand how it arrives at its predictions. Will Knight, 'The Dark Secret at the Heart of AI' (2017) 120 *MIT Technology Review* 54, 57.

34 Yilun Wang and Michal Kosinski, 'Deep Neural Networks Are More Accurate Than Humans at Detecting Sexual Orientation from Facial Images' *OSF* (Research Project, updated 26 May 2020) <https://osf.io/zn79k/>.

35 Bridianne O'Dea and others, 'Detecting Suicidality on Twitter' (2015) 2 *Internet Interventions* 183.

36 Anya E. R. Prince and Daniel Schwarcz, 'Proxy Discrimination in the Age of Artificial Intelligence and Big Data' (2020) 105 *Iowa Law Review* 1257, 1263–64.

does not mean the outcome is correct for a specific individual. Accuracy is also heavily dependent on training data provided.[37]

3. Challenges to Financial Law and Regulation

3.1. Overview of Potential Consumer Harms

AI and Big Data technologies used in automated decision-making in the context of retail financial services may lead to consumer harm. Several reasons for this can be identified. First, harm may partly stem from characteristics of the technology discussed, such as opacity and unreliable inferences. Second, new technologies are opening doors to new possibilities in terms of financial products being offered, especially personalised products, which may affect consumers in negative ways. Third, use of technologies and the promised benefits incentivises wide-reaching collection of consumers' data by financial firms, which again may (potentially) have negative consequences for consumers. We discuss specific instances of consumer harm below.

Various areas of law and regulation can potentially address some harms. In many cases current rules, when applied to factual scenarios arising in the context of the use of AI and Big Data analytics, should provide a high level of consumer protection. Areas of potential relevance include:

- financial services law, applying to consumer contracts such as banking contracts, insurance, investment contracts, and especially rules requiring consumer-centric approaches to design, advertising and selling of financial products;
- consumer protection rules, especially rules:
  - introducing fairness standards for treatment of consumers, either generally, or specifically in the financial services context (including concepts such as 'good faith' and 'utmost good faith', 'fair dealing', 'fairness', etc);
  - protecting consumers from unfair commercial practices, misleading conduct, and related concepts;
  - related to consumer contracts in general, including formation, information duties, withdrawal or termination, online contracting;

37 Guihot and Bennett Moses (n 14) 31-41.

- privacy and data protection rules, including rules aimed at providing consumers with information and control over automated processing of their data;
- anti-discrimination laws, relevant to provision of financial services to consumers.

Sometimes, however, current law and regulation may be inadequate in addressing some potential harms. There are two reasons for this. First, it may be because use of new technologies exacerbates issues arising previously or independently from technology use. For instance, if financial services firms have already been engaged in misconduct harming consumers,[38] either by breaking the law or taking advantage of legal loopholes, there are reasons to believe they will continue doing so, especially where technology makes such conduct easier to hide, cheaper, or more efficient. The examples discussed below, in particular regarding algorithmic bias and discrimination, and excessive data collection, provide useful illustrations.

Second, use of this technology by the financial services industry can also bring about new challenges for consumer protection legal frameworks. For example, certain uses of technology can enable firms to manipulate consumers more efficiently and in new ways. It can also provide means to personalise financial services to a point not possible before. Although this may benefit some consumers on price or terms, others may find themselves totally excluded from accessing financial services such as insurance or bank loans.

3.2. Algorithmic Bias and Discrimination

A concern often raised in the context of AI tools being used for decision-making is the possibility of algorithmic bias and resulting discrimination.[39] Discrimination in provision of financial services is not strictly related to the use of AI models. It is actually an 'old' problem,[40] but it can potenti-

---

38 Systemic misconduct of financial services firms towards consumers has been evidenced, eg, in Australia, see Royal Commission into Misconduct in the Banking, Superannuation and Financial Services Industry, 'Final Report' (1 February 2019).

39 Centre for Data Ethics and Innovation (CDEI), 'Review into Bias in Algorithmic Decision-Making' (Report, November 2020) 21; Eirini Ntoutsi and others, 'Bias in Data-Driven Artificial Intelligence Systems: An Introductory Survey' [2020] *WIREs Data Mining and Knowledge Discovery* 1, 2.

40 See eg practices such as 'redlining': Robert Barlett and others, 'Consumer-Lending Discrimination in the FinTech Era' (2019) National Bureau of Economic

ally be *exacerbated* through use of new technologies.[41] With the increasing volume of data held by financial services firms, rapid technological advancements and promised benefits, more and more consumers may become affected.[42]

Algorithmic bias can result from perpetuating human biases embedded in datasets used for training and testing of models.[43] For example, historically women were underrepresented in banks' clients bases. Men would traditionally be the income earners, consequently using bank services such as loans. A ML model trained on such historic data could therefore learn that more loans, with lower default risk, were granted to men, and then reproduce this in its outcomes.

Use of AI models may also lead to creating new biases. Even where a 'protected attribute' under discrimination law has been removed from an automated decision-making algorithm, where the attribute correlates with a particular risk on historical data, AI-enabled tools may nevertheless find proxies for this protected attribute, and outcomes will be based on these proxies.[44] These may be more difficult to discover than decisions based directly on the protected attribute. For example, if data processed by an AI model discovered a correlation that people with a commonly protected attribute, such as a disability, were more likely to default on a loan, the model may base its decisions on the *proxies* for disability found in the dataset. These could be very diverse information items, such as

---

Research Working Paper 25943, 5 <https://www.nber.org/papers/w25943>, and 'cherry-picking' and 'lemon-dropping': Marshall Allen, 'Health Insurers Are Vacuuming Up Details About You: And It Could Raise Your Rates', *NPR* (17 July 2018) <https://www.npr.org/sections/health-shots/2018/07/17/629441555/health-insurers-are-vacuuming-up-details-about-you-and-it-could-raise-your-rates> accessed 26 May 2021.

41 Australian Human Rights Commission (AHRC), 'Using Artificial Intelligence to Make Decisions: Addressing the Problem of Algorithmic Bias' (Technical Paper, 2020) 26, 31, 40; Prince and Schwarcz (n 36) 1267–68; CDEI (n 39) 7; Frederik J. Zuiderveen Borgesius, 'Strengthening Legal Protection Against Discrimination by Algorithms and Artificial Intelligence' (2020) 24(10) *The International Journal of Human Rights* 1572, 1577; Ntoutsi and others (n 39) 9.

42 CDEI (n 39) 24.

43 AHRC (n 411) Scenarios 2 and 3.

44 ibid 32; Prince and Schwarcz (n 36) 1273.

membership in certain Facebook groups,[45] grocery shopping history,[46] or Google search history.

The risk of algorithmic bias is exacerbated by lack of reliable datasets for training and testing of models. Ironically, this derives in part from operation of data protection rules requiring anonymisation or de-identification of data to protect individual identity.[47] This often results in sensitive or protected attributes, such as gender-, health-, or ethnicity-related data being removed, which means bias may become unmeasurable.[48]

However, two considerations need to be made. First, some form of discrimination, and especially indirect discrimination,[49] will almost always exist in any decision-making procedure,[50] including automated decision-making. Second, some types of discrimination are not always unlawful, due to exemptions for industries such as insurance.

3.3. Excessive Data Collection

There is growing evidence that various organisations, including financial services firms, are obtaining consumers' data from external sources.[51] Such

---

45 Moana Mononoke and Fred Trotter, 'Strict Inclusion Closed Group Reverse Lookup (SICGRL) Attack', *Missing Facebook Patient Consent* (Report, 16 February 2019) <https://missingconsent.org/downloads/SicGRL_initial_report.pdf>.

46 See eg observations made in Australian Competition and Consumer Commission, 'Customer Loyalty Schemes' (Final Report, December 2019) 45ff.

47 Christine M O'Keefe and others, 'The De-Identification Decision-Making Framework' (CSIRO Data61 Report, 18 September 2017) 18–20.

48 This is a very real-life problem, as the example of Onfido, a company providing remote biometric identity verification technology for banks, demonstrates: Information Commissioner's Office UK, 'Regulatory Sandbox Final Report: Onfido' (A summary of Onfido's participation in the ICO's Regulatory Sandbox Beta, September 2020).

49 Which is when a seemingly neutral rule leads to discriminatory outcomes, see eg European Court of Human Rights, 'Guide on Article 14 of the Convention (Prohibition of Discrimination) and on Article 1 of Protocol No. 12 (General Prohibition of Discrimination)' (Report, updated 31 December 2020) 11–12.

50 And especially in processes such as underwriting of insurance, Anti-Discrimination Working Group of the Actuaries Institute, 'The Australian Anti-Discrimination Acts: Information and Practical Suggestions for Actuaries' (Paper Presented to the Actuaries Institute 20/20 All-Actuaries Virtual Summit, 3-28 August 2020) 28.

51 See eg Mohammed Aaser and Doug McElhaney, 'Harnessing the Power of External Data', *McKinsey Technology* (3 February 2021) <https://www.mckinsey.com/business-functions/mckinsey-digital/our-insights/harnessing-the-power-of-external-data> accessed 26 May 2021.

external sources may include, for example, consumers' social media, Internet browsing history, website cookies, retail loyalty schemes, credit cards, smartphone applications, wearable devices, connected cars, smart home devices, voice assistants such as Alexa – the list is potentially endless. Financial firms may directly engage in collection of such data, which includes practices such as sharing of data between various entities belonging to the same company group or aggregating and repurposing information collected previously. They may also purchase consumers' data from data brokers.[52]

The financial services industry has always been concerned with data analytics and statistics, and it has quickly adopted the new technologies. AI models need huge amounts of data to work, as they become increasingly accurate with more training and testing data available. The reverse is also true: AI models provide means to analyse massive amounts of data and create value for corporations.

Such large-scale data collection presents important challenges for privacy and data protection regimes. Various questions arise, such as:

- how consumers' data should be collected;
- to what extent consumers should be able to control what happens to their data;
- whether sharing of personal data can be a condition of access to services; and
- how re-identification of data should be treated.

These issues, already of concern in online advertising,[53] are becoming increasingly relevant in the context of financial services.

Data collection from external sources also raises ethical questions. AI tools make it possible to analyse data without an easily identified link to customer's financial value, such as peoples' lifestyles, hobbies, and behaviours.[54] They may infer, and thus reveal, facts that individuals would prefer to keep private, for example their sexual orientation,[55] mental health

52 Wolfie Christl, 'Corporate Surveillance in Everyday Life: How Companies Collect, Combine, Analyze,
Trade, and Use Personal Data on Billions' (Report by Cracked Labs, Vienna, June 2017).

53 See eg Forbrukerrådet, 'Out of Control: How Consumers Are Exploited by the Online Advertising Industry' (Report, 14 January 2020).

54 Allen (n 40).

55 See Wang and Kosinski (n 34).

issues,[56] or pregnancy.[57] Finally, abundant data collection potentially exposes the data, including inferences, to cyber security breaches.[58]

3.4. Digital Consumer Manipulation

There is a concern that increasing use of AI and Big Data tools will support a significantly increased capacity not only to discover consumer preferences, but also to use data combined with insights from behavioural research to *exploit* consumer vulnerabilities, emotions and individual cognitive biases for commercial benefit. This type of 'digital consumer manipulation'[59] may be used to manipulate consumers to buy particular products or services, hand over additional data, pay higher prices or recommend particular brands to other consumers.

In a financial services context, digital consumer manipulation may take the form of 'margin optimisation', a 'process where firms adapt the margins they aim to earn on individual consumers'.[60] Reviews of EU, UK and US insurance firms' practices demonstrated how, when setting prices, firms may look at a consumer's willingness to pay based on their personal characteristics gained from the insights that external data provides.[61] The use of data analytics means that the firms, instead of taking into account the cost a consumer generates for the firm, examine the consumer's price sensitivity and propensity to switch to a different product. This may be inferred by an AI model from, eg, the analysis of consumers' behaviour on a website or app controlled by the financial firm, the time an individual spends reading terms and conditions, or websites visited before applying

56 See O'Dea and others (n 35).

57 Brigid Richmond, 'A Day in the Life of Data: Removing the opacity surrounding the data collection, sharing and use environment in Australia' (Consumer Policy Research Centre Report, 2019) 34 describes how US retailer Target inferred a customer's pregnancy based on shopping history and sent them pregnancy- and baby-related advertising and products.

58 Kayleen Manwaring and Pamela Hanrahan, 'BEARing responsibility for cyber security in Australian financial institutions: The rising tide of directors' personal liability' (2019) 30 *Journal of Banking and Finance Law and Practice* 20, 25.

59 Manwaring, 'Will emerging information technologies outpace consumer protection law?' (n 27). See also Ryan Calo, 'Digital Market Manipulation' (2014) 82 *George Washington Law Review* 995.

60 Financial Conduct Authority UK, 'General Insurance Pricing Practices: Interim Report' (Market Study MS18/1.2, October 2019) 21.

61 ibid, EIOPA (n 30) 12, 39.

for (or enquiring about) a financial product. This type of conduct by financial firms is particularly concerning for regulators, as it may amount to unfair pricing or unfair commercial practices in some jurisdictions.[62]

3.5. Personalisation of Financial Services

Personalisation of financial services is hailed as one of the main benefits, both to consumers and financial firms, that advancements in data analytics can provide, as consumers will be offered products tailored to their needs.[63] However, for 'lower value' customers, it may create additional difficulty in accessing financial services.

Consumer insurance contracts provide a useful example. Greater granularity and availability of data, paired with means to analyse it, translates into a possibility of individualised risk assessment of prospective insureds. In voluntary lines of insurance, this in turn may lead to a situation in which insurance firms will only offer insurance to consumers who present very low risk and exclude those who may potentially generate higher costs.[64] However, these excluded customers may be in most need of insurance. Similar scenarios could occur in context of other financial services, such as loans, as consumers who need the loan most, will be least likely to have it granted.

Clearly, a delicate balance must be struck with rules relative to responsible lending or, more generally, provision of fit-for-purpose financial services for consumers. The problem, however, lies in the fact that using AI and Big Data tools may bring about such granular assessment of individuals, that affordability of financial services offered to them, and ultimately their access to financing, investment, and insurance, may be inappropriately limited. What makes this potentially worse is when the automated decision-making process is opaque and possibly discriminatory or based on inaccurate inferences produced by an AI model.

---

62 ibid.

63 CCAF (n 2) 32.

64 EIOPA (n 30) 30; Financial Conduct Authority UK, 'Sector Views' (Report, 2020) 35.

4. Conclusions

Sociotechnical change does not arise in a regulatory vacuum, so much of it will be regulated under current rules. Legislative overreaction to sociotechnical change runs the risk of restricting beneficial innovation. Nevertheless, some rules in the new context may be under- or over- inclusive, uncertain, or sometimes the change is so truly new that it may amount to an unregulated 'new harm'.[65] Therefore any legal and regulatory framework should allow and promote courts, legislators and other rulemakers to be both swift and flexible in their responses to sociotechnical change, particularly in development and application of legal rules,[66] and the provision of accessible opportunities for consumer redress. Rules that aim to prevent consumer harm in a traditional setting should be interpreted, as much as possible, to achieve that rationale in a new sociotechnical reality.

Some of the harms discussed may not be intentional. For example, algorithmic bias and resulting discrimination may be difficult to discover due to ML opacity and be unintended by well-meaning financial services firms using AI and Big Data tools. This lack of intention may or may not have legal consequences, depending on the context and relevant legal system and applicable rules. For example, the law may impose specific consequences when harm is inflicted knowingly, or with an intention to profit from, and a disregard for the interests of, affected individuals. However, intention in some cases may be irrelevant. Therefore, financial services firms must be particularly diligent in implementing these technologies to avoid situations in which consumer harms may arise.

Use of emerging technologies brings about a risk of various harms to consumers. These harms are especially concerning in the context of retail financial services, where discrimination and digital manipulation may result in financial exclusion, disproportionately affecting already disadvantaged and vulnerable consumers. As AI and Big Data tools bring significant gains to financial firms, expectations of their conduct and the fairness of decision-making processes they implement increase.

The digital transformation of financial services, including the use of advanced AI and Big Data tools is here to stay. Policymakers, regulators and courts, in addition to industry bodies and associations, need to be

65 Lyria Bennett Moses, 'Recurring Dilemmas: The Law's Race to Keep Up with Technological Change' (2007) 2 *University of Illinois Journal of Law, Technology & Policy* 239, 269.

66 Manwaring, 'Will emerging information technologies outpace consumer protection law?' (n 27).

ready to deliver a legal and regulatory framework that is fit for purpose, and allows both financial firms and consumers to reap the benefits of the technological revolution.

New Technologies as Exclusion Instrument in the Social Security System. The Brazilian Covid-19 Pandemic Case

Renato Bernardi <bernardi@uenp.edu.br>

Heloísa Pancotti <hpancotti@gmail.com>
JACAREZINHO (Parana), Brasil

Abstract
The covid pandemic 19 had negative effects worldwide, however, the Brazilian case, among many others, was marked by errors and by the way technology ended up promoting the exclusion of the poorest portion of the population from government benefits for income maintenance. Some Brazilian particularities need to be highlighted, such as the fact that the right to connect is not yet seen as a fundamental right. Likewise, an administrative policy of budgetary restrictions related to investments in social security - which in Brazil encompasses health, assistance and social security - promoted the dismantling of a structure that had been consolidated for years and that supported social development. The article intends to study the phenomenon that arose at a time when access to benefits capable of ensuring income were made available only digitally, due to the need for social distance, to a population marked by increasing in poverty rates and with a considerable portion of the population in a situation of food insecurity, having an opposite effect to what was intended.

Keywords:
Technology, Pandemic, Social Security Benefits.

Introduction

Brazil´s population is very diverse and marked by very long-term standards of inequality. As result, digital inclusion still challenges effectiveness of a public policies. In the past, though up providing access to new technologies should be enough to increase social inclusion, but as Covid pandemic reached the country, urging social security system to create distributive policies to fight hungry and unemployment, it became very clear that is no simple solution to urgent national risks in informational societies of underdeveloped countries.

Social security in Brazil has been neglected and suppressed by an increasing alignment with neoliberal interests, to the detriment of the late welfarist national understanding. Access to some benefits has been hindered by successive legal modification.

In the other hand, the necessity to create ways of provide attendance with social distance, accelerated deployment of new technologies that enabled access to social programs through data crossing, facial and digital recognition.

However, poor Brazilian population- goodwill`s policies customer- due to low schooling and familiarity to technological tools, failed to access programs and formed endless lines in front of bank offices searching of redeeming amounts made available by the government.

As result, poor citizens were exposed to greater risks of contamination and faced grater difficulties to receive government emergencies income, increasing the already huge gap between economically active and vulnerable citizens.

Brazilian social security failed to protect because its vulnerable population has no ways of accessing new technologies and it´s been used as instrument for suppression of constitutionally guaranteed state obligations.

It seems very clear that the use of new technology to provide access to public policies must be made in addition to a strong instrumentalization and training population on how to operate this, something unthinkable for highly developed countries with lower social inequality patterns.

For better observation of this particular case, which seems to reveal that new technologies can be instrument of exclusion in inequality societies, if poorly inserted in certain contexts, especially on public policies issues, is important to analyze some social contexts.

Thus, from some structuring axes, the socio-political context, the social security prism, the first challenge to the global social security systems - Covid 19 and what it revealed, the social economic markers and the number of precarious workers, the virtual inclusion in Brazil, this paper search to explain what went so wrong to the point of presenting the reverse result of what was intended in Brazilian model of using technological instruments to protect vulnerable population.

The methodological path followed is also a timeline, in which the contexts from the structuring axes intertwine, allowing to understand structural failures to improve the use of technology in future policies.

From the analysis of official surveys that measure inequality and income in opposition to the requirements for emergency benefits to face the social risk of the pandemic, it was possible to verify that the virtual inclusion is still a challenge in countries that are still struggling to fight poverty and hunger as Brazil.

In a state struggling with severe budgetary restrictions for investments in this area, due to the issuance of a constitutional amendment that plastered investments for the sector, based on a beckian reading of contingency of modern risks, the study points to the need to resume investments in education and social promotion, under the risk that the technological instrumentalization of public policies ends up digging an even greater gap between the economically active and vulnerable population, increasing exclusion and creating a legion of subordinate citizens, without government protection.

1.1 The social political context.

As the word faces your worst enemy in the twenty first century, COVID 19 pandemic, nations are trying to help they´re citizens thru the difficulty. People were put to work home and, at the beginning, one thing seem to be very clear in our national reality: some workers can`t adapt themselves to the new scenario. In Brazil, it became very clear real fast, revealing the urgency to rethink the Brazilian educational system, to adapt the very archaic model and incorporate new technologies.

Some sectors in which there is a concentration of individuals with longer schooling, such as the judiciary, which had been incorporating technology in routine for a long time, managed to properly adapt itself, after a brief interruption of services, existing in virtual environment, ensuring maintenance of jurisdictional activity.

On the other hand, pandemic revealed an enormous contingent of workers unable of adapt to adverse situations. They´re mostly under educated citizens, product of public education deterioration, schooling dropout, facing great difficulty in maintaining their jobs and guaranteeing income. To the members of this working class, manual workers and in non-intellectualized activities, technology represents an additional obstacle.

By this time, is still uncertain predict when and if things will be back from pre pandemic times in the work system, and if it will be.

Since the end of the second half of the twenty century, in the late 80´s, is expected that labor will evolute to two very distinct kinds of work.

The first one, patronized, attaches to old pillars that is the company in which the worker are switched on the place where labor happens, profession and the wage work.[1]

The second one was very close to what we know today as the precary workers, the apps workers, known in Brazil as "trabalhadores uberizados", something like "uberizated workers" in a free translate of the terminology.

In modern capitalized world, the second group is expected to grow and swallow the first, because the flexibility of the pillars which sustained the work was also evoluting at technology evolution´s rhythm.

This, don´t have traditional guarantees as work environment protection, salary, health care, access to pensions and take themselves the risk of the economic activities.

Our social context hasn´t prepared workers to adapt to the rapidly increasing technological developments that operate mutations in the protective fabric and exposing protective weaknesses and economic vulnerabilities.

Un addiction, since 2016, we have experienced a constant decrease of registered workers and consequent increase of informal workers and "entrepreneurs[2]". It´s necessary to clarify that what Brazilian data calls éntrepreneurs is a very large group that reunites low-income workers who receive their wages as if they´re a company (pejotizados) and small and micro entrepreneurs with annual incomes not exceeding R$ 81.000,00[3] (USD 15.055,00) maximum in 2020.

Brazil couldn't deal with the old unemployment problem, so started to consider full employment this precary situations and threat as full protected workers, citizens in potential vulnerability situation and who, in any negative fluctuation in economic indexes, will need state intervention to maintain their subsistence.

So, when official research pointed to very high rates on unemployment[4] - 11,9 % by the end of 2019 - we are referring to unsuitable workers, people

---

1 Ulrich Beck, '*Sociedade de Risco, Rumo a uma outra modernidade*'. (Editora 34, 2010) 206.

2 Instituto Brasileiro de Geografia e Estatística-IBGE, 'Síntese de Indicadores Sociais. Uma análise das condições de vida da população brasileira'(IBGE, 2020) <https://biblioteca.ibge.gov.br/visualizacao/livros/liv101760.pdf> accessed 21 January 2021.

3 In January, 21, 2021 R$ 81.000,00 equals USD 15.055,76.

4 Marcelo Silva and Elaine C. F Volpato, 'Trabalho escravo contemporâneo e a Pandemia SARS-COV2: Reflexões sobre o Biopoder, A Biopolítica e a Necropolítica' (2020) 14 CDA 256 <http://www.cadernosdedereitoactual.es/ojs/index.php/cadernos/article/view/561/307> accessed 2 January 2021.

without ability to work, who need capacitation and couldn´t adapt to technological transformation ongoing in labor work. This people, for lack of a better policy, make up a large contingent of served by social assistance program, which distributes income to the vulnerable population considered unable to work.

In addition to this mass, all other low-income workers are added, outside norms of labor protection and which have guarantees against unemployment. In general, it is possible to stablish that this social group have low levels of education, great difficulties adapting to incorporate new technologies into everyday life.

In the same way, especially after 2016, year in which new forms of exercise of paid activity were regulated with less guarantees, there was a migration from the group of protected workers to the group of precarious workers[5].

Beck believes the unemployment problem could be fixed by the decrease rates of births, which could provide some stability in Europe[6].

But in inequality's countries, it´s not so simple. Brazil also experiences a decrease in the number of births; however, the age pyramid inversion has resulted in an actuarial problem for the social security system, which is structured in intergenerational solidarity and in the simple non-capitalized distribution system[7]. Government reacts with large changes in constitutional text that broke with the welfarist tradition and inaugurated rules that aim to decrease the participation of the State, relativizing rights, reducing and limiting investments in social rights, creating a state of unconstitutional affairs.

That´s the social political contexts when COVID 19 pandemic hit Brazil.

1.2 The social security context:

Brazilian´s social security system is based in solidarism and the whole society participation in the funding form. The collection base is broad,

---

5 In regard, it´s worth to mention the creation of the intermittent work contract, which regulated the workday without guaranteeing minimum hours, resulting in a drop in incomes.

6 Beck (n 3) 207.

7 Brasil, Ministério da Fazenda, 'Envelhecimento da população e Seguridade Social' (2018) 37 MF 8 <http://sa.previdencia.gov.br/site/2018/06/colprev37.pdf> accessed 2 January 2021.

ranging from social contributions to taxes levied on contests of forecasts and sale of assets captured by the courts and arising from criminal actions, such as drug trafficking.

In these terms, for the sustainability of this simple share social security system, with the exception only of what concerns social security, of a contributory nature and only accessible to its list of beneficiaries and dependents, it is extremely important to maintain constant economic and social development, increase in full employment, or at least, voluntary affiliation of precarious workers to the social security system through social inclusion programs.

The Federal Constitution of 1988, had incorporated in its text the fundamental social rights, being thus labor and social security that should be regulated through the intervention of the State, along the lines of that Welfare State outlined in the first half of the 20th century by William Beveridge.

The social security issue in Brazil is the major cause of legal disputes in all instances of Justice and it is umbilically linked to the achievement of an ideal of full employment that some theorists already predicted to be overcome even in the 1980s[8], since the flexibility and precariousness labor relations was already underway in much of the world and it was a matter of (little) time that it also spread here.

The wide financing network is what ensures that we have free public health care accessible to everyone on national soil and also what guarantees the population exposed to the situation of long-term vulnerability - which has been agreed to measure in two years here - a minimum income capable of guaranteeing subsistence.

Thus, it also incorporated the commitments assumed in international treaties, establishing its position in the world.[9]

The public policies to be developed by the State to bring about this state of social welfare pursued in national lands, gained the constitutional text, the basic principles being located in the fundamental guarantees and their organization throughout our long constitutional text, in the chapter on Security Social, Economic and Social Order, Social Security and sparse infra-constitutional legislation.

The intricate legal tangle, sometimes conflicting, that created several zones of opacity and exclusion, which segregate the beneficiaries of the

---

8 [10] Beck (n 3) 205.

9 Marco Aurélio Serau Junior, *Seguridade Social e Direitos Fundamentais* (4th edn, Editora Juruá, Curitiba 2020).

social security system into first- and second-class citizens, the first to be protected and the second not to.

When the first measures to support the population, whose income was suppressed by the restrictions on circulation, necessary to combat COVI-D19, were announced, the Brazilian social security implanted implanted an access system through data crossing, facial and digital recognition to request aid through mobile applications, tablets and virtual platforms.

As soon as the platforms were on, it became evident that as the public administration would make its service available exclusively remotely, di-sadvantaged citizens (those with the greatest need) would not have access to benefits. They were excluded. People in severe deprivations as people who live in streets, in areas not covered by connections services were simply ignored.

This is because the right to connection is not a homogeneous right in Brazil, it is only accessible to those who can pay for it. The community use of the internet is also carried out in person, whether in libraries, service stations or something similar.

This has not discouraged the public administration from adopting a progressive restructuring of the public service which, in some modalities, such as social security, is only accessible through the internet or telephone.

In fact, it is noticeable that the denial of access and the creation of what we call "social security limbo" has been used for the benefit of the public administration, as a way to lower the costs of social assistance in Brazil.

In a clear demonstration of this, in November 2019, there was a broad reform in the part of the Brazilian Constitution that deals with social security, through the approval of Constitutional Amendment 103/2019.

In this way, all benefits required before the social security agency, who-se policyholders had implemented access conditions as of November 12, 2019 should follow the new rules, however the social security platform only adapted to the new rules in April 2020[10]. In this *vacacio temporis*, no benefit subject to the new rules was granted whatsoever.

Another factor that remained evident is the educational deficit of the population that qualified to receive the benefit, since for many Brazilian citizens, the registration rules were incomprehensible.

---

10 Ana Paula Branco, 'Simulador do INSS volta a funcionar e adaptado à reforma da previdência' (Agora, 3 April 2020) <https://agora.folha.uol.com.br/grana/2020/04/simulador-do-inss-volta-a-funcionar-e-adaptado-a-reforma-da-previdencia.shtml> accessed 4 June 2020.

The worst factor, the one that the Brazilian Social Security did not count on, was the number of people who registered to receive the benefit called emergency aid, which consisted of an income of about 120 dollars a month for, in principle, three months.

More than 101 million people registered to request the payment of the benefit[11] and the processing capacity of the orders fell far short of people's needs.

Brazil has a population of about 209 million people, which means that around half believed they were in a poverty situation, or at list incapable to manage his own maintenance.

This is because the requirements for access to the benefit were outlined to serve the vulnerable population with a *per capta* income of half the minimum wage or total family income of up to about 3 minimum wages.

Thus, the result of the schizophrenic social security policy adopted which places one foot in neoliberalism and the other in welfarist state, coupled with the increasingly accentuated number of precarious workers, as seen in first topic, produced a nation of poor people.

Relaxation of employment protection rules, developed since 2016, the increase of info proletarians - those who exercise their activities through applications- generated an unprotected working class with low-incomes.

Deregulation of this type of activity encourages the evasion of social contributions from individual taxpayers, which would not happen if the employment relationship were recognized, since the retention of contributions would become mandatory. This policy results, was the spread of distrust and the judicialization of social rights which increased 140%[12]. It´s captured the CNJ- Conselho Nacional de Justiça- attention, because since 2011, INSS- Instituto Nacional do Seguro Social- is the major litigant of all Brazilian justice system[13].

---

11 Caixa Econômica Federal, 'Auxílio Emergencial clique aqui para ver os últimos números' <https://caixanoticias.caixa.gov.br/noticia/20795/auxilio-emergencial-clique-aqui-para-ver-os-ultimos-numeros> accessed 4 June 2021.

12 Luciana Otoni, 'Debate aborda dados preliminares sobre judiciaização da previdência' (Agência CNJ de notícias, 30 April 2021) <https://www.cnj.jus.br/debate-aborda-dados-preliminares-sobre-judicializacao-da-previdencia/> accessed 6 June 2020.

13 Luiza de Carvalho, 'INSS lidera numero de litígios na Justiça' (Agência CNj de notícias,31 March 2011)<https://www.cnj.jus.br/inss-lidera-numero-de-litigios-na-justica/> accessed 6 June 2020.

A study conducted by França[14] demonstrated this and warned of the malign effects that the suppression of social security benefits would cause in the national economy. Not to mention the creation of an almost insoluble problem for social security to fix: the poorest regions of the country, depends too much of social security money. In 70 % of Brazilian cities, the largest source of income comes from the benefits of social security.[15]

Some Brazilian cities would become unfeasible if the money injected by social security stopped flowing. So, it became commonplace in Brazil, therefore, to suppress the protection of social security, driven by the reproduction of the neoliberal discourse translated in a violent way against the population that these expenses could potentially break the country.[16]

To 1988 until 2015, it seems possible to coexist some welfare and neoliberalism practices, because the State had a visible commitment to the eradication of poverty and the distribution of incomes by programs like "Bolsa Familia", "Benefício de Prestação Continuada" among others, that have established standards of service to the poorest population, providing minimum income to the vulnerable people.

But as of 2015, with the start of the mass review and cancellation of assistance and social security benefits, the Brazilian paradox of defending a social welfare model and in the economy a neoliberal model, destabilized both, vulnerable people and economy.

The virtual environment was used, in addiction to standardizing restrictions to access, excluding the most marginal people, final recipients of income distribution programs.

1.3 *The first global risk to the social security system at the XXI century: What came up?*

The Covid 19 pandemic arrived in Brazil in the middle of this social security chaos, with newly structured programs at the federal level, as well

---

14 Álvaro Sólon de França, 'A Previdência Social e a Economia dos Municípios' (ANFIP, 2019) <https://www.anfip.org.br/wp-content/uploads/2019/04/2019-Economia-dos-munici%CC%81pios_b.pdf> accessed 7 June 2020.

15 Central Unica dos Trabalhadores, 'Municípios também serão afetados com a reforma da previdência' (Brasil de Fato e edição da Redação Spbancários, 7 February 2018) <https://spbancarios.com.br/02/2018/municipios-tambem-serao-afetados-com-reforma-da-previdencia> accessed 6 June 2020.

16 Lizandro Mello, 'Discurso de Ódio Neoliberal: o feitiço do malfare state' in José Ricardo Caetano Costa, Marco Aurélio Serau Junior and Hector Cury Soares (eds) *O "Estado de Mal-Estar Social" brasileiro* (Belo Horizonte, IEPREV, 2020)69.

as state programs in full restructuring - Brazil is a Federative Republic and each federated state enjoys autonomy to regulate related issues to the welfare of its employees - including rules related to the costing and actuarial balance of the entire system.

Generally, the modifications occurred to suppress access and benefits values, as we seen before in this paper.

To worsen, the already chaotic scenario, the social security system has a queue of requests to be examined that exceeds two million[17]digital requests and does not have the capacity to process in a timely manner, which leads to two obvious problems: a) a large number of beneficiaries it does not get access in an acceptable time, remaining outside the protection. b) frustrated, the beneficiaries seek justice to claim what the social security agency should have provided.

Fisty-five million people asked for emergency assistance, for an overloaded virtual system with an unacceptable delay. After processing the major part of the demands, some serious misunderstandings came up. For reason still not explained, the virtual data crossing has often failed, allocating emergency resources to a part of the population that wasn´t in the need.

The most important one, military forces workers received the emergencies benefit without even request it. They don´t have paychecks interrupted and don´t fit the legal hypothesis for granting. Till now it´s uncertain how it happened.

The defense ministry informed that more than seventy-three thousand military workers[18] irregularly received the benefit. The same happened with aleatory people, including the son of a very well-known and wealthy anchorman and a Brazilian billionaire entrepreneur. The Federal Audit Office - TCU determined the irregular pay had to be returned, without, however, determining the way of return or when it had to be done.

It´s clear, in the most challenging moment for the Brazilian's XXI century social security system, everything went wrong. The principle of distributivity, which guides the target of public policies, was not observed.

---

17 Jéssica Otoboni, 'Entenda o motivo das filas para a concessão de benefícios do INSS' (CNN, 14 March 2020) <https://www.cnnbrasil.com.br/nacional/2020/03/14/entenda-o-motivo-das-filas-para-a-concessao-de-beneficios-do-inss> accessed 6 June 2020.

18 'Bolsonaro diz que militares que receberam auxílio emergencial serão punidos' (UOL ECONOMIA, 14 May 2020) <https://economia.uol.com.br/noticias/redacao/2020/05/14/bolsonaro-diz-que-militares-que-receberam-auxilio-emergencial-serao-punidos.htm> accessed 6 June 2020.

Since 2019, when the virtual platform needed to be restructured, many difficulties presented themselves.

Incomprehensible applications, difficult data processing, access barriers, fraud and errors prevented resources from being used more efficiently. So, the most needed were excluded by this disastrous scenario of bad management.

In a nation of poor, precarious workers, needy people who didn´t have access to emergency benefits, it was very difficult to achieve adherence to the purposes of the Ministry of Health, to prevent as much as possible, circulation of people. Hungry and fearful for their incomes people, cannot afford to remain in seclusion.

It costs so many lives, and now[19] we faced more than 210.000 losses.

The strategy of seclusion and financial support to the population is not well regarded by the Federal Government, much more inclined to the neoliberal proposal, to protect the market at any cost, even human lives.

So, in the exponential growth of the number of lost lives in the pandemic, federal governments, state governments, city halls are all trying to reopen shops, fabrics, restaurants, schools as nothing happens. By the way, the favela´s population question is unique, since it is about fulfilling social distancing in small super habited spaces.

Harari[20] points out that there is no way to contain pandemic risk without restricting the movement of people, without quarantines. But the paralysis of cities, affects the local economies very strongly. Security in international cooperation is what would motivate the adoption of restrictive measures in a timely manner to avoid excessive mortality.

Brazilian case is indeed peculiar since it exposes new technologies offers to users, an extra power that distinguish them to those who can't afford it. In inequality societies, these individuals end up being gradually banned and made invisible. What actually happened was that the pandemic caused the need for adaptation and them was leaved behind. Had no longer access to essential incomes, public services, legal services and education. So, for the most vulnerable part of Brazilian population, the use of new technologies in the public services increased vulnerabilities, promoting exclusion and maximizing social problems.

---

19 Till January 21 th 2021, 212.831 people died.

20 Yuval Noah Harari, '*Na Batalha Contra o Coronavírus, Faltam líderes à humanidade*' (Companhia das Letras, 2020) 7.

It revealed the urgency to promote a serious debate on the essentiality of the right to connection, as well as digital inclusion in public education, a very distant reality to Brazilian's classrooms and its analog devices.

1.4 The digital inclusion challenge in Brazil

To trace the geography of digital inclusion in Brazil, professor Marta Arretche, holder of the Political Science Department at the University of São Paulo, published a study from the perspective of regional inequalities in the city of São Paulo- the major Brazilian city[21]. She found evidence to support the following hypothesis:

[...] the new digital technologies have revolutionized the economy, politics and knowledge production, on the other the speed of the expansion of its use would be marked by inequalities, due to the opportunities opened up by the digital world isn´t equally accessible to everyone.[22]

The digital world is capable to became different realities depending of the engagement of the use. Professor Arretche measured it, identifying the diversity of the activities carried out online. Two kinds of users came up. The first-class user, and the second-class user.

The first group had unlimited online activities, complexes online engagement. They receive widest opportunities to education and to economic activities, even civic participation. The second group is more associated with domestic broadband access, with cellphones and using social medias. They´re less connected with simple interaction with digital content and unable to do complex operations in virtual environment. For this group, internet can´t provide the same opportunities.

It reveals a stratification of users, a new component to make more complex distributive solutions in inequality societies.

As internet access depends of the broadband, devices and connections costs, is very plausible to suppose that low-income individuals had more difficulty to reach the same opportunities as those who can afford for it.

As a matter of fact, the overlap between stratification of the offline world and the online world, turning inequality ever worse. This can easily

21 Marta Arretche, `A geografia digital no Brasil: um panorama das desigualdades regionais´, in *Desigualdades digitais no espaço urbano: um estudo sobre o acesso e o uso da internet na cidade de São Paulo* (NIC.br, 2019)55-80 <https://cetic.br/media/docs/publicacoes/7/11454920191028-desigualdades_digitais_no_espaco_urbano.pdf> accessed 21 January 2021.

22 Marta Arretche, A geografia.... (2019, 60).

explain why a country with large internet coverage has so many citizens unable to access digitally available services.

In the Brazilian case, therefore, it is not true that the technologies have eliminated spatial barriers to the integration of individuals to economic opportunities and civic engagement that the place where you live affects opportunities for inclusion digital. In addition to the division between rural and urban areas that, in good measure, reveals genuinely physical barriers, the territorial inequalities in internet access and use are an expression the spatial concentration of low-income individuals, that is, not they are only physical, but also social and economic; in the case Brazil, the territorial inequalities of the offline world are still a strong predictor of inequalities in the online world.[23]

The urgency in making public policies to attend pandemic necessities caused a rupture in the face-to-face service model, segregating the access of the less favored from emergency services and policies, including emergencial income.

The digital difficulties of the most vulnerable population are the result of poverty, low income and educational deficit, indicators that Brazil has struggled to improve for decades.

In the current moment, in which the Brazilian state seeks to discharge its social obligations, as has been demonstrated in the previous items by the limitation of investments, the ideal digital inclusion, which provides broad access to the same quality of exploitation to the digital environment, is unthinkable.

The evolution, dissemination and use of new technologies will not be interrupted due to Brazilian difficulties, which projects for a future in which the overlaps of real and virtual stratification promise to increase social inequalities and income distribution.

Conclusions

The pandemic situation highlighted the importance of progressive social rights in times of crisis. Its slowdown in Brazil is reflecting on state's capacity to limit this social risk and the effect on the population.

Brazilian State faces an important budget constraint in order to offer the population the necessary income to face the moment of paralysis and restriction of movement and economic activity.

23 IDEM (2019, 60-61).

The post-modern context of our society revealed, as Ulrich Beck had predicted, a future of uncertainty, unpredictability, more flexible working relationships and an increase in social inequalities.

The greatest social risk of the 21st century has materialized globally, in the form of the COVID 19 pandemic, which required restrictive measures of freedom and the paralysis of economic activities.

At this time, social security systems were challenged and the State was faced with the need for intervention to guarantee the safety and well-being of its citizens.

The social security Brazilian model had been under intense deconstruction, simultaneously to a serious economic and political crisis that has been intensifying towards an authoritarian and ineffective model, unable to efficiently process even when emergency requirements presented.

As social detachment was initiated and essential services had to adapt themselves forcefully to the most advanced technologies to provide emergency and essential services, it ran into the digital access, which in Brazil, overlaps traditional models of social exclusion, virtually repeating them.

As a result, the most vulnerable were unable to access the available resources and, desperate, exposed themselves even more to the risks of contamination, crowding in search of face-to-face assistance, for lack of conditions to access the new technologies. In the Brazilian case in particular, the progressive adherence to new technologies without solving important obstacles to their equal incorporation into society, made it accelerate processes of exclusion, segregating social segments.

The Future of e-Voting. Some Remarks from the Perspective of the Polish Law

Beata Stępień-Załucka <beata@kpmz.pl>
RZESZÓW, Poland

Abstract
The life of modern man is different from that of twenty or even ten years ago. Over the Internet, we work, we talk, we do our shopping, we check our account balance, we pay, but we still do not vote, and yet elections are the basis of democracy. The introduction of Internet voting, especially in times of pandemics, has shown that it is our future. However, its introduction requires further obstacles to be overcome, both legal and technical. In this paper, I will present the legal requirements that e-voting would have to meet, from the perspective of the validity of the electoral principles contained in the Constitution. At the same time, I will present arguments indicating that the introduction of e-voting will not require amendments to the Constitution of the Republic of Poland, but only changes to the Electoral Code concerning the way of voting. In terms of the technical requirements that e-voting would have to meet, I will point to the problems and shortcomings revealed in the countries that have decided to introduce e-voting. Observing revealed errors and shortcomings in the operation of e-voting in other countries is a natural way to prevent them in Poland. Addressing these problems will allow us to avoid the mistakes that other countries introduction of e-voting.

1. Introduction

Elections are the foundation of democracy.[1] They allow the society to choose representatives who will exercise power on its behalf.

---

1 Joseph L. Hall, *Policy Mechanisms for Increasing Transparency in Electronic Voting*, (Barkeley 2008) 11 <https://josephhall.org/papers/jhall-phd.pdf> accessed 30 June 2021.

This process currently takes different forms, sometimes based on the traditional method of casting a vote on a piece of paper, or it reaches more innovative forms such as e-voting, which means electronic voting, which is a collective term for a form of voting using electronic means of communication. This can be divided into three types of voting: electronic visualization of voting results, electronically assisted voting (voting machines) and Internet voting, which, like the entire section, is also sometimes referred to as e-voting (or Internet voting, ivoting, e-voting: full, complete, proper). This type of voting is characterized by the fact that votes are cast remotely over the Internet, from any location, and are received and counted by a central computer election system. [2]

Nowadays, when the world faces a pandemic, it has become clear that the current form of voting, let's call it - paper-based, in the long run will require changes in the on-line direction. This direction raises questions firstly about the legal, social, technical requirements and secondly about the risks associated with its introduction.

In this article I will present the legal framework related to the possible introduction of e-voting in Poland and I will bring closer the problems faced by the countries that have already introduced e-voting, so that the possibly introduced form in Poland will contain technical answers to them. Their technical elimination will make it possible not to repeat the doubts and mistakes that have already been overcome or with which other countries are still struggling.

We must remember that e-voting is still associated with innovation, which is followed by new solutions, but also hitherto unknown problems, both legal and otherwise.

2 Beata Stępień-Załucka, 'E-voting. Sukces czy porażka na przykładzie Estonii i Szwajcarii' in Paweł Kuczma (ed) *Aktualne wyzwania demokracji partycypacyjnej w Polsce i na świecie* (Wydawnictwo Uczelni Jana Wyżykowskiego) 2017 244.

2. *Definition of e-voting*

E-voting[3] is a collective term for a form of voting that uses electronic means of communication.[4] This form of voting can be divided into three types of electronic voting:

- electronic visualization of voting results. In this form, computer systems play an auxiliary role in collecting and visualizing the results of voting conducted by traditional means;[5]
- electronically assisted voting, in which case computer systems are the main tool for receiving and counting votes. Votes are cast by voters in person at polling stations on specialized voting machines. [6]Such

3 I wrote more about that in: Beata Stępień-Załucka *E-voting a Konstytucja RP* in Jerzy Jaskiernia and Kamil Spryszak (eds) *Dwadzieścia lat obowiązywania Konstytucji RP. Polska myśl konstytucyjna a międzynarodowe standardy demokratyczne* (Wydawnictwo Adam Marszałek 2017) 223-225.

4 Andreu R. Jorba, Josè A. Ortega Ruiz and Paul Brown, 'Advanced Security to Enable Trustworthy Electronic Voting' (2003) Scytl Online World Security 2-3 <https://www.scytl.com/wp-content/uploads/2013/04/Advanced-Security-to-Enable-Trustworthy-Electronic-Voting.pdf> accessed 30 June2021]; Lilian Mitrou, 'Constitutional And Legal Requirements For Evoting' (2004) Electronic Voting Observatory II Votobit (Leon, 3-4.10.2004) 2 ff. <http://www.Icsd.Aegean.Gr/Website_Files/Metaptyxiako/65983061.Pdf> accessed 30 June2021; Lelia Barlow, *An Introduction to Electronic Voting*, 2003, 2-13 <http://citeseerx.ist.psu.edu/viewdoc/download?doi=10.1.1.136.2993&rep=rep1&type=pdf> accessed 30 Jue 2021.

5 International Idea. International Institute for Democracy and Electoral Assistance: Peter Wolf, Rushdi Nackerdien and Domenico Tuccinardi, *Introducing Electronic Voting: Essential Considerations* (IDEA 2011) 7<http://www.idea.int/publications/introducing-electronic-voting/upload/PP_e-voting.pdf> accessed 30. June 2021.

6 Barbara Simons, 'Electronic Voting Systems: the Good, the Bad, and the Stupid' (2004) 2, 7 QUEUE 3-11.
<http://www.openvotingconsortium.org/files/voting_good_bad_stupid.pdf> accessed 30 June2021.More about that, Ben Goldsmith and Holly Ruthrauff, 'Chapter 2.3: Implementing Electronic Voting or Electronic Counting in an Election Lead' in NDI and IFES, *Implementing and Overseeing Electronic Voting and Counting Technologies* (2013) 36 ff. <https://www.ndi.org/files/2.3.pdf> accessed 30 June 2021. IFES, 'Electronic Voting Machines (EVMs), „Pakistan Factsheet'(IFES, 2014) 1-5, <https://www.ifes.org/sites/default/files/electronic_voting_machines.pdf> accessed 30 June 2021.

a system can be found in Australia, Brazil, Canada, France,[7] India,[8] Japan, Kazakhstan,[9]Peru, Russia, the United States, the United Arab Emirates and Venezuela;[10]

- voting via the Internet (due to the fact that it is currently the most complete form of electronic voting available, it is also generally referred to as -ivoting, e-voting, e-voting proper, full, complete, Internet voting). This type of voting occurs when votes are cast remotely from any location via the Internet[11] and are received and counted by a central computerized election system.[12] This is the case in Estonia and Switzerland,[13] for example, and a number of countries have non-binding plans, with varying degrees of progress, to implement it. Among them are Argentina, Azerbaijan, Belarus, Bulgaria, Chile, Czech Republic, Finland, Greece, Italy, Latvia, Lithuania, Mexico, Nepal, Nigeria, Norway, Portugal, Romania, Slovakia, Slovenia, South Africa, Spain, South Korea and Sweden.[14]The diffusion of Internet voting is currently growing fastest in Canada and Norway.[15] It is also worth nothing that while some countries are planning to implement e-voting, others, for

---

7 Jordi B. Esteve, Ben Goldsmith and John Turner, 'International Experience with E-Voting. Norwegian E-Vote Project' (IFES, 2012) 12 <https://www.parliament.uk/documents/speaker/digital-democracy/IFESIVreport.pdf> accessed 30June 2021.

8 ScottWolchok, Eric Wustrow, J. Alex Halderman, Hari K. Prasad, Arun Kankipati, Sai Krishna Sakhamuri, Vasaya Yagati and Rop Gonggrijp, 'Security Analysis of India's Electronic Voting Machines' (2010) CCS . 1-14, <https://jhalderm.com/pub/papers/evm-ccs10.pdf> accessed 30June 2021.

9 Douglas W. Jones, 'Kazakhstan: The Sailau E-Voting System' in Michael Yard (ed) *Direct Democracy: Progress and Pitfalls of Election Technology* 4-6 <http://homepage.cs.uiowa.edu/~jones/voting/IFESkazakhstan.pdf> accessed 30 June 2021.

10 The Electoral Knowledge Network, 'E-voting' <http://aceproject.org/ace-en/focus/e-voting/countries> accessed 30 June 2021.

11 Andrzej Kisielewicz, Komentarz do art. 2 Kodeksu wyborczegoin Kazimierz W. Czaplicki, Bogusław Dauter and others, *Kodeks wyborczy Komentarz LEX* (Wolters Kluwer 2014) 22.

12 Kazimierz W. Czaplicki, 'Alternatywne sposoby głosowania. (Zarys problemów)' in Sabina Grabowska and Radosław Grabowski (eds) *Międzynarodowa konferencja naukowa. Alternatywne sposoby głosowania a aktywizacja elektoratu. Rzeszów 26-27 marca 2007 r.*, 29.

13 The Electoral Knowledge Network, *E-Voting*, <http://aceproject.org/ace-en/focus/e-voting/countries>, [Access by day 30.06. 2021].

14 ibid.

15 Alexander H Trechsel, *Can introducing the internet as a means of casting votes lead to distortions in the political sphere? How neutral is this new technology?* Seminarium from 4th February 2013, described by Rosie Scammell, 'Internet voting a success in two European countries' (European University Institute, 12 February 2013)

various reasons, are at the stage of stopping projects of its implementation. These include Germany, Ireland, the Netherlands and the United Kingdom.[16] And it is this type of voting that will be the subject of further consideration.

3. *Standards and regulations that e-voting has to face*

The answer to the question, which is the title of the subsection, is contained in H. Kelsen's pyramid. According to its idea, all legal acts must be consistent with the highest one - the Constitution.[17] In this case, it is important to note that the Constitution of the Republic of Poland does not indicate the form of conducting elections. E-voting as a method of voting would be determined at the level of the election code, i.e. the law. Therefore, while e-voting would be consistent with the constitutional election principles, i.e. universality, equality, directness, proportionality and secrecy of voting, as well as the sometimes overlooked principle of free elections, its possible introduction would not require a change to the Constitution. The only change would be made at the level of the law. At the same time, this compliance with electoral principles is important because their implementation is a condition sine qua non for recognising the validity of elections. Therefore, their non-fulfilment automatically translates into a lack of democracy in filling the seats in representative bodies and leads to invalidation of the elections by the Supreme Court.[18]

Implementation of the principle of universality of elections will boil down to guaranteeing all eligible persons the opportunity to vote, but also to overcoming the problem of digital exclusion, i.e. the lack of equal opportunities in access to the Internet, information and communication

---

<http://www.eui.eu/News/2013/02-12-InternetvotingasuccessintwoEuropeancountries.aspx> accessed 30 June 2021.

16 The Electoral Knowledge Network, *E-voting*, http://aceproject.org/ace-en/focus/e-voting/countries, [Access by day 30.06. 2021]; Tadayoshi Kohno, Adam Stubblefield, Aviel D. Rubin and Dan S. Wallach, 'Analysis of an Electronic Voting System' (IEEE 2004) 3-7 <http://avirubin.com/vote.pdf> accessed 30 June 2021. More about that, Beata Stepień-Załucka, 'E-voting. Sukces czy porażka na przykładzie Estonii i Szwajcarii'in Paweł Kuczma (ed) *Aktualne wyzwania demokracji partycypacyjnej w Polsce i na świecie* (Wydawcnitwo Uczelni Jana Wyżykowskiego 2017).

17 Mirosław Granat, *Prawo konstytucyjne w pytaniach i odpowiedziach*, (LexisNexis 2010) 40.

18 I wrote more about that in (n 3) 223-225.

technology (ICT) infrastructure, or computer skills.[19] Therefore, this form of voting, if introduced, could be only optional in relation to the traditional voting method. Internet voting requires also compliance with the criterion of equality, which in the case of e-voting would boil down to the necessity to exclude the risks associated with the possibility of multiple voting, family voting, forced voting, voting by a non-voter and selling the vote, and at the same time to introduce technical solutions that would guarantee the casting of only one vote and protect against the possibility of repeated voting. Equality, on the other hand, should also guarantee the accessibility of the ballot in terms of access to it and the simplicity of voting. [20]Another determinant of the constitutionality of Internet elections

---

19 Michał Wróblewski, 'Cyfrowy analfabetyzm ante windows? O wykluczeniu społecznym i projekcie DIGI.COM/YOUTH #37' (Medium, 31 January 2017) <https://medium.com/@wiedziecwiecej/cyfrowy-analfabetyzmem-ante-windows-o-wykluczeniu-spo%C5%82ecznym-i-projekcie-digi-com-youth-406d4fadfecb#.o003zj2ma> accessed 30 June 2021.
Henry E. Brady and Iris Hui, *Accuracy and Security in Voting Systems*, (Berkeley 2008) 1 ff. <https://www.princeton.edu/csdp/events/Election050108/BradyElection.pdf> accessed 30 June 2021.

20 *Ibidem.*
The American Congress countered the irregularities related to the Internet vote count in the 2000 presidential election with the HAVA law reforming the electoral process, signed by President Bush on 29 October 2002. Its essence was, on the one hand, an order to fund the replacement of outdated voting technologies such as punch cards and replace them with more modern ones such as optical scanners and electronic direct voting machines. On the other hand, and more importantly, HAVA included a requirement, allowing for voter identification in certain situations, to allow for manual audits of voting results, which directly implicated the inability of the voter and anyone else, in an audit, to verify to which candidate in 2000 their vote was actually attributed. A. Roseman, *State constitutional law—equal protection—the Indiana Supreme Court's less than rational basis review of equal protection claims resulted in the validation of the Indiana voter id law. League of Women Voters of Indiana, inc. v. Rokita*, 929 n.e.2d 758 (ind. 2010), (2013) 43, 2Rutgers Law Journal. 873 ff. <http://lawjournal.rutgers.edu/sites/lawjournal.rutgers.edu/files/issues/16RosemanVol.43.4_v3.pdf> accessed 30 June 2021. FinLaw's Team, 'Federal Voter ID Requirements: The Help America Vote Act (HAVA)' (Findlaw, 18 March 2021) <http://civilrights.findlaw.com/other-constitutional-rights/federal-voter-id-requirements-the-help-america-vote-act-hava.html> accessed 30 June 2021.; Gloria Lin and Nicole Espinoza, 'Florida Congressional Elections: November 2006' (Standford 2007) <https://cs.stanford.edu/people/eroberts/cs181/projects/2006-07/electronic-voting/index_files/page0004.html> accessed 30 June 2021; See too, New Study of E-Voting Effects in Florida, https://freedom-to-tinker.com/blog/felten/new-study-e-voting-effects-florida/;Study accessed 30 June 2021. Robert McMillan, 'finds e-voting irregularities in Florida' (Computerweekly.com,

is directness.[21] In the practice of online elections, this principle would be realized through the direct registration of the ballots online, but the counting of the ballots would have to take place at the very end of the voting procedure so as to eliminate any possible influence of the knowledge of the partial results on the turnout and the final outcome of the election.[22] The principle of proportionality in the case of e-voting is the least relevant to a possible claim of constitutionality, since while this method of voting allows for the establishment of accurate data, the distribution of seats obtained on the basis of such data is carried out by means of a specific distribution method. In Poland, this is the d'Hondt method.[23] Another electoral attribute that e-voting would have to meet is the secrecy of the vote,[24] which in the case of Internet voting would have to guarantee the secrecy of the election at all stages and at the same time allow for verification of the vote cast, which would be particularly important in the case of situations such as selling votes or voting under pressure from other voters - parents or spouses.[25] E-voting would also have to meet the requirements of the principle of free elections, guaranteeing each voter the ability to exercise his or her active and passive electoral rights without any physical or mental coercion or constraints, ensuring freedom of expression[26] but

---

23 November 2004) <http://www.computerweekly.com/feature/Study-finds-e-voting-irregularities-in-Florida accessed 30 May 2021.

Mitrou (n 4) 8 ff. <http://Www.Icsd.Aegean.Gr/Website_Files/Metaptyxiako/65983061.Pdf>, accessed 30 June 2021.

21 Dorota Lis-Staranowicz, 'Kodeks wyborczy. Wyrok z dnia 20 lipca 2011 r., K 9/11', in Leszek Garlicki, Marta Derlatka and Marcin Wiącek (eds) *Na straży państwa prawa. Trzydzieści lat orzecznictwa Trybunału Konstytucyjnego* (Wolters Kluwer 2016) 819-838.

22 Mitrou, (n 4)15. More about that, Gábor Toka, *The impact of partial results on election*, <http://www.personal.ceu.hu/staff/Gabor_Toka/Papers/Toka04Chicago.pdf> accessed 30 June 2021.

23 Jeremiasz Salamon, 'Polityczne konsekwencje wyboru metody dystrybucji mandatów na przykładzie elekcji do Sejmu RP z 21 października 2007 roku' (2014) 4-5 Studia Politicae Universitatis Silesiensis 139 i n.

24 Blerim Rexha, Vehbi Neziri and Ramadan Dervishi, 'Improving authentication and transparency
of e-Voting system – Kosovo case' (2012) 1, 6 International Journal Of Computers And Communications 84 <http://www.universitypress.org.uk/journals/cc/17-858.pdf> accessed 30 June 2021.

25 Mitrou (n 4) 12.

26 BartłomiejOpaliński, 'Wolność wyborów parlamentarnych i jej gwarancje na gruncie Konstytucji Rzeczypospolitej Polskiej' (2012) 2 Przegląd Prawa Konstytucyjnego 59 ff; http://www.marszalek.com.pl/przegladprawakonstytucyjnego/ppk10/03.pdf accessed 30 June 2021.

also the possibility of casting an invalid vote, which is a kind of manifesto of the voter. [27]

4. Threats connected with introduction of e-voting.

Apart from changes in the Electoral Code, introduction of e-voting in Poland would also require elimination of threats to its operation noticed in practice in countries where this form of voting already works. Eliminating them, or at least minimizing them, will allow the system to operate without the errors that have been noticed.

The Netherlands is a country that has faced up to the shortcomings of e-voting. This country tried to conduct elections in the form of e-voting in 2008. The choice of this way of voting was aimed at increasing voter turnout, but it soon turned out that it contains shortcomings that undermine the integrity of elections. The first argument in favor of incorrect operation system concerned the encryption of the votes cast. According to the tests, the chosen encryption method protected the secrecy of the vote any for some time, in the best case, the votes will be secret until the end of 2030. However, the testers themselves stated that even before this date it will be possible to know the votes cast. In other words, it will become possible to know for whom a given voter voted. Another argument in this regard was the possibility of multiple voting. The election lasted 14 days, the system processed the vote for 20 hours, and this means that during the election, each voter could cast 16 defective votes. There were also concerns about the possibility of the system being hacked. Faced with these threats, on June 30, 2008, the Dutch government decided to halt certification of the system. [28]The more so because another problem that arose concerned

---

27 An example of how important a role invalid votes can play in the electoral system can be Australia. More on this topic, Jessica Irvine, 'Informal vote makes mockery of democrasy'(smh.com, 28 August 2010) <http://www.smh.com.au/federal-politics/informal-vote-makes-mockery-of-democracy-20100831-14fc3.html> accessed 30 June 2021. More on this topic: (n 3) 226 ff.

28 Leontine Loeber, 'E-voting in the Netherlands; past, current, future?' <https://www.researchgate.net/publication/301547849_E-voting_in_the_Netherlands_past_current_future> accessed 30 June 2021. More on that subject, Ben Goldsmith and Holly Ruthrauff, 'Implementing and Overseeing Electronic Voting and Counting Technologies. Case Study Report on Electronic Voting in the Netherlands'(NDI, 2013) 268-274 https://www.ndi.org/sites/default/files/Implementing_and_Overseeing_Electronic_Voting_and_Counting_Technologies.pdf accessed 30 June 2021.

the system's counting of so-called "air votes," i.e. votes that were included in the system even though they were not cast by voters.[29]

For years, Estonia has been an international model country that has implemented and in which functions on the basis of e-voting. In Estonia, e-voting is carried out by providing voters with a certificate (digital signature) with which they can vote on the website of the State Electoral Commission. The voter is thus identified by a digital signature. The choice is that once the voter is identified, the voting text is displayed to the voter on the website so that the voter can cast a vote. The voters are then informed on the website whether their vote has been added.[30] It is important to note that voters can change their votes until the voting is complete, the last vote cast is the one that counts.[31]

Based on the above, it is necessary to note the following problem regarding voter identification. On the one hand, the Estonian voting mechanism consists of a password and an electronic signature that allow the voter to cast a ballot. On the other hand, this password and signature may not necessarily be used by the voter. One should be aware that both the password and the electronic signature can be used by third parties. So if Poland decided to go ahead with e-voting, the system would also have to face this threat.[32]

This raises another problem of how to verify the accuracy of the vote cast so that the secrecy of the ballot is not compromised. This is particularly true in systems which perform both voter authentication and vote casting. At this point, it should be noted that the system based on anonymity is not a solution to the above dilemma, because it completely eliminates any possibility of verifying the correctness of the system's operation. Thus, e-voting would remain beyond real control, which I find unacceptable.[33]

---

29 Krzysztof Skotnicki, *Kilka słów o i-votingu*, <http://repozytorium.uni.wroc.pl/Content/89856/35_K_Skotnicki_Kilka_slow_o_i-votingu.pdf> accessed 30 June 2021.

30 Michał Czakowski, 'E-voting na przykładzie Estonii i Brazylii' (2011) 3, 27 Studia BAS 130.

31 Daniel Lohrmann, 'Could Estonia Be the Model for Secure Online Voting?' (govtech.com, 25 September 2020) https://www.govtech.com/blogs/lohrmann-on-cybersecurity/could-estonia-be-the-model-for-secure-online-voting.html accessed 30 June 2021.

32 Magdalena Musiał-Karg, 'Challenges of i-voting – practices, rules and perspectives. Examples from Estonia and Switzerland' (2017) 4, 17 Przegląd Polityczny <http://przeglad.amu.edu.pl/wp-content/uploads/2018/07/pp-2017-4-06.pdf> accessed 30 June 2021.

33 Stępień-Załucka (n 3) 232.

However, regardless of the lack of spectacular moments of failure Estonian of this system, there is a problem that cannot be completely eliminated - namely hackers. The risks associated with a hacking attack simply need to be, as much as possible, prepared for.[34]

This issue was vividly outlined in the 2020 elections in the United States. For it showed that the use of e-voting must go hand in hand with cybersecurity, the provision of which remains a major concern. This is because online voting opens the door to hackers collaborating, in the case of the aforementioned 2020 election, with U.S. opponents i.e. Russia and China. Skilled hackers can influence and manipulate the electoral outcome in their favor, several audits conducted against previous online U.S. elections, have shown, revealing many security vulnerabilities. For example, in 2020, "In February, MIT reported finding serious flaws in the online election system of Voatz, the company that ran the first mobile election in West Virginia, allowing a hacker to alter, stop or reveal a user's vote. Another study by MIT and the University of Michigan also found security problems with Omniballot, the system Delaware uses for online voting."[35]

Cybersecurity experts emphasize that there is not and never will be a 100 percent guarantee for the security of any given website, app, or system. This is because every single one of these tools relies on humans to manage their software, and this makes it impossible to ever rule out the possibility that another human will break the software. The hacking of Twitter is a case in point. Another example is the operation of voting machines in the United States, which have repeatedly show to be not fully secure and a hacker is able to change, add or remove votes.[36]

With that said, beyond the hacking attack itself, e-voting is a system that also raises the risk of massive voter fraud.[37] An example of this can be found in the literature on the use of electronic voter registration and voting systems in Alvarez and Hall in U.S., which pioneered the use of electronic voting and subsequently faced allegations of malicious software

---

34 Lohrmann (n 31).

35 Nathaniel Lee, 'Here's why most Americans are not able to vote online in 2020' (CNBC, 23 September 2020) <https://www.cnbc.com/2020/09/23/why-us-cant-vote-online-in-2020-presidential-election-trump-biden.html> accessed 30 June 2021.

36 Jasmine Webb, 'Security Experts Say Online Voting Is a Bad Idea. Here's Why' (Digital Diplomacy, 20 July 2020), <https://medium.com/digital-diplomacy/security-experts-say-online-voting-is-a-bad-idea-heres-why-1792c9a876b0> accessed 30 June 2021.

37 Skotnicki (n 29).

and hardware tampering. Another example is the anomalies revealed during the referendum in Venezuela in the state of Delta Amacuro, for which, after statistical studies, it was found that at different stages of the election the data differed and had a different distribution of turnout. Municipalities were singled out in this state that had a very large and out of bounds coefficient related to the proportion of "yes" votes.[38]

The experience of Ireland should also be kept in mind when introducing e-voting. In 2004, the government of this country purchased for about 50 million euros from a Dutch company specialized equipment - Nedap, which was used in some constituencies. However, curiously, the Irish authorities responsible for the proper conduct of elections decided to order, an independent audit of the system's security. What transpired was that the auditing company questioned the quality of the security of the equipment purchased against potential fraud. As a result, the expensive pilot system became an expensive-to-maintain (generating annual maintenance costs running into hundreds of thousands of euros) digital dud.[39]

5. Summary

E-voting is one of the most modern instruments used in a democracy. Its introduction takes a country to a new, higher level of innovation and use of new technologies. However, its introduction is not only connected to legal changes, which in Poland would have to take place at the statutory level, as the basic regulations concerning the method of voting are still regulated at the statutory level, but also would have to overcome a number of technical problems that other countries have already faced or are still facing. These problems relate to issues such as security, the digital divide or, as the recent example shows, inadequate, excessive funding in relation to the product obtained, i.e. a system which, in the case of Ireland, proved to be flawed.

---

38 Inés Levin, Gabe Cohen, Peter Ordeshook and M. Alvarez, 'Detecting Voter Fraud in an Electronic Voting Context An Analysis of the Unlimited Reelection Vote in Venezuela' (2009) 83 Voting Technology Project

39 Marek Kowalski, 'Głosowanie przez internet – dlaczego jeszcze nie w Polsce? Korzyści i zagrożenia związane z wyborami elektroncznymi' (Softonet.pl, 25 October 2015) <https://softonet.pl/publikacje/poradniki/Glosowanie.przez.internet-dlaczego.jeszcze.nie.w.Polsce.Korzysci.i.zagrozenia.zwiazane.z.wyborami.elektronicznymi,1383> accessed 30 June 2021.

The question that remains to be answered is whether the above risks associated with e-voting therefore preclude its introduction? In answering this question, account must be taken, on the one hand, of these risks and, on the other, as the pandemic period in particular has shown, of the fact that modern man's life is moving online. This raises another question: how do banking operations differ from e-voting operations? After all, both of them are key to the functioning of societies, so they must use the highest security, and if banks can operate online, can't evoting? Although in theory the answer to the above seems simple, it is not. And it is also not true that bank security is the highest, because as the example of recent years shows, many banks have fallen victim to hackers. However, the difference between banking operations and e-voting is that while banks are businesses and can compensate for losses, e-voting is much worse, because democracy cannot be compensated for possibly rigged elections. Does this mean that there is no future for e-voting and concerns about its dangers will outweigh the desire to introduce it in Poland? In my opinion, no. E-voting is the future not only for Poland but also for the legal systems of other countries. The risk associated with it is high, but this does not mean that it cannot be minimised and I think that this is the right direction for change.

Regulation and Control of Algorithmic Codes – a Necessity of our Times (?)

Ewa Rott-Pietrzyk
<ewa.rott-pietrzyk@us.edu.pl>
KATOWICE, Poland

Dariusz Szostek
<dariusz.szostek@szostek-bar.pl>
KATOWICE, OPOLE, Poland

Marek Świerczynski
<m.swierczynski@uksw.edu.pl>
WARSZAWA, Poland

Every technology has a good and a bad side,
and the use people make of the fruits of their knowledge
depends on themselves[1]
Stanisław Lem

Abstract
For many years, the issue of algorithmic codes and implementation was not more widely addressed by lawyers. The development of blockchain, smart contract but above all artificial intelligence has changed this situation. Algorithms not only support human work, but more and more often replace human actions, including decisions affecting the rights of individuals. There is an emerging need to control and verify algorithmic codes. In this article we intend to show what changes in this area are taking place in Europe and inspire other countries.

Keywords:
Algorithm, software, artificial intelligence, blockchain, implementation of law in codes.

---

1 While 2021 is Lem's year, it is symbolic to remind readers that Stanisław Lem's statement can be found in his collection of his short stories titled: Dziury w całym, Znak 1997 [in English: A hole in the whole].

1. Introduction

One of the most serious challenges, not so much for the internet or the development of the digital economy, but more broadly for the maintenance of human rights at the current level, is the need to control not only the content placed on the Internet (e.g. hate speech, sexual abuse of children, violation of personal rights, etc.), but also the algorithmic codes, which are no longer just the carriers of such content, but tools that have an increasing influence on people and their rights.[2] At the end of the last century, Prof. L. Lessig published a concept of law functioning as an algorithm – law incorporated into software – which seemed futuristic at the time, but which is now being implemented – the law consisting of "puzzles" that can be combined and shaped in cyberspace.[3] Reading the chapters of this monograph indicates the increasing role of algorithms. This not only refers to the shaping of cyberspace, but also to their direct impact on people and their rights. We are no longer just witnessing pilot projects or academic concepts, but actually implemented IT systems in which human language (written or spoken) is transformed into algorithmic codes readable by machines equipped with processors and directly executed by them. This process has been increasingly taking place, but in a way that can be directly perceived by humans, transcribing computer code into symbols, letters, words, phrases and sentences.[4] A provision of a law or a contract is beginning to function as a computer program, rather than as a text of legal provisions consisting of letters and grammatical signs presented in natural language.[5] Law and technology are increasingly interacting with

---

2 See also Robert Seyfert, 'Algorithms as regulatory objects' (2021) Information, Communication & Society 2021.

3 Lawrence Lessig, '*Code and other laws of cyberspace*' (Basic Books 1999) 3 ff.

4 Anderas Wiebe, *Die elektronische Willenserklarung* (Tubingen 2002) 350; see also Mirko Pečarič 'Lex Ex Machina: Reasons For Algorithmic Regulation' (2021) Masaryk University Journal of Law and Technology 85 ff.

5 For more on the transcription of spoken language into algorithmic codes, see: Michał Araszkiewicz, 'Algorithmization of legal thinking. Models, possibilities, limitations' in Dariusz Szostek (ed) *Legal Tech* (C.H. Beck 2021) 57-83.

each other.[6] Code is the architecture of cyberspace and pieces of code are the building material of this architecture. Everything we see online is delivered through code, only code can allow the regulation of social rules in cyberspace. In this way, code functions as a regulator of cyberspace.[7]

It was more than 20 years ago that L. Lessig drew attention to the problem of algorithmic code as a regulator:

> *"Every age has its potential regulator, its threat to liberty. Our founders feared a newly empowered federal government; the Constitution is written against that fear. John Stuart Mill worried about the regulation by social norms in nineteenth-century England; his book On Liberty is written against that regulation. Many of the progressives in the twentieth century worried about the injustices of the market. The reforms of the market, and the safety nets that surround it, were erected in response. Actuality this regulator is code--the software and hardware that make cyberspace as it is. This code, or architecture, sets the terms on which life in cyberspace is experienced. It determines how easy it is to protect privacy, or how easy it is to censor speech. It determines whether access to information is general or whether information is zoned. It affects who sees what, or what is monitored. In a host of ways that one cannot begin to see unless one begins to understand the nature of this code, the code of cyberspace regulates."*[8]

Even that early, he pointed towards the need for the certification and authorisation of algorithms. Nowadays, when algorithms are not only creating cyberspace, but also making decisions that have an effect on human life, implementing legal regulations in themselves[9] and increasingly boldly

6 Rohan Nanda, Giovanni Siragusa, Luigi Di Caro, Guido Boella, Lorenzo Grossio, Marco Gerbaudo and Francesco Costamanga, 'Unsupervised and supervised text similarity systems for automated identification of national implementing measures of European directives' (2019) 27 Artificial Intelligence and Law Romain Boulet, Pierre Mazzega and Danièle Bourcier 'Network approach to the French system of legal codes part II: the role of the weights in a network' (2018) 26 Artificial Intelligence and Law 23 ff.

7 Sergii Schrebak, 'Integrating Computer Science into Legal Discipline: The Rise of Legal Programming' (SSRN, 15 September 2014) 4 <https://papers.ssrn.com/sol3/papers.cfm?abstract_id=2496094> accessed 5 July2021.

8 Lawrence Lessig, 'Code is Law. On Liberty in Cyberspace'(Harvard Magazine, 2000), <https://www.harvardmagazine.com/2000/01/code-is-law-html> accessed 6 July 2021.

9 Sergii Schrebak, 'Integrating Computer Science into Legal Discipline: The Rise of Legal Programming' (SSRN, 14 September 2014) 1 <https://papers.ssrn.com/sol3/papers.cfm?abstract_id=2496094> accessed 5 July 2021.

participating in law enforcement[10] or even issuing court judgments, their control becomes important and even more necessary, both at the regional level (EU), but also, in our opinion, at the international level (Convention).

It seems to be a paradox that we humans are building a powerful tool (covering various NewTech instruments), making great progress in coming up with improvements and it is only as almost the "last step" that we notice that its regulation has grown not only necessary, but urgent. Therefore it seems that this is a good time, as it is possibly the last time, to create some regulations that protect many values in the human environment in the era of new technologies that is influencing almost all (if not all) spheres of life. The need for the certification and authorisation of algorithms is very urgent at both national and international level, not only local (EU) but global. There is a question as to what would be the best body to establish that? And what would be the best way to create it (in terms of procedure, methods and content)? For now, the creation of universal norms at global level (no matter their nature: binding force or *soft law*) is kind of fiction in the near future. However, some solutions have to be found. What we have currently on the European stage is not sufficient, but it can be perceived as a vital step. It sounds banal, but there is no return to the old world, and the new world needs to have some protection against the products of its own making. In the frame of Europe, the regulatory process has started, which is itself of great value.

The aim of this article is to present the European approach, way of thinking and dealing with the issue covered in its title with some general reflections on the need for a regulation and control over algorithmic codes.

---

10 An example of this is the increasing prevalence of smart contracts. Daniel Hellwig, Goran Karlic and Arnd Huchzermeier, '*Build Your Own Blockchain*' (Springer 2020) 74 ff., Maria G. Vigliotti and Haydn Jones, *The Executive Guide to Blockchian* (Pagrave Macmillan 2020) 133; Eranga Bandara, Wee Keong, Nalin Ranasinghe and Kasun de Zoysa, 'Smart contract Made Smart' in (ed) Zibin Zheng, Hong-Ning Dai, Mingdong Tang and Xiangping Chen, *Blockchain and Trustworthy System* (Springer 2020) 431; Robert Wilkens and Richard Falk, *Smart Contracts, Grundlagen, Anwedungsfelder und rechtliche Aspekte* (Springer 2019) 3 ff; Riccardo de Caria, 'Definitions of Smart Contracts' in Larry A. DiMatteo, Michel Cannarsa and Cristina Poncibo (eds) *Smart contracts, blockchain technology and digital platforms* (Cambridge Law Handbooks 2019) 19-36.

2. *Control over codes at EU level*

The European Union has recognised the problem of code control and has taken a great deal of legislative action in this area. In a number of documents it has pointed to the need for transparency and accountability – initially of algorithms acting as AI, and eventually also of other algorithms. It has been pointed out, including in the resolution on civil law provisions in the field of robotics and AI adopted by the European Parliament on 16 February 2017, in the resolution of the European Parliament and the Council of 20 October 2020 containing recommendations to the European Commission on a civil liability regime for artificial intelligence (AI), in the White Paper for AI,[11] and more comprehensively in the Report Artificial Intelligence and Fundamental Right (2020),[12] that, when creating algorithms, it is necessary to take into account: human dignity, the right to privacy and data protection, access to justice, equality and non-discrimination and consumer protection. A recent European Commission report "Safety over Liability Related Aspects of Software" prepared by Prof. Christiane Wenderhorst[13] identifies recommendations for the regulation of algorithms as follows: 1. Introduce a new semi-horizontal and risk-based regime on software safety (accompanied by further steps to modernise the safety-related acquis), 2. Revise the Product Liability Directive, 3. Introduce a new regulatory framework for AI, 4. Introduce a new instrument on AI liability, and 5. Continue the digital fitness check of the whole acquis. Particularly worth quoting is the justification to introduce a new semi-horizontal and risk-based regime on software safety:

> "*The European legislator should introduce a new regime on software safety. This regime would be semi-horizontal in nature as it would apply only to software, but to all software (e.g. whether embedded, accessory or standalone), in a very broad and technologically neutral sense and including, e.g., SaaS. It would overcome shortcomings in the existing safety legislation, which does either not cover software, in particular not standalone software, or is poorly equipped to deal with software. The European legislator might*

---

11 <https://ec.europa.eu/info/sites/default/files/commission-white-paper-artificial-intelligence-feb2020_en.pdf> accessed 7 July 2021.

12 <https://fra.europa.eu/sites/default/files/fra_uploads/fra-2020-artificial-intelligence_en.pdf> accessed 8 July 2021.

13 See also Christine Wendehorst's approach in her article, 'Strict Liability for AI and other Emerging Technologies'(2020) 11, 2 Journal of European Tort Law: https://www.degruyter.com/journal/key/jetl/html, 150-180.

thus consider introducing a new Software Safety Directive (SSD), which would have to be accompanied by selected further steps towards modernisation of the safety-related acquis.

The relationship of the SSD with existing and future sectoral legislation would be one of complementarity. The SSD would be dealing with cross-cutting issues such as the delineation between products with software elements, add-on software for other products, and standalone software that otherwise interacts with other products, and the division of responsibilities between the different producers in either case. It would deal with privacy by design, cybersecurity (until/unless addressed by other acts developed under the Cybersecurity Act), post-market surveillance duties, issues arising in the context of updates, and similar questions."

The European Union goes further than simply referring to the regulation and control of algorithmic codes in its reports and recommendations. In its most recent legislative proposals, it explicitly proposes appropriate solutions. At present, the following ideas deserve particular attention: Proposal for a Regulation Of The European Parliament And Of The Council On Machinery Products,[14] Proposal For A Regulation Of The European Parliament And Of The Council Laying Down Harmonised Rules On Artificial Intelligence (Artificial Intelligence Act) And Amending Certain Union Legislative Acts,[15] and Proposal of Regulation of the European Parliament and the Council amending Regulation (EU) No 910/2014 a regards establishing o framework for a European Digital Identity.[16]

The broadest proposal for the regulation of algorithmic codes is the proposed Artificial Intelligence Act. Its scope covers not only AI in the narrow sense, but also other codes indicated in its Annex 1. According to the proposed definition in Article 3(1), artificial intelligence system (AI system) means software that is developed with one or more of the techniques and approaches listed in Annex I and can, for a given set of human-defined objectives, generate outputs such as content, predictions, recommendations, or decisions influencing the environments they interact with. Whereas according to Annex 1, AI includes: machine-learning approaches, including supervised, unsupervised and reinforcement learning, using a wide variety of methods including deep learning; logic- and knowledge-based approa-

14 <https://ec.europa.eu/docsroom/documents/45508> accessed 5 July 2021.

15 <https://eur-lex.europa.eu/legal-content/EN/TXT/?uri=CELEX:52021PC0206> accessed 6 July 2021.

16 <https://op.europa.eu/pl/publication-detail/-/publication/5d88943a-c458-11eb-a925-01aa75ed71a1/language-en/format-PDF/source-search> accessed 6 July 2021.

ches, including knowledge representation, inductive (logic) programming, knowledge bases, inference and deductive engines, (symbolic) reasoning and expert systems; statistical approaches, Bayesian estimations, as well as search and optimization methods. This means that, once the regulation comes into force, not only AI, but also a number of other algorithms may be covered by the regulation.

Some very interesting proposals, indirectly introducing code control, are contained in the proposal for an amendment of Regulation eIDAS (beyond eIDAS2). The European Commission proposes to introduce into the European legal order a definition of "electronic ledger" where "electronic ledger" means a tamperproof electronic record of data, establishing the authenticity and integrity of the data it contains, the accuracy of the date and time, and the chronological ordering. It is proposed to link the legal effects to the entry in the electronic register. As proposed in Article 45h of eIDAS2, an electronic ledger would not be denied legal effect and admissibility as evidence in legal proceedings solely on the grounds that it is in an electronic form, or that it does not meet the requirements for qualified electronic ledgers. More relevant is the introduction of a legal presumption linked to an entry, but not so much to a 'ordinary' electronic ledger as to a qualified electronic ledger. As proposed in Article 45h(2), a qualified electronic ledger would enjoy the presumption of the uniqueness and authenticity of the data it contains, of the accuracy of the date and time, and of the sequential chronological ordering within the ledger. In other words, it is proposed to equate the entry of data into a qualified register kept by a qualified entity providing certification services as a trust service with the original of a document, or even more broadly, with the original of data not necessarily constituting a document in the traditional sense. The presumption will only apply to electronic registers previously verified and audited as a qualified trusted service. Qualified electronic ledgers must meet the following requirements: (a) they are created by one or more qualified trust service provider or providers; (b) they ensure the uniqueness, authenticity and correct sequencing of data entries recorded in the ledger; (c) they ensure the correct sequential chronological ordering of data in the ledger and the accuracy of the date and time of the data entry; (d) they record data in such a way that any subsequent change to the data is immediately detectable. This concept is not novel. Similar legal solutions already exist in many countries, e.g. Malta, Singapore and the State of New York in the USA.

The Proposal for a Regulation of The European Parliament And Of The Council On Machinery Products, as proposed in Annex 1, considers as hazardous products, among other things, software ensuring safety functions, including AI systems and machinery embedding AI systems ensuring safety functions. As in the proposed AI Act, these systems will be subject to control and supervision depending on the level of risk associated with them.

These are not the European Commission's only proposals for legislation involving the control of algorithms. They are only an example of the legislative changes taking place in this area.

3. *Artificial Intelligence Act & Council of Europe*

3.1. *General remarks*

It is not only the European Union that is taking action on code control regulation. The Council of Europe has also taken initiatives in this area. The draft Artificial Intelligence Act aims to build an ecosystem of trust based on a legal framework for trustworthy artificial intelligence. As noted above, this includes the regulation and control of algorithmic codes. It contributes to ensuring that users trust and accept new solutions based on algorithmic codes and that entrepreneurs are more willing to develop such solutions.[17] It also addresses challenges such as the *black box* effect,[18] complexity, bias, unpredictability and the possible autonomy of algorithmic code-based solutions.

It is also clear that the development of innovations based on algorithmic codes, based to an even wider extent than just on AI itself, requires

---

17 Jenna Burrell, 'How the Machine 'Thinks': Understanding Opacity in Machine Learning Algorithms' (2016) 3, 1 Big Data & Society <https://papers.ssrn.com/sol3/papers.cfm?abstract_id=2660674> accessed 12 July 2021.

18 Rosario Girasa, *Artificial Intelligence as a Disruptive Technology. Economic Transformation and Government Regulation* (Palgrave Macmillan 2020) 4; see also Octavio Loyola-González: https://www.researchgate.net/profile/Octavio-Loyola-Gonzalez, 'Black-Box vs. White-Box: Understanding Their Advantages and Weaknesses From a Practical Point of View' IEEE Access; Yavar Bathaee, 'The Artificial Intelligence Black Box And The Failure Of Intent And Causation' (2018) 31, 2 Harvard Journal of Law & Technology 889-938.

convergence with the proposed Data Governance Act,[19] the Open Data Directive[20] and other initiatives that are part of the European Data Strategy.[21]

The developers of the draft AIA aim to ensure its consistency with the provisions of the Charter of Fundamental Rights of the European Union and applicable Union secondary law. In particular, in the area of algorithmic codes, it is crucial to ensure consistency with the provisions of the General Data Protection Regulation (Regulation (EU) 2016/679) and with the provisions of the Enforcement Directive (Directive (EU) 2016/680). Indeed, the draft Regulation complements the provisions of these acts by introducing a set of harmonised rules applicable to the design, development and use of algorithmic codes.

The draft also supplements the current legislation with specific requirements to minimise the risk of algorithmic discrimination, in particular with regard to the design and quality of datasets used to develop solutions based on algorithmic codes. This involves the introduction of specific testing, risk management, documentation and oversight obligations for algorithmic codes.

3.2. A risk-based approach

When regulating algorithmic codes, there should be a clear preference for a risk-based approach. The use of a risk-based framework is preferable to a general regulation of all possible solutions based on algorithmic codes. Risks and threats should be determined on a case-by-case and sector-by-sector basis. Risks should also be calculated taking into account the impact on users' rights and safety. Risks should be calculated taking into account the impact on the rights and safety of users

For these reasons, the draft AIA sets out harmonised rules for the development, marketing and use of algorithmic code-based solutions in accordance with a proportionate risk-based approach.

This approach entails detailed solutions involving algorithmic codes.

---

19 Proposal for a Regulation on European data management (Data Management Act) COM(2020) 767.

20 Directive (EU) 2019/1024 of the European Parliament and of the Council of 20 June 2019 on open data and re-use of public sector information, PE/28/2019/REV/1 [2019] OJ L172/56.

21 Commission Communication 'A European Data Strategy', COM(2020) 66 final. "A European data strategy", COM(2020) 66 final.

First of all, it should be stressed that the project has adopted a very broad definition of artificial intelligence, which also includes algorithmic codes. This is because the definition is based on the key functional characteristics of software, in particular, taking into account a set of human-defined goals, the ability to generate outputs such as content, predictions, recommendations or decisions that affect the environment with which the system interacts, whether physical or digital. Algorithmic code-based systems can be designed to operate at various levels of autonomy and can be used as stand-alone solutions or as part of a product, regardless of whether the system is physically integrated into the product (embedded) or whether it serves a product function although not integrated into it (non-embedded). The definition is complemented by a list of specific techniques and approaches used in the development of algorithmic codes. However, it should be stipulated that this list should be updated in the perspective of market developments and technological progress in the field of algorithmic codes.

The draft AIA also provides for a prohibition on certain particularly harmful practices using algorithmic codes that are contrary to EU values, and proposes specific restrictions and safeguards for certain applications of remote biometric identification systems for law enforcement purposes.

Obligations are also placed on the providers and users of such solutions to ensure security and respect for existing legislation on the protection of fundamental rights.

The proposed rules will be enforced through a governance system at Member State level based on already existing structures and a cooperation mechanism at EU level, for which a European AI Council will be established. Furthermore, the draft proposes additional measures to support innovation, including in particular regulatory sandboxes and other measures to reduce the regulatory burden and to support small and medium-sized enterprises and start-ups.

3.3. Evaluation of Artificial Intelligence Act

The introduction of new EU legislation concerning algorithmic coding entails a high risk of overlap with existing legislation, conflicting obligations and overregulation in this area. It is therefore crucial to introduce a proportionate, technology-neutral regulatory framework.

It must be accepted that the nature of algorithmic codes, which are often based on large and diverse data sets and which can be used in virtually any product or service traded freely in the internal market, means that individual countries will not be able to draw up a coherent regulation on their own.

The potential thicket of divergent national laws will hinder the marketing of products and services based on algorithmic codes. It will be ineffective in ensuring security and protecting fundamental rights. A national approach to solving these issues will only create additional legal uncertainty and barriers and will slow down the introduction of new technologies into the market.

These objectives can be better achieved at EU level. This avoids fragmenting the Single Market into potentially conflicting national frameworks preventing the free circulation of AI-enabled goods and services.

The choice of a regulation as a legal instrument is justified by the need for the uniform application of the new rules, prohibitions on certain harmful practices associated with the use of algorithmic codes and the classification of certain solutions based on them. A regulation, as an instrument directly applicable under Article 288 TFEU, will reduce legal fragmentation and facilitate the development of the Single Market. This can be achieved, in particular, by introducing a harmonised set of essential requirements for algorithmic code-based solutions and obligations for their providers and users.

It should be accepted that the draft AIA sets out a balanced and proportionate horizontal regulatory approach to algorithmic codes that is limited to the minimum requirements necessary to address the risks associated with their use, without unduly restricting or impeding technological development or otherwise causing a disproportionate increase in the cost of bringing new products and services to market.

3.4. The Council of Europe's role in regulating algorithmic codes

The Council of Europe plays a key role in ensuring the further development of algorithmic code-based solutions at the global level, ensuring their compatibility[22] with human rights protection standards .

The resulting output can be divided into four areas: 1) Recommendations, guidelines and other instruments issued by the Council of Europe

22 A study of the implications of advanced digital technologies (including AI systems) for the concept of responsibility within a human rights framework. Prepared by the Expert Committee on human rights dimensions of automated data processing and different forms of artificial intelligence (MSI-AUT). Rapporteur: Karen Yeung, DGI(2019)05.

bodies or committees established to look into AI – recommendations, guidelines and other instruments issued by Council of Europe bodies or AI committees; recommendations of the Committee of Ministers to Member States on the human rights impacts of algorithmic systems; recommendations on developing and promoting digital citizenship education; a declaration of the Committee of Ministers on the manipulative capabilities of algorithmic processes; a European Ethical Charter on the use of artificial intelligence in judicial systems and their environment; and a recommendation of the Parliamentary Assembly of the Council of Europe about technological convergence, artificial intelligence and human rights; 2) Studies, reports and conclusions of key events – a feasibility study on the establishment of a certification mechanism for artificial intelligence tools and services (CEPEJ, 8 December 2020); Artificial Intelligence in the Audiovisual Industry – a summary of a workshop (European Audiovisual Observatory, 17 December 2019); Artificial Intelligence and its Impact on Young People – a seminar report (European Youth Centre, 4-6 December 2019); proceedings of the Roundtable on Artificial Intelligence and the Future of Democracy (CDDG-Bu(2019)17, Democratic governance department, 20 September 2019); conclusions from the conference "Governing the Game Changer – impacts of artificial intelligence development on human rights, democracy and the rule of law" (Finnish Presidency of the Committee of Ministers and Council of Europe, Helsinki, 26-27 February 2019); 3) Reports of the Parliamentary Assembly of the Council of Europe: a report on "Artificial Intelligence and Labour Markets: Friend or Foe?"; a report on Artificial Intelligence in Healthcare: medical, legal and ethical challenges ahead; a report on Justice by Algorithm (the role of artificial intelligence in policing and criminal justice systems); a report on Preventing Discrimination Caused by the Use of Artificial Intelligence; a report on the Need for Democratic Governance of Artificial Intelligence, 4) other initiatives: a concept note on Artificial intelligence and Criminal Law Responsibility in Council of Europe Member States – the case of automated vehicles; the development of a recommendation and a study on the Impacts of Digital Technologies on Freedom of Expression; youth policy standards and other institutional responses to newly emergent issues affecting young people's rights and transition to adulthood, including AI; a report on AI in the Audiovisual Industry; a draft declaration of the Committee of Ministers of the Council of Europe on the risks of computer-assisted or artificial-intelligence-enabled decision making in the field of the social safety net.[23]

The importance of work on algorithmic codes is underlined by the Council of Europe creating the *Ad hoc Committee on Artificial Intelligence* (hereinafter: CAHAI) in 2019.[24] The purpose of CAHAI is to examine, based on broad stakeholder consultation, the issue of artificial intelligence, based on the Council of Europe's promoted standards on human rights, democracy and the rule of law.[25]

In summary, the Council of Europe acquis to date takes into account current needs arising from the use of algorithmic code-based tools. The guidelines of the Council of Europe, as an instrument of soft law, lend themselves to easy changes and additions, along with technological progress. Code-based technologies are global in nature. Multilateral cooperation among countries is therefore required to establish uniform international standards.

---

23 To the details see: <https://www.coe.int/en/web/artificial-intelligence/work-in-progress> accessed 12 July 2021.

24 <https://rm.coe.int/cahai-2020-2021-rev-en-pdf/16809fc157> accessed 12 July2021.

25 The CAHAI is composed of: representatives of the 47 member states, appointed by their governments, who have recognised expertise in digital governance and the legal implications of various forms of AI; representatives of observer states (Canada, the Holy See, Israel, Japan, Mexico and the United States of America); and representatives of other Council of Europe bodies, in particular the Secretariat of the Parliamentary Assembly, the Office of the Commissioner for Human Rights and the intergovernmental commissions dealing with issues related to AI. Representatives of other Council of Europe bodies, in particular the Secretariat of the Parliamentary Assembly, the Office of the Commissioner for Human Rights and the intergovernmental commissions dealing with issues related to artificial intelligence; representatives of other international and regional organisations working in the field of artificial intelligence, such as the EU, the UN (in particular UNESCO), the OECD, the OSCE; representatives of the private sector, including companies and associations with which the Council of Europe has exchanged letters in the framework of the Digital Business Partnership; representatives of civil society, research and academic institutions who have been admitted by CAHAI as observers. More: <https://www.coe.int/en/web/artificial-intelligence/cahai#{%2266693418%22:[0]}> accessed 12 July 2021; <https://rm.coe.int/list-of-cahai-members-web/16809e7f8d> accessed 12 July 2021.

4. Conclusions

Over the last ten years, it has become obvious that the legal framework must be extended into the various uses of automated decision-making software creeping into every layer of our lives. As the evidence continues to accumulate, it is also obvious that automation does not equal justice, and the greater the autonomy of the autonomous system, the greater the possibility for creating a prejudicial framework that would discriminate against specific groups of people.[26] It is an undisputable issue that the same prejudices and biases that have haunted society for decades, could now possibly be incorporated into pseudo-objective algorithms.[27]

This can be announced in a symbolic way: welcome to a new world where mankind is joining forces with machines through digital technology(!).[28] As we noted in the introduction, there is no return to the old world. However, the new (digitalised) world has to be devised in a proper way so as not to destroy its creator. This world covers a new system of social ordering, in other words – algorithmic regulation. This regulation refers to decision-making systems that regulate the domain of activity in order to manage risk or alter behaviour through the continual computational generation of knowledge by collecting data in real time on a continuous basis, emitted directly from numerous dynamic components concerning the regulated environment, in order to identify and, if necessary, automatically refine the system's operations to attain a pre-specified goal.[29] In other words, it employs the idea of controlling a population by means of feedback mechanisms, based on the threefold requirement of standard-setting, monitoring and behaviour modification. It is grounded and explained in a behaviourist perspective on human intercourse and

26 Terence Shin, 'Real-life examples of Discriminating Artificial Intelligence' (Towards Data Science, 4 June 2020) <https://towardsdatascience.com/real-life-examples-of-discriminating-artificial-intelligence-cae395a90070> accessed 12 July 2021.

27 Alina Köchling and Marius C. Wehner, 'Discriminated by an algorithm: a systematic review of discrimination and fairness by algorithmic decision-making in the context of HR recruitment and HR development' (2020) 13 Bus Res 795–848 . <https://doi.org/10.1007/s40685-020-00134-w> accessed 12 July 2021.

28 These words were used by Lina Willatte in the foreword to Jérôme Béranger's book titled: *The Algorithmic Code of Ethics: Ethics at the Bedside of the Digital Revolution*, vol. 2, as a part of Science and New Technologies Series. Technological Prospects and Social Applications Set, London-Hoboken 2018, p. vii.

29 For more detail, see Karen Yeung, 'Algorithmic regulation: A critical interrogation' (2017) 12, 4 Regulation & Governance 505-523.

displays an external perspective on human action.[30] At a first glance, this may sound not very optimistic, taking into consideration the possible negative effects of human freedoms and rights. Humankind as a species is at this point.[31] We could contest the algorithmic regulation doing nothing or undertake serious action. In our opinion, serious action is absolutely essential. During this serious action, two areas of consideration are absolutely vital: the area of law and the area of ethics. Both areas have to be combined. There are important voices establishing the extent to which ethics could create a background for the legal regulations concerning the regulation and control of algorithmic codes.[32]

Proper testing of new solutions implies built-in contestation – in science as in law. Therefore new ideas, concepts and proposals always provoke heated discussion, critique and contestation. This all is natural. However, in our opinion it cannot stop nor delay the mentioned serious action that has already started and is continued at the European level, as we present in the article. It was not our intention to discuss specific solutions proposed in all the various documents that have been prepared in Europe. We intend to underline the urgent need to regulate and control algorithmic codes using every lifesaving measure currently at our disposal, for example using *soft law* or various legislative proposals. This creates a background for binding solutions at the level of the European Union and the Member States, and may simultaneously inspire national legislators to start work in internal legislation.[33] Therefore, even if what we have now at the European level is not perfect and can be perceived by some to be chaotic, or even negative for the classic civilists, the action that has been commenced cannot be stopped. Instead, it should be supported by scientists and practitioners rep-

---

30 For more detail, see Mireille Hildebrandt, 'Algorithmic regulation and the rule of law' (2018) 376, 2128 Philosophical Transactions of the Royal Society A Mathematical, Physical and Engineering Sciences <https://royalsocietypublishing.org/doi/pdf/10.1098/rsta.2017.0355> accessed 12 July 2021.

31 See also Karen Yeung, *Algorithmic regulation* (footnote 27), who quotes *Tim O'Reilly, CEO of O'Reilly Media Inc.* 2013, p. 291 and takes his sentence as her motto: *It's time for government to enter the age of big data. Algorithmic regulation is an idea whose time has come.*"

32 A good example of this writing is Jérôme Béranger's book titled: The Algorithmic Code of Ethics: Ethics at the Bedside of the Digital Revolution (footnote 28).

33 The same is with the case of the Draft Common Frame of Reference (DCFR) which states a model law for many national legislators, for example Polish, see Ewa Rott-Pietrzyk and Mateusz Grochowski, 'Regulacja umów o pośrednictwo w DCFR (wzorcem dla ustawodawcy polskiego?)' (2017) 3 Transformacje Prawa Prywatnego 49-81.

resenting a wide range of disciplines. This is definitely not only a matter of action (in terms of producing law) taken by the lawyers and EU officials, it is a serious interdisciplinary task for a large number individuals who could be engaged for the benefit of all.

The conclusion can be covered in one sentence – we should regulate algorithms, otherwise the algorithms will end up regulating and controlling us. It is obvious that we cannot go back to a world without algorithms, but we can overcome algorithmic hegemony.[34] Thinking this way, mankind will try to follow Stanisław Lem's thought: *Every technology has a good and a bad side, and the use people make of the fruits of their knowledge depends on themselves.*

34 See also the position of Fabian Ferrari and Mark Graham, 'Fissures in algorithmic power: platforms, code, and contestation' (2021) Cultural Studies 13, 14.

Section Two.
Internet, New Technologies and the Justice System

The Legal Tech and the Legal Profession – the New Technology Enters the Lawyers' Offices

Fryderyk Zoll <fryderyk.zoll@uj.edu.pl>
OSNABRÜCK, Germany and KRAKÓW, Poland

Abstract
The article refers to the potential of artificial intelligence technology in the lawyer's profession, as well as the objections to its application. Firstly, the article presents the business model of law firms based on AI, focusing the way in which such law firms operate, taking into consideration employment and investment structure. Secondly, the challenges in the legal ethics are discussed. In this regard problems of confidentiality, conflict of interests as well as obligation of further study are tackled. Thirdly, the question about the necessity of a new education model is raised.

Keywords:
AI, artificial intelligence, legal profession, code of conduct

1. *New technology impacts the way in which the legal profession operates*

For a long time lawyers have felt exempted from a need to care about the development of the modern technology and of the IT.[1] Majority of lawyers seemed to disregard the impact the newest technologies have or might have on their profession.[2] The old-fashioned habits were well-established and the daily routine of legal professionals seemed to be immune to the

---

1 The different AI systems supporting legal services are presented by Ed Walters, 'The Model Rules of Autonomous Conduct: Ethical Responsibilities of Lawyers and Artificial Intelligence' (2019) 35.4 Georgia State University Law Review 1077.

2 It is not a solely Polish phenomenon: for the USA see: Drew Shimshaw, 'Ethical Issues in Robo-Lawyering: The Need for Guidance on Developing and Using Artificial Intelligence in the Practice of Law' (2018) Hastings Law Journal 185 and 195; Mark McKamey, 'Legal Technology. Artificial Intelligence and the Future of Law Practice' (2017) 22.45 Appeal Law Journal 6.

digital revolution.[3] This conservative approach was not only a result of the general reluctance towards the spread of the modern technology but also an attempt to defend a traditional business model of this profession – the new technology requires its investment scheme to be reshaped. The adjustment to the modern technology would mean that also the manner in which lawyers tend to think needs to evolve.[4] A revised approach to the lawyers' duties towards their clients is required.[5] The AI-supported process of the decision-making imposes different requirements as to the education of lawyers. The AI-supported legal profession will be a very different one. As a rule, these changes cannot be observed in the lawyers' community yet and there is little awareness among legal practitioners of how dramatic they are likely to be. We, as lawyers, are not prepared to face upcoming challenges. The process of transition will be painful because the march of the AI would require the full re-organization of the law firm, including changing the well-established way of earning money. The expansion of the AI would require redesigning legal framework governing the legal profession. It is also necessary to think about modernizing legal education, ethics, and business model. The purpose of this paper is to examine the content of the existing Polish codes of conducts of the two Polish legal professions: the advocates' and the so-called legal advisers (with practically this same status as advocates) from the perspective of the growing AI usage in the daily work of lawyers. Even if in Poland this revolution is only beginning, it will bring about enormous changes. Probably we will face immense difficulties when unprepared professionals will have to pursue their profession in a completely new environment.

Another effect of the development of the AI designed for the legal services may be the increase of the availability of the "self-help" devices.[6] This matter will be not further examined in this paper. However, in countries like Poland, with its common distrust to the lawyers and general unwillingness to ask for legal services, such self-help (namely, use of AI-based devices) may be problematic. The tendency to avoid asking for the human-driven legal services will grow as people will be looking for the alternative sources of „legal advice".

---

3 On the discussion concerning the conservative reluctance towards the technological innovation in the law offices see: Mark McKamey, 'Legal Technology' (n 2) 16. Such kind of reluctance seems to be an international and intercultural phenomenon.

4 ibid 11.

5 Shimshaw (n 2) 178.

6 ibid 181.

Nevertheless, the impact of the AI-supported legal services depends primarily on abilities of the AI itself. The scale of the revolution/potential revolution depends very much on the sophistication of the AI (weak or – still being rather *in statu nascendi* – strong AI.[7]

1.1. The AI-supported decision-making

In this introductory part of my article, I would like to comment shortly on the way in which AI may impact the manner of exercising legal professions. It is necessary to make the ethical standard understandable.

Devices that are designed to support the work of lawyers become more sophisticated and can substitute the work of many paralegals and even lawyers within a law firm. These devices facilitate not only the administration of files, but they are able to perform a lot of tasks, also these requiring an intellectual involvement.[8] Advanced systems can e.g. produce legal writings. The AI may also suggest the case theory by shaping the strategy and suggesting the best possible solution for the client.[9] Eventually, the role of lawyers may be reduced to controlling and supervising.[10] The essence of the AI is an ability to modify its own algorithms in line with the obtained input data. The systems supporting legal decision-making process of lawyers are likely to have different level of autonomy and require varied intensity of the participation of lawyers to achieve the outcome.[11] Finally, the AI-based software may force senior partners of the law firm to reorganize completely the structure of the law firm. In the law firm of the future, numerous junior partners, associates and paralegals might

---

7 On this difference ibid 188-189.

8 Gabriela Bar, 'Sztuczna inteligencja w kancelarii prawnej przyszłości' in Dariusz Szostek (ed), *Legal Tech. Czyli jak bezpiecznie korzystać z narzędzi informatycznych w organizacji, w tym w kancelarii oraz dziale prawnym* (C. H. Beck 2021) 609.

9 There is still a question to what extend the AI will be able to function within the environment of the law. McKamey (n 2) 12-13 indicates the technical constraints of the AI which may impede it from finding reasonable answers for the legal questions, but the Author himself does not find this pessimistic approach as to the abilities of the AI in legal matters convincing.

10 Richard Susskind and Daniel Susskind, *The Future of the Professions. How Technology Will Transform the Work of Human Experts* (Oxford University Press 2015) 187.

11 For an overview see: Daniel Kluttz and Dreidre Mulligan, 'Automated Decision Support Technologies and the Legal Profession' (2019) 34 Berkeley Technology Law Journal, 853.

no longer be necessary.[12] Instead, a person supervising the accuracy of the system's operation[13] and the senior partner who would assess the results generated by the AI-algorithms would be needed.[14]

The usage of the AI-based support systems keeps growing and, eventually, it will profoundly reshape the way in which the legal profession operates. This process of changes challenges the organization of the law firms, traditional investment models, the duties of the lawyers, including the ethical duties, and may even render the traditional legal education model obsolete. In this paper I would like to discuss briefly this process in order to provide an overview of how it would impact the picture of the legal profession in Poland in a very close future. Lawyers in Poland tend to be unaware of how deeply the implementation of the AI changes law firms. The first stage of the encounter with the AI applied in the law offices could be shocking for lawyers who would have to practise law under entirely new conditions.

Various systems based on the AI and used in the law offices are able to substitute work of many lawyers.[15] These systems prepare drafts of the legal writings, are able to monitor and apply the case law and the doctrine, to support the decision-making process and to make prediction concerning the outcome of the case, which is useful when developing a case theory. Systems based on the AI perform also a lot of other tasks, supporting the organization of the lawyering process in the law firm.

---

12 See however: Shimshaw (n 2) 190.

13 Phillip Leith and Amanda Hoey, *The Computerised Lawyer* (Springer 1998) 317; Iga Kurowska and Kamil Szpyt, 'Legal Tech w kancelariach prawnych oraz pracy prawników in-house' in Dariusz Szostek (ed), *Legal Tech. Czyli jak bezpiecznie korzystać z narzędzi informatycznych w organizacji, w tym w kancelarii oraz dziale prawnym* (C. H. Beck 2021) 167.

14 John Armour and Horst Eidenmueller, 'Self-Driving Corporations' (2019) 475 European Corporate Governance Institute - Law Working Paper 6 and 11. The authors describe also the AI of the future with the ability of so-called unsupervised learning, p. 12. At this moment it is premature to examine such systems. It is unlikely that the final assessment of the supervising lawyer would not be required in the foreseeable future.

15 McKamey (n 2) 7. The author refers to the Moravec's paradox according to which in highly specialized professions, relying on the high-intelligence requirement, it will be much easier to replace humans than in less intense professions. The legal profession could be then a victim of this development.

1.2. New business model

The impact of the AI on the traditional business models of the law firms will be far-reaching.[16] The regular scheme of earning money by medium or large law firms was the billing of hours,[17] which have been generated mostly by the junior partners and associates.[18] The business model of the law firm is based on the relatively small investment at the beginning of the commercial activity and then requiring a relatively high level of investment through the existence of the law firm, resulting e.g., from rising salaries of highly qualified members of the law firm. The expansion of the AI in the legal work changes this model dramatically: to start a law firm equipped with highly efficient AI-systems a substantive investment[19] would be required at the beginning (it could be a simplification depending on various payment schemes) and then the costs of the further functioning of the law firm would be reduced, due to the savings on the staff.[20] This reality would have an impact on the career of the young lawyers. In the future it will be extremely difficult to start a legal career. There will be no need to hire young lawyers due to the fact that exactly their work[21] will

16 (n 2) 179. The author expects the lowering of the legal services costs and improvement of the conditions of the access to the legal services (USA). It is probably a correct assumption from the long term perspective, but the necessity of the large investment at the beginning of the operation might reduce this effect.

17 Leah Wortham, 'The Future of the Legal Profession and Legal Services Delivery' in Leah Wortham and others (eds), *Learning from Practice. A Text for Experiential Legal Education* (West Academic Publishing 2016) 763; John Armour, Richard Parnham and Mari Sako, 'Augmented Lawyering' (2020) 558 European Corporate Governance Institute - Law Working Paper 24.

18 Richard Susskind, *Tomorrow's Lawyers. An Introduction to Your Future* (Oxford University Press 2017) 60.

19 Iga Kurowska, Kamil Szpyt, 'Legal Tech w kancelariach prawnych' (n 13) 162; Mark McKamey, 'Legal Technology' (n 2) 14-15. The author argues against with the view (Chester) according to which the lawyers' environment will be reluctant to change the traditional business approach in this respect. McKamey claims that such reluctance could appear in reality, but only in the short term. Finally, the advantages resulting from the AI would also prevail in this conservative environment.

20 Tomasz Zalewski, Podstawowe zasady skutecznego wykorzystania narzędzi Legal Tech in Dariusz Szostek (ed), *Legal Tech. Czyli jak bezpiecznie korzystać z narzędzi informatycznych w organizacji, w tym w kancelarii oraz dziale prawnym* (C. H. Beck 2021) 216.

21 Susskind and Susskind (n 10) 69. It is, however, disputed, how strong this impact on the legal profession will be. Some authors predict much lower reduction of the need for the staff – (n 2) 190. The author predicts that the outcome will

be replaced by the AI-based supporting systems.[22] A systematic rethinking of the design the future career models would be crucial in order not to lose the development opportunities for the younger generations of lawyers.[23]

2. *The ethical challenge*

The broad application of the AI in the law offices will require an adaptation of the professional code of conducts,[24] too. It would involve a revision of the interpretation of the codes' rules as well. The usage of the AI will mean that a different kind of skills would be necessary. A lawyer benefitting from the AI-support systems must understand well the way in which these systems function, and the way how the algorithms are designed to produce results.[25] Such lawyer should also know the limits of the system used. He or she should not blindly rely on the results which are produced by AI tool, and be able to verify whether the system used secures the required confidentiality of the services provided to the client.

The existing professional codes of conducts in Poland do not deal with the challenges of the AI-systems directly, even though the usage of the electronic systems has already been observed.[26] However, it should be taken into account that the existing codes of conduct apply also to the

---

be rather that lawyers would be able to conquer new fields of the activity. It is possible, but it does exclude the observation that in the core business this need will be reduced. It may encourage the further expansion of the business, but in case of the quite conservative legal businesses, at least from the perspective of such countries like Poland, it is likely that legal services would not expand to the new territories but the opportunity will be used to reduce the staff related expenses. Armour,Parnham and Sako (n 18), 3-4 stress that the AI would not replace lawyers in the law firm.

22 Susskind (n 19), 87; Armour, Parnham and Sako (n 18) 22.

23 On different career prognoses for young generation lawyers – Tony King, 'The Future of Legal Education from the Profession's Viewpoint: A Brave New World?' in Hilary Sommerlad and others (eds), *The Futures of Legal Education and the Legal Profession* (Hart 2015) 192.

24 Some attempts may be expected due to interest of e.g. Warsaw Attorneys-at Law's Bar – see: https://www.oirpwarszawa.pl/izba-warszawska-powoluje-komisje-ds-legaltech/.

25 Shimshaw (n 2) 196.

26 § 19.6 of the advocates' code of conduct (Zbiór Zasad Etyki Adwokackiej i Godności Zawodu (Kodeks Etyki Adwokackiej) from 27 February 2018) and Article 23 sentence 3 of the attorneys-at-law code of conduct (Kodeks Etyki Radcy Prawnego from 22 November 2014) refer to the safety of electronic documents.

AI-related concerns. It is necessary to interpret them having in mind the fundamental changes of the reality of the lawyering under the influence of the AI.[27]

2.1. Confidentiality

Both codes of conducts require keeping the confidentiality.[28] It is understood as a basis for the client's reliance towards the lawyers. A duty to keep all information regarding the client and his or her cases confidential[29] encompasses also the documents produced in the frame of providing the service to the client. The duty of confidentiality may be difficult to fulfil if the AI-systems are used.[30] A lawyer using the AI-supported systems must be sure that the use of a particular software does not endanger the data of their clients.[31] It depends mainly on the algorithms used, especially the details of how the self-learning mechanism really works and whether other users of this AI-based software get access to the data processed for the previous user.[32] It means that the lawyer must understand well the setting of the system within the Internet, in particular be aware of how the processing of data looks like.[33] He must know how the system works

27 Comment 8 to the Rule 1.1 to the American Bar Association of Model Rules of Professional Conduct on the lawyer's duty to provide competent representation to a client makes it clear that to maintain the requisite knowledge and skill, a lawyer should keep abreast of changes in the law and its practice, including the benefits and risks associated with relevant technology.

28 § 19.1 of the advocates' code of conduct and Article 15.1 of the attorneys-at-law code of conduct.

29 Although e.g. data about criminal convictions and offences (that are frequently processed by lawyers) are not within the utmost sensitive data under Article 9 GDPR, due to their particular meaning they are subject to special protection according to Article 10 GDPR – Mariusz Krzysztofek, 'Commentary to Article 10' in *Ochrona danych osobowych w Unii Europejskiej po reformie. Komentarz do rozporządzenia Parlamentu Europejskiego i Rady (UE) 2016/679* (Legalis 2016) para 7.

30 Leith and Hoey (n 14) 324; Shimshaw (n 2) 198.

31 About the technology challenges in regards to processing clients' data – Jerzy Nauman, Commentary to § 19 in *Zbiór Zasad Etyki Adwokackiej i Godności Zawodu* (Legalis 2020) para 63.

32 About the duty of care in the context of processing data with the use of technology on the example of personal data – Dariusz Szostek, Przechowywanie danych kancelarii w chmurze in Dariusz Szostek (ed), *Bezpieczeństwo danych i IT w kancelarii prawnej. Czyli jak bezpiecznie przechowywać dane w kancelarii prawnej* (C.H. Beck 2018) 300.

33 Walters (n 1) 1080-1082.

and whether the self-learning process of the AI does not endanger the observance of the confidentiality principle, what may happen if the external resources are also used for the self-learning process of the artificial intelligence.[34] It means that a lawyer must not use the system without being able to understand its functioning or without knowing what kind of data are used further. The principle behind the duty of confidentiality must apply regardless of the technology used – the AI-system must not utilize the data which are covered by the duty of confidentiality.

2.2. *Conflict of interests*

The above-mentioned remarks concern also the matter of the conflict of interests. An online AI system may use the resources gathered on the Internet. It means that the system may use also the data generated in one law firm for the purposes of the other law firm. It may create a situation of the conflict of interests, for instance if the data transmitted from the one law firm to another, even anonymised, are used to generate a better outcome for a possible opponent law firm, even in a different case. Of course, such data are converted into the Big Data and there is no possibility to identify the data of individual clients. Probably the AI-systems with self-learning ability based on the collected data from various law firms shall be regulated by the codes of conduct. The rule should probably allow for the usage of the AI-data, if there is no possibility to identify individual clients in any way and the self-learning process is based on the high amount of the data, coming from different sources, so that it is technically proven that the self-learning process is based on the material which is so differentiated that there is no technical possibility that the information harvested by the AI-based system from one case may support the opposing party to this case.

2.3. *Acting based on the professional skills and knowledge*

Acting for the client and on behalf of the client requires knowledge and skills which are adequate to the provided service. This rule, though written

34 Shimshaw (n 2) 200; On the use of the internal and external data (but not in the specific context of the law firm see: John Armour, Horst Eidenmueller, 'Self-Driving Corporations' (n 14) 17.

in different words, is found in both Polish code of conducts.[35] The usage of the AI-based systems would require lawyers to acquire abilities which differ from the abilities which traditionally have been expected from the these professionals.[36] A lawyer advising clients must understand well the logic behind the functioning of the system and must be aware of its limitations. The case theory designed with the support of the system must be verified by the lawyer. He or she must have the soft abilities[37] helping the client to make the final decision. It must be understood that the AI-based system cannot replace all factors which are considered by the judges in the courtroom or must be taken into consideration when looking for the real improvement of the client's situation.[38] It must be understood that the machine, even if very advanced and equipped with the perfectly developed self-learning systems, after analysing thousands of cases and doctrinal views still does not replace a human understanding and evaluation.[39]

3. *Changing the legal education of lawyers in the AI-age*

The above-mentioned abilities of lawyers require completely new approach to the process of legal education.[40] During the legal education in Poland there are very few opportunities to learn about the highly innovative systems supporting the lawyering work in the law firm. The lack of understanding how this technology works yields into being unprepared[41] to face the emerging challenges for the profession. Also, the professional

---

35 § 13 of the advocates' code of conduct and Article 12.1 of the attorneys-at-law code of conduct.

36 Armour Parnham and Sako (n 18) 5.

37 About the increased meaning of soft skills in lawyer's profession –Susskind (n 19) 75; Leah Wortham, 'The Future of the Legal Profession' (n 18) 789.

38 Shimshaw (n 2) 204. Author stresses the importance of the "soft" moral, social and political factors which even an advanced system cannot consider and sufficiently take into account.

39 Walters (n 1) 1079.

40 Wiesław Staśkiewicz and Tomasz Stawecki, 'Legal Databases and Their Functions in the Process of Interpreting and Applying the Law' (2012) 1 Archiwum Filozofii Prawa i Filozofii Społecznej 103, mentions the challenges to legal education due to distortion of theories of interpretation of law and decreased knowledge about law outside provisions of law.

41 On meaning of practical skills in legal education during studies Fryderyk Zoll, 'Przyszłość kształcenia prawników w Polsce' (2010) 6 Państwo i Prawo 25.

association of lawyers[42] must think how to organize the paths of the legal career, due to the diminished need for the young lawyers in the law firm using the AI-based systems. It is necessary to create a vision for the legal career of lawyers in the Legal Tech dominated world.

4. Conclusions

This short overview shows only a small number of issues which will emerge when the technological progress finally reaches the law firms. The vast application of the AI will deeply change the profession, requiring different set of skills from lawyers on one hand, and on the other – reshaping the organisation model of the law firm. The law schools and the professional association of lawyers should rise to the challenge and adjust the profession to new AI-fuelled environment. They must also adjust the rules of conducts, so that not only the legal knowledge is required but also clear understanding of the technology supporting the lawyers. The future of the legal profession is beginning, even in Poland.

42 The importance of legal education both during university studies and after them, in formula of lifelong learning is underlined in Polish doctrine by e.g. Arkadiusz Radwan, 'Edukacja prawnicza wobec wyzwań XXI wieku' in Ryszard Czarny and others (eds), *Państwo i prawo wobec wyzwań u progu trzeciej dekady XXI wieku. Księga jubileuszowa z okazji 70. urodzin Profesora Jerzego Jaskierni* (Wydawnictwo Adam Marszałek 2020) 206.

The Impact of Law Tech on the Future of Lawyers

Gabriela Bar <gabriela.bar@szostek-bar.pl>
WROCŁAW, Poland

Silvia A. Carretta <silvia.carretta@ipandtechlab.com>
STOCKHOLM, Sweden

Shobana Iyer <shobana.iyer@swanchambers.com>
LONDON, England

Abstract
The future belongs to rapidly evolving technologies. The most fascinating and capable of revolutionising legal industry is likely to be with the use of Artificial Intelligence (AI). It will be the main driver of changes in the legal profession. In the digital world of the future, human lawyers will need to demonstrate emotional intelligence and a deep understanding of how technology can help them to provide better services. These qualities and skills will undoubtedly be just as valuable as formal legal knowledge. The lawyers of tomorrow should focus on cooperating with AI, making sure it is developed and used legally, so as to augment their services rather than fearing being replaced by it. The future partner of law firms may be the leader of a multi-disciplinary team of professionals in which AI is substantially used. Legal teams consisting of people and AI could be a dynamic and very effective structure where humans have an important role to play thanks to their unique features and abilities: intellective judgment, empathy, creativity and adaptability.

Keywords:
LawTech, legal technology, future, lawyers of the future, artificial intelligence, AI, algorithms, machine learning, blockchain, technology, legal analytics, transparency, discrimination, judges, law firm, court.

1. Introduction

The revolutionary changes within the legal industry due to new technologies date back to the 1990s with the arrival of the Internet. With it, the possibility of faster communication via e-mail arrived, the creation of digital libraries, the primordial document management systems and early contract lifecycle management platforms which started to be used by lawyers to facilitate their daily activities.

In recent years there has seen a surge in innovation and investment in legal tech solutions. Lawyers have started using more key technologies such as electronic payments, client portals, and client intake and CRM products[1]. This is because exploiting the advantages of legal tech solutions enables them to be more efficient and productive, more in control of their businesses and acknowledge better the legal needs of clients.

The COVID-19 pandemic had brought about an unprecedented and accelerated adoption of technology by lawyers. The Clio LTR 2020[2] report indicates that the vast majority (82 %) of law firms are using software to manage their practice, 79 % of lawyers rely on cloud technology to store their firm's data, 62 % of firms allow clients to securely share and sign documents electronically, 73 % allow clients to pay invoices electronically, and 83 % of firms are conducting meetings with clients through remote video conferencing applications.

Remote hearings are nothing new to civil proceedings in some countries like UK (particularly in commercial cases where an international element/party is involved), but the COVID-19 pandemic has forced courts and tribunals in all areas of practice to proceed rapidly to another level, pushing judges, counsels, and participants out of their normal comfort zone. There were three major elements that had caused difficulties to arise: firstly, the lockdown had made the move towards 'full' remote hearings where all participants (including the judge, judge's clerk, counsel, witnesses etc.) are all appearing remotely from separate locations; secondly the speed at which this transition had to take place, and finally, the use of remote hearing in practice areas where remote hearings were uncommon. The use of technology to conduct court hearings had become an inevitable requirement to keep access to justice open and to reduce the backlogs

---

1 Clio, 'Legal trends for solo law firms' (Clio.com, 2021), <https://www.clio.com/resources/legal-trends/2021-solo-report/?utm_source=press&utm_medium=web&utm_campaign=solo-ltr-2021>, accessed: 13 April 2021.

2 Clio, 'Legal Trends Report' (Clio.com,2020) <https://www.clio.com/wp-content/uploads/2020/08/2020-Legal-Trends-Report.pdf> accessed: 13 April 2021.

and delays created by adjournments. The same can be said also for those countries where the use of such technology in the judiciary system has so far been viewed more sceptically (such as in Poland).

The legal profession has undergone fast technological changes but there is so much more that technology can do for lawyers to improve their daily activities, businesses and serve their clients' needs and expectations. The trends indicate that lawyers will be expected to embrace technology even further as technology develops in using LawTech tools. Lawyers will be required to develop their know-how in the use of the underlying technology, and have more advanced digital and computational competences. There is clearly economic pressure for ever-greater use of artificial intelligence (AI) in both low-end and high-end consumers of legal services. The last decade or so has seen a dramatic increase in the capabilities of AI based systems and their application has potential to bring about significant change in the legal sector.

The future for lawyers will substantially be impacted with the use of LawTech tools: it will not only affect the automation of activities and the possibility of replacing certain tasks (e.g. performing routine and repetitive activities or recommendation systems) but it will also see the use of advanced autonomous systems that can cooperate with, and augment certain tasks to deliver greater efficiencies, improve access to know-how and provide better services.

2. *New Means of Production*

The legal ecosystem has evolved through trends taking hold within the industry, and they include data exploitation to enable effective project management, new LawTech products, use of blockchain solutions and AI technologies for the simplification of legal works. These new means of productions have become key drivers of quality and investment in legal technology with in-house legal teams, in law firms, in government legal departments.

A survey from Gartner presented that the proportion of budgets spent by legal departments on technology is set to increase threefold by 2025, as legal tech solutions have driven lawyers' appetite to expand their use of technology to support workflows and meet productivity demands[3]. Lawy-

3 <https://www.gartner.com/smarterwithgartner/5-legal-technology-trends-changing-in-house-legal-departments> The Gartner's survey states that legal departments will

ers are keener to exploit technology primarily to drive efficiency by using it for deal management tools, intellectual property portfolio management, eDiscovery, M&A due diligence procedures, contract negotiation, data collection and dashboard building, compliance reviews, legal research and more.

Another important area that lawyers will need to learn to exploit is with data. IBM had calculated in 2016 that 90 % of all world's stored data has been created in the past two years[4], creating new challenges and opportunities for analysis. Data relevant to legal work is no longer just within the sole ambit of accredited legal professionals and is becoming accessible, searchable and analysable to non-lawyers, which means wider competition. Data shows patterns that reveal recurring problems and inefficiencies, and shows insights into how the work is being managed, divided within the office's resources and with which costs. Understanding the value of data will help lawyers rethink who does their work and learn significant information about how to offer better value to their clients and where to look for quality improvement. AI is an invaluable aid in the processing of these huge amounts of data, in searching for hidden correlations that elude the human eye, and in choosing the best solutions.

Blockchain and distributed ledger technology (DLT) are another set of technology that can be used by lawyers to improve their services[5]. DLT can help the legal services become more accessible, transparent, automated and cost efficient. Law firms are leveraging DLT to streamline and simplify their transactional work, to be able to digitally sign documents and to store legal agreements in an immutable way.

For instance, DLT creates a shared ledger accessible by all parties to an agreement, it contains coded-in compliance obligations (through smart contracts, automated contractual terms run by code, embedded in the chain), removing the risk for non-compliance and leaving less room for misinterpretation. Another advantage is the ability to record events for

---

have automated 50 % of their legal work related to major corporate transactions by 2024, accessed 13 April 2021.

4 <https://www.ibm.com/blogs/watson/2016/05/biggest-data-challenges-might-not-even-know>, accessed 13 April 2021.

5 In brief blockchain is a type of distributed ledger technology (DLT) that allows for peer-to-peer transactions without the need for a trusted authority (if a public blockchain), creating an immediate, immutable, transparent record of the transaction. They are effective because the transaction is based on a distributed consensus between all nodes on the chain.

a long period of time, without the possibility for them to be modified without trace or losing any of the judicial authority.

There is a wide range of areas where blockchain could become a major player, from supporting the changing nature of legal work to enabling new lines of business and differentiating service offerings. Practical examples of DLT uses in the legal industry include the recording of music works to protect copyright[6], safe storage of real estate deeds transforming documents into immutable tokenised assets[7], time stamp certification of agreements with verifiable digital signature, automation of payments (e.g., management of escrow accounts at a fraction of the cost of manual labour through smart contract)[8]. In short, the transparent, immutable and secure nature of DLT will allow lawyers to solve various types of legal matters, streamline and simplify their transactional work, digitally sign and immutably store legal agreements. Further DLT can also provide more transparency as the shared ledger is accessible by relevant parties, and any such contracts can embed regulatory and/or compliance information, reducing the risk for misinterpretation and/or non-compliance issues. Apparently, lawyers can spend up to 48 % of their time on administrative tasks, including information between software or updating client trust ledgers[9] which can be significantly eliminated with the use of DLT.

In 2017, PwC revealed that 70 % of surveyed law firms would be open to utilise smart contracts for transactional legal services[10]. What is known, however, is that today there is still a current scepticism around DLT and

---

6 Silvia A. Carretta, *Blockchain challenges to copyright: Revamping the online music industry* (Stockholm University 2019) <http://urn.kb.se/resolve?urn=urn:nbn:se:su:diva-173248> accessed 13 April 2021.

7 Shelter Zoom, based in New York, is the first real estate technology startup to incorporate blockchain technology within the real estate industry's infrastructure using Docuwalk, a blockchain-based platform that transforms documents and contracts into immutable, interoperable tokenized assets on the Blockchain.

8 Neel Kirit and Priya Sarkar, 'EscrowChain: Leveraging Ethereum Blockchain as Escrow in Real Estate', (2017) 5, 10 International Journal of Innovative Research in Computer and Communication Engineering, <https://www.researchgate.net/publication/325392683_EscrowChain_Leveraging_Ethereum_Blockchain_as_Escrow_in_Real_Estate> accessed 21 June 2021.

9 <https://www.clio.com/resources/legal-trends/2018-report> accessed 20 April 2021.

10 PwC, 'Time for change PwC Law Firms' Survey 2017' (pwc.fr, 2017) <https://www.pwc.fr/fr/assets/files/pdf/2017/12/law-firms-survey-report-2017.pdf> accessed 13 April 2021. Out of the analysis of total legal firms interviewed, 41 % will use blockchain for transactional legal services, 21 % for business support and 31 % for providing high-value legal services.

blockchain which now holds little practical appeal for lawyers due to the lack of a minimal viable ecosystem. Until such an ecosystem is created law firms and in-house legal departments will not be able to take full advantage of this technology.

Lawyers could obtain many advantages by embracing the latest technologies involving artificial intelligence (AI). In the last five years there has been a hype around the implementation of AI in every industry and the legal industry is no exception. AI is posed to develop fast and to bring together an incremental change for lawyers that are willing to increasingly embrace these new opportunities offered by AI to jump-start automation, efficiency, and interconnectivity of its operations.

For example, legal AI tools have been developed to help lawyers review a large number of documents in instances of M&A procedures.[11] But that is not just it: the speed at which AI algorithms are developing, becoming better and faster at learning, promises a fast journey into the reality of natural language processing tools for leveraging legal text data, to extract more quickly and precisely information from a huge data set of legal documents (saving lots of hours of manual labour). Through both machine learning and deep learning, AI systems have the ability to mimic, to some extent, human decision-making. These AI tools could be used for text summaries, extracting attributes and relations, document relevance scoring, predicting outcomes (e.g. likelihood of certain crimes being committed in the future or to infer statistical commonalities between judgements to decide how to proceed on a case) and also for answering legal questions.[12]

In commercial transactions, AI is employed to scan voluminous documentation to identify unusual, unexpected, or disadvantageous contractual clauses[13]. In a recent study, experienced US corporate lawyers were pitted against the LawGeex AI to spot issues in non-disclosure agreements. The

11 Philip Hacker, Ralf Krestel and Sstefan Grundmann and others, 'Explainable AI under contract and tort law: legal incentives and technical challenges' (2020) 28 Artificial Intelligence Law 415–439 <https://doi.org/10.1007/s10506-020-09260-6> accessed 20 April 2021.

12 John Nay, 'Natural Language Processing and Machine Learning for Law and Policy Texts' (7 April 2018), <https://ssrn.com/abstract=3438276> accessed 21 June 2021.

13 Joe Dysart, 'AI Removes the Drudgery from Legal Due Diligence' (Communications of the ACM, 8 January 2019) <https://cacm.acm.org/news/233886-ai-removes-the-drudgery-from-legal-due-diligence/fulltext> accessed 19 April 2021; Lauri Donahue, 'A Primer on Using Artificial Intelligence in the Legal Profession' (JOLT Digest, 3 January 2018) <https://jolt.law.harvard.edu/digest/a-primer-on-using-artificial-intelligence-in-the-legal-profession> accessed19 April 2021;

lawyers achieved an 85 % success rate, against the AI's 94 %; lawyers took 92 minutes on average to complete the task which took the AI 26 seconds[14]. Advances in AI have encouraged non-lawyers in the US to offer services that were otherwise the exclusive domain of lawyers. Several US states have begun to consider licensing non-lawyers to provide some limited legal services: a practice known as "Limited-License Legal Technicians" (LLLTs)[15].

It is noteworthy that e-disclosure in common law litigation has advanced significantly since the simple keyword search method. Now algorithms are used efficiently for predictive coding, where the capacity of the AI system is employed to learn to respond to unprogrammed situations by the lawyer. This process has been endorsed by the English High Court[16] as appropriate to consider in reducing costs and increasing efficiency, avoiding necessary delays to the effective resolution of cases. In the US it has been claimed that AI discovery has a better track record than human review[17].

The CaseCruncher Alpha program[18] took a challenge between 100 lawyers and the CaseCruncherAI system in predicting the outcome of 775 Payment Protection Insurance Claims likely to be made by the Financial Ombudsman. The CaseCruncher AI System won not only in speed but with an accuracy rate of 86.6 % compared with 66.3 % by the lawyers. AI systems have been trained to predict the outcome of court proceedings[19]. Im-

---

Chris Goodman, 'AI/Esq: Impacts of Artificial Intelligence in Lawyer-Client Relationships' (2019) 72 Okla. L. Rev. 149.

14 LawGeex, 'Comparing the Performance of Artificial Intelligence to Human Lawyers in the Review of Standard Business Contracts' (LawGeex, 2018), <http://ai.lawgeex.com/rs/345-WGV-842/images/LawGeex%20eBook%20Al%20vs%20Lawyers%202018.pdf> accessed 20 April 2021.

15 B. Sheppard, 'Incomplete Innovation and the Premature Disruption of Legal Services' (2015) 1797 Mich. St. L. Rev. 1842. A State of California task force called for the bar to consider a pilot programme for LLLTs: <http://board.calbar.ca.gov/docs/agendaItem/Public/agendaitem1000013042.pdf> accessed 19 April 2021.

16 *Pyrrho Investments Ltd v MWB Property Ltd* [2016] EWHC 256 (Ch) and *David Brown -v- BCA Trading Ltd & Others* [2016] EWHC 1464 (Ch). The learning strategy of predictive coding is described in: Richard Bolton and David Hand, 'Unsupervised profiling methods for fraud detection' (2001) Proceedings of credit scoring and credit control VII , 235–255.

17 *Federal Housing Finance Agency v HSBC North America Holdings Inc*, Nos 11 Civ. 6189 (DLC), 11 Civ, 2014 WL 1909446, at 1 (S.D.N.Y. May 13, 2014).

18 <https://www.case-crunch.com/#challenge> accessed 20 April 2021.

19 Reed C. Lawlor, 'What computers can do: analysis and prediction of judicial decisions' (1963) 49 American Bar Association Journal 337 cited in: Nikolaos

pressive results have been achieved in predicting decisions of the European Court of Human Rights[20], and of the US Supreme Court[21]. Such statistical analysis is sometimes used by law firms to decide whether to take on cases[22]. However, it is questionable how accurate these AI systems will play when it comes to assessing the exercise of judicial discretion or dealing with novel or complicated cases. Machine Learning systems are developing legal research skills by employing user-feedback to train algorithms to move beyond keyword searches and perform ever more demanding tasks[23].

3. *Hybrid Disruption Through Lawtech*

We are in the middle of a 'hybrid disruption' in terms of implementation of new technologies within the legal industry. LawTech empowers lawyers in better doing their work, reducing repetitive works, allowing them to focus more on their specialisations, and bringing better value to their clients. Brian Zubert, Director of Ecosystem Development of Thomson Reuters, when asked about the past and present of the legal profession, stated that:

> *"Investment in Legal Tech has grown substantially in recent years, and so too have the number of solutions and services available. Although law firms and corporate legal departments have more choices than ever, the reality is that there are more options available than purchasing budget, procurement capacity, integration capability, rollout management, and investment*

Aletras and others , 'Predicting Judicial Decisions of the European Court of Human Rights: A Natural Language Processing Perspective' (2016) Peer J. Comput. Sci. <https://peerj.com/articles/cs-93.pdf> accessed 19 April 2021.

20 Aletras and others, (n 22).

21 Matthew Hutson, 'Artificial Intelligence Prevails at Predicting Supreme Court Decisions', (Science, 2 May 2017), <https://www.sciencemag.org/news/2017/05/artificial-intelligence-prevails-predicting-supreme-court-decisions> accessed 19 April 2021.

22 Deloitte, 'Objections Overruled: The Case for Disruptive Technology in the Legal Profession' (Deloitte, 2017), available <https://www2.deloitte.com/content/dam/Deloitte/uk/Documents/corporate-finance/deloitte-uk-technology-in-law-firms.pdf> accessed 19 April 2021.

23 Brian Sheppard, 'Does Machine-Learning-Powered Software Make Good Research Decisions? Lawyers Can't Know for Sure' (Legal Rebels, 22 November 2016) <http://www.abajournal.com/legalrebels/article/does_machine-learning-powered_software_make_good_research_decisions_lawyers> accessed 19 April 2021.

> *needed to drive meaningful user adoption. 2020 magnified the operating constraints and competing for technical priorities"*[24].

While automation may substitute some tasks for lawyers, the ability to undertake other tasks augmented by AI technologies becomes more valuable[25]. As AI acquires more advanced skills it may reach a stage where it would be seen as an alternative to many lawyers' tasks[26]. We suggest that: (a) some legal tasks will remain beyond the capabilities of AI for the foreseeable future and continue to be performed by lawyers; (b) some tasks (predominantly the repetitive and/or administrative) will be substituted by AI systems; and (c) new tasks will be created in order to be delivered through AI systems legitimately, which will be carried out by multidisciplinary teams consisting of lawyers and other experts working together.

Professor Brian Sheppard outlined the possible effects of AI's "disruptive innovation" on legal services[27]; in his view AI will not entirely replace lawyers in the foreseeable future, but it could make sufficient inroads to disrupt the economics of the legal profession; a process which he refers to as 'premature disruption, since it would provide only some, but not all, legal services. Premature disruption would affect the profitability of the legal profession without offering an alternative to the core services that lawyers offer. Core services consist of the creative intellectual tasks of the lawyer like arguing difficult cases, advancing novel legal interpretations, developing legal concepts and generally advancing the study of the law.

AI could reduce demand for lawyers' core services or lead to a fall in their profitability or bring down the number of lawyers needed to provide such services[28]. Demand for core lawyer services could diminish because

---

24 Kenneth Jones and Matthew Jones, 'Strategies supporting the development and deployment of high-quality legal software 221)' (Legal evolution blog, 31 January 2021) <https://www.legalevolution.org/2021/01/tactics-supporting-the-development-and-deployment-of-high-quality-legal-software-221> accessed 20 April 2021.

25 Andrew McAfee and Erik Brynjolfsson, 'Human Work in the Robotic Future: Policy for the Age of Automation' (2016) 95, 4 Foreign Affairs 139-150 <https://www.jstor.org/stable/43946940> accessed 21 June 2021.

26 John O. McGinnis and Russell G. Pearce, 'The Great Disruption: How Machine Intelligence Will Transform the Role of Lawyers in the Delivery of Legal Services' (2013) 82 Fordham L. Rev. 3041.

27 Sheppard (n 18). See generally, Clayton Christensen, 'Disruptive Innovation' (2020), <http://www.claytonchristensen.com/key-concepts> accessed 20 April 2021.

28 It seems that this process is already underway with large firms restricting recruitment: The Law Society, 'Law Society report, Legal services sector forecasts 2017–2025' (Law Society of England and Wales, 2018) <https://www.lawsociety.org.uk

clients may be content with the limited but cheaper services offered by AI. For example, instead of litigating, parties may settle in accordance with AI-approximated predictions of the outcome of litigation. The profitability of litigation services themselves may fall as profits from peripheral activities decline due to automation; because, for instance, disclosure and document review have been fully automated, or mediation is conducted by machines.[29]

However, the development and implementation of AI systems in LawTech to perform tasks (whether they be substituted or augmented tasks) will require human capital and intelligence for it to be legitimately functional so as to have sufficient trust and confidence in the AI system. This will create new roles for lawyers working in multidisciplinary teams with other professionals, not excluding AI itself (i.e. centaurs AI)[30].

Further, the use of LawTech and AI in society generally will bring about novel legal issues and challenges, for example in the way intellectual property laws may have to be adapted and applied. These will need more intellectual input from lawyers to steer proper evolution and governance of laws.

/support-services/research-trends/legal-services-sector-forecasts>/ accessed 20 April 2021.; Jane Croft, 'More than 100,000 legal roles to become automated' (Financial Times, 15 March 2016), <https://www.ft.com/content/c8ef3f62-ea9c-11e5-888e-2eadd5fbc4a4>, accessed 20 April 2021. Consultancy firm McKinsey estimates that 22% of a lawyer's job and 35% of a paralegal's job can be automated: Michael Chui, James Manyika and Mehdi Miremadi, 'Four fundamentals of workplace automation' (McKinsey Digital, 1 November 2015) <https://www.mckinsey.com/business-functions/mckinsey-digital/our-insights/four-fundamentals-of-workplace-automation> accessed 20 April 2021.

29 E.g. mediation: University of Southern California, 'Do we trust artificial intelligence agents to mediate conflict? Not entirely' (Science Daily, 16 October 2019) <https://www.sciencedaily.com/releases/2019/10/191016094909.htm> accessed 21 June 2021.

30 Nicky Case, 'How To Become A Centaur' (Journal of Design and Science MIT Media Lab, 02 February 2018), <https://jods.mitpress.mit.edu/pub/issue3-case/release/6> accessed 12 April 2021.; Hilary G. Escajeda, 'The Vitruvian Lawyer: How to Thrive in an Era of AI and Quantum Technologies' (2020) XXIX Kansas J. of Law & Pub. Pol'y 421-521 , 463), <https://ssrn.com/abstract=3534683> accessed 14 March 2021.

4. New Challenges Posed by the Use of AI

While the benefits of AI are clear - e.g. cost-effective legal services, faster outcomes, greater consistency - there are also novel challenges and risks that have to be considered by lawyers.

Dr. Paola Cecchi-Dimeglio, a behavioural scientist and senior research fellow for Harvard Law School's Centre on the Legal Profession, stated in an interview that it's very important for legal organisations or companies in general to determine why they are using AI in the first place: "*You have to remember that with many legal organisations, the data they are looking at is either what is publicly available or data they have gathered from working with their clients. And when artificial intelligence starts working with this data, it can be a very positive thing for a law firm*"[31]. She noted that this process allows firms to make better decisions about jurisdictions, judges' decisions, and client matters in comparable situations. But wisely she added that "*problems arise, especially problems with biases, when the organization isn't careful about where it's taking its data from or about what portion of data it's using and not using. Because if you start out with a biased history, you're going to have biased results.*"[32]

A classic example of how incompetency in the use of technology can cause substantial injustice is illustrated in the case of the COMPAS algorithm,[33] which was used by US judges for assessing the probability of reoffending. The algorithm was based on questions which indirectly discriminated against black humans, who were given relatively disproportionate sentences in comparison to white humans. Algorithm bias can be a troublesome problem which has attracted considerable criticism.[34]

---

31 Thomson Reuters Institute, *Ask Dr. Paola: Detecting & Battling Biases in Artificial Intelligence & Machine Learning (Part 2)*, March 29, 2018. <https://www.legalexecutiveinstitute.com/ask-dr-paola-battling-ai-biases-march> accessed 13 April 2021.

32 Thomson Reuters Institute (n. 34).

33 <https://www.propublica.org/article/machine-bias-risk-assessments-in-criminal-sentencing>, accessed 29 April 2021.

34 Law Society Commission on the Use of Algorithms in the Justice System, *Algorithms in the Criminal Justice System* (2019) <https://www.lawsociety.org.uk/topics/research/algorithm-use-in-the-criminal-justice-system-report> accessed 23 September 2021. Liberty have called for a ban on the use of such algorithms. See: I. Iberty, 'Liberty Report Exposes Police Forces' Use of Discriminatory Data to Predict Crime'(libertyhumanrights.org.uk, 4 February 2019), <https://www.libertyhumanrights.org.uk/issue/liberty-report-exposes-police-forces-use-of-discriminatory-data-to-predict-crime> accessed 20 April 2021.

The main challenges to be address by the use of AI systems include:

Bias and discrimination: the data sample used to train and test the AI system can often be insufficiently representative of the populations from which they are drawing inferences. This creates real possibilities of biased and discriminatory outcomes, because the data being fed into the systems is flawed from the start. Secondly, it should be noted that as AI technologies gain their insights from the existing structures and dynamics of the societies they analyse, so data-driven technologies can reproduce, reinforce, and amplify the patterns of marginalisation, inequality, and discrimination that exist in these societies. Further, because many of the features, metrics, and analytic structures of the models that enable data mining are chosen by their designers, these technologies can potentially replicate their designers' preconceptions and biases.

Lack of transparency, black box effect: transparency of legal decision-making is a requirement of fairness and accountability, it bolsters public confidence and promotes legitimacy[35]. Many machine learning models generate their results by operating on high dimensional correlations that are beyond the interpretive capabilities of human scale reasoning. In these cases, the rationale of algorithmically produced outcomes that directly affect decision subjects remains opaque to those subjects. While in some use cases, this lack of explainability may be acceptable, in some applications, where the processed data could harbour traces of discrimination, bias, inequity, or unfairness, the opaqueness of the model may be deeply problematic. Quite apart from considerations of fairness and accountability, lack of transparency may conceal overestimation of the reliability of AI algorithms' outcomes. Facial-recognition results, for instance, could be taken as conclusive, overlooking the fact that the system produces false positives in 20 to 34 % of cases[36]. Solutions to the

35 More on AI Transparency: Gabriela Bar, *Explainability as a legal requirement for Artificial Intelligence*, (Medium.com, November 2020) <https://medium.com/womeninai/explainability-as-a-legal-requirement-for-artificial-intelligence-systems-66da5a0aa693>, accessed: 12/04/2021.

36 Alice Feng and Shuyan Wu, 'The myth of the impartial machine' (Parametric Press, 1 May 2019) <https://parametric.press/issue-01/the-myth-of-the-impartial-machine>. Margot Kaminski, 'Binary Governance: Lessons from the GDPR's approach to Algorithmic Accountability' (2019) 92 S. Cal. L. Rev. 1529); Monika Zalnieriute, Bennett Moses and George Williams, 'The Rule of Law and Automation of Government Decision-Making' (2019) 82 M.L.R. 425. European Parliamentary Research Service, 'A governance framework for algorithmic accountabi-

explainability of AI algorithms have been considered with the use of counterfactuals which identify the prime factors that lead to the outcome, in order to identify and neutralise any unfairness.[37] It is also to be discussed whether it would be easier to deal with algorithm bias than with human unconscious bias[38].

Privacy and Data Protection: with the use of big data, protecting privacy, client confidentiality, and legal professional privilege have to be carefully considered when designing, and using AI systems.

Isolation and Disintegration of Social Connection: Excessive automation might reduce the need for human-to-human interaction limiting exposure to worldviews and peer coordination and might polarise relationships and views. This may reduce the development of emotional interactive skills for future lawyers as well as the quality of client relationships.

Lawyers will have to be constantly aware of the challenges and ethical concerns on the uses of AI in both the legal sector and in any client sector specific technology used, (e.g., FinTech, InsurTech) as well as the growing laws and regulations surrounding the use and deployment of the technology. It is particularly important in the context of compliance with the principles of professional ethics and professional secrecy. An interesting idea may be a system of conformity assessment (digital certification) for lawyers using advanced AI systems to provide legal services.

Although the full adaptation of AI is still in its infancy in many areas of the law, as mentioned above there are already issues around the use of AI that have raised to the surface with regard to ethics, data protection, fundamental rights, discrimination and bias passed down from humans to the AI. Like many similarly situated industries across world markets, it may be wise for the legal industry to pause before jumping blindfolded on

---

lity and transparency', Panel for the Future of Science and Technology (STOA 2019)), p.64, <http://www.europarl.europa.eu/stoa/en/document/EPRS_STU(2019)624262> accessed 20 April 2021.

37 Sandra Watcher, Brent Mittelstadt and Chris Russel, 'Counterfactual explanations without opening the black box: automated decisions and the GDPR' (2018) 31, 2 Harvard Journal of Law and Technology <https://jolt.law.harvard.edu/assets/articlePDFs/v31/Counterfactual-Explanations-without-Opening-the-Black-Box-Sandra-Wachter-et-al.pdf> accessed 20 April 2021.

38 Holger Spamann and Lars Klöhn, 'Justice is Less Blind, and Less Legalistic, Than We Thought: Evidence from an Experiment with Real Judges' (2017) 45 J.L.S. 255. They found that judges' decisions were affected by irrelevant characteristics of defendants but that they had failed to mention these in their judgments.

using a new technology that is not fully understood. The implementation of AI innovative solutions in the legal industry has really only just started. We need to see how it will play out over the next decade or two, to see whether AI will truly bring a disruptive transformation to the legal sector.

5. Innovation as a Must on the Long Run

LawTech solutions are a key part of the disruption and development within the legal industry. But technology alone cannot be the sole disruptive factor. Lawyers are expected to integrate the use of technology with specialised knowledge with regard to how each new technology works. The lack of training in tech innovation and related disciplines makes it challenging for lawyers to be able to make conscious and long-lasting decisions to their business models and be successful in the long run. Lawyers will have to master the basics of legal technologies available on the market and this requires enormous talent, energy, commitment and skill.

This is also the approach supported by bar associations, which understand the need for their members to become more knowledgeable in terms of new technologies. For instance, the American Bar Association changed its rule on lawyer competency to requiring that lawyers have duty to "*keep abreast of changes in the law and its practice, including the benefits and risks associated with relevant technology*"[39] to maintain the requisite knowledge and skill. The Law Society and the Bar Council of England and Wales takes a continuing view to keep members informed of relevant guidance and training, and work with relevant authorities to deal with novel use of technologies.

The next few years will require from lawyers a rethinking of the legal profession as we know it. It will be necessary to fully understand how the changed picture of our post-2020 society may have also changed the nature of the legal profession (not only from a technological perspective) with new services that must replace traditional ones and new market areas that are emerging on the horizon. Alongside, there are the issues of the necessary digitalisation of large spaces of the legal profession and the automation of various routine processes. In addition to the vexed

39 American Bar Association, 'Model Rules of Professional, Rule 1.1 – Competence, Comment' (American Bar Association, August 2020) <https://www.americanbar.org/groups/professional_responsibility/publications/model_rules_of_professional_conduct/rule_1_1_competence/comment_on_rule_1_1> accessed 20 April 2021.

question of liberalisation, due to the emergency of a saturated market and high competition, it will be necessary to rethink how lawyers offer their services virtually, modernising their billing and payment structures, including price transparency and flexibility, unbundling legal services offline, and offering specialised services.

At the end of the day, meeting the needs of firms, legal departments, technology companies, vendors, and so on, requires a team effort in pursuit of a joint ambition: getting legal work done simply, efficiently, and accurately. This is a great first step, but it must be substantiated with action and engagements discussion in detail. Until lawyers are willing to invest in gaining legal tech knowledge, knowhow and solutions, there will be a large delay in the development for LawTech solutions in the legal industry.

The future direction of LawTech development is worth considering now. Even if AI becomes solid enough that we can be sure that the AI applies the right rules, takes all circumstances into account, and is impartial, will we be able to understand the logical argument carried out by the algorithm to trust its decision? Will AI ever be able to consider the thousands shades of grey that human life generates, which have a significant impact on the interpretation of declarations of will and the resolution of litigation?

It seems that the lawyers of tomorrow should focus on using AI to augment their services rather than the fear of being replaced by it. The future partners of the law firm may be leaders of a multi-disciplinary, multi-diverse team of professionals in which AI is substantially implemented and used. Legal teams consisting of people using AI could be a dynamic and very effective structure where humans have an important role to play, thanks to their unique features and abilities: intellective judgment, empathy, creativity and adaptability.

A Quest for Technological Competence: Raising the Bar

Doug Surtees <doug.surtees@usask.ca>

Craig Zawada <craig@zawada.ca>
SASKATOON, Canada

Abstract
The necessity for legal professionals to acquire and maintain a minimum standard of technological competence for lawyers has never been higher. Regulators of the legal profession in several jurisdictions have imposed a duty of technological competence on lawyers. The authors argue that law societies and law schools have an obligation to work together to include appropriate technological education in law school. This requires teaching not only Law of Technology (LOT) concepts such as Intellectual Property but also Law Practice Technology (LPT) concepts.

Keywords:
educating lawyers, technological competence , tech competence
technological education, tech education, tech ed, lawyers' duties, code of conduct, law of technology, law and tech, law practice technology, law practice tech, law school curricula, law school reform, continuing legal education, legal ed, law society duty, legal education reform, legal ed reform, legal education, legal ed, professional development

Lawyers are the original knowledge workers. An absolute statement like this invites debate and disagreement. Other professions depend on their own specialized know-how, after all. But there is no doubt that law rests almost entirely on information and its application.

So it is odd that lawyers have not been the vanguard of the Information Age. Somewhat the opposite, actually. Law and lawyers have been criticized for not keeping up with the internet, mobile computing and other commonplace technologies.[1] Despite its reliance on information and its application, the legal profession has not been a high-tech leader.

The landscape is not entirely bleak. Some lawyers' codes of conduct have adopted a duty of technological competence. The American Bar Association approved a such a duty in 2012. It has since been implemented by a majority of US states. The Federation of Law Societies of Canada's Model Code added a comparable duty in 2019. It has been adopted by several Canadian jurisdictions. This duty now exists on the same plane as duties of confidentiality, civility and other fundamental elements of ethical legal practice.

Mandating a duty is just the first step. Although the ultimate result could be sanctions and penalties for non-compliance, that is clearly not the goal.[2] The purpose of adopting the duty at the outset was undoubtedly to elevate lawyer skills so they were "competent"[3] when delivering services in the Information Age.

Competence does not just happen. All skills required by codes of conduct, regulator rules or otherwise rely on an infrastructure to provide sufficient education and training to learn those skills. The duty of technological competence is no different.

All participants in the education of legal practitioners have a responsibility to support the new duty. This includes not only the regulators, through their continuing professional development (CPD) programs, but also law schools and private providers of legal training. This paper will review the new requirements, the delivery of legal education in Canada, and barriers to bringing technology education into the current system.

---

1 Jordan Furlong, *Law is a Buyer's Market: Building a Client-First Law Firm* (Law21 Press 2017) 60

2 Many regulators, including the Law Society of Saskatchewan, have intentionally moved to a first mindset of coaching rather than discipline. This recognizes that prevention is usually easier than remedy, and that the ultimate goal is not penalties but public protection.

3 Measuring competence is fraught with issues, and they will not be discussed here.

Adoption of a Duty of Technological Competence

The list of reasons cited to require lawyers to possess a duty of technological competence includes:[4]

- The constant need to maintain and improve efficiency when delivering legal services
- Client and societal demand for modern delivery of services
- The increasing digitalization of society's institutions and their delivery of services

Technology related issues, including such diverse topics as blockchain, privacy and intellectual property protection have emerged in all legal fields. In response, the Federation of Law Societies of Canada (FLSC) adopted a duty of technological competence in October, 2019.[5] The FLSC is the national coordinating body of the 14 law societies mandated by provincial and territorial law to regulate Canada's 130,000 lawyers, Quebec's 3,800 notaries and Ontario's 11,300 licensed paralegals. The FLSC maintains a Model Code of Professional Conduct. This Code has been implemented in whole or part by most Canadian law societies, including our home jurisdiction of Saskatchewan.[6]

In November, 2019, the Law Society of Saskatchewan adopted changes to its Code of Professional Conduct based on the Model Code. The language adopted in Saskatchewan reads:

3.1-2 …

> *[4A] To maintain the required level of competence, a lawyer should develop an understanding of, and ability to use, technology relevant to the nature and area of the lawyer's practice and responsibilities. A lawyer should under-*

---

4 See <https://flsc.ca/wp-content/uploads/2014/10/Consultation-Report-Draft-Model-Code-Amendments-for-web-Jan2017-FINAL.pdf> accessed 1 September 2021. See also Stacey Blaustein, Melinda McLellan and James Sherer, 'Digital Direction for the Analog Attorney-Date Protection, E-Discovery, and the Ethics of Technological Competence In Today 's World of Tomorrow'(2016) 22, 4, 1 Richmond Journal of Law & Technology.

5 The addition was added as a Commentary item to the existing duty of competence: "A lawyer must perform all legal services undertaken on a client's behalf to the standard of a competent lawyer."

6 Saskatchewan is one of 10 provinces which, along with 3 territories, form the Canadian federation. Like all other provinces and territories (except Quebec, which implements a dual common law / civil law system), Saskatchewan is a common law jurisdiction.

stand the benefits and risks associated with relevant technology, recognizing the lawyer's duty to protect confidential information set out in section 3.3.

[4B] The required level of technological competence will depend upon whether the use or understanding of technology is necessary to the nature and area of the lawyer's practice and responsibilities and whether the relevant technology is reasonably available to the lawyer. In determining whether technology is reasonably available, consideration should be given to factors including: a) The lawyer's or law firm's practice areas; b) The geographic locations of the lawyer's or firm's practice; and c) The requirements of clients.

As of May, 2021, many Canadian regulators have adopted the Model Code changes, or issued separate practice advisories.[7] These changes followed similar additions to the American Bar Association's Model Rules of Professional Conduct. Comment 8 to Model Rule 1.1 was amended in 2012 to add the emphasized text:

To maintain the requisite knowledge and skill, a lawyer should keep abreast of changes in the law and its practice, *including the benefits and risks associated with relevant technology*, engage in continuing study and education and comply with all continuing legal education requirements to which the lawyer is subject.[8]

As of May, 2021, 39 US states have formally adopted the revised Comment. At least one other state (California), while not formally adopting the Comment, has issued an ethics opinion requiring the duty.[9]

The passage of regulations creating a duty of technological competence establishes a specific requirement which will require attention by all lawyers, and upgrading by some. We will have to wait for future interpretation of the regulation to fully define its scope. The duty, however, has arrived.

7 For example, Saskatchewan, Alberta, Nova Scotia, Manitoba and Yukon Territory adopted the FLSC commentary. Other jurisdictions, including Ontario and Northwest Territory, have issued guidance on technological competency.

8 <https://www.lawsitesblog.com/tech-competence> accessed 1 September 2021.

9 ibid.

Legal Education in Canada

The education of lawyers typically combines elements of academia, regulator-sponsored CPD[10] and private training. For most lawyers,[11] the process begins with a University education. Law school applicants generally require a minimum of 60 university level credit units. This is equal to two years of full-time study. All Canadian law schools have many more applicants than seats available. As a result, many applicants have completed one or more university degrees prior to being accepted as a law student. The typical law school program is three years, with law schools accredited by the FLSC.

Following law school convocation, would-be lawyers must complete articles of clerkship. This normally involves a year-long engagement with a private law firm, or lawyer.[12] Alongside this articling period, the prospective lawyer must successfully complete a bar admission course, typically administered by the relevant law society. The length, content and format of this course differs among jurisdictions. After completing articles and the bar admission course, the individual is eligible for admission to the law society as a full member.

All lawyers are entitled to practice virtually any type of law and act for any client. However, few lawyers would consider themselves fully proficient upon admission. Depending on circumstances including the areas of law, it may be years before someone would be considered fully "competent."[13] The training in that period is a combination of the continuing professional development (CPD) provided under the auspices of the regulator, as well as on the job instruction and mentoring received while providing legal services to clients. Ideally, lawyers are life-long learners.

---

10 The Law Society of Saskatchewan provides many hours of CPD opportunities through in-person and online instruction, some free and some fee-based. Members can pick and choose topics of interest, subject to a requirement of a minimum number of hours annually. In addition, lawyers can take courses from other providers, or prepare their own programs, with LSS approval. While details vary, most Canadian jurisdictions operate under a similar framework.

11 Canada does offer a program, the National Committee on Accreditation, which permits lawyers from other countries or who have obtained civil law accreditation, to obtain the right to become law society members without attending a Canadian law school.

12 Articles can also be served with various courts or government justice ministries.

13 Of course, depending on the level of self-awareness or self-doubt, some might never consider themselves at a required level.

The merits and disadvantages of this educational system are open to debate, but there are obviously many opportunities available to upgrade and obtain necessary skills. One striking feature is the importance of experiential training, usually through private sources such as law firms. Law firms can enhance their market competitiveness by providing its lawyers with a high level of education and experience, including in technology.

There are also incentives for the academy and the regulator to enhance further technological competence. Regulators strive to reduce discipline in their role of protecting the public interest. Enhanced technological skills in lawyers will assist in this goal. Law schools seek to graduate the best students from their programs. Law schools can enhance their reputation by teaching their students greater technology skills.

But these considerations may not be enough to guarantee the new duty is properly embraced, with enough content to ensure both new and existing lawyers possess the minimum skills required by Codes. It is important for educators and regulators to recognize their responsibilities in providing education in all critical competencies, including technology.

The existing landscape is obviously not barren. There are already courses and CPD offerings in certain aspects of technology. For example, the Law Society of Saskatchewan and the University of Saskatchewan's College of Law have recently partnered in a program to educate students in practice matters, including technology.[14]

Law schools might also argue that the increasing impact of the Information Age has led to new technology courses. This may be true, but it is also important to recognize the difference between courses on the law of technology (LOT) and those on law practice technology (LPT). Both are important, but they are not the same.

LOT courses have existed for many years. These courses include topics such as intellectual property and licensing. In recent years, schools have created courses on emerging technologies such as blockchain, biotechnology and internet law.[15] Some of these topics, such as the integration of blockchain into smart contracts, make their way into traditional law courses like Contract Law. While important, these classes do not directly impact the duty of technological competence. In fact, it may be that

14 This course, *Transformation in Practice: Building the Future Lawyer*, began in the Winter term of 2021.

15 Examples include the Osgoode Hall *Certificate in Blockchains, Smart Contracts and the Law,* Harvard's cluster of courses devoted to Health Law, Biotechnology, and Bioethics, and Stanford Law School's Center for Internet and Society.

students taking such courses are above the norm in technical knowledge and would already meet the newly prescribed duty.

It is the LPT courses which are more aligned with the new duty of technological competence, since they deal with actually using and benefiting from technological aids. These courses might teach something as fundamental as the various e-discovery packages for purposes of a civil litigation practice. They might be specifically aimed at enhancing all aspects of technology use in a law practice, ranging from accounting to document management, client management and more. There has been some resistance to including these courses in the standard law school curricula. However, as law schools incorporate concepts of LPT courses, their graduates will enter the profession with a significantly higher baseline of knowledge. This in turn will support the development of adequate knowledge by all lawyers.

Challenges

While few would challenge the desirability of providing law students and lawyers more education on using relevant technology, there are obstacles to overcome. One impediment is simple conservatism. Lawyers are often criticized for being change-averse, perhaps a consequence of being immersed in a profession which literally depends on precedent. They do not have a monopoly on traditionalism, however. The academy also changes slowly. An often bureaucratic administrative structure and huge sunk-cost investments are two factors mitigating against rapid change. In fairness to these institutions, humans are generally not change-receptive at the best of times. Moving from the *status quo* represents a risk.

There are other challenges to change. Law professors tend to stay in their position for many years. Not all professors practised law before becoming full time law teachers. Professors being hired today are more likely to hold a doctorate than in the past. Individuals with a doctorate have clearly demonstrated their academic credentials, but this is not the same thing as practicing law. Many law professors have not practiced law in a way, or at a time, which required the technologies being explored in LPT courses.

There are also resource issues, particularly as post-secondary institutions around the world struggle with rising costs and indifferent public funding. Creating new programs requires funds.

We will address five typical arguments likely to be put forth as reasons to not move forward with enhancing education on technological competence: the 'trade school' objection; the 'competing resources' objection; the 'limited faculty' objection; the 'ever-changing technology' objection and the 'difficulty in measuring competence' objection.

The Trade School Objection

Law schools and the legal profession seem to have a close relationship, given the former's role as the principal source of new lawyers. The actual situation, however, is more nuanced.

Law schools exist in an academic setting and are not merely factories producing lawyers. The law school atmosphere is highly theoretical. The partnership forged over many decades has law school primarily focused on providing students with an academic education rich in theory and including a robust exchange of ideas, while the profession, through articling and bar admission courses, has primarily focused on teaching individuals the practice skills they need to be effective lawyers. A lawyer's education is received partly through law school and partly through articles and post-graduation professional development courses. But this does not mean the law school and the regulator need be in conflict.

Casting the relationship between law schools and regulators as a choice between whether a law school education should be academic or practical does a disservice to law schools and regulators, as well as to the concepts of 'academic' and 'practical' education. Law schools and regulators certainly do look through different lenses, and it is true their interests or objectives do not always align. However, they share a common goal that law school education be "both intellectually rigorous and professionally useful."[16]

The law school journey is intimately concerned with teaching skills, but not necessarily teaching practice skills. Consider a Wills and Estates class as an example. Such a course would typically consider the various ways in which jurisdictions provide for the orderly transfer of property upon a person's death. Matters including Will validity, correction of errors, Wills interpretation issues, obligations to dependents, and admissibility of evidence would be considered. Successful students would gain the skills and knowledge to recognize common Wills issues and be able to identify relevant legislation in their jurisdiction. In short, students would be 'functionally literate' in Wills in that they would know how to learn to adminis-

16 Beth Bilson, 'Prudence Rather than Valor: Legal Education in Saskatchewan 1908-23' (1998) 61 Sask L Rev 341, 342.

ter an estate in various jurisdictions and would have the skills to adapt to changes in the law. No competent law school would consider a Wills and Estates course complete if it solely consisted of teaching students how to complete probate forms in its jurisdiction – although some exposure to those forms, or at least awareness that such forms exist would presumably be useful to students.

Similarly, LPT courses must provide students with the skills and knowledge required to not only identify common LPT issues, but also to be functionally literate using that technology. This means they would not only be familiar with examples of LPT, but would also know how to learn to become skilled with emerging technology. The law school mission and the regulator mission would both seem to support such outcomes. As with other areas, law school courses on LPT would be expected to take a broader, more academic approach whereas professional development courses would likely have a somewhat more practical approach. The approaches are complementary, and each has a role in developing competent lawyers.

A competent lawyer must understand substantive law, interpret and communicate complex principles, and demonstrate empathy and mental resilience. We are not diminishing any of these elements. Our point is that technological competence is also a critical skill. This is particularly so in the Information Age when IT tools are augmenting or replacing traditional lawyer functions.

Law schools and regulators should not see themselves in a 'turf war' where one defends academic standards and the other promotes lawyer skills. To do so would miss the point that the ground being contested is not theirs. The real purpose of educating lawyers during and after law school is to provide legal assistance to citizens. It is their interests which are paramount. Lawyers are a means to that end.

The proper educational balance between theory and skill development depends upon purpose. There may be a range of views as to the best place to draw the precise line. In truth, it is impossible to train lawyers without a healthy dose of substantive law *and* training in delivery of information. Law schools have always tried to bridge this divide. There are already many examples of classes at every North American law school that go beyond substantive law into technique and practical matters.[17] The real question is where the balance should rest.

17 For example, courses on negotiation, awareness of Indigenous issues and clinical programs for delivery of legal services to underserved populations.

That balance will always be shifting. Given the importance of information technology to all phases of society and everyday life, it is hard to argue against providing at least a modicum of such knowledge for lawyers. The duty of technological competence cements this necessity. It is simply inconceivable that technology will become less important in everyone's lives. Lawyers must not only accept it, but be able to benefit from it.

Competing Resources

A common objection to adding anything to law school curricula is that there is no available time or financial resources to support new initiatives. Introducing LPT courses comes down to priorities. Is technological competence as important as, say, learning criminal law?

The law school curriculum and pedagogy has changed over recent decades. This change has been driven in part by a recognition of the evolving needs of lawyers and society.[18] Most law schools have avoided a 'one-size fits all' approach to legal education. This is appropriate as not all law graduates practice law, and those who do have a tremendous variance in the scope of their practice.[19] While it is difficult to compare the importance of *any* substantive area against others, an ongoing assessment of the appropriate concentration of various topics is necessary to avoid stagnation. We submit that technological competence exists on a plane above most substantive law. It covers all practice areas and practitioners. If the goal is universal utility, a far better case can be made for the need to understand technical aids over many substantive areas which a lawyer may never experience in their career. In other words, technology cannot be viewed in isolation. It infuses itself into literally all facets of society, and all substantive areas of law. This means that courses outside of LPT should incorporate technology instruction into their syllabi. Examples include teaching online platforms in an alternative dispute resolution course, or blockchain and smart contract technology in a contracts course.

---

18 James R Maxeiner, 'Educating Lawyers Now and Then: Two Carnegie Critiques of the Common Law and the Case Method' (2007) 35 Int'l J Legal Info 1.

19 Most regulators do not restrict new lawyers from practicing any area of law, whether or not they were trained on the subject. This "murder to merger" practice model is in itself a competency issue which regulators have not yet been able to adequately handle -but this issue is beyond the scope of this paper.

Limited Faculty

The world seems to be divided into two types of people: those who revel in technology, and those who put up with it. For every person who delights in technology for its own sake, there are others who only want to use technology to get things done, without understanding bits, protocols and internet minutiae.

This impacts teaching in a couple of ways. For one, if we are trying to integrate technology into existing courses like civil procedure or contracts, teachers with knowledge in those topics might not have sufficient technology skills to teach those aspects. There is no inherent intersection between knowledge of contracts and knowledge of blockchain. An expert in the former may be completely illiterate in the latter. This does not mean they are a poor contracts educator. They may be world-renowned in the substantive topic, but they could benefit from introducing guests with specific knowledge and skills. A benefit of the massive increase in online teaching during the Covid-19 epidemic was the increased use of guest lecturers, including non-local teachers. Devoting a class or two to specific technology in a substantive area, with world-class experts who deliver the information remotely, has proven to be an effective way to supplement the substantive law skills of classroom instructors.

Introducing dedicated LPT courses presents a different challenge. Only the most fortunate law schools will have the ability to hire additional instructors with both a deep understanding of technology as well as familiarity with the substantive law.

Many law schools may address this challenge through the use of adjunct professors.[20] LPT courses by definition involve practice matters. The melding of substance and practice is a fundamental aspect of these courses. Lawyers with a working knowledge of the technology itself can be extremely effective educators.

Changing Technology

Another objection raised to teaching technological competence is the ever-shifting terrain of technology itself. Although there has always been a progression of tools, and obsolescence of old ways of doing things, this has

---

20 Sometimes referred to as sessional lecturers in Canada. For these purposes, an adjunct/sessional is a person, often a lawyer, who is not part of tenured faculty and is paid on a per-course or per-student basis.

accelerated in the Information Age. Legacy support of old technologies can adapt to a point, but new paradigms arise which kill old ways of doing things.

This will never change. New ways of doing things inevitably arise. Sometimes they are evolutionary and adaptation is in order. In other cases a revolutionary advancement requires an entirely new mindset and set of skills to cope. This has happened with the printing press, the photocopier and the fax machine. The difference today is in the speed of change, and the shrinking life cycles of products. While we used fax machines for 3 or 4 decades, newer technologies may be measured in years or even months.

The answer is obvious. We cannot stem the advancement of technology, in law or society as a whole. We must embrace the mindset that change *will* happen and we must be flexible enough to accept and implement the change. Individuals adapt to technologies at varying speeds. Wherever teachers, students, lawyers and regulators are along this innovation adoption curve,[21] a key concept in technological competence courses is that we must accept that change will occur, and we must adapt.

This requires teaching concepts rather than specific technologies. This does not mean ignoring the tools themselves. Technology such as word processing and collaborative software packages like Microsoft Teams will be around a long time, at least long enough to make it worthwhile to learn about them. But getting comfortable with technology concepts inherent to the internet and mobile computing, to use a couple of examples, is critical in competence education.

Measuring Competence

Objectors to the addition of technological competence emphasize the difficulty of measuring capabilities. Even in the vaguely worded duties adopted in Canada, one wonders how a meaningful assessment of a minimum standard can be achieved.

Every aspect of legal competence is subject to the same objection. How does one measure substantive law knowledge, or ability to communicate information to clients? The former is arguably assessed through law school

21 See Joe M. Bohlen and George M. Beal 'The Diffusion Process' (Special Report No. 18. 1, Iowa State College, May 1957) 56–77, where the authors categorized users of new innovations as innovators, early adopters, early majority, late majority, and laggards.

and bar course exams,[22] but there are no meaningful ongoing testing procedures in place in Canada or most other jurisdictions. This is not just a legal education problem.[23] However, the difficulty of valid and reliable competency measurement is not an excuse to avoid teaching technological competence. We ought to teach it, and we ought to strive to develop valid and reliable competency evaluation tools. Perhaps if we are successful in the second of these, we will improve our ability to evaluate all strata of competence. There may be nothing inherently different about measuring technological competence from measuring other skill-based competencies. A new rigor applied to evaluating technological competence may provide a lesson of how to perform assessment of other types of lawyer competence.

Conclusion

It is beyond the scope of this paper to describe what a well-formed system teaching life-long technological competence would include. We would suggest that legal educators and regulators must work together to create such a system. Law schools can benefit from the expertise of practitioners and regulators as they seek to imbed such education within the law school. Practitioners and regulators can benefit from legal educators embracing the goal of providing appropriate LPT and LOT education as a standard part of a law school education.

The competence of legal practitioners is at the heart of legal education, legal practice and the regulatory system which oversees it. The public interest depends on knowledgeable practitioners delivering sufficient legal services. The hardware and software that form the backbone of the Information Age is a critical category of knowledge necessary for competence. As law societies and legal educators recognize this, they must also recognize their respective obligations to actively promote and supply that education.

---

22 Although it is also arguable that this measures only one's skill in writing exams or essays, not the actual work of being a lawyer.

23 There is a rich literature in evaluation and assessment in education generally, as evidenced by the wide variety of academic journals focusing on the topic.

The Road to Modern Judiciary. Why New Technologies Can Modernise the Administration of Justice?

Mariusz Załucki <mzalucki@afm.edu.pl>
KRAKÓW, Poland

Abstract
The future of administration of justice is an issue increasingly often discussed in the literature. Representatives of the doctrine wonder about the greater use of new technologies in the judiciary, so as to, among other things, shorten the waiting time for a case to be decided by the court. Changes taking into account the wider use of new technologies are indispensable. Such a future has already been foreseen in the literature. The author reviews selected reported and functioning ideas, presents how the judicial field has changed recently and reflects on possible future solutions. The result of his observations is a conclusion about the need to discuss the future of justice on a broad, global scale.

Keywords:
Judiciary, justice, administration of justice, courts, new technologies, AI

1. Introduction

Today's judiciary is a complex structure, with specialised courts and judges, although there is no consensus in individual states on how judicial power should be exercised. It is the political system of a given state, regulated by acts of the highest rank, usually in the form of a constitution, which defines the subject of state authority, including judicial authority, delineates its scope and indicates the main directions of state activity. According to the traditional division, derived from ancient thought developed by Enlightenment thinkers, the judiciary is one of the authorities, independent from the executive and legislative powers.[1] The position of

1 Mehrdad Payandeh, *Judikative Rechtserzeugung: Theorie, Dogmatik und Methodik der Wirkungen von Präjudizien* (Mohr Siebeck 2017) 2 ff.

the judiciary in the system of a tri-partition of powers is largely based on the isolation of the judicial power, the competence monopoly of the judiciary in the exercise of that power, one of the basic tasks of which is to administer justice.[2] The organs of the judiciary are to resolve disputes arising in connection with the application or making of law, they decide on citizens' rights and obligations. One of the basic elements of a legal state is the citizen's access to court, the existence of a judicial sphere for resolving disputes.[3]

The judiciary, in the course of several centuries of evolution, has developed a specific model of the organisation of the judiciary, which is now reflected primarily in the provisions of fundamental laws, as well as in legal regulations of a lower order defining the system of the judiciary in a given state. For the courts to function properly within the system of state bodies, it is necessary to ensure respect for and observance of the independence of the judiciary, which is, inter alia, the duty of state bodies. Of great importance for assessing the proper functioning of courts is the access of citizens to a court, understood primarily as the right to have a case heard within a reasonable time by an independent and impartial court. Interestingly, according to the OECD, is that only 46 % of people live in conditions which can be said to be subject to such legal protection, while, for example, over 50 % of all people today have access to the Internet.[4] Access to the court is therefore more limited than access to the Internet, which may raise and raises important questions.

One of the greatest problems of the justice system, related to the access of citizens to the court, is the lengthiness or even protraction of examination of individual cases.[5] Legal regulations on the protection of human rights, including e.g. the European Convention on Human Rights, have for a long time created a standard for the so-called fair trial (Article 6 ECHR), which consists, inter alia, of the right to a fair and public hearing within a reasonable time.[6] However, individual countries of the world

---

2 Lech Garlicki, *Polskie prawo konstytucyjne. Zarys wykładu* (Wolters Kluwer Polska 2020) 75 ff.

3 Cf. Paul Craig and others, *Rule of Law in Europe Perspectives From Practitioners and Academics* (European Judicial Training Network 2020) 43 ff.

4 Cf. Richard Susskind, *Online Courts and the Future of Justice* (Oxford University Press 2019) 27.

5 José María López Jiménez, 'Sistemas Judiciales Justos Y… Eficientes' (2013) 2013 eXtoikos 31.

6 William A Schabas, *The European Convention on Human Rights: A Commentary* (Oxford University Press 2015) 264 ff.

have problems with the implementation of this standard, as evidenced, for example, by the various legal remedies brought against these countries for violation of this standard, including, inter alia, complaints to the European Court of Human Rights about the so-called lengthiness of judicial proceedings.[7] As one may think, and as the available data show, also the recent period of functioning of the justice system in the era of the COVID-19 pandemic has revealed a number of difficulties related to adjudication of court cases within a reasonable time.[8] However, social expectations in this respect are significant. Basically, everyone would like their case to be heard quickly.

In this light, it should be noted that lawyers all over the world are considering improvements to the functioning of the judiciary. Recent years have seen an increasingly bold use of solutions based on new technologies, which can be categorised as LegalTech 1.0, 2.0 and 3.0.[9] Courts have started to operate on the Internet, algorithms have appeared to support their work, and even solutions based on artificial intelligence have appeared, which in some categories of cases make it possible to replace a traditional judge.[10] All these solutions were and undoubtedly are intended to improve the efficiency of the justice system. Looking at some of these solutions, it is necessary to reflect on the further possible direction of changes in judicial proceedings, using new technologies, so that, while respecting the standards in force in this area, the functioning of the courts is modernised and improved. What can and should the courts of the future be like?

2. *The current state and recent developments in the judiciary*

The issue of lengthiness or protraction of proceedings is widely commented upon in the doctrine and judicature.[11] It is not only of theoretical importance. First of all, it is a practical problem. Lengthiness of proceedings, which can be understood as violation of a party's guarantee to have its

7 Schabas (n 6).

8 David Freeman Engstrom, 'Post COVID Courts' (2020) 68 UCLA Law Review Discourse 246, 249 ff.

9 Cf. Dariusz Szostek (ed) *LegalTech. Czyli jak bezpiecznie korzystać z narzędzi informatycznych w organizacji, w tym w kancelarii oraz dziale prawnym* (C H Beck 2021) passim.

10 Cf. Paulo Cezar Neves Junior, *Judiciário 5.0. Inovação, Governança, Usucentrismo, Sustentabilidade e Segurança Jurídica* (Edgard Blücher 2020) passim.

11 Susskind (n 4).

case heard within a reasonable time, is a problem of many countries.[12] The pursuit of efficient and speedy examination of a case cannot be an aim in itself. Nevertheless, inefficiency is undoubtedly one of the key factors disrupting the proper functioning of the justice system and hampering the assertion and protection of rights. The negative consequences of lengthy court proceedings are evident. For example, in civil cases, lengthiness not only undermines the sense of justice actually being done, but can also result in the merely illusory nature of the legal protection provided. For example, there may be a loss of value resulting from the devaluation of money in payment cases, or the debtor losing property to which enforcement can be directed, or its value decreasing. In cases for the surrender of property, the loss of its usefulness associated with the passage of time and technological progress may occur, another example is the inability of entities, the resolutions of which have been challenged (e.g. companies) to function properly.[13] Generally speaking, it may be pointed out that with the passage of time, a decision may lose its significance for the parties due to changes in the socio-economic reality or technological progress.[14] It is therefore obvious that the lengthiness of court proceedings is an undesirable state of affairs, and that a court proceeding lasting as short as possible is optimal.

The efficiency of the justice system is stimulated at various levels, although the effect of the various measures stimulating the judiciary is not always correct.[15] It should be remembered that when resolving cases, speed of proceedings should not overshadow other procedural guarantees of the parties.[16] This can be seen against the background of modern legal systems, where the right to a court and the right to a fair trial (and thus the requirement of a speedy resolution of the case) are constitutional principles of a democratic state under the rule of law, being protected under the constitution. For example, the Polish Constitution in the content of Article 45 par. 1 indicates that everyone has the right to a fair and public hearing without undue delay by a competent, independent and impartial

12 Szymon Rożek, *Sprawność sądowego postępowania cywilnego na tle rozstrzygania spraw spadkowych* (Krakowska Akademia 2020).

13 ibid.

14 ibid.

15 Richard Susskind, *Tommorow's Lawyers. An Introduction to Your Future* (Oxford University Press 2017).

16 Janneke Gerards, *General Principles of the European Convention on Human Rights* (Cambridge University Press 2019); Amal Clooney and Philippa Webb, *The Right to a Fair Trial in International Law* (Oxford University Press 2021).

court.[17] This striving for the absence of delay in the examination of cases is noticeable in the mechanisms available to the parties and related to combating protraction. In this context, the already mentioned Polish law, as early as in 2004,[18] following the case-law of the ECHR,[19] introduced the mechanism of a complaint against the lengthiness of court proceedings, which consists in bringing a complaint to a court superior to the court before which the proceedings are pending, in which the court may declare that in the proceedings to which the complaint relates, there has been a lengthiness of proceedings. The court may, inter alia, at the request of the party or of its own motion, order the court with jurisdiction over the substance of the case to take appropriate action within a specified period of time, but such directions shall not extend to the factual and legal assessment of the case. The court may also award the applicant an appropriate sum of money. However, this mechanism has not resulted in any significant decrease in the length of court proceedings. Current media reports and available data indicate that the average length of court proceedings has increased by around 3 months from 2010 to 2020.[20] Currently, selected categories of cases are heard in first instance on average after approximately 7 months.[21] Waiting times have therefore increased by 75 %. Statistics of this kind are not unknown in other countries either.[22] The increase in the number of cases, their increasingly complex subject matter, the growing number of legal regulations, their complexity, etc., all lead to an impaired functioning of the judiciary. Court cases are taking longer and longer to be heard.

This must therefore mean that the threat to the efficiency of judicial proceedings is increasing. In the era of the COVID-19 pandemic, when the courts were not working for a period of time, adjusting to the demands of social isolation, the waiting period for a party to have the case heard continued to increase.[23] The justice system did not function for some time, or only heard urgent cases, including those related to crime or family pro-

---

17 Garlicki (n 2).

18 This is when the Act of 17 June 2004 on Action for Infringement of a Party's Right to Judicial Proceedings without Undue Delay was enacted.

19 The introduction of the complaint to the Polish legal order is commonly associated with the implementation of the ECHR judgment of 26.10.2000 in the case of Kudła v. Poland, case No. 30210/96.

20 Cf. Report of the Ministry of Justice: Średni czas trwania postępowania sądowego w latach 2011-2020, <https://isws.ms.gov.pl/pl/baza-statystyczna/opracowania-wieloletnie> accessed 23 June 2021.

21 ibid.

22 Jiménez (n 5).

23 Engstrom (n 8).

blems, especially involving minor children. Traditional civil cases, especially those with a high number of small claims, were not heard. Lawyers all over the world thought about modifying court procedures and prepared solutions that would make it possible and, to a large extent, unblocked the resulting bottlenecks.[24] The judicial process has changed, certain simplifications have been introduced into the procedures, including, among others, the large-scale use of means of distance communication. Hearings went online, judges started using IT solutions that had been available for years to question witnesses and parties.[25] Although this was supposed to be a temporary solution, it is already clear that the old analogue instruments will be and are being replaced by instruments based on new technologies.

Judicial procedures have changed.[26] Before the pandemic, many countries had a model according to which the party and witnesses, as well as other persons important for the examination of the case, met in the court building, in the courtroom, where the case was examined. The obligation of social isolation forced the search for other solutions. It soon turned out that a different course of the trial was possible and that the parties and other persons did not have to stay in the same building to have the case heard. These solutions were becoming more and more daring, which, among other things, led to the tendency to hear cases in closed sessions. As a rule, a regulation was introduced, according to which, where the court deems it sufficient, it passes a sentence without the presence of the parties. The possibility for third parties (the public) to participate in a court hearing and observe its proceedings has also been significantly restricted or completely eliminated.[27] Meanwhile, openness of proceedings is also, at least according to current standards, one of the basic values taken into account when assessing whether the standard of the so-called fair trial was observed in a given case. The law and values may therefore change under the influence of various impulses. And there is no doubt that they are changing.

As is well known, some countries have gone further.[28] The need for the use of new technologies in the field of justice has long been discussed, and

---

24 ibid.

25 Szostek (n 9).

26 Mlle Andreea Mirela Staicu, *La réforme du système judiciaire roumain dans le processus d ' adhésion de la Roumanie à l ' Union européenne Mémoire présenté par* (ENA, 2006).

27 Such a future has already been foreseen in the literaturę, cf., e.g.: Susskind (n 4).

28 AD Dor Realing, 'Courts and Artificial Intelligence' (2020) 11 International Journal for Court Administration 1.

following the tests made of some technological solutions in the judiciary, it is going even further.[29] Here, as is also well known, the impetus for basing the judiciary on new technologies came from, among other things, two high-profile incidents around the world involving the use of artificial intelligence. In 2016, 584 cases pending before the European Court of Human Rights were subjected to an experiment involving artificial intelligence.[30] The algorithm, after analysing the case documents, predicted 79 % of the decisions of this court. These settlements concerned claims under Article 3 (prohibition of torture, inhuman and degrading treatment), Article 6 (right to a fair trial) and Article 8 (right to respect for private and family life) of the European Convention on Human Rights.[31] In turn, in 2017, a similar test was conducted in the United States of America, among others.[32] There, in turn, artificial intelligence analysed, on the basis of a created algorithm, more than 28 thousand cases pending before the Supreme Court there. The algorithm was able to predict 70.2 % of cases decided between 1816 and 2015.[33] At the same time, the spectrum of cases was much broader than in the case of the test concerning the application of the standards of the European Convention on Human Rights in specific cases. Therefore, it is not surprising that the results of these experiments were widely echoed in the scientific space.[34]

It is worth explaining that the above tests were based primarily on the method of natural language processing, where the predictive model of artificial intelligence operating on text data was used.[35] Extensive amounts of data were analysed to accurately predict the actual outcome. The results of the tests are interesting in that a large proportion of the errors in the

---

29 Mariusz Załucki, 'AI and dispute resolution' in Javier García González, Álvaro Alzina Lozano and Gabriel Martín Rodríguez (eds) *El derecho público y privado ante las nuevas technologías* (Dykinson 2020).

30 Nikolaos Aletras and others, 'Predicting Judicial Decisions of the European Court of Human Rights: A Natural Language Processing Perspective' (2016) 19 PeerJ Computer Science 93, 93 ff.

31 Masha Medvedeva, Michel Vols and Martijn Wieling, 'Using Machine Learning to Predict Decisions of the European Court of Human Rights' (2020) 28 Artificial Intelligence and Law 237.

32 Daniel Martin Katz, Michael J Bommarito II and Josh Blackman, 'A General Approach for Predicting the Behavior of the Supreme Court of the United States' (2017) 12 Plos One passim.

33 Katz, Bommarito II and Blackman (n 32).

34 Cf., e.g.: Haoxi Zhong and others, 'Legal Judgment Prediction via Topological Learning' (2018) 1 Proceedings of the 2018 Conference on Empirical Methods in Natural Language Processing; Realing (n 28).

35 Cf. Aletras and others (n 30).

predictions related to similar legal standards, where only nuances in the jurisprudence determined a different outcome in reality. It should therefore be noted that a system dealing with the automation of the analysis, understanding, translation and generation of natural language by a computer in the context of the processing of specific decisions made in reality may be an interesting starting point for further research.[36] Certainly, such experiments open up the controversial debate as to whether the traditional judge can be replaced by a computer.[37] In this context, it should be noted that such views appear more and more frequently and boldly in scientific discourse, where, among other things, theses are formulated according to which, at least in some categories of cases, it seems possible.[38]

Such tests show that artificial intelligence, sometimes referred to as LegalTech 3.0, may be an interesting tool to assist in the administration of justice, and may one day be able to replace "real" judges. It is against this background that a number of possibilities, and at the same time doubts, arise. Are new technologies the future of justice?

3. Selected solutions from around the world

The above experiences with predictive systems show that changes in the administration of justice are possible.[39] New technologies have already taken over the justice system. Just as in the past simple solutions were used in this area (the so-called LegalTech 1.0),[40] today nobody can imagine further work in the judiciary without extensive legal information systems containing not only provisions of law, but also case law, commentaries and broad statements of doctrine and other instruments supporting the work of judges (the so-called LegalTech 2.0).[41] All this, in the form of relevant data systematised in an appropriate way, is an important tool supporting

---

36 Cf. *Study on the Use of Innovative Technologies in the Justice Field. Final Report* (European Commission 2020).

37 Paul Bennett Marrow, Mansi Karol and Steven Kuyan, 'Artificial Intelligence and Arbitration: The Computer as an Arbitrator — Are We There Yet?' (2020) 74 Dispute Resolution Journal 35.

38 Załucki (n 29).

39 Mark Mckamey, 'Legal Technology: Artificial Intelligence and the Future of Law Practice' (2017) 22 Appeal: Review of Current Law and Law Reform 45.

40 Szostek (n 9).

41 ibid.

the judiciary.[42] This trend will continue, especially as it is predicted that around 2050 the development of technology will mean that the average computer will have a greater capacity to process data than the combined brains of all the inhabitants of the earth.[43] It is therefore certain that the transfer of information resources to the digital world will continue, slowly replacing the use of traditional tools.

This trend has recently been visible, among others, in the context of communication with the courts. This is because it is increasingly bold to move to the virtual world. Individual legal systems are slowly abandoning traditional delivery of court correspondence and electronic delivery is appearing, which will slowly replace traditional court letters.[44] An example of such a trend is that which can be observed, inter alia, in China, where a new system of communication with the courts is taking its first steps. Adoption of the Rules on the Provision of Online Case Service for Parties to Cross-border Litigation on 3 February 2021[45] has changed the image of communication with courts. These Rules require Chinese courts to provide services that include guidance on initiating online cases, responding to enquiries, providing testimony via video, and initiating cases for parties in cross-border litigation. This is certainly the path that other countries will follow. Surely this is also a path from which there is no turning back.

China, however, has more to boast about in this regard. As of today, the country already has three internet courts that operate in Hangzhou, Beijing and Guangzhou,[46] in which the settlement of cases is based, among others, on algorithms using artificial intelligence, or where the "Shanghai Intelligent Assistive case-handling system for criminal cases - System 206" operates, which is useful for solving criminal cases.[47] The use of IT tools in the judiciary, with minimal human intervention, is already a standard. But is it possible to go even further in the transformation of the judiciary and, for example, replace the human being?

---

42 Cf., e.g.:Konrad Zacharzewski and Mariusz Tomasz Kłoda, *Przegląd zastosowania technologii blockchain w wymiarze sprawiedliwości w wybranych państwach* (Instytut Wymiaru Sprawiedliwości 2019).

43 Ray Kurzweill, *The Singularity Is Near: When Humans Transcend Biology* (Viking Press 2005).

44 Michał Araszkiewicz and Victor Rodriguez-Doncel (eds), *Legal Konwledge and Information Systems* (IOS Press 2019) passim.

45 (关于为跨境诉讼当事人提供网上立案服务的若干规定).

46 Changqing Shi, Tania Sourdin and Bin Li, 'The Smart Court – A New Pathway to Justice in China?' (2021) 12 International Journal for Court Administration 4.

47 Yadong Cui, *Shanghai Intelligent Assistive Case-Handling System for Criminal Cases - System 206* (Springer 2020) 43 ff.

Interesting solution is being tested in the Netherlands, where a court in collaboration with research units is investigating the possibilities of artificial intelligence in the context of traffic offence cases in which a citizen appeals (contesting the validity of the penalties imposed for the offence).[48] The aim of this work is to develop an artificial intelligence mechanism that would resolve such cases autonomously.[49] Putting this tool into practice would mean the need for a serious rethinking of the judicial system. Such a task, one would think, has already been done in Estonia, for example. In this country, the first steps are being taken by a mechanism that assists judges by collecting certain data necessary to decide a case and analysing it in order to decide the case in the most equitable manner.[50] This mechanism is intended, among other things, as a response to the courts' inability to cope with the growing number of cases, so one of the motivations for working on this solution is the desire to improve the efficiency and effectiveness of case resolution. Its first task is to resolve the so-called minor cases, where the value of the subject of a dispute does not exceed the amount of 7000 EUR. Traditional judges are not involved in these settlements. The system is based on the parties providing documents supporting their positions, which are analysed by an algorithm which then issues the decision. Only an appeal against this decision is heard in the traditional way. This is certainly another step towards taking seriously solutions of this kind based on artificial intelligence, where the involvement of a human judge is minor (minimised).[51] Thus, while traditional case disposal has its values, reaching for modern solutions based on artificial intelligence and other technologies also seems to be a direction from which there is and will be no turning back.

This technological future for the judiciary will undoubtedly present new challenges for legislators.[52] These challenges, however, should not be feared, but rather, based on existing solutions, develop further possibilities

48 Manuella van der Put, 'Kan artificiële intelligentie de rechtspraak betoveren' (2019) 2 Rechtstreeks 50, 50 ff.

49 Put (n 48).

50 Franciska Z. Gyuranecz, Bernadett Krausz and Dorottya Papp, 'The AI Is Now in Session. The Impact of Digitalization on Courts' (European Judicial Training Network 2019) 8 ff.

51 Tanel Kerikmäe and Evelin Pärn-Lee, 'Legal Dilemmas of Estonian Artificial Intelligence Strategy: In between of e-Society and Global Race' (2020) 36 AI & Society 561 ff.

52 David Freeman Engstrom and Jonah B Gelbach, 'Legal Tech, Civil Procedure, and the Future of American Adversarialism' (2020) 169 University of Pennsylvania Law Review 1.

of technologies that will certainly appear. Here, for example, the solutions planned in Poland to be used in arbitration appear to be very interesting. The arbitration court operating at the Polish Notaries' Association in Warsaw already conducts completely electronic proceedings, and its IT system is largely automated, verging on AI mechanisms.[53] In the future, it is planned to conduct analysis of case documentation and their assignment to specific legal norms by artificial intelligence, which is to be advisory and prepare draft awards with justifications. The system is also to support the arbitrator during the proceedings by providing him with information on the course and outcome of other similar cases. It is also supposed to present excerpts from the justifications of other judgments, which best explain a particular problem or legal issue. The announcements related to this are therefore promising.[54] In this context, one wonders whether common courts could not also follow this path? The above-mentioned mechanisms, both those already operating in China or Estonia and those planned e.g. in Poland, would certainly make it possible to finally deal with the greatest problem of the judiciary of our times - the lengthiness of court proceedings. As one may think, this is an interesting avenue to pursue. New technologies can and should modernise the administration of justice.[55]

4. Towards the modernisation of the judiciary (instead of a conclusion)

Consequently, as one may think, a judge, the judiciary, and the administration of justice are concepts that require redefinition and a modern outlook through the prism of the possibilities and effectiveness of new technologies.[56] The justice system is confronted with a number of ills, and the most important one in recent times, the protraction or lengthiness of individual court proceedings, is an area where solutions are already visible. The Internet as a channel of communication, algorithms as tools supporting and sometimes replacing the traditional judge, is already a model that marks a

---

53 Cf. <https://ultimaratio.pl/sztuczna-inteligencja-w-ultima-ratio-czy-roboty-zastapia-arbitrow> accessed 23 June 2021.

54 Tania Sourdin and Archie Zariski (eds), *The Responsive Judge: International Perspectives* (Springer 2018) passim.

55 Riikka Koulu and Laura Kontiainen (eds) *How Will AI Shape the Future of Law?* (University of Helsinki Legal Tech Lab publications 2019) passim.

56 Cf. Martin Ebers and Susana Navas (eds) *Algorithms and Law* (Cambridge University Press 2020); Susskind (n 15).

new history for the judiciary.[57] Relying on new technologies can be, and in an increasing number of cases already is, a solution thanks to which the time required to resolve a case is shorter. It therefore seems that individual legislators will follow this path and build their solutions on modern technologies. Modernisation of the justice system in this direction is essential.[58] Those opinion groups and those discussants taking part in the discussion on the future of justice who advocate such a necessity, however, at the same time see a number of new challenges that technological changes in the administration of justice may bring about. After all, there is no doubt that part of the world, as has already been mentioned, does not use IT tools, is digitally absent (as I pointed out 50 % of people in the world do not have access to the Internet). Modernisation of justice in this direction must not become a problem for this social group. What is needed, therefore, are intermediate, transitional mechanisms that guarantee not only efficiency and speed, but also the other elements that make up the so-called right to a fair trial. A fair trial is only fair if the case of an individual is heard within a reasonable time by an independent and autonomous court, taking into account existing standards of the rule of law.[59] These standards will have to evolve, and the main challenge for them, which can already be foreseen today, will be to reconcile the role of the traditional judge with the automated world of administering justice. The possibility of a human judge being replaced by a computer is not a "naive euphoria"[60] but a future reality. It is therefore not only possible to envisage various technological solutions supporting judicial activities and performing judicial activities in this way, but also the further development of courts, especially online courts (which could be called second-generation courts in the modern judiciary), where the tasks of the judge will be performed in a virtual environment by machines, based on functioning algorithms.

Applications, smartphones, portals, chat bots, livechats, webcasts - all these tools can help non lawyers to interact with the court, and the court itself will also rely on technology. Justice 2050 will reflect technological trends. The use of artificial intelligence and other technologies in the

57 Judit Glavanits and Péter Bálint (eds) *Law 4 . 0 – Challenges of the Digital Age* (Széchenyi István University 2019).

58 Cf. Report: *Possible Introduction of a Mechanism for Certifying Artificial Intelligence Tools and Services in the Sphere of Justice and the Judiciary: Feasibility Study* (European Comission 2020).

59 Schabas (n 6) 264 ff.

60 As indicated by Aneta M Arkuszewska, *Informatyzacja postępowania arbitrażowego* (Wolters Kluwer 2019) 39 ff.

judiciary on a wider scale is only a matter of time. Today is the time for a wider global discussion on these standards. The courts of the future should make use of new technologies; legislators must make this possible.

The Use of Artificial Intelligence in the Field of Justice

Wilfried Bernhardt <bernhardt-wi@t-online.de>
LEIPZIG, Germany

Abstract
The expectations on the judiciary remain high. In particular, the judiciary is expected to use modern IT in a manner like institutions in civil society. In addition, the situation is exacerbated by the fact that large platforms operated by the private sector have managed to use data to bring enormous new volumes of cases into the court system. Debt collection agencies send AI enabled automated filings of cases against people for debt to the courts. Thus, AI tools are leading to a flood of cases into the courts, calling for the courts to also use the tools to manage this volume of applications and automatically evaluate the cases received. And finally, the pressure is also growing due to competition from private arbitration courts and mediation bodies, online dispute resolution platforms and automated decision-making, which can produce much faster decisions than the courts due to intensive AI use. If one tries to catalog the AI under consideration for the judiciary, three main categories classification/analysis, translation/anonymization and interaction can be considered.
For example, AI can help to structure incoming documents and assign them to relevant areas of law and responsible judges, connections between different documents can be found or essential factual or legal aspects can be tracked down to provide essential insights for the court to prepare civil law decisions or to categorize crimes . AI can also help with machine translation and anonymization of court judgments. AI-powered chatbots can help citizens seeking legal protection. Although AI can assist judges in their work in a variety of ways, it is very doubtful whether AI can be used to make fully automated judicial decisions. Several principles of fundamental and human rights as well as the rule of law oppose a robot judge insofar as it removes judicial decisions from human control. But prudence is also called for when judges rely on AI-supported proposals in making their decisions.

Keywords:
Artificial Intelligence judiciary, automated filings, private arbitration courts, online dispute resolution platforms, faster decisions, Legal Tech 3.0, prosecution authorities, structure incoming documents, information Retrieval, data extraction, automated analysis, statistical evaluation, legal aspects, prepare civil law decisions, categorize criminals, machine translation, anonymization of court judgments, detect child pornography, predicting the outcome of proceedings, machine learning AI, AI-powered chatbots, effective legal protection, fully automated judicial decisions, robot judge, fundamental rights, human rights, right to human dignity, protection of personal data, principle of non-discrimination, principle of the natural and independent judge, right to the legal judge, transparency principle, fair trial, principle of the right to be heard, trustworthy AI, certification systems, European AI regulation, risk-based approach, human control, AI-supported decision.

1. *Introduction*

The use of artificial intelligence (AI) has become widespread in many areas of the economy, and to some extend also in the administration. Some countries have taken the first steps to use AI in the area of justice.[1] It is therefore worth examining how information technology, in particular the use of artificial intelligence make judicial work more user-friendly and efficient without disregarding fundamental constitutional principles and values.

2. *Definition of AI*

There is no uniform definition of AI.[2] In the glossary of the Ethics Guidelines for trustworthy AI of the High Level Expert Group on Artificial Intel-

---

1 Jenny Gesley, 'Comparative Summary', Law Library of Congress (ed) *Regulation of Artificial Intelligence in Selected Jurisdictions* (January 2019) 1 <https://www.loc.gov/law/help/artificial-intelligence/regulation-artificial-intelligence.pdf> accessed 24 June 2021.

2 Isabelle Biallaß, 'Legal Tech und künstliche Intelligenz' in Ory and Weth (ed), *jurisPK-ERV* vol 1, 1st edition, chapter 8, status 28 August 2020, para 206.

ligence (AI)[3] set up by the EU Commission, the following definition is used: „Artificial intelligence (AI) refers to systems designed by humans that, given a complex goal, act in the physical or digital world by perceiving their environment, interpreting the collected structured or unstructured data, reasoning on the knowledge derived from this data and deciding the best action(s) to take (according to pre-defined parameters) to achieve the given goal. AI systems can also be designed to learn to adapt their behavior by analyzing how the environment is affected by their previous actions". The definition in Art. 3 of the EU Commission's proposal for an AI Regulation[4] is: „'artificial intelligence system' (AI system) means software that is developed with one or more of the techniques and approaches listed in Annex I and can, for a given set of human-defined objectives, generate outputs such as content, predictions, recommendations, or decisions influencing the environments they interact with". And also important the definition of the Commissioner for Human Rights[5]: "An AI system is a machine-based system that makes recommendations, predictions or decisions for a given set of objectives. It does so by: (i) utilising machine and/or human-based inputs to perceive real and/or virtual environments; (ii) abstracting such perceptions into models .anually or automatically; and (iii) deriving outcomes from these models, whether by human or automated means, in the form of recommendations, predictions or decisions."

3. *Stages of development of IT support for the judiciary*

IT support for the judiciary and communication with users of the judiciary ("E-JUSTICE") can look back on a history of more than twenty years – also for example in Germany. Machine-readable data has long played an

3 <https://ec.europa.eu/digital-single-market/en/news/draft-ethics-guidelines-trustworthy-ai> accessed 30 May 2021.

4 COM (2021) 206 final <https://digital-strategy.ec.europa.eu/en/library/proposal-regulation-laying-down-harmonised-rules-artificial-intelligence> accessed 30 May 2021.

5 Council of Europe Commissioner for Human Rights: *Recommendation Unboxing Artificial Intelligence: 10 steps to protect Human Rights* (2019) <https://rm.coe.int/unboxing-artificial-intelligence-10-steps-to-protect-human-rights-reco/1680946e64> accessed 31 May2021.

important role in this. From today's perspective, IT support in the judiciary or the legal profession is often divided into three groups[6]:

"Legal Tech 1.o" refers to simple programs that facilitate the daily work of lawyers, such as legal databases or programs for document management and organization. It empowers the human players within the current system with computer assisted legal research, document production and case or customer management systems that store information. In Germany, legal online publishers such as Juris, founded in 1985, play an important role. Today, there are several online legal databases, some of them international. A convenient search in case law and literature, a linking of essays and online books with court decisions characterize legal online publishers today. Then, however, many courts also use programs that calculate, for example, obligations to pay alimony or pension equalization, the question of legal aid, or attorney and court fees. In Australia, the AI system "Split-Up" supports family court judges in divorce disputes: It identifies the parties' assets to be divided and based on a calculation, suggests a percentage that the respective party should receive. Legal Tech 2.0 refers to more complex programs that perform narrowly defined steps independently, such as the automated creation of legal documents (for example statements of claim) on the basis of predefined patterns and rules. Legal Tech 2.0 replaces an increasing number of human players. Automated order for payment procedures also belong to this category. Twenty years ago, it was already possible to transmit a German application for a payment order to the courts electronically. Since 2008, for example, lawyers have been obliged to send them electronically. The further processing of the procedure before the courts is also carried out electronically, even if the *Rechtspfleger* (legal officers) are still officially involved in the individual steps. The machine checks compliance with the formal legal requirements for the applications. It generates a corresponding payment order. However, the machine itself does not learn anything new; it does not check substantive legal and evidentiary issues. The machine does not decide whether the applicant is entitled to the claim. A similar situation applies to the European order for payment procedure. In this procedure, creditors can assert their uncontested civil and commercial claims according to a uniform procedure based on electronic standard forms across borders and with automated translations into all official EU languages.

---

6 The classification can be found at Oliver R. Goodenough, 'Legal Technology 3.0' (HuffPost, 6 April 2015) <https://www.huffpost.com/entry/legal-technology-30_b_6603658> accessed 29 May 2021.

While the process is largely automated, ultimate responsibility for the outcome remains with a natural person of the court. A fully electronic procedure ranging from the electronic submission of applications to fully automated decision without human intervention have not yet been provided for by the German legal system. However, there are corresponding projects in other European countries: In Estonia, for example, there are plans to have an AI-based program autonomously decide on civil contract disputes with a value in dispute of less than 7000 euros, although these decisions can then be appealed to a human judge.[7] In this context, the term "robot judge" is then used.

In contrast, in administrative procedures, a basis for the regulation of an automatic administrative act has existed since Jan. 1, 2017 (Section 35a of the German Administrative Procedure Act) and allows the administration to issue an administrative act entirely through automatic devices (without a human decision maker) provided this is permitted by another legal provision and neither discretionary.

Finally, Legal Tech 3.0 refers to highly complex programs in the sense of the use of cognitive systems and deep neural networks. Here, large parts of the content of legal decision-making are automated, e.g., by AI -assisted analysis of the content of files and subsequent autonomous generation of pleadings and decisions. Some of the systems can also (partially) replace legal work. In this context, artificial intelligence is to be understood in the sense of machine-understandable data, i.e., automatisms. Legal Tech 3.0 includes systems also located outside the judiciary, such as online air passenger portals, which initially perform automated checks free of charge to determine whether compensation is likely to be due for certain flights in the event of a cancellation or long delay. On this basis, a user can then instruct the respective provider online to enforce his claims against the airline on his behalf or to buy them directly from him. Other online platforms relate, for example, to reviews of rental claims. For example, the

7 Der Standard (Internet edition), 'Estland will Richter durch künstliche Intelligenz ersetzen' (Der Standard, 3 April 2019) <https://www.derstandard.at/story/2000100613536/justiz-estland-will-richter-durch-kuenstliche-intelligenz-ersetzen> accessed 29 May 2021; Wissenschaftliche Dienste Deutscher Bundestag *„Künstliche Intelligenz in der Justiz - Internationaler Überblick“* WD 7 -3000 -017/21,7 <https://www.bundestag.de/resource/blob/832204/6813d064fab52e9b6d54cbbf5319cea3/WD-7-017-21-pdf-data.pdf> accessed 29 May 2021; Lukas Staffler and Oliver Jany, 'Künstliche Intelligenz und Strafrechtspflege –eine Orientierung' (2020) 164 Zeitschrift für Internationale Strafrechtsdogmatik 170. <http://www.zis-online.com/dat/artikel/2020_4_1357.pdf> accessed 25 June 2021.

German Federal Court of Justice (BGH) ruled in a basic decision dated April 8, 2020 (Ref.: VIII ZR 130/19) that the portal does not violate the statutory regulations, in particular the provisions of the Legal Services Act (RDG). Algorithms also check claims of people threatened with losing their jobs, the amount of accident payments or possibilities of appealing against social welfare notices.

4. *AI support for the judiciary and prosecution authorities*

In the following remarks, I will focus on AI support for the judiciary and prosecution authorities. This is because the judiciary faces a major challenge: Ordinary people without lawyer representation are often not able to use the system clearly or efficiently. They do not understand the legal system without outside help and often cannot afford specialized lawyers. For their part, in the face of an increasingly complex legal system, the courts face the problem that they are hardly able to efficiently process the huge amounts of legal norms, information and arguments in a quick manner, given a very difficult resource situation (financial constraints, too few judges due to budget cuts). Nevertheless, the expectations on the judiciary remain high. In particular, the judiciary is expected to use modern IT in a manner like institutions in civil society. In addition, the situation is exacerbated by the fact that large platforms operated by the private sector have managed to use data to bring enormous new volumes of cases into the court system. Debt collection agencies send AI enabled automated filings of cases against people for debt to the courts. Thus, AI tools are leading to a flood of cases into the courts, calling for the courts to also use the tools to manage this volume of applications and automatically evaluate the cases received. And finally, the pressure is also growing due to competition from private arbitration courts and mediation bodies, online dispute resolution platforms and automated decision-making, which can produce much faster decisions than the courts due to intensive AI use.

4.1 *Categories*

If one tries to catalog the AI under consideration for the judiciary, three main categories classification/analysis, translation/anonymization and interaction can be considered:

Classification and analysis involve the structuring of incoming documents: It is conceivable that documents received by the court can be analyzed with artificial intelligence and assigned to different areas of law, such as criminal law, civil law, and labor law. In criminal cases, texts can be automatically differentiated into categories such as " interrogation of defendants", "statements of witnesses" or "criminal complaint". In this way, documents and parts of documents can be classified, at least provisionally, which in turn can relieve the judge in his decision-preparing activities.

4.1.1 Information Retrieval, Data Extraction

Within a document, in addition to the simple search functions used so far, certain content-related contexts can also be found, motions or requests for evidence can be filtered out and assigned to certain facts or legal arguments. This is a particularly useful tool when the data coming in with a document is unstructured. These possibilities for electronic analysis of specific data in larger data collections found its origin in so-called e-discovery in the context of electronic forensic data analysis, later also in criminal or administrative investigation proceedings. [8] And content-related connections can also be made clear in pleadings, even if they cannot be recognized by a human without further effort. This is particularly helpful in mass proceedings, where it is necessary to find commonalities and possibly individual differences in the documents. Such tools could also be used to analyze the pleadings of litigants to determine the extent to which they relate to one another, where differences in content exist, where repetitions can be identified, and where redundancies can be eliminated.

Some active, intelligent AI based case management systems like the smart court management system of the Hebei High Court in China automatically scan and digitize filings, transfer documents into electronic files, match incoming documents to existing files, identify relevant laws, cases, and legal documents to be considered, automatically generate all necessary court procedural documents and distribute cases to judges for them to be put on the right track.[9] In various courthouses, AI-equipped robots are also being used that can retrieve and communicate information on judges, court employees, procedural rules, and procedural actions. It is also possible to use AI to extract arguments from lawsuits and other

8 Jens Wagner, *Legal Tech und Legal Robots* (SpringerGabler2nd edn 2020) 43.

9 Jonah Wu, 'AI Goes to Court: The Growing Landscape of AI for Access to Justice' (Medium, 2019) <https://medium.com/legal-design-and-innovation/ai-goes-to-court-the-growing-landscape-of-ai-for-access-to-justice-3f58aca4306f> accessed 29 May 2021.

motions and compare them to similar legal cases. In Brazil, an AI program called "Socrates" analyzes new incoming cases at the highest federal court in Brazil (Superior Tribunal de Justiça) for commonalities based on data from 300,000 closed cases and forms groups of similar cases, so that they can be judged in blocks. [10] This program can also automatically review incoming appeal documents to gain knowledge regarding the jurisdiction of the court. Similarly, the Brazilian Constitutional Court (Supremo Tribunal Federal) has an AI program called "VICTOR" developed that can automatically analyze incoming cases for jurisdictional requirements for the court.[11]

4.1.2 Automated analysis and statistical evaluation of sentencing considerations in criminal judgments.

In Germany, a "Smart Sentencing Task Force" of the Legal Tech Lab Cologne[12] is working on the automated analysis and statistical evaluation of sentencing considerations in criminal judgments. The aim is to create a publicly accessible database with a search function that will, for example, enable the criminal judge to find those decisions from a large number of judgments that are similar to the case to be decided by the judge. In addition, it will be possible to analyze the considerations that have an impact on the sentence level or to filter out, based on statistical material, what impact the presence of a certain characteristic has on the sentence level decision.[13]

AI-based systems that can predict decisions are also becoming increasingly important. On the one hand, this could be used to give the litigants better opportunities to formulate their arguments. This could possibly

---

10 Flavio Fereira, 'Artificial Intelligence Makes its Mark in the Brazilian Judicial System' (Folha de S.Paulo, 10 March 2020) <https://www1.folha.uol.com.br/internacional/en/brazil/2020/03/artificial-intelligence-makes-its-mark-in-the-brazilian-judicial-system.shtml> accessed 31 May2021; Wissenschaftliche Dienste Deutscher Bundestag (n 7) 8.

11 Wissenschaftliche Dienste Deutscher Bundestag (n 7) 8; Daniel Becker and Isebela Ferrari, *Artificial Intelligence and the Supreme Court of Brazil –Beauty or a Beast?* (22 June 2020) 2 <https://sifocc.org/app/uploads/2020/06/Victor-Beauty-or-the-Beast.pdf> accessed 31 May 2021.

12 Under the scientific direction of Prof. Rostalski, Chair of Criminal Law, Criminal Procedure Law, Philosophy of Law and Comparative Law at the University of Cologne <https://legaltechcologne.de/smart-sentencing/> accessed 30 May 2021.

13 Isabell Biallaß (n 2) para 206.

even be integrated into online court platforms to give potential plaintiffs a chance to have their legal options checked, for example at the legal application offices. On the other hand, it could also be used by judges to improve their decision preparation or, in extreme cases, even to install a robot judge.

In a study, the University College of London (UCL) explored the possibilities of predicting the outcome of proceedings before the European Court of Human Rights based on the decision text of 584 cases alone.[14] The aim was to obtain a prediction as to whether there had been a violation of Art. 3, 6 or 8 of the European Convention on Human Rights. For this purpose, parts of the text that did not contain the decision were extracted from the judgments. The correct outcome of the proceedings was predicted with a 79 percent probability, which is not very high.

AI experts and lawyers in Australian Family Law have developed a split-up system based on neural networks to predict outcomes for property disputes in divorce and other family law cases.[15] However, the Split-Up system is only used by judges to support their decision-making, by helping them to identify some relevant aspects that should be taken into account in maintenance or provision decisions. The system will above all present the proposals transparently to the judge.

Since court files are subject to a high degree of confidentiality and files on ongoing proceedings cannot, for the most part, be used as material for artificial intelligence programming, it is a particular challenge to extract learning material for artificial intelligence from court files.

---

14 Nikolaos Aletras, Dimitrios Tsarapatsanis, Daniel Preoţiuc-Pietro and Vasileios Lampos, 'Predicting judicial decisions of the European Court of Human Rights: a Natural Language Processing perspective' (PeerJ Computer Science 2016) <https://peerj.com/articles/cs-93/> accessed 20 May 2021); Chris Johnston, 'Artificial intelligence judge developed by UCL computer scientists' (The Guardian, 29 October 2016)<https://www.theguardian.com/technology/2016/oct/24/artificial-intelligence-judge-university-college-london-computer-scientists> accessed 25 June 2021.

15 John Zeleznikow and Andrew Stranieri, 'Split Up: An Intelligent Decision Support System Which Provides Advice Upon Property Division Following Divorce'(1998) 6, 2 International Journal of Law and Information Technology 190–213.

4.1.3 *Use of AI for criminal investigative services to detect child pornography and child abuse.*

It can also be very useful for criminal investigative bodies to have cognitive systems technology for their work. Image, video, and audio material can be analyzed in an automated way to determine whether a person is visible and if so, which person, whether the person is a juvenile or older, which is potentially relevant for sexual criminal law, child pornography. Thus, on May 25, 2021, the Minister of Justice of North Rhine-Westphalia and the project partners presented a hybrid cloud scenario ZAC - AIRA ("AI enabled Rapid Assessment"), which is intended to revolutionize the work of public prosecutors.[16] Together with Prof. Dr. *Sorge* and Prof. Dr. *Brodowski* (Saarland University), the AI specialist Dr. *Krohn-Grimberghe*, the German EDV- Gerichtstag and Microsoft as a business partner, ZAC NRW had developed an AI-based tool kit that can classify image material into the categories child pornography, juvenile pornography, non-criminal adult pornography and other image material with an accuracy beyond 90%. The AI used is not intended to replace the human evaluator and the legal evaluator, but to help filter out quickly and effectively from a large amount of data at a very early stage of the investigation those pieces of evidence that are necessary to examine the urgent suspicion of the crime required for pre-trial detention.

In white-collar criminal cases, documents can be checked to see if a particular word is used that could be significant in further clarifying any criminal charges.

4.1.4 *Use of AI to categorize offenders*

In the United States, a software program developed by the company Equivant in 1998 with an algorithm called COMPAS (Correctional Offender Management Profiling for Alternative Sanctions) is used by criminal justice institutions to categorize offenders according to a risk score. This risk score calculates the probability of criminal recidivism. The calculated probability, in turn, is used to make decisions about sentence levels or possible early release from prison. The software obtains decision insights from

16 <https://www.sueddeutsche.de/panorama/justiz-duesseldorf-ergebnis-kuenstliche-intelligenz-erkennt-kinderpornografie-dpa.urn-newsml-dpa-com-20090101-210524-99-725248> accessed 30 May 2021.

court records and from answers to questions posed to the defendant.[17] However, the use of this software has also revealed problems, as one study points out. For example, dark-skinned people were apparently assigned higher recidivism risks in principle than white people. *Angwin/Larson/Mattu / Kirchner* cite a case in which the computer program spat out a score predicting the likelihood of each committing a future crime. One person - who was black - was rated a high risk. Another person - who was white - was rated a low risk. Two years later, the computer algorithm got it exactly backward. The black person was not charged with any new crimes. The white man was serving an eight-year prison term for subsequently breaking into a warehouse and stealing thousands of dollars worth of electronics. This was not the only case where, in retrospect, the prognosis proved to be wrong. This was not the only case where, in retrospect, the prognosis proved to be wrong. The forecasts in the use of COMPAS were only 65 percent correct, far too low to be able to attach significant legal consequences to them. [18]

By using machine learning AI, there is a risk of a vicious circle: In a district that is frequently affected by burglaries, the police will increasingly patrol. As a result, more crimes will be detected there than elsewhere in the city. This, in turn, makes it necessary for the AI system to consider an even stronger police presence, which increases the described effect of crime detection and may lead to exclusion zones. People living there will then no longer be able to sign contracts or find jobs. And the fact that this person lives in such a district makes prognosis with such programmed AI to experience a future without committed crimes unfavorable. Something similar can happen with dark-skinned people, who are usually more and more suspected under the influence of AI. This risk of discrimination, which is inherent in the programming of AI, must be considered when deploying AI.

Furthermore, with the help of artificial intelligence, the chronological events in a case, a historical description, i.e. a timeline, can be created.

---

17 Julia Angwin, Jeff Larson, Surya Mattu and Lauren Kirchner, 'Machine Bias. There's software used across the country to predict future criminals. And it's biased against blacks', (ProPublica, 23 May 2016) https://www.propublica.org/article/machine-bias-risk-assessments-in-criminal-sentencing accessed 25 June 2021.

18 Franziska Wahedi, *Verfassungsrechtliche Anforderungen an die Automatisierung der Justiz*, (Dr.Kovac 2021) 25 ff; Aleš Završnik, 'Criminal justice, artificial intelligence systems and human rights' (Springer 2020) <https://link.springer.com/article/10.1007/s12027-020-00602-0> accesssed 31 May 2021.

Citations of standards or case law can be linked to standards and case databases, or citations can be checked for accuracy.

4.1.5 Automated Translation

Very useful could be the use of AI for translation in the field of justice. Especially in the European Union with 24 different official languages, it is often necessary to translate foreign-language texts into the court language in cross-border legal cases, which results in significant costs. Often, once translations are made, they are not reused for other proceedings. Professional translators today often work with machine translation programs and then adapt the automatic translation proposal to the requirements of the specific translation job. Or translators develop their own translation memories as patterns for specific text fragments. Neural machine translation is based on neural network modeling, which is modeled after the human brain. The neural machine learns from texts available in both languages, recognizes users and adapts further translations to these requirements. The German European Council Presidency in the 2nd half of 2020 had released a website - the EU Council "Presidency Translator"[19] - and in this way kept various automatic translation programs available. It can be seen from the analysis that the different programs vary in terms of the subject area in which they are used.

4.1.6 Anonymizing court judgments

AI can also be used to anonymize court judgments. This is because it is sometimes not enough to just black out personal names to prevent rapid de-anonymization. AI may be able to use context analysis here to figure out what further anonymization needs to be done.

4.1.7 Interaction

Another category of application areas for AI is interaction. Online dispute resolution procedures already exist - outside the narrow scope of the judiciary - which largely automate the submission of requests and the responses

---

19 <https://www.presidencymt.eu> accessed 25 June 2021.

of the dispute resolution body.[20] However, since they do not generally produce binding decisions automatically, their use is not yet problematic unless they increasingly take the place of the judiciary. Newer forms of legal action such as the "Musterfeststellungsklage" are also based on - at least simple forms of - artificial intelligence.

In countries as the UK and in provinces in China, there is a noticeable tendency to virtualize processes, although not to automate all steps. In Germany, a working group on "Modernization of Civil Procedure" has drawn up proposals for the judiciary on behalf of the presidents of the Higher Regional Courts, the Court of Appeal, the Bavarian Supreme Regional Court and the Federal Court of Justice[21]: According to these proposals, an accelerated online procedure in the form of a form-based procedure is to be introduced, which as a rule is to be conducted entirely by means of electronic communication. It can be concentrated at certain courts and is to be introduced for amounts in dispute up to € 5,000. The first consideration here is mass disputes between consumers and defendant companies, but a later expansion could be considered. Such an accelerated online procedure will also be accompanied by the introduction of automated mechanisms, again relying on AI.

Theoretically, AI is also capable of automatically generating decision documents. First, so-called legal generators are created which, after the facts of the case have been entered, perform a subsumption under the legal norm. In its simplest form, this is already done by electronic fee and deadline calculators or - as already illustrated - in the process of creating automatic payment orders. Such subsumptions can be prepared by means of dynamic electronic forms or questionnaires, which in turn are linked to a programmed legal result, as is already happening with the online platforms for checking any claims for flight delays..[22] Finally, documents - decisions - possibly also with justifications are automatically produced from the found legal result.

Since tools already exist that are used, for example, by online arbitration boards which automatically produce certain decision proposals, it is also technically conceivable to fully automate processes.

However, this is currently not planned, at least in Germany. It is true that in administrative proceedings it is possible to issue a so-called automa-

---

20 Franziska Wahedi (n 18) 178 -179

21 <https://www.justiz.bayern.de/media/images/behoerden-und-gerichte/oberlandesgerichte/nuernberg/thesenpapier_der_arbeitsgruppe.pdf> accessed 25 June 2021.

22 Jens Wagner (n 8). 47.

tic administrative act - provided there is no discretion or scope for assessment on the part of the authority, see § 35a Administrative Procedure Act. However, the court decision is not comparable to an administrative decision. There are legal remedies against an automatic administrative act that people decide on. But who decides on automatic court decisions?

There is only sparse discussion in Germany about whether a parallel provision to § 35a VwVfG (Administrative Procedure Act) should be created for court decisions. If one takes up the basic idea of § 35a VwVfG, then an automatic decision only comes into consideration in very strongly structured procedures such as the order for payment procedures or the small claims procedures, i.e. in the enforcement of minor claims, if a decision is already based only on formal criteria. Politicians, such as the German Conference of Ministers of Justice, decided against such automatic court decisions.

4.1.8 Further possibilities of AI use in the judiciary

Chatbots based on artificial intelligence could also be used.[23] In this way, applications or responses to complaints could be recorded in a structured manner via information systems, thus relieving or replacing the lawyers' offices. Attorney applications could be checked for conclusiveness by chatbots.

4.2 Use of AI by the European Union

The outlined use scenarios for AI in the judiciary have also attracted the attention of the European Union. The new multi-annual action plan for E-JUSTICE 2019-2023 adopted in December 2018 [24] provides the following:

One project aims to define "the role that AI could play in the field of justice and to develop an AI tool for the analysis of court decisions." Another project is planned to develop a chatbot for the E-JUSTICE portal "that will assist users and guide them to the information they are looking for". Of course, these EU projects do not cover all possible scenarios for the use of artificial intelligence in the judiciary. But it is a first step.

---

23 Franziska Wahedi (n 18) 77 ff.
24 OJ 2019/C 96/05.

5. Legal assessment of the use of artificial intelligence in the judiciary

5.1 GDPR

Incidentally, within the scope of application of the GDPR of April 2016[25], with Europe-wide validity, Art. 22 (1) GDPR standardizes that a data subject has a right to action by a human being, a machine decision is not sufficient - unless the data subject has consented to such an automatic decision or national law provides otherwise.

5.2 Principles of national constitutions, European Charter of Fundamental Rights, Universal Declaration of Human Rights (United Nations), International Covenant on Civil and Political Rights

In any case, some principles must be observed laid down in national constitutions, but also in supranational law such as the European Charter of Fundamental Rights. The Universal Declaration of Human Rights proclaimed by the United Nations General Assembly on 10 December 1948 is not a treaty, so it does not directly create legal obligations for countries. Because countries have consistently invoked the Declaration for more than sixty years, it has become binding as a part of customary international law and has given rise to a range of other international agreements like the International Covenant on Civil and Political Rights (ICCPR) which are legally binding on the countries that ratify them. In particular, the obligations of each State Party to the Covenant mentioned in Article 2 are significant in this context: "undertakes to respect and to ensure to all individuals within its territory and subject to its jurisdiction the rights recognized in the present Covenant, without distinction of any kind, such as race, colour, sex, language, religion, political or other opinion, national or social origin, property, birth or other status". "Each State Party to the present Covenant undertakes: (...) (b) to ensure that any person claiming such a remedy shall have his right thereto determined by competent judicial, administrative or legislative authorities, or by any other competent authority provided for by the legal system of the State, and to develop the

25 Regulation (EU) 2016/679 of the European Parliament and of the Council of 27 April 2016 on the protection of natural persons with regard to the processing of personal data and on the free movement of such data and repealing Directive 95/46/EC [2016] OJ L119/89 (General Data Protection Regulation).

possibilities of judicial remedy; (c) To ensure that the competent authorities shall enforce such remedies when granted."

5.2.1 Constitutional principles that suggest the use of artificial intelligence

There are constitutional principles that suggest the use of artificial intelligence in certain cases.

For example, it follows from national constitutional law (Article 19 (4) of the German Basic Law) that effective legal protection must be guaranteed. This includes the guarantee of legal protection within a reasonable time, which is based on the specific circumstances of the case. If courts are unable to provide legal protection within a reasonable period due to inadequate equipment, technical means must also be used to increase efficiency. The aspect of the judiciary's ability to function (Article 20 (3) of the German Constitution) must also be considered. It also dictates that information technology tools should not be denied to the judiciary if this is the only way to maintain its ability to function.

5.2.2 Principles that could oppose the use of AI

On the other hand, however, constitutional principles must also be considered that could oppose the use of AI in individual cases:

(1) Right to human dignity

Above all, the right to human dignity must be observed.[26] In conjunction with Article 2 (1) of the German Basic Law, this gives rise to the right to protection of personality, the right to informational self-determination, which has been given its own form in Article 7 of the European Charter of Fundamental Rights in the form of the right to determine the use of information about one's personal life.

---

26 Art. 1 para. 1 German Basic Law, Art. 1 European Charter of Fundamental Rights, Art. 2 sentence 1 TEU, Art. 1 of the Universal Declaration of Human Rights of the United Nations of 10.12.1948.

(2) Principle of non-discrimination

The obligation to observe the principle of equality and the principle of non-discrimination[27] has already been pointed out. Caution is required if judges use software for their decision whose programming is not disclosed and therefore discriminatory input - as in the case of the COMPAS software - is not visible to the judge. The transparency requirement also follows from the principle of the rule of law (Article 20 of the German Basic Law).

(3) Principle of the natural and independent judge

It is established the guiding principle of the natural judge (according to Art. 92 German Basic Law), the independent judge, who must at all times retain control over his own decision, i.e. must not leave it to a self-learning machine, the result of which no one can foresee or concretely influence. The judge, when using IT assistance software, to be able to recognize which data material has been used, in order to be able to make his or her own, responsible, and if necessary to be able to make a decision that will further develop the law. [28]

Art. 10 Universal Declaration of Human Right[29] can also only be understood in such a way that the independent judge cannot mean a machine programmed by technicians.

(4) The right to an effective remedy

The right to an effective remedy implies the right to a reasoned and individual decision. Article 13 of the European Convention on Human Rights: "Everyone whose rights and freedoms as set forth in this Conventi-

27 Art. 3(1) sentence 1 German Basic Law; Art. 20, 21 European Charter of Fundamental Rights, Art. 9 TEU, Art. 14 European Convention on Human Rights, Art. 2 United Nations Universal Declaration of Human Rights.

28 Wilfried Bernhardt and Christina-Maria Leeb, 'Elektronischer Rechtsverkehr' in Dirk Heckmann and Anne Paschke (ed) *jurisPK-Internetrecht* 7th edition, chapter 6 (status: 01 June2021), para 860.

29 "Everyone is entitled in full equality to a fair and public hearing by an independent and impartial tribunal, in the determination of his rights and obligations and of any criminal charge against him."

on are violated shall have an effective remedy before a national authority (…)" The Study on the Human Rights Dimensions of Automated Data Processing Techniques[30] rightly emphasizes: "Automated decision-making processes lend themselves to particular challenges for individuals' ability to obtain effective remedy. These include the opaqueness of the decision itself, its basis, and whether the individuals have consented to the use of their data in making this decision or are even aware of the decision affecting them. The difficulty in assigning responsibility for the decision also complicates individuals' understanding of whom to turn to address the decision. The nature of decisions being made automatic, without or with little human input, and with a primacy placed on efficiency rather than human-contextual thinking, means that there is an even larger burden on the organisations employing such systems to provide affected individuals with a way to obtain remedy."

(5) Fair trial

The requirement of a fair trial (Art. 47 para. 2 European Charter of Fundamental Rights, Art. 6 European Convention on Human Rights) gives the parties to the proceedings the opportunity to influence the course and outcome of the proceedings. This, too, is likely to be difficult to realize in the case of a self-learning, unsupervised AI. Also Art. 14 ICCPR (…" everyone shall be entitled to a fair and public hearing by a competent, independent and impartial tribunal established by law") reveals the essential obligations that are difficult to fulfill by a machine.

(6) Right to the legal judge

In addition, the right to the legal judge requires that certain responsibilities be observed and that the competent judge or court panel be clearly determined before the dispute begins. But who is responsible for a machine deciding a case? The question of legal responsibility is a core issue in

30 Committee of Experts on Internet Intermediaries (MSI-NET), Study on the Human Rights Dimensions of Automated Data Processing Techniques (in Particular Algorithms) and Possible Regulatory Implications (6 October 2017) 23, <https://rm.coe.int/study-hr-dimension-of-automated-data-processing-incl-algorithms/168075b94a> accessed 31 May 2021; Aleš Završnik (n 18).

the use of artificial intelligence. Generally, the question is asked: Who is responsible for artificially intelligent, self-controlling machines? The buyer or owner of the robot that caused the damage? The manufacturer? The robot itself? Translated into the world of courts, this means: Who is then responsible for the court decision? The program manufacturer for the automatic court decision? The judiciary that provided for the use of the program? The court/judge that specifically arranged for the use of the program? Or the machine itself?

(7) Transparency principle

The verifiability of the decision in the sense of effective legal protection also suffers when a non-transparently operating machine decides. The transparency requirement follows from the principle of the rule of law.[31] Thus, the already known dangers of discrimination must be considered, which can always occur when an AI takes existing discrimination as inventory data as a reason to perpetuate discrimination in the future.

(8) Principle of the right to be heard

Furthermore, the principle of the right to be heard (Art. 103 German Basic Law) as well as effective legal protection with the right to inspect the documents on which the judicial decision is based must be observed: For example, the use of AI could lead to the right to be heard running dry because certain bases for the decision are not known either to the litigants or to the court because the results of the AI use remain untransparent.

Care must be taken if the programming of the AI may have incorporated values from other legal systems that are inconsistent with the fundamental values of the European Constitutions and European specifications.

31 Franziska Wahedi (n 18) 40 et seq.; Jürgen Bröhmer, *Transparenz als Verfassungsprinzip* (Mohr Siebeck 2004) 147 ff.

6. *European Commission for the Efficiency of Justice*

2018 the European Commission for the Efficiency of Justice adopted certain principles that must also be observed for AI support.[32] Accordingly, the following basic principles must be observed:

The design and implementation of AI tools and services must be compatible with human rights as laid down in the European Convention on Human Rights (ECHR) and in the Council of Europe Convention for the Protection of Personal Data. The development or intensification of any discrimination between individuals or groups of individuals must be prevented. Judicial institutions should be able to develop an understanding of data processing methods. External expertise should be brought in, and the use of certification systems with short certification intervals would also be useful. AI users should be informed and maintain control over their decisions. The judge should also always feel responsible for his decision. He should always have access to the data on which the decision is based. And he should always have the option to withdraw from the solution proposed by the AI, taking into account the specifics of the case.

7. *Proposal for a Regulation laying down harmonized rules on artificial intelligence.*

On April 21, the EU Commission presented the Proposal for a Regulation laying down harmonized rules on artificial intelligence.[33] The proposal is "based on EU values and fundamental rights and aims to give people and other users the confidence to embrace AI-based solutions, while encouraging businesses to develop them. AI should be a tool for people and be a force for good in society with the ultimate aim of increasing human well-being. Rules for AI available in the Union market or otherwise affec-

---

32 European Commission for the Efficiency of Justice (CEPEJ), *European ethical Charter on the use of Artificial Intelligence in judicial systems and their environment* <https://rm.coe.int/ethical-charter-en-for-publication-4-december-2018/16808f699c> accessed 31 May 2021. See also the report on the CEPEJ Conference "Artificial intelligence at the service of the Judiciary"(27 September 2018) <https://www.coe.int/en/web/cepej/justice-of-the-future-predictive-justice-and-artificial-intelligence> accessed 31 May 2021.

33 COM(2021) 206 final; <https://digital-strategy.ec.europa.eu/en/library/proposal-regulation-laying-down-harmonised-rules-artificial-intelligence> accessed 30 May 2021.

ting people in the Union should therefore be human centric, so that people can trust that the technology is used in a way that is safe and compliant with the law, including the respect of fundamental rights (...) The proposal sets harmonized rules for the development, placement on the market and use of AI systems in the Union following a proportionate risk-based approach". The aim of this proposed regulation is to improve and promote the protection of the rights protected by the EU Charter of Fundamental Rights:[34] the right to human dignity (Art. 1), respect for private life and the protection of personal data (Arts. 7 and 8), the prohibition of discrimination (Art. 21), and equality between women and men (Art. 23). The intention is to prevent interference with the rights to freedom of expression (Art. 11) and freedom of assembly (Art 12). It also seeks to ensure protection of the right to an effective remedy and to a fair trial, the rights of the defense and the presumption of innocence (Arts. 47 and 48), and the general principle of good administration. The proposed regulation provides harmonized rules for the development, placing on the market, and use of AI systems in the Union using a risk-based approach. Particularly harmful AI practices will be banned for violating Union values. AI technologies with "high risk" that pose significant threats to the health and safety or fundamental rights of individuals can only be approved if they meet the requirements for trustworthy AI, if providers present a risk assessment and intended safeguards, and if they have undergone a review process with quality management and conformity assessment procedures (Art. 17) before they can be placed on the Union market and ensure the establishment, implementation and maintenance of a post-market surveillance system. [35]

The Proposed Regulation also comments on the use of a remote biometric recognition system "in real time" in publicly accessible premises for law enforcement purposes. [36] "This should be subject to an explicit and specific authorization by a judicial authority or an independent administrative authority of a Member State, to be obtained in principle before use." However, in a duly justified urgent situation, the use of the system may start without authorization, and the authorization may be requested only during or after the use.

Recital 40 mentions AI systems intended for the administration of justice and democratic processes. These "should be classified as high-risk, considering their potentially significant impact on democracy, rule of law,

---

34 3.5. of the Explanatory Memorandum of the proposed regulation.

35 In detail Art. 8 et seq. of the proposed regulation.

36 Recital 21.

individual freedoms as well as the right to an effective remedy and to a fair trial." Given the "risks of potential bias, error, and opacity," "AI systems intended to assist judicial authorities in researching and interpreting facts and law, and in applying the law to a specific set of facts" should be classified as high-risk. But - according to the proposed regulation - this classification does not extend to" purely ancillary administrative activities " with no impact on "the actual administration of justice in individual cases, such as anonymization or pseudonymization of judicial decisions, documents or data, communication between personnel, administrative tasks or allocation of resources".

The use of high-risk AI systems (when used, for example, in the administration of justice) require effective "human oversight" under Article 14. This means that judges, for example, would need to be aware of the possible tendency to automatically rely or over-rely on the output generated by a high-risk AI system ("automation bias"), especially when AI is used to provide information or recommendations for decisions. Such "human oversight" would also need to be able to " to correctly interpret the high-risk AI system's output, taking into account in particular the characteristics of the system and the interpretation tools and methods available."[37]As a consequence, the "human" must then also be able to not use the high-risk AI system or otherwise ignore, override, or reverse the output of the high-risk AI system.

8. *Conclusion*

The planned European AI Regulation is likely to oppose automatic court decisions (robot judges) using artificial intelligence, especially if such court decisions are beyond human control. This can also be derived from the German constitution. It is therefore unrealistic to expect the establishment of robot judges in the foreseeable future.[38]

However, the planned AI regulation is not only aimed at automatic decision-making systems of the judiciary, but also at AI systems for the preparation of decisions by judges. Thus, transparency about the risks

37 Art. 14 para 4 (c) of the draft.

38 Cancio Fernández, 'La sustitución directa de la actividad humana en la decisión judicial, al día de hoy, es puramente quimérica a corto y medio plazo' (Legal today, 11 September2020) <https://www.legaltoday.com/legaltech/nuevas-tecnologias/la-realidad-y-el-deseo-inteligencia-artificial-y-decision-judicial-2020-09-11/> accessed 31 May 2021.

of AI must be established in this respect as well. Judges should not be allowed to rely rashly on the decision proposals; rather, they should use AI responsibly and also be able to "switch it off" once in a while.

But even if AI systems only support the courts, caution is required because - as explained - AI systems can reinforce discriminatory evaluations. Judges must therefore handle the systems with responsibility. The training and continuing education of judges must also enable them to do so.[39]

Nevertheless, the discussions surrounding the "robot judge" must not obscure the fact that AI can also provide valuable support in the judiciary - for example, in the areas of classification/analysis, translation and anonymization - which should not be dispensed with in view of the increasingly complex legal system, competition from online platforms and the scarcity of judicial resources.

39 UNESCO and partners are developing the program for capacity building of judicial actors concerning the use of AI in courts and by law enforcement, as well as to address the legal implications of AI judicial decisions based on international human rights standards: UNESCO, *AI and the Rule of Law: Capacity Building for Judicial Systems* <https://en.unesco.org/artificial-intelligence/mooc-judges> accessed 31 May 2021.

Towards a Right to Digital Justice? The Constitutionalization of Digital Justice in Mexico

Mauro Arturo Rivera León <arturo.riverale@gmail.com>

Rodrigo E. Galán Martínez <rodrigo.galanmtz1@gmail.com>
MEXICO CITY, Mexico

Abstract
Mexico introduced elements of digital justice in the 2013 Amparo Act. The 2020 COVID pandemic forced a full transition to digital justice to address the forced suspension of activities. However, the lack of a full normative framework and the disparity between the Federal and State Judicial Powers present strong challenges to digitalization. In 2020, the Mexican Senate approved an amendment to constitutionalize digital justice. Even though a constitutional right to digital justice would be a pioneer innovation, the authors conclude that many challenges lie ahead.

1. Introduction

Law is a predominantly conservative discipline. It is often said that normative provisions tend to "chase" social reality and societal change rather than fostering them. The usage of new technologies in judicial proceedings has not been the exception. Digital justice has been an increasing challenge in the world, especially in the last fifteen years. Many countries have developed mechanisms adjusted to their adaptation pace and technological possibilities, in a constant struggle between evolution and resistance to change.

The 2020 outbreak of the COVID-19 Pandemic turned out to be a tough test on the world's capacity to perform remote working, distant activities, and the transition into the digital sphere. Given the risks associated with physical activities, digital justice was suddenly not only seen as "desirable" but as "necessary."

This article will analyze Mexico's evolution from the struggle to provide digital justice to the likelihood of establishing a constitutional right to digital justice. Section II) will analyze the 2020 full transition to online procedures, accelerated by the COVID-19 Pandemic. We will present the argument that as of the 2013 Amparo Act, Mexico has advanced notably in the possibility of providing digital procedures, notwithstanding restricted to a single type of case. It will be shown that the Federal Judiciary relied on such legal framework and experience to extend online procedures in 2020-2021 as a response to the issues associated with the forced suspension of activities. Section III) will analyze the explanatory memoranda, content, and feasibility of the recent constitutional amendment approved by the Mexican Senate to institutionalize a constitutional right to digital justice. In section IV), we set the challenges ahead, concluding that even after the amendment's potential approval, a constitutional right to digital justice will require more than normative provisions.

2. *A Forced Transition: Online Justice at the Federal Level*

a) Constitutional justice and digital justice: the pre-pandemic beginning. Mexico possesses a mixed constitutional justice system[1] with elements of both the diffuse and concentrated constitutional control models. At the federal level, the constitutional control procedures are the Amparo trial[2], actions of unconstitutionality, constitutional controversies, and a peculiar procedure, introduced by the 2011 constitutional amendment, the so called "general declaration of unconstitutionality".

As of 2013, Mexican constitutional justice has implemented elements of digital justice. The 2013 Amparo Act established the possibility of electronically filing Amparo suits. The Amparo Act regulated creating a digital system through which documentation could be filed employing an electronic signature[3].

---

1 Prior to 2011, only the Supreme Court and Federal Judges were permitted to perform constitutional control (mostly through Amparo). However, the Supreme Court changed its doctrine in the ruling "Varios 912/2010" affirming the ability of every judge to perform a diffuse constitutional control.

2 Amparo is a procedure pertaining to the defense of human rights with universal legal standing. The Supreme Court, Circuit Courts, Unitary Courts and District Courts are all competent to solve Amparo in a complex system of competence distribution. For the Supreme Court perspective see Arturo Zaldívar, *Hacia una Nueva Ley de Amparo* (1st ed. IIJ-UNAM 2002) 122.

3 This was considered a great innovation by the Amparo Act. See Rosa González, 'Sobre la competencia' in Guadalupe Tafoya (ed), *Elementos para el estudio del Juicio de Amparo* (Suprema Corte de Justicia de la Nación 2017) 191.

The Supreme Court and the Federal Council of the Judiciary further developed the normative provisions by creating FIREL (the Federal Judiciary's electronic signature). FIREL is the digital instrument replacing the autograph signature, enabling access to digital case files, and additionally permission to serve documents and receive official notifications[4], *inter alia*. In the case of judges/judicial clerks, it allows them to sign official resolutions electronically and to create an electronic case file for each case. [5]

A FIREL may be obtained through an electronic request to the Federal Council of the Judiciary, by attaching a digitalized form of the applicant's identification. Subsequently, the Federal Council of the Judiciary will grant the applicant an official administrative appointment to review the original documentation and record their biometric data. If the validation is successful, the procedure concludes by issuing the digital electronic signature sent by an authorized e-mail to the applicant[6]. As the digital filing of documents is non-compulsory for the parties, the option of filing documents either physically or digitally (or through both modalities) has been upheld.

Electronic case files are also extensively regulated. Digital records of every case file are produced by the digitally filed documents and physically filed documents (which Courts are under obligation to scan). Parties are also entitled to request the official serving of documents within the digital system.[7]

Electronic files pertaining to the Supreme Court developed in slower motion. All parties were expressly allowed to access the Supreme Court's electronic files relating to Amparo trials only until 2015, under the stipulation that an authorized request was provided[8]. In fact, initiating access to interlocutory decisions or judgments through the electronic files by any party automatically performs an official serving of the notice of entry by

---

4 Adriana Campuzano, *Manual para entender el Juicio de Amparo* (1st edn Thomson Reuters 2016) 67.

5 See "Acuerdo General Conjunto número 1/2013 de la Suprema Corte de Justicia de la Nación, del Tribunal Electoral del Poder Judicial de la Federación y del Consejo de la Judicatura Federal, relativo a la Firma Electrónica Certificada del Poder Judicial de la Federación (FIREL) y el expediente electrónico".

6 ibid.

7 ibid.

8 See "Acuerdo General Conjunto de la Suprema Corte de Justicia de la Nación, del Tribunal Electoral del Poder Judicial de la Federación y del Consejo de la Judicatura Federal, que regula los servicios tecnológicos relativos a la tramitación electrónica del juicio de amparo, las comunicaciones oficiales y los procesos de oralidad penal en los Centros de Justicia Penal Federal".

generating a digital record of such access, thus putting the wheels of any appeal or legal action into motion[9].

Therefore, the 2013 Amparo Act laid the foundation for digital justice at the federal procedural level. However, its usage was rather scarce given that the non-compulsory nature of digital procedures allowed the favoring of manual procedure by traditional lawyers. Additionally, even though Amparo is a key constitutional control procedure, the normative provisions failed to quickly expand the scope of digital justice to include ordinary procedures.

b) The impact of the pandemic on digital justice. The COVID-19 pandemic increased the need for digital justice in Mexico substantially. As a preventative measure, the Federal Judiciary declared a work suspension on health and safety grounds in March 2020. However, the case backlog forced concrete actions. In June 2020, the Federal Judiciary extended the application of the electronic signature, electronic case files, and digital service of documents to all procedures within its jurisdiction[10].

The administrative regulations issued also established the possibility of holding remote hearings, videoconference proceedings, and remote Court sessions. The Federal Judiciary Council itself justified the measure to deal with the pandemic while continuing procedures "on a large scale"[11].

Before the pandemic, there was scarce regulation of the digital nature of Supreme Court proceedings, with the exception of Amparo. This was to change radically. The Supreme Court determined[12] that all procedures may be filed and solved digitally through the usage of FIREL. Therefore, the Supreme Court extended the Amparo regulation to all procedures

---

9 Extensively analyzed in Yuritza Castillo, "Las notificaciones" in Juan González and Fernando Sosa and others (eds) *Teoría y Práctica del Juicio de Amparo* (Tribunal Superior de Justicia de la Ciudad de México 2020) 89-94. For a concrete analysis on the abovementioned digital record of the access, see 95-96.

10 See "Acuerdo General 12/2020, del Pleno del Consejo de la Judicatura Federal que regula la integración y trámite del expediente electrónico y el uso de videoconferencias en todos los asuntos de competencia de los órganos jurisdiccionales".

11 ibid.

12 See "Acuerdo General número 13/2020, de trece de julio de dos mil veinte, del Pleno de la Suprema Corte de Justicia de la Nación, por el que se cancela el período de receso que conforme a lo previsto en el artículo 3o. de la Ley Orgánica del Poder Judicial de la Federación tendría lugar del dieciséis de julio al dos de agosto de dos mil veinte y, para este período, se prorroga la suspensión de plazos en los asuntos de su competencia y se habilitan los días que resulten necesarios para las actuaciones jurisdiccionales que se precisan".

such as actions of unconstitutionality[13], constitutional controversies, competence conflicts, and other cases[14].

The Supreme Court also advanced on implementing digital case files, thus permitting access to all parties and Supreme Court clerks[15]. The Court additionally authorized migrating procedures to remote Court sessions via the Zoom platform, thereby being instantly transmitted on YouTube and the Judicial Channel (Justicia TV) [16].

c) The problematics of digital justice in Mexico. As noted, despite some traits of digital justice pertaining to constitutional control through Amparo prior to the pandemic, ordinary procedures in district courts lacked a digital procedure at the federal level. In addition, a substantial percentage of services of court documents and notices of entry were issued personally through actual clerks. The pandemic forced the Federal Council of the Judiciary and the Supreme Court to a rather fast and forced transition to digitalization.

Digital justice faces two current problems in Mexico. In the first case, while the measures taken by the Federal Judiciary represent a step towards digital justice, it should be considered that, due to their reactive nature, their true effectiveness remains the necessary subject of future assessment. A thorough evaluation process is required, which should be accompanied with technical training for a section of the law clerks[17]. For example, it has been common practice that Federal Courts, unfamiliar with the

---

13 See "Acuerdo General 8/2020, de veintiuno de mayo de dos mil veinte, del Pleno de la Suprema Corte de Justicia de la Nación, por el que se regula la integración de los expedientes impreso y electrónico en controversias constitucionales y acciones de inconstitucionalidad, así como el uso del sistema electrónico de este Alto Tribunal para la promoción, trámite, consulta, resolución y notificaciones por vía electrónica en los expedientes respectivos".

14 See "Acuerdo General 9/2020, de veintiséis de mayo de dos mil veinte, del Pleno de la Suprema Corte de Justicia de la Nación, por el que se regula la integración de los expedientes impreso y electrónico de los asuntos de la competencia de este Alto Tribunal, salvo las controversias constitucionales y acciones de inconstitucionalidad, así como el uso del sistema electrónico de la Suprema Corte de Justicia de la Nación para la promoción, trámite, consulta, resolución y notificaciones por vía electrónica en los expedientes respectivos".

15 ibid.

16 See "Acuerdo General 5/2020 de trece de abril de dos mil veinte, del Pleno de la Suprema Corte de Justicia de la Nación, por el que se regula la celebración de las sesiones de la Salas de este Alto Tribunal a distancia, mediante el uso de herramientas informáticas".

17 México Evalúa, *Guía de Buenas Prácticas en el uso de nuevas tecnologías para la impartición de justicia* (1st edn Tinker Foundation 2020) 43.

digital procedure, render interpretations of the law or the administrative regulations that hinder the procedure's effectiveness or require the involved parties to appear unnecessarily in Court physically. Furthermore, the current normative provisions are still largely based on employing technological tools to adapt the current procedures to the digital sphere instead of creating procedural designs to operate online fully[18].

In the second case, there is a disparity between the Federal Judiciary and the local judiciaries. In 2021 only 24 of the 32 local judiciaries held electronic case files, while only 18 allowed electronic filing and service of documents[19]. Within these statistics the levels of development also vary notably in every State. It can definitively be argued that the Federal Judiciary has been more effective in implementing digital justice than its local counterparts.

3. *The Constitutionalization of Digital Justice: A Future Fundament Right or a Characterization of Justice in Mexico?*

The abovementioned scenario illustrates that Mexico started proactive efforts towards the digitalization of judicial proceedings in 2013. Nonetheless, the 2020 Pandemic produced an immense number of technical challenges to the Justice system and particularly to the Courts. After a couple of months, the initial absolute suspension was quickly discarded as a potential solution after the "new normality" showed that the impact of the Pandemic would be felt in the years to come. The Federal Public Administration and governmental bodies centered their efforts on remote working and informatics as the only means to proceed with the otherwise suspended physical activities. We have analyzed that the Federal Judiciary also undertook similar efforts. The Federal Judiciary was fortunate enough to have a base from which to build a progressive digitalization. Having the normative framework of the 2013 Amparo Act and a (rather minimal) four years' experience on its functioning, the path was eased. It is noteworthy that these measures were designed to mitigate the effects of the forced suspension and not to provide a reliable solution, which is undoubtedly

---

18 A similar observation by Arturo Ramos and Laura Márquez, *Observatorio: Avances de Justicia Abierta en línea en México 2020* (1st edn Escuela Libre de Derecho 2020) 74.

19 Laurence Pantin and Sandra Escamilla, 'La justicia digital en México: el saldo a un año del inicio de la Pandemia' (animalpolitico.com, 11 March 2021) <https://bit.ly/3sTibJi> accessed 27 April 2021.

required. Such a solution may have come in the shape of a constitutional amendment.

In July 2020, Senator Ricardo Monreal (a member of "MORENA", the Parliamentary majority) sponsored a constitutional amendment to article 17 of the Constitution[20], considering digital justice as a component of the right to access justice itself. Three months later, Senators Zepeda and Galvez (from the "PAN" party) sponsored their own proposal in similar terms[21].

Article 17 of the Mexican Constitution provides a set of rights concerning access to justice (the right to free access to courts, the right to an anti-formalist nature of court proceedings, class actions as collective rights, the right to alternative dispute solution mechanisms, et cetera[22]). Constitutionally in Mexico, therefore, access to justice is characterized as free of charge, impartial, complete, fast, and expeditious (ensuring rulings are rendered within a reasonable time). The amendment would imply a further adjective to justice: "digital". Can digital justice become a fundamental right? Can justice itself be digital or not be deemed so?

a) *Reasons for the amendments.* The explanatory memorandum for Monreal's amendment explored the correlation between access to the internet and access to justice. The proposal dwells on the Joint Declaration on Freedom of Expression and the Internet[23], the Mexican legal framework pertaining to access to the internet, and the right to access justice.

---

20 Ricardo Monreal, 'Iniciativa con Proyecto de Decreto por el que se reforma el artículo 17 de la Constitución Política de los Estados Unidos Mexicanos, en materia de digitalización de procesos judiciales' <https://bit.ly/31ZgRth> accessed 9 April 2021). See also the official website of the Senate concerning the parliamentary procedure's data of the proposed amendment: <https://bit.ly/3dPRpMs> accessed 9 April 2021.

21 Damián Zepeda and Xóchitl Gálvez, "Iniciativa con Proyecto de Decreto por el que se adiciona un párrafo cuarto al artículo 17 de la Constitución Política de los Estados Unidos Mexicanos en materia de Justicia Digital" <https://bit.ly/327x5Ra> accessed 10 April 2021). See also the official website of the Senate concerning the parliamentary procedure's data of the proposed amendment: <https://bit.ly/3wQG V7U> accessed 10 April 2021.

22 A reference is Fernando Pérez, 'Artículo 17. Párrafo segundo' in José Ramón Cossío (ed) *Constitución Política de los Estados Unidos Mexicanos Comentada*" (Tirant lo Blanch 2017) 378-389.

23 See Joint Declaration on Freedom of Expression and the Internet by the United Nations (UN) Special Rapporteur on Freedom of Opinion and Expression, the Organization for Security and Co-operation in Europe (OSCE) Representative on Freedom of the Media, the Organization of American States (OAS) Special Rapporteur on Freedom of Expression and the African Commission on Human

Moreover, the amendment analyzes several mechanisms in Europe, Asia, and the American continent concerning artificial intelligence and e-justice. Regarding the national framework, the initiative discusses the RR 1554/2019, in which the Supreme Court dismissed a claim pertaining to the need to provide digital justice in all judicial procedures.[24] After providing a comprehensive analysis of the legal framework concerning digital procedures at the federal level, the amendment proposal stated the need to implement such mechanisms at a general level given the challenges presented by the Pandemic.

The Zepeda-Galvezes amendment dwells on the benefits that digital justice may provide in terms of quality and efficiency. The amendment analyzed the works of "Transparencia Mexicana" and "Tojil" which concluded[25] that after 100 days from the outbreak of the Pandemic, while the Mexican Federal Judiciary allowed full online procedures, only 16 of the 32 local judiciaries allowed a proper digital procedure. Zepeda's proposal also analyzed some of the examples in comparative law regarding digital justice, such as H@bilus (Portugal), NGCS (Israel) or XHIBIT (England), EFS (Singapur), et cetera.

b) *Relevant changes.* Monreal's amendment proposed introducing a progressive system to provide online justice, establishing virtual Courts through information and communication technology. It also stated that such regulations should comprise establishing full online procedures, regulating electronic case files and electronic signatures, and specify an elective or non-compulsory nature of online justice to the parties considering a progressive increase in internet access. Monreal's amendment proposed to force Federal and State Congresses to issue such legislation within 180 days of issuing the amendment.

---

and Peoples' Rights (ACHPR) Special Rapporteur on Freedom of Expression and Access to Information (adopted 1 June 2011).

24 Recurso de Reclamación 1554/2019 (04/09/2019), First Chamber of the Supreme Court. The Court dismissed the claim (pertaining to the admissibility of a "recurso de revision"). In its dissenting opinion, Justice González Alcántara stated that even though the Code did not foresee the digitalization of the procedure in commerce disputes, the Court should have analyzed if digital justice was a part of the access to justice itself and whether the omission of providing digital justice in certain procedures was rational or not. The amendment's proposal strongly highlights Justice González Alcántara's position.

25 See: Transparencia Mexicana, '¿Cómo será la justicia digital en la Nueva Era: Episodio 2' (www.tm.org.mx, 17 June 2020) <https://bit.ly/3sl4UsG> accessed 10 April 2021.

In turn, Zepeda's amendment regulated in greater detail the inclusion of concepts such as digital files, videoconferences concerning hearings, and creating a general electronic filing system pertaining to filing and serving court documents. Therefore, both amendments' proposals seemed to draw inspiration from comparative experiences and recognized the need to force the states to implement digital justice to the same degree as the Federal Judiciary. As expected, the pandemic emergency played a notable role in both proposals.

c) *From Senatorial approval to the road ahead: Feasibility of the amendment.* The Joint Senatorial Legislative Committees of "Constitutional Amendments" and "Legislative Studies" after having studied both amendment proposals, issued a favorable opinion introducing certain changes[26] , and moved it forward for consideration by the full Chamber. The Senate approved the amendment by a solid 97 votes (out of 120 senators) on March 2021. The approved amendment includes a transitory regime that binds the General and Local Congress to issue secondary legislation within 180 days and forces local and Federal Parliaments to foresee a budgetary reserve to implement digital justice "progressively."

After the Senate's approval, the constitutional amendment would need to pass a 2/3 qualified vote in the Chamber of Deputies and attain a simple majority of the State Parliaments (17/32). Is it a possible road?

The introduction of such a fundamental right at the constitutional level may seem complicated though there are at least two factors, which may decisively tilt the scales. In first place, the recent discussion in Mexico towards digital environments prompted by the Constitution's recognition of a right to internet and telecommunications in the Constitution, and in second place, the political nature of the Mexican constitutional amendment procedure.

Regarding the first factor, article 6 of the Constitution was amended in 2013 to establish a right to access broadcasting and telecommunication services "including broadband and internet". Not only was the right recognized, but also the State was bound to establishing proper competence

26 The amendment approved by the Senate is: "Article 17 (...) To guarantee access of justice in a fast, timely and inclusive way, the Federal and local Judiciary Power, the Federal and local Administrative Courts, Agrarian Courts, Labor Courts, local and Federal Electoral Courts shall implement digital justice systems employing Information and communications technology to provide full digital trials and electronic access and serving of documents in the terms prescribed by the law. A Law shall establish the type of hearings that must be physical to ensure an adequate administration of justice".

conditions in order to provide the services[27]. Both amendment proposals dwelled upon the right to access the internet and therefore deemed that a natural relationship between such a right and access to justice must recognize digital justice as an essential constitutional component of all court procedures.

In relation to the second factor, Mexico's Constitution has often been described as formally rigid (in Brycean terms[28]) but materially flexible[29]. Prof. Valadés famously stated that constitutional amendments seemed to be in Mexico "a living testimony of what the country has deemed the most relevant content of a temporary political program[30]."

The Pandemic will certainly be one of the most significant events during López Obrador's Presidency and MORENA's parliamentary majority: an amendment certainly would be expected under the political conception of the Constitution by the political actors. Senator Monreal belongs to the "MORENA" party, the majoritarian party in both the Chamber of Deputies and the Senate. After the 2018 election, MORENA has performed exceptionally well with passing amendments consolidating its main policies, and this one might not be the exception.

Morena holds a solid 51.4 % majority in the Chamber of Deputies. In turn, Senators Zepeda and Gálvez belong to the "Partido Acción Nacional" (PAN) party, the first minority in the Chamber of Deputies, holding a 15.6 % and therefore very few votes are practically required to pass the amendment in the lower Chamber. That is, both parties combined (67 % of the Chamber) hold more than the 2/3 qualified majority required to approve the amendment. It is worth noting that the Federal Entities generally approve all constitutional amendments passed by Congress[31]. Therefore, in terms of Mexican reality, approving the amendment in the Chamber of

---

27 The transitory regime (Article 14) even stated that the Federal Executive shall guarantee broadband access to internet in every building and entity of the Federal Public Administration.

28 James Bryce, *Flexible and Rigid Constitutions* (1st edn Oxford University Press 1905) 7.

29 *Inter alia*, Mauro Arturo Rivera, 'Understanding Constitutional Amendments in Mexico: Perpetuum Mobile Constitution' (2017) 2 Mexican Law Review 3, 6. The accelerated amendment rhythm of the Mexican Constitution has been a source of academic fascination.

30 Diego Valadés, *La Constitución reformada* (1st edn IIJ-UNAM 1987) 12.

31 Mauro Arturo Rivera, 'De Directores y Orquestas: Análisis comparado de la posición institucional del Consejo de la Judicatura Federal en México' (2020) 159 Boletín Mexicano de Derecho Comparado 1139, 1143.

Deputies would practically ensure that the Constitution would be definitively amended in 2021.

4. More Challenges than Certainties: A Provisional Conclusion

Our analysis has shown that the first solid steps towards digital justice in Mexico were taken in 2013 only concerning Amparo. However, the COVID-19 Pandemic forced the Federal Judiciary to rely on that legal framework to provide online justice in other procedures. The transition was forced and unplanned, a tough necessity given the pressing circumstances as shown by the substantial differences visible between the Federal Judiciary and the local Judiciaries of the States.

The Senate's approval of the Monreal/Zepeda&Galvez amendment to article 17 of the Constitution proved that the legislative branch learned from the Federal Judiciary measures and tried to further expand on the remedial actions taken. The amendment would imply either creating a fundamental right to digital justice or, at the very least, constitutionally stating that "digital" is an intrinsically necessary characterization of justice.

The amendment procedure in Mexico and the strong support attained by the Senate's proposal render such an amendment feasible to be approved in 2021. Mexico would become one of the very first countries to guarantee digital justice constitutionally. The scenario certainly might look promising, however, we need to bear in mind that any further recognition of rights does not necessarily expand the rights *per se*. Of course, constitutionalization in itself would imply the possibility of submitting to judicial review cases in which digital justice is not provided[32] or imposing budgetary obligations to the Federation and the States to guarantee full online procedures. However, constitutionalizing digital justice will not create this if not followed by an intensive intervention at both the federal and state levels.

At the federal level, it would imply creating an enduring legal framework and not relying on the provisionary regulations issued by the Supreme Court and the Federal Council of the Judiciary. A comprehensive approach might require formal amendments to procedural regulations. At

32 The Mexican Supreme Court holds a firm doctrine allowing to appeal legislative omissions through amparo. For example AR 1359/2019 by the First Chamber (also known as the "Artículo 19" case) or AR 805/2018 (hate speech case), by the First Chamber.

the state level, the struggle widens. While some states are at an advanced level, others will require intensive intervention to develop functional models.

Introducing a constitutional provision guaranteeing digital justice would probably position Mexico as a pioneering country in pure normative terms: nonetheless, a tough road will still lie ahead.

Online Dispute Resolution and the Form of an Arbitration Agreement

Przemysław Polański[1] <*polanski@kozminski.edu.pl*>
WARSZAWA, Poland

Jacek Gołaczyński[2] <*jacek.golaczynski@uwr.edu.pl*>
WROCŁAW, Poland

Introduction

ODR or online dispute resolution systems could become the cornerstone of the next incarnation of e-commerce revolution. In the offline world it takes various forms, but the lessons from the past are rarely a blueprint in the online world. Online arbitrage is about settling a dispute in a way similar to a traditional court. The decision of arbiters is binding upon the parties and is enforceable, although courts may overrule the decision, if challenged. Mediation is the process of resolving issues between parties with the assistance of a third party, which helps to find a solution to the problem. Conciliation method, on the other hand, requires appointment of an expert to propose a solution to the dispute between the parties.

It is natural to expect the development of such services with the growth of electronic commerce. Developing information systems for online, out-of-court resolution of disputes over illegal content on the Internet has several advantages. It may help to speed up proceedings in general and modernize the judiciary by creating state-independent online dispute resolution systems. Latest legal developments on the EU level seem to expect the provision of such services by online service providers. It seems that such an approach is necessary also due to the changing expectations of the young generation of residents of our country, brought up in the era of ubiquitous Internet. This approach is also supported by the COVID-19 pandemic, which has accelerated the transformation of the Polish economy and administration to the digital age.

1 Author of Part I.
2 Author of Part II.

It is worth mentioning here that although out-of-court dispute resolution encounters cultural barriers and is breaking through with great difficulty, Poland is the first place in Europe, and the second after Japan, where an electronic court for blockchain technology disputes has been launched. The blockchain arbitration court was established at the Polish Chamber of Commerce for Blockchain and New Technologies and its main goal is to "provide an efficient, fast and industry-specific way of binding dispute resolution".

In this article we are going to present a challenge of solving disputes in modern Internet era relying on online, out-of-court dispute resolution mechanisms rather than traditional court systems. Modern challenges require modern solutions and a sheer volume of illegal or dubious content in cyberspace requires a more decisive action from international community, policymakers as well as nation states.

Out-of-court dispute settlement can be also categorized as the so-called alternative dispute resolution (ADR)[3]. Initially, the ADR movement was referred to as "alternative forms of dispute resolution", "out of court settlement techniques", "new voluntary mechanisms of resolving dispute"[4]. One of the characteristics of alternative dispute resolution methods is that they depart from absolute application of the provisions pertaining to a specific normative system in favor of equitable forms of resolving conflict between the parties. What is important in arbitration is the greater influence on the proceedings enjoyed by the parties if compared to state court proceedings (e.g. in the selection of arbitrators, methods of submitting and receiving evidence, etc.).[5] Legal scholars assume that the concept of "alternative forms of dispute resolution" can be defined in three ways:

As forms of court proceedings, which, however, are alternative also to traditional court proceedings, i.e. an alternative to contentious proceedings will be non-contentious proceedings;

3 Karol Weitz and Katarzyna Gajda-Roszczenialska, 'Alternatywne metody rozwiązywania sporów ze szczególnym uwzględnieniem mediacji' in Andrzej Torbus (ed) *Mediacja w sprawach gospodarczych. Praktyka-teoria-perspektywy* (Ministerstwo Gospodarki Departament Doskonalenia Regulacji Gospodarczych 2015) 13.

4 Andrzej Kobyrski, *Alternatywne rozwiazywanie sporów w USA. Studium teoretyczno-prawne* (Wydaw. UMCS 1993) 10; zob. także Aneta Arkuszewska, *Informatyzacja postepowania arbitrażowego* (Wolters Kluwer 2019) 50.

5 Aneta Jakubiak-Mirończuk, 'Zmiany zachodzące w charakterze form alternatywnego rozwiązywania sporów sądowych rozwój idei „zarządzania sporem"', (2008) 4 ADR. Arbitraż i Mediacja 12 ff.

As forms of court proceedings, which, however, do not have adjudicatory character, e.g. mediation, settlement call, conciliation etc.

As all other extrajudicial forms regulated outside of state institutions competent to resolve disputes, conflicts between parties, but which are related to judicial activity, such as arbitration[6].

Ultimately, it can be concluded that ADR is a method of dispute resolution alternative to courts (proceedings before state courts), conducted with the participation of a neutral, impartial party, which also includes arbitration. ODR is a subset of ADR methods that rely on Internet technologies to achieve similar goals. In the first part, written by P. Polański, the notion of online dispute resolution will be presented outlining an already functioning, early model of such regulatory mechanisms established on the EU level. In the second part, written by J. Gołaczyński, a detailed analysis of an arbitration agreement and its electronic form under Polish law will be analysed.

Part I. Online Dispute Resolution

Background

A flood of illegal content, including in particular hate speech and defamation, as well as other forms of law violations in Poland has already become a fact.[7] This phenomenon only deepens the division of society caused by the results of the political elections. It will also come as no surprise that this is not just a problem in Poland, but to a greater or lesser extent around the world. The Polish Ministry of Digitalisation has already taken the first, very modest but noteworthy steps in this regard, formulating key questions as part of the consultation on the European Commission's Re-

---

6 Lech Morawski, *Główne problemy współczesnej filozofii prawa. Prawo w toku przemian* (PWN 2000) 228 ff; Łukasz Błaszczak, 'Mediacja a inne alternatywne formy rozwiazywania sporów (wybrane zagadnienia)' (2012) 2 ADR. Arbitraż i Mediacja 14.

7 The article is a result of the NCN grant nr 2014/15/B/HS5/03138 titled "Fighting illegal and harmful content on the Internet" as well as the NCN grant nr 2016/22/E/HS5/00434 "Ensuring web accessibility in accordance with national and international law as well as WCAG 2.0 guidelines." The idea described in the above article is being currently implemented practically thanks to the NCBiR grant nr 274091 "System for dispute resolution concerning illegal speech in cyberspace (eletronic arbitrage)" as part of the Tango Project led by prof. ALK dr hab. P. Polański.

commendations on combating illegal content on the Internet, including "how should a model for out-of-court dispute resolution function?"[8]

The current legal situation places online intermediaries such as website administrators in the role of judges who must make decisions regarding the removal of a particular post or file of a website user. Privatisation of justice leads to the chilling effect on speech, promoting removal or blocking of potentially dangerous content just in case. This may lead to the erosion of the protection of civil liberties guaranteed by Polish and European law and burdens the intermediaries themselves with costs and administrative duties.

One of the solutions is to streamline the operation of courts, another - of administrative bodies, in order to provide users with the maximum level of protection of their rights. Taking into account, however, the current burden on courts, it is highly unlikely that developing specialized courts would help to swiftly adjudicate disputes in cyberspace.

Instead, it is proposed to create a model of removal of unlawful content by arbitration bodies independent of content providers (e-arbitration) - a form of ODR or online dispute resolution. These still novel types of information society services can be encountered mainly in a traditional world of legal dispute settlement, although the Domain Name dispute resolution mechanism operated by ICANN[9] could be regarded as a frontrunner of such cyber-mechanisms in an area where conflicts frequently arise.

---

8 The European Commission has set the online community to understand the main regulatory challenges in this area, see <https://www.gov.pl/cyfryzacja/konsultacje-zalecen-komisji-europejskiej-dotyczacego-walki-z-bezprawnymi-tresciami-w-internecie> accessed 5 December 2018.
1. "How should the actions taken by hosting providers to effectively combat illegal content on the Internet, affect the exclusion of their liability (Article 14 of Directive 2000/31/EC)?
2) How should the conditions and criteria for recognition of trusted flaggers be defined by hosting providers in order to achieve a plurality of entities?
3. if there is illegal content on the Internet, is it possible to protect it effectively if it is reported anonymously and at what stage should it be reported? How to prevent abuse of reporting?
4) How should a model for out-of-court dispute resolution work?
What are the EC recommendations (in addition to those mentioned in the above recommendation) that should be taken up by hosting providers in order to effectively fight illegal content on the Internet?
6. what is the most convenient form of collecting reports on notifications and decisions of hosting providers on illegal content on the Internet?

9 <https://www.icann.org/resources/pages/dndr-2012-02-25-en> accessed 20 July 2021.

Online Dispute Resolution is a form of ADR (ang. Alternative Dispute Resolution) where a quarrel is settled out-of-court or without a judge.[10] It make take a form of an arbitrage, mediation or conciliation but other modes are also possible. Typically, parties to the dispute have a greater freedom with respect to selection of arbiters, mediators or conciliators as well as the evidentiary rules and the proceedings usually are shorter and less expensive than traditional court adjudication. It is of particular value in the context of potentially large volume, low-cost dispute characteristics of disputants in modern cyberspace.

ODR has many additional advantages, ranging from removing from large and medium-sized entities the difficult responsibility of deciding what is lawful and what is not - to strengthening the fundamental rights of natural and legal persons in cyberspace. Furthermore, quasi-judicial bodies, independent from national states are also a direct reference to medieval arbitration courts resolving disputes between entrepreneurs based on lex mercatoria - trade customs - whose greatest advantage was speed.

The European Union already has some experience in setting up Internet-based out-of-courts systems. Already in 2013, Regulation 524/2013 on ODR in consumer disputes was adopted[11], which led to the creation of the first electronic arbitration in the European Union. Recital 8 of the Regulation stresses that "ODR offers the possibility of simple, effective, fast and low-cost out-of-court resolution of disputes arising from online transactions. However, there is currently a lack of mechanisms that allow consumers and traders to resolve such disputes by electronic means; this works to the detriment of consumers, constitutes an obstacle to cross-border online transactions in particular, and creates an uneven playing field for traders and consequently hinders the overall development of online commerce."

The new platform was developed and is being used by the EU citizens in their local languages. However, the architecture is not based on the idea of centralised, online dispute resolution website, but is outsourced to national bodies settling a dispute. Despite a significant growth in the number of complaints, reaching an average of 2000 cases per month[12], the statistics

---

10 g*erm. Alternative Streibeiegungm, French:* le reglement extajudiciaire des litiges).

11 Regulation (EU) No 524/2013 of the European Parliament and of the Council of 21 May 2013 on online dispute resolution for consumer disputes and amending Regulation (EC) No 2006/2004 and Directive 2009/22/EC [2013] OJ L165/1–12 (Regulation on consumer ODR).

12 <https://ec.europa.eu/consumers/odr/resources/public2/documents/trader_info_stats/ODR_Trader_Info_stat_EN.pdf> accessed 20 July 2021.

have not been updated for more than three years, raising questions as to its accuracy. Although the ODR consumer disputes platform in the EU has not brought about any major breakthrough in the number of cases recognized, it has laid the foundations for upcoming developments.

The situation may fundamentally change with undergoing legislative efforts to introduce new rules to combat unlawful online content. The European Commission's draft Regulation of 15 December 2021 on the Single Market for Digital Services[13] (Digital Services Act), which is intended to repeal Articles 12-15 of the E-Commerce Directive, envisages establishment of an online dispute resolution system.

The introduction of mandatory mechanism for online providers may drastically improve the situation of people whose content or accounts had been blocked by the platform provider. Online traders operating on a larger scale will both have to establish an internal dispute resolution system (Article 17 of DSA), and users of information society services will be entitled to submit their dispute to dispute resolution by providers of electronic arbitration services established and certified in Member States (Article 18 of DSA).

The DSA does not seek to replace the right to a court with the right to electronic out-of-court dispute settlement, but only complements this right. Hence, the idea of incorporating ODR as a new mechanism for online dispute resolution is to be welcomed, refreshing the optional call for Member States to develop such solutions expressed in Article 17 of the E-Commerce Directive, which has never materialised in practice.

Requirements for ODR

It is particularly important to set out the general principles expressed in Article 5(1) of the DSA. "The ODR platform shall be user-friendly. The development, operation and maintenance of the ODR platform shall ensure that the privacy of its users is respected from the design stage ('privacy by design') and that the ODR platform is accessible and usable by all, including vulnerable users ('design for all'), as far as possible)."

There are two principles expressed in the aforementioned provision. Firstly, it is important to note the need to create an ODR platform based

13 Proposal for a Regulation of the European Parliament and of the Council on a Single Market For Digital Services (Digital Services Act) and amending Directive 2000/31/EC, COM/2020/825 final

on the privacy standard introduced by the GDPR[14], especially privacy by design and privacy by default. These principles may be challenging to implement in the context of a dispute management as it will require managing sensitive data originating from many users, especially comments revealing ethnic origin or health status. Transfer of data to third countries, particularly the USA, may also turned out the be problematic.

Secondly, the ODR platform should be accessible to everyone, including people with special needs. This requires that the platform be created taking into account the principles developed from the bottom up by the international community, i.e. the WCAG 2.1 principles (Web Content Accessibility Guidelines). The aforementioned guidelines require that interactive elements, such as forms are accessible to blind people as well as people with other types of limitations.

Apart from the privacy and accessibility-friendly requirements, the draft of DSA regulation outlines general organisational obligations for the operator of a platform. The dispute resolution service provider should (1) be independent, (2) have the knowledge and skills to resolve disputes related to unlawful content, (3) provide a fast, low-cost and impartial process (4) operate under procedural rules that are transparent and fair, and (5) provide easy access to the functionalities offered by the dispute resolution platform. The fulfilment of the above requirements is to be confirmed by an appropriate certificate issued by the national Digital Services Coordinator envisioned by the project.

Theoretically, there is nothing to prevent such a dispute resolution system from relying on automated decision-making using machine learning. Neither the draft regulation on combating unlawful content (DSA) nor the new draft on harmonized rules for artificial intelligence create fundamental obstacles in this regard.[15]

However, one should bear in mind that such automated systems would be classified as highly risky under the draft Artificial Intelligence Act. This, in turn, could seriously impede the efforts of system creators to rapidly introduce such solutions on the EU market. Secondly, in light of the

14 Regulation (EU) 2016/679 of the European Parliament and of the Council of 27 April 2016 on the protection of natural persons with regard to the processing of personal data and on the free movement of such data, and repealing Directive 95/46/EC [2016] OJ L119/1–88 (General Data Protection Regulation).

15 Proposal for a REGULATION OF THE EUROPEAN PARLIAMENT AND OF THE COUNCIL LAYING DOWN HARMONISED RULES ON ARTIFICIAL INTELLIGENCE (ARTIFICIAL INTELLIGENCE ACT) AND AMENDING CERTAIN UNION LEGISLATIVE ACTS of 21 April 2021 r. COM(2021) 206 final

GDPR the data subject shall have the right not to be subject to a decision based solely on automated processing, including profiling, which produces legal effects concerning him or her or similarly significantly affects him or her (art. 22 par. 1). Therefore, AI-based approaches should rather be used as a complementary element to the traditional IT systems operated by human experts.

A very important element of the proposed ODR architecture is the definition of how to ensure financial stability of such platforms. After all, they have to support their operations as well as to ensure the quality of their judgments and the smooth functioning for a longer period of time. The DSA provides for the possibility of establishing public ODR by Member States but the functioning of private entities is far less clear.

The DSA regulation provides for the possibility of charging fees for dispute resolution. These these fees should not be excessive and should not exceed the cost of providing the service. This, in turn, may turn out to be a challenge in building sustainable online dispute resolution systems, as it is simply hard to tell at this point, what is the cost of providing such service. There are too few examples to draw conclusions from.

The draft DSA also made some important stipulations changing the burden of costs associated with loosing a case. If the dispute is resolved in favour of the online trader's counterparty, the counterparty will be obliged to reimburse the entire cost of dispute resolution incurred by the trader, whereas if the professional entity wins, the counterparty will not be obliged to reimburse the expenses incurred by the online trader (Article 18(3) of the draft DSA).

Features of the ODR platform

The proposed model of the European Commission in the DSA is quite generic and will therefore require a lot more planning and engineering effort to develop a comprehensive set of features for such a platform to function well. Even the most basic features of the proposed out-of-court ODR are missing. Therefore, it is worthwhile to revisit the older, already mentioned Regulation 524/2013 to see what requirements the European legislator has envisaged for ODR platforms for consumer disputes to see if they could be adapted for settling disputes related to unlawful content. It is worth pointing out that the aforementioned Regulation often uses a more generic term ADR (Alternative Dispute Resolution) rather than a more restrictive, purely Internet-based ODR (Online Dispute resolution).

According to Article 5(4) of the Regulation 524/2013 on ODR in consumer disputes, the ODR platform should offer the following features:

(a) providing an electronic complaint form that can be completed by the complainant. This is a self-evident requirement; moreover, the complaint form should be accessible to persons with various disabilities, including visual impairments;
(b) informing the party against whom the complaint is made about filing of the ODR complaint. This is also an integral part of the due process, which should be the cornerstone of the information flow envisaged by the unlawful content dispute resolution platform;
(c) identifying the relevant adjudicator (i.e. arbitrator, mediator or conciliator). The Regulation 524/2013 uses a more generic term "ADR entity"[16] instead and mandates forwarding the complaint to the ADR entity that the parties have agreed to use. This requirement can be seen as an extension of the due process principle by requiring that the case be referred to another entity as indicated in the agreement concluded between the complainant and the online trader;
(d) the provision, free of charge, of an electronic case handling tool that will enable the parties and the adjudicator (ADR entity) to conduct their online dispute resolution proceedings through the ODR platform. In fact, the above requirement is so broad that it will need to be spelled out in detail in terms of the detailed functionalities of the platform, including how the "hearing rooms" will be visualized, the scope of information provided to the parties, the adjudicator and the administration of the platform, etc. On the other hand, with regard to payments, draft DSA regulation provides for the possibility of charging fees, which is one of the main differences with respect to the consumer dispute resolution model;
(e) provide the parties and the adjudicator (ADR entity) with a translation of the information that is necessary for the resolution of the dispute and that is exchanged through the ODR platform. This is an interesting requirement, the implementation of which should also be

---

16 'ADR entity' means any entity, however named or referred to, which is established on a durable basis and offers the resolution of a dispute through an ADR procedure and that is listed in accordance with Article 20(2) of the Directive 2013/11/EU of the European Parliament and of the Council of 21 May 2013 on alternative dispute resolution for consumer disputes and amending Regulation (EC) No 2006/2004 and Directive 2009/22/EC (Directive on consumer ADR) [2013] OJ L165/ 63–79 (Directive on consumer ADR).

recommended to all ODR platforms. It may give raise to the possibility of additional fees being charged, of which the complainant would have to be informed of before initiating the dispute. Alternatively, such translation service could also be provided by a machine learning solution;

(f) making available mechanisms, such as an electronic form, by means of which adjudicator (ADR entity) can share with other participants the details of the complaint at hand, namely: (i), the date of receipt of the complaint file; (ii), the subject matter of the dispute; (iii), the date on which the procedure was concluded; (iv), the outcome of the procedure. The Regulation 524/2013 presupposes handling of such administrative duties by a relevant entity rather than an administrative unit within an ODR platform. This, however, can be adapted to the needs of centralised, purely-online service providers.

(g) the provision of a feedback system allowing the parties to express their views on the functioning of the ODR platform and on the adjudicator (ADR entity) that handled their dispute. This is also an interesting requirement concerning on the level of service offered by the ODR platform, which was not imposed with respect to e.g. traders dealing with consumers. It would be interesting to see what kind of information can be gathered and distributed via such feedback forms. Especially, to what extent critical remarks concerning verdicts and/or adjudicators should affect the functioning of the ODR system;

(h) making publicly available statistical data on the outcome of disputes and general information on how to resolve disputes out of court, an online guide on how to lodge a complaint and contact information.

The above requirements provided by the 2013 Regulation are quite vague, especially in critical areas, such as"case handling tool" or mechanisms for sharing data with other participants. Nevertheless, it is necessary to foresee functional solutions in sufficient detail, such as issues related to the flow of necessary information in the dispute resolution system ranging from the registration of the case through its transfer to the adjudicators, the conduct of voting, the registration of the process to the announcement of the award and its transmission to the participants. In addition, platforms should be prepared to cover the details in the general terms and conditions of an ODR platform.

Procedural requirements

The features or functional requirements envisaged in Regulation 524/2013 are a good starting point for further elaboration of the characteristics of the unlawful content dispute resolution model. In this context, it is worth a second block of functional solutions provided in Articles 8 and 9 of the Regulation on consumer ODR, which can be described as procedural or workflow architecture requirements.

1) Complaint form

In order to submit a complaint to the ODR platform, the complainant shall fill in an electronic complaint form and the European Commission has been obliged to define an electronic complaint form by means of implementing acts. The complaint form should be user-friendly and easily accessible on the ODR platform. This means that the form must be accessible within the meaning of WCAG 2.1 principles, in particular the fields of the form must be constructed in such a way that .e.g. a visually impaired person can enter and submit the information stored therein to the ODR system.

The information to be submitted by the complaining party must be sufficient to determine the competent entity (an adjudicator) that will deal with the complaint (in the context of consumer disputes, this is the designation of the relevant ADR entity that will actually deal with the dispute using ODR platform).[17] In the context of illegal content, this may entail an elaboration of the algorithm for selecting relevant adjudicators specialising in a given area of illegal content.

The complainant should be able to attach documents in support of their complaint. This means building an infrastructure to upload and store files, including both text files, photos and scans of paper documentation. One should consider expanding the document retrieval functionality to include

17 In the Consumer Disputes Regulation, ADR entities handling complaints must comply with the relevant requirements. Article 8 of the Regulation provides that in order to take into account the criteria on the basis of which ADR entities listed in accordance with Article 20(2) of Directive 2013/11/EU and handling disputes covered by this Regulation define their respective scopes of competence, the Commission shall be empowered to adopt delegated acts in accordance with Article 17 of this Regulation adapting the information listed in the Annex to this Regulation.

screenshots for evidentiary purposes along with the date of the screenshot and perhaps a digital signature.

2) Collection and retention of personal data contained in the complaint

Article 8(5) of the Regulation 524/2013 provides that the electronic complaint form and its attachments shall only be processed in respect of data that is accurate, relevant and not excessive in relation to the purposes for which it was collected. The above provision is not well structured taking into account the entirety of the personal data protection standards, and therefore its meaning should be decoded in the light of the general principles relating to the processing of personal data contained in the GDPR, i.e. in particular the principle of lawfulness, the principle of purpose limitation, the principle of data minimization, the principle of short period of data retention and the security of data processing, as well as the necessity to demonstrate the way in which the above principles are implemented.

Particularly noteworthy are the principle of prohibiting the processing of sensitive data and the principles of privacy by design and privacy by default. The first principle concerns the prohibition of the collection, storage and processing of data that leads to facilitating discrimination against people on the basis of skin color, gender, health status, sexual preference, political opinions, etc., unless the processing is permitted by one of the exceptions set out in Article 9(2) of the GDPR. On the other hand, the second group of principles concerns the consideration of all technical ways to minimize privacy risks by using mechanisms such as encryption, data minimization, and data anonymization (or pseudonymization) to increase the resilience of data sets to the effects of loss of access to data.

3) Pre-dispute information

The Regulation 524/2013 provides that a complaint submitted via the ODR platform shall be considered if all required fields of the complaint form are completed. If the complaint form is not filled in completely, the complainant shall be informed that the complaint cannot be further processed unless the missing information is provided (Article 9(2) of the Regulation).

In accordance with Article 9(3) of the Regulation, upon receipt of a fully completed complaint form, the ODR platform shall clearly and promptly transmit to the party complained against, in any official language of the Union institutions chosen by that party.[18]

4) Handling of the case by the ODR entity

The ODR platform should automatically and immediately forward the complaint to the adjudicator appointed by the parties in accordance with their agreement. The ADR entity to which the complaint has been transmitted is obliged to inform immediately the parties whether it agrees to deal with the dispute or declines to do so (which it may do in accordance with Article 5(4) of Directive 2013/11/EU). The ADR entity that has agreed to deal with the dispute shall also inform the parties of its procedural rules and, where applicable, of the costs of the dispute resolution procedure in question.

In accordance with Article 8(9) of the Regulation 524/2013, where within 30 calendar days of the submission of the complaint form the parties have not reached an agreement with the ADR entity or the ADR entity refuses to deal with the dispute concerned, the complaint should not be processed further. The complainant shall be advised to contact the ODR adviser for general information on other means of redress.

---

18 The complaint should be sent together with the following (a) an indication that the parties must agree on an ADR entity in order for the complaint to be transmitted to it, and that in the event of disagreement between the parties or failure to identify an appropriate ADR entity, the complaint shall not be processed further;
(b), information on the ADR entity or entities that are competent to deal with the complaint, insofar as such entity or entities have been named in the electronic complaint form or have been identified by the ODR platform on the basis of the information provided in that form;
(c) if the party against whom the complaint is lodged is a trader, a request to determine within 10 calendar days
- whether the trader is obliged or has committed itself to use a specific ADR entity to resolve disputes with consumers, and
- if the trader is not obliged to use a specific ADR entity, whether he is willing to use one or more ADR entities referred to in point (b);
(d) where the party against whom a complaint has been lodged is a consumer and the trader is obliged to use a specific ADR entity, a request to agree within 10 calendar days to that ADR entity or, if the trader is not obliged to use a specific ADR entity, a request to select one or more ADR entities referred to in point (b);
(e) the name and contact details of the ODR contact point in the Member State of the complainant's habitual residence or place of establishment and a brief description of the functions referred to in Article 7(2)(a).

Recommendations concerning ODR systems

The proposed model for online dispute resolution with respect to illegal content in the draft DSA has one major drawback. ODR as a service is available only to customers of larger Internet entities, rather than to all online entrepreneurs. Such approach may deprive the contractor of smaller and medium-sized enterprises of access to online out-of-court dispute resolution, such as online arbitration, mediation or conciliation.

It is proposed to offer access to out-of-court dispute settlement to a broader category of customers. The right to review a decision made by an online businesses should be accessible to a greater number of customers. One should keep in mind that out-of-court dispute resolution service should not be a burden for the small and medium-sized enterprise (SMEs) in the sense that it is provided by a third party and relieves them from strategic legal risks. On the other hand, this may entail some further deliberations on how to ensure proper financing of the ODR platforms. Consequently, Article 18 of the DSA draft should be placed earlier, i.e. in Section 1 of the DSA.

Financing of ODR systems should be given a second thought. A model envisaged in the draft DSA regulation relieves the users of online platforms from reimbursing the costs of the proceedings. Although the proposal seems appropriate with respect to large online platforms, it would be hard to accept for SMEs operating in cyberspace. This may be a reason why a right to out-of-court dispute settlement in case of illegal content was not extended to customers of smaller online businesses. But this is not a good solution, either. A clear model should be developed, which incentivizes providers of online services to support independent online dispute resolution centers to relieve them from a burden of self-deciding about the legality of blocking or removing questionable content.

The existing legal framework(s) do not presuppose arbitration, mediation or conciliation as methods of alternative dispute resolution in cyberspace. It is therefore up to the creator of such platform to assume one or all of the defining characteristics of online dispute resolution model. ODR systems developed on the basis of the draft DSA legislation to handle illegal content should take into account the EU legislation that established some early requirements for handling disputes online. In particular, the Regulation 524/2013 could be a good a starting point for the development of detailed requirements that ODR systems should fulfil in the area of tackling illegal content, such as privacy by design and privacy by default.

One important requirement for ODR system to be potentially borrowed from the Regulation 523/2013 should be a feedback system. A majority of modern information society services provide functionality for assessing sellers or service providers. Such feedback mechanism could also be a part and parcel of the ODR model as it would help to provide a better service in future. There are, however, challenges related to the impartiality of adjudicators that should be more thoroughly examined.

All web forms, including text boxes, text areas, radio buttons and other user interface components should be accessible by design. This entails the necessity to develop ODR systems with the Web Content Accessibility Guidelines in mind to make sure that people with various disabilities can access both content as well as user interface elements in a non-discriminatory manner. Content of ODR systems should be perceivable to all humans, operable not only by mouse but also by keyboard and similar input devices, understandable both to humans and assistive technologies and technically robust, including compatibility with older devices and technologies.

Privacy by design and privacy by default should be the guiding principles when constructing user forms and databases for storing user-defined content. On one hand side, ODR system should enable processing of not only harmful message(s) but also its context (e.g. not only a harmful comment but the whole thread in a discussion forum). On the other hand, the collection and processing of personal data should be minimised and kept for a set period of time. Other obligations resulting from the GDPR and the future ePrivacy regulation should be also taken into account. In any case, the EU lawgiver should give a second thought to exemptions for processing personal data in the context of online dispute resolution systems in order to ease its functioning.

The EU legal framework for ODR in consumer disputes assumes that the ODR platform does not need to provide dispute solving functionalities and can act as an integrator of verdicts issued by independent, national ADR entities. In other words, the online consumer dispute resolution model is not based on a philosophy of resolving problems through a dedicated online platform, but on referring the dispute to third-party entities (ADR entities) that may or may not take on the challenge of resolving the dispute. Such an architecture has its advantages, in particular if it is assumed from the outset that the system should operate in all EU countries simultaneously, and that the ODR platform should serve as the basic mechanism for routing and exchanging information. But the drawback is that legal requirements are vague.

A lot of technical issues would still need to be clarified in future legislation concerning ODR in order to build a full-fledged online dispute resolution system based on an IT centralized model for resolving legal issues in cyberspace, such as:

the content of forms for different categories of cases (including from the GDPR perspective), also for evidentiary purposes,
the way disputes are resolved through the platform,
how voting and decision-making will be documented, how "second instance" review of decisions will be carried out, and
how and to what extent information is communicated externally to dispute participants as well as to the public.

An important aspect of creating the architectural framework for such systems will be to take into account the recruitment of arbitrators, including the possibility of relying on so-called trusted third parties, e.g. NGOs fighting pathologies in cyberspace, or law firms specializing in these issues. An important issue from the perspective of resolving disputes in the area of freedom of speech on the Internet will also be the question of recognition of such awards by national courts, but this is an area where it is difficult to have any influence.

Part II. Arbitration covenant. The concept

In the Polish Code of Civil Procedure, Title II of Part V regulates the arbitration covenant. The provision of Art. 1161 section 1 of CCP defines this concept, indicating that submitting a dispute to an arbitration court requires an agreement between the parties in which the subject of the dispute or the legal relationship from which the dispute has arisen or may arise must be specified. In Polish literature it is indicated that the arbitration covenant in the Polish procedural law corresponds to the German Schiedsvetrag and combines the French clause compromissoir and compromis. However, this term is characteristic of Polish law only because international law uses the term arbitration agreement[19]. The term is thus used in the Polish Act on International Private Law of 2011[20].

19 E.g., Art. II paragraph 1 of the New York Convention, which does not use the term "arbitration agreement" but specifies that each contracting state will recognize a written agreement which the parties agree to submit to arbitration. On the other hand, the term "arbitration agreement" is used by the UNCITRAL Model Act in Art. 7 in options I and II.

20 Act of 4 February 2011 – International Private Law, Journal of Laws of 2015, item 1792, where even chapter 8 was titled Arbitration Agreement.

In arbitration proceedings, it is possible to resolve not only disputes that have already arisen between the parties, i.e., post litem natam, but also disputes that may arise in the future from a specific legal relationship. Hence, under Polish law, two types of arbitration agreement can be distinguished: a compromise[21], i.e., an arbitration covenant in the strict sense of the word, and an arbitration clause[22].

The essence and inseparable feature of an arbitration agreement in Polish law is its connection with a binding resolution of an arbitration court, and therefore an arbitration covenant is not an arbitration agreement, which does not provide for a judicial function for the arbitration court. This is due to the fact that the jurisdictional element is a feature of an arbitration covenant, i.e., submission of a dispute to an arbitration court[23]. The essence of the arbitration covenant also results from the provision of Art. 1161 section 1 of CCP which indicates that submitting a dispute to an arbitration court must be included in the arbitration covenant itself. The settlement of a dispute is an arbitrary, imperative process based on coercion or authority and consisting in imposing the decision on the parties[24].

Therefore, the resolution of a dispute in arbitration is the authoritative imposition of a decision ending a dispute on the parties to the proceeding by a third party, i.e., an arbitrator or a panel of arbitrators. Therefore, the subject does not have the power to make imperative decisions. However, it should be noted that the purpose of arbitration and its adjudicative character do not invalidate its amicable nature, which means that arbitration belongs to one of the forms of ADR (Alternative Dispute Resolution). However, the Polish Act on ADR uses a different term, namely out-of-court resolution of consumer disputes[25].

---

21 Michał Janowski, 'Zapis na sąd polubowny de lege lata i w świetle projektowanych zmian' in Józef Skoczylas (ed) Prace laureatów konkursu im. Prof. J. Jakubowskiego (PWN 2005) 33 ff.

22 M. Tomaszewska in Andrzej Szuamński (ed) *System Prawa Handlowego. Arbitraż handlowy, vol. 8* (C. H. BECK 2015) 325 ff.

23 Grzegorz Żmij, 'Zapis na sąd polubowny' (2014) e-Przegląd Arbitrażowy special edition after the conference on Diagnosis of Arbitration. Functioning of the law on arbitration and directions of the postulated changes 95; also: judgment of the Supreme Court of 11 July 2001, V CKN 379/00, OSNC 2002, No 3, item 37; Robert Kulski 'Glosa do wyroku SN z dnia 17 listopada 2000 r., V CKN 1364/00' (2002) 11 PiP 103.

24 Arkuszewska (n 4) 231; Korybski (n 4) 32.

25 Arkuszewska (n 4) 232.

Legal nature of an arbitration agreement

In order to determine the form in which an arbitration covenant may be concluded in Polish law, it is essential to initially determine what the legal nature of this clause is. The problem of the nature of the arbitration covenant arises from the very essence of arbitration. Arbitration is less formal than common courts in terms of the way a case is examined. As a result of this assumption, the Polish Procedural Act does not contain detailed solutions concerning the course of arbitration proceedings. The legal nature of the arbitration covenant is the reason for numerous disputes in the Polish doctrine of civil law, civil procedure law and private international law. And so, it is assumed that the arbitration covenant is the so-called procedural contract[26]; legal transaction, i.e., an action subject to the regime of substantive civil law[27]; an action of a material and procedural nature[28] or a sui generis action[29]. Recently, other views have also emerged, namely that an arbitration covenant is a special type of a private-procedural agreement[30], or a legal action taken to pursue claims (action to pursue rights)[31].

---

26 Bogusław Sołtys, 'Forma umowy o arbitraż' in Maksymilian Pazdan, Wojciech Popiołek, Eewa Rott-Pietrzyk and Maciej Szpunar, *Europeizacja prawa prywatnego, vol. 2*, (Wolters Kluwer 2008) 408; Maciej Tomaszewski, 'Umowa o arbitraż. Podstawowe problemy prawne' (1994) 1 PUG 15; Tadeusz Ereciński and Karol Weitz, *Sąd arbitrażowy*(LexisNexis 2008) 85; Robert Kulski, *Umowy procesowe w postepowaniu cywilnym* (Wolters Kluwer 2006) 167.

27 Elwira Marszałkowska-Krzes and Łukasz Błaszczak, 'Zapis na sąd polubowny. A czynności materialne (wybrane zagadnienia)' (2007) 9 Rejent 12 ff.; Łukasz Błaszczak, *Wyrok sądu polubownego w postepowaniu cywilnym* (Wolters Kluwer 2010) 104; Łukasz Błaszczak, 'Charakter prawny umowy o mediacje' (2008) 1 ADR. Arbitraż i Mediacja 1-27.

28 Roman Kuratowski, *Sądownictwo polubowne. Studium teoretyczno-praktyczne z uwzględnieniem prawodawstwa obowiązującego w trzech dzielnicach Rzeczypospolitej i polskiego kodeksu postepowania cywilnego z roku 1930* (Księgarnia F.Holesicka 1932) 23-35.

29 Marian A. Myrcha, *Sądy polubowne w prawie kanonicznym. Studium prawoporównawcze* (KUL 1948) 186 ff.; Maksymilian Pazdan, Prawo właściwe dla oceny zapisu na sąd polubowny (2003) 10 Rejent 176; arbitration agreements.

30 AndrzejW. Wiśniewski, *Międzynarodowy arbitraż handlowy w Polsce. Status prawny arbitrażu i arbitrów* (Wolters Kluwer 2011)77 ff.

31 Aleksandra Budnik-Rogala, *Charakter prawny zapisu na sąd polubowny w postepowaniu cywilnym* (Uniwersytet Wrocławski 2015) 107 ff. The Author considers that an arbitration agreement does not fulfil the requirements specific to procedural actions. It cannot be assumed that it is a substantive law agreement or a substantive law action. The provisions of the Code of Civil Procedure, i.e., the proce-

It has been assumed in the jurisprudence of the Supreme Court that an arbitration covenant combines the features of a substantive and procedural agreement. Although in the decision of 7 November 2013 the Supreme Court stated that the arbitration covenant concerns the broadly defined jurisdiction of the court to examine the case, and its main effect is the exclusion of the jurisdiction of the state court. Therefore, this goal falls within the broadly understood functionality of the definition of a procedural action. An arbitration covenant has a procedural effect by excluding the state judiciary from examining the case covered by the covenant[32]. Thus, regardless of the adopted concept of assessing the legal nature of an arbitration covenant, it is necessary to determine which provisions will be applicable to assess the validity of an arbitration covenant, therefore, in Polish doctrine it is assumed that the provisions on the arbitration covenant contained in the Code of Civil Procedure should be applied first, and in unregulated matters, the provisions of the Civil Code on legal transactions should be considered[33]. A similar view was also expressed by the Supreme Court in the resolution of 8 March 2002, where it stated that when adopting the substantive nature of the arbitration covenant, the provisions of the Civil Code should undoubtedly be applied to it, nevertheless, also in a situation when the arbitration covenant is assigned the form of a procedural agreement, in matters not regulated in the Code of Civil Procedure, the provisions of the Civil Code on legal transactions should be applied[34]. Of course, when an arbitration covenant is included in a commercial contract, as an arbitration clause, it is necessary to assess, for example, the legal capacity of the parties to perform a substantive action in accordance with the provisions of the Civil Code, and the assessment of the capacity to establish the covenant – court capacity, procedural capacity[35].

dural act, apply to an arbitration covenant, but in matters not regulated by CCP, the provisions of the Civil Code in the scope of legal actions can be applied.

32 Cf. decision of the Supreme Court of 22 February 2007, IV CSK 200/06, OSNC 2008, No 2, item 25; decision of the Supreme Court of 7 November 2013, V CSK 545/12, Lex No 1422127.

33 Zbigniew Radwański, 'Glosa do postanowienia SN z 13.06.1975 r., II CZ 91/75' (1977) 5 OSPiKA 204; Andrzej Jakubecki, 'Poddanie się egzekucji w akcie notarialnym' (1998) 12 Rejent 67.

34 Resolution of the Supreme Court of 8 March 2002, III CZP 8/02, OSNC 2002, No 11, item 133.

35 Jakubecki (n 33) 67.

Form of arbitration agreement

Written form

The above considerations will now allow us to discuss the form of an arbitration covenant according to the Code of Civil Procedure in Poland. Therefore, determining in what form the arbitration clause should be concluded is of fundamental importance for the assessment of its validity. The provision of Art. 1162 section 1 of CCP stipulates that the arbitration covenant should be concluded in writing, i.e., pursuant to Art. 78 section 1 et seq. of CC.

The jurisprudence[36] assumes that the method of concluding an arbitration covenant, specified in Art. 1162 § 2 sentence 1 of CCP is an alternative method to the principles set out in Art. 1162 § 1 of CCP. There was even an opinion that the provision of Art. 1162 § 2 of CCP is a lex specialis in relation to Art. 78 of CC because it aims at the liberalization of form[37].

In a situation where the dispute arises from an agreement which requires a special form to be valid (e.g., the form of a notarial deed), the regular written form is sufficient for the arbitration covenant to be valid[38].

It is worth reminding that the written form of ab arbitration agreement has also been provided for in other legal systems. And so, section 1031 paragraph 1 of ZPO requires a written form when drawing up the arbitration agreement, although unlike in Art. 1162 § 1 of the Polish CCP. According to its wording, the arbitration covenant must be concluded either in a document signed by the parties or in letters, faxes, telegrams, or other means of distance communication exchanged by them, which secure the proof of concluding the agreement. Therefore, this provision contains two alternatives. The first one corresponds to the content of Art. 1162 § 1 of CCP. The

---

36 Judgment of the Court of Appeal in Warsaw of 27 October 2010, I ACa 498/10, LEX No 1643011.

37 Beata Gessel-Kalinowska vel Kalisz in Beata Gessel-Kalinowska (ed) *Postępowanie przed sądem sądem polubownym. Komentarz do Regulaminu Sądu Arbitrażowego przy Konfederacji Lewiatan* (Wolters Kluwer 2015) 61.

38 Judgment of the Supreme Court of 23 April 1936, II C 110/36, PPC 1936/19, 605; Sławomir Dalka, *Sądownictwo Polubowne w PRL*(Wydawnictwo Prawnicze 1987) 58; Robert Kulski, Umowy procesowe w postępowaniu cywilnym, (Wolters Kluwer 2006) 213; Łukasz Błaszczak and Małgorzata Ludwik, *Sądownictwo. Polubowne (arbitraż)* (C. H. BECK 2007) 114; Aleksandra Budniak, 'Forma zapisu na sad polubowny w świetle polskiego i niemieckiego postepowania cywilnego - zagadnienia prawnoporównawcze' (2009) 4 ADR. Arbitraż i Mediacja 19.

second one contains a regulation similar to Art. 1162 § 2 of CCP. Due to the significant similarity to the provisions of substantive law on the form of a legal transaction, the norm contained in § 1031 section 1 of ZPO is often referred to as "the modified written form of § 126 of BGB" ("Modifizierte Schriftform des § 126 BGB")[39]. The signatures of the parties to the arbitration covenant do not have to be placed on the same document. If the arbitration agreement was drawn up in the form of several identical documents, it is enough for each party to sign a copy intended for the other party (§ 126 paragraph 2 of BGB)[40].

There is a divergence of views in German literature – whether a signature has to be handwritten or not[41]. The legal form provided for in § 1031 serves, like all formal requirements, legal certainty. The German literature indicates that the form of an arbitration agreement covers two main areas. The legislator separates an arbitration agreement involving a consumer from the one used in professional trade. In the case of an agreement involving a consumer, stricter formal requirements are intended, in particular, to protect the consumer within the meaning of the so-called warning function, while in business transactions the normal written form is more flexible (paragraphs 1-4)[42]. In cases without the participation of the consumer, the legislator did not recognize that there are special protective mechanisms to protect the parties from themselves. Arbitration, which plays a large role in economic life, would be very limited if such formalism were practiced[43].

Similarly, in § 583 of ZPO, the arbitration covenant must be contained either in a document signed by the parties, or in letters, faxes, e-mails, or

---

39 Cf. Karl H. Schwab, Gerhard Walter and Adolf Baumbach, Schiedsgerichtsbarkeit Kommentar (C. H. BECK 2005) 37 ff.; Wilhelm Harmann, 'Zum Schriftformererfordernis fur Schiedsvereinbarungen' in Stefan Grundmann and others, *Festschrift fur Klaus J. Hopt zum 70. Geburtstag am 24. August 2010: Unternehmen, Markt und Verantwortung* (De Gruyter 2010) 2777-2778; Rolf A. Schutze in Rolf A. Schutze and Bernhard Wieczorek, *Zwilprozessordnung und Nebengesetze. Grofikommentar* (De Gruyter 2014) 383; Budniak (38) 19.

40 Schwab, Walter and Baumbach (n 39) 38.

41 Cf. Schutze and Wieczorek (n 39) 384, indicate that, according to § 126 of BGB, the signature must be handwritten or certified by a notary. A mechanical reproduction in writing of the signature specimen, e.g., by a matrix or facsimile, is not a handwritten signature; differently Adolf Baumbach, Wolfgang Lauterbach, Jan Albers and Peter Hartmann, *Zivilprozessordnung* (C. H. BECK 2007) 2600.

42 Hanns Priitting and Markus Gehrlein, *Zivilprozessordnung. Kommentar* (Luchterhand Verlag 2016) 2393 et seq.; cfSchwab Walter and Baumbach, (n 39) 43-44.

43 Schiitze and Wieczorek (n 39) 386.

other forms of transmission of messages exchanged by them, which constitute evidence of the conclusion of the covenant.

In French law, the issue of the form of an arbitration agreement is included in Art. 1443 of the French Code of Civil Procedure. According to this provision, the arbitration agreement must be in a written form in order to be valid. This form is observed, if it follows from written correspondence, in a document to which it relates, contained in the main agreement[44]. Similarly, the Italian Code of Civil Procedure in Art. 807 assumes that the arbitration agreement should be, otherwise null and void, concluded in writing and specify the subject of the dispute. The written form is also considered to be observed when the will of the parties is expressed by means of a telegraph, teletype, fax, or electronic communication, in compliance with the standards, including the regulations, regarding the sending and receiving of documents transmitted remotely[45].

On the other hand, in Spanish law, the arbitration laws also stipulate that the arbitration agreement should be concluded in writing, in a document signed by the parties, or in the exchange of letters, telegrams, telexes, faxes or other means of distance communication that make it possible to record the content of the agreement (Art. 9 paragraph 3)[46].

---

44 Cf. JeanL. Delvolve, Jean Rouche and Gerald H. Pointon, *French Arbitration Law and Practice* (Wolters Kluwer 2003) 297.

45 Art. 807 Italian of CCP is a kind of a fiction of keeping the written form in the circumstances specified in this provision – Michał Bieniak, 'Polska regulacja postępowania arbitrażowego na tle przepisów włoskiego Kodeksu postępowania cywilnego' (2009) 3ADR. Arbitraż i Mediacja 9.

46 Gorgonio M. Atienza, *Comentarios a la Ley de Arbitraje* (Editorial v Lex 2011) 104-118.

Electronic form of an arbitration agreement

Under Polish law, an arbitration agreement may be drawn up in an electronic form with the use of a qualified electronic signature. Article 781 § 1 of CC states that in order to maintain the electronic form of a legal transaction, it is sufficient to submit a declaration of will in an electronic form and affix a qualified electronic signature to it[47]. After the entry into force of the Regulation of the European Parliament and of the Council on electronic identification and trust services for electronic transactions in the internal market[48] on 1 July 2016 (Art. 52 paragraph 2 of the Regulation) and the Act of 5 September 2016 on trust services and electronic identification[49] for the application of this Regulation, the terminology of this signature was changed in order to align the term used in it with the nomenclature adopted in the eIDAS Regulation. As a reminder, it can be noted that pursuant to Art. 3 point 12 of the eIDAS Regulation, "qualified electronic signature" means an advanced electronic signature that is created by a qualified electronic signature creation device, and which is based on a qualified certificate for electronic signatures. A qualified electronic signature creation device can only rely on the configured software, not on the device and software. Qualified electronic signature creation devices as well as qualified electronic signature certificates[50] must meet the requirements speci-

---

47 Until 2016, this signature was called "secure electronic signature verified with a valid qualified certificate".

48 Regulation (EU) No 910/2014 of the European Parliament and of the Council on electronic identification and trust services for electronic transactions in the internal market and repealing Directive 1999/93/EC [2014] OJ L257/73 (eIDAS). The eIDAS regulation introduces a uniform terminology in all Member States, increases the requirements for liability in terms of security, expands the catalogue of trust services, and provides for clear rules for supervision over trust service providers. It is interdisciplinary, cross-sectoral, and pan-European, based on two key elements: security and trust. At the same time, the eIDAS regulation is open to innovative solutions and services such as mobile signatures – cf. Magdalena Marucha-Jaworska, *Rozporządzenie eIDAS. Zagadnienia prawne i techniczne* (Wolters Kluwer 2017) 15; Maria Siemaszkiewicz, 'Rozporządzenie eIDAS - nowe ramy prawne w zakresie identyfikacji elektronicznej i usług zaufania w Unii Europejskiej' (2016) CYII AUWr PPiA 212.

49 Journal of Laws of 2019, item 162.

50 A qualified certificate is the basic tool for verifying the identity of the person signing an electronic document. It is the equivalent of an online identity card, but it is issued by a qualified trusted entity, however, it must be recognized by all EU entities, the administration or the broadly understood system of justice. In the event of its revocation, this fact is registered in the database of a qualified trust

fied in Annexes II and I, respectively, to the eIDAS Regulation. A qualified electronic signature may be issued only by a trusted entity within the meaning of eIDAS, and in Poland it also must meet the requirements of the Act on trust services and needs to be entered on the list of trusted entities.

The court should not analyse technological solutions, but limit itself to formal issues, as the eIDAS Regulation introduced a rule that a qualified electronic signature, which is on the list of notified e-signatures, complies with the Regulation and must be recognized in legal transactions. Examination, whether a given qualified e-signature meets the requirements of an EU legal act is carried out at the stage of entering it on the certification list kept by any of the Member States. If the e-signature is already included in such a list, it is presumed to be compliant with the eIDAS Regulation. The court could therefore limit itself to checking the register of qualified trust services kept by the National Certification Centre.

Document-like form

In Polish law, the concept of a document has been defined very broadly in Art. 773 of CC, thus, a division is made into evidence from documents containing text, enabling the identification of issuers and other documents[51]. The concept of a document is sometimes used on a par with other terms, such as "letter", "written form of legal transactions", "receipt" or "notarial deed", so the main purpose of this definition is to organize the terminology[52]. The constitutive feature of a document is its intellectual content – information, content, which includes various statements, including a declaration of will. The content of the document should be recorded in an appropriate way that allows it to be recreated, so there is no need to sign the document.

---

service provider and published online. In practice, everyone from that moment on, in the case of verification of a qualified certificate, when a signature is made after its revocation, sees its invalidity in the signed document – more: Krzysztof Kamiński in Dariusz Szostek (ed), *Bezpieczeństwo danych i IT w kancelarii prawnej radcowskiej/adwokackiej/notarialnej/komorniczej. Czyli jak bezpiecznie przechowywać dane w kancelarii prawnej* (C. H. BECK 2018) 411-412.

51 Jacek Gołaczyński, 'Wpływ rozporządzenia eIDAS na polskie prawo prywatne. Wybrane zagadnienia' in Kinga Flaga-Gieruszyńska, Jacek Gołaczyński and Dariusz Szostek (eds) *Media elektroniczne. Współczesne problemy prawne* (C. H. BECK 2016) 7.

52 Justification for the draft act on trust services and electrical identification, 8th term of office, Sejm paper No 713, p. 3.

Hence, it is ultimately considered that the signature is not a necessary element of a document[53]. After all, the content of the document may be disclosed in any way – e.g., by graphic symbols, image, or sound, and remains technologically neutral in accordance with the adopted European and international rules[54]. The content of the document can be recorded on any medium – it can be a file or paper, by any means, such as a computer or a mobile phone. The evidentiary function of a document limits technological neutrality – the method of recording information should enable its preservation and reconstruction. The information should therefore be properly recorded on the medium so that it can be reproduced. Thus, a document consists of two elements in total – information that can be reproduced and the medium on which its content has been recorded[55].

In Polish law, the electronic form pursuant to Art. 78 (1) section 1 of CC is not a qualified form for the written form, however, it may replace the document-like form of a legal transaction, and it will not replace qualified written forms[56]. Consequently, drafting an arbitration covenant in an electronic form will be equivalent, in terms of legal consequences, to drafting a covenant in writing. It is emphasized in the literature that it is equivalent to the form, specifically to the written form[57], which means that the reciprocal substitutability would refer to the reservation of the form in the act, although not necessarily in a pactum de forma[58][59].

For example, in German law there is also an electronic form of an arbitration covenant. Pursuant to § 126 of BGB, it is used to interpret the provisions governing the form of an arbitration covenant. However, at the same time § 126 paragraph 3 of BGB indicates that, unless the Act provides otherwise, a written form may be replaced by an electronic form, thus there are no obstacles to use an electronic form in relation to an arbitration agreement.

---

53 Magdalena Marucha-Jaworska, *Rozporządzenie eIDAS zagadnienia prawne i techniczne* (Wolters Kluwer 2017) 180.

54 See more: Magdalena Marucha-Jaworska, *Podpisy elektroniczne, biometria, identyfikacja elektroniczna* (Wolters Kluwer 2015) 282 ff.

55 Marucha-Jaworska (n 46) 181; for more on the concept of a document, see the considerations on the document-like form of the arbitration covenant.

56 Grzegorz Stojek, 'Art. 78' in Mariusz Fras (ed) Kodeks cywilny. Komentarz. Tom I. Część Ogólna (Wolters Kluwer 2017).

57 Radosław Strugała 'Art. 78' in Edward Gniewek and Piotr Machnikowski (eds) *Kodeks cywilny. Komentarz* (C. H. BECK 2017)section 1.

58 Mateusz Grochowski, *Skutki braku zachowania formy szczególnej oświadczenia woli* (C. H. Beck 2017) 21.

59 Kamiński (n 50) 415.

It should be remembered that when the written form reserved by the act is replaced by the electronic form, the issuer must attach his or her name to it and the document must be signed with a qualified electronic signature in accordance with the Act on electronic signatures. In a case of an agreement, the parties must submit an electronic signature on a superposable document issued in the above-mentioned manner (§ 126a of BGB)[60].

Before the entry into force of the Act of 10 July 2015[61], which introduced two new forms into the legal system – electronic and document-like – there were two terms present in the literature[62]: "qualified electronic form" in legal transactions, which required the use of a secure electronic signature; and "regular" electronic form of legal transactions, which did not require such a signature[63]. Thus, it was assumed that an arbitration covenant could be concluded in "a special form", which is a qualified electronic form[64], as well as in "regular" electronic form (Art. 1162 § 2 first sentence of CCP)[65].

However, currently, i.e., based on the Civil Code in the wording established by the Act of 2015, it is reasonable to assume that the previously indicated "regular" electronic form may now be regarded as a document-li-

60 Cf. also § 1031 paragraph 5 of ZPO.

61 The Act of 10 July 2015 amending the Act – Civil Code, the Act – Code of Civil Procedure and some other acts (Journal of Laws, item 1311, as amended).

62 Jacek Gołaczyński, 'Wykorzystanie środków komunikacji elektronicznej w arbitrażu. W prawie polskim' in Andrzej Janik (ed) *Studia i rozprawy, księga pamiątkowa dedykowana profesorowi Andrzejowi Całusowi* (Szkoła Główna Handlowa 2009) 674; Dariusz Szostek and Marek Świerczyński, 'Arbitraż elektroniczny' (2009) 16 MoP 479; Berenika Kaczmarek-Templin, 'Kilka uwag o elektronicznej postaci umowy o arbitraż w kontekście przepisów regulujących formę zapisu na sąd polubowny' (2010) 3 ADR. Arbitraż i Mediacja 23; Ereciński, Weitz, (n 24) 127; Karol Weitz 'Art. 1162' in Tadeusz Ereciński (ed) Kodeks postępowania cywilnego. Komentarz. Tom 3 (Wolters Kluwer 2017), Art. 1162; Justyna Balcarczyk, 'Zagadnienie formy umowy o arbitraż w świetle art. II (2) Konwencji nowojorskiej o uznawaniu i wykonywaniu zagranicznych orzeczeń arbitrażowych oraz w świetle regulacji wewnętrznych'(2008) 4 ADR. Arbitraż i Mediacja 4.

63 Cf. Zbigniew Radwański, 'Elektroniczna forma czynności prawnej' (2001) 22 MoP 1107 et seq.; Ewa Wyrozumska, 'Elektroniczne oświadczenie woli w ustawie o podpisie elektronicznym i po nowelizacji kodeksu cywilnego' (2003) 8 PPH 45; WojciechJ. Kocot, Elektroniczna forma oświadczeń woli (2001)3 PPH 1 ff.; Bogusław Sołtys, 'Zawarcie umowy o arbitraż w formie elektronicznej' in Jacek Gołaczyński, *Prawo umów elektronicznych* (Wolters Kluwer 2006) 126-127; Sołtys (n 26) 408.

64 Cf. Kaczmarek-Templin (n 62) 23.

65 Szostek and Świerczyński (n 62) 479; Ereciński and Weitz (n 24) 127; Weitz (n 62).

ke form[66]. A similar position can be adopted with regard to an arbitration covenant in the case of a covenant included in letters exchanged between the parties or statements made by means of distance communication that make it possible to record their content, i.e., it can be assumed that it is classified as a special form – document-like form of the arbitration covenant.

Therefore, Art. 772 of CC, concerning submitting a declaration of will in the form of a document, Art. 773 of CC, defining the term "document" and Art. 1162 § 2 first sentence of CC should be assessed collectively.

The provision of Art. 772 of CC stipulates that in order to maintain the document-like form, it is sufficient to submit a declaration of will in a manner enabling the identification of the person submitting the declaration in one of the forms of the document defined in Art. 773 of CC. If it is possible to identify the author of the declaration of will, it is not possible to consider that it was submitted in document-like form. However, it is enough that the addressee may be able to identify the person making the declaration, as the legislator has not determined the necessity of identifying the person making the declaration by persons other than the addressee[67].

The need to identify the person submitting the declaration is not explicitly provided for in Art. 1162 § 2 first sentence of CCP, which, however, clearly indicates that "the covenant was included in the letters or statements exchanged between the parties"[68], therefore it specifies that the co-

---

66 Cf. Dariusz Szostek, 'Nowelizacja formy czynności prawnej wprawie cywilnym' (2017) 2 PME 47 – The document-like form is something between the written form and equivalent electronic form, and the fleeting, unregistered oral utterance. It leaves some kind of trace, evidence (although weak, but still much stronger than a fleeting oral statement), such as: e-mail message, SMS, internet portal, electronic banking.

67 Dariusz Szostek in Jacek Gołaczyński and Dariusz Szostek (eds) *Informatyzacja postępowania cywilnego*(C. H. Beck 2016) 65; Piotr Konik and Maciej Pannert, 'Materialnoprawne i procesowe aspekty formy dokumentowej i dokumentu' (2017/2018) 2Kwartalnik EP 38.

68 Cf. Art. 65' of CC. Conclusion of an arbitration agreement, pursuant to Art. 1162 § 2 first sentence of CCP requires the exchange of declarations by two parties made by means of electronic means of distance communication, however, such an agreement is concluded in the form of an offer, negotiation or using agreement templates made available in electronic form. The condition for the successful submission of an offer in electronic form is immediate confirmation of its receipt (Art. 66' § 1 of CC). However, the confirmation of receipt of the offer expressed in electronic form, as well as the acceptance of the offer may be made by any behaviour sufficiently revealing the fact of receiving the offer and its acceptance, so it

venant is to be drawn up between the parties to the dispute, and this makes it necessary to identify these subjects – to determine whether the parties have entered into an arbitration agreement[69]. Hence, as a result of the liberalization of the form of legal transactions, pursuant to Art. 772 of CC and Art. 1162 § 2 first sentence of CCP, the legislator does not provide for signatures by given entities when submitting declarations.

The provision of Art. 1162 § 2 first sentence of CCP uses the term "means of distance communication", but at the same time does not define this concept[70]. However, such a definition is contained in Art. 4 point 34 of Directive (EU) 2015/2366 of the European Parliament and of the Council of 25 November 2015 on payment services in the internal market[71], according to which "means of distance communication" means a method which, without the simultaneous physical presence of the payment service provider and the payment service user, may be used for the conclusion of a payment services contract. Thus, it can be assumed that it will be any type of means that only allows communication between the parties without the simultaneous physical presence of the parties in the same place or even time. Moreover, the Act of 18 July 2002 on the provision of electronic services in Art. 2 point 5 defines the term "means of electronic communication", which are technical solutions, including ICT devices and software tools cooperating with them, enabling individual communication at a distance using data transmission between ICT systems, in particular electronic mail.

Similarly, Art. 4 paragraph 1 point (g) of the ODR Regulation defines the term "electronic means", which means electronic equipment for the processing (including digital compression) and storage of data which is entirely transmitted, conveyed, and received by wire, by radio, by optical means or by other electromagnetic means.

---

does not have to be expressed in the same form as the offer – Sołtys, (n 26) 413-414.

69 Cf. decision of the Supreme Court of 22 February 2007, IV CSK 200/06, OSNC 2008/2, item 25, which assumed that the conclusion of an arbitration covenant pursuant to Art. 1162 § 2 first sentence of CCP must identify the sender. In contrast, Sołtys (n 26) 412, believes that in order to record the fact and content of an action, it is not always necessary to establish the identity of the person performing the action, but it is enough to confirm the authenticity of the action itself.

70 Journal of Laws of 2012, item 1225.

71 Directive (EU) 2015/2366 of the European Parliament and of the Council of 25 November 2015 on payment services in the internal market, amending Directives 2002/65/EC, 2009/110/EC and 2013/36/EU and Regulation (EU) No 1093/2010, and repealing Directive 2007/64/EC (OJ L337/35, as amended).

Still, the most traditional and common means of distance communication are mobile phones (e.g., recording a covenant through a short text message, the so-called SMS, or recording a conversation) and electronic mail (e-mail).

In the Polish doctrine, there is a view that, for example, an audio or videophonic recording forwarded to the other party via the Internet or (recorded on a CD) by post does not meet the requirements of Art. 1162 § 2 of CCP.

In this case, we are dealing with the recording of the party's statement, but the statement is made orally. Therefore, just like a videophonic recording of the oral statements of the parties submitted simultaneously cannot be considered as maintaining a written form of an arbitration covenant (Art. 1162 § 1 of CCP), the parties providing each other with an audio or videophonic record of their statements should not be considered as maintaining the form specified in Art. 1162 § 2 of CCP. It seems that the Author's view is justified when it comes to the exchange of information carriers with audio or videophonic recording, but the inability to pass an audio or videophonic recording to the other party via the Internet seems to narrow the scope of the concept of "means of distance communication" only to the possibility of recording them in writing, which may be questionable. The indicated "means" include any type of communication, including oral, written or even through a video only.

Recommendations concerning arbitration agreement

1. The arbitration agreement should be treated as a mixed, substantive and procedural agreement. Its purpose is to resolve a dispute arising from an obligation relationship by an arbitration court by selecting an arbitration court. It is also necessary to assume that the purpose of the arbitration agreement is to exclude the jurisdiction of the state court in the case from the dispute covered by the arbitration agreement.
2. A consequence of this assumption of the mixed nature of an arbitration agreement is that it is possible to determine which law will be applicable to the agreement. If an arbitration agreement is only a procedural concept, the admissibility, form and scope of the arbitration agreement will be governed only by the procedural law of the fori state, in accordance with the legis fori processualis principle.
3. The form of the arbitration agreement is therefore governed by the law applicable to the agreement. It seems that at present, a fairly liberal approach to formal requirements prevails and usually, in conventions, na-

tional law (e.g. in the Polish Code of Civil Procedure) allows, apart from the written form, forms based on electronic communication, provided that the parties' declarations of intent are required to be preserved. This approach refers to the Polish document form contained in Art. 77 (2) of the Civil Code

Section Three.
Internet, New Technologies and Sustainable Development

Digitally Transforming the Web into an EcoSphere of EcoSystems

Charlie Northrup <Charlie.Northrup@neursciences.com>
BEDFORD, HN, United States of America

Abstract

This paper explores the possibilities of membership in a hyperconnected framework where every individual, household, and organization is represented by a digital twin – an intelligent software agent responsible for managing their digital ecosystem. The framework provides for the identification, authentication, authorization, and auditing of the people, places, and things involved in the exchange of value within and across these ecosystems.

1. Beyond the Web

In 1990 the World Wide Web emerged as a disruptive technology opening a new digital frontier. Thirty years later, consumers would spend over $25.6 trillion online.[1] Like every disruptive technology before it, the Web would forever change society. With 30 years of historical data to look upon, we can now consider what we got right and what can be improved. This analysis will help us evolve the digital world for the next generation.

The World Wide Web started at the National Center for Supercomputing Applications (NCSA) at the University of Illinois. In 1990 Tim Berners Lee proposed a document information sharing system as a way for members of academia to share research papers.[2] The system would become the Web. Back then, you simply entered a URL, and it displayed a web page. There were no logins or passwords, and you did not have to prove you are not a robot.

---

1 United Nations Conference on Trade Development, "UNCTAD Estimates of Global e-commerce 2018" (2020) <https://unctad.org/system/files/official-document/tn_unctad_ict4d15_en.pdf> accessed 7 July 2021.

2 Tim Berners Lee, 'Information Management: A Proposal' (w3.org, 1989-1990) <https://www.w3.org/History/1989/proposal.html> accessed 7 July 2021.

From the beginning, the Web has evolved despite its largest weakness and most pervasive problem, the lack of a membership model. The Web's own architecture provided the features that enable bad actors and also causes its inability to universally prevent nefarious and fraudulent presentations and conveyances.

The original architect of the Web consisted of a collection of stateless document-sharing Web servers. The Web browser connected to the server identified by a Domain Name System lookup of the host name to request a document. The clients were identifiable and addressable only within the scope of the server to which they were connected. The stateless architecture of the Web meant each time the browser connected to a server; it was as if the two had never interacted before.

Four years later, a startup company which became Netscape licensed the web technology from the university's licensing company. Headed by CTO Marc Andreesen, who developed the popular NCSA Mosaic web browser, Netscape offered the first consumer-ready version of the web browser for the Microsoft Windows operating system. By 1994 Netscape began exploring a way to change the stateless document sharing system into an e-commerce platform through the use of "cookies".

Cookies enabled the server to store state information with the client browser. For example, cookies enabled the server to know if the client had previously visited the website and what items were in its shopping cart. The public became more aware of the privacy concerns when the Financial Times published a store in February 1996.[3] After much discussion and public hearings held by the Federal Trade Commission, cookies became standardized in 1997.[45]

There are valuable lessons to be learned here. Firstly, 1997 marked the "end of free." The use of cookies enabled websites to erect paywalls. As a result, it was now possible to provide subscription-based services. Secondly, 1997 marked the moment every server could collect, own and

---

3 Tim Jackson, 'This Bug in Your PC is a Smart Cookie' (Financial Times, 02 December 1996).

4 Federal Trade Commission, 'Consumer Privacy on the World Wide Web' (FTC,1998) <https://www.ftc.gov/sites/default/files/documents/public_statements/prepared-statement-federal-trade-commission-consumer-privacy-worldwide-web/privac98.pdf> accessed 7 July 2021.

5 David Kristol and Lou Montulli, 'HTTP State Management Mechanism' (1997) IETF RFC 2109 <https://datatracker.ietf.org/doc/html/rfc2109> accessed 7 July 2021.

store information about the client. Monetization of that data began slowly and quickly accelerated as businesses realized the value.

Initially, the general public tolerated the use of cookies between the browser and a given server. However, people soon discovered they were being tracking across different websites through third-party cookies creating a significant privacy risk. For example, why would a social network need to know what medications a person ordered from an online pharmacy? Would a employer learn that an employee was purchasing a pregnancy test?

Over 130 jurisdictions across the world have since added some form of data privacy laws to address digital data privacy concerns.[6] The United States currently has a patchwork of laws at the federal level, such as FISMA and HIPAA, to address sensitive verticals, but no overall national privacy law, leaving each state to define its own.[7] [8] As more jurisdictions add their own specific laws, compliance could pose significant risk and cost to small and medium-sized businesses.

2. Lack of a universal self-validating/authenticating membership model

Perhaps the single most significant limitation of the client-server architecture of the Web is the lack of a universal membership model. In general, the lack of a membership model exacerbated the Web's profound identity and trust crisis. This forced service providers to rely on 3rd party unauthenticated email addresses as a imperfect indicator of identity and the basis of trust. In the current situation, when users cannot remember a password, they select a reset password button which sends a hyperlink to your email account. The disadvantage is that over 3B fake emails go out every day, including numerous phishing attacks trying to trick people into clicking a link to a bogus website.

A recent Coveware report indicated nearly 80 % of the ransomware events in the first quarter of 2021 were started with email phishing at-

---

6 Morrison Forester, 'Catch Up on Privacy Around the World on Data Privacy Day 2021' (Morrison Foerster, 2021) <https://www.mofo.com/resources/insights/210127-data-privacy-day.html> accessed 7 July 2021.

7 Federal Information Security Management Act of 2014, (2014) <https://www.congress.gov/113/plaws/ publ283/PLAW-113publ283.pdf> accessed 7 July 2021.

8 Health Insurance Portability and Accountability Act of 1996, (1996) <https://www.congress.gov/104/plaws/ publ191/PLAW-104publ191.pdf> accessed 7 July 2021.

tacks.[9] Verizon noted 94% of malware was delivered through an email phishing attack vector.[10] Checkpoint describes the email phishing attack vector as the biggest threat in the online world today.

In summary, Web users are not, nor ever have been members, or citizens of the Web or the larger digital world. Users are limited in scope and sense of agency. They persist only within the closed digital ecosystem of the domain they are connected to. Users do not own their addressable identities, nor do they have a discoverable personal point of presence outside of the closed ecosystem. They lack the set of keys that comes with membership.

Membership, in the NeurSciences' context, gives users an identifiable and addressable point of presence, a set of personal keys to lock and unlock their resources, and a personal assistant application to manage those keys. The personal assistant is an intelligent software agent that uses the member's keys for identity, authentication, authorization, and audit. This eliminates the need for the end user to remember complex passwords. Instead, the agent manages the digital complexity for the member. The agent and the member's keys provides the mechanism for the user to protect or manage the privacy of their data and the means to automate the exchange of value within and across all digital ecosystems.

3. Disintermediating the Intermediaries

The emergence of the P2P Bitcoin Blockchain in 2009 is notable for several reasons.[11] Firstly, it introduced a digital commodity that could be bought and sold. Secondly, it disintermediated the intermediaries. Thirdly, it allowed anybody and everybody to participate as a peer.

A Bitcoin is a digital commodity. It is not a currency in the true sense of the word. Instead, it is a commodity valued at precisely what somebody is willing to pay for it at a given moment in time. In many jurisdictions, individuals need to keep track of the value when they purchased the

---

9 Coveware, 'Ransonware Costs Double in Q4 as Ryuk, Sodinokibi Proliferate' (Coveware.com, 2020) <https://www.coveware.com/blog/2020/1/22/ransomware-costs-double-in-q4-as-ryuk-sodinokibi-proliferate> accessed 7 July 2021.

10 Verizon, '2021 Data Breach Investigation' (Verizon.com, 2021) <https://www.verizon.com/business/resources/reports/dbir/> accessed 7 July 2021.

11 Satoshi Nakamoto, 'Bitcoin: A Peer-to-Peer Electronic Cash System' (Bitcoin.org, 2008) <https://bitcoin.org/bitcoin.pdf> accessed 7 July 2021.

Bitcoin and the value when they sold the Bitcoin. They are then taxed on the gain or loss accordingly.

The Bitcoin platform eliminated the need for intermediaries such as central banks. Instead of having a central bank to clear transactions, anybody could participate and get paid in Bitcoins for clearing the transaction. Eliminating the intermediaries removes the central authority's monopoly on controlling the money supply. Central banks typically increase the money supply to grow an economy and decrease the money supply when the economy grows too fast.

Bitcoin is based on a public ledger. The benefit of a completely open ledger is that anybody can inspect and prove its correctness. In addition, the open ledger enables everybody to see the current balance of each account.

A series of public and private key pairs are used in each transaction to ensure security. In simple terms, if Alice wants to send Bob a Bitcoin, then Alice would use her private key to sign off that she is sending the Bitcoin to Bob's public key. Anybody can use Alice's public key to authenticate the transaction. Bob would then use his private key to gain access to the Bitcoin.

To satisfy government regulations on Know Your Customer, Alice should know who Bob is. However, with the Bitcoin blockchain, there is no individual identity. Therefore, Alice would not know with any certainty who Bob is. The only thing that Alice would know is his address which Bob could change as frequently as he wants.

Some jurisdictions may require anybody involved in the exchange of Bitcoins and fiat currencies to be registered and licensed. In the United States, the laws can sometimes conflict between member states and even between the states and federal government. For example, the state of New Hampshire (NH) required Bitcoin exchanges operating in their state to acquire a Money Service Business license. A subsequent NH law changed that by exempting Persons conducting business using transactions conducted in whole or in part in virtual currency. At the Federal level, however, the Internal Revenue Service classifies and taxes Bitcoins as a commodity.

To prevent money laundering and other nefarious acts, the Governments typically monitor the traffic and impose specific rules. For example, to purchase a Bitcoin, you may be required to go through a licensed exchange that imposes strict Know Your Customer rules. The rules may require you to provide a photo ID, a driver's license, a utility bill, and so on. In addition, the central exchange may record and report your transactions to ensure compliance with tax laws in your jurisdiction.

The general perception is that fiat currency and central banks will retain their power for the foreseeable future. This is because the banks play an integral role in government and are not going away anytime soon. Yet, in the digital world, the word "soon" is somewhat relative to perspective. From the viewpoint of the central banks, they want to retain control on the money supply. Yet from the perspective of the cryptocurrency advocates, the role of the central bank will diminish.

4. Disintermediating the Web Browser

The inventors of disruptive technology enjoy the power shifts it enables, while those that follow the status quo find their markets collapsing around them. The smartphone was one such disruptive technology. It helped service providers to disintermediate the need for the web browser.

The Apple app store, released in 2008, along with voice-activated assistants such as Siri in 2011, played critical roles in disintermediating the need for the browser.[12] Firstly, the apps provided a direct connection between the end-user (client) and the app provider. Notifications enabled the app providers to alert the user of pending actions and events. Secondly, the convenience of voice-activated requests and audible responses eliminated the need to use the browser for simple tasks such as requesting today's weather forecast. The disruption occurs by eliminating online advertisement monetization events that would have otherwise occurred through the client-server web browser.

Amazon released their voice-activated Echo product in 2016, followed by Google Home later that year. Both products allowed the consumer to use voice recognition to interact with the devices. As more smart devices come online, it further reduces the reliance on a web browser for interacting in the digital world.

5. The Benefits of Membership

Membership provides you a set of keys and a software agent to manage those keys for you. The agent uses the keys to unlock your point of presence and manage your digital ecosystem. Each member has its own digital

---

12 Apple, 'The App Store Turns 10' (Apple.com, 2018) <https://www.apple.com/newsroom/2018/07/app-store-turns-10/> accessed 7 July 2021.

ecosystem which collectively are referred to as a Digital EcoSphere. Identity within the Digital EcoSphere is enabled by the MultiKey infrastructure (MKI) which is a key based version of the public key infrastructure.

Your agent uses your keys to secure your content and secure your communications. Each member uses multi factor authentication to pair with their agent. Your agent guards your digital ecosystem and manages all the digital complexities so you do not have to.

6. We are at the beginning of the beginning

Neal Stephenson's 1992 science fiction novel "Snow Crash" introduced the metaverse as a threedimensional space where people, as digital avatars, interact with each other and other software agents.[13] Although it was limited to the digital world, it did set the stage for thinking differently about augmented reality. It also raised questions about integrating the digital world with the physical world at the same time.

In 2014 Kevin Kelly of Wired Magazine stated: "We are at the beginning of the beginning." It was the first time Kelly described a meta organism he referred to as Holos, which forms from the combination of Gaia (the aggregate of Earth's like), Humanity, and Technium.[14] The meta organism Kelly was referring to is different from the metaverse introduced in Neil Stephenson's "Snow Crash". Stephenson's metaverse was focused on virtual reality while Kelly's meta organism encompassed everything.

In 2016 Klaus Schwab, founder of the World Economic Forum, suggested we are entering a 4th Industrial Revolution that will blur the distinction between the physical, biological, and digital spheres.[15] In Schwab's view it is more about the fact that everything will be interconnected than how the interconnection works at the technical level. Although he did not elaborate on "how," he did note that when it occurs, it will change everything about the way we live, work, and play.

The common theme is that of a hyperconnected world extending well beyond the Web as we know it today. However, the idea of a hyperconnec-

---

13 Neal Stephenson, *Snow Crash* (Bantam Books (US) 1992)

14 Danielle Engelman, 'Kevin Kelly Holos Rising' (2014) <https://blog.longnow.org/02014/12/01/kevin-kellyseminar-media/> accessed 7 July 2021.

15 Klaus Schwab, 'The Fourth Industrial Revolution: What it means and how to response' (weforum.org, 2014) <https:// www.weforum.org/agenda/2016/01/the-fourth-industrial-revolution-what-it-means-and-how-to-respond/> accessed 7 July 2021.

ted world is not without its concerns. Some people fear it will lead to intelligent machines overtaking the world. Ray Kurzwell, a futurist and Chief Technical Officer at Google, refers to it as the technological singularity – the moment in time in which technological growth has unforeseen changes to human society.

While some futurists believe the singularity will always be near, others believe it is already happening. With 30 years of history, we can now look back to consider some of the unforeseen changes in human society brought about by the Web. For example, cyberbullying, malware, ransomware, social isolation, and others. Yet, we also achieved enormous benefits, such as government accountability, immediate access to information, e-commerce, telehealth visits, and the ability to work from home.

7. Fiefdoms to Hyperconnectivity

When history looks back at this stage of the Web, it might describe it as similar to the fiefdoms of feudal lords. Each website is owned and operated in isolation. The domain owner dictates who can participate in the ecosystem and what role(s) they can perform, such as buyer, seller, distributor, broker, or consumer of content. The owner carefully controls what their subjects (subscribers) can and cannot do within their walled domain and decides the monetization events. The client-server model enables the owner to maintain a monopoly and assert total control over their domain.

Looking beyond the Web, we see companies such as Pizza Hut planning pizza deliveries by drone and Amazon envisioning large-scale drone delivery systems. Flying drones is one thing, but getting the drones to independently and autonomously interact with a physical environment is more complex. Not only would the drone need to interact with the physical environment, but the drone will also encounter other entities independently and autonomously operating in the environment.

Tesla and Google expanded the concept to unmanned autonomous vehicles driving on our streets. The challenge is the potential harm such vehicles could cause to life and property. Given that a human-operated vehicle could accidentally take the life of a driver, passenger, or pedestrian, so too could an independent, autonomous vehicle. The implication is simple. It is no longer sufficient to think of independent, autonomous cars and trucks without considering how these machines can interact with each other.

The idea of autonomous, independent entities is a very different model from the Web as we know it today. In the real world, a visitor can enter a city, shop at any number of stores, dine at various restaurants, and ultimately return to their home town. In today's client-server Web, the client must provide a secret password to gain entry. Upon exit, the client immediately returns to their home. They must repeat this process over and over again. You can see how the digital world and the natural world models do not align.

8. The Need for a New Framework

The Web's client-server framework precludes the client from participating as an independent addressable collaborative member of a global ecosystem. The client is neither identifiable nor addressable outside of the scope of its current domain. In a peer-to-peer framework, however, the client could easily be represented and participate as a member.

In the P2P blockchain model, each peer has a digital wallet. The wallet itself is a collection of private and public key pairs. Each private and public key pair plays an essential role. The private key, as the name implies, is meant to be kept a secret. A Bitcoin address is derived from the public key. When somebody sends a Bitcoin to your Bitcoin address, you will be the only person in the world with the corresponding private key to unlock it. The best common practice is to use a different Bitcoin address (hence a different public-private key pair) for each transaction. It is essential to understand that each transaction on the P2P Bitcoin blockchain is publicly available. That is, anybody and everybody can view the ledger and see the balance of each address. What they cannot tell is who owns the address as that information is kept private.

Any new framework must ensure the privacy of its participants while operating with the laws of the participant's host country. Certain government's such as Canada, India, Ireland, Norway, and the UK, along with those of the EU are at the forefront of data privacy. At the same time, taxing authorities require access to certain information. Similarly, justice departments want to ensure there is no illegal activity occurring. It is a delicate balance between the needs of privacy, finance, and the rule of law.

The design of a new framework must also consider the speed of adoption. After 30 years, the Web's client-server architecture will not simply be replaced. On the other hand, the adoption of digital currency is on the horizon, with its decentralized peer-to-peer model gaining attention.

This implies both the client-server model and the peer-to-peer model must persist in a single unified framework – a framework of everything.

Furthermore, the new framework has to provide and manage the keys that allow it to extend beyond the Web and the Internet as we know it today. It must be able to incorporate everything: independent, autonomous vehicles, machines, and even robotic devices with and without mobility. In certain cases, these machines may have no network connectivity at all. In other cases, the machines will untether from the network and reconnect at a later time. Depending on their form factor, communication may be limited to a speaker, a microphone, and optical devices such as a camera and/or an infrared transceiver. Most importantly, the framework must support the ad-hoc dynamic connections and communications to support even one-off transactions.

The new framework provides each user with sets of keys to associated keyed resources. This enables each participant to independently manage their own private digital ecosystem while being interconnectable with all other ecosystems under agreed rules. The individual decides who can participate in their ecosystem, similar to managing a contact list. Unlike a simple contact list, the participants have active direct connections with that individual's ecosystem. In this regard, the new framework enables collaborative ecosystems that are collections of independently owned and operated ecosystems. This collection of uniquely addressable ecosystems is a digital ecosphere.

A smart city is a type of digital ecosphere. It includes one or more digital ecosystems independently operating within the smart city. For example, the departments within the city government are independent of each other but collectively must adhere to and operate within the rules of the city charter.

The extents of the smart city are defined by the property boundaries. Each property can be independently owned and operated. The digital twins of these properties can be managed by software agents. Some of these agents work for the city, while others work for individuals, households, and organizations. Unlike the Web, these agents are peers that persist across digital ecosystems. At times the smart city will also have guests and anonymous visitors, each represented by digital twins that are peers.

The smart city must provide a dynamic mesh infrastructure enabling the peers to traverse and interact with the various shared services provided by the city workers as well as those services offered by the city's participants. It must do this while ensuring the peers persist across the digital ecosystems within the smart city. Just as there are peers representing people, there will also be peers representing places and things.

A smart vehicle will have a peer. When the vehicle enters the smart city, its peer can register its point of presence. In this manner, the city's Intelligent Transportation System can communicate with the smart vehicle agent independently of identifying the vehicle occupants. Meanwhile, the vehicle occupants can interact with the smart city grid to locate nearby points of interest such as restaurants, stores, doctors, parking, or other services. The smart city can help provide a direct connection between the occupant and the service provider.

In this hyperconnected view of the world, a truck entering the smart city can communicate with the city, notify its destination, and properly time its arrival. The destination can communicate with the truck to determine the bill of lading detail, the type, and size of the truck, and notify the truck which loading dock it should arrive at. The destination building can adjust its energy utilization within the loading dock area by calculating how long it will take to unload the content, which exposes the building to outside temperatures and humidity during that process.

9. The Transformation

On the one hand, we can build a new independent decentralized framework as a standalone platform and integrate a web front end. That, however, does not solve the problem of the closed central authority model of the Web. Alternatively, we can build a parallel decentralized framework where the entire Web is represented as a resource available to the agents working for individuals, households, and organizations. We refer to this as the Universal Framework of Things (UFT).

The UFT views everything as a "Thing." This is distinct from the view of objects in the object oriented world, where an object is an instance of a superclass. Instead, a "Thing" is simply something a machine can do, act upon, or otherwise use. The simplicity of the model is that it allows us to represent people, places, and things of the real world as Things in a digital world. For example, you are represented by an intelligent software agent (a Thing).

The framework enables us to abstract away issues of languages and grammar, protocols, and syntax as Things. For example, some machines use the Internet and others communicate using sound and optics. Yet, both machines have a known identity and can collaborate as machines in a smart city.

In the UFT, identity is modeled as a Thing. This allows various identity models to be incorporated for different purposes. For example, a machine can be identified by a serial number independently of identifying its owner and/or operator. The operator may simply be identified as the operator of the machine with this serial number. On the other hand, when completing a financial transaction, the operator may be identified by name, driver's license, and, when required, even their taxpayer identification number. Other identity models include biometrics.

Today the majority of identities represented on the Web are based on third-party unauthenticated email services which are prone to abuse and attack. Industry titans such as Google are working hard to require multi-factor-authentication (MFA) as a default option. The FIDO-2 standard is being promoted as a solution to proving a human is on the other end of the connection. Yet, in the new digital world, we will have more agent-to-agent communications.

In a hypothetical exchange, an offering agent will disclose a set of acceptable identity models to the potential accepting agent. The agent accepting the offer will use an acceptable identity model with the least identifiable information required. The sending of any identifying information must be authorized by the individual, household, or organization the agent is working for.

10. MultiKey Infrastructure (MKI)

The agents can participate in a MultiKey Infrastructure to augment the use of the Public Key Infrastructure. Each MultiKey Key provides an agent with over 2^{512} cryptographically derived keys, any one of which can be used as another MultiKey Key. This creates a hierarchical arrangement of derived keys, all of which are cryptographically linked to the starting MultiKey Key.

In a simple view, the agent acts upon components of data, such as the components of a URL, to derive the hierarchical cryptographic keys from the starting MultiKey Key. For example, "https:" would generate one cryptographic key. Similarly, www.neursciences.com would generate another cryptographic key within the https MultiKey Key, and so on. By providing each agent a unique MultiKey Key to start, the agent can immediately generate unique keys for each and every URL of the Web.

MultiKey Keys can be distributed in digital form or in a physical form factor such as an ablated Holographic Memory ID (HMID) tag. The HMID tags are impervious to EMP attack and inert to radio frequency interrogation. Instead, the HMID tag requires line of sight optical interrogation, such as with an LED light of a smartphone camera. With 3.4 billion smartphones in use today, anybody can participate.

11. Summary

A new digital world is emerging where people, places, and things, need to be irrefutably identified, verified, and authorized in order to interconnect safely. The current Web framework of isolated domains is unable to easily support the required interoperability as only the servers are identifiable and addressable. In this paper, we describe transforming the Web into a Digital Ecosphere of independently owned and operated interconnected digital ecosystems. It is transformational in that it enables every individual, household, and organization to be represented as first class members of the digital world.

The Sarbanes-Oxley Act and ist Influence Upon the Internal Context of Brazilian Companies

Felipe Garcia Telò <felipetelo@hotmail.com>

Ricardo Pinha Alonso <ripial1@gmail.com>
MARÍLIA, Brasil

Abstract
Using bibliographic, jurisprudential and comparative review methodologies, as well as the scientific deductive method, this work intends to approach the subject of compliance, specially through the corporate, accounting and legal scope, with an emphasis on the reflexes of the Sarbanes-Oxley Act (SOX) upon Brazilian companies. It approaches the concept of compliance, as well as the history of this activity as we know it, analysing the historical context that led to the promulgation of the Sarbanes-Oxley Act, namely, the scandals of Enron Corporation and Arthur Andersen, in the early 2000s. After a thorough analysis of the Sarbanes-Oxley Act main sections, this paper sustains the need of implementing the best practices of corporate governance in publicly-held companies, instigating and ethical culture revolution, aiming to attack in a more comprehensive way corporate wrongdoings and encourage the adoption of the highest standards of compliance, accountability, disclosure and fairness. Finally, it undertakes case studies to report the process of adaptation of two Brazilian companies to SOX regulations, aiming to demonstrate the challenges of the implementation of such compliance programs.

Keywords:
Compliance. Controllership. Corporate Governance. Sarbanes-Oxley Act.

Introduction

In recent times, Brazil has been plagued by an avalanche of political and ethical scandals that have placed the issues of law enforcement and the fight against corruption on the agenda of civil society's concerns. Although Brazilians are used to corrupt practices, the systemic extension of the sophisticated corruption schemes investigated and dismantled by the Brazilian authorities shocked the local population, especially because these acts involved joint action with public authorities and large multinational corporations, whose top executives are currently in prison.

At this point, the indignation of the Brazilian population also resides in the lack of adequate means of controlling the financial and equity balance sheets of these companies, which would enable the identification, through accounting audits, of adulterations, fraud and illicit acts committed by their directors and executives, preventing such criminal practices from reaching such an extent.

Although these issues are only on the rise now in the Brazilian public debate, they were already extensively addressed and studied by the United Nations (UN), which has already issued reports on the global cost of corruption, and by the Organization for Economic Cooperation and Development (OECD), in which the Convention on Combating the Corruption of Foreign Public Officials in International Business Transactions (1977) was signed.

In other countries, the topic was also widely discussed, with special emphasis on the United States of America, where, since the edition of the Foreign Corrupt Practices Act (FCPA), in 1977, and, more intensely, since the promulgation of the Sarbanes-Oxley Act (SOX), in 2002, a broad legal framework on anti-corruption practices in the private sector was established, with special emphasis on accounting compliance.

The aforementioned standards have ample potential for application outside the United States of America, requiring companies from around the world to adapt their provisions, implementing the highest standards of corporate governance for the promotion of business integrity, preventing illegal practices and guarantying the market confidence in companies listed on the stock exchanges.

Therefore, given the importance and diffusion of this matter, in this paper we will address aspects related to the Sarbanes-Oxley Act, especially with regard to its influence in the internal context of Brazilian companies, the levels of implementation of such legislative requirements in the Brazilian corporate context and eventual conflicts between the Brazilian and American standards to which these companies are subject.

We will make a brief analysis of the compliance theme, seeking to define and present its modalities, among which is the legal and accounting compliance, going on to analyse the historical context of the Sarbanes-Oxley Act, as well as its main provisions and its influence in the internal context of Brazilian companies, with special emphasis on those that trade securities on the New York Stock Exchange. In this endeavour, we will make use of bibliographic sources and the deductive scientific method, starting from general arguments to particular arguments, connected by a logical causal relationship.

2. Compliance

The numerous corruption scandals that have surfaced in recent years have caused a renewed social outcry for the institutionalization of higher ethical and moral standards, causing an increase in interest in compliance programs, which seeks to guarantee ethical conducts. In fact, the fight against corruption, money laundering, terrorism and extremism is closely linked to compliance programs, which unfold, in the corporate sphere, in corporate governance and risk management, optimizing confidence of the market in the corporations that implement them.

2.1. Definition

Etymologically, the English noun "compliance" has its root in the verb "comply", which means to act according to an order, set of rules or request. In this way, literally, compliance can be understood as the act of obeying an order, rule or requisition. According to Bertonccelli,

> the term compliance originates from the English verb to comply, which means to act according to the law, an internal instruction, a command or an ethical conduct, that is, to be in compliance is to be in compliance with the internal rules of the company, in accordance with ethical procedures and current legal rules. However, the meaning of the term compliance cannot be reduced only to its literal meaning. In other words, compliance is more than just formal rules. Its scope is much broader and must be understood in a systemic way, as an instrument for risk mitigation, preservation of ethical values and corporate sustainability, preserving business continuity and stakeholder interest.[1]

Therefore, the meaning of the expression goes far beyond its literal one, since the compliance activity has spread and is today an institutionalized concern at the corporate level, integrating the very concept of corporate

---

1 Rodrigo de Pinho Bertonccelli, 'Compliance' in André C. Carvalho, Tiago C. Alvim, Rodrigo P. Bertoccelli and Otavio Venturini, *Manual de Compliance* (1th ed., Forense 2019) 15.

governance and consisting of a set of internal mechanisms whose function it is to guarantee and promote good practices, encourage the private autonomy of economic agents and promote the business ethics of all employees.

Consequently, compliance could also stand for "enforcing" or "integrity", since it consists of an activity that seeks to encourage accordance with pre-stablished standards, promoting compliance with laws, regulations, internal rules, codes, policies and avoiding the occurrence of fraud, corruption and illegal acts. According to the Compliance Programs Guide, edited by the Brazilian Administrative Council for Economic Defence (CADE, in the Portuguese abbreviation),

Compliance is a set of internal measures that makes it possible to prevent or minimize the risk of violating the laws resulting from an activity practiced by an economic agent and any of its partners or collaborators. Through compliance programs, agents reinforce their commitment to the values and objectives explained therein, primarily with accordance with legislation. This objective is quite ambitious and for this reason it requires not only the elaboration of a series of procedures, but also (and mainly) a change in the corporate culture. The compliance program will have positive results when it is able to instil in employees the importance of doing the right thing.[2]

Hence, compliance can be defined as an activity that seeks to establish and implement mechanisms of internal control, self-regulation, self-responsibility and self-surveillance, which encourage ethics, transparency and due diligence, and which monitor compliance with laws, rules and internal regulations of corporations, avoiding the occurrence of fraud, corruption, immorality and illicit acts or, if they have already occurred, provide the means for an immediate return to the context of normality and legality .

2.2. Modalities

The historical facts that have driven the growth of attention on compliance programs in Brazil in recent years, notably the corruption scandals

---

2 Vinicius Marques de Carvalho and Eduardo Frade Rodrigues (organizers), "Guia Programas de Compliance: Orientações sobre estruturação e benefícios da adoção dos programas de compliance concorrencial" [Compliance Programs Guide: Guidance on the structuring and adoption of concurrence compliance programs] (1th ed., CADE 2016) 9.

that "Operation Lava Jato" has brought to light, have inevitably led the national legal community to devote special emphasis to compliance in the public sector and anti-corruption. Although anti-corruption integrity programs are undeniably important, the scope of compliance programs is not limited to public sector anti-corruption, with developments in numerous areas. In fact, according to Carvalho and Rodrigues, a compliance program will rarely cover legislation relevant to just one sector or address just one type of concern. The most common is that the programs deal simultaneously with different aspects and normative diplomas. Therefore, each economic agent must take into account their own particularities when implementing a compliance program. [...] As an example of a compliance area other than that of competition, but which can be integrated into it, it is worth mentioning the anti-corruption compliance, of Law 12.846/2013.[3]

The extent of compliance programs and the complexity of social and technological relationships mean that the areas in which integrity programs unfold expand far beyond mere fields of law, which is why large corporations have set up separate multidisciplinary teams whose focus is on different compliance modalities. In recent years, for instance, technological development has led to a broad development of data protection compliance, the study of which requires interdisciplinarity between Law, Economics and Information Technology (IT). This is also the case for the compliance modality regulated by the object of study in this article, namely the Sarbanes-Oxley Act, which establishes rules relating mainly to accounting and managerial compliance.

3. *The Sarbanes-Oxley Act*

The Sarbanes-Oxley Act is an American law, passed in July 2002 by the Congress of the United States of America as a response to numerous corruption scandals involving companies listed on that country's stock exchanges, whose aim was to re-establish ethics in the corporate field and reinforce confidence in the capital markets.

3 Vinicius Marques de Carvalho and Eduardo Frade Rodrigues (organizers) (n 1) 9-10.

3.1. Historical Context

The historical context that preceded the publication of the Sarbanes-Oxley Act in August 2002, was set against the backdrop of a series of corporate scandals unveiled after the discovery of irregularities within the scope of Enron Corporation, a Texas electricity giant. The company, headquartered in Houston, Texas, was the first to create a nationwide piped natural gas system and, in 1989, revolutionized the energy sector market by launching Gas Bank, a program under which, at fixed prices, natural gas buyers could secure long-term supplies[4].

This model, which was known as "structured finance" or “hypothetical future value accounting”, was devised by Enron's then Chief Executive Officer (CEO), Jeffrey Skilling, allowing it to account and trade rights to exploit infrastructures and technologies that did not even exist[5]. In the end, it was this system that allowed the company to grow dramatically, to the point of becoming the largest company in the energy sector in the world, with annual revenues exceeding US $ 100 billion[6], as well as the sixteenth largest company on the planet and the seventh largest company in the United States of America[7].

However, the Enron quickly went bankrupt in November 2001, after accusations of accounting fraud, with a debt that exceeded thirteen billion US dollars[8]. The Enron case is considered by many financial analysts to be the corporate crime of the century, since it involved a complex actuarial scheme that took advantage, among other things, of gaps in the sector's regulatory framework in the United States of America.

Throughout the 1990s, Enron rapidly expanded its operations to numerous areas, such as the development of gas pipelines and power plants, an expansion that required a long gestational period and a considerable investment. By doing that, the company accumulated large debts, which should affect its credit score. However, “special arrangements” were made to keep its debts and losses off its financial statements, allowing its credit

4 Seied Beniamin Hosseini and R Mahesh, ‘The Lesson from Enron Case – Moral and Managerial Responsibilities’ in (2016) 8, 8 International Journal of Current Research .

5 ‘Enron: The Smartest Guys in the Room’ (Directed by Alex Gibney Magnolia Pictures 2005).

6 Hosseini and Mahesh (n 6) 37451-37460.

7 Luciana de Almeida Araújo Santos and Sirlei Lemes, ‘Desafios das empresas brasileiras na implantação da Lei Sarbanes-Oxley’ (2007) 4, 1 BASE – Revista de Administração e Contabilidade da Unisinos 37-46.

8 Santos and Lemes (n 9) 37-46.

score not to be lowered[9]. This was mainly due to the use of Special Purpose Entities (SPEs), used for hiding and dumping its losses in those subsidiary companies. The responsible for this strategy was Enron's Chief Financial Officer (CFO), Andrew Fastow[10].

Under the then-current rules of the United States Securities and Exchange Commission (SEC), if a holding company finances less than 97 % of the initial investment in a Special Purpose Entity (SPE), it would not need to carry out consolidation on its financial statements, provided that two conditions are met, that is, that the assets are legally isolated from its transferor (in this case, Enron) and that a third independent owner makes a "substantial capital investment" of at least 3 % of the total capitalization of the SPE[11].

Therefore, the solution found by Enron was to find external "investors" willing to enter into an "agreement" with them and start numerous independent SPEs. In addition, in order to allow these entities to borrow money from the market, in many cases Enron offered credit guarantees from the company itself[12]. The main beneficiary of this scheme was its own creator, Andrew Fastow, who was also the CEO of an investment fund called LJM Investiments, responsible for controlling most of these SPEs. In fact, Enron itself did raise money in the market for LJM and some of its main investors were the largest investment banks in the United States of America[13].

The absence of adequate regulatory mechanisms has allowed Enron to co-opt financial analysts from the major North American investment banks, offering gifts, bonuses and benefits as a reward for good recommendations and using influence peddling to obtain the dismissal of those who refuse to do so[14]. The case was also characterized by the occurrence of the so-called regulatory capture, since Enron made significant electoral donations to both the Republican and the Democratic Party, leading to the possibility of nominate friendly candidates, especially for the Federal Energy Regulatory Commission (FERC)[15]. Therefore, Enron's case can be classified as "synergistic corruption", since the irregularities that happened in the company were, to some extent, known to shareholders, investors,

9 Hosseini and Mahesh (n 6) 37451-37460.
10 (n 7).
11 Hosseini and Mahesh (n 6) 37451-37460.
12 ibid.
13 (n 7).
14 ibid.
15 Hosseini and Mahesh (n 6) 37451-37460.

brokers, directors, investment banks, analysts, accountants, lawyers, politicians and public officials, who remained silent because they profited from the situation.

The first suspicions that something abnormal was happening at Enron were only raised by journalist Bethany McLean, from Fortune Magazine, in a report entitled "Is Enron Overpriced?"[16], In which the reporter raised a seemingly simple question, but that no one could manage to answer, which was "how does Enron earn its money?". Following the report, an investigation was opened by the SEC and the chief auditor of Arthur Andersen, the company responsible for accounting and financial auditing at Enron, David Duncan, ordered the destruction of more than a ton of documents that could compromise those involved[17].

Arthur Andersen was the oldest actuarial company in the United States[18] and one of the five largest auditing and accounting companies in the world[19], with more than 85 thousand employees operating in 84 countries[20]. Since its founding in 1913, the company has had a reputation for providing the highest quality services. However, a shift in emphasis in the 1970s introduced a new generation of auditors who advocated for clients in exchange for consulting fees, and, in time, the company's consulting division started to generate significantly higher profits than the audit division (COLLINS, 2018). According to Denis Collins[21], the combination of more complex financial statements, more aggressive accounting techniques, greater concern for customer satisfaction, greater dependence on consulting fees, and smaller cost-effective sampling techniques created many problems for auditing firms. Arthur Andersen's Houston office was billing Enron $1 million per week for auditing and consulting services, and David Duncan, the lead auditor, had an annual performance goal of 20% increase in sales. Duncan favorably reviewed the work of Rick Causey, Enron's chief accounting officer and Duncan's former colleague at Andersen. Duncan let Enron employees intimidate Andersen auditors,

---

16 Bethany McLean, 'Is Enron Overpriced? It's in a bunch of complex businesses. Its financial statements are nearly impenetrable. So why is Enron trading at such a huge multiple?'(Fortune Magazine, 5 March 2001).

17 Hosseini and Mahesh (n 6) .

18 (n 7).

19 Hosseini and Mahesh (n 6) 37451-37460.

20 Denis Collins, 'Arthur Andersen: American Company' in Encyplopaedia Britannica (2018).

21 ibid.

such as locking an Andersen auditor in a room until he produced a letter supporting a $270 million tax credit.

Thus, the bankruptcy of Enron in November 2001, which started as the centre of an unprecedented crisis, ended up becoming a mere backdrop for a series of corporate scandals in other large Arthur Andersen customers, such as World Com, AOL Time Warner, ImClone, Tyco, Adelphia, Bristol-Myers, Squibb and Global Crossing[22]. As a result of these facts, Arthur Andersen was charged and convicted of obstruction of justice, which effectively led to the closure of the company, since the SEC is prohibited to accept audits of criminal convicts. The company delivered its Certified Public Accountant license on August 31, 2002 and 85,000 employees lost their jobs. Although the conviction was later reversed by the United States Supreme Court, in theory allowing the company to resume operations, the damage to its reputation was so great that it would not be a viable business[23].

As such, the Enron case was the largest of a series of cases that affected the reputation of the American financial market, forcing the United States Congress to endeavour to pass a law with bipartisan support, making corporate executives criminally responsible, closing regulations gaps that allowed accounting frauds and establishing safer rules to avoid the occurrence of future similar cases. It was against this background that, in July 2002, the United States Congress passed the Sarbanes-Oxley Act, a law whose name refers to its two main defenders, Democratic Senator Paul Sarbanes and Republican Representative Michael Oxley[24].

3.2. General Background

The Sarbanes-Oxley Act is a United States of America law, signed on July 30, 2002 by President George W. Bush, whose structure is divided into sections. It is no exaggeration to say that SOX, as the law is also known, is a true Corporate Governance Code, especially if we consider its significant length, of 1,107 sections.

As a reflection of the historical context that predated its elaboration, the SOX has as its main goal to impose new management parameters, to stimulate the best corporate governance practices, to foresee a strict internal

22 Hosseini and Mahesh (n 6) 37451-37460.

23 ibid.

24 Fabiana Farias, 'Principais impactos da Sarbanes-Oxley Act' (2004) 4, 6 Revista ConTexto.

control of processes, to stipulate risk management standards, to restrain manipulation of accounting reports and to compel its full disclosure. As such, SOX created a new corporate governance environment. According to Oliveira and Linhares, corporate governance is understood as the practices and relationships between shareholders, board of directors, executive officers, independent auditors and fiscal council, in order to optimize the performance of companies, facilitate access to capital and return to shareholders.[25]

Therefore, Sarbanes-Oxley sought to introduce a true cultural revolution at the corporate level, forcing companies to implement corporate governance policies that, due to their high cost, would hardly be implemented if this legal imposition did not exist. Among these policies, there is an emphasis on internal controls and the disclosure of financial reports, as a way to encourage corporate transparency and increase confidence in this sector[26].

SOX is considered one of the most stringent regulations in the corporate sector in the United States of America, being also applicable to all foreign companies with certificates of deposit admitted to trading on United States stock exchanges[27]. That is to say, SOX is applicable not only to US companies, but also to foreign companies that have bounds registered with the SEC, such as, for example, Brazilian companies that have American Depositary Receipts (ADRs) admitted to trading on the United States stock exchanges.

ADRs are an instrument created in the 1920s in the United States of America to allow the shares of foreign companies to be traded on US stock exchanges in an easy and safe way for the acquirer[28]. They act as a kind of receipt of shares of foreign companies, which are purchased by banks in the country where the stock was issued, which are responsible for their custody. In the United States, an investment bank issues receipts for these papers and trades them, over the counter or on stock exchanges, indivi-

25 Marcelle Colares Oliveira and Juliana Silva Linhares, "A implantação de controle interno adequado às exigências da Lei Sarbanes-Oxley em empresas brasileiras – Um estudo de caso", (2007)4,2 BASE – Revista de Administração e Contabilidade da Unisinos 161.

26 Marlon Messias Peixoto de Souza and Mariana Dórea Figueiredo, 'A Lei Sarbanes-Oxley e Sua Importância para as Companhias Abertas Brasileiras a partir do Ano de 2004' (2008) 10, 42 Revista Pensar Contábil 31-35.

27 Marcelle Colares Oliveira and Juliana Silva Linhares (n 27) 161.

28 Rita Azevedo, 'Entenda o que é ADR' Criados há 70 anos, os American Depositary Receipts permitem que investidores dos EUA coloquem recursos em empresas estrangeiras' ((2017) 4 Revista Exame,.

dually or in bundles of shares, with values in US dollars[29]. In the Brazilian case, there are three levels of ADRs available, namely, levels 1, 2 and 3:

Level 1 ADR can only be sold on the non-organized over-the-counter market. In level 2 receipts, the company transforms Brazilian papers into ADRs and trades on the New York Stock Exchange. At level 3, the company makes primary issuance and negotiates shares in the secondary market. These receipts may represent preferred (non-voting) or common (voting) shares. But most of the issued papers correspond to preferred shares. Usually, only large and medium-sized companies are able to launch ADR programs in the USA, as the volume of trading is high.[30]

Level 1 ADRs are offered exclusively on the over-the-counter market, which is why the company is subject to few information disclosure obligations. In turn, Level 2 ADRs are traded on a stock exchange, forcing the issuing company to disclose its financial information in the manner imposed by the SEC. Finally, at Level 3, ADRs are backed by new shares, with primary issuance of stocks by the issuing company, so that they are then traded on the US stock exchanges. The prestige of Level 3 ADRs, which is practically equated with the shares of American companies, is accompanied by the requirements to which they are submitted, since they are linked to the provisions of SOX and the regulations issued by the SEC[31].

This is significantly important because in Brazil, contrary to what happens in more developed economies, it is not yet common for middle class people to invest in the capital market, which ends up forcing the biggest companies in the country to resort to the United States financial market, so that their stocks are traded in that country, through ADRs, as a way of raising capital. Talking about this situation, Souza and Figueiredo teach that due to cultural, political and economic factors, the Brazilian middle class still does not trust the capital market. As the solution to this problem is neither easy nor resolvable in the short term, the foreign capital market is crucial and extremely important for the approximately 40 national companies that operate on the New York Stock Exchange. Thus, adapting to the new SOX rules has become an extremely stressful, but healthy, process for the financial health of these companies.[32]

For this reason, large Brazilian companies resort to the trading of ADRs in the United States capital market, such as Ambev (ABV), Gerdau

29 Rita Azevedo (n 30).
30 Agência Estado, 'Entenda melhor os ADRS' (Estadão, 20 November 2000).
31 Rita Azevedo (n 30).
32 Marlon Messias Peixoto de Souza and Mariana Dórea Figueiredo (n 28) 33.

(GGB), Petrobrás (PBR and PBR-A), Vale (VALE), Brazil Foods (BRFS), Eletrobrás (EBR), National Steel Company (SID), Embraer (ERJ), Gol (GOL), Net (NETC), Sadia (SDA), Vivo (VIV), Itaú Unibanco (ITUB) and Bradesco (BBD)[33]. Therefore, there is a need for Brazilian companies like these to comply with the requirements of the Sarbanes-Oxley Act, so that they can continue offering shares in the US market without being subject to sanctions, fines or investigations.

3.3. Main dispositions

As previously stated, the Sarbanes-Oxley Act is a true code, with 1,107 sections, equivalent to articles of Brazilian law. Although the act as a whole is of fundamental importance, it is possible to identify utmost important dispositions, such as those contained in Titles I, II, III, IV, VIII and IX.

In Title I, Sections 101 to 109 establish the creation of a supervisory body for independent auditing companies, called Public Company Accounting Oversight Board (PCAOB), which operates under the Securities and Exchange Commission (SEC) and has as its main function the supervision of public company auditors. It also provides for the registration of auditors, quality control of audits and standards for assessment and inspection.

In Title II, Sections 201 to 209 deal with independent auditors, establishing standards for the provision of services not included in the scope of audit practices and imposing a rotation scheme for external auditors in company inspections subject to the Sarbanes-Oxley Act. It also addresses conflicts of interest, approval requirements for independent audits and reporting.

In Title III, Sections 301 to 308 deal with corporate responsibility, imposing the creation of Audit Committees on companies submitted to SOX. It also establishes corporate responsibility for financial statements, situations that characterize improper influence on the conduct of auditors, rules regarding the distribution of bonuses and the imposition of penalties.

Among the Sections of Title III, the number 302 is particularly relevant, especially for Brazilian companies, which determines that the CEO and the CFO must personally declare that they are responsible for disclosure controls and procedures[34]. Therefore, senior executives of companies that

33 Jeff Reeves, 'BRIC Investing – ADR List for Brazil, Russia, India and China' (Investor Place, 16 June 2010).

34 Oliveira and Linhares (n 27) 164.

file financial reports with the SEC, even though foreign and small, must attest and be responsible for the thorough review of the balance sheets.

It is also in Title III that one of the most controversial provisions of the Sarbanes-Oxley Act is found, namely, Section 307, which establishes rules of professional liability for corporate lawyers. This Section obliges the lawyers to notify the Chief Legal Counsel (CLC) or the CEO when they encounter material evidence of violation of the rules of the capital markets by the company itself or its agents. If there is no adequate response to the reported evidence, the lawyer must then report it to the Independent Audit Committee or the Board of Directors. This is highly controversial because of its flagrant conflict with the duty of professional secrecy.

In Title IV, Sections 401 to 409 establish the obligation to disclose in-depth financial statements, through periodic reports. They also contain provisions on conflicts of interest, requiring broad disclosure of transactions involving the company's board of directors and large shareholders. It also deals with internal controls and the cases exempted from them, the need to create a Code of Ethics and the audit of balance sheets by financial experts, with subsequent disclosure of their reports, among other provisions.

Among the Sections of Title IV, the number 404 is particularly relevant, which also requires the Chief Executive Officer (CEO) and the Chief Financial Officer (CFO) to periodically evaluate and attest to the effectiveness of internal controls and the compliance of financial reports to SOX, SEC and PCAOB rules, under penalty of imprisonment of up to 20 years and a fine of up to US $ 5 million for each untrue statement made. In addition, the company's independent auditor must issue a parallel report, attesting the effectiveness of internal controls and procedures for issuing financial reports[35]. Also in Title IV, Section 406 instituted the mandatory elaboration of an Ethics Code, which must be widely disclosed by the company to its employees, officers and directors.

In Title VIII, Sections 801 to 807 establish corporate and criminal liability for accounting fraud, defining crimes and establishing their respective penalties. It establishes criminal penalties for altering documents and for fraud against shareholders, as well as rules regarding statute of limitations, parameters for the imposing of penalties and plea bargains by employees of companies traded on the stock exchange that provide evidence of fraud.

In Title IX, Sections 901 to 906 stablish increased penalties for white collar crimes, applicable in the event of attempts or conspiracy to commit

35 Oliveira and Linhares (n 27) 164.

fraud and crimes against employee pension funds. It also establishes sentencing parameters for some white-collar crimes and corporate responsibility for financial reporting.

4. The impact of the Sarbanes Oxley Act upon Brazilian companies

One of the most important impacts of the Sarbanes-Oxley Act is its application in jurisdictions of several other countries around the world, considering the approximately 14.000 non-American companies listed on stock exchanges in the US through ADRs[36]. Hence, the challenge is to reconcile the SOX with the interests and norms of other sovereign states, sometimes in open conflict with it. In the specific Brazilian case, there were initial difficulties in adapting to local rules, especially regarding the independence of the members of the Board of Directors[37].

As a consequence, the SEC has made some concessions to address legitimate concerns from outside the US. Taking advantage of these concessions, the Brazilian Securities and Exchange Commission (CVM) and the Brazilian Association of Publicly-Held Companies (ABRASCA) asked the SEC for authorization for the Audit Committee to be replaced by the Fiscal Council[38]. Referring to the Audit Committee, Souza and Figueiredo state that, the main purpose of creating this committee is to eliminate the possibility of coexistence between the company and the independent audit; its assignment is to provide conditions so that complaints about fraud related to auditing and accounting controls can be presented without risk to the whistle-blower. Once these complaints are filed, they should be investigated by this committee with complete independence and impartiality vis-à-vis the company's management.[39]

Despite the SOX insistence that the Audit Committee perform advisory and recommendation functions, the SEC accepted the request of CVM and ABRASCA, considered that the performance of the Fiscal Council was considered adequate to the existing corporate balance in Brazil[40]. However, despite this concession, numerous Brazilian companies with papers traded on the American stock exchanges, such as Petrobras and Vale, still

36 Farias (n 26).
37 ibid.
38 ibid.
39 Souza and Figueiredo (n 28) 33.
40 Farias (n 26) 9.

prefer to fully comply with the requirements of the SOX, establishing independent Audit Committees[41].

In fact, the CVM recommends the creation of an Audit Committee, "composed of members of the board of directors with experience in finance and included at least one director who represents minority shareholders, who must supervise the relationship with the external auditors"[42]. In addition, as a way of adapting to the requirements of the Sarbanes-Oxley Act, a series of regulatory measures were issued by Brazilian public bodies, among which a Resolution from the Brazilian Central Bank (BACEN), which regulated, in a manner compatible with SOX, the requirement of independent audit services for financial institutions.

Another requirement of the Sarbanes-Oxley Act, unparalleled in Brazilian legislation, but easy to adapt, is the mandatory elaboration and disclosure of an Ethics Code among the company's employees, directors and board members. The majority of Brazilian companies with papers traded on US stock exchanges have this code, although more often than not in a purely *pro forma* manner, with little to none internal disclosure[43].

After almost 18 years of the Sarbanes-Oxley Act, it can be said that most publicly traded companies in the country have already adapted, albeit partially, to its provisions, instituting internal control structures, adapting processes and implementing corporate governance practices as a way of encouraging business ethics. In addition, many of the requirements of SOX are already in effect in Brazil through local laws and CVM's Instructions. Hence, few changes will be necessary to comply with American regulations[44].

Another aspect that deserves to be highlighted is the tendency that even companies not directly subject to SOX adapt to its standards of compliance, as a consequence of an imposition of the market itself, implemented as way of obtaining a competitive advantage. According to Almeida and Duarte Junior, there is no way back for Brazilian companies other than to follow these steps. Local investors are more interested and informed and, therefore, more careful when it comes to investing their savings in companies with no commitment to transparency, risk management and corporate governance. In other words, Brazilian companies that spontaneously decide to satisfy SOX may obtain, for example, a reduction in

41 Souza and Figueiredo (n 28) 33.
42 Oliveira and Linhares (n 27) 165.
43 Souza and Figueiredo (n 28) 31-35.
44 Oliveira and Linhares (n 27) 165.

financing costs, a better perception of investors regarding their products, and a reduction in operational and legal losses. Even privately held companies can benefit from adhering to the best risk management practices and in line with the demands of SOX.[45]

Forecasts about the future aside, let us see, briefly, some case studies regarding the impacts of the Sarbanes-Oxley Act on Brazilian companies subject to it.

4.1. Case study 1: Enel Distribution Ceara (EDC)

Enel Distribution Ceara (EDC), is an electric power company based in Fortaleza that was privatized on April 2, 1998 through an auction held at the Rio de Janeiro Stock Exchange (BVRJ), in which it was acquired by the Endesa Group, through Investluz SA, a subsidiary of the Italian company Enel SpA, based in Rome, which has securities traded on the New York Stock Exchange[46]

As a consequence, EDC is subject to the provisions of SOX, such as inspections by the SEC, which is why the company has been promoting a progressive structuring to the corporate governance practices, as well as the adequacy of its structures and internal controls[47]. The case of EDC is paradigmatic, since the company does not have ADRs traded directly on US stock exchanges, but, as a subsidiary of a foreign company traded in America, it must comply with both SOX and SEC standards.

This restructuring aims to promote transparency and accountability, with special emphasis on the disclosure of annual reports, which have been progressively improved since its privatization. Also, with regard to internal controls, there was a significant adaptation of management practices, specially upon external audits[48]. According to Carioca, De Luca and Ponte, thus, since the implementation of the SOX Project, COELCE has

45 Luiz Claudio Schleder Sampaio de Almeida and Antonio Marcos Duarte Júnior, 'Desafios e soluções da Petrobras em seu projeto de atendimento à Lei Sarbanes-Oxley' (2010/2011) III, 1 RAUnP – Revista Eletrônica do Mestrado Profissional em Administração da Universidade Potiguar 37.

46 Karla Jeanny Falcão Carioca, Márcia Martins Mendes de Luca and Vera Maria Rodrigues Ponte, 'Implementação da Lei Sarbanes-Oxley e seus Impactos nos controles internos e nas práticas de governança corporativa: um estudo na Companhia Energética do Ceará – COELCE' (2010) 6, 4 Revista Universo Contábil 50-67.

47 Oliveira and Linhares (n 27) 165.

48 Carioca, Luca and Ponte (n 48) 50-67.

performed the analysis of all its processes, aiming at adapting to the requirements of the Law and improving its internal controls. Control activities became known and monitored, always aiming at the correct functioning and mitigation of the risks involved, as a way of enabling changes in the company's control culture, with an impact on the control environment [...].[49]

So, it is possible to verify that the adequacy of EDC's internal practices to the SOX provisions is very relevant, consisting of real cultural changes in the organization and directly impacting the management practices and management of the company's internal processes.

4.2. Case study 2: Petrobras

Petroleo Brasileiro S.A., better known by the name Petrobras, is a publicly traded company whose largest shareholder is the Brazilian Federal Government, headquartered in the city of Rio de Janeiro. Although its credibility has been severely affected by the recent scandals unveiled by "Operation Lava Jato", Petrobras remains the largest company in Brazil and Latin America, one of the thirty largest companies in the world and one of the ten largest companies in terms of market capitalization on US stock exchanges[50].

Petrobras has shares on the New York Stock Exchange, which are sold through Level 3 ADRs. As such, the company is fully subject to the provisions of SOX and the regulations issued by the SEC since 2006, the deadline for adjustments to these rules by companies based outside of America[51]. Due to its size and importance, it is important to analyse the process of adapting Petrobras to SOX, the main challenges faced by the company in this endeavour and the solutions adopted by it in order to meet legal requirements.

In September 2004, Petrobras began the process of adapting its internal structures to SOX, creating the Integrated Project for Internal Controls Assessment Systems (PRISMA), with an impact on all the company's operating units, including its subsidiaries and controlled companies. Initially, PRISMA was created within the Internal Audit Unit of Petrobras, being monitored by the Internal Controls Management Committee. In this first

49 Carioca, Luca and Ponte (n 48) 65.
50 Almeida and Júnior (n 47) 27-40.
51 Almeida and Duarte Júnior (n 47) 27-40.

stage, a mapping and evaluation of the company's internal processes was carried out, with risk and control assessments[52]. In April 2006, PRISMA was replaced in its duties and responsibilities by the General Management of Internal Controls (GGCI), linked to the Executive Management of Corporate Finance and reporting to the CFO. The reason for this change is explained by Almeida and Duarte Junior in the following terms: it is important to mention that a common mistake made by Brazilian companies when setting up the group responsible for SOX certification was repeated at Petrobras: lack of segregation of functions between PRISMA and Internal Audit. In other words, the untying of tasks that were later allocated to the GGCI, and that could not be subordinated to Internal Audit, required that at least two distinct units be involved between proposing, evaluating and monitoring the self-assessment of controls on the one hand, and the verification of the effectiveness of the controls in practice, on the other side. Thus, the creation of the GGCI - outside the Internal Audit - solved the problem of lack of segregation of activities.[53]

Consequently, it is possible to verify that the fact that the SOX was a legislative novelty to which few were accustomed, especially in Brazil, caused some problems to arise in the process of initial adaptation to the requirements of the American regulations. Within this panorama, the identification and recruitment of trained internal personnel to conduct the first certification related to SOX was one of the main initial obstacles to PRISMA's activities[54].

With that in mind, Petrobras hired one of the largest consultancies in the world in November 2004, Deloitte, through a bidding process. The company's expertise, which had already acted in the certification processes of companies based in the US, whose initial period of adaptation to SOX was earlier, that is, December 2014, was fundamental in this process of adaptation[55]. Also, in accordance with SOX requirements, Petrobras had to contract an external audit, to certify the regularity of the work of PRISMA and Deloitte itself, and the company KPMG was chosen for this purpose, also through bidding, in December 2005[56].

Petrobras had to adapt not only internal and cultural processes, but also the acquisition of compatible technological resources, consistent with structures of internal controls and information technology, thus increasing

52 ibid.
53 Almeida and Duarte Júnior (n 47) 30.
54 Almeida and Duarte Júnior (n 47) 27-40.
55 ibid.
56 ibid.

the financial cost of adapting to SOX to levels even higher[57]. As is to be expected in the face of the imposition of new corporate cultural paradigms, the first reaction of all parties to SOX was its perception as a mere high-cost additional bureaucracy. Initially, this was also the case. However, in the long term, the consensus has been consolidated in the sense that SOX is a valuable resource for the management of corporate risks, helping to secure corporate longevity[58].

5. Conclusion

Corruption is a human phenomenon with economic, legal, historical and cultural dimensions, which cannot be neglected. It is not restricted to developing countries, constituting a universal human fact, which is why there is a growing global concern about the development and implementation of effective strategies to combat the practice of illegal acts. For these reasons, compliance has grown significantly in importance at a global level, being considered fundamental in the fight against corruption, terrorism, organized crime and extremism. Basically, compliance consists of the activity that seeks to stimulate accordance with legal standards, self-surveillance, ethics, transparency and due diligence, consisting, in the private sphere, of a pilar of corporate governance.

This worldwide phenomenon, which has been stimulated by the OECD, has its roots in important regulatory acts in the US, among which the FCPA (1977) and the SOX (2002), aimed at combating acts of corruption in the public and private sectors, respectively. Mainly due to the importance of the financial and capital markets of the United States of America, US compliance standards have a wide potential for extraterritorial application, forcing public officials and economic agents from around the world to promote adjustments.

Within this panorama, Brazil, although with some delay, has come to recognize the importance of implementing compliance programs, stimulating their adoption, initially in the public sector, but with increasing importance in the corporate sector. Business managers are increasingly aware of the importance of compliance as a catalyst for corporate longevity itself.

57 ibid.
58 ibid..

SOX is of crucial importance in this process of disseminating corporate governance practices, since its primary objective is to re-establish ethics in the business sphere, serving to reinforce the reliability of capital markets. The Act is a true Corporate Governance Code, establishing, throughout its 1,107 Sections, strict procedures applicable to the business environment, with special emphasis on the accounting and ethical aspects.

SOX is also applicable to foreign companies, provided that they have securities registered with the SEC, what, in the case of Brazilian companies, is made possible through the negotiation of American Depositary Receipts (ADRs). That is, large Brazilian companies, listed on US stock exchanges, need to submit to SOX requirements so that they are not subject to sanctions, fines or investigations by the authorities of that country. This is the case for numerous Brazilian business conglomerates and companies that are subsidiaries of groups somehow listed on US' stock exchanges.

Thus, large Brazilian corporations, as well as thousands of companies around the world, must conform to the standards established by SOX, implementing audit policies and adapting their internal organization charts, in order to promote legal compliance, accountability, transparency and a sense of justice, in a true revolution of corporate culture.

Eco Smart City Method of Promoting Environmental Sustainability and Sustainable Development in an Industralised and Digitalized Society

Alexandra R. Harrington <arharrington@gmail.com>
NEW YORK, USA

Magdalena Stryja <magdalena.stryja@us.edu.pl>
KATOWICE, Poland

1. Introduction

When starting to consider the ecological smart city ("eco smart city") as a method of promoting sustainable development, it is worth emphasising the interdisciplinary nature of this issue, which makes it difficult to discuss urban development in isolation from the environment and its protection. Many scientists and researchers emphasise that the idea of the smart city should be looked at in a holistic way. This approach requires a systematic approach to the elements and phenomena occurring within it, but it also suggests analysing the processes that shape it, taking into account the past, present and future. And here we enter a new, more and more commonly used terminology, i.e. smart city.[1]

The antecedents of the concept of smart growth can be found in Agenda 21,[2] an international document on sustainable development, which was adopted during the "Environment and Development Conference" on the initiative of the United Nations in 1992 at the Second Conference in Rio de Janeiro. The Agenda contains 21 Millennium Goals with a timeframe of 2000 to 2015. The document outlined how to develop, implement and enforce sustainable development programmes in local life. Agenda 21 defines sustainable development as "...social and economic development, which is the process of integrating political, economic and social activities while maintaining natural balance and permanence of basic natural processes

1 Agnieszka Sobol 'INTELIGENTNE MIASTA VERSUS ZRÓWNOWAŻONE MIASTA' (2017) 320 Studia Ekonomiczne. Zeszyty Naukowe Uniwersytetu Ekonomicznego w 76.
2 Action Programme – Agenda 21

in order to guarantee the possibility of satisfying basic needs of particular communities or citizens of the present and future generations".[3]

This idea carried through to the concept of smart growth and smart cities, the ideal version of which should be an eco smart city or a sustainable smart city. Such a city is a smart city, which acts in a sustainable way or is created in such a way.[4] It is a city that, through the cooperation of many entities, by integrating infrastructure, services, production, education and recreation, ensures the most optimal functioning of the city as a whole.[5] Future cities thus appear as a joint venture of many social partners: inhabitants, authorities, local entrepreneurs and other institutions, making use of the wealth of diversity of knowledge and the roles played by different local actors.[6]

One of the definitions is proposed by Robert Horbaty, who calls an intelligent city a city that offers its inhabitants the maximum quality of life while minimising the use of resources through an appropriate combination of infrastructural systems, such as transport or energy transmission. [7] Jeninifer Belissent, on the other hand, points out that a smart city uses information and communication technologies to make key services and urban infrastructure elements such as administration, education, security, public transport more efficient[8]. From the perspective of the present deliberations, the most desirable concept is that of the eco smart city, i.e. a city in which protection and concern for economic, social and spatial aspects extends and is equally important to protection of the environment, natural resources, air or climate, which can be seen, for example, in actions aimed at limiting carbon dioxide emissions, reducing water consumption or switching the energy sector to less harmful renewable sources. Following this line of thought, it can be said that the reason for the development of the eco smart city concept are the following: climate change, instability of the global economic system, urbanisation, digitalisation of life, greater expectations of the public in terms of quality of life, demographic trends

3 Agenda 21

4 Peter Newman, *Sustainable Cities of the Future: The Behavior Change Driver*, (2010) 11, 7 Sustainable Dev. L & Pol'y.

5 ibid.

6 Walter Castelnovo, Gianluca Misuraca and Alberto Savoldelli, '*Smart Cities Governance: The Need for a Holistic Approach to Assessing Urban Participatory Policy Making*' (2015) Social Science Computer Review <https://doi.org/10.1177/0894439315611103> Accessed 2 July 2021.

7 Cf. <https://ideologia.pl/smart-city-jak-inteligentne-miasta-poprawiaja-zycie-mieszkancow/> accessed 2 July 2021.

8 Cf. ibid.

and growing social awareness of the need to take care of the natural environment for the benefit of our own and future generations.

In each configuration of the eco smart city, it is clear that there are significant connections between the ways in which law, regulation, policy and technology intersect to create the ideally functioning entity and the ability of a State in which such a city is located to fulfill the obligations undertaken by Member States of the international community through the 2015 Sustainable Development Goals (SDGs). As this chapter explains, the eco smart city is deeply rooted in the terms of the SDGs, and vice versa, such that achieving one would significantly further the achievement of the other. This was true when the SDGs were agreed to in 2015, however, in the continuously unfolding context of the Covid-19 pandemic and the design of post-pandemic recovery plans and solutions, the symbiosis in relationships has only been reinforced. Indeed, as discussed throughout Section III, which overlays the various SDGs and associated targets with lessons from the eco smart city model, the pandemic has shed further light on the need for interconnections that are environmentally and societally sound, technologically advanced and focused on perpetuating durable communities in which all are regarded as valuable members with voices, merits and contributions to make. This requires a complex set of legal, regulatory and technological tools, which the SDGs and eco smart city model can provide.

2. *SDG Background and History*

Adopted in September 2015 during a meeting of the United Nations (UN) General Assembly, the Sustainable Development Goals (SDGs) represent the second set of goals used by the international community to address the most pernicious and threatening issues facing it.[9] To fully understand the SDGs, however, it is essential to view them as part of a history that began with the turning of the millennia.

In 2000, the UN General Assembly adopted the first such set of goals, the Millennium Development Goals (MDGs) in order to acknowledge the critical issues following the international community into the new

9 United Nations General Assembly, Transforming our world: the 2030 Agenda for Sustainable Development, A/RES/70/1 (25 September 2015).

millennium.[10] The MDGs were significantly fewer in number than the SDGs – 8 overall – and have been criticised for being overly aspirational in nature rather than setting achievable and quantifiable standards.[11] In an innovative step, the MDGs were given a lifespan, 15 years, during which to accomplish their mission.[12] The MDGs were focused on poverty elimination, building partnerships, addressing gender issues, addressing communicable diseases and disease in general, improving maternal health, child health, advancing access to basic education, and promoting "environmental sustainability."[13] Each of these goals was accompanied by several targets to provide a more tangible layer for assessing implementation, although these were not as detailed as the targets set forth in the SDGs.[14] Key to the topic of the Eco-Smart City was MDG 7 on environmental sustainability. In this MDG, the international community focused specifically on the importance of preserving forests and natural resources, combatting air pollution and carbon emissions, increasing access to drinking water and proper sanitation, and assisting those defined as "slum dwellers."[15]

The MDGs established the pattern of international community acceptance of and efforts to implement what are essentially soft law mechanisms as part of national laws and policies, international and regional organization policies and undertakings, and international practice.[16] However, they have been openly criticized for lacking enforcement and oversight mechanisms and for their generality, combined with their aspirational nature, which can be seen in the small number of targets used and the lack of calculable measures of implementation.[17] When the MDGs were set to expire in 2015, official UN evaluations indicated that, although there had been some important successes, including in increasing access to drinking water, overall the MDGs had not been achieved.[18]

With the lessons of the MDGs in mind, the international community engaged in a multi-year and multi-stakeholder process of drafting the

10 United Nations Millennium Development Goals, <https://www.un.org/millenniumgoals/> accessed 2 July 2021; Alexandra R. Harrington, *International Law and Global Governance: Treaty Regimes and Sustainable Development Goals Implementation* (Routledge 2021).
11 See Millennium Development Goals, (n 10).
12 ibid.
13 ibid.
14 ibid.
15 ibid.
16 ibid; see also Harrington, (n 10).
17 ibid.
18 ibid.

successor entities, ultimately the SDGs. The SDGs, encapsulated in the larger Agenda 2030 document adopted by the UN General Assembly, recognize the need to address the three pillars of sustainable development – economic, social and environmental – as part of a concerted effort to address the most pressing issues facing global society in the short and long-term.[19] This includes the recognition of the inherent connections with environmental issues that extend beyond the concept of environmental sustainability promotion as enshrined in the MDGs.[20]

In total, there are 17 SDGs, which are accompanied by 169 targets and several hundred indicators, keyed to specific targets and intended to provide methods of measuring their implementation at set intervals.[21] The 17 elaborated goals range from poverty to education to infrastructure to environment and beyond and, as discussed below,[22] there are areas of intersection between elements of each of these goals and the concept of the Eco Smart City.

3. *Intersections of the SDGs and Eco Smart Cities*

SDG 1 – End poverty in all its forms everywhere

The MDGs echo soundly throughout the parameters of SDG 1 in terms of the continued global goal of eradicating poverty, a goal that also underlies many aspects of the Eco Smart City. While Target 1.1 provides a definition of "extreme poverty," namely USD 1.25 per day, and sets the goal of eradicating extreme poverty by 2030, Target 1.2 seeks to address all forms of poverty and allows for the use of a national definition of poverty as created by each State.[23] Taken together, these targets are intended to set the floor of extreme poverty while at the same time allowing each State to define poverty levels above it commensurate with national standards.[24] This can be seen as providing flexibility for the development phases of the Eco Smart City while at the same time endorsing the social benefit aspects of it in the short and long-term.

---

19 See Agenda 2030, (n 9).
20 ibid.
21 ibid.
22 ibid.
23 United Nations, Sustainable Development Goal 1 <https://sdgs.un.org/goals/goal1> accessed 2 July 2021.
24 ibid.

Target 1.4 provides that "By 2030, [States] ensure that all men and women, in particular the poor and the vulnerable, have equal rights to economic resources, as well as access to basic services, ownership and control over land and other forms of property, inheritance, natural resources, appropriate new technology and financial services, including microfinance."[25] There are many areas of law and policy implicated by this target, and it seems that many aspects of the Eco Smart City could be used as methods of fulfill these requirements, ranging from ensuring that all citizens have access to reliable services to providing citizens with access to technology and technological developments.

SDG 2 – end hunger, achieve food security and improved nutrition and promote sustainable agriculture

Target 2.1, "By 2030, end hunger and ensure access by all people, in particular the poor and people in vulnerable situations, including infants, to safe, nutritious and sufficient food all year round," provides a critical area in which the Eco Smart City can advance the SDGs by providing information on food needs and access to food services.[26] By coordinating this type of information and attempting to ensure that cities are ecologically sustainable through efforts such as urban gardening, the Eco Smart City represents a way in which to advance Target 2.1 throughout an often overlooked and underserved population in terms of food production and access – those in urban areas, especially the urban poor.

SDG 3 – ensure healthy lives and promote well-being for all at all ages

Target 3.3, "By 2030, end the epidemics of AIDS, tuberculosis, malaria and neglected tropical diseases and combat hepatitis, water-borne diseases and other communicable diseases,"[27] was important in 2015 but, in the wake of the Covid-19 pandemic, has taken on an entirely increased sense of urgency in 2021. As has been observed in cities across the globe, the pandemic has spread rapidly in congested living and working areas, as well as those that

25 ibid.
26 United Nations, Sustainable Development Goal 2 <https://sdgs.un.org/goals/goal2> accessed 2 July 2021.
27 United Nations, Sustainable Development Goal 3 <https://sdgs.un.org/goals/goal3> accessed 2 July 2021.

are hubs for travel and transportation.[28] The lessons from the Covid-19 pandemic have yet to be fully concluded, however it is clear that there is an inherent tie between environmental degradation, the growth of zoonotic diseases, and the spread of these diseases.[29] By focusing on Target 3.3 and increasing the ability of cities to use technology as a means to track and analyze upticks in illnesses, the Eco Smart City has a significant role to play in the achievement of the SDGs.

Concomitantly, the importance of Target 3.4, "By 2030, reduce by one third premature mortality from non-communicable diseases through prevention and treatment and promote mental health and well-being,"[30] has been emphasized in the Covid-19 pandemic's impacts on mental health and the marked relationship between the imposition of social distancing, lockdowns and quarantines and declines in mental health statuses of populations across the globe.[31] In this context, there is a direct tension between the mental health needs of members of a population and the legal policies generated by States to address the public health needs of the population as a whole.[32] One of the key methods of overcoming the underlying elements of mental health stresses during the pandemic – namely, isolation – has been through the use of technology to connect patients with their mental health providers.[33] This highlights a critical role that technology and the interconnectedness fostered by the Eco Smart City can play in the pandemic and post-pandemic recovery from the mental health perspective as well as the achievement of SDG 3. Similarly, the ability of physicians and healthcare providers to continue delivering at least basic levels of care to patients in the pandemic through technological capacities such as telemedicine allows for further progress toward implementing SDG 3 to be sustained in areas with technological capacity.[34]

Further, Target 3.9, "By 2030, substantially reduce the number of deaths and illnesses from hazardous chemicals and air, water and soil pollution and contamination,"[35] highlights the importance of ties between environmental degradation and illness in a non-zoonotic capacity. Given the his-

---

28 See Global Pandemic Network Ecological Rights Working Group, *Position Paper: Environmental Protection and Human Rights in the Pandemic* (2021).
29 ibid.
30 (n 26).
31 See Global Pandemic Network, (n 28).
32 See ibid.
33 See ibid.
34 See ibid.
35 (n 26).

toric role of cities as agents of pollution, leading to zoning and other legal regimes which attempt to regulate pollution in urban areas, and the tendency of urban populations to demonstrate significant illness rates, for example respiratory and cardiac illnesses,[36] there is a direct connection between achieving Target 3.9 and effectively implementing the goals and function of the Eco Smart City.

SDG 4 – ensure inclusive and equitable quality education and promote lifelong learning opportunities for all

Education is the foundation for future generations. It determines the level of education in society, the awareness of citizens of their role in public life, and in the life of the State overall. Quality education is a guarantee of a better life, a decent job, a happy and fulfilling private life, and of full participation in social life. As SDG 4 highlights, this concept of education does not end at a certain age or with the attainment of a certain level of education, but rather is envisioned as something that exists throughout one's life.

The concept of universality in education begins in Target 4.1, "By 2030, ensure that all girls and boys complete free, equitable and quality primary and secondary education leading to relevant and effective learning outcomes,"[37] and is supplemented by Target 4.2, "By 2030, ensure that all girls and boys have access to quality early childhood development, care and pre-primary education so that they are ready for primary education."[38] Recognizing the many forms education may take and the many skills needed by individuals and society, Target 4.3 provides "By 2030, ensure equal access for all women and men to affordable and quality technical, vocational and tertiary education, including university,"[39] Target 4.4 provides "By 2030, substantially increase the number of youth and adults who have relevant skills, including technical and vocational skills, for employment, decent jobs and entrepreneurship,"[40] and Target 4.6 provides "By 2030, ensure that all youth and a substantial proportion of adults, both

36 Global Pandemic Network, (n 28).

37 United Nations, Sustainable Development Goal 4, <https://sdgs.un.org/goals/goal4> accessed 2 July 2021.

38 ibid.

39 ibid.

40 ibid.

men and women, achieve literacy and numeracy."[41] Finally, Targets 4.5 and 4.7 directly address the potential forms of discrimination faced by members of society, especially vulnerable members of society, across all levels of educational access and opportunity and requires States to create meaningful ways to work around this.[42]

Only with a well-educated society can the implementation of the eco-smart city be successful. The young people of today should be seen as the future implementers of the smart city idea, and at the same time the need for education of those at all ages is essential for the implementation and acceptance of smart city-based technologies.[43] From the perspective of climate change in particular, the introduction of environmentally friendly technology and the creation of spaces that are friendly to everyday life, raising awareness in society should begin with appropriate education.

At the same time, the ability of technology to connect students and educators at all levels has been emphasized during the Covid-19 pandemic, in which the majority of education has become online to some extent.[44] This has created many benefits, particularly in terms of allowing students to keep up with lessons, advance within and graduate through their academic programs, and maintain social cohesion with their fellow students and teachers.[45] Conversely, the reliance on technology for education – be it in the midst of a global crisis or as a means of providing temporary education during emergencies or in lieu of absences from school for illness – has brought to light a serious issue of access and equity. From the beginning of the pandemic onward, there was an assumption in many laws and policies that students and families would have the technological capacity to connect to classes and participate in lessons.[46] This assumption has been proven incorrect in developed and developing States alike, and many students in urban settings as well as rural areas have found that they are further stigmatized by being unable to access the technology necessary to remain in school.[47] In this context, the emphasis of the eco smart city on ensuring access to technology for all citizens of an urban area becomes extremely impactful for students and their families, educators, communities and States. Understanding this relationship and the ways in which it can

41 ibid.
42 ibid.
43 ibid.
44 See Global Pandemic Network, (n 28).
45 ibid.
46 ibid.
47 ibid.

contribute to the many targets established under SDG 4 offers the ability to advance the achievement of the SDGs as well.

SDG 6 – ensure availability and sustainable management of water and sanitation for all

One of the core benefits of the eco smart city model is the ability to deliver basic services and resources to all citizens of the city, including water resources and hygienic sanitation. Thus, SDG 6 is particularly relevant in the eco smart city context and, at the same time, the eco smart city model can be seen as a method through which is achieve the terms of the SDG and associated targets.

Target 6.1, "By 2030, achieve universal and equitable access to safe and affordable drinking water for all,"[48] addresses the needs of all populations, including those in urban areas, for sustainable and sustained water resources. As has been demonstrated in cities, especially large cities, during the Covid-19 pandemic, living in urban areas makes communities and especially vulnerable communities susceptible to water shortages and lack of access to water resources when there are disruptions in the water supply chain.[49] The eco smart city model would assist States in fulfilling Target 6.2 through the use of technology and the encouragement of sustainable practices for the use of water resources. This also ties into the terms of Target 6.4, "By 2030, substantially increase water-use efficiency across all sectors and ensure sustainable withdrawals and supply of freshwater to address water scarcity and substantially reduce the number of people suffering from water scarcity,"[50] and, through the continued use of adaptive technologies and updated information capacities, would allow for the perpetuation of a sustainable city model from the perspective of water resource consumption and water scarcity potential. Relatedly, Target 6.3, "By 2030, improve water quality by reducing pollution, eliminating dumping and minimizing release of hazardous chemicals and materials, halving the proportion of untreated wastewater and substantially increasing recycling and safe reuse globally,"[51] can be advanced through the ecological and

48 United Nations, Sustainable Development Goal 6, <https://sdgs.un.org/goals/goal6> accessed 2 July 2021.
49 See Global Pandemic Network, *supra* note 28.
50 (n 48).
51 ibid.

technical aspects of the eco smart city model, in which increased awareness, transparency and technological capacity come together.

Target 6.2, "By 2030, achieve access to adequate and equitable sanitation and hygiene for all and end open defecation, paying special attention to the needs of women and girls and those in vulnerable situations,"[52] correlates to the aims of promoting safe and efficient waste management services – as part of infrastructural services – that are responsive to the needs of the community at the same time as they are geared toward promoting environmentally friendly solutions.

SDG 7 – ensure access to affordable, reliable, sustainable and modern energy for all

When thinking of the eco smart city model, perhaps one of the most common areas of sustained improvement which comes to mind is the energy sector given the focus of the model on environmental and technological convergence for improved innovation. This convergence echoes in key elements of SDG 7, Target 7.1, "By 2030, ensure universal access to affordable, reliable and modern energy services,"[53] and Target 7.3, "By 2030, double the global rate of improvement in energy efficiency."[54] It must be admitted that the eco smart city model will not, without more, result in the latter target of increases in global energy efficiency. However, as cities which have adopted the eco smart city model into their frameworks, such as Amsterdam and Masdaru, UAE, demonstrate, the changes in energy use and consumption patterns within large urban areas have significant impacts and can act as drivers for the larger energy sector.[55]

SDG 8 – promote sustained, inclusive and sustainable economic growth, full and productive employment and decent work for all

Economic growth and decent work in the smart city at a time of overlapping phenomena: the fourth revolution, the global trend of decarbonisa-

52 ibid.

53 United Nations, Sustainable Development Goal 7, <https://sdgs.un.org/goals/goal7> accessed 2 July 2021.

54 ibid.

55 See Newman, (n 5); Christian Iaione, *The Right to the Co-City*, 9 Italian J. Pub. L. 80 (2017).

tion in the service of climate protection and environmental protection. Work is one of the greatest values in human life. Decent work, decently paid, is the source of human balance and the fuel that gives energy to establish a family, self-development, fulfilment of passions and joy in many aspects of life. It also brings with it individual dignity and mobility, especially for jobs in the technology sector, and also allows communities to benefit from the skills and expertise of their members. Full and productive employment and the ability to access decent work is critical to implementing the eco smart cities model at the foundational level in terms of design, regulation, construction and maintenance as well as the fundamental level in terms of the philosophy behind the model.

Given the necessary symbiosis between SDG 8 and the elements needed for the eco smart city model, it is perhaps not surprising that the majority of articulated targets for SDG 8 intersect. Target 8.1, "Sustain per capita economic growth in accordance with national circumstances and, in particular, at least 7 per cent gross domestic product growth per annum in the least developed countries,"[56] Target 8.2, "Achieve higher levels of economic productivity through diversification, technological upgrading and innovation, including through a focus on high-value added and labour-intensive sectors,"[57] Target 8.3, "Promote development-oriented policies that support productive activities, decent job creation, entrepreneurship, creativity and innovation, and encourage the formalization and growth of micro-, small- and medium-sized enterprises, including through access to financial services,"[58] Target 8.4, "Improve progressively, through 2030, global resource efficiency in consumption and production and endeavour to decouple economic growth from environmental degradation, in accordance with the 10-year framework of programmes on sustainable consumption and production, with developed countries taking the lead,"[59] and Target 8.5, "By 2030, achieve full and productive employment and decent work for all women and men, including for young people and persons with disabilities, and equal pay for work of equal value,"[60] all relate to the foundational and fundamental elements of the eco smart city model in which there is a focus on sustainability of employment, community

56 United Nations, Sustainable Development Goal 8, <https://sdgs.un.org/goals/goal8> accessed 2 July 2021.
57 ibid.
58 ibid.
59 ibid.
60 ibid.

and individuals as well as on environmental concerns and technological development *per se*.

SDG 9 – build resilient infrastructure, promote inclusive and sustainable industrialization and foster innovation

Each of the targets listed under SDG 9 is of considerable importance as a separate objective and at the same time they are inextricably linked in the context of furthering infrastructure, industrialization and innovation as well as advancing the laws, policies and systems needed for the implementation of the eco smart city model. Without technology and innovation there will be no industrialisation, which in turn promotes industrialisation and innovation. All aspects of the smart city concept, better education, decent work, income growth, health care, economic growth, environmental protection, development and strengthening of scientific research, are highly dependent on investment in infrastructure, industrial development and investment in innovation.

Target 9.1, "Develop quality, reliable, sustainable and resilient infrastructure, including regional and transborder infrastructure, to support economic development and human well-being, with a focus on affordable and equitable access for all,"[61] highlights that infrastructure should be durable and of good quality, it should be sustainable but at the same time reliable, it should give people equal access to it but at an affordable price. These are on the surface seemingly difficult to reconcile, let alone to achieve, and yet in many cities they have been turned into action and implemented.[62] This has been achieved by launching a fundamental assumption that infrastructure, modern technologies and good management should form a coherent organism with the inhabitants.[63] Further, it must be remembered that modern infrastructure influences environmental protection, where its intelligent systems, sensor networks, collect data and process them, continuously perform measurements, analyse them automatically creating messages that warn, inform, recommend, about failures, collisions, air quality, or an increased state of harmful substances. Thus, an intelligent city can monitor and react to undesirable phenomena, can

---

61 United Nations, Sustainable Development Goal 9, <https://sdgs.un.org/goals/goal9> accessed 2 July 2021.

62 See, e.g., Newman, (n 5); Iaione, (n 55).

63 See ibid.

identify their sources, can perceive and warn, and as a result counteract and prevent such phenomena in the future.

Target 9.2, "Promote inclusive and sustainable industrialization and, by 2030, significantly raise industry's share of employment and gross domestic product, in line with national circumstances, and double its share in least developed countries,"[64] Target 9.3, "Increase the access of small-scale industrial and other enterprises, in particular in developing countries, to financial services, including affordable credit, and their integration into value chains and markets,"[65] Target 9.4, "By 2030, upgrade infrastructure and retrofit industries to make them sustainable, with increased resource-use efficiency and greater adoption of clean and environmentally sound technologies and industrial processes, with all countries taking action in accordance with their respective capabilities,"[66] and Target 9.5, "Enhance scientific research, upgrade the technological capabilities of industrial sectors in all countries, in particular developing countries, including, by 2030, encouraging innovation and substantially increasing the number of research and development workers per 1 million people and public and private research and development spending"[67] represent a holistic method of understanding the needs of individuals and communities as they strive for industrialization and innovation in sustainable and mutually beneficial ways. The considerations concerning infrastructure, sustainable industry and supporting innovation should be accompanied by a few examples of the implementation of the Smart City concept, where Smart Economy, Smart Living and Smart Governance remain in symbiosis with care for the environment and climate, and where the residents are not only the beneficiaries of intelligent solutions, but are also often their initiators. It is worth emphasising that a large role in the development of sustainable smart cities is played by social capital, which, unlike human capital, is collective in nature, since it defines a community, including interpersonal relations, and not the sum of individual units [68].

---

64 (n 61).
65 ibid.
66 ibid.
67 ibid.
68 Aleksandra Kuzior and Bartosz Sobotka, 47 <https://www-arch.polsl.pl/wydzialy/ROZ/ZN/Documents/smart%20city%202019/Rozdzia%c5%82%203.%20Aleksandra%20Kuzior,%20Bartosz%20Sobotka,%20SPO%c5%81ECZNY%20WYMIAR%20SMART%20CITY.pdf> accessed 2 July 2021.

SDG 11 – make cities and human settlements inclusive, safe, resilient and sustainable

In creating and implementing the eco smart city model, one of the essential elements of law, policy and practice is that the entities being created can provide a place of protection and support for those living and working in them. This is perhaps obvious for any settlement area and even more so given the importance of all aspects of sustainability to the eco smart city model. Thus, SDG 11 represents a key nexus between the SDGs and the eco smart city, particularly for the inclusion and protection of all populations and communities living in such cities.

There is perhaps no better way of understanding this nexus than to examine the articulated targets for SDG 11, namely: Target 11.1, "By 2030, ensure access for all to adequate, safe and affordable housing and basic services and upgrade slums,"[69] Target 11.2, "By 2030, provide access to safe, affordable, accessible and sustainable transport systems for all, improving road safety, notably by expanding public transport, with special attention to the needs of those in vulnerable situations, women, children, persons with disabilities and older persons,"[70] Target 11.3, "By 2030, enhance inclusive and sustainable urbanization and capacity for participatory, integrated and sustainable human settlement planning and management in all countries,"[71] Target 11.6, "By 2030, reduce the adverse per capita environmental impact of cities, including by paying special attention to air quality and municipal and other waste management,"[72] and Target 11.7, "By 2030, provide universal access to safe, inclusive and accessible, green and public spaces, in particular for women and children, older persons and persons with disabilities."[73] Each of these targets represents a fundamental concern of the international community in adopting the SDGs and Agenda 2030, while at the same time represents a critical concern for inclusiveness, protection and responsiveness for all members of an urban community.

---

69 United Nations, Sustainable Development Goal 11, <https://sdgs.un.org/goals/goal11> accessed 2 July 2021.

70 ibid.

71 ibid.

72 ibid.

73 ibid.

SDG 13 – take urgent action to combat climate change and its impacts & SDG 15 – protect, restore and promote sustainable use of terrestrial ecosystems, sustainably manage forests, combat desertification, and halt and reverse land degradation and halt biodiversity loss

At the heart of the eco smart city model is the understanding of how vital environmental preservation and conservation is for all of society, as well as the unique role that cities and urban areas plan in efforts to address climate change. Without this understanding, the model would be very much technology driven but would lack the ability to ensure that technology is used in a way that addresses the key issues facing local, national and international communities.

Taken together, SDG 13 on climate change, which is intended to function in conjunction with the United Nations Framework Convention on Climate Change system, and SDG 15 on life on land have generated a set of targets that inform – and can be implemented by – the eco smart city model. Target 13.2, "Integrate climate change measures into national policies, strategies and planning,"[74] encourages the entrenchment of laws and rules relating to the eco smart city and climate change efforts in a way which offers these cities the opportunity to serve at the forefront of generating new and responsive governance systems alongside technology systems. Much the same is true of Target 13.3, "Improve education, awareness-raising and human and institutional capacity on climate change mitigation, adaptation, impact reduction and early warning,"[75] which can be advanced through the lessons of the eco smart city model.

Additionally, SDG 15 sets out goals for many of the environmental challenges faced by city and urban settlement areas, namely, Target 15.1, "By 2020, ensure the conservation, restoration and sustainable use of terrestrial and inland freshwater ecosystems and their services, in particular forests, wetlands, mountains and drylands, in line with obligations under international agreements,"[76] Target 15.2, "By 2020, promote the implementation of sustainable management of all types of forests, halt deforestation, restore degraded forests and substantially increase afforestation and reforestation globally,"[77] Target 15.3, "By 2030, combat desertification, restore

74 United Nations, Sustainable Development Goal 13, <https://sdgs.un.org/goals/goal13> accessed 2 July 2021 .
75 ibid.
76 United Nations, Sustainable Development Goal 15, <https://sdgs.un.org/goals/goal15> accessed 2 July 2021.
77 ibid.

degraded land and soil, including land affected by desertification, drought and floods, and strive to achieve a land degradation-neutral world,"[78] and Target 15.4, "By 2030, ensure the conservation of mountain ecosystems, including their biodiversity, in order to enhance their capacity to provide benefits that are essential for sustainable development."[79]

SDG 16 – promote peaceful and inclusive societies for sustainable development, provide access to justice for all and build effective, accountable and inclusive institutional at all levels

SDG 16 is one of the fundamental elements of Agenda 2030 and SDGs overall in that it covers such important areas as the protection of life, health, combating violence against children, sexual violence and human trafficking, as well as ensuring access to justice and the rule of law.[80] The concept of Smart Growth, which includes development, support for infrastructure, Smart Living and the Smart Economy, can only come about if the rule of law is taken for granted and the protection of life, health, human rights and the sense of security of the individual is an undisputed overriding good. Without a legal system that provides effective mechanisms of legal protection, without legal security of all areas in a sustainable way, the attempts to implement the concept of Smart City cannot have a chance to succeed.

SDG 17 – strengthen the means of implementation and revitalize the global partnership for sustainable development

The concept of wide-ranging partnerships is critical to SDG 17 and also to implementing the eco smart city model, which requires all aspects of innovation and consumption to work together. In particular, several aspects of SDG emphasise the ability of the eco smart city model to work in tandem with and promote the achievement of the SDGs. These include Target 17.7, "Promote the development, transfer, dissemination and diffusion of environmentally sound technologies to developing countries on favourable terms, including on concessional and preferential terms, as mutually

78 ibid.
79 ibid.
80 United Nations, Sustainable Development Goal 16, <https://sdgs.un.org/goals/goal16> accessed 2 July 2021.

agreed,"[81] Target 17.16, "Enhance the global partnership for sustainable development, complemented by multi-stakeholder partnerships that mobilize and share knowledge, expertise, technology and financial resources, to support the achievement of the sustainable development goals in all countries, in particular developing countries,"[82] and Target 17.17, "Encourage and promote effective public, public-private and civil society partnerships, building on the experience and resourcing strategies of partnerships Data, monitoring and accountability."[83]

4. *Conclusion*

The concept of the eco smart city is constantly developing and this requires a certain amount of flexibility, which intersects well with the spirit and contents of the SDGs as soft law instruments that are intended to be implemented by each State in ways that advance the economic, social and environmental needs of the State's population and the international community. Indeed, the focus of the eco-city concept on "how cities can achieve a better environment through the reduction in air, water and soil pollution and smart waste generation"[84] and on incorporating "a wide range of approaches aiming to turn cities in environmentally sustainable places and at developing communities that respect . . . nature and have sustainable behaviors"[85] corresponds directly to the terms and structure of the SDGs and Agenda 2030. This is true across the swathe of SDGs, although there are necessarily some which are cross-cutting in nature and have more firmly entrenched connections to the eco smart city model.

In promoting the method of environmental sustainability, sustainable development with the parallel implementation of the eco-smart city concept, the chronology of action must not be forgotten. Firstly, quality education, sustainable economic development and, as a result, decent work, which will thus be the natural outcome of such a smart policy. This is also directly linked to economic growth that is shaped in a sustainable way. The promotion of mobility is conducive to the development of an open, multicultural society, and contributes to the removal of mental barriers.

81 United Nations, Sustainable Development Goal 17, <https://sdgs.un.org/goals/goal17> accessed 2 July 2021.
82 ibid.
83 ibid.
84 Iaione, (n 55) at 89.
85 ibid.

From the perspective of the development of smart cities, the implementation of Goal 4 should include appropriately constructed educational programmes, scholarships, training of teachers and academic staff, but also, above all, infrastructure that supports this. It is not only modern school or academic teaching, but the entire urban environment (parks, modern campuses, sports facilities, cultural zones, green zones, etc.) which will support the implementation of the postulate of high-quality education.

An economy based on modern, environmentally friendly technologies, with a high labour intensity rate, a productive economy providing jobs, supporting entrepreneurship and creativity are the basic goals that should guide governments in implementing the Smart City idea. According to Agenda 2030, over the next nine years governments should ensure full productive employment and decent work for all women and men, should strive to ensure employment for young people and people with disabilities. In parallel, programmes should be developed, based on the Just Transition concept, aimed at retraining workers currently employed in sectors related to coal mining. We must not lose sight of the fact that most of the workers currently employed in coal mines, for example, are highly skilled and specialised professionals in occupations such as welders, machine operators, crane operators, electricians. These are skills that can be successfully applied in the eco-industry, especially since they are possessed by workers who are tenacious, accustomed to hard work, resilient, unafraid of the challenges and risks they face on an almost daily basis in the mining industry.

SDG 16 is directly linked to SDG 5 - gender equality - and to SDG 17 - partnership for the achievement of the 2030 Agenda goals, which together form a plan that is very difficult to implement in view of the political situation in the world, conflicts, human rights violations, the isolation of certain areas, and especially if a new challenge is added to this, namely the post-pandemic reality with which the whole world is confronted, and the struggle to stabilise this state of affairs will be spread over the coming years. SDG 16 has thus become even more wide-ranging and capacious, and if we try to put SDG 16 in a short definition, it can be characterised as the protection of the rule of law.

Finally, it must be noted that responses to the pandemic at the legal and policy levels have given rise, arguably with necessity, to a world in which connection and interconnection is a good that is at once intangible and yet highly sought after. This has impacted the ability achieve every aspect of the SDGs, from health to poverty reduction to gender protections to partnerships and beyond. The eco smart city model stands as a potential source of support as the global community emerges from the Covid-19 pandemic, seeks to address the core legal and scientific drivers of the pandemic and its fallout, and attempts to fulfil the obligations it undertook in 2015 as part of the SDGs.

Criminal Liability in the Context of the Functioning of a Smart City

Wojciech Filipkowski <w.filipkowski@uwb.edu.pl>

Rafał Rejmaniak <r.rejmaniak@uwb.edu.pl>
BIAŁYSTOK, Poland

Abstract

The United Nations 2030 Agenda for Sustainable Development goals concern the functioning of individuals, societies, states, and the economy, and human interference with the environment. A smart city concept makes it possible to demonstrate and analyze many problems related to sustainable development in urban areas. This also applies to the use of artificial intelligence, which will manage such a city together with humans or without their active participation. All these issues are challenges for legal science. Moreover, the researchers (including lawyers) must not lose sight of the negative aspects of the actions taken by people and their organizations within that complex environment (including issues of criminal responsibility of humans).

The Authors rise general research questions: What is the concept of a smart city and what is the role of criminal law in this context? Their first goal is to present different roles of humans and AI concerning the functioning of smart cities as well as criminal acts that may be committed. There are e.g., end-users, manufacturers, developers, people responsible for implementing and maintaining services. The Authors present three concepts of attribution of criminal responsibility: decision loop, trustworthy artificial intelligence, and Human-Centered Automation. The criminal aspects related to the operation of completely autonomous AI systems are included in the consideration. Another goal is to present the solutions, reported in the doctrine, to evaluate human behavior in interaction with AI. The Authors discuss two major concepts: man-in-the-loop and man-on-the-loop.

Although these considerations are carried out in the context of the smart city, the Authors are convinced that the conclusions will be useful wherever such interaction is taking place or will take place in the future.

Keywords:
artificial intelligence, smart city, criminal responsibility

1. *Introduction*

The United Nations 2030 Agenda for Sustainable Development contains seventeen laudable goals that the international community would like to achieve over the next decade[1]. These include goals that concern the functioning of individuals, societies, states, and the economy, and human interference with the environment. Of key importance is proper understanding of the term "sustainable" in the context of social development, economic growth, and environmental development. By reference to the 1987 Report of the World Commission on Environment and Development entitled "Our Common Future," the term can be defined as improving the quality of life of people around the world without pillaging the earth's natural resources[2]. These are the two core priorities that are broken down into more specific priorities in the 2030 Agenda. They require differentiated action in different regions of the world in key areas, such as protection of natural resources and the environment, economic growth and equitable distribution of benefits, and human development. The key is to find the right balance between these priorities and areas.

A *smart city* concept, especially one including the environmental aspect of functioning of cities, makes it possible to demonstrate and analyze many problems related to sustainable development in urban areas. This also applies to the use of artificial intelligence in this area, which to a greater or lesser extent will "manage" such a city together with humans or without their active participation[3]. On the other hand, it is beyond dispute that conducting ongoing multidirectional activities (even by dynamically responding to the changes taking place) in order to improve the functioning of a city and the quality of life of its inhabitants will require the support of artificial intelligence.

1 About the Sustainable Development Goals - 'Take Action for the Sustainable Development Goals' <https://www.un.org/sustainabledevelopment/sustainable-development-goals> accessed on 14 April 2020.

2 World Commission on Environment and Development, 'Our Common Future. From one earth to one world' (Report, Annex A/RES/42/187, 11 December 1987).

3 United Nations, 'Artificial intelligence summit focuses on fighting hunger, climate crisis and transition to 'smart sustainable cities' (UN News, 28 May 2019) <https://news.un.org/en/story/2019/05/1039311> accessed on 14 April 2020.

The above idealistic, but also pragmatic, constructive, and progressive, view of the world and interstate relations, which underlies the 2030 Agenda, is a challenge for the legal science. However, while conducting research on a whole range of interrelated problems, one must not lose sight of the negative aspects of the actions taken by people and their organizations[4]. The question that arises is: What is the role of criminal law in this context? To answer this question, reference should be made to classical principles, such as subsidiarity and proportionality. The former indicates the role of criminal law as additional and complementary to the functioning of the legal system created by other branches of law[5]. It is used when other regulations have proved insufficient, but also to strengthen them. If one resorts to criminal law, its impact should be proportional to the criminal act committed[6]. Moreover, a detailed analysis must be made as to whether the application of criminal law norms has any undesirable side effects.

Taking into account the above assumptions, the goal that the authors set for themselves is to indicate the existing principles of criminal law in relation to cases of criminal acts committed by persons performing different roles in the system falling under the general term *smart city*. However, we do not lose sight of the fact that reality - and technology in particular - is changing, and the role of criminal law is also to respond to these changes. Therefore, another goal is to present the ways, reported in the doctrine, to evaluate human behavior in interaction with artificial intelligence. Although these considerations are carried out in the context of the *smart city*, we are convinced that the conclusions will be useful wherever such interaction is taking place or will take place in the future. On the other hand, we will not consider the question of criminal liability of artificial intelligence, because of our firm belief that this is premature[7].

---

4 Sławomir Redo, 'Chapter II. Priorytety Agendy na rzecz Zrównoważonego rozwoju 2030' in Emil Walenty Pływaczewski, Sławomir Redo, Ewa Monika Guzik-Makaruk, Katarzya Laskowska, Wojciech Filipkowski, Ewa Glińska, Emilia Jurgielewicz-Delegacz and Magdalena Perkowska, *Kryminologia, Stan i perspektywy rozwoju, Z uwzględnieniem założeń Agendy ONZ na rzecz zrównoważonego rozwoju 2030* (Wolters Kluwer 2019) 846-847.

5 Jan Kulesza, *Problemy teorii kryminalizacji. Studium z zakresu prawa karnego i konstytucyjnego* (Wydawnictwo Uniwersytetu Łódzkiego 2017) 156; Andrew Ashworth and Jeremy Holder, *Principles of Criminal Law* (7th edn., Oxford University Press 2013) 56.

6 Kulesza (n 5) 37-38; Ashworth and Holder (n 5) 33 (this principle is also referred to as "Criminalization as a last resort").

7 See: Ryan Abbott and Alex Sarch, 'Pushing Artificial Intelligence: Legal Fiction or Science Fiction' (2019) 53 University of California, Davis Law Review 332ff;

2. Assumptions of the smart city concept

2.1. Smart city and the 2030 Agenda

The term *smart city* was first used only in about 1992[8]. It seems, however, that the ranges of meanings presented by particular authors, or those contained in various types of documents issued to date, are different and have changed over the years. It depends on the authors' points of view, their education, the field of science they represent, and the goals set for these publications.

Many authors have made attempts to define the *smart city* concept[9]. One can try to put them on several levels. Smart cities are characterized by widespread presence of innovation processes that lead to creation of new products or improvement of existing products, technological processes, and organizational systems. Innovation as a process goes through a series of stages from idea to application to dissemination. Thus, this is a dynamic phenomenon that is gradually and unevenly implemented in the areas of functioning of a city (or many cities). Its course and intensity also depend on the degree of involvement of stakeholders, i.e. public authorities, inhabitants, private entities (municipal companies, businesses, start-ups), and non-governmental organizations. Another development factor is resources, primarily capital. On the other hand, an important feature of solutions that are being implemented is the aim to improve the quality of life of a city's inhabitants, but also of investors and tourists, through social and economic development. As we recall, these are the priorities of the 2030 Agenda.

Artificial intelligence - being an innovative tool in its own right - can be used to bring innovation to such areas as, for example[10]:

- management of the public sphere of the city - public management;
- offering products or services - e.g. public transport, technology parks;

Gabriel Hallevy, 'The Criminal Liability of Artificial Intelligence Entities - from Science Fiction to Legal Social Control' (2016) 4 Akron Intellectual Property Journal 177ff.

8 'Smart city. What is a smart city?' (Official website of the City of Vienna) <https://www.wien.gv.at/stadtentwicklung/studien/pdf/b008403j.pdf> accessed 14 April 2020.

9 Leonidas G. Anthopoulos, *Understanding Smart Cities: A Tool for Smart Government or an Industrial Trick?* (Springer 2018) 7-12; Alicja Korenik, *Smart cities, Inteligentne miasta w Europie i Azji*, (CeDeWu 2019) 19ff.

10 Korenik (n 9) 21.

- implementation and application of technological solutions - e.g. computerization of the city; and
- financial management - e.g. the provision of services in the form of a public-private partnership.

As the literature rightly points out[11], this concept is usually strongly identified only with implementation of a modern solution of a technological nature (especially IT). This is incorrect and is used by city authorities to serve marketing and promotional purposes. This can also happen with the use of artificial intelligence. The adjective *smart* should mean a greater ability to learn, collaborate, and above all solve problems of cities[12].

When describing the *smart city* concept in the context of the 2030 Agenda, it is impossible not to mention Goal 11, which is to make cities and human settlements inclusive, safe, resilient, and sustainable, and to involve all inhabitants in their functioning. This goal can be achieved by:

- ensuring access for all to adequate, safe, and affordable housing and basic services, and upgrading slums (11.1);
- providing access to safe, affordable, accessible and sustainable transport systems for all, improving road safety, notably by expanding public transport. Special attention should be paid to the needs of those in vulnerable situations, women, children, persons with disabilities and older persons (11.2);
- enhancing inclusive and sustainable urbanization and capacity for participatory, integrated and sustainable human settlement planning and management in all countries (11.3);
- strengthening efforts to protect and safeguard the world's cultural and natural heritage (11.4);
- significantly reducing the number of deaths and the number of people affected, and substantially decrease the direct economic losses relative to global gross domestic product caused by disasters, with a focus on protecting the poor and people in vulnerable situations (11.5);
- reducing the adverse per capita environmental impact of cities, including by paying special attention to air quality and municipal and other waste management (11.6);

---

11 ibid 24.

12 Waleed Ejaz and Alagan Anpalagan, *Internet of Things for Smart Cities* (Springer 2019)2ff; Łukasz Kowalski, 'Inteligentne miasta - przegląd rozwiązań' in Maria Soja and Andrzej Zborowski (eds), *Miasto w badaniach geografów* (Wydawnictwo Uniwersytetu Jagiellońskiego 2015) 105.

- providing easy and universal access to safe, inclusive, and accessible, green and public spaces, in particular for women and children, older persons and persons with disabilities (11.7);
  - supporting positive economic, social and environmental links between urban, suburban, and rural areas by strengthening national and regional development planning (11.a);
  - significantly increasing the number of cities and human settlements adopting and implementing integrated policies and plans towards inclusion, resource efficiency, mitigation and adaptation to climate change, resilience to disasters; and developing and implementing, in line with the Sendai Framework for Disaster Risk Reduction 2015-2030, holistic disaster risk management at all levels (11.b).

It can be assumed that artificial intelligence can make a significant contribution to achievement of these goals. This is due to the fact that having adequate computing power, access to data and information, as well as appropriate algorithms, it is able to forecast the effects of possible actions to be taken and to estimate to what extent these actions will achieve the objectives[13].

2.2. *Smart areas*

For a more complete analysis of the problem, it is also necessary to point out specific areas that allow evaluating the quality of services provided by cities and the quality of life in cities. In this respect, reference can be made to the set of ISO 37122:2019 standards (and earlier the ISO 3720:2014 standards), which are the result of cooperation between the European Union, the International Organization for Standardization in Geneva, and national standardization bodies. This is also an object of analyses carried out by experts[14]. Of the dozens of possible indicators, the following 17 are listed: education; fire and emergency response; safety; environment; economics; finance; recreation; health; telecommunications and innovation;

---

13 Thales, 'Secure, sustainable smart cities and the IoT' <https://www.gemalto.com/iot/inspired/smart-cities> accessed 27 February 2021.

14 Ejaz and Anpalagan (n 12) 2ff.

transportation; governance; energy; shelter; solid waste; water and sewers; wastewater; and urban planning[15].

All of them are important for raising the quality of life of city dwellers. What can be defined as the legal interests protected by criminal law are availability, integrity, and confidentiality in relation to a service in the broadest sense, updating the position represented in the doctrine of computer criminal law[16]. Firstly, it is in the interest of both the inhabitants themselves and the providers of services in these areas that they are available for use at any time and in the manner expected. Secondly, the integrity of a service (and in particular its associated data and information) is that no changes are made to it by unauthorized persons. They should be exactly as their suppliers assume and complete so as to perform some tasks effectively and keep them in proper condition. Thirdly, only authorized persons may have access to them. Modern information technology systems provide for different roles and associated ranges of authorizations to make changes to services, including, for example, entering, changing, or deleting data and information.

From the point of view of criminal law, four questions are relevant: To what extent were the above-mentioned interests violated or were they put at risk of indirect or direct infringement (state of danger)? What socially unacceptable consequences did the behavior cause? Who committed this act and what was his or her role in the system? How should the behavior be classified?

3. *Selected technological issues*

In the legal considerations being carried out, certain assumptions have to be made regarding technological issues:

- building a *smart city* will be done in a various ways for each area; at the moment individual cities around the world are implementing elements

15 'ISO 3720:2018. Sustainable development of communities — Indicators for city services and quality of life' (*International Organization for Standardization*, July 2017) <https://www.iso.org/standard/68498.html> accessed 14 April 2020.

16 Cf.: Andrzej Adamski, *Prawo karne komputerowe* (C. H. Beck 2000) 41-42.

of such systems[17], but so far they are choosing those that are most important to them[18];

- certainly, the very architecture of the system will have a modular nature: individual *smart* areas will ultimately constitute a functional whole, but at the same time they will be based on common data or will exchange data for more efficient functioning; individual modules will be upgradeable or exchangeable with others;
- the system will be distributed and network-centric;
- the implemented solutions will have different levels of automation and, in the future, different levels of artificial intelligence[19].

It seems that at the moment, the following technologies will be crucial for the functioning of current and future *smart cities*[20]:

- energy management on the scale from individual appliances, buildings, neighborhoods, up to the critical infrastructure of the city, which determines the use of any processes[21];
- transport management in the public spaces of cities, e.g. smart traffic lights, parking lots, and vehicles, all the way to synchronization of a multimodal transport system in the city and its surroundings[22];

---

17 Ejaz and Anpalagan (n 12) 11-14.

18 Richard van Hooijdonk, 'Top 10 smart cities that use tech to transform urban life' (Richard van Hooijdonk blog, 9 December 2019) <https://www.richardvanhooijdonk.com/blog/en/top-10-smart-cities-that-use-tech-to-transform-urban-life> accessed 14 April 2020.

19 Thomas B. Sheridan and Raja Parasuraman, 'Human-Automation Interaction' (2006) 1 Reviews of Human Factors and Ergonomics 89-129.

20 Cf. Mahashreveta Choudhary, 'Six technologies crucial for smart cities' (Geospatial world, 19 November 2019) <https://www.geospatialworld.net/blogs/six-technologies-crucial-for-smart-cities> accessed 14 April 2020; Teena Maddox, 'Smart cities: 6 essential technologies' (TechRepublic, 1 August 2016) <https://www.techrepublic.com/article/smart-cities-6-essential-technologies> accessed 14 April 2020./

21 George Koutitas, 'The Smart Grid: Anchor of the Smart City' in Stan McCleallan, Jesus A. Jimenez and George Koutitas (eds) *Smart Cities, Applications, Technologies, Standards, and Driving Factors* (Springer 2018) 53 ff.

22 Jesus A. Jimenez, 'Smart Transportation Systems' in Stan McCleallan, Jesus A. Jimenez and George Koutitas (eds) Smart *Cities, Applications, Technologies, Standards, and Driving Factors* (Springer 2018) 123 ff.

- efficient and secure (using e.g. *blockchain*) acquisition, collection, and analysis of large amounts of data (*big data*) and real-time decision-making (e.g. cloud computing[23]);
- *smart internet of things* - individual modules will have different levels of autonomy in their functioning in the system[24]; their basic functions are to acquire data and information (sensors[25]) or to put it into the system, transfer it to the elements dealing with collecting and further processing, as well as manipulators and switches, which make changes in the real world[26].

Each of the above technologies, in addition to its advantages, also leads to certain challenges, and in its extreme form also to dangers[27]. When used not in accordance their intended purpose, they can violate socially acceptable interests. This includes, for example, the life and health of their users; their freedom or privacy; the availability, integrity, and confidentiality of services, or the safety of individual users (or groups of users). It does not matter whether the perpetrator of these violations is public authorities, criminals, or other users of the elements that make up the entire *smart city* system. Besides, due to the interconnections between individual modules and areas, violations and threats in one part of the system can relatively easily spread to others and affect every person or organization operating in it. If only for this reason, research should be undertaken into the shaping of the criminal liability of the system participants.

---

23 Brad Booth, 'The Cloud: A Critical Smart City Asset' in Stan McCleallan, Jesus A. Jimenez and George Koutitas (eds) *Smart Cities, Applications, Technologies, Standards, and Driving Factors* (Springer 2018) 97 ff.

24 Ejaz and Anpalagan (n 12) 5 ff.

25 Soumia Bellaouar, Mohamed Guerroumi, Abdelouahid Derhan and Samira Moussaoui, 'Towards Heterogeneous Architectures of Hybrid Vehicular Sensor Networks for Smart Cities' in Zaigham Mahmood (ed) *Smart Cities, Development and Governance Frameworks* (Springer 2018)51 ff.

26 Raja Parasuraman, Thomas B. Sheridan and Christopher D. Wickens, 'A Model for Types and Levels of Human Interaction with Automation' (2000) 30 IEEE Transactions on Systems Man and Cybernetics - Part A Systems and Humans 286-97.

27 Amrita Ghosal and Subir Halder, 'Chapter 5. Building Intelligent Systems for Smart Cities: Issues, Challenges and Approaches' in Zaigham Mahmood (ed) *Smart Cities, Development and Governance Frameworks* (Springer 2018) 119-120.

4. *Basic problems of liability of smart city component users*

4.1. *Concepts of attribution of responsibility for a result to a human*

Cooperation of a human with particular *smart city* modules can be shaped in different ways depending on the level of autonomy of the systems used in them: from treating such system as mere tools in the hands of a human, through cooperation of a human with the systems, to complete autonomy of the systems in making decisions and their implementation. Defining the role of humans and the tasks they are charged with is one of the fundamental challenges in the design and use of smart systems. One of the key issues in this regard is the problem of assigning responsibility - of whatever nature - for the effects caused by the operation of such systems. In the following sections, the decision loop, the concept of trustworthy artificial intelligence, and Human-Centered Automation will be presented.

4.1.1. *Decision loop*

The decision loop concept is used mainly to define the relationship between humans and the so-called systems with progressive autonomy of a military nature (*Lethal Autonomous Weapon Systems - LAWS*)[28], but it can also be successfully applied to *smart city* components. It distinguishes three models of the relationship between humans and systems. The first model, called man-in-the-loop, describes a situation in which systems have no freedom of action. Humans, on the other hand, control the systems and make decisions[29] or authorize them before they are implemented[30]. Humans are directly responsible for the operation of the systems. The systems themselves are a tool in the hands of the operators, like a hammer or a screwdriver. An example of this type of cooperation between humans and systems is the use of a remotely controlled drone by its operator.

---

28 Jeffrey J. Caton, *Autonomous Weapon Systems: A Brief Survey of Developmental, Operational, Legal, and Ethical Issues* (United States Army War College Press 2015) 3-4; Ajey Lele, 'Debating Lethal Autonomous Weapons Systems' (2019) 13 Journal of Defense Studies 55-56; William C. Marra and Sonia K. McNeil, 'Understanding "The Loop": Regulating the Next Generation of War Machines' (2012) 36 Harvard Journal of Law & Public Policy 1141-1142.

29 Noel Sharkey, 'Saying 'No!' to Lethal Autonomous Targeting' (2010) 9 Journal of Military Ethics 370.

30 Lele (n 28) 55-56.

The second model describes a situation where systems act autonomously: they make and implement "decisions" without an active role played by humans. Humans do not take part in the decision-making process, but they supervise the operation of the system and can interrupt it ("veto") when they consider it necessary. In this model, referred to as man-on-the-loop, humans are responsible for preventing the systems from implementing wrong decisions.

This concept is further distinguished by a third model, referred to as man-out-of-the-loop. In this model, the system operates completely autonomously with no human oversight. The role of humans is merely to give the system commands or define its tasks. However, humans do not have the power to stop its operation. This model is controversial as it raises significant problems in terms of the possibility of attributing responsibility for the "actions" of the systems to humans. Humans do not know how the systems will perform the set tasks, and have no way to react when unforeseen circumstances arise or when the systems behave differently than in the assumed scenario. Advocates of full autonomy of the systems try to create algorithms to ensure proper operation of the systems in unforeseen circumstances[31].

In characterizing this concept, it should be added that the systems may exhibit different levels of autonomy in their performance of different tasks. The decision-making process can be decomposed into smaller parts, e.g., based on Boyd's loop ("OODA Loop")[32], which divides the decision-making process into 4 components: observe (data collection), orient (analysis), decide, and act. At the different stages of the decision-making process, the system may have varying degrees of autonomy. For example, it can be completely autonomous in the observe and orient stages, and supervised by a human in the decide and act stages[33].

31 Ronald C. Arkin, Patrick Ulam and Brittany Duncan, 'An Ethical Governor for Constraining Lethal Action in an Autonomous System' (Technical Report GIT-GVU-09-02, Georgia Institute of Technology Atlanta Mobile Robot Lab, 2009).

32 A diagram of the Boyd's loop is available at: Boyd JR, 'The Essence of Winning and Losing' (September 2012) <https://fasttransients.files.wordpress.com/2010/03/essence_of_winning_losing.pdf> accessed on 14 April 2020.

33 Marraand McNeil (n 28) 1146-1147.

4.1.2. Trustworthy artificial intelligence

As for determination of the appropriate entity and the grounds for attributing criminal liability to it for the negative effects on legal interests caused by the operation of *smart city* components, it should be emphasized once again that these components usually use artificial intelligence systems to a greater or lesser extent. It is the characteristics of artificial intelligence systems, which may be their advantages, that also cause significant difficulties in determining the entity responsible for their actions. These systems have the capacity to learn and exhibit autonomy from the human interacting with them[34]. Furthermore, it is sometimes impossible to determine why an AI system made a particular decision[35].

Recognition of these problems has led the European Union to formulate and practically develop the concept of "trustworthy artificial intelligence". Seven requirements have been formulated as a part of the development of basic European standards for the design and use of AI systems[36]:

- human agency and oversight;
- technical robustness and safety;
- privacy and data governance;
- transparency;
- diversity, non-discrimination, and fairness;
- social and environmental wellbeing; and
- accountability.

With respect to conditions directly related to accountability for the actions of such systems, the European Commission indicated that one of the key requirements is to ensure an appropriate degree of control measures depending on the specific AI system and its area of application[37]. In addition, such systems should be assessed by both internal and external auditors,

34 See: Tomasz Zalewski, 'Definicja sztucznej inteligencji' in Luigi Lai and Marek Świerczyński (eds) *Prawo sztucznej inteligencji* (C. H. Beck 2020) 11.

35 See for example: Anna Kasperska, 'Problemy zastosowania sztucznych sieci neuronalnych w praktyce prawniczej' (2017) 11 Przegląd Prawa Publicznego 25.

36 Commission, 'White Paper on Artificial Intelligence. A European approach to excellence and trust', COM (2020) 65 final 11.

37 Commission, 'Communication from the Commission to the European Parliament, the Council, the European Economic and Social Committee and the Committee of the Regions - Building Trust in Human Centric Artificial Intelligence', COM (2019) 168 final 5.

and any potential adverse effects of the use of such systems should be identified, assessed, and documented[38].

The High Level Expert Group on Artificial Intelligence established by the European Commission in 2018, with respect to the condition of ensuring a oversight human role, indicated that such oversight can take place in different ways, according to the principle of human participation (*human-in-the-loop* (HITL) - assuming the possibility of human intervention in each decision cycle of the system), the principle of human intervention (*human-on-the-loop* (HOTL) - assuming the possibility of human intervention during the system design cycle and monitoring of the system operation), or the principle of human control (*human-in-command* (HIC) - the possibility of only supervising the general functioning of the system and deciding when and how the system will be used)[39]. The need to meet the condition of ensuring an oversight role for humans was also indicated in the Policy for the development of artificial intelligence in Poland until 2020[40].

4.1.3. Human-Centered Automation

Another concept that should be pointed at is *Human-Centered Automation* (HCA). Its basis is the assumption that systems must be designed to cooperate with humans or to interact with them in other ways[41]. According to this concept, humans are responsible for proper functioning of systems. Consequently, systems should be designed in such a way that the human operator is in command in this collaboration (although the implementation of this assumption in individual cases may cause some difficulties[42]). This is possible when the operator is involved in the operation of the sys-

---

38 ibid 7.

39 High-Level Expert Group on Artificial Intelligence, 'Ethics Guidelines for Trustworthy Artificial Intelligence' (2019) 20.

40 Resolution no. 196 of the Council of Ministers of 28 December 2020 on establishing the "Policy for the development of artificial intelligence in Poland until 2020," Monitor Polski 2021, item 23, Annex, 66.

41 Sheridan and Parasuraman (n 19) 94.

42 Toshiyuki Inagaki, 'Design of human-machine interactions in light of domain dependence of human centered automation' (2006) 8 Cognition, Technology & Work 164.

tem and is duly informed of the principles of its operation[43]. This concept also requires that the operation of the system is predictable and that the human ability to monitor it is real[44]. In addition, the system should also monitor human behavior and both the system and its operator should communicate their "intentions" in the task undertaken (what they intend to achieve)[45].

4.2. *The question of full autonomy of systems*

In addition to the concepts of human-system interaction presented above, other stances can be found. It seems reasonable to mention the increasingly clear view that the most desirable state is full autonomy of systems, especially with regard to artificial intelligence. Although it is difficult to assume nowadays that full autonomy could characterize cooperation of humans with various systems in general, this assumption can be developed in some fields.

The idea of striving for a fully autonomous system guides, for example, developers of the concept of autonomous vehicles that drive, sail, or fly[46]. Developing this concept may be important for the functioning of *smart cities*[47]. Dissemination of such vehicles will change the urban landscape (less space will be used for parking), reduce emissions, decrease congestion, and the vehicles themselves can also be used for public transport[48]. At the same time, the problem of legal regulation of the functioning of such solutions is becoming more and more urgent. The legal solutions obtained

---

43 Charles E. Billings, 'Human-Centered Aviation Automation: Principles and Guidelines' (NASA Technical Memorandum 110381, Ames Research Center, February1996) 8 ff.

44 See for example: Cheng Zhang and others, 'Human-centered automation for resilient nuclear power plant outage control' (2017) 82 Automation in Construction 182.

45 Billings (n 43) 11 ff.

46 Cf.: Tomasz Neumann, 'Perspektywy wykorzystania pojazdów autonomicznych w transporcie drogowym w Polsce' (2018) 19 Autobusy 787-788; 'Dronomat zamiast paczkomatu. Czy wkrótce niebo zaroi się od dronów?' (*Rozmowy Instytutu Nowej Europy* on Anchor.fm, 10 June 2020) <https://anchor.fm/instytutnowejeuropy/episodes/Dronomat-zamiast-paczkomatu--Czy-wkrtce-niebo-zaroi-si-od-dronw-ef77ru> accessed 27 February 2021.

47 Testing of autonomous vehicles is one of the indicators for evaluating smart cities in the *Global Smart City Performance Index*. See: Korenik (n 9) 32.

48 Neuman (n 46) 789-790.

in this way can provide experience and possibly be a starting point for the development of further standards for other systems of this type.

However, it should be emphasized that the concept of full autonomy currently faces a number of difficult and as yet unresolved issues concerning the question of attribution of responsibility for the effects caused by such systems[49]. In a situation where there is no human being who could bear responsibility for the damage caused by such a system, the following questions arise: Can the system itself be a subject capable of bearing responsibility? On what principles would it be liable? Would it be entitled to any guarantees and rights? What sanctions could be imposed on it? Although the discussion regarding these problems has already begun, it seems premature to consider the possibility of attributing legal liability (including criminal liability) to the system itself in the current conditions[50]. However, the issue of manufacturers or suppliers of such solutions and their liability remains open.

4.3. Scope of responsibilities of system users

The entity involved in performance of the tasks of a smart system is its user. The user can be defined as the entity that has purchased and implemented, and is using the system (a legal person, e.g. a company under private law or local government bodies). Typically, the functioning of such a system is further based on its cooperation with or supervision by a human (operator). Another category of system users is people who only use products or services that have already been implemented, e.g. residents of *smart cities*. In the following discussion, we will analyze the first example, because people act on behalf of the legal entity that implements a system.

The responsibilities of an entity that uses an information-technology system can be divided into responsibility to ensure proper operation of the system itself, responsibility to ensure competence of the operators and supervisors of the system, and responsibility to establish appropriate security procedures in case of a threat. The first category of responsibilities includes ensuring proper control and authorization of access to the system,

---

49 See for example: Sabine Gless, Emily Silverman and Thomas Weigend, 'If Robots Cause Harm, Who is to Blame? Self-Driving Cars and Criminal Liability' (2016) 19 New Criminal Law Review 412–436.

50 Cf. Gabriel Hallevy, *Liability for Crimes Involving Artificial Intelligence Systems* (Springer 2015) 229; Woodrow Barfield and Ugo Pagallo, *Advanced Introduction to Law and Artificial Intelligence* (Edward Elgar Publishing 2020) 120-121.

use of encryption (e.g. *blockchain*), regular security audits by an external entity[51], and making sure to update the system and maintain it.

The second category of responsibilities on the part of the entity that uses a system is to ensure that the people who work with or oversee it are adequately prepared. It is therefore necessary that these persons are properly trained and have sufficient skills to carry out the tasks they are charged with. This is the necessary condition of real, and not only formal, human participation in the decision-making process carried out by the system. The literature on human interaction with smart systems analyzes many undesirable phenomena that need to be addressed. These include:

- excessive confidence in the operation of the system (*overreliance*)[52];
- lack of situation awareness when a human oversees the system[53], and
- loss of the skills needed when taking control of the system's tasks (*deskilling*)[54].

The entity that implements a smart system should also define the internal procedures to deal with malfunctions that[55] should be communicated to those working with it.

Another important responsibility of the entity that using a smart system is to collect and secure logs. In a situation where the operation of the system has caused damage, analysis of previously stored data may make it possible to determine the cause of the event, to detect anomalies in the operation of the system, and to trace and evaluate the actions taken by the operator[56].

In contrast, the responsibilities of a human interacting with an smart system may take different forms depending on the characteristics of the system in question. If the system shows a low degree of autonomy, e.g. it only suggests taking an action on the basis of analyzed data, the human

---

51 Indu B. Singh and Joseph N. Pelton, 'The cyber city of the future' (2013) 47 The Futurist 23.

52 Sheridan and Parasuraman (n 19) 98-100.

53 Mica R. Endsley, 'Automation and situation awareness' in Raja Parasuraman and Mustapha Mouloua (eds) *Automation and Human Performance. Theory and Applications* (reprint, CRC Press 2009) 178.

54 John D. Lee and Bobbie D. Seppelt, 'Human factors and ergonomics in automation design' in Gavriel Salvendy (ed) *Handbook of Human Factors and Ergonomics* (John Wiley & Sons 2012) 1616, 1617.

55 Zubair A. Baig and others, 'Future challenges for smart cities: Cyber-security and digital forensics' (2017) 22 Digital Investigation 7.

56 Ben Shneiderman, 'Human Responsibility for Autonomous Agents' (2007) 22 IEEE Intelligent Systems 61.

make the decisions, while the system itself should be treated as a mere tool used to perform its tasks. Assuming that the system works properly and collects the appropriate data, it will act as an "adviser", but making the final decision and taking the right action (or giving instructions for such action) will be the responsibility of the operator[57]. It is therefore important for the human to be aware of the role of the smart system as a decision support and its limitations (e.g., in terms of the tasks for which it was designed or the probability of the forecasts it formulates). Otherwise, the operator who formally decides to take certain actions will in fact be just a "human stamp" authorizing the decisions of the system, without the possibility of their assessment. However, the use of an advisory system may give rise to the temptation for its users to treat the system as a decision-making authority. Such a system would thus provide a mental "moral buffer" against responsibility for making difficult decisions, giving the illusion that it is the system, and not the person, that is responsible for the consequences of the choice made[58]. Depending on the specific nature of the operator's tasks and the purpose of the system used[59], the content of his or her duties should be defined in an agreement with his or her employer.

The situation is slightly different when the system has greater autonomy. The human then plays the role of a supervisor and his or her primary task is to monitor whether the system is functioning properly. The responsibilities of such a person should therefore include interrupting the system when it performs its tasks incorrectly (*mitigating the failure*). Depending on the specific characteristics of the system, this may involve, for example, an obligation to turn off the system, stop the implementation of the decision made by the system (*veto*)[60], or take control of the task and implement it "manually" (in systems that use *adaptable automation*[61]). Again, however, it is important to note that the supervisor must be properly trained and competent. Lack of sufficient knowledge and experience can lead to situations where the supervisor fails to notice an existing problem in the performance of the system, although he or she should notice it (*omission error*), or, without due verification, considers the operation of the

57 Mary L. Cummings, 'Automation and Accountability in Decision Support System Interface Design' (2006) 32 The Journal of Technology Studies 28.

58 ibid 26.

59 Ben Wagner, 'Liable, but Not in Control? Ensuring Meaningful Human Agency in Automated Decision-Making Systems' (2019) 11 Policy & Internet 115, 117.

60 Shneiderman (n 56) 60-61.

61 Lee and Seppelt (n 54) 1626-1627.

system to be correct when, in light of other existing data, it would appear to be faulty (*commission error*)[62].

5. *Selected specific problems of criminal liability of users of smart city components*

The issue of assignment of criminal liability for exposure or infringement of legal interests caused by smart systems is a challenge for the science of criminal law. The tendency to blame the operator for any malfunctions of the system also causes difficulties[63]. When examining the issue of criminal liability of a system operator or supervisor (understood as an individual) for the operation of the system, two models of interaction between humans and smart systems must be distinguished. Using the decision loop concept, these can be referred to as *man-in-the-loop* and *man-on-the-loop*.

When analyzing the principles of criminal liability of the user of a smart system for the effects caused by that system, it should be noted that liability incurred by a human operator or supervisor is only one possibility. There is also the possibility of civil liability of both individuals and legal persons. However, this issue is beyond the scope of this paper.

5.1. *Man-in-the-loop*

In the first case, it is the human who is in control of the system and who makes the decisions, so he or she is directly responsible for the effects caused by the decisions. An offence committed in such conditions is generally be a crime of commission. The effect of exposing or violating a legal interest to danger is the result of the perpetrator's active behavior. Depending on the specific situation, the user's criminal liability may take different forms.

If the operator consciously made a decision, knowing that its execution would cause the damage (he or she knew it and wanted to commit a criminal act, or although he or she did not want to commit it, he or she

---

62 Linda J. Skitka, Kathleen Mosier and Mark D. Burdick, 'Accountability and automation bias' (2000) 52 International Journal of Human-Computer Studies 701-702.

63 Karen Hao, 'When algorithms mess up, the nearest human gets the blame' (MIT Technology Review, 28 May 2019) <https://www.technologyreview.com/2019/05/28/65748/ai-algorithms-liability-human-blame> accessed on 26 April 2020.

accepted it), he or she committed an intentional act and used the system as an instrument of crime. Examples of such offences are murder, causing loss of health, causing a disaster, or putting in danger.

Much more difficulties are caused by a situation in which the user acted unintentionally, i.e. when he or she anticipated the possibility of committing a prohibited act and groundlessly believed that he or she would manage to avoid it, or did not anticipate such a possibility at all, although he or she could have and should have foreseen it (provided that the legislator allows for the possibility of incurring criminal liability for an unintentional offence). The user, by contract (or certain regulations), assumes the obligation to perform certain tasks (*task responsibility*)[64]. If, nevertheless, the constitutive elements of the offence are present and a cause and effect relationship has been established between the operator's conduct and the result, it is necessary to examine whether the operator complied with the precautionary rules required in these circumstances. They may be defined by e.g. the rules of system use defined by its supplier or internal procedures to be followed when carrying a given task. An example is the requirement to verify the system's suggestions on the basis of independent data instead of unreflective acceptance of the recommended solutions[65].

Determination of criminal liability for unintentional crimes, however, involves significant challenges that need to be met. The first is the possibility of assigning criminal responsibility to the operator when the required response time in a dynamic environment has exceeds the biological capabilities of a human being. Various smart systems can perform tasks at different speeds. According to the criterion of the system response time, tasks can be divided into strategic - in which the time of task completion is specified in minutes-days, tactical - in which the response time is from 5 seconds to several minutes, and operational - which are performed in less than 5 seconds[66]. Systems (primarily those using artificial intelligence) that perform the tasks assigned to them in real time may require extremely fast human response. On the one hand, it is the task of the system supplier to design a system suitable for the human perceptual capabilities. On the other hand, it is impossible to predict all situations in the dynamic environment in which the system will be used. For example, it may be

64 Giuseppe Contissa, 'Automation and Liability: an Analysis in the Context of Socio-Technical Systems' (2017) 11 i-lex 20-21.

65 ibid 23.

66 Lee and. Seppelt (n 54) 1625.

necessary to suspend instructions given to the system due to an unforeseen change in the situation that requires a change in the operator's decision. It seems that in such cases it should be examined whether the operator was objectively able to avoid the effect, because if this was not the case, the operator is not liable under criminal law, because one cannot require him or her to do something that is impossible.

Further problems may arise from multiple operators and smart systems working in parallel. It may happen that an isolated decision of a particular operator does not in itself turn out to be wrong. Instead, only in a specific situational setting created by a simultaneous operation of multiple systems and operators its fallacy becomes apparent. System malfunctions can be the result of the sum of independent errors made by different operators or people on different levels of the organizational hierarchy. In other words - a theoretically correct decision made in a certain factual situation can cause a damage resulting from the existence of a network of interdependencies between different elements of the system (systems) that created at a given moment an arrangement that is conducive to the occurrence of damage ("*a many hands problem*")[67].

5.2. Man-on-the-loop

The second category of cases are situations where the system has a higher degree of autonomy and makes decisions on its own, while the human monitors the performance of the task. Thus, the user assumes the position of a supervisor, passively observing the system, and is obliged to interrupt its operation in case of a threat (and possibly to take control manually).

Where the operation of the system puts in danger or violates interests protected by criminal law, the supervisor may be accused of failing to stop the operation when he or she could and should have done so. Failure to fulfill the duties (breach of precautionary rules) imposed on the supervisor constitutes grounds for attributing criminal liability to him or her. The human is thus the guarantor of non-occurrence of the effect. Under criminal law, a guarantor is a person who is under a specific legal obligation to prevent an effect that is a constitutive element of a given type of crime. The specific nature of the obligation means that its addressee is not everyone, but only those who have certain characteristics that distinguish them

67 Contissa (n 64) 29.

due to the relation to the interest protected by a legal norm[68]. The legal nature, on the other hand, indicates that the obligation must be grounded in law[69]. Although there is a dispute in the doctrine of criminal law as to what may be the source of such a duty, the catalog of such sources indicates a statute and a voluntary acceptance of a duty to prevent an effect (e.g. an employment contract)[70].

If the supervisor allows a damage caused by the smart system to occur by failing to stop its operation, he or she may be criminally liable for a crime of omission. The accusation against the supervisor, however, does not concern the fact that he or she caused the effect, but the fact that he or she did not take the necessary steps to prevent such an effect, although he or she was legally obliged to do so. It should be emphasized that such liability could be incurred by the supervisor only if the effect[71] could have been objectively foreseen and prevented[72]. This is because a guarantor cannot be required to do something that cannot be done[73]. Otherwise the form of his or her responsibility would be dangerously close to the construction of objective responsibility, independent of the existence of fault, which has been gradually abandoned since the Middle Ages[74]. Liability for culpable acts, on the other hand, is the foundation of modern criminal law, expressed synthetically in the *nullum crimen sine culpa* principle[75].

---

68 Maciej Kliś, 'Źródła obowiązku gwaranta w polskim prawie karnym' (1999) 2 Czasopismo Prawa Karnego i Nauk Penalnych 173.

69 Alicja Grześkowiak, 'Komentarz do art. 2 k.k.' in Alicja Grześkowiak, and Krzysztof Wiak (eds.), *Kodeks karny. Komentarz* (6th edn, C. H. Beck 2018) 50-51;Kliś (n 68) 170.

70 Grześkowiak (n 69) 51.

71 Jacek Giezek, 'Teorie związku przyczynowego oraz koncepcje obiektywnego przypisania' in Ryszard Dębski (ed.), *System prawa karnego, tom 3: Nauka o przestępstwie. Zasady odpowiedzialności* (C. H. Beck 2017) 547-548.

72 Andrzej Zoll, 'Komentarz do art. 2 k.k.' in Włodzimierz Wróbel and Andrzej Zoll (eds) *Kodeks karny. Część ogólna. Tom I. Komentarz do art. 1-52* (Wolters Kluwer 2016) 89; Damian Tokarczyk, 'Obowiązek gwaranta w prawie karnym' (2014) 76 Ruch Prawniczy, Ekonomiczny i Socjologiczny 211.

73 Tokarczyk (n 72) 208.

74 Robert Zawłocki, 'Pojęcie przestępstwa' in Ryszard Dębski (ed.), *System prawa karnego, tom 3: Nauka o przestępstwie. Zasady odpowiedzialności* (CH Beck 2017) 52; Wacław Urszczak, *Historia Państwa i Prawa Polskiego. Tom I (966-1795)* (Wolters Kluwer 2013) 115.

75 Andrzej Zoll, 'Komentarz do art. 1 k.k.' in Włodzimierz Wróbel and Andrzej Zoll (eds.), *Kodeks karny. Część ogólna. Tom I. Komentarz do art. 1-52* (Wolters Kluwer 2016) 76.

It should be emphasized that the guarantor's liability does not exclude the possibility that the manufacturer of the system is also liable for the effect caused. However, determination of whether, in fact, the circumstances in which the system made a faulty decision could have been objectively foreseen at the system design stage continues to be a challenge[76].

The legal consequences of a system supervisor's omission may vary depending on whether the guarantor took any measures to counteract the effect and whether these were adequate to eliminate the danger, what his or her intent was, what effect materialized, whether it is possible to assess from a hindsight perspective how the danger would have been affected if he or she had taken appropriate action[77].

However, if the supervisor takes over the tasks of the system to perform them manually, the he or she assumes the role of a direct operator (*man-in-the-loop*), with all the consequences this entails.

6. Conclusion

As has been shown, the basic issue that determines the scope of criminal liability of an individual is the specific design of the system in which human interaction with artificial intelligence takes place. In the case of the *smart city* concept, we assumed that the system will have a modular structure and its individual components (services, products) will be at different levels of implementation of automated solutions up to those using artificial intelligence. This assumption results from an observation and analysis of the practice of implementation of this concept to date. The human role in each module may vary depending on the level of autonomy of the systems used in them.

This influences the specification of the duties of a human operator or supervisor of such smart modules, subsystems, services, products, etc. At the same time, it is a challenge for both the designers of individual system components (e.g. by defining the principles of task allocation between the human and the system and of conflict resolution - if any conflicts are allowed) and the entity that implements and uses them (e.g. ensuring proper system configuration, training for operators, and counteracting negative

76 Wojciech Filipkowski, 'Prawo karne wobec sztucznej inteligencji' in Luigi Lai and Marek Świerczyński (eds) *Prawo sztucznej inteligencji* (C. H. Beck 2020) 124-125.

77 Tokarczyk (n 72) 211-212.

phenomena occurring during cooperation between the human and the system).

So far, various concepts have been developed to define the principles of human-system interaction. Some of them require constant present of a human in the decision-making process of the system and the human's responsibility for the system's operation (Trustworthy Artificial Intelligence, *Human-Centered Automation*). There are also proposals to develop full autonomy of systems. *Human-out-of-the-loop* is one of the models in the decision loop concept; this direction is also adopted in the design of autonomous vehicles. From the standpoint of criminal law, which is based on human responsibility for prohibited acts and requires the presence of guilt (a person is accused the fact that in the situation in which he or she found himself, he or she could and should have behaved differently than he or she did), allowing fully autonomous systems to function would generate hitherto unresolved significant problems in determining the subject to whom responsibility should be attributed if the constitutive elements of a crime are in place.

For systems with a low degree of autonomy (falling within the *man-in-the-loop* model), the operator is responsible for the effects they cause. In such a situation, a systems is used as a tool (e.g. an "adviser" in decision making or an "executor" of a command given by a human). When humans cooperate with systems with higher levels of autonomy, humans assume the role of supervisors. The concept of a guarantor present in criminal law can be successfully used to determine the principles of a human's liability. This concept makes it possible to accuse the supervisor of failing to prevent the occurrence of an effect in a certain situation when he or she was legally obliged to do so (the so-called guarantor of non-occurrence of an effect).

However, there are some challenges associated with the issue of criminal liability of users of smart systems, such as those related to the cooperation and interdependence of different systems ("*many hands problem*") and to biological limitations of humans. In addition, there is the problem of examination of the level of awareness of the operator or the supervisor of the smart system, his or her knowledge of the procedures, and the principles on which the solution that makes up the *smart city* concept is based.

In conclusion, it should be emphasized that it is necessary to conduct research in this area of criminal law. Moreover, this research must be interdisciplinary. Lack of expert knowledge from different areas makes it difficult to establish communication between researchers, but can also lead to ill-considered and unforeseen consequences. However, it is beyond dispute that such research is necessary if we want to achieve Goal 11 of the 2030 Agenda, which is to make cities and human settlements inclusive, safe, resilient, and sustainable, and to involve all inhabitants in their functioning with the use of artificial intelligence.

The Use of Governance and Mediation for Disaster Prevention and Environmental Risk Management

Gabriela Soldano Garcez <gabrielasoldano@unisantos.br>

Renata Soares Bonavides <renata.bonavides@unisantos.br>
SANTOS, São Paulo, Brasil

Abstract
This essay aims to demonstrate the cleary interconnection of the themes of economic development and environmental protection. Such connection is present especially when analyzing the need for the implementation of compliance mechanisms by the business sector, such as how to obtain the Sustainable Development Goals (SDGs), of the 2030 Agenda, formulated by the United Nations (UN), mainly with regard to SDG 17. Because, how this essay concludes, through collective participation mechanisms, it is possible to reconcile interests between all the actors involved in business processes, implemented by socio-environmental mediation in the search for the most appropriate and, currently, most sustainable solution.

Keywords:
Mediation; Governance; Risk management; Compliance; 2030 Agenda.

Introduction

Development cannot be understood (nor measured) only from an economic perspective. In a contemporary view (guided by the needs of today's complex and plural society), it should include the social and environmental dimensions. This implies that it is essential to maintain adequate environmental levels for human life for present and future generations.

The Brazilian Federal Constitution of 1988 follows this same line, by imposing the defense and protection of the environment on both the Public Power and the community, in a combination of collective efforts to maintain the environmental quality and the dignity of the human person. Therefore, it is necessary to seek a peaceful coexistence between elements of environmental protection, social resources and economic development.

In this context, and in accordance with a socio-environmental model of State (which tries to direct economic activity in order to become more environmentally responsible), the instruments implemented by the business sector called environmental compliance gains prominence, as an instrument that allows the political and public management of the company combined with environmental protection, adding value to the sector in question through mechanisms of transparency, accountability and codes of conduct, in a real stimulus to risk management and prevention of environmental disasters.

This compliance instrument can be applied in practice through the pillars of governance and socioenvironmental mediation, in an attempt to allow, at the same time, the participation of everyone involved and interested in the discussions of adequate and sustainable environmental management.

In this line of reasoning, this article aims, at first, through a critical-deductive analysis carried out by a bibliographic reference survey on the main topics of this theme, to analyze the socio-environmental responsibility of companies for maintaining environmental quality levels, taking into account in view of the current experienced Risk Society. Then, it discusses how the implementation of instruments provided for compliance can contribute to the achievement of the SDGs of 2030 Agenda, especially with regard to SDG 17 (which deals with partnerships for sustainable development).

Finally, it correlates compliance with governance and socio-environmental mediation, considering that, for its adequate use, it is necessary to allow the broad participation of all actors involved in the theme (such as, for example, investors, partners, shareholders, banks, employees, consumers, among others, through governance) in the search for joint solutions, based on consensus, that serve the interests of all (through mediation).

As a successful example of this correlation, this article mentions the online platform "SDG Action Manager", created by B.Lab and the United Nations Global Compact, which does, for free and confidentially, a risk analysis of the actions of companies for its proper management.

2. *Social and Environmental Responsibility of Companies*

Currently, due to a plural and complex society, which also can be considered a Risk Society[1], companies must guide its socioeconomic decision-making according to environmental issues, bearing in mind the need to implement standards aimed at sustainability, because the effects of globalization mark the emergence of a world in which the risks produced by human activity that cannot be immediately perceived, measured and understood[2].

For this reason, business decisions are so important, because it can cause innumerable reflexes internal and/or external impacts (which even go beyond generations, in a true "boomerang" effect[3]).

There are several examples of disastrous activities located in this risk area, such as the Dañana ecological disaster, the so-called BSE disease (bovine spongiform encephalopathy), the famous "Lederspray" case or the "Colza" case, not to mention yet the Chernobyl disaster and the many questions that are frighteningly asked about animal and human cloning, genetic manipulation etc. Such risks, which are produced according to a market logic, where the greater gain prevails in a faster financial return, with the lowest possible production costs, covering the largest possible number of consumers, follows production and efficiency criteria never previously experienced, which makes those risks unpredictable and uncontrollable.[4]

This is because, "in fact, more than a mere object of political and academic discussions, the environmental cause has become a matter of great concern of all society"[5], from the The United Nations Conference on the Human Environment (in 1972), that has generated internal consequences for the States from the need to incorporate environmental issues in the respective Constitutions. As was the case with the 1988 Federal Constitution of Brazil, which, more than a decade later, was inspired by Principle nº.

---

1 Ulrick Beck, *Sociedade de risco: rumo a uma outra modernidade* (OUP 2011).

2 BAHIA, Carolina Medeiros Bahia, Ester de Carvalho and Suélen Cristina Beninça, *Sociedade de Risco, mudanças climáticas e a função reguladora do Direito Ambiental* (OUP 2017) 705.

3 Beck (n 3).

4 Paulo Silva Fernandes, *Globalização, Sociedade de Risco e o futuro do Direito Penal* (OUP 2001) 20.

5 Felipe Santos Ribas and Arlei Costa Junior, 'A importância do compliance ambiental para as empresas: Interfaces entre governança corporativa e impactos socioambientais' (*Revista Jurídica Luso-Brasileira*, 2019) <http://www.cidp.pt/revistas/rjlb/2019/3/2019_03_0581_0610.pdf> accessed 12 November 2020.

1, of the Stockholm Declaration, to formalize an entire chapter dedicated to environmental protection, recognizing the healthy environment as a fundamental right.

It is also worth noting that, the 1988 Federal Constitution of Brazil (nicknamed as "citizen's constitution", considering that its creation process was part of a symbol of Brazil's period of re-democratization after the end of the military dictatorship)[6] was the first Brazilian constitution to mention the expression "environment" and to address the issue (and its protection), classifying it as a "good for the common use of the people" and "essential to a healthy quality of life" (according to article 225), "insofar as the quality [and the existence] of a greater legal good depends, that is, human life"[7].

On the other hand, the 1972 Stockholm Declaration also recorded the importance of raising awareness of the social and environmental responsibilities of "by individuals, enterprises and communities in protecting and improving the environment in its full human dimension", in Principle 19.

In this way, the intensity of environmental risks caused the awakening of international society (including transnational enterprises) to the emergency in discussing new mechanisms and instruments for the defense and protection of the environment (including on command and control issues) to minimize the negative impacts when complete mitigation of environmental damage is not possible, because the degradation of the ecologically balanced environment can reach (and cause serious damage) to other places, cities, regions, countries, "causing the deterioration of environmental conditions at an unknown pace and scale"[8].

Take, for example, environmental disasters, emission of pollutants, oil spills, acid rain, accidents with radioactive or nuclear materials, increased Earth temperature, greenhouse effect or hole in the ozone layer, chemical waste, organic waste, among other events.

Thus, it is necessary to have a truly effective management for the protection of the environment, since it is fundamental for the construction of a sustainability model that there is an integrated management of the right to an ecologically balanced environment and of all the instruments and mechanisms made available to its adequate defense and protection, which favors cooperation (at national and international level), forming a very

---

6 Istoé, *A constituição cidadã* (2011) <https://istoe.com.br/161883_A+CONSTITUICAO+CIDADA/>. accessed on 09 December 2020.

7 Gilberto Passos de Freitas, *Ilícito Penal ambiental e reparação do dano* (OUP 2005) 111.

8 Édis Milaré, *Direito do Ambiente* (OUP 2013) 52.

important beneficial cycle for building sustainable development, with a view to ensuring the compatibility of the socioeconomic aspect with the protection of environmental quality.

It's about perception that environmental protection has come to be considered a concrete obligation, directed towards the State's duty and law, but also imposed on individuals. That is, environmental standards must be consolidated, including by the business sector.

So, to be socioenvironmentally responsible, a enterprise has to be concerned with the management of the risks it may cause to the environment (through tools that allow planning and implementing, as well as evaluating and supervising the mapping of measures capable of minimizing or even mitigating environmental damage, avoiding any damage to society), since its actions (economic and social) can generate consequences for present and future generations, mainly in the face of disasters and impacts that have been caused to nature by the business sector (take, as an horrible example, the disasters of Brumadinho and Mariana, in Brazil).

Especially because, according to the "National Guidelines on Business and Human Rights", implemented by Decree 9.571, of 2018, in Brazil[9], which influences the risk management posture of enterprises when determining that the entire business sector has an obligation to be responsible for human rights, implementing mechanisms to repair those rights that have been affected (article 2), monitoring the production chain related to the company for its adequacy to respect for human rights (article 5), among other important guidelines established in the Decree, and also, must identify "the risks of impact and the violation of human rights in the context of its operations, with the adoption of appropriate and effective prevention and control actions" (article 9), as well as "develop and permanently improve the procedures for controlling and monitoring risks, impacts and violations, and, repair the negative consequences on human rights that provoked or have contributed to provoke "(article 9, item II).

Therefore, social and environmental responsibility implies a series of benefits for the companies themselves, which will adopt a more assertive environmental adequacy process, avoiding non-compliance of sustainable standards and commitments (which, in addition, enhances the brand and

9 Decreto 9.571/2018 <http://www.planalto.gov.br/ccivil_03/_ato2015-2018/2018/Decreto/D9571.htm> accessed on 12 December 2020.

adds value to the enterprise, demonstrating a more sustainable image for consumers and potential investors[10]).

It is about transforming the company into a "citizen company" (alluding to the "citizen constitution" mentioned above), with correction of socio-environmental ethical values, fulfilling its ethical and legal responsibility, in addition to being useful and profitable (in the economic sense), but also sustainable, avoiding and minimizing environmental impacts with the assumption of its productive role in society (which clearly imposes determining rules of conduct).

In other words, it is a posture and social behavior that recognizes not only the profitable importance of the enterprise itself, but also a socio-environmental responsibility, which imposes a concern for social well-being, in order to meet society's expectations about of sustainability, because "the peculiarity of the debate on the State of Environmental Law requires that reflection on the preservation of the environment cannot be restricted to isolated States only"[11].

Thus, the awareness of the business sector about the importance of actions that positively impact the environment is a strategic measure for reaching global partnerships with respect to sustainable development, which can contribute significantly to the advancement of environmental protection, and, in an ultimately analysis, allows for an improvement of socio-environmental issues (mainly with regard to the mitigation and minimization of environmental disasters), but also for the achievement of the Sustainable Development Goals (SDGs), under the terms of the 2030 Agenda, of the United Nations (UN).

3. *The Contribution of Environmental Compliance to the Reach of the Sustainable Development Goal 17*

The role played by the private sector is extremely important for the due achievement of the SDGs, of the 2030 Agenda, formulated by the UN, mainly with regard to SDG 17, which is entirely connected to the conduct of positive behaviors (as is the case, for compliance).

10 José Carlos Barbieri and Jorge Emanuel Reis Cajazeira, *Responsabilidade social e empresarial e empresa sustentável* (OUP 2010) 03.

11 José Rubens Morato Leite, 'Sociedade de risco e estado' in José Canotilho and José Rubens Morato Leite (eds), *Direito constitucional ambiental brasileiro* (OUP 2015) 179.

The 2030 Agenda has the proposal of reflecting the new challenges of the current globalization and the Risk Society[12], with the final purpose of achieving the dignity of the human person (in all its aspects, including environmental), by providing programs, actions and guidelines, also with a view to sustainability, on a new standard of development, by reconciling environmental protection with social justice and economic efficiency.

To this end, world leaders adopted the SDGs (through UN General Assembly Resolution 70/I[13], with the title "Transforming our world: the 2030 Agenda for Sustainable Development")[14], at the UN Summit, from 25 to 27 September of 2015, with the purpose of succeeding the Millennium Development Goals (MDGs), of the former Agenda 21, signing, thus, a new and current commitment among all UN members that proposes to provide programs, actions and guidelines for an ambitious development Agenda by 2030, aiming at strengthening consensus among signatory countries on environmental cooperation.

Thus, the new Sustainable Development Agenda calls for poverty eradication, environmental protection, gender equality, disease prevention, universal education, inclusive economic growth and good governance, through 17 SDGs (subdivided into 169 targets, which now include social, economic and environmental aspects with the indispensable application of public policies aimed at such areas, for the creation of a healthy relationship between society and the environment), acting as a means of guiding actions and international cooperation by next 15 years.

Each of the 17 Goals has a specific content, therefore, its own purposes. The demand is so high that the UN involves all actors in its development, governments, the private sector, civil society and individuals. This leads to collaborative strategies to achieve sustainability and the improvement of life for future generations.[15]

Therefore, it is true that the document includes, for the first time in an international agreement of this type, a commitment to the need for new mechanisms to implement the goals brought about by the SDGs.

---

12 Beck (n 3).

13 Assembleia Geral da Organização das Nações Unidas, *Transformar nuestro mundo: la Agenda 2030 para el Desarrollo Sostenible* (A/70/L.1, 2015) <https://unctad.org/meetings/es/SessionalDocuments/ares70d1_es.pdf> accessed on 21 December 2020.

14 Organização das Nações Unidas, *Agenda 2030* (OUP 2015) <https://nacoesunidas.org/pos2015> accessed on 10 December 2020.

15 José Júlio Rodriguez, *ODS 16: paz, justicia e instituciones flertes* (OUP 2018) <http://www.ieee.es/Galerias/fichero/docs_investig/2018/DIEEEINV18-2018ODS.pdf> Accessed on 09 December 2020.

Among such Goal is the 17, which has as its guideline "Partnerships and Means of Implementation: Strengthen the means of implementation and revitalize the global partnership for sustainable development", especially with regard to the specific goals of nº. 17.14, 17.16 and 17.17[16].

It is, in fact, an axis of SDG 17 focused on systemic issues thought of mechanisms of "institutional policy sciences" (which seeks joint and stable efforts), "multisectoral partnerships" (in which there is a search for partnerships of the Public authorities with non-state actors and civil society to mobilize and share knowledge, expertise, resources and technologies) and "data, monitoring and accountability" (through the training of developing countries, to increase the availability of high quality data, which are reliable, according to their national contexts on the implementation of the goals of the other SDGs).

This is because cooperation between the international community, interested sectors and people affected by development processes is an essential requirement for growth on new sustainable standards.

Thus, SDG 17 is the path to the effective realization of all other SDGs in the 2030 Agenda, in a true coordination of national and international efforts, which requires the participation of all, including companies (by allowing expanded participation as a vital mechanism for good governance, in the new terms of non-state actors and subjects of Public International Law).

Currently, one of the biggest mechanisms that make such a commitment possible on the part of enterprises is the so-called compliance, which refers to acting with pre-stipulated internal rules, such as a command or corporate norms.

By the definition of article 7, item VIII, of Law nº. 12.846/2013 (which provides "about administrative and civil liability of legal entities for the practice of acts against public administration, national or foreign")[17], and also programs "are internal mechanisms and procedures integrity, auditing, incentive to report irregularities and the effective application of codes of ethics and conduct within the scope of the legal entity"[18], with the applicable rules (including environmental) to the business sector in question (whether standards are imposed or voluntarily adhered to).

---

16 Organização das Nações Unidas, *Parcerias e meios de implementação* (OUP 2015) <http://www.agenda2030.org.br/ods/17/> Accessed on 05 December 2020.

17 Lei 12.846/2013. <http://www.planalto.gov.br/ccivil_03/_ato2011-2014/2013/lei/l12846.htm> Accessed on 14 December 2020.

18 Ribas and Costa Junior (n 7) 14.

In other words, it is the set of actions and internal activities carried out by companies that allow a true mapping of positive behaviors, in order to prevent and/or minimize the risk of violations of environmental standards, as well as to monitor and inspect the implementation progress of such actions and activities in order to avoid environmental damage, for example, by sharing information and promoting transparency actions in order to avoid lawsuits, imposing penalties and any consequences harmful to society.

It is an imperative of conduct which imposes control (through monitoring and inspection) of the attitudes taken by the enterprises in order to obtain environmentally appropriate behaviors, in accordance with pre-established ethical and moral principles (including 2030 Agenda), effective both for the public and private sectors, a true prevention and precaution mechanism within organizations.

Thus, environmental compliance aims to avoid irregularities or violation of any standards that may cause damage and/or disasters (often irreparable to the population), through the effective implementation of environmentally appropriate strategies to enhance compliance with standards, transparency and implementation of measures preventive and precautionary measures, in addition to internal environmental education training for partners and employees (which, in turn, generates the production of a cycle of positive behaviors, based on strengthening the building of environmental education). And, ultimately, it allows the maintenance of the enterprise's positive image towards society (and possible consumers).

However, the creation of this scenario is only possible through the opening of constructive, inclusive and resilient communication channels, what is possible to be done through social and environmental mediation mechanisms.

3.1. Mediation as an instrument of compliance and prevention of environmental disasters: Negotiated conflict resolution strategy for environmental risk management, through governance

It is clear, therefore, that the pursuit of social responsibility from the perspective of sustainability requires concrete attitudes that enable environmental protection promoted by intense debate and, later, consensus on the issues.

That is why, as mechanisms for implementing compliance (which aims to map risks for a preventive and precautionary consensual action), governance should be used through its socio-environmental mediation instrument, which presents itself as an important tool for environmental and business policy, effective in protecting the ecologically balanced environment, and which adds value to enterprises.

Governance has become a common expression, since the beginning of the 21st century, in the areas of Humanities, Applied and related Social Sciences, as being essential for the processes of economic and social development, since it covers several areas, such as, for example, political, technological, cultural, among others, as it is the "set of interrelated processes that operate through all the primary fields of social power"[19].

The current concept of "Global Governance" emerged through the Commission on Global Governance, by the United Nations (UN) in 1992 (with an official report in 1994), as the totality of the different ways in which individuals and public and private institutions manage their common problems. It is an ongoing process by which it is possible to accommodate conflicting interests and carry out cooperative actions. Governance concerns not only institutions and formal regimes authorized to impose obedience, but informal agreements that serve the interests of people and institutions[20].

It is, therefore, considered a solution to common problems between States and non-State actors with the intention of formulating principles and guiding actions and activities that allow the designation of capacities required for an adequate and sustainable management of the environment, "adopting stricter social and environmental policies, and, guaranteeing a more active role for citizens and local agents"[21], bearing in mind that there is an increasing concern to establish forms and mechanisms of shared power management in a transparent manner, where States, international organizations, multinational companies and civil society organizations can play a relevant role.

Thus, in order for an integrated solution to common problems to be possible, it is necessary to create new formulas, which enable the expansion of participation in all phases of the decision-making procedure (discussion, execution, monitoring, inspection etc.).

With regard to an action-oriented approach, authors have characterized governance as a multi-actor system which extends beyond traditional actors (such as states and international organizations) and includes non-go-

---

19 David Held and Anthony McGrew, *Prós e Contras da Globalização* (OUP 2001) 18.

20 Comissão sobre Governança Global, *Nossa comunidade global* (OUP 1996) 2.

21 Alcindo Gonçalves, "Governança Global e o Direito Internacional Público" in Liliana Lyra Jubilut (eds), *Direito Internacional Atual* (OUP 2014) 84.

vernamental organizations, in particular, activist groups, networks of scientist, business associations and policy research institutions. While states, at least formally, are still the primary actors within this framework, there is a growing number of non-governmental organizations (NGOs), societal movements and other private actors which are transforming the character of the whole system. (...) Last but not least, the individual has become increasingly involved as an actor.[22]

Thus, "governance is a means, tool, instrument for solving problems"[23], designed to encompass new decentralized relationships, seeking to go beyond of simply solving problems, to also encompass much broader discussions with States, civil society and the business sector.

However, for this phenomenon to be properly employed, it is necessary to build mechanisms for participation and dialogue in the search for consensus in decision-making and environmental management through joint procedures for diagnosis and, from there, building the solution and subsequent implementation and monitoring, that is, in the search for a final result after processes of discussion and interaction between all those involved in that problem (instead of coercion and imposition).

The consensus is present "when it is able to articulate the different actors - State and non-State - to face challenges acting and articulating from the construction of consensus and forging cooperation to solve problems"[24], considering that it must be understood as the search for viable solutions and accepted by the majority, after the discussion between all involved.

It refers, therefore, to activities that support common goals, which may or may not derive from legal and formal prescriptions, but which, due to its intrinsic condition, should be accepted and/or supported by the majority.

This new relationship of management and discussion of common problems, based on constructive and respectful interaction, can be implemented through socioenvironmental mediation, because if governance is oriented towards the search for consensus, it can be translated (and implemented) by mediation of different interests, being one of the main governance

---

22 Ulrich Beyerlin and Thilo Marauhn, *International Enviromental Governance.* (OUP 2011) 244.

23 Alcindo Gonçalves and José Augusto Fontoura Costa, "Governança Ambiental Global: possibilidades e limites" in Maria Luiza Machado Granziera and Fernando Cardozo Fernandes Rei (eds), *Direito Ambiental Internacional: Avanços e retrocessos* (OUP 2015) 109.

24 ibid 25.

instruments when providing precisely the expanded participation in the decision-making processes, since several actors play decisive roles in the resolution of conflicts of interest.

In this way, mediation allows the negotiated solution process, in order to facilitate the approach of the parties involved (through their active participation) so that they find, in a consensual way, through stimuli from a third party (who only has powers to assist the conflicting interests in the construction of the solution), a satisfactory result that will be built throughout the process.

The Law nº. 13.140/2015, which constitutes a true legal framework on the subject, dispose of mediation as a means of dispute settlement, considers the concept of this instrument to be (according to article 1): "Mediation is considered to be the technical activity performed by impartial third party without decision-making power, which, chosen or accepted by the parties, assists and encourages them to identify or develop consensual solutions to the controversy"[25].

In other words, through mediation as an instrument of governance, it is possible to improve the relationships between those involved (thus allowing the broadened participation of all stakeholders), through dialogue, to move forward in building cooperation between the parties to find consensus on a more appropriate solution for all, in a dynamically way by empowering the actors involved in decision-making and execution of business management, providing satisfaction and security to the parties, in addition to reestablishing personal relationships.

It can be seen that mediation plays an important role in combining the interests of everyone involved in the enterprise: investors, partners, shareholders, banks, employees, consumers, among others, through the opening of constructive communication channels, inclusive, resilient and, why not, now facing the 2030 Agenda, also sustainable.

Therefore, it is an important mediation process for the management of environmental and business interests "between social actors who act on the physical-natural and built environment, aiming to guarantee the right to an ecologically balanced environment, as determined by the Brazilian Federal Constitution"[26].

Thus, compliance, as a mechanism of responsibility, integrity and risk management, depends on the proper performance of socio-environmental

25 Lei 13.0140/2015 <http://www.planalto.gov.br/ccivil_03/_ato2015-2018/2015/lei/l13140.htm> accessed on 16 December 2020.

26 José Silva Quintas, *Introdução à gestão ambiental pública* (OUP 2006) 30.

mediation (as a mechanism for strategic management of environmental, economic and social interests) for its effectiveness.

In other words, mediation, as a compliance instrument, can be used for issues involving socioenvironmental conflicts in the search for negotiated solutions among all interested and involved actors, aiming at the protection of environmental quality, under the terms of the 1988 Brazilian Federal Constitution, according to article 225, to ensure an ecologically balanced environment for all.

An example of this possibility of applying governance and socio-environmental mediation is the online platform called "SDG Action Manager", created by B.Lab and the United Nations Global Compact[27], which has the purpose to assist enterprises in determining better and more positive actions for the environment, directing them within the reach of the SDGs, of the 2030 Agenda, with the adoption of significant measures for this, and, of course, ultimately, social welfare. It is a free and confidential tool for the impact of risk and socioenvironmental management (by allowing the measurement of socioenvironmental impact, defining objectives for the improvement of concrete actions), and it is capable of actively contributing to the combination of interests in the business sector, with the union of efforts towards a common goal: to improve the business performance related to sustainable development for all, rethinking models and promoting sustainable collective actions.

To this end, the platform works by studying the alignment of strategies and operations (already implemented and/or still in delimitation, but which, in any case, are registered on the website) of enterprises with the SDGs. When analyzing the information provided (with the support of experts in business sustainability, including the UN and the scientific community), the site indicates risks, business opportunities and current trends for that particular sector (all in accordance with the SDGs, provide what the objetive of each Goal are most important according to the enterprise's performance profile), in addition to proposing objetives (of high impact) that can serve as the basis for an action plan in order to become more sustainable by encouraging a corporate action and self-assessment, that is, a proposal for reform in performance so that activities and environmental management are in line with the search for adaptation to new global scenarios and the demands of society of sustainability. In the end, it is

27 Global Pact, *Sdg Action Manager* (OUP 2020) <https://www.pactoglobal.org.br/pg/sdg-action-manager> accessed on 01 December 2020.

also possible to share the results obtained, in order to generate even more positive impact on the enterprise.

It is a platform (which requires a simple registration, made free of charge and completely confidential) that gives companies an opportunity to "learn, manage and directly improve their performance"[28], according to the SDGs of 2030 Agenda, which is umbilically connected to issues of governance and socioenvironmental mediation (by allowing everyone to participate and discussions together).

4. Conclusions

Sustainable development seeks to combine quantitative and qualitative factors in the search for social integration and economic growth, in addition to preserving the environment so that present and future generations can enjoy quality of life.

This is because, the environmentally harmful effects of the risks produced by the current society are enormous and incalculable, since it doesn't respect borders and reach several generations (in a true sense of transnational and intergenerational). A long-term relationship of social and legal responsibility arises to define actions in favor of the environmental quality, life and dignity of the human person, by all members of international society, whether it be a classic subject of Public International Law (such as States and International Organizations), an non-State actor, as is the case with transnational companies (alongside others, for example, academic institutions, non-governmental organizations, individuals, among others).

This is because, governments alone are no longer able to achieve the SDGs of 2030 Agenda in a current Risk Society. Joint and effective action by other public and private actors is necessary in order to make sustainable development feasible.

Because of this, it is extremely important to understand and practice concrete, effective and strategic actions to reach the SDGs of 2030 Agenda, by the signatories of this global pact, demonstrating the responsibility for the dignity (including environmental) of future generations, which brings benefits to the international society, but also, in the long term, to the enterprises themselves (improving its image, and adding value), which start promoting social welfare with financial balance.

28 ibid 29.

This involves, for example, the use of the tool known as compliance (which seeks to map risks in order to minimize with action plans and internal policies in the prevention and precaution of environmental risks), with pre-defined objectives that need consensus and constructive dialogue for its implementation.

This reality can be implemented through mechanisms provided by socioenvironmental mediation, which allows the participation of all those interested in the discussions, in order to make it effectively inclusive, resilient and sustainable, helping to guide more positive behaviors in relation to the environment, implementing SDG 17, of 2030 Agenda, through partnerships for sustainability.

Section Four.
Internet, New Technologies and Privacy

Privacy by Design – Searching for the Balance Between Privacy, Personal Data Protection and Development of Artificial Intelligence Systems[1]

Zanda Davida <zanda.davida@hotmail.com>
RIGA, Latvia

Dominik Lubasz <dominik.lubasz@lubasziwspolnicy.pl>
ŁÓDŹ, Poland

Abstract

The growing use of artificial intelligence systems has put them under the regulatory spotlight all around the world. The EU considers to regulate artificial intelligence systems as a part of initiative of creating ethical and legal framework for trustworthy artificial intelligence. It is no secret that data is the fuel of artificial intelligence systems, but the problem with the insufficient protection of data subjects is remaining. The article aims to analyze the interaction between the GDPR and the draft of Artificial Intelligence Act and search for the balance between privacy, personal data protection and development of artificial intelligence systems. The article analyses the legal framework and compare many guidance documents issued by the international organisations. The authors reveal that the draft of Artificial Intelligence Act does not contain instruments for the insufficient protection of data subjects, especially in aspects concerning control and transparency, and that it lacks the promised horizontality of the draft legislation and the creation of a legal framework for all artificial intelligence systems and not just selected ones. Moreover, the article proposes solutions on how to minimize the privacy risks associated with the development and use of artificial intelligence systems. It suggests to develop further guidance and regulation and to consider a more horizontal approach.

---

1 The research leading to this publication was supported by the National Science Centre (*Narodowe Centrum Nauki*) in Poland on the basis of decision no. 2018/31/B/HS5/01169.

Keywords:
data protection, privacy, privacy by design, artificial intelligence, AI systems, data protection by design.

1. Introduction

With the expansion of artificial intelligence, trust deficits in both the technology and its developers are becoming an important issue. Concerns arise about the application of technology in an instrumental way, arbitrary or discriminatory effects of automated decisions made using it. As new technologies gain importance and become easier to implement, it becomes necessary to analyse whether these technologies may violate the law or ethical standards. One of the main areas of concern is the area of data protection and privacy implications, especially since the demand for data due to the development and use of AI-based solutions is greater than ever. In this context, the availability, quality, and quantity of data is an issue of concern, as they are the basis for self-learning systems to fulfil their original purpose, i.e. to find relationships between information allowing to draw specific conclusions, make decisions, and through them, influence the environment. The accuracy of the algorithms themselves is also not without significance. Algorithm bias can independently generate cognitive deficiencies that intensify the negative effects on data subjects.[2].

Thus, there is a need to identify solutions to minimize the risks related to the use of techniques based on artificial intelligence, particularly from the perspective of the possibility of a discriminatory effect, harming human dignity and privacy, and leading to restrictions on freedom of expression, access to information, and manipulation of opinions.[3].

---

2 On the subject of potential risks, see further: Tjerk Timana and Zoltan Manna (ed) 'Data Protection in The Era of Artificial Intelligence. Trends, existing solutions and recommendations for privacy-preserving technologies' (GDVA, 2019), 11. Overview of trends in AI guidelines in different countries and organizations: see: Anna Jobin and Marcello Ienca, 'Artificial Intelligence: the global landscape of ethics guidelines' (2019) AL/Digital ethics project <https://www.researchgate.net/publication/334082218_Artificial_Intelligence_the_global_landscape_of_ethics_guidelines> accessed 22 June 2021.

3 ibid; Advisory Board on Artificial Intelligence and Human Society, Report on Artificial Intelligence and Human Society, (2017) <https://www8.cao.go.jp/cstp/tyousakai/ai/summary/aisociety_en.pdf> accessed 22 June 2021.

The need to build, or essentially support the recovery of trust in technology was also seen as an important element. Trust in technology or trustworthiness of technology ultimately became a key element in the search for a target regulatory framework.

In the field of privacy and data protection, for the legal assessment of the social and ethical implications of AI, it was obvious to reach for the mechanisms developed in the creation of Regulation (EU) 2016/679 of the European Parliament and of the Council of 27 April 2016 on the protection of natural persons with regard to the processing of personal data and on the free movement of such data, and repealing Directive 95/46/EC (General Data Protection Regulation)[4]. It had to be assessed whether legal instruments such as risk-based approach, privacy by design, data protection by design, data protection impact assessment or privacy impact assessment more broadly could form the basis for a legal framework for artificial intelligence. This assessment had to be done in the context of a European AI strategy supporting "the creation of ethical, secure and state-of-the-art AI solutions in Europe" based on three pillars: (i) increasing public and private investment in AI for its wider deployment, (ii) preparing for socio-economic change, and (iii) providing an appropriate ethical and legal framework to strengthen European values[5]. This vision is presented in the communications issued by the European Commission on 25.4.2018. "Artificial Intelligence for Europe".[6] and in the "Coordinated

---

4 European Parliament, Regulation (EU) 2016/679 of the European Parliament and of the Council of 27 April 2016 on the protection of natural persons with regard to the processing of personal data and on the free movement of such data, and repealing Directive 95/46/EC [2016] OJ L199/1–88 (General Data Protection Regulation).

5 See also European Commission, 'Member States and Commission to work together to boost artificial intelligence „made in Europe"' (Press release, 7 December 2018) <http://europa.eu/rapid/press-release_IP-18-6689_en.htm> accessed 6 March 2019. See more Agnieszka Jabłonowska, Maciej Kuziemski, Anna Maria Nowak, Hans-Wolfgang Micklitz, Przemysław Pałka and Giovanni Sartor, 'Consumer law and artificial intelligence. Challenges to the EU consumer law and policy stemming from the business' use of artificial intelligence' (EUI Working Papers, 2018) 4-11; Sandra Wachter and Brent Mittelstandt, 'A Right to Reasonable Interferences: R-thinking Data Protection Law in the Age of Big Data and Ai' (2019) Columbia Business Law Review 1.

6 Commission to the European Parliament, the European Council, the Council, the European Economic and Social Committee and the Committee of the Regions, 'Artificial Intelligence for Europe' (Communication) COM (2018) 237 final.

Plan on Artificial Intelligence" of 7.12.2018.[7], as well as in the "Declaration of Cooperation on AI" signed on 10.4.2018.[8] and in the White Paper On Artificial Intelligence – A European approach to excellence and trust issued on 19.2.2020 r.[9]

The first result of the work initiated in the above documents was the establishment of the High-Level Expert Group on AI (HLEG), which was first tasked with developing ethics guidelines for trustworthy artificial intelligence, followed by policy and investment recommendations. In the guidelines developed in April 2019, HLEG pointed out the need to create conditions for the development of human-centric artificial intelligence in Europe primarily by giving it the characteristic of "trustworthy" artificial intelligence. A trustworthy artificial intelligence should have certain characteristics[10], which revolve around providing guarantees of autonomy and control, as well as protection, to human beings subjected to the influence of AI-enabled processes. These principles are:

1. Human Agency and Oversight;
2. Technical Robustness and Safety;
3. Privacy and Data Governance;
4. Transparency;
5. Diversity, Non-discrimination and Fairness;
6. Societal and Environmental Well-being;
7. Accountability[11].

---

7 Commission to the European Parliament, the European Council, the Council, the European Economic and Social Committee and the Committee of the Regions, 'A coordinated plan for artificial intelligence' (Communication) COM (2018) 795 final.

8 European Commission, 'EU member states sign up to cooperate on artificial intelligence' (News, 8 March 2020) <https://ec.europa.eu/digital-single-market/en/news/eu-member-states-sign-cooperate-artificial-intelligence> accessed 6 March 2019.

9 Commission, 'White Paper on Artificial Intelligence – A European approach to excellence and trust' (Communication), COM (2020) 65 final.

10 European Commission, 'Assessment list of trustworthy artificial intelligence' (Study, 1 March 2021) <https://digital-strategy.ec.europa.eu/en/library/assessment-list-trustworthy-artificial-intelligence-altai-self-assessment> accessed 27 April 2021.

11 To assess compliance with these principles, the High Level Expert Group on Artificial Intelligence has developed and made available the ALTAI tool – High Level Expert Group on Artificial Intelligence, 'The Assessment List on Trustworthy Artificial Intelligence' <https://futurium.ec.europa.eu/en/european-ai-alliance/pages/altai-assessment-list-trustworthy-artificial-intelligence> accessed 27 April 2021.

Viewed individually, each of these characteristics is necessary but not sufficient to achieve trustworthy artificial intelligence. Under ideal conditions, all seven characteristics interact harmoniously with each other, and their scopes overlap. However, if in practice it turns out that the interactions between these features lead to conflicts, society should make efforts to correct them accordingly.

The analysis carried out in the European Union led to the presentation by the European Commission on 21 April 2021 of a draft regulation laying down harmonised rules on artificial intelligence (Artificial Intelligence Act) and amending certain Union legislative acts[12]. This Regulation is to lay down harmonised rules on artificial intelligence, providing rules applicable to the design, development and use of certain high-risk AI systems and restrictions on certain applications of remote biometric identification systems. Non-discrimination legal solutions are also to be implemented by introducing requirements aimed at minimising the risk of algorithmic discrimination, in particular with regard to the design and quality of datasets used for developing AI systems, complemented by obligations for testing, risk management, documentation and human oversight throughout the life cycle of AI systems. Although the Regulation on AI is intended to be horizontal and, despite its broad definition of AI systems, it only regulates certain aspects related to the operation of AI systems and only certain systems. This is also important in the context of the planned relationship of this regulation to the GDPR. According to paragraph 1.2 of Explanatory Memorandum, the AI Regulation is only intended to supplement the General Data Protection Regulation (Regulation (EU) 2016/679) and the Law Enforcement Directive (Directive (EU) 2016/680) with a set of harmonized rules applicable to the design, development and use of certain high-risk AI systems and restrictions on certain applications of remote biometric identification systems.

Under EU law, the GDPR is thus to remain the basis for assessing the horizontal compatibility of AI systems in the area of personal data. The objectives of this legal act, which are to ensure a high level of protection of individuals' rights and a technology-neutral approach in which the implementation of the requirements is based on a risk analysis of the processing from the perspective of the rights and freedoms of data subjects, and the

12 Commission, 'Proposal for a Regulation of the European Parliament and of the Council Laying Down Harmonised Rules on Artificial Intelligence (Artificial Intelligence Act) and Amending Certain Union Legislative Acts' COM 2021 206 final.

elements of proper implementation of the regulation are not only the security of processing (Article 32 RODO) but also the principles of processing (Article 5 RODO), such as transparency, fairness, data minimisation and purpose limitation[13], are in line with the trends in the development of technology and the assumptions of the legal framework of trustworthy and human-centric artificial intelligence defined in the above mentioned documents[14]. Also the legal mechanisms and instruments used in this act, which allow the assessment of technical solutions from the perspective of their impact, both at the design stage as well as during implementation and use, on data subjects, i.e. the obligation to take into account data protection by design, data protection by default or to conduct a data protection impact assessment, which have a technology-neutral mechanism, allows the assessment of fit for purpose.

2. *Concepts of privacy by design and data protection by design*

The original concept of privacy by design was originally created by Ann Cavoukian, during her time as Privacy Commissioner for the State of Ontario[15]. This concept is the result of work to consolidate the practice of incorporating privacy protection into new infrastructure projects currently underway in Canada and as a specific, both philosophical and practical response to the difficulties of guaranteeing adequate privacy protection in

---

13 See more: Piotr Drobek in Edyta Bielak-Jomaa and Dominik Lubasz (eds) *RODO. Ogólne rozporządzenie o ochronie danych. Komentarz* (Wolters Kluwer 2017) 340.

14 Dominik Lubasz and Katarzyna Witkowska, 'Europejska reforma ochrony danych osobowych z perspektywy pełnomocnika przedsiębiorcy' in Kinga Flaga-Gieruszyńska, Jacek Gołaczyński and Dariusz Szostek (eds) *Media elektroniczne. Współczesne problemy prawne* (C. H. Beck 2016) 176.

15 IPC, 'Privacy by Design. The 7 Foundational Principles' <https://www.ipc.on.ca/wp-content/uploads/Resources/7foundationalprinciples.pdf> accessed 23 March 2021. See also Dominik Lubasz and KatarzynaWitkowska, *RODO. Ogólne rozporządzenie o ochronie danych. Komentarz* (LEX/el., comments on Art. 25 No 5), see also Wojciech R. Wiewiórowski, 'Privacy by design jako paradygmat ochrony prywatności' in Grażyna Szpor and WojciechR. Wiewiórowski (eds) *Internet. Prawno-informatyczne problemy sieci, portali i e-usług* (C. H. Beck 2012) 13–29 and the literature referred to therein, and Michał Bienias, 'Ochrona danych w fazie projektowania oraz domyślna ochrona danych (privacy by design oraz privacy by default) w ogólnym rozporządzeniu o ochronie danych' in Grzegorz Sibiga (ed) *Ogólne rozporządzenie o ochronie danych. Aktualne problemy prawnej ochrony danych osobowych 2016* (2016) 20 Monitor Prawniczy 53–57.

light of rapidly developing technology[16]. It is based on seven principles: proactive rather than reactive ; privacy as the default setting; privacy embedded into design ; full functionality understood as achieving positive sum, not zero sum; protection of privacy from the beginning to the end of the information life cycle; visibility and transparency and respect for user privacy[17].

A strategy for privacy by design in the implementation of new technological solutions was also presented by ENISA (European Union Agency for Network and Information Security) in its report Privacy and Data Protection by Design. It indicated two possible approaches, i.e. data-oriented - aiming at limiting the negative impact by, among others, data minimisation, separation or generalization, and process-oriented concerning mainly organizational aspects and procedures ensuring the realization of the right to autonomy, in particular by informing data subjects, enabling data control, enforcing protection and, finally, demonstrating compliance[18].

These approaches allow to put the data subject in the centre of attention when designing personal data processing processes with the use of modern technologies, including artificial intelligence, especially because of their technological neutrality. The applied procedure of focusing the evaluation perspective on a human being allows, at the same time, to realize the postulate of striving to regain trust by technology and to include mechanisms to ensure this in the design (trust by design)[19].

---

16 It is worth noting that in the context of artificial intelligence, A. Cavoukian modified the original concept indicating the need for ethical construction of tools using artificial intelligence mechanisms (AI Ethics by design). The core elements of this concept have become: transparency and accountability of algorithms; application of ethical principles to the processing of personal data; ensuring oversight and accountability for the performance of algorithms; respect for privacy as a fundamental human right; data protection as a default setting; proactive identification of security risks, thereby minimising risks; robust documentation to facilitate ethical design and data symmetry - Ann Cavoukian, 'Ethics by design' <www.ryerson.ca/pbdce> accessed 23 March 2021.

17 This concept was subsequently adopted in the Resolution on Privacy – Design Data Protection and Privacy Commissioners, 'The Resolution on Privacy by Design' (32nd International Conference of Data Protection and Privacy Commissioners, Jerusalem, 27–29 October 2010. <http://www.giodo.gov.pl/pl/1520084/3830> accessed 13 May 2021.

18 ENISA, 'Privacy and Data Protection by Design – from policy to engineering' <https://www.enisa.europa.eu/publications/privacy-and-data-protection-by-design> accessed 23 March 2021.

19 Witold Chomiczewski and Dominik Lubasz, 'Privacy by design a sztuczna inteligencja' (2020) 20 MoP 67 ff.

The concept of privacy by design implemented as a regulatory instrument in Article 25 of the General Data Protection Regulation shows some particularities resulting from the subject of protection related to the scope of its provisions, namely the protection of natural persons in relation to the processing of their personal data (data protection by design). According to the adopted structure, Article 25 RODO imposes an obligation on controllers to implement appropriate technical and organisational measures designed to effectively implement data protection principles, in particular the principle of data minimisation and to provide the processing with the necessary safeguards in order to meet the requirements of the General Data Protection Regulation, and in particular to protect the rights of data subjects in a specific context of processing. The context of the processing, on the other hand, is to be determined taking into account the state of the art, the costs of implementation and the nature, scope, context and purposes of the processing, which are to be the basis for examining the likelihood of risks of the violation of the rights or freedoms of natural persons by the processing under consideration, in order to assess which technical or organisational measures should be implemented to mitigate those risks, both in determining the modalities of the processing and at the time of the processing itself[20].

Notwithstanding the above requirements formulated in Article 25(1) of the GDPR, Article 25(2) adopts a principle that was originally part of the privacy by design concept of Ann Cavoukian, i.e. privacy by default, in the form of the data protection by default principle. According to this principle, the controller is obliged to implement appropriate technical and organisational measures to ensure that, by default, only those personal data are processed that are necessary for each specific purpose of the processing. This obligation relates to the amount of personal data to be collected, the extent of their processing, their storage period and their availability.

The analytical process underlying this obligation shall have a multistage character, starting from determining the full context of the processing, i.e. defining the assumptions and determining the circumstances, the scope, the tool-layer and the manner of performing the data operations, through assessing the impact of the above factors on the rights and freedoms of data subjects to be processed, in particular whether any undesirable effects

20 European Data Protection Board, 'Guidelines 4/2019 on Article 25 Data Protection by Design and by Default' (20 October 2020) <https://edpb.europa.eu/sites/edpb/files/files/file1/edpb_guidelines_201904_dataprotection_by_design_and_by_default_v2.0_en.pdf> accessed 13 May 2021.

of the processing occur or are likely to occur in relation to the proposed processing from the perspective of the data subject, e.g. discrimination. This assessment shall take place in the context of the proper implementation of the principles of processing contained in Article 5 of the GDPR, in particular the principle of data minimisation and the rights of data subjects (Article 25(2) and 12-22 of the GDPR), and finally the analysis of the adequacy of organisational and technical measures to ensure the implementation of the principles of processing and the protection of the rights of data subjects, including ensuring their security.

3. *Functional use of data protection by design model in the design of AI systems*

The assumptions of the privacy by design concept adopted in Article 25 of the GDPR, in the form of data protection by design requirements, referring in particular to the assessment perspective, i.e. humonocentric approach in the performance of obligations, taking into account principles such as reliability, transparency and, in particular, data minimisation, and finally, the necessity to ensure data subjects' control over their data prima facie, seem to correspond to the basic problematic issues formulated when designing solutions using artificial intelligence. They address regulatory concerns about the application of technology in an instrumental way, arbitrary or discriminatory effects of automated decisions made with the use of AI, both in the context of the designed algorithms and the possibility of their corruption (algorithm bias), as well as the data necessary to teach AI to make decisions in the designed area, which is primarily related to the availability, quality and quantity of input data[21]. The importance of the issue of using this regulation in an increasingly digital world is highlighted by the European Data Protection Board in its Guidelines 4/2019 on the application of the Article 25 principle of data protection by design, pointing out that this principle plays a key role in promoting privacy and the protection of personal data in society. For these reasons, it is important that controllers take this responsibility seriously and implement the obligations

21 Slomit Yanisky-Ravid and Sean K. Hallisey, 'Equality and Privacy by Design: Ensuring Artificial Intelligence (AI) is Properly Trained & Fed: A New Model of AI Data Transparency & Certification as Safe Harbor Procedures' <https://ssrn.com/abstract=3278490> accessed 13 May 2021.

under the General Data Protection Regulation when designing processing operations[22].

The regulation of Article 25 of the GDPR applies to all controllers regardless of their size, organisational complexity or the level of complexity of the planned processing operations. The provision of Article 25(1) of the GDPR implies first of all that compliance with the data processing requirements is to be an equivalent goal to the business purposes for a controller designing new processing operations[23]. Data protection must therefore be embedded first in the R&D project and then in the implementation and maintenance and be an inherent part of the whole process in its individual phases. This principle is therefore not only about the compliance aspect, but also, and perhaps above all, about developing a specific organisational culture of working on new solutions to ensure compliance[24].

The primary obligation is to implement appropriate measures and necessary safeguards to ensure the effective implementation of data protection principles and, consequently, the rights and freedoms of data subjects. Article 25 sets out both design and default elements to be taken into account, addressing the context, the nature of the processing purposes and scope, as well as the state of the art and the cost of implementation, and the risks to data subjects, of varying probability and severity. The analysis of these elements should be made at an early stage of planning a new processing operation and repeated during the processing, through regular reviews of the effectiveness of the chosen measures and safeguards.

As emphasised by the European Data Protection Board in the abovementioned Guidelines, effectiveness is at the heart of the concept of data protection by design. The requirement for effective implementation means that any measure should produce the intended results in terms of the processing designed by the controller from the perspective of the data subject. For this reason, the provision of Article 25 does not introduce a catalogue of required measures and leaves the decision on adequacy from an effectiveness perspective to the controller. Whether specific measures are effective will therefore depend on the context of the processing in question and an assessment of the relevant elements to be taken into

22 European Data Protection Board, 'Guidelines 4/2019 on Article 25 Data Protection by Design and by Default' (20 October 2020) <https://edpb.europa.eu/sites/edpb/files/files/file1/edpb_guidelines_201904_dataprotection_by_design_and_by_default_v2.0_en.pdf> accessed 13 May 2021.

23 Monika Susałko in Dominik Lubasz (ed) *Meritum Ochrona danych osobowych* (Wolters Kluwer, 2020) 227.

24 Chomiczewski and Lubasz (n 19) 67 ff.

account when determining the modalities of the processing. This approach implies that controllers should be able to demonstrate that they have ensured adequacy and that the implemented measures and safeguards achieve the desired effect in terms of personal data protection by minimizing the risks for data subjects related to the envisaged forms of processing. To this end, as underlined by the European Data Protection Board, the controller may define appropriate key performance indicators (KPIs), or provide a justification of its assessment of the effectiveness of the chosen measures and safeguards, in order to demonstrate their effectiveness, in line with the accountability principle (Article 5(2))[25].

In developing a model approach for the use of data protection by design instruments in the design of IS systems, reference can be made to already developed guidelines[26]. Particularly noteworthy is the concept developed by the Norwegian Data Protection Supervisory Authority in its guidelines on Software Development with Data Protection by Design and by Default[27]. This is primarily supported by the AI definition proposed in the draft AI Regulation, which indicates that 'artificial intelligence system' (AI system) means software that is developed with one or more of the techniques and approaches listed in Annex I and can, for a given set of human-defined objectives, generate outputs such as content, predictions, recommendations, or decisions influencing the environments they interact with[28]. Consequently, the logic of proceeding in the design and development of AI systems will be similar to that presented in the aforementioned Guidelines, taking into account and adapting the model to the particular characteristics of AI.

In the above mentioned Guidelines, the implementation plan is divided into 7 phases:

1. Training,
2. Requirements,
3. Design,

---

25 European Data Protection Board, 'Guidelines 4/2019 on Article 25 Data Protection by Design and by Default' (20 October 2020) <https://edpb.europa.eu/sites/edpb/files/files/file1/edpb_guidelines_201904_dataprotection_by_design_and_by_default_v2.0_en.pdf> accessed 13 May 2021 7.

26 ibid.

27 Norwegian data protection supervisory authority, 'Software development with Data Protection by Design and by Default' (Guidelines) <https://www.datatilsynet.no/en/about-privacy/virksomhetenes-plikter/innebygd-personvern/data-protection-by-design-and-by-default/?print=true> accessed 13 May 2021.

28 ibid, Art. 3(3).

4. Coding,
5. Testing,
6. Release
7. Maintenance.

The key to the correct implementation of the presented approach in the development of IS systems is the prior definition of the nature and purpose of the project. It is important to determine the full context of the activity, and from the point of view of personal data protection, the processing of data, the determination of the scope of data, the sources of their acquisition and the manner, needs, and therefore the purpose of processing, the manner of performing particular operations, the tools used, both internal and provided by external entities. Defining the project framework in the above-mentioned scope shall allow to perform the compliance analysis and the risk analysis of the designed solution in the subsequent steps of planning and implementation.

4. Training

In the presented model, the first phase is a training allowing, in accordance with data protection by design requirements, to determine the level of knowledge, including personal data protection and processing security and cyber security, which needs to be absorbed in the organisation in order to be able to properly carry out the subsequent steps. The end result is to reach, by means of appropriate staff qualification improvement, a state in which, when starting to work on a new solution, everyone in the organisation understands both the need for and the risk of data protection and security, and knows what requirements apply, what they should pay attention to and what tools enable them to transform their knowledge of data protection and information security into instruments, technical and organisational measures that secure them. This applies both to internal requirements, including policies, procedures, including risk assessment procedures, and to external requirements, in particular relevant legislation in the area of personal data and information security or cyber security[29]. It is important to consider that external requirements may include sectoral regulations. For example, the requirement to comply with best practices, standards, code of conduct for the chosen technology, business practices.

29 (n 27).

The data subject is entitled to rely on the due and professional care of the AI system developer. Namely, if there is a generally accepted good practice in the industry, then the data subject can be sure that this will also be taken into account in the training activity. The exception may be where sectoral rules (e.g. business practices) are not mandatory, in which case the AI system developer may ignore them, but must sufficiently inform the data subject that normal business practices have not been followed.

5. *Requirements*

The next phase is the identification of data protection and information security requirements for the final product. The correctness and completeness of the requirements identification will have a significant impact on the correctness of the end result, and from this perspective it is a key step. In order to define correct requirements, it is necessary to establish the context, i.e. to determine the data requirements starting from the scope, sources, the categories of data subjects, the identification of the user and the owner, i.e. the future controller, as well as the further entities involved in the processing, i.e. the processors and other recipients. This will allow to identify the relevant legislation, both general and sectoral, guidelines, applicable codes of conduct, norms and standards. The analysis of the requirements, as in the first stage, must be both external and internal and from the perspective of personal data protection include regulations, in particular provisions of the General Data Protection Regulation, but also business practices and policies, internal procedures such as control, audit, compliance procedures, etc.

In relation to the implementation of data protection by design model, among the legal requirements at the forefront is ensuring compliance of the solution to be developed with the principles of personal data processing formulated in Article 5, i.e. the principles of lawfulness, fairness and transparency, purpose limitation, data minimisation, accuracy, storage limitation, integrity and confidentiality. Already in this phase of the analysis the controller will have to demonstrate its assessment as well as its decision on how to ensure compliance in accordance with the principle of accountability, which should be included in the compliance procedure by creating appropriate documentation, check lists, etc.

From the perspective of the construction of AI-based mechanisms, the intensity of compliance difficulties may vary, but in particular the verification of the principle of legality, fairness, transparency, data minimisation, and security embedded in the principle of confidentiality and integrity will be crucial[30]. This is also indirectly related to the direction of the conceptual work on the legal framework for AI indicated in the European Commission and HLEG studies related to the expectation of constructing trustworthy human-centric artificial intelligence.

The primary issue relates to the requirement for AI developers to ensure compliance with the principle of lawfulness and fairness. It is not limited to the determination of an adequate legal basis, but also requires that AI algorithms or models are constructed in such a way as to ensure the correctness and non-discriminatory character of the processing or the effect of such operations, as well as to exclude the possibility of basing on them biased or detrimental automated decisions affecting the rights and freedoms of data subjects. It is an element of the assumption of the necessity to take into account the interests of the data subject in shaping the processing, including the expectation that the interference with privacy caused by the data processing is not excessive. Consequently, it results from the controller's obligation to introduce measures to prevent arbitrary and discriminatory treatment of data subjects and to implement solutions and self-learning mechanisms to exclude from the processing which is the basis of the decision data which are incorrect, unduly processed or inadequately processed, as well as those which ensure the correction of factors causing the inaccuracy of personal data and which will be oriented at the maximum reduction of the risk of errors and at securing personal data in a way which takes into account the potential risks for the interests and rights of the data subject. This applies both to the algorithms themselves and to the data used , in particular their quantity and quality.

The transparency principle, on the other hand, is aimed at ensuring that the data subject is aware of the purpose, scope and context of the processing, in order to enable him to exercise control over his own data[31]. The challenges in ensuring compliance with the principle of transparency are mainly related to the assessment of the extent to which it is possible to explain how AI systems work, from the perspective of the person whose

---

30 Dominik Lubasz and Monika Namysłowska in Dominik Lubasz (ed) *Meritum Ochrona danych osobowych* (Wolters Kluwer, 2020) 1013.

31 The WP29 indicates that consent should also specify the consequences of the processing - see WP29, 'Opinion 15/2011 on the definition of consent' (13 July 2011, WP 187), <http://www.giodo.gov.pl/pl/file/5341> accessed 13 May 2021 18. See also Arwid Mednis, 'Cechy zgody na przetwarzanie danych osobowych w opinii Grupy Roboczej Art. 29 dyrektywy 95/46 Nr 15/2011 (WP 187)' in Grzegorz Sibiga (ed) *Aktualne problemy prawnej ochrony danych osobowych* (2012) 7 MoP 26. Łuczak (n 13) 466.

data are to be processed. In specific cases, it may prove difficult to provide sufficient information to the data subject, mainly when the AI system is based on deep learning, unsupervised or only partially supervised, when learning is not based on methods using symbolic reasoning principles. The selection of methods to underpin the operation of AI mechanisms, taking into account the requirement of their explainability, is consequently one of the elements of assessing compliance with the principle of transparency. This is because the choice of a particular technological solution should not exclude a priori the possibility of implementing this principle already at the design stage. Technological difficulties cannot exempt one from the obligation of transparency. Therefore, the core of the issue is to find a solution that will allow the proper exercise of data subjects' rights and to provide them with relevant information about the principles of operation of the algorithm so that the data subject can understand the scope and the consequences of the processing of his/her data as well as contest the decisions taken with regard to him/her.

The assessment of the compliance of the AI systems with the data protection by design requirements will also be influenced by the designated purpose of the data processing, which determines the individual parameters of the processing, such as the scope of the data or the time limits, underlying the principle of purpose limitation and data minimisation. The identification and indication of the purpose must therefore take place before the processing starts, and properly informing the data subject about it is one of the elements that allow the data subject to act within his autonomy and control over the processing. The purpose will be different for the different phases of the development of AI systems, starting from the learning phase, validation, testing and finally implementation. It has a significant impact because the correlation between the purpose and the scope of data resulting from the data minimisation principle determines which data fall under the notion of data necessary to fulfil the purpose and which do not. This scope will vary from one phase to another, and will also be case-specific. In the design phase of the AI the main difficulty lies in the fact that at the stage of data acquisition its developers are not always able to predict, especially in models that are not based on symbolic principles of reasoning, how much data will be necessary to achieve a satisfactory learning outcome of the AI in order for it to reach practical applicability[32]. Thus, it can be extremely difficult to draw the line between adequate and inadequate data. It may be even more difficult to demonstrate this

32 Chomiczewski and Lubasz, (n 19) 67ff.

relationship based on measurable criteria. The identification of solutions can start with analysing the possibility of using prepared data and test environments in the learning phase of the AI, and in the application phase performing regular reviews of the area of its operation and adjusting the scope of the data as it changes[33].

The scope of the data as one of the factors also affects the risks of the processing to the data subjects, the more data and individual personal information is collected about the data subject and the more individuals are assessed in the processing, the greater the risks to those individuals[34]. Consequently, it is necessary to search for adequate safeguards corresponding to the increased risk, the level of which must increase as the risk increases. These safeguards are subject to the confidentiality and integrity principle enshrined in Article 5(1)(f). The construction of this principle is based on a risk-based approach and is concretised in particular in the provisions of Articles 25 and 32 of the GDPR. Its essence is the obligation to ensure that personal data are processed in a way providing adequate security, including protection against accidental or unlawful destruction, loss, alteration, unauthorised disclosure of, or access to personal data transmitted, stored or otherwise processed.

Security requirements will be determined by identifying the threats to which AI systems may be exposed, the correlated vulnerabilities of these threats, and the likelihood and severity of the impact on data subjects. These factors influence the parameters for selecting adequate and appropriate security measures. In order to identify risks and make decisions on mitigating them, it is necessary to conduct a risk analysis focused on identifying and addressing the above-mentioned factors affecting the level of risk. This assessment shall be made from the perspective of the impact of the risk on the data subjects. Furthermore, it shall take into account the state of the art, the cost of implementation, and the nature, scope, context and purposes of the processing affecting the risk of violation of the rights or freedoms of natural persons with varying degrees of likelihood and severity arising from the processing by the particular system. The flexibility of the choice of measures is therefore limited by their adequacy to the potential risks of the processing operations and in particular to their security[35].

---

33 ibid.

34 ICO, Guidance on AI and data protection, op. cit., p. 60.

35 Norwegian data protection supervisory authority, 'Software development with Data Protection by Design and by Default' (Guidelines) <https://www.datatilsynet.no/en/about-privacy/virksomhetenes-plikter/innebygd-personvern/data-protection-by-design-and-by-default/?print=true> accessed 13 May 2021.

The proactive identification of security risks, a feature still derived from Ann Cavoukian's original privacy by design principle, and thus the minimisation of risks, technical robustness, are important qualities when designing AI-based solutions, in the data protection by design model of Article 25 of the GDPR.[36]

The specific nature of the technologies used in connection with the development of AI systems, taking into account the requirements of Article 35(1), (3), and (4) of the GDPR, makes it obligatory in some cases, and advisable in others, to implement the specific requirement of conducting a data protection impact assessment. It consists in assessing the impact that the envisaged solution or processing operation may have on the rights and freedoms of natural persons whose data are or will be used. Deepening the analysis in this mode is one of the elements that may be key to prove the fulfilment of the principle of fairness, which, as it was mentioned, requires the limitation of the negative impact of the processing on data subjects.

Equally important from the perspective of the legal requirements that AI developers need to take into account is the issue of designing software, algorithms, and processing, including decision-making processes using AI mechanisms, to ensure that the rights of data subjects, as enshrined in Articles 12-22 of the GDPR, are respected[37]. This includes both the appropriate design of the information policy, in particular in the context of the proper implementation of the principle of transparency, and the preparation for the exercise of specific rights under the GDPR, i.e. the rights of access to data, rectification of data, erasure of data, restriction of processing, data portability, objection and not to be subject to decisions based solely on automated processing of data. In the latter case, the possible authorisation of decisions based solely on automated processing of data, including profiling, with the effects of Article 22 requires the fulfilment of additional requirements of legitimacy and an in-depth analysis.

Notwithstanding the above regulations, from a privacy and personal data protection perspective, the requirements formulated in the draft regulation presented by the European Commission on 21 April 2021 establishing harmonised rules on artificial intelligence (Artificial Intelligence Act) and amending certain Union legislative acts will have to be taken into account

---

36 High Level Expert Group on Artificial Intelligence, 'The Assessment List on Trustworthy Artificial Intelligence' <https://futurium.ec.europa.eu/en/european-ai-alliance/pages/altai-assessment-list-trustworthy-artificial-intelligence> accessed 27 April 2021, *op. cit.*, p. 20.

37 Susałko (n 23) 230.

in the future[38]. As I mentioned, this regulation is intended to lay down harmonised rules on artificial intelligence, providing for rules applicable to the design, development and use of certain high-risk AI systems and restrictions on certain applications of remote biometric identification systems. If this Regulation is finally adopted, there will therefore be new requirements for certain AI systems, additional to the GDPR, as the AI Regulation is only intended to complement and not replace the regulation of the General Data Protection Regulation.

In the context of the scope of the analysis, if this is the final form of the AI Act, an analysis will have to be made as to whether the proposed solution does not fall under the black list of AI-related practices which are prohibited in Article 5 of the AI Regulation. Subsequently, it will also have to be analysed whether the designed AI system will not qualify as a high-risk AI system, as referred to in Article 6 of the draft AI Regulation. In the case of such qualification, a number of additional obligations to be imposed on both manufacturers and users of IS systems will be actualised.

At the end of the deliberations concerning the verification of the requirements to be met by the designed AI system, it is worth returning to the HLEG guidelines on trustworthy and ethical artificial intelligence, and the follow-up to these guidelines in the form of The Assessment List For Trustworthy Artificial Intelligence (ALTAI) For Self Assessment, which provides a system for verifying the compliance of designed AI systems with the principles of trustworthy and ethical artificial intelligence formulated by HLEG and indicated above. In order to facilitate the analysis, a web application for assessing compliance has also been prepared - ALTAI - The Assessment List on Trustworthy Artificial Intelligence[39].

6. *Design*

In the design phase the mechanisms that address the diagnosed requirements should be taken into account and appropriately designed, in parti-

---

38 Commission, 'Proposal for a Regulation of the European Parliament and of the Council Laying Down Harmonised Rules on Artificial Intelligence (Artificial Intelligence Act) and Amending Certain Union Legislative Acts' COM 2021 206 final.

39 High Level Expert Group on Artificial Intelligence, 'The Assessment List on Trustworthy Artificial Intelligence' <https://futurium.ec.europa.eu/en/european-ai-alliance/pages/altai-assessment-list-trustworthy-artificial-intelligence> accessed 27 April 2021.

cular by ensuring compliance with the implementation of the principles of processing, security of processing and the rights of data subjects. In the last mentioned point it is not only about ensuring that these rights are respected and fulfilled, but also that these rights are easily realisable, accessible and intuitive, and that the impact of the processing is limited to what is necessary to achieve reliable results.[40]

These requirements must be precisely reflected in the design. It needs to be assessed and designed by which means these requirements are to be achieved. The means must be adequate for each specific requirement, and this adequacy can be measured e.g. using instruments such as data protection impact assessments. Among the measures proposed by the Norwegian supervisory authority in the aforementioned study on the principle of data protection by design are, inter alia, measures such as minimisation and limitation of the processing and scope of data, security, storage separation, data aggregation, default data protection, i.e. configuring privacy settings in such a way that they are most conducive to ensuring privacy by default.

AI system developer should implement appropriate technical and organisational measures to ensure that, by default, only personal data which are necessary for each specific purpose of the processing are processed. AI system developer and user are accountable for implementing default processing settings and options in a way that only processing that is strictly necessary to achieve the set, lawful purpose is carried out by default. The basic requirement is that data protection is built into the processing by default.

Process requirements for design, on the other hand, include informing, i.e. designing an appropriate level of transparency of the processing for the data subject, ensuring control through the right of access, update, erasure of one's own data, enabling the exercise of rights, and finally designing in such a way that the controller can document how the requirements of the General Data Protection Regulation have been implemented. It is important to emphasize that the General Data Protection Regulation aims to protect not only privacy, but also fairness and other fundamental rights including private life. Therefore data protection law is protecting people also against abuse of information asymmetry.[41] The position of the data subject in relation to data controllers is improved by the transparency of

40 Chomiczewski and Lubasz, (n 19) 67 ff.

41 Paul De Hert and Serge Gutwirth, 'Privacy, data protection and law enforcement: Opacity of the individual and transparency of power' in Erik Claes, Antony Duff and Serge Gutwirth (eds) *Privacy and the Criminal Law* (Intersentia, 2006).

processing activities.[42] The principle of transparency is one of the key principles also in consumer law. Therefore, the inadequate compliance with the requirements may lead to both – breach of data protection law and consumer law. The GDPR contains more detailed transparency obligations than the EU consumer law. Nevertheless, requirements for design must be fulfilled in a broad manner because data are important not only for data protection but also for consumer policy. For example, AI system developer must see the distinction between the terms and conditions and the privacy policy. It must be clear to the data subject and communicated in plain and intelligible language that terms of use of AI system are related to the rights and obligations of the data subject as consumer and the trader under the contract, while a privacy policy provides information about what the AI system does with the personal data[43]. It must also be ensured that data subjects are motivated to read by encouraging interaction. The more interaction is provided, the more data subject choice would be meaningful. Similar methods are used in consumer law.[44] The GDPR makes explicit reference to pictograms – „standardized icons in order to give in an easily visible, intelligible and clearly legible way a meaningful overview of the intended processing".

The design phase is the last moment when AI system developer must objectively assess usage methods regarding to protect specific groups of the data subjects, namely vulnerable persons including children. For example, profiling children should be avoided. It is prohibited to do direct exhortation to children.

7. *Coding*

A project that takes into account the defined requirements, both data- and process-oriented, enables it to be coded correctly. The knowledge base, absorbed in the organisation and then designed in detail taking into account all requirements, should be translated into an appropriate execution level in which all designed requirements are addressed and then tested.

---

42 Natali Helberger, Frederik Zuiderveen Borgesisu, and Agustin Reyna, 'The Perfect Match? A Closer Look at the Relationship between EU Consumer Law and Data Protection Law' (2017) 54, 5 Common Market Law Review 11.

43 General Data Protection Regulation, Recital 42.

44 BEUC, 'EU Consumer Protection 2.0 Structural Asymmetries in Digital Consumer Markets' (March 2021) <https://www.beuc.eu/publications/beuc-x-2021-018_eu_consumer_protection.0_0.pdf> accessed 13 May 2021.

In this context, consideration must also be given to excluding the use of specific functions and modules that may prove to be unsafe. Furthermore, the guidelines point out the need to perform static code analysis and code reviews on a regular basis, which ensures that guidelines for secure coding are being followed and can be measured to ensure controls are working.

8. *Testing*

The testing phase is aimed at verifying whether the data protection and information security requirements have been implemented as planned and properly met. In the case of software, it is indicated that it needs to be tested for vulnerabilities using dynamic tests, fuzz tests and penetration tests[45]. It is important to clearly define the requirement for testing for data protection and information security, in particular in high risk and specific AI systems, for example facial recognition, product safety components, immigration and border control AI systems[46]. In line with a risk-based approach, high-risk AI systems will need to include the implementation of adequate risk correlated mitigation measures. The data subject has a legitimate right to expect that higher data protection requirements will be met in the testing of higher risk AI.

9. *Release*

A successfully completed testing phase allows the decision to launch the product on the market. In this phase, it is important to plan not only the sales and marketing strategy, including communication, but also the strategy for managing incidents that may occur after the release and the procedure for updating the designed and implemented security features. At release phase it is also important to have strategy how to react to individual complaints of data subjects. The AI system basically operates

---

45 Norwegian data protection supervisory authority, 'Software development with Data Protection by Design and by Default' (Guidelines) <https://www.datatilsynet.no/en/about-privacy/virksomhetenes-plikter/innebygd-personvern/data-protection-by-design-and-by-default/?print=true> accessed 13 May 2021.

46 Irena Nesterova, 'Mass data gathering and surveillance: the fight against facial recognition technology in the globalized world' (SHS Web of Conferences 74, 03006, 2020) 6.

independently, so human supervision is essential in specific and individual cases that may indicate general data security risks regarding AI system.

Finally, it is the responsibility of the AI system controller to demonstrate compliance with data protection principles. If the principle of accountability is not effectively implemented, trustworthy AI cannot be achieved.

10. Maintenance

The last-mentioned elements ultimately become the goal of the maintenance phase. In this phase, business continuity, incident and security breach management plans are implemented, the purpose of which is to guarantee the ability to continuously ensure confidentiality, integrity, availability and resilience of the processing systems and services, as well as the ability to quickly restore the availability of and access to personal data in the event of a physical or technical incident. On the basis of observed incidents, work is to be undertaken to ensure that identified non-conformities are resolved, as well as to initiate further product development activities. For these activities, the same strategy should be applied as in the development of the project based on the requirements of data protection by design, starting with the development of the concept and the context allowing the identification of knowledge needs, and therefore the training stage, as the first stage of the cycle. This process is not a one-off, but a continuous process in which it is necessary to update the conclusions, taking into account changing factors, above all those related to the context of processing.

11. Summary and conclusions

The risks related to the development and application of solutions using artificial intelligence mechanisms, as well as the search for and definition of protective objectives, especially in the area of fundamental rights, in particular the right to privacy and the protection of personal data, clearly directs the analysis, among other things, to the search for and evaluation of the fit for purpose of existing legal regulations. In the area of personal data protection, which is also a fundamental right according to Article 8 of the CFR, and in the context of the will to create human-oriented artificial intelligence, the potential should be seen in the provisions of Regulation 2016/679, at the regulatory basis of which lies the will to ensure a high level of protection of the rights of natural persons through, inter alia, the legal instruments data protection by design and data protection by default[47]. Objective of taking into account the perspective of the data subject in the creation process, as an immanent element of the assessment, and at the same time will allow to perform the analysis from the perspective of the principle provided for in the GDPR, to ensure the realization of the rights of data subjects and the security of the processing.

The adoption and process-oriented implementation in the development of new technological solutions of a personal data protection strategy in the design phase based on Article 25(1) and (2) of the GDPR, using both data-centric and process-oriented approaches, addresses the main concerns related to the application of technology in an instrumental way, arbitrary or discriminatory effects of automated decisions made using AI. It allows reflection, definition of requirements and appropriate design of solutions to avoid discriminatory bias of algorithms as well as problems of availability, quality and quantity of input data, through the use of a federated learning model[48]. At the same time, applying this method to AI projects should allow trust in the technology to be rebuilt and this goal to be woven into the design (trust by design), which is ultimately a key element in creating human-centric AI.

In the context of the submission by the European Commission on 21 April 2021 of a draft regulation laying down harmonised rules on artificial intelligence (Artificial Intelligence Act) and amending certain Union legislative acts[49], the regulatory environment for artificial intelligence will evolve. However, if the strategy of building a trustworthy human-centric AI in the European Union based, inter alia, on the principles of human agency and oversight, technical robustness and safety, transparency, diversity, non-discrimination and fairness is upheld, the GDPR will remain the only leading regulation in this area, and data protection by design

---

47 High Level Expert Group on Artificial Intelligence, 'The Assessment List on Trustworthy Artificial Intelligence' <https://futurium.ec.europa.eu/en/european-ai-alliance/pages/altai-assessment-list-trustworthy-artificial-intelligence> accessed 27 April 2021, p. 26.

48 Shlomit Yanisky-Ravid and Sean K. Hallisey, 'Equality and Privacy by Design: Ensuring Artificial Intelligence (AI) is Properly Trained & Fed: A New Model of AI Data Transparency & Certification as Safe Harbor Procedures' <https://ssrn.com/abstract=3278490> accessed 13 May 2021.

49 Commission, 'Proposal for a Regulation of the European Parliament and of the Council Laying Down Harmonised Rules on Artificial Intelligence (Artificial Intelligence Act) and Amending Certain Union Legislative Acts' COM 2021 206 final.

mechanisms will have to be embedded in the design and use of AI. This corresponds with the outlined intentions of the proposed AI Regulation, which is merely to complement the General Data Protection Regulation with a set of harmonised rules applicable to the design, development and use of certain high-risk AI systems and restrictions on certain applications of remote biometric identification systems.

The discussion on the regulation of artificial intelligence is now going to gain momentum, and the European Commission's proposal should be seen as an encouragement for this. However, voices are already being raised that the draft does not contain instruments for the insufficient protection of data subjects, especially in aspects concerning control and transparency, and that it lacks the promised horizontality of the draft legislation and the creation of a legal framework for all AI systems and not just selected ones.

There is an urgent need to develop further guidance and regulation and to consider a more horizontal approach. While Europe is still debating this, the effective use of data protection instruments in the design phase of AI systems is becoming increasingly important. The article proposes solutions on how to minimize the privacy risks associated with the development and use of AI systems.

Privacy by Design in China's Digital Privacy Laws and its Application in Smart Cities

Hongyu Fu

Chong Liu
BEIJING, China

Abstract
The rapid development of internet and data technological tools gravely endangers people's privacy in China, triggering legislative response to provide more protection. Private by Design is embodied in recent Chinese digital privacy laws and applied in Chinese smart cities. It provides a balance between digital privacy protection and the need of utilization of personal private information to make cities more intelligent, efficient and environment friendly.

Keywords:
Private by Design, digital privacy law, smart cities

1. *Privacy by Design: Principles and Its Application in EU and U.S.*

1.1 *Introduction of Privacy by Design and Its Foundational Principles*

"Privacy by Design" is a paradigm developed by Dr. Ann Cavoukian, in the 1990s, to address the emerging and growing threats to online privacy. The main idea is to inscribe the privacy protection into the design of information technologies from the very start. This paradigm represents a significant innovation with respect to the traditional approaches of privacy protection because it requires a significant shift from a "reactive model to proactive one."[1]

1 See Anna Monreale, Salvatore Rinzivillo, Francesca Pratesi, Fosca Giannotti and Dino Pedreschi, Privacy-by-design in big data analytics and social mining (EPJ Data Science 2014) 3.

According to Dr. Ann Cavoukian, “Privacy by Design advances the view that the future of privacy cannot be assured solely by compliance with regulatory frameworks; rather, privacy assurance must ideally become an organization’s default mode of operation.”[2] The Private by Design paradigm consists of seven foundational principles: (1) Proactive not Reactive; (2) Privacy as the Default Setting; (3) Privacy Embedded into Design; (4) Full Functionality; (5) Full Lifecycle Protection; (6) Visibility and Transparency; (7) Keep it User-Centric.[3] Therefore, Private by Design highlights the proactive protection of privacy, the end-to-end and full lifecycle protection by using the protection system embedded into design. Besides, user-friendly characteristics, the increased data transparency, and a “win-win” result are critical elements, based on the seven principles of Private by Design.

1.2 An Overview of the Application of Private by Design in EU and U.S.

EU and U.S. have incorporated Privacy by Design in their digital privacy protections laws, though in different manners. EU insisted to enact an comprehensive and far-reaching digital privacy law, and adopted Data Protection Directive in 1995 to protect individuals’ personal data and the free movement of such data.[4] In 2012, the European Commission proposed a comprehensive reform of the EU’s 1995 data protection rules to strengthen online rights of privacy and boost Europe’s digital economy.[5] After more than four years’ legislation efforts, the EU passed the General Data Protection Regulation (GDPR) in 2016, which superseded the Data Protection Directive and became enforceable in 2018.

The GDPR reflects the seven basic principles of Private by Design in many parts. Firstly, GDPR protects natural persons’ fundamental rights to protect their personal data and shows the respect for their privacy. Secondly, GDPR reflects the transparent, full-life cycle protection on individuals’

---

2 See Anne Cavoukian, ‘Private by Design. The 7 Foundational Principles. Originally’ <https://www.ipc.on.ca/wp-content/uploads/resources/7foundationalprinciples.pdf> accessed on April 25 2021.

3 *Ibid.*

4 European Parliament, Regulation (EU) 2016/679 of the European Parliament and of the Council of 27 April 2016 on the protection of natural persons with regard to the processing of personal data and on the free movement of such data, and repealing Directive 95/46/EC [2016] OJ L199/1 (General Data Protection Regulation).

5 Full text available at https://edps.europa.eu/data-protection/data-protection/legislation/history-general-data-protection-regulation_en

personal data. Thirdly, Article 25 specifies on "Data protection by design and by default" explicitly, making it a settled legal principle.

In U.S., legal protection of privacy is based on a combination of the Constitutional protection, federal legislation, industry self-regulations and the state laws. The Fair Information Practice Principles (FIPPs) published by the U.S. Department of Health, Education and Welfare in 1973 has been the foundation of the U.S. legislation on personal data protection. In recent years, with a rising tide of privacy blunders on social networking sites and platforms, U.S. is also searching for a new regulatory approach, i.e., private by design.[6]

The Federal Trade Commission first rolled out Private by Design as an official policy in its 2010 privacy report, as one of three components of a proposed framework for data security. The other two components are "simplified choice" and "greater transparency."[7] And in its 2012 Report, FTC proposed the final FTC privacy framework and implementation recommendations, incorporating "Privacy by Design"; "Simplified Consumer Choice" and "Transparency" principles.[8] According to the 2012 FTC report, Privacy by Design requires companies to promote consumer privacy throughout their organizations, and at every stage of the development of their products and services. The FTC report further requires the companies to assure data security, take reasonable collection limits, make sound retention practices, and keep data accuracy by adopting appropriate procedural measures.[9]

2. *Private by Design in China*

2.1 *The Chinese Legal Regime of Digital Privacy Protection*

Unlike EU and U.S., digital privacy protection legal regime in China can be characterized as (1) coordinated from multiple areas of law, (2) comprehensive in enacting an integrated legislation, and (3) supplemented by lower-level legal documents. China in recent years have enacted several legislations, the provisions of which provide criminal, civil, and adminis-

6 Deirdre K. Mulligan and Jennifer King, 'Bridging the gap between privacy and design' (2012) 14 U. Pa. J. Const. L. 989.
7 FTC, Protecting Consumer Privacy in an Era of Rapid Change (FTC 2010) 9.
8 FTC, Protecting Consumer Privacy in an Era of Rapid Change (FTC 2012) 7-8.
9 See *ibid.*, 22-34.

trative sanctions or remedies for breach of privacy and personal information in digital era. The criminal, civil and administrative law provisions provide a full-scale legal network addressing digital privacy protection issues, though the relationship among them is not well delineated. In 2020 a major legislation was proposed, named Personal Information Protection Law. The draft law marks an attempt by China's legislators to enact an encompassing, comprehensive law covering most aspect in this matter, changing the landscape of digital privacy protection from the coordinated approach to a unified approach. Besides such specific legislative provisions, departments in charge of privacy protection and digital society administration published lower-level legal documents supplementing the legislation, which, together with privacy protection provision in other areas of laws, provided clearer guidance for different participants to fulfill their legal responsibilities.

2.1.1 China's Coordinated Legislative Approach to Digital Privacy Protection

The Criminal Code provides sanctions against intentional infringement on a person's personal information and privacy since 2009, making it punishable by imprisonment and fine. The scope of criminal punishment has been gradually expanded, and severity extended in recent years as of some personal infringement cases leading to severe harm to the victim. For example, since the case of Xu Yuyu, the Supreme People's Court and the Supreme People's Procuratorate published the judicial interpretation of "crime of infringing on citizens' personal information" (the Interpretation)[10]. The Interpretation shows the determination of the highest Chinese Judicial Institutions, which is to put emphasis on protecting citizens' important private personal information and exert the punishment in severe and lenient manner depending on different circumstances.

With respect to the civil law, the Civil Code of the People's Republic of China (the Civil Code), which is a foundational, systematic, and comprehensive code in the area of private law. Firstly, the Civil Code's protection on digital privacy is manifested in Article 111: "The personal information of a natural person shall be protected by law." Neither the illegal collec-

---

10 Xu Yuyu case involves a telephone fraud against Ms. Xu, a high school graduate student from a less wealthy family, who was going to college. Ms. Xu's personal information was hacked and was defrauded to wire out several thousand RMB prepared for her college study. She committed suicide, and the case generated an outcry in China for criminal punishment of personal information invasions.

tion, use, process and transmission, nor the illegal deal, provision, and publishment of the personal information of other persons are allowed. Secondly, the Civil Code made specific stipulations to protect the right of privacy and personal information in Book Four, Personality Rights. According to Articles 1032 and 1034, a natural person enjoys the right of privacy, and the Civil Code protects a natural person's personal information. Remarkably, the Civil Code keeps balance between protection and processing. For example, an actor shall not assume any civil liability if the processing is for protecting the public interest or the lawful rights and interests of the natural person. Thirdly, although the Civil Code is a private law, it can also prevent the administrative decision, management, and supervision from violating a natural person's private right. In other words, the Civil Code can impose certain restrictions on the administrative power.

Concerning the administrative law, the Cybersecurity Law of the People's Republic of China (the Cybersecurity Law) provides the foundational legal protection on cybersecurity and the lawful rights and interests of citizens, legal persons and other organizations. Firstly, the Cybersecurity Law emphasizes on constructing a comprehensive state governance system on the cyber area. According to Articles 6, 9, 10, 11 and 12, the system needs the state's legal measures. However, the cyber security cannot be realized with the mere efforts from the state. The participation of the entire society, the intensify industry self-discipline by network-related industry organizations and any individual or organization's legal usage of the internet are also essential. Secondly, the Cybersecurity Law completes cyber security obligations and responsibilities of network operators, who are the owners and administrators of the network as well as network service providers. Thirdly, in Chapter VI, Legal Liability, the penalties for illegal acts have been raised, which is conducive to ensure the implementation of the Cybersecurity Law.

2.1.2 China's Recent Endeavor to a Unified Digital Privacy Protection Law

The draft of Personal Information Protection Law was issued on October 21, 2020 for public comment. The draft assimilates the relevant laws and regulations of the Cybersecurity Law, Law on the Protection of Rights and Interests of Consumers, the Civil Code, the E-Commerce Law and so on. Besides, the draft also assimilates some good rules of foreign legislation, for example GDPR. In conclusion, there are five main highlights of the draft:

(1) The expansion of the applicable territorial scope. According to Article 3, the draft law shall not only be applied within the territory of the People's Republic of China, but also be applied to the processing outside the territory of the People's Republic of China, under certain circumstances. Article 3 is similar to the stipulations in Article 3 of GDPR.
(2) The emphasis on the preliminary explication and the consent of a natural person. Most of the rules on personal information processing are stipulated in Chapter II. In Article 14, the draft law clearly clarifies the definition of "consent to the processing of personal information", i.e., an individual shall express his consent voluntarily and explicitly on the premise of being fully informed. However, being excessive with the explication on premise and the consent of a natural person can sometimes be the enemy of the good. According to Article 13, the lawmakers have decreased the limitation on information processing, which is beneficial for the balance between personal information protection and usage. In the era of big data and cloud technology, this new balance can promote the economy vitality.
(3) The emphasis on the obligation of the personal information processors. The draft law has increased the personal information processors' freedom on processing personal information. Thus, comparatively, it is necessary for the processors to bear more responsibilities on protecting individuals' personal information. The specific stipulations are in Chapter V, Obligations of Personal Information Processors.
(4) The explicit statement of individuals' rights in personal information processing activities. According to Articles 44 to 48, individuals shall have the following five main rights, i.e. the right to know and the right to decide on the processing of their personal information; the right to consult and duplicate their personal information; the right to request personal information processors to correct or supplement relevant information; the right to delete his or her personal information; the right to request personal information processors to interpret the personal information processing rules they develop.
(5) The strengthening on monitoring of the states' departments. "Personal information protection is different from industry to industry." Therefore, Article 56 stipulates on three kinds of states' departments performing the function of protecting personal information, which have

formed a system, in order to make sure every individual can receive the legal protection on their personal information.[11]

2.1.3 Supplementing Rules to Digital Privacy Legislation

In addition to the four main legislations hereinberfore, there are various separate rules on personal information in different departmental laws and regulations. For example, Article 12 in Law of the People's Republic of China on Prevention and Treatment of Infectious Diseases; Article 16 in Regulation on the Handling of Medical Accidents; Article 4 in Provisions on the Technical Measures for the Protection of the Security of the Internet, and so on.

2.2 The Application of Private by Design under Current China's Digital Privacy Protection Laws

Although there is no explicit term "Private by Design" appearing in the Chinese legislations, the seven foundational principles of Private by Design have been embodied in the Chinese digital privacy laws.

2.2.1 The "Proactive not Reactive" Principle Is Embodied in the Chinese Criminal and Administrative Legislations

First of all, the criminal law naturally has a deterrent effect, with the legal power to impose fine, limit individuals' person freedom and even take one's life. To protect citizens' data privacy, the Amendment IX to the criminal law revised the criminal law from two aspects.

In the first place, the Amendment added a new crime called "crime of infringing on citizens' personal information", which expanded the scope of the criminal subjects. Before the Amendment IX became effective, according to the Amendment VII, the criminal subjects of crimes on personal information were enumerated as "the staff member of a state organ or an entity in such a field as finance, telecommunications, transportation, education or medical treatment". While in the Amendment IX, all citizens

11 Full text available at <https://m.mpaypass.com.cn/news/202010/22144504.html> accessed on April 25 2021.

could be the criminal subjects. The Amendment also expanded the scope of "personal information". The "personal information" is no longer limited within the scope of personal information that is obtained during the organ's or entity's performance of duties or provision of services. According to the Amendment VII, any act of infringing on citizens' personal information, if with serious circumstances, is under the criminal law's jurisdiction; In the next place, the criminal law also clarifies that the network service provider has the obligation to perform the information network security management.

Secondly, the judicial interpretation in 2017 made explicit interpretation on "serious circumstance". The Interpretation set different standards for different kinds of personal information. According to Article 5, paragraph 3, the crime standard is 50 pieces for "the citizen's whereabouts, communication contents, credit investigation information and property information"; while for "accommodation information, communication records, health and physiological information, transaction information and other personal information", the crime standard is 500 pieces. Also, the Interpretation adopts the fair principle. For example, with respect to the punishment, Article 12 stipulates that the punishment will be considered based on the hazards caused by the crime, the amount of illegal income involved in the crime, and criminal record and confession and repentance attitudes of the defendant.

In conclusion, the criminal code and the interpretation expanded the scope of the criminal subjects and the criminal acts on personal information, which can protect the personal information and prevent crimes before-the -fact. In addition to the criminal code, the Cybersecurity Law also shows the preventative measures on protecting personal information. The Cybersecurity Law stipulates on the regular conduction of data protection reviews. According to Article 21, it is important for the network operators to establish safe and effective protection system; to choose a appropriate technical solution; to strengthen the data protection capacity according to the Cybersecurity Law. In addition, according to Article 25, the Cybersecurity Law also focuses on making emergency response plans for cybersecurity incidents.

2.2.2 The "Privacy as the Default Setting" Principle Is Embodied in the Relevant Stipulations on Mobile Internet Application Program (APP).

"Privacy as the Default Setting" means that the protection on citizens' privacy has been built into the system with the default setting. Being applied to the apps operation, it means that the privacy policy and other collection and usage rules showed to the users have adopted the strictest protection on personal privacy as a default setting, being built into IT systems, technology infrastructure or business practices by default.[12] In other words, it is similar to the "opt-out" regime on personal privacy protection. Only if a user chooses not to consent the policy or the rules, will their privacy lose protection. In fact, this automate protection on users' privacy is also embodied in the Chinese legislation. Taking Provisions on the Administration of Mobile Internet Applications Information Services (the Provisions) as an example, the Provisions not only stipulates on a mobile internet apps provider's obligation, but also emphasizes on an internet apps service provider's obligation.

According to Article 7, a mobile internet apps provider shall establish and improve the users' information security protection mechanism. For example, encrypting and protecting the users' data; preventing unrelated people from obtaining the data; preventing the data from being downloaded and stolen and recording the operation on important documents and so on.[13] Article 8 stipulates that an internet apps service provider shall perform management and supervision responsibilities for apps providers. For example, urging apps providers to establish and improve the security examination mechanism to protect users' information; to provide complete explanations on the obtaining of apps and users' information, and to present them to users. If apps providers violate the Provisions, the internet apps service providers shall adopt measures, such as warning, suspension of launching, and removal of apps, keep relevant records, and report to the competent department.

2.2.3 The Principles of "Privacy Embedded into Design" and "Full Lifecycle Protection" are Applied in The Civil Code and The Cybersecurity Law

The principles of Privacy Embedded into Design and End-to-End Security have connections on personal information protection. These two principles both focus on a comprehensive security mechanism to protect personal information. However, the former one focuses on the preventative

12 Full text available at <https://www.pwc.com/us/en/services/consulting/library/gdpr-embedding-data-protection.html> accessed on April 25 2021.

13 Full text available at <http://www.ip-guard.net/blog/?p=1818> accessed on April 25 2021.

measures, while the latter one puts emphasis on the later-stage management. Therefore, these two principles will be introduced together.

Firstly, the Civil Code provides a basic "End-to-End Security" system for personal information and privacy protection. According to Book Four, Personality Rights, Chapter VI, Right of Privacy and Protection of Personal Information, the Civil Code protects a natural person's personal information and privacy from six aspects, i.e. (1) the definition of privacy and personal information; (2) the principles of processing the personal information; (3) the obligations of a information processors; (4) the strict restrictions on exemption excuses for processing a natural person's information; (5) the three main rights of a natural person; (6) the confidentiality of the state organs, statutory institutions and their staff members. These stipulations have established a comprehensive firewall for a natural person's privacy and personal information. [14]

Secondly, the Cybersecurity Law mainly protects network users' personal information from two aspects, i.e., network operation security and network information security. According to Articles 15 and 40, the state shall establish and improve the system of cybersecurity standards and the system for the protection of users' information.[15] The network operation security is the premise of the network information security, just like the relationship between Privacy Embedded into Design and End-to-End Security.

2.2.4 The Full Functionality Principle Is Applied in The Civil Code and The Personal Information Protection Law.

Full Functionality principle means that Private by Design seeks to accommodate a "win-win" manner rather than a dated, zero-sum approach. In other words, this principle is seeking for a balance. This principle is embodied in many legislations by increasing the legitimacy for operators to process the personal information.

Firstly, according to Article 1036 in the Civil Code, there are three circumstances under which an actor does not need to obtain the natural person's consent. The three circumstances are (1) under the consent by the natural person or his or her guardian; (2) with the initiative publishment

14 Full text available at <https://m.mpaypass.com.cn/news/202006/11113115.html> accessed on April 25 2021.

15 The Cybersecurity Law of China.

of the natural person or the legal publishment; (3) for protecting the public interest or the lawful rights and interests of the natural person.

Secondly, according to the Personal Information Protection Law, Article 13, there are six circumstances under which a personal information processor to process personal information without the preliminary consent.[16] The draft law decreases the limitation on the personal information processing, which is beneficial for the balance between personal information protection and usage.

2.2.5 The Visibility and Transparency Principle Is Embodied in Preliminary Informing and Later-stage Processing.

The principle of Visibility and Transparency is embodied in two aspects, namely, to inform users clearly before collecting their information and to process personal information transparently. The first aspect is always explicitly indicated as the principles of openness and transparency in laws and regulations. For example, in Article 7 of the Personal Information Protection Law; Article 1035 of the Civil Code; Article 7 of the Cybersecurity Law; Article 17 of the E-commerce Law; Article 29 of Law of the People's Republic of China on the Protection of Consumer Rights and Interests and so on. Besides, after receiving individuals' personal information, the transparency of processing and retention on personal information shall also be guaranteed.

2.2.6 The Keep It User-Centric Principle Is Applied in Confirming Users' Right by Laws and Regulations.

Most of the Chinese laws and regulations explicitly stipulate on an individual's right to protect his or her personal information. For example, the Personal Information Protection Law makes a conclusion on individuals' rights in personal information processing activities in Articles 44-48, which shows the priority to users' privacy.

Also, the Chinese legislative institution enacts laws and regulations in key areas concerning citizens' personal information protection. For example, the E-commerce Law was enacted to safeguard the lawful rights and interests of all parties to e-commerce. According to Article 18 and 19,

16 See the specific stipulations in the Personal Information Protection Law.

the E-commerce Law adopts the "opt-in" regime, stipulating that an e-commerce business shall provide the consumer with options not targeting his or her identifiable traits; and shall not set the said tie-in sale as a default option, which show respect and equally protection for the lawful rights and interests of consumers. Besides, the E-commerce Law also increases e-commerce businesses' burden of proof in order to help the consumer defend his or her lawful rights and interests. According to Article 62, over the course of handling an e-commerce dispute, an e-commerce business shall provide the original contract and transaction records to ascertain the facts. Otherwise, the e-commerce business shall assume corresponding legal liability.

In conclusion, the Chinese legislations on personal information, from the public laws to the private laws, have contained the spirit of the seven principles of Private by Design. In the future, with the Personal Information Protection Law becoming effective and more and more departmental laws being enacted in key areas, the Chinese legal protection on personal information will become more complete.

3. *Application of Privacy by Design in China's Smart Cities, with A Case Study of Face Recognition Technology*

3.1 *China's Smart City Building and the Entailed Privacy Concerns*

The overarching concept of smart city rests on internet that connects various end users and their appliances, as well as the vast amount of data that are being generated and processed for system control and decision making. China has been building up internet and data infrastructure which facilitate the construction of smart cities, especially with the rollout of 5G and gigabit network. The application of internet over things (IoT) has increased significantly in China, not only in first tier cities like Beijing, Shanghai, and Shenzhen, but also in so-called New First Tier cities including Hangzhou and Chengdu, as well as cities in lower tiers. The fast pace in smart city building reflects China's momentum in all three layers of IoT logical architecture, including application layer, transport layer and sensing layer.[17]

17 For the discussion about the layers of IoT, see Li Ling, Li Shancang, Zhao Shanshan, 'QoS-aware scheduling of service-oriented Internet of things' (2014) 10 2 IEEE Trans on Industial Informatics 1497-1505[12]; Wu Chunkun. Security Fundamentals for Internet of Things (Science Press 2013).

The sensing layer, which includes the sources of data like RFID, GPS, environment detectors, cameras, etc., has infiltrated not only into industrial settings, but also to average offices and households. Intelligent device manufactures compete fiercely on this level, producing cutting edge end user devices that fit into different scenes. Thanks to the fast pace of urbanization and booming in real estate market, newly built home and offices are generally equipped with such data collecting devices providing basic input for the community and city IoT infrastructure. The utilization of wireless technologies over WiFi, Bluetooth and other energy-signal transforming mechanisms also enables intelligent innovation for older buildings. In the transport layer, the bandwidth of mobile communication networks and computer networks increases significantly in the 5G era, expanding the transmittable data into more applicable scenes and enabling new technologies including autonomous driving. In the application layer, major platform providers provide services to various users including governments and public entities, allowing the latter to engage in smart decision based on big data and AI. The public sector also pushes for the utilization of new technologies, under the requirements of Fang, Guan, Fu reform.[18] Big data and AI are also used for managing traffic and most importantly, in recent COVID-19 pandemic prevention and control.[19] To give more room to the private sector and to positively engage with new technologies, municipal governments in China are weighing themselves in transforming mega cities into smart cities.

The fast expansion of the utilization of IoT and AI technologies has generated concerns over the breach of privacy in various settings. In smart homes, the intelligent devices make privacy exposure more easily, where leaking of private information could happen over the internet by means of security breach or inadvertent maneuvers by residents. Hacking into home cameras has been prevalent in China because of weak security protocols.[20] The inter-connected nature of smart devices further exacerbates the problem. In addition, the face recognition technology has been developed to an extent that customer's face information could be captured far a certain

---

18 *Fang, Guan, Fu* in Chinese means government agency shall return power to market, to provide better management and to serve well the needs of market participants.

19 For a summary of the application, see "What are the roles of Big Data in Pandemic Control and Management", available at <https://www.thepaper.cn/newsDetail_forward_9806802> accessed on April 25 2021.

20 See media report, available at <https://www.sohu.com/a/150861985_182299> accessed on April 25 2021.

distance, creating concerns over her privacy as well as financial security. It also raises a contract law issue, where the customer may dispute whether she gives actual and voluntary consent to the payment request, thus finalizes the transaction. In another instance where smart utility devices are applied, a user's real time electricity, water and other utility usage are constantly monitored and processed. The big data generated from these smart utility devices assists the utility providers to adjust their services to better meet users' demand, reduce unnecessary production and make energy consumption greener. Yet utility consumption data may reveal users' personal lifestyle. Improper use of such information may create social inequality among groups with different income, as household income level in general positively correlates with its utility consumption. The data may also reveal information regarding personal habits and recreational activities which is private. On a broader level, the inter-connectivity of numerous IoT devices make the smart cities more susceptible to data breaches, and the invasion in end user device may cause large scale privacy incidents to ensure utility data being anonymous and identified. It is crucial to secure privacy. Therefore, a more comprehensive legal framework covering each layer and every participant is needed, to address privacy concerns from using smart utility devices to the technologies used in smart cities.

3.2 The General Application of Privacy by Design in China's Smart Cities

The Private by Design principles, when actively applied, can provide illustrative solutions to above challenges against privacy protection in smart city building in China.

Firstly, Private by Design requires privacy protection to be incorporated throughout the life cycle of smart city planning, building, operation, and management. Privacy protection therefore is considered as part of the major functions of a smart city, which is a requirement must be met not a cost to be ignored. The incorporation of privacy protection can mitigate the risk of privacy invasion, especially considering that the remedies provided by privacy laws apply ex post to privacy infringement and may not be sufficient to prevent large scale privacy invasion in city level.

Secondly, the concept of Privacy by Default makes residents and users more confident about the privacy protection. Currently privacy protection legal regime premises on the notion of self-determination, where a user gives informed consent to the collection and use of her personal information and private data. The proliferation of IoT devices in smart cities brings convenience and efficiency to its residents, but it makes users more difficult to make meaningful decisions on whether to allow the collection or use of their private information. Privacy by Design requires each participant in smart cities, when collecting and using users' private information, must respect users' right of privacy and personal information, must by default protect users' relevant rights without users' further or additional action. Thus, users are not required to go through voluminous amounts of informed consent documents, as they can expect every informed consent document by default provides sufficient protection for their privacy. This will also in turn facilitate the collection and use of private data, as more users are willing to voluntarily allow data access.

Thirdly, Private by Design can generate positive results in smart city planning, building and management, creating win-win for various participants. In the past decades, China has been developing fast in internet and data technologies, at the cost of users' personal information and privacy. Recently the legislation made it clear that privacy and personal information are strictly protected by civil law, administrative law and criminal law, overcoming the concerns that stringent legal protection on privacy may choke technology development and innovation process. The application of Private by Design principles provides good illustration that the need of privacy protection and the interest of technology innovation can both be met. In smart cities where Private by Design principles are applied, privacy can be attained together with efficiency, cleanliness, and convenience. The positive sum result will in turn attract more residents and more capital, creating more competitiveness for the city.

3.3 Case Study: Applying Privacy by Design in Face Recognition Technology

Face recognition technology serves as the nexus between human and machine, where a person who intends to access and control the machine is identified and authorized. Comparing to the other biometric identification technologies, it is more accurate with recent development in image capture and analysis technologies. In addition, it doesn't require the cooperation of the users, and can identify an user remotely without his or her actual knowledge of being identified. Thus it enables quick and mass surveillance, especially for security purposes. Smart cities in China have vastly used face recognition technologies to provide identification in public places, especially where security is of concern, including transportation hubs and major gatherings. Privately, face recognition has been used in mobile apps when a user intends to get access to his or her private information, always to his or her financial information, where mobile bank is used.

Recently, the application of face recognition technology later goes into different urban areas, including public spaces where security is of less concern like parks and zoos, workplaces; where the working hours of the employees are monitored; and vending machines where the identity of a purchaser is verified and an automatic charge against her account is made. The wide application of face recognition technology by government and businesses in cities in China reflects the need of a more accurate, efficient, and convenient mechanism, which can be used to verify the identity of a user intending to have access to the city's services, public or private. Some municipalities used the face recognition technology to identify people who violated traffic rules.[21] In some parks, people must scan their faces to get toilet paper.[22] And in some universities, students were required to make face recognition before they engaged in sports activities. However, the necessity of such pervasive use and negative implication to user's personal information and privacy are not properly and adequately addressed.

In the vast and fast process of urbanization, commercial pragmatism, few concern went over the need for protection of personal rights, leading to outcries in society where people object the proliferation of unnecessary use of face recognition technology. In 2019, a case was brought by Professor Guo Bing who intended to enter Wide Life Park in the City of Hangzhou but required to go through face recognition. Professor Guo considered his facial information as extremely sensitive and private, and sued the zoo in the city's Fuyang district court.[23] The district court decided that the zoo violated its contract with Professor Guo and ordered nominal compensation. The intermediate court of Hangzhou upon appeal (where court sessions were streamed online) made a landmark decision, which emphasized on the nature of personal facial information as sensitive information protected under the then applicable civil laws, and the misuse of personal facial information might cause substantial personal and financial

21 "A man in the City of Zhengzhou declined to provide ID number, and the Police used Face recognition to identify", available at <https://new.qq.com/omn/20191108/20191108A0NP7R00.html> accessed on April 25 2021.

22 "One uses face recognition to get toilet paper in public restrooms", available at <https://baijiahao.baidu.com/s?id=1637066496072386885&wfr=spider&for=pc> accessed on April 25 2021.

23 Guo Bing v. Hangzhou Wildlife Park Co., Ltd, Zhe0111MinChu No.6971(2019).

injuries. The court asked the zoo to delete the face photo taken from Professor Guo, as well as his fingerprint information.[24]

The decisions were rendered before the application of the Civil Code, but the judicial recognition marked a fundamental step towards the balance between the proliferation of facial recognition technology and the urgent need of personal information protection. On one hand, the two courts' decline to decide whether the compulsory use of face recognition technology, without informed consent from the user, violates the statutory protection of personal information, leaving the uncertainty on the legality of such use intact. On the other hand, the decisions do confirm that if there is a legal basis for the protection of personal information (in this case, a breach of consumer's contract), the grieved party can sue for damages as well as specific performance including requesting the deletion of any unauthorized personal information obtained and retained by a commercial party. It can be argued that the case was not decided under the Civil Code, therefore it lacks the authority as a precedent for subsequent disputes on face recognition technology. Nevertheless, the development of this case generates great public attention to the abuse of face technology in current Chinese cities. It also calls for a better legal framework to address the need for privacy and personal information protection.

Compared with similar cases, for example, the Swedish Data Inspection Authority imposed fines on the Swedish Data Inspection Authority, because this school uses face recognition technology to monitor its student attendance, which is against the GDPR. However, the decisions from the courts in China did not invoke a tort theory, thus not giving a direct answer to whether a person in China has the priority to use his or her facial information over any authorized commercial use; and whether he or she can claim any remedies in case his or her right is infringed. And what is more important is, since facial recognition technology is widely used by public entities, which also retains most accurate and full-scale facial information, how to restrict the use of the technology by public entities for ill-defined public purposes is far from being raised and contested in courts.

Privacy by Design can be used in the application of face recognition technology in building smart cities in China. The policy goal is to make a proper balance between the need of swift and accurate identification

---

24 The decision was officially announced, but the full opinion is not currently available. The abstract can be accessed at <https://www.chinacourt.org/article/detail/2021/04/id/5956124.shtml> accessed on April 25 2021.

in certain situations, to enhance security and efficiency, to reduce congestion and prevent identify fraud, and the need to protect people's privacy and personal information as basic civil rights, against unintended and unauthorized use either by commercial entities or by public entities. The principle on preventing abuse has been acknowledged in practice. City of Hangzhou, in response to the Wild Life Park case, proposed a municipal regulation to forbid compulsory use of face recognition technologies in commercial and residential properties.[25] One of the new national standards requires more secured systems involving remote face recognition.[26] The principles of Privacy Embedded into Design and Full Lifecycle Protection are also critical to strengthening privacy protection when face recognition technology is applied. Face information is considered sensitive and pertains not only to privacy but also to user's financial and other security. Another national standard requires full assessment and risk prevention before handling sensitive information, providing comprehensive and reliable protective mechanism above data minimization and necessity principles.[27] It can be argued that although the fast urbanization and wide application of face technologies in China bring privacy concerns, recent judicial cases and technology standards incorporated Privacy by Design principles while attempting to reconcile the competing interests of efficiency and privacy protection. The decisions and soft rules supplement China's legislative regime on privacy protection, making face recognition technology more privacy-friendly and less invasive to user's rights.

4. Conclusion

China in recent years is advancing in its digital privacy protection laws, learning from EU and U.S., and more importantly reacting to domestic pressure as of the proliferation of internet technologies which have gravely threatened people's privacy. It has incorporated Privacy by Design in its legal provisions and applied in its smart city planning and building. Priva-

---

25 Draft City Regulation on Property Management (2020) Full text available at <http://sf.hangzhou.gov.cn/art/2020/9/10/art_1659435_57186813.html> accessed on April 25 2021.

26 Information security technology—Technical requirements for remote face recognition system (2020), available at <http://std.samr.gov.cn/gb/search/gbDetailed?id=A47A713B767814ABE05397BE0A0ABB25> accessed on April 25 2021.

27 'GB/T39335-2020 Information Security Technology Personal Information Security Assessment Guidelines', China Standard Press, 2020 (in Chinese).

cy by Design provides meaningful guidance and solutions to the balance of privacy protection and better utilization, especially considering the interconnectivity of IoT devices in smart cities. The application of Privacy by Design, like digital privacy laws, remain to be tested in court. However, it can be argued that China's recent legislative response to provide a better and more comprehensive digital privacy protection framework, applying Privacy by Design principles in smart cities and other situations, could be illustrative in regime and constructive in experience.

Cloud Computing Issues: A Possible Solution

Maddalena Castellani <castellani@triberticastellani.com>
MILANO, Italia

Roberto Giacobazzi <roberto.giacobazzi@univr.it>
VERONA, Italia

Cesare Triberti <triberti@triberticastellani.com>
MILANO, Italia

Abstract
While the current Pandemic has accelerated the strong link between IT and enterprise, it has also shown how current technology systems are increasingly at risk of cyberattacks.

In this article we will deal with Cloud Computing systems, whose use is increasingly central to enterprises, first analyzing the legal aspect within the larger set of outsourcing contracts, highlighting the strengths and weaknesses (especially regarding the need to comply with the rules provided by the GDPR), and then offer a possible technologically advanced solution (Homomorphic encryption) to the problem of data protection, confidentiality and security of data stored in systems based on the Cloud.

Keywords:
cloud computing; Outsourcing; Virtual Organization; Saas, Iaas; Daas; Privacy; GDPR; *homomorphic encryption*; cybersecurity; Cryptography; Man-At-The-End (MATE) attack; obfuscation

1. Cloud Computing, Outsourcing

The IT world is continuously evolving.

Its relationship with the business world has a twofold impact: on one hand, Information Technology allows economic relations to evolve, on the other, the business world is always looking for new technological solutions that allow continuous development and improvement.

An example of this is the increasing dissemination of software solutions in the marketplace: first through licensing and software development contracts, then through service contracts, spread around the world by the Internet[1].

In this continuously evolving world, the development of service contracts such as Outsourcing, Facility Management and Disaster Recovery fits perfectly with notions of Cloud Computing.

In the second part of this paper, we will examine the IT aspect of Cloud Computing and identify a possible solution to the problems raised in the first part, in which some of the legal risks of Cloud computing will be analyzed, focused mainly on security risks to data stored in Cloud-based systems.

The protection and confidentiality of data, as well as the need for companies to comply with the General Data Protection Regulation[2], has put the "privacy" issue squarely at the door of Cloud computing, due to the technological structure underpinning this service.

Great attention must be paid to the "privacy" risk since most online trials are now conducted on Cloud platforms.

Civil law, unlike common law, allows parties to stipulate contracts governed by the Italian Civil Code, which lays down precise rules for standard contracts. Non-standard contracts can also be stipulated, on condition that they comply with all the mandatory regulations[3].

IT contracts can be categorized both as typical (for example, software development and IT services) and atypical: in the latter case, the parties may use the principle of analogy, with software licenses as the template.

The codified system has also enabled the creation of a series of criminal laws against computer crimes, thereby overcoming the prohibition on the use of analogy in criminal cases.

Let us return to the central issue.

---

1 Cesare Triberti and Giuseppe Carrella, *Internet ,aspetti tecnici, tematiche sociali, incidenze giuridiche civili e penali*, (Edizioni Maros Milano (ITA), 2000).

2 European Parliament, Regulation (EU) 2016/679 of the European Parliament and of the Council of 27 April 2016 on the protection of natural persons with regard to the processing of personal data and on the free movement of such data, and repealing Directive 95/46/EC [2016] OJ L199/1 (General Data Protection Regulation).

3 Art. 1322 c.c. (ITA) in <https://www.gazzettaufficiale.it/atto/serie_generale/caricaArticolo?art.progressivo=0&art.idArticolo=1322&art.versione=1&art.codiceRedazionale=042U0262&art.dataPubblicazioneGazzetta=1942-04-04&art.idGruppo=163&art.idSottoArticolo1=10&art.idSottoArticolo=1&art.flagTipoArticolo=2> accessed 1 August 2021.

Cloud computing is remarkably like an outsourcing contract, since it operates on the same technological and legal bases[4].

Outsourcing underpinned the spread of computer services throughout the industrial and commercial world, cutting labor costs (initially in the IT departments of the banking and assurance sector, then within big business).

This economic and technological boost paved the way for Cloud Computing.

There was a gradual transition from Grid systems to Cloud Computing, which is essentially an elaborate Grid system.

This is a complex infrastructure of dispersed computing power that was the driving force in the bulk processing of data.

This backstory and its parallel technological evolution are reflected in a single virtual computational system that offers the maximum potential in the use of shared applications, the concept behind the notion of the Virtual Organization.

A Virtual Organization is a set of human and technological resources that can best exploit this kind of asset sharing.

Users can view all the resources and access modes, benefitting from a high standard of security and authentication.

These resources are integrated in a Database that does not depend on a central repository but is generated by a network of independent servers, which keep records of the transactions carried out and can aggregate this information in multiple ways.

The Grid coordinates and shares all the resources using different procedures and does not need centralized control.

It employs differentiated protocols able to guarantee users a quality service center (so-called QoS, quality of service)[5].

Users can make use of the different computing resources "on demand" and can access and manage reams of data, even if such data are distributed in different ways.

So the Grid is an ASP, Application Service Provider, the Service Level Agreement of which is contractually regulated both in terms of the services offered online, and the levels of management and security.

4 Triberti and Carrella (n 1) 132-139.

5 Yang Yong, Dumas-Menijvar Marlon, Garcia-Banuelos Luciano, Polyvyanyy Artem and Zhang Liang, 'Generalized aggregate Quality of Service computation for composite services' (2012) 85, 8 Journal of Systems and Software 1818-1830.

While there may be structural differences, it is but a short step from the Grid to Cloud Computing.

The National Institute of Standards and Technology (NIST) defines it as:

> "Cloud computing is a model for enabling ubiquitous, convenient, on-demand network access to a shared pool of configurable computing resources (e.g., networks, servers, storage, applications, and services) that can be rapidly provisioned and released with minimal management effort or service provider interaction.".

NIST offers five specific features of Cloud Computing, as follows[6]:

1. On-demand self-service.
2. Broad network access.
3. Resource pooling.
4. Rapid elasticity.
5. Measured service.

Here is a brief analysis.

On-demand self-service allows instant, automatic access to Cloud Computing resources without human interaction with the provider.

Broad Network Access makes possible the access and use of resources through the network (such as the Internet) using standard mechanisms compatible with uniform platforms, such as personal computers and intelligent telephony systems with their multiple applications.

Resource Pooling offers the possibility of placing the resources of a specific provider at the service of multiple users, taking advantage of the service's multi-tenancy and virtualization features, so that the consumer accesses them depending on specific needs.

Rapid Elasticity identifies the immediate flexibility in providing and releasing resources based on user demand. The consequence is that the requested resources are provided immediately, and without limitation on "consumption", multiplying in line with requirements.

Measured Service provides the Cloud system with the ability to control and make the best use of resources, delivering what each individual needs,

6 Eric Simmon, 'Evaluation on cloud computing servicesbased on NIST 800-145' (National Institute of standards and Technology (NIST), February 2018) 4 <https://doi.org/10.6028/NIST.SP.500-322> accessed 1 August 2021 , <https://www.nist.gov/system/files/documents/2017/05/31/evaluation_of_cloud_computing_services_based_on_nist_800-145_20170427clean.pdf> accessed 1 August 2021.

simultaneously measuring the use and cost, while increasing the service's transparency.

2. *Features of the Services*

All the services that can be delivered through Cloud Computing have been universally identified: increasing the possibility of new applications and improving the quality of the services.

Software-as-a-service (SaaS) is a software distribution model in which customers pay a periodic subscription or licensing fee and a third party, typically the software vendor, makes the application available over the internet. SaaS is one of the primary commercial applications of Cloud computing. In the SaaS model, rather than buying a physical copy of an application and installing it on a local server, the software vendor gives customers access to the application via the internet, hosting and maintaining it on their own servers.

What's more, any maintenance and troubleshooting of the underlying infrastructure remain the sole responsibility of the Software-as-a-Service provider, leaving the customer with more time to focus on strictly business-related matters. Another vital aspect of SaaS products is that they are constantly evolving and are regularly updated.

This category also includes the hardware (known as the Virtual Machine (VM)), consisting of large-scale servers.

With this service (anticipating the definition of Computer Service, the legal aspects of which will be examined below), a customer accessing the Cloud needs no technical knowledge or specific hardware/software resources.

It offers centralized access to an application via the Web.

Extensive IT knowledge or the downloading of updates or new files are not required since they are part of the contract.

A single application can operate with many users, maintaining the logical separation of each user's data.

Platform as a Service (PaaS) is a complete development environment hosted in the Cloud that enables application developers to create apps quickly and easily. It usually includes an Operating System, web server, tools, programming language, database, network, servers, storage and more. The PaaS provider hosts and maintains the system and may often construct its own solutions tailored to the unique needs of the customer. Users retain control of the applications and many providers offer pay-as-you-go and other online pricing models.

This is a type of Cloud service that is particularly suitable for developing, managing and distributing applications.

By offering a platform equipped with all the necessary tools for the testing, development and deployment of applications in the same environment, PaaS eliminates the need to be concerned about anything other than development through the full underlying infrastructure, using the advantages of security, server software and backup, programming languages, libraries, services and dedicated tools, all developed by the provider.

Infrastructure as a service (IaaS) is a form of Cloud computing that provides virtual computing resources over the internet[7].

In the IaaS model, the Cloud provider manages IT infrastructures such as storage, server and networking resources, and delivers them to subscriber organizations via virtual machines accessible through the internet. IaaS offers many benefits for organizations, potentially making their work faster, easier, more flexible and cost efficient.

In an IaaS service model, a Cloud provider hosts the infrastructure components that are traditionally present in an in-house data center, including servers, storage and networking hardware, as well as the virtualization or hypervisor layer.

IaaS providers also supply a range of services to accompany the infrastructure components. These can include detailed billing, monitoring, access logs, security, load balancing,

clustering and storage resiliency, such as backup, replication and recovery.

These services are increasingly policy-driven, enabling IaaS users to implement greater levels of automation and orchestration for important infrastructure tasks. For example, a user can implement policies to drive load balancing in order to maintain application availability and performance.

Data Storage as a Service or DaaS (also known as Desktop as a Service) is directly related to the concept of virtualization on demand.

The service is based on the development of deduplication technologies that, in turn, deploy a hypervisor, that is, a particular technique of storing a computer's operating system configuration as if it were an image (snapshot) making it possible to issue the same type of configuration to one or more locations.

The data are made available via the Web and users can access them through any application, ensuring the best the provider can offer on the network, including storage, backup, and security systems. The customer

7 Xenofon Kontargirys, *IT laws in the era of cloud computing*, (Nomos, 2018).

does not have to pay the whole cost of a database license, only for what is used.

It is clear that the Cloud service features examined above have several points in common, like the ease of access, maintaining data separation even on a multiple-user service, cost savings for software supply and updating. These are borne by the provider, as well as the proper maintenance for remote access to services and the option of using services available on multiple Clouds.

They also differ, insofar as there is a Private Cloud and a Public Cloud.

With a Private Cloud, infrastructure use occurs only within a single operational structure/company that manages it directly or delegates management to a third party.

In the case of an in-house service, this means better use of the company's internal resources, the management of security and privacy of data and a reduction of costs compared to the use of a Public Cloud.

In-house management involves the configuration of servers in terms of hardware and software, plus the virtualization.

Conversely, in the Public Cloud, the Provider is responsible for the management and ownership of the entire structure, where they operate directly on the servers used by customers and manage the use of resources required by each client, providing them with ease of use and lower costs.

Finally, there is the Hybrid Cloud, a combination of private and public Clouds. The user can benefit from the greater flexibility of the Public Cloud, while maintaining their own data inside the company.

This type of solution demands a careful distribution of the different processing loads by combining the two architectures, private and public.

3. *Advantages and Disadvantages of Cloud Computing*

A special outsourcing contract with a supplier specialized in the management of computer resources via the Web means no costs for employees, hardware or software updates.

The costs and infrastructure remain the burden of the provider offering an on-demand service.

The individual contracts establish the appropriate clauses and the different costs of the service on a periodic basis or depending on use (on-demand).

They also offer peace of mind. The risk of interruptions due to system failures is non-existent since, even if a node fails, the service will still be available and someone else will be worrying about maintenance and restoration costs.

The downside is the issue of the privacy and security of customer data, which requires careful risk assessment in the management and storage.

4. Legal Aspects: Security and Risk in Cloud Computing

In such a highly innovative and functional system, featuring a vast range of available services, the problem arises of guaranteeing the security and integrity of the data of customers or third parties.

So, what is Cloud Computing in the eyes of the law? This must be understood on order to allow users to take appropriate security measures to prevent breaches of network integrity and data security.

Under civil Italian law, the Cloud is a computer service contract (Outsourcing).

It is a procurement contract (art. 1655-1677 c.c.)[8], which can also be qualified as a "mixed" procurement contract, that is, it covers the service itself and supplementary software developments or additional applications, which have no effect on the legal definition.

All contracts involve a series of mutual guarantees between the client and the contractor, with prevalence given to the protection of the client. These guarantees established by the Civil Code "must" be specifically mentioned in the contract between the client and the Cloud provider.

In particular, all possible critical situations in the performance of the service must be regulated in detail.

There are "general contractual clauses" that are common to all IT contracts.

For example:

- Hardware Structure
- Software Structure
- Specialist Resources
- Limits on the Use of other Structures and/or Resources without Charge or a Reduction in the Quality of Service for the "User".

---

8 Art. 1655 c.c. (ITA) in <https://www.gazzettaufficiale.it/atto/serie_generale/caricaArticolo?art.versione=1&art.idGruppo=208&art.flagTipoArticolo=2&art.codiceRedazionale=042U0262&art.idArticolo=1655&art.idSottoArticolo=1&art.idSottoArticolo1=10&art.dataPubblicazioneGazzetta=1942-04-04&art.progressivo=0> accessed 1 August 2021.

But there are also "special" clauses for the Cloud, designed to protect and guarantee this specific type of IT service. Firstly, risks may arise from specific criminal actions carried out by third parties against the customer's data and systems, the negative effects of which obviously extend to the Cloud provider.

The regulations on Computer Crimes are an example. They cover unauthorized access to a computer system or remaining on it without authorization, the damaging or extraction of data or the unlawful discovery of information, especially business information.

Special attention must be paid to the European Privacy Code and, in particular, to the regulations laid down by the GDPR, which governs the correct use of data and penalizes any behavior in breach of its provisions[9].

In summary, a list of critical issues is given below:

- the secure transfer of data from the customer to the Cloud;
- the secure management of data within the Cloud;
- the secure management, in accordance with agreed methods, of restoring data to the client;
- the coordination of data management, data transfer or sharing between different Clouds, particularly if they are located in distant geographical areas and subject to different jurisdictions;
- the accurate identification of each customer's data within the Cloud and the secure extraction of only the data required;
- the technological guarantee of interconnectivity related to the Virtual Network;
- problems of jurisdiction and applicable laws (divergent regulations between States and conflict between civil and common law) without precise contractual definition;
- the responsibilities of the Administrative Bodies of companies towards the shareholders for security breaches and consequent damage;
- the correct use of encryption as the primary guarantee against unlawful data access.

The foregoing highlights the need both for correct contractual management and technological advances, not only in the ordinary management phase of the Cloud, but also for the effective defense against cyberattacks, given that the pervasiveness of Cloud-based IT systems is now well established.

9 Kontargirys(n 7) 181.

5. A Possible Solution

As mentioned above, every Cloud-based system needs secure data management on the part of Cloud providers and the problem of privacy protection lies with them. These issues are impeding the deployment of Cloud services when large volumes of sensitive data are involved. The ultimate frontier of data security and privacy for Cloud computing is represented by *homomorphic encryption*. Homomorphic encryption is intended to solve the problem of malicious misuse of data in remotely executed algorithms, such as the Cloud. In a Man-At-The-End (MATE) attack scenario[10], the security, the integrity, and in particular the privacy of sensible can be compromised. A MATE attack scenario is characterized by two parties, say Alice and Bob, that are supposed to cooperate in order to achieve a given result. In this scenario, we may assume Alice to be a trusted entity, while no trust can be ensured for the case of Bob. In our setting, Alice can be a user of a Cloud service and Bob can be the Cloud service itself, here specified by a set of functionalities that operate on Alice' data in order to produce a result that can be useful for Alice. A MATE attack holds when Bob intentionally, or because he has been hacked, performs a malicious misuse of Alice' data, with the specific intent of breaking privacy and integrity constraints on the information provided by Alice. Here Bob' Cloud service corresponds to perform some operation op on Alice' private (or partially private) data set D. Examples are the analysis of financial data to evaluate specific assets, or a machine learning-based analysis of a CT Scan image for specific medical diagnosis. In a Cloud computing environment we can imagine that the operation op will be performed remotely on the Cloud servers under the control of Bob' Could algorithms. Alice, who can be a trusted financial advisor or an MD at your trusted medical center, provides the data D to the Cloud (Bob) and receives back an analysis. If this protocol has been attacked in a MATE attack, an adversary (e.g., Bob or a hacker) gains the control of Alice' private data at the Cloud level. This could violate the privacy and integrity of Alice' medical records and other sensitive personal data. On a larger scale, this phenomenon could cripple a national infrastructure and national security.

Several solutions have been put forward in Computer Science (CS) to overcome MATE attacks. It is clear the difference between a MATE attack

10 Christian Collberg, Jack Davidson, Roberto Giacobazzi, Yuan Gu, Amir Herzberg, and Fei-Yue Wang, 'Towards Digital Asset Protection' (2011) 26(6)IEEE Intelligent Systems 8-13.

and a Man-In-The-Middle (MITM) attack. In the latter a standard encryption mechanism can be extremely effecting to protect all communications between Alice and Bob. In MITM attacks, both parties Alice and Bob are trusted entities and only the communication has to be protected, while in MATE attacks it is one of the two parties of the protocol that can be untrusted. Code/Data obfuscation, white-box cryptography and (fully) homomorphic encryption are solutions designed specifically in order to solve the problems of privacy and integrity in MATE attacks.

Code/Data obfuscation and White-Box Cryptography are partial solutions to this problem[11]. In code/data obfuscation and white-box cryptography, the structure of our asset is intentionally morphed in order to maintain the sensible information secret and protected. This can be performed easily and usefully in many contexts, such as in code protection against reverse engineering or for hiding cryptographic keys for protecting digital assets (e.g., DRM in music, video etc). This technology has a major drawback: the information that is made secret cannot be used by the third party, e.g., the Cloud, simply because the same existence of this information is hidden to the Cloud.

In a (fully) homomorphic encryption (FHE) mechanism[12], the operation op operates homomorphically with respect to the primitives of encryption Enc_k and decryption Dec_k for some private key k, if the following equation holds for any possible (private) data set D:

$Dec_k(op(Enc_k(D))) = op(D)$.

In a sentence: the operation op can operate on encrypted (hence protected) data set D producing a cyphertext that, once decrypted (e.g., by a private key) results in the correct application of the operation op to D. FHE enables the design of programs for any desirable functionality, which can run on encrypted inputs and produce an encryption of the expected result. The key point is that the private key k is unknown to the operation op. Therefore, such programs never really decrypt their inputs, i.e., they never reveal to the untrusted user the private data set D and can therefore run by any untrusted party without compromising privacy, security or integrity. This *magical* mechanism is reality and several solutions are known in this field with an endless effort by scientists and engineers to make it available

11 Obfuscation: Finn Brunton and Helen Nissenbaum, *A User's Guide for Privacy and Protest* (MIT Press 2015).

12 Craig Gentry, 'Fully Homomorphic Encryption Using Ideal Lattices' (the 41st ACM Symposium on Theory of Computing (STOC) 2009).

as service to users[13]. Two are the main issue of FHE: *Scalability* and *expressivity*. Scalability means that the current technology can handle relatively small amounts of data with e relatively high computational effort. While scalability can be overcome by the advancements of the technology or by weakening the FHE paradigm, by restricting the full privacy only to portions of the data set D, the expressivity issue is more fundamental. We know that we can implement any Boolean circuit in FHE, but can we imagine to run in FHE any program? Namely can we imagine of having a FHE interpreter that can run an arbitrary program? If we impose limitations on the way programs run (e.g., in the amount of memory used or computational time complexity) the answer is yes. It is still not clear whether a FHE system can run an arbitrary program. This means that, while Alice can keep secret her data set D to Bob, yet achieving the desired result op(D) but computed by Bob on $Enc_k(D)$, hence without knowing D, if D is itself a software component and the operation op that Bob is required to perform is just its remote execution, then it is not clear whether Bob can provide this service in FHE for all programs D. Therefore, while data protection can be and will eventually be protected by FHE, the protection of software assets is way more complex and probably impossible.

13 Homomorphic Encryption Standardization: <https://homomorphicencryption.org> accessed 1 Auugust 2021.

Liability of Hosting ISPs: the Czech Perspective

Matěj Myška <102870@mail.muni.cz>

Pavel Koukal <pavel.Koukal@law.muni.cz>

Zuzana Vlachová <Zuzana.Vlachova@law.muni.cz>

Ondřej Woznica <445915@mail.muni.cz>
BRNO, Czech Republic

Abstract
This paper deals with the issues of liability of the hosting ISPs under Czech law with focus on copyright infringement. It introduces the Czech transposition of the E-commerce Directive (EU Directive No. 2000/31) and discusses the theoretical questions of establishing and limiting the civil non-contractual liability of the hosting ISPs. Furthermore, the rather scarce case law dealing with these issues is presented and analysed. Finally, the paper offers a glimpse into the possible changes vis-à-vis the transposition of the Copyright on the Single Digital Market Directive (EU Directive No. 2019/790).

Keywords:
copyright infringement; information society service provider; liability; case law

This paper utilizes the answers given by the authors in the Questionnaire for national experts within the study "Mapping of national remedies against online piracy of sport content" (European Audiovisual Observatory (Council of Europe)). The original source is available at: https://www.obs.coe.int/en/web/observatoire.

Introduction

In copyright infringement cases on the Internet consisting of unauthorized communication of the protected content to the public via various services allowing users to do so, rightsholders often find it challenging to pursue their claims against the actual infringers – the uploading users – successfully. For this reason, attempts are made to take action against third parties, namely intermediaries offering these services, who, although not being direct infringers, have nevertheless contributed to the infringement, i.e., have indirectly caused it by providing the needed infrastructure and service. However, the liability of these intermediaries is limited by the so-called safe harbour regulated in the article 14 E-commerce Directive.[1] As noted by *Husovec*, the regulation thereof *"is akin to conditional liability-free zone, in which you can move freely as long as you respect its predefined boundaries"*.[2] The establishing of the liability, i.e., what happens outside "the zone" is a matter national law of the Member State.[3]

This paper aims to present the situation "outside the European law zone" in Czech civil law. It introduces the transposition of the E-commerce Directive and discusses the theoretical questions of establishing and limiting the civil liability of hosting intermediaries. Furthermore, the relatively scarce case law dealing with these issues is presented and analysed. Finally, the paper offers a glimpse into the possible changes vis-à-vis the transposition of the Copyright on the Single Digital Market Directive (hereinafter as "Digital Single Market Directive")[4] into the Czech law.

1. *Transposition of the E-commerce Directive and the System of Safe Harbours*

The article 14 E-commerce Directive has been transposed to the Czech law into the Section 5 of the Act No. 480/2004 Sb., on Certain Information Society Services and on Amendments to Certain Acts (Act on Certain Information Society Services; hereinafter as "ISSPA"), in a peculiar way.[5]

---

1 Directive 2000/31/EC of the European Parliament and of the Council of 8 June 2000 on certain legal aspects of information society services, in particular electronic commerce, in the Internal Market [2002] OJ L178/1.

2 Martin Husovec, *Injunctions against Intermediaries in the European Union: Accountable but Not Liable?* (Cambridge University Press 2017) 50.

3 Husovec (n 2) 50. Also see Matthias Leistner, 'Structural Aspects of Secondary (Provider) Liability in Europe' (2014) 9 Journal of Intellectual Property Law & Practice 75, 76.

4 Directive (EU) 2019/790 of the European Parliament and of the Council of 17 April 2019 on Copyright and related rights in the Digital Single Market and amending Directives 96/9/EC and 2001/29/EC [2019] OJ L130/92.

5 It must be noted that this is not the only peculiarity since the prohibition of the monitoring set in Section 6 ISSPA is as such also rather peculiar. As *Polčák*

Whereas the E-Commerce Directive sets out conditions under which hosting ISPs cannot be held liable due to the applicable safe harbour protection, the Czech transpositions may be interpreted as *"providing specific grounds for the liability of service providers for user conduct"*.[6] Namely, the Section 5 ISSPA is formulated in such a way that the ISP *is liable* only if certain conditions are fulfilled, i.e. in the case of the hosting ISP that it either could have known (constructive knowledge) about the illegal nature of the information or actually knew about the illegal nature of the information and did not act upon it (actual knowledge). The provision of Section 5 ISSPA must be, however, interpreted in conformity with the E-commerce Directive correctly as actual "safe harbour", i.e. setting limits on the liability of the ISPs.[7] This means that Section 5 ISSPA, does not impose any separate liability on hosting ISPs, but represents a waiver of liability arising under civil, administrative or criminal law.[8]

Unfortunately, even the courts seem to be confused by this wording.[9] In the *Prolux* case,[10] the website operator (qualified as hosting ISP) as defendant has been sued by reality estate company (*Prolux*) for comments under one of its posts where many involved individuals commented on

---

notes, the fact that ISPs do not have such a duty can be deduced merely from the absence of the explicit regulation of the duty [Radim Polčák, 'Information Society Between Orwell and Zapata: A Czech Perspective on Safe Harbours' in Graeme B Dinwoodie (ed), *Secondary Liability of Internet Service Providers* (Springer International Publishing 2017), 263].

6 Polčák (n 5) 263.

7 Martin Maisner, *Zákon o Některých Službách Informační Společnosti: Komentář* (C H Beck 2016) 69–70; František Korbel, Roman Cholasta and Alexandra Molitorisová, 'Safe Harbour: Vyloučení Odpovědnosti Poskytovatelů Hostingových Služeb Za Obsah Vložený Uživateli Internetu' [2016] Soudce 9, 15.

8 Martin Husovec, 'Zodpovednosť na Internete: podľa českého a slovenského práva' (CZ.NIC 2014) 114; Korbel, Cholasta and Molitorisová (n 7) 9, 16.

9 As noted by Husovec (translated by the authors): *"Many courts have interpreted this concept to mean that, in the event of a loss of safe harbours, liability for third party content is presumed. But the exclusion of liability institute is not intended to establish liability. Its purpose is merely to determine, across–the–board, the point at which liability for damages and other property claims does not or cannot arise. If the exclusion of liability is not applied, it only means that the liability of the provider is to be assessed on the basis of the principles mentioned above (under domestic law)."* [Husovec (n 8) 93]. Similar conclusions are also expressed by Polčák [Radim Polčák, 'Odpovědnost ISP' in Radim Polčák and others, *Právo Informačních Technologií* (Wolters Kluwer ČR 2018) 74].

10 Municipal Court in Prague, 17 March 2010, file no. 10 Cm 47/2009; High Court in Prague, 2 March 2011, file no. 3 Cmo 197/2010–82, and Supreme Court of the Czech Republic, 31 July 2013, file no. 23 Cdo 2623/2011.

their experience with *Prolux*. *Prolux* has requested take-down of comments and compensation. The Municipal Court in Prague, however, ordered only the take-down of the whole post and refused to grant the compensation due to *Prolux's* controversial business activities. However, the High Court in Prague limited this injunction only to obviously unlawful (indecent) words. Interestingly, both the trial court[11] as well the appeal court[12] mentioned the section 5 ISSPA as the *"sole reason for the liability of a discussion board service provider who, despite receiving a notice from a defamed corporation, refused to remove the defamatory statement"*.[13]

Apart from the discrepancy in the wording, however, Section 5 ISSPA follows the wording of the E-commerce Directive in the conditions of safe harbours rather closely.

The first safe harbour (Section 5 para. 1 let. a) ISSPA) shields the hosting ISP in cases where it could have not, with regard to the subject of its activity and the circumstances and nature of the case, known that the contents of the information stored is illegal. This provision thus aims at manifestly illegal content such as child pornography or terrorist content[14]. In the already mentioned *Prolux* case,[15] the courts dealt not only with the question of knowledge of the ISP that the information exists but rather with the knowledge of illegal nature of this information.[16] As aforementioned, the courts incorrectly based the liability of the provider on the Section 5 ISSPA. However, they stated that the provider has to remove information that is evidently illegal automatically, i.e., when there is no doubt about its illegal nature [i.e., where the constructive knowledge might be established pursuant to Section 5(1)(a) ISSPA]. If the illegal nature is not evident, the actual knowledge of a provider is established by informing the provider about the unlawful information pursuant Section

---

11 Martin Husovec, 'Zodpovednosť poskytovateľa za obsah diskusných príspevkov' (2011) 2 Revue pro právo a technologie 40, 41 <https://journals.muni.cz/revue/article/view/4015> accessed 10 June 2021.

12 Confirmed by the Supreme Court of the Czech Republic, 31 July 2013, file no. 23 Cdo 2623/2011.

13 Polčák (n 5) 264. Confirming this view Ján Matejka and Alžběta Krausová, 'Odpovědnost poskytovatelů hostingových služeb se zřetelem k povaze a druhu přenášeného obsahu' (2017) 156 Právník 751, 754.

14 Polčák (n 9) 86.

15 Municipal Court in Prague, 17 March 2010, file no. 10 Cm 47/2009; High Court in Prague, 2 March 2011, file no. 3 Cmo 197/2010–82, and Supreme Court of the Czech Republic, 31 July 2013, file no. 23 Cdo 2623/2011.

16 Similar conclusions were expressed in the Google France case, see: Joined Cases C-236 to 238/08 *Google France and Google* [2010] ECR I–2417, para 109.

5(1)(b) ISSPA. As the High Court in Prague noted, this criterion covers a broader spectrum of situations – the unlawful nature of the information could be decided upon by a court in a decision or proven by other means to the ISP.[17] *Parlamentní listy* case[18] concerned infringement of personality rights by racist and xenophobic comments posted by the readers in the discussion forum under an article on a webpage operated by the defendant. The defendant, qualified as hosting ISP, did not remove the respective comments for a substantive amount of time (years). The liability was based on the constructive knowledge due to the highly controversial topic; thus, the ISP should act proactively and have either be more active regarding the content[19] or simply not allow the discussion.

The second safe harbour is thus lost as soon as the ISP knows about the illegal nature of the content and does not act upon it [Section 5(1)(a) ISSPA]. There is no general regulation of notice and take-down (or stay-down for that matter) procedure under the Czech law vis-à-vis hosting ISPs, e.g., legal requirements as to who, how and in what form this notice shall be executed.[20] To establish the (actual) knowledge of the ISP, the notification shall identify accurately the content that is, according to the notifier, of unlawful nature, indicate precisely in what consists the unlawfulness of the content.[21] If the notification does not identify sufficiently on what grounds the unlawfulness of the content rests, it shall not be qualified as precise enough.[22] As to the person entitled to submit such a notice, the doctrine opines that it could be anyone.[23] However, usually the notice will be sent by the rightsholder or representative thereof. The ISP must examine the notification and respond to it in order not to be held liable.[24] In reaction to the notification, the provider can remove the content or deny access to it.[25] If not, the liability of the ISP could be established.

17 High Court in Prague, 2 March 2011, file no. 3 Cmo 197/2010–82.

18 Municipal Court in Prague, 12. 1. 2015, file no. 66 C 143/2013.

19 The defendant operating the website failed to respond to notice and, as noted, did not remove the respective comments for a substantive amount of time (years).

20 Polčák (n 9) 86.

21 It must be sufficiently precise or adequately substantiated as the CJEU ruled in C-324/09, *L'Oréal v eBay*, ECR [2011] I-06011, para 122.

22 Matejka and Krausová (n 13) 751, 762.

23 Polčák (n 9) 86.

24 It seems impossible to establish a uniform reaction time of the ISP. It is necessary to assess its proportionality according to the circumstances of individual cases, depending on the type of a service, the nature of unlawfulness or on the person/type/nature of a provider [Polčák (n 9) 87–88].

25 Husovec (n 8) 115–119.

However, ISP liability would be based on different provisions (as will be discussed below) than the ISSPA provisions.

As regards to civil liability, the safe harbours cover the issues of liability for third-party content/conduct. As *Husovec* generally notes,[26] as soon as the ISP accepts the third-party content as its own, the safe harbours do not apply since the ISP is to be treated as a direct infringer (section 2910 of the Act no. 89/2012 Sb., Civil Code, as amended, further referred as "CC")[27] and all the sanctions, remedies, and injunctions available to the rightsholder do apply.[28] However, the concept of safe harbour and its effect is still unclear in terms of Czech tort law. It is not sufficiently clear whether it is a defence precluding illegality ("grounds for justification"; "Rechtfertigungsgründe"; see article 7:101 PETL) or whether the requirements of article 14(1) E-commerce Directive are directed at the subjective aspect of the tort and define the requirements of responsible care.[29]

---

26 Ibid (n 8) 44.

27 English translation of the CC available from <https://obcanskyzakonik.justice.cz/images/pdf/Civil-Code.pdf> accessed 10 June 2021. Quotations of the English translation of the CC stem from this source.

28 The situation is obfuscated by the fact that the respective articles of the E-commerce Directive stipulating the possibility of the Member States to set up a system of injunctions to terminate or prevent an infringement or remove or disable access to the unlawful information were not implemented generally into the Czech Law. In cases of copyright infringement, the Czech Copyright Act [Act no. 121/2000 Sb., on Copyright and Related Rights and on Amendment of Certain Other Acts, as amended (zákon o právu autorském, o právech souvisejících s právem autorským a o změně některých zákonů)] in section 40(1)(f) stipulates that the rightsholder whose rights were *"unlawfully infringed or are in danger of unlawful infringement may demand (…) prohibition of providing the service that is used by third parties for breaching or endangering the rights."* (English translation of CA quoted and if needed adapted stems from the Legal Information System ASPI, Wolters Kluwer ČR, 2021).
Similarly, following the argumentum *a maiore ad minus* rightsholders may demand prohibition of providing segments/parts of the respective service. [Husovec (n 8) 168]. In civil law proceedings, this injunction is a measure resulting from a decision on the merits of the case. Therefore, it is to be accomplished in formal civil proceedings where the rightsholder must also claim and prove the infringement or exposure of infringement via the service provided (Ivo Telec and Pavel Tůma, *Autorský Zákon: Komentář* (2nd edition, C H Beck 2019) 503).

29 On applying different standards of care in safe harbour limitation of tort liability, see Husovec (n 8) 89 ff.

2. *Establishing the Liability of ISPs*

As mentioned above, if the safe harbour is lost for the ISP, its liability for third-party content and conduct must be established based on general tort law liability as stipulated by the CC, not on specific liability which the ISSPA provisions would have prescribed.

The primary liability for copyright infringement rests with the user, i.e., the person who unlawfully uploads the copyrighted work or other protected subject matter to the relevant platform. This liability is based on interference with the absolute right of the injured party, as follows from section 2910 CC.[30] As was noted, the exact primary liability also applies to the intermediary if it takes over someone else's content as its own.[31]

A question that has not yet been uniformly resolved in Czech doctrine is whether Czech law establishes secondary liability for intermediaries, i.e., whether it is possible to consider their position as "several concurrent tortfeasors" similar to German law.

Unlike German law, where the liability of intermediaries for infringement of intellectual property rights is based on the concept of *Störerhaftung* (Breach of Duty of Care),[32] the establishing of intermediaries' liability in

---

30 Husovec (n 8) 53; Roman Cholasta and others, 'Safe Harbour: Režim Vyloučení Odpovědnosti Poskytovatelů Služeb Informační Společnosti v Kontextu Pasivní Role Poskytovatele' (2017) Právní rozhledy 399 <www.beck-online.cz> accessed 10 June 2021.

31 Husovec (n 8) 41 ff.

32 Breach of duty (*Störerhaftung*) is a unique form of third-party liability for indirect infringements outside the categories of direct infringement and participation (cooperation). Breach of Duty of Care involves a party's own responsibility for contributing to another party's infringement of the law. Initially, the prerequisite for liability as a "Störer" (secondary infringer) is an infringement of the law. Claims can only be asserted against the secondary infringer if it is established that an infringement has occurred at all. Accordingly, a person is liable as a secondary infringer if he or she has in some way intentionally and adequately causally contributed to the creation or maintenance of an unlawful infringement, it is legally and factually possible and reasonable for him or her to prevent the direct infringement and has breached reasonable inquiry obligations. The concept of *Störerhaftung* is well developed in German tort law (see e.g. BGH, 26 September 1985, I ZR 86/83; BGH, 22 April 2009, I ZR 216/06; BGH, 12 July 2012, I ZR 18/11; Thomas Hoeren and Silviya Yankova, 'The Liability of Internet Intermediaries – The German Perspective' (2012) International Review of Intellectual Property and Competition Law, 501; Jan Bernd Nordemann, 'Liability for Copyright Infringements on the Internet: Host Providers (Content Providers) - The Geman Approach', 2 JIPITEC 37 <https://nbn-resolving.org/urn:nbn:de:0009-29-29629> accessed 10 June 2021; Christina Angelopoulos, 'European Intermediary Liability

the Czech law is still subject to doctrinal disputes. Generally, two doctrinal streams of thoughts discussed later in detail might be identified. The ISP might be liable as an indirect (secondary) infringer [Section 2915 (1) and (2) CC] or addressee of the prevention duty and duty to act to avoid (Section 2900 and 2901 CC).

As regards the liability as an indirect (secondary) infringer as the person participating in this delict, it must be noted as a general remark that the Czech tort law does not expressly operate with the concept of secondary liability.[33] However, the position of intermediaries acting as secondary infringers in Czech tort law can be derived from Section 2915 (1) CC.[34] This

---

in Copyright: A Tort-Based Analysis' <https://dare.uva.nl/search?identifier=a406e67d-b537-49ae-9f46-80e831b988d4> accessed 10 June 2021 148 ff.). *Husovec* suggests that the conclusions of the German doctrine on *Störerhaftung* may also be applicable in Czech law and that Czech courts may be inspired by them [Husovec (n 8) 170]. It should also be highlighted, that according to the Czech tort law, stricter criteria apply to professionals regarding their intentional or negligent conduct than to ordinary users. In its general part, the Czech Civil Code already sets out two basic rational assumptions for acting subjects of private law. The first is the standard of reasonable conduct of an average person (Section 4 CC), the second is the standard of conduct of a professional (Section 5 CC). Both standards are then reflected in tort law by the fact that the CC establishes rebuttable presumptions of negligent conduct. Section 2912(1) CC provides that "*if a tortfeasor does not act as a person of average character might reasonably be expected to act in private, he shall be presumed to have acted negligently.*" As to the standard of a professional, the Civil Code in Section 2912 (2) CC regulates that "*if the tortfeasor displays special knowledge, skill, or care, or undertakes an activity for which special knowledge, skill, or care is required, and fails to exercise those special qualities, he shall be deemed to have acted negligently*". If we accept that the concept of *Störerhaftung* is applicable in Czech law and that the liability of intermediaries is based on a failure to comply with the requirements of the duty of care, we would also apply the rebuttable presumption regulated in section 2912 (2) CC.

33 Polčák (n 5) 257; Husovec (n 8) 54.

34 Sec. 2915 reads as follows: "*(1) If several tortfeasors are obliged to provide compensation for damage, they shall do so jointly and severally; if any of the tortfeasors has the duty under another statute to provide compensation only up to a certain limit, he is obliged jointly and severally with the other tortfeasors within that scope. This also applies where several persons have committed separate unlawful acts, each of whom may have caused a harmful consequence with a high degree of certainty, and if the person who caused the damage cannot be ascertained.*
(2) Where there are reasons deserving special consideration, a court may decide that the tortfeasor shall provide compensation for the damage in proportion to his participation in the harmful consequences; if the participation cannot be determined accurately, account is taken of the degree of probability. Such a decision may not be made if a tortfeasor knowingly participated in causing the damage by another tortfeasor, or instigated or supported it, or if the entire damage can be attributed to each tortfeasor,

provision, in accordance with article 9:101 PETL Principles establishes solidary liability for those persons whose joint conduct led to the damage. Nevertheless, this provision affects the relationship of these persons to the injured party. It does not in any way address the nature of the liability of the tortfeasors.[35] Thus, it is possible that a user who uploads a file to a platform provided by the ISP may be liable under different principles than the ISP. If the actions of both have led to the damage, they will be jointly and severally liable for compensation.

Husovec implies that the ISP might also be held liable for the breach of its preventive duty.[36] This concept can be derived from Section 2900 and subsequent provisions CC[37] and aims at active (commission: Section 2900 CC) or passive (ommission: Section 2901 CC)[38] of an obliged person in three specific situations.

Passive liability is limited only to the person (i.) who created or controlled dangerous situation, (ii.) with a personal relationship with the perpetrator, or (iii.) for whom the intervention is cheaper in comparison to imminent damage.[39] The subsumption of a specific person under this

---

even where they acted independently, or if the tortfeasor is to pay for the damage caused by a helper where the helper also incurred the duty to provide compensation."
As for the conclusion that Czech tort law recognizes secondary participants to a tort, see Husovec (n 8) 86, Filip Melzer In: Filip Melzer and Petr Tégl, Občanský Zákoník: Velký Komentář. Svazek IX: § 2894-3081 (Leges 2018) 384. Concurrently, *Polčák* rejects this conclusion and suggests that section 2915 (1) CC establishes only the liability of joint tortfeasors. Polčák (n 5) 257, 258.

35 Melzer in Melzer and Tégl (n 34) 376, 384.

36 Husovec (n 8) 73 ff.; Husovec (n 2) 51 ff.

37 Section 2900 CC reads as follows: *"If required by the circumstances of the case or the usages of private life, everyone has the duty to act so as to prevent unreasonable harm to freedom, harm to life, bodily harm or harm to the property of another."*

38 Section 2901 CC reads as follows: *"If required by the circumstances of the case or the usages of private life, the person who produced a dangerous situation or who has control over it, or where it is justified by the nature of the relationship between the persons, has the duty to intervene to protect another. The person who can, according to his potential and skills, easily avert harm of which he knows or must know that its impending gravity clearly exceeds what must be exerted for the intervention has the same duty"*. This provision was inspired by article 4:103 of the PETL Principles and applies to so-called non-genuine omissions. It means that a person is liable for damages if the circumstances show that there is a duty to act to avert the impending harm. In these situations, we do not reproach the person for having caused the damage, but we reproach him or her for not having prevented the damage [Melzer in Melzer and Tégl (n 34) 92].

39 Husovec (n 8) 80.

obligation as an indirect (secondary) infringer must be thus decided on a case-by-case basis.

However, the application of the preventive duty as a ground for establishing ISP liability is not uncontroversial. Namely, the doctrine differs whether the safe harbours also cover the prevention duty. On the one hand, *Telec*[40] opines that the ISPs are actually taking advantage of the unlawful situation that they have created and under which they have control which directly contravenes the Section 6(2) CC.[41] *Maisner*, on the other hand, concludes that application of such broad prevention duty *ex-ante* would basically annul the safe harbours and the specific liability regime set in ISSPA.[42] *Polčák* concluded in 2017 that it is unclear whether the safe harbours also shield from the liability arising from preventive duty.[43] Nevertheless, it might be claimed that the ISSPA regulation serves as *lex specialis* and, thus, the liability of ISPs for preventive duty is limited.[44]

It can also be argued against *Husovec's* concept of preventive obligations under Section 2901 CC that the general preventive provision cannot be applied where a preventive obligation would result from a specific provision of a statutory norm.[45] As the duty to act is set out in Section 5 (1) ISSPA, it might not be entirely appropriate to consider the Section 2901 CC applicable to the liability of intermediaries.[46]

---

40 Ivo Telec, 'Zakázané těžení a nebezpečná situace na elektronických úložištích dat' 1–2 (2015) Bulletin advokacie 19, 20.

41 "*No one may benefit from acting unfairly or unlawfully. Furthermore, no one may benefit from an unlawful situation which the person caused or over which he has control*" [Section 6 (2) CC]. Moreover, *Harašta* claims that the preventive duty may arise as to the specific content that has been already notified to the respective ISP in the extent of keeping it off its service. (Jakub Harašta 'Obecná Prevenční Povinnost Poskytovatele Služeb Informační Společnosti ve Vztahu k Informacím Ukládaným Uživatelem' (2014) Právní rozhledy 590 <www.beck-online.cz> accessed 10 June 2021).

42 Martin Maisner, 'Snaha o Zakázané Těžení Ze Zdánlivé Absence Výslovné Legislativní Úpravy a Nebezpečná Situace pro Poskytovatele Služeb Informační Společnosti' (Bulletin advokacie, 24 September 2015) <http://www.bulletin-advokacie.cz/snaha-o-zakazane-tezeni-ze-zdanlive-absence-vyslovne-legislativni-upravy> accessed 10 June 2021.

43 Polčák (n 5) 266.

44 Polčák (n 5) 266.

45 This provision is not applicable in cases where the law imposes a specific duty to act for the protection of another. Such an obligation is in the nature of a special protective norm, which has the nature of a special law (*lex specialis*). Section 2901 has a place where the subject has neither a contractual nor a specific legal obligation to act to protect another. Melzer in Melzer and Tégl (n 34) 92.

46 See also Cholasta and others (n 30) 399.

We believe that the new Czech tort law contained in the new Czech Civil Code recognizes, similarly to German law, the tort of "several concurrent tortfeasors" and therefore the joint and several liability of ISP for damages resulting from copyright infringement is based on Section 2915 (1) CC (in connection with 2910 CC). This is a typical example of a tort where two persons, by separate acts, cause damage and are jointly and severally liable for it, although the nature of their liability is different.

On the other hand, we must agree with *Husovec* that even if the ISP is not liable, this does not mean that it cannot be targeted with specific injunctions/remedies as a "non-infringing" ("non-obligated") intermediary.[47] These include interlocutory injunctions (section 74 Act No. 99/1963 on the Civil Procedure Code, as amended), information claim [section 40(1)(c) CA] and prohibition of providing the service that third parties use for breaching or endangering the rights.[48]

3. *Conclusion and Outlook*

As apparent from this paper, the situation regarding the liability of ISPs for copyright infringement is rather challenging under Czech law.[49] The peculiar "reverse" transposition of the E-commerce Directive and the need to interpret it in conformity with EU law, the doctrinal disharmonization on basic concepts and the relatively scarce case law that is still in the stage of "delimitation" of the playing field do not bring much legal certainty and predictability for the ISPs.[50] Furthermore, no system of best practices as regards the limitations of liability has been established.[51] Unfortunately, the fundamental issues of ISP liability and its limitation have not yet been tested extensively by the national courts and are, as shown above, still debated in the doctrine.

A significant change in this area will be the transposition of the Digital Single Market Directive. The available preparatory legislative documents show that the Czech Republic opted for a rather literal translation of the

47 Husovec uses the term "accountable, not liable". See in general Husovec (n 2) and specifically Husovec (n 8) 163 ff.

48 Husovec (n 8) 168.

49 As already observed generally by Polčák (n 5).

50 Polčák (n 5) 271. *Husovec* notes that the judgment of the Appellate Court in the *Prolux* case was actually one of the first judgments dealing with ISP liability for comments in forum [see also Husovec (n 11) 40]

51 Polčák (n 5) 269.

article 17 Digital Single Market Directive.[52] Consequently, any online content sharing service provider communicating the protected subject-matter uploaded by users of this service will be liable as an indirect (secondary) infringer if the conditions of the special liability exemption regime will not be fulfilled.

Even though that the Commission guidelines explicitly advise the Member States to do so, the proposed Czech transposition does not take specifically into account the recital 62, i.e., that the *"liability exemption mechanism should not apply to service providers the main purpose of which is to engage in or to facilitate copyright piracy"*.[53] Thus, this should be derived from the legislative definition of the online content sharing service provider and by interpreting the regulation in conformity with the EU.

It is obvious that the Czech Republic will not meet the transposition deadline. As of May 2021, the transposition amendment has not started its way through Parliament yet. In October 2021, the general legislative elections to the Chamber of Deputies in the Czech Republic will result in, among other things, constituting new government. As a result, the legislative fate of the transposition is thus yet unknown. The above described and explained mechanism of establishing the liability of hosting ISPs will thus be still relevant for years to come.

---

52 The documents are available in Czech from <https://apps.odok.cz/veklep-detail?pid=KORNBV4HKCRN> accessed 10 June 2021.

53 Commission (EC) 'Guidance on Article 17 of Directive 2019/790 on Copyright in the Digital Single Market Guidelines' (Communication) COM (2021) 288 final 4.

Cybersecurity Resilience in Digital Society – the Practical Approach

Ewa Niewiadomska-Szynkiewicz <ewan@nask.pl>,

Marek Amanowicz <marek.amanowicz@nask.pl>,

Agnieszka Wrońska <agnieszka.wronska@nask.pl>,

Paweł Kostkiewicz <pawel.kostkiewicz@nask.pl>
WARSZAWA, Poland

Abstract
Modern societies are deeply dependant on information technology, which means that threats to the availability, integrity, and confidentiality of information and communications infrastructure can significantly impact the functioning of the state and the safety of citizens.

This chapter intends to present the threats connected with the widespread use of digital technologies and the mechanisms for protecting states, institutions, and citizens against these threats. It gives an overview of national and international activities and those of the European Commission to increase security and situational awareness. The authors discuss commonly used protection techniques and mechanisms and safeguard systems to increase society's resilience to cybercrime and give examples of such solutions developed and implemented in Poland. They pointed out the importance of cybersecurity certification procedures and conformity assessment schemes for increasing the resilience to cyberthreats. The chapter concludes with some remarks on the future and challenges.

Keywords:
information and communication technologies, cyber threats, society resilience, cybersecurity protection, security certification, situational awareness

1. Introduction

Information and communication technologies (ICT) have become an indispensable component of modern societies. They are deeply dependent on information and communication infrastructures in all forms of their activities, from governance and economics to the entire exercise of civil rights and freedoms. The rapid development of telecommunication and information networks, systems and applications contribute to creating new, more effective work organisation and process management forms. Advances in mobile technologies, providing anytime, anywhere access to systems and resources, support effective management and business operations and stimulate the development of novel organisational, procedural and socio-economic solutions. By facilitating broad access to global information resources, ICT becomes a stimulator of innovative forms of human communication and leads to significant reassessments in social behaviour. The numerous social networks are becoming a primary source for disseminating information and expressing opinions and views. The use of electronic means of communication is an increasingly common form of human contact.

The reliance on information technology means that threats to the availability, integrity, and confidentiality of ICT infrastructure can significantly impact the functioning of the state and the safety of citizens. At the same time, due to their complexity, modern ICT systems are increasingly vulnerable to cyber-attacks. Individual protection of autonomous systems using a simple analysis of transmitted messages is becoming insufficient. There is a clear need to create new, holistic solutions utilising a fusion of data obtained from multiple sources, integrating different methods, mechanisms and algorithms. Volume, quality, reliability and timeliness of data and information on the situation in the network, and the speed of its processing, determine the effectiveness of protection by preventing threats and identifying the type of attack and responding to their occurrence. Government institutions and commercial companies use many safeguards to protect their networks, but these are often limited in scope.

The challenge is to increase situational awareness by detecting known threats and recognising anomalies on the computing systems that may be symptomatic of malicious activities. It requires advanced frameworks and tools for distributed monitoring, reporting, and aggregation capabilities, to derive events, measures, metrics for deeper processing and analysis. Data fusion, advanced statistics, machine learning techniques and deep learning are often used to correlate a broad range of security contexts for cyber threat intelligence. A further challenge is to extend trust and integrity of data and the execution environment by including access control, identity management, privacy and accountability in executing all processes and trust mechanisms that ensure a high level of security. When building security systems, it is essential to remember the human being in the loop. Therefore, behavioural, social and human aspects must be included in the engineering process to avoid the risk of neglecting or underestimating security threats.

The transfer of activities to the Internet and problems associated with assuring cybersecurity and the reliable functioning of states have led to significant international and national efforts. The activities included legislation, policies and cybersecurity agendas, roadmaps at the national and international levels, and initiating national and international research projects that result in innovative solutions.

On the 6th of July 2016, the European Parliament and the Council of the European Union passed the Directive on the security of network and information systems, colloquially called the NIS Directive [NIS, 2016]. The European Union Member States has issued the relevant legislation implementing the NIS Directive and adapting it to their local legal systems. On the 5th of July 2018, the Polish Parliament passed the Bill on the National Cybersecurity System (NCS) [NCS,2018] to create an efficient and secure system that should increase the protection against computer threats in Poland and enable effective cooperation with the EU Member States. NCS implements into the Polish legal system the NIS Directive. The Act on NCS appoints three institutions to serve as response teams – the Internal Security Agency (GOV CSIRT[1]), NASK – National Research Institute (NASK CSIRT[2]) and the Ministry of National Defence (MON CSIRT[3]). All these institutions work with one another and with other organs responsible for cybersecurity. Together, they constitute a coherent and complete national risk management system, combating cybersecurity threats, both sector-specific and cross-border, as well as coordinating the handling of all reported incidents. The institutions making up the national cybersecurity system form a cohesive whole, making it possible to take a wide range of practical actions to counteract threats and successfully respond to hazards. They are active participants in various national programmes and cross-border initiatives. The NASK CSIRT receives and analyses reports, takes actions and coordinates responses to incidents occurring in

1 <https://csirt.gov.pl> accessed 1 June 2021.

2 <https://cert.pl> accessed 1 June 2021.

3 <https://csirt-mon.wp.mil.pl/pl> accessed 1 June 2021.

Polish civilian cyberspace reported by key service operators, digital service providers, local authorities and individuals. It also responds to incidents involving the uploading of illegal content or poses a hazard to children and monitoring online threats and the level of cybersecurity in individual sectors and the entire country.

In 2018, the European Commission presented a proposal for establishing a European Cyber Security Competence Centre for industry, technology and research with national coordination centres. The proposal aims to stimulate the European technology and industry ecosystem and strengthen cooperation on cybersecurity between different industries and research communities. The centre is supposed to become the main body that would manage EU financial resources dedicated to cybersecurity research under the two proposed programmes: Digital Europe and Horizon Europe for 2021-2027. The book [Felkner, 2020] gives an overview of the most important findings related to cybersecurity research analysis for two exampled regional entities, the Europe Union and Japan, in the last two decades. It highlights the progress in the legal and regulatory area within the privacy and cybersecurity domain and the number and diversity of research funding initiatives. On the other hand, the book points the potential blockers and issues to strengthen the cooperation between different regions. One of the crucial blockers is sharing data and knowledge due to the need to protect sensitive, private data and protect national interests.

Information sharing between national stakeholders and countries are significant activities to improve a security level. It is desirable for the parties concerned to provide each other with knowledge on tackling attacks, incident response and protection and mitigation methods. These are essential tasks of Information Sharing and Analysis Centers[4] (ISACs), non-profit organisations that provide a central resource for gathering information on cyber threats and sharing experience, knowledge and analysis. The NIS Directive groups the operators of vital services in sectors and tasks them to implement incident and threats reporting requirements. Both the Cybersecurity Act and the NIS Directive nourish the creation of sectoral ISACs within the EU. In the many EU Member States, ISAC or similar initiatives have already existed. ISACs are trusted entities to foster information sharing between the public and the private sectors about security incidents and threats, focusing on critical infrastructure. In 2018 ENISA published a report on cooperative models and best practices for ISACs [ISAC, 2018].

---

4 <https://www.enisa.europa.eu/topics/national-cyber-security-strategies/information-sharing> accessed 1 June 2021.

The authors intend to present the threats connected with the widespread use of digital technologies and the mechanisms for protecting states, institutions and citizens against these threats. In this chapter, we present national and international activities, and those of the European Commission, to increase security and situational awareness. We discuss commonly used techniques and mechanisms of protection and defence systems. We present examples of early warning and fraud detection systems developed and implemented in Poland.

2. *Society Resilience*

Internet originating and usage caused the greatest, since printing development, cultural change of real character, encompassing social, economic, political, and personal phenomena. The Internet has changed society and the way of learning and interacting with others. Virtual space is more and more strongly integrating with reality. Many infrastructural, economic, and social factors connected both with easier access to the web and the benefits resulting from using it comprises fast growth of Internet popularity. The development of technology made it possible to connect with the Internet from anywhere, at any level, using every device equipped with specific technology. The Internet is attractive thanks to obtaining current information fast, communicating with others, and getting access to different content sources.

What seems to be interesting is the social dimension of Internet use. With the everyday use of this tool, the borders of countries and languages disappeared. Users from all over the world can communicate with each other at any place and time. The latest data shows that digital, mobile, and social media constitute inevitable and more extensive and significant parts of daily human lives worldwide. Over 50 % of the world's population use the Internet, and the number of people who use social media exceeded 3,8 billion [ITU 2020, Digital Report 2020][5]

What is observed is the influence of the Internet on society and its particular group behaviour patterns (Wrońska, Lange 2016). The dimension of the changes is determined by habits, practices, and ways of using the Internet. That applies to both population in general and young users, which is the group that is seen as one of the most active online. Access

5 <https://www.itu.int/en/ITU-D/Statistics/Pages/stat/default.aspx> accessed 1 June 2021.

to its content has two aspects. On the one hand, the web arranges free time and becomes a prime mover of personal development, initiative, and creativity, and is the place and tool of social communication.

On the other hand, it is a territory full of traps and threats with a more complex character. It has been almost thirty years since information technology had been transferred to everyday social use and has become a universal ecosystem in which children worldwide exist. As quantity studies show [Livingstone 2014, Bąk 2015, Livingstone 2017, Pyżalski et al. 2019, Lange et al. 2020], the internet initiation age in the last decade has dramatically lowered. A few years ago, the average age was ten while currently, children begin to use the Internet on their own still before starting primary school [Kirwił 2011, Tanaś 2016, Kamieniecki et al. 2018, Wrońska, Lange, et al. 2018, Pyżalski et al. 2019, Lange et al.2021]. The studies show that the vast majority of Polish teenagers use the web every day, staying online between 4 and 6 hours on average [Kamieniecki et al. 2017, Pyżalski et al. 2019, Lange et al. 2021]. They engage in various types of online activities, in which they have been ever since and constitute an inseparable element of their lives and virtual space accompanies them in their cognitive, recreational, and interactive activities [Wrońska, Lange 2016]. The Internet attracts young people because it is easy to use, it is multimedia, interactive, and hypertext.

Nearly all young internet users commonly use social communicators and services (just 0,7 % point out that they do not use the Internet this way). The young so-called 'digital natives' – quoting the famous Prensky's statement [Prensky, 2001a; 2001b] – with courage and ease, move around intuitively within the expanse of the Internet. From an anthropologist's point of view, we can talk about developing global prefigurative culture [Mead, 2020]. Younger generations presenting needs, attitudes, and behaviour and transmitting their knowledge to older ones somehow give direction to civilisational changes. Of course, it cannot happen without the participation of older generations – experts who have specific competencies provide users with technological solutions. The Internet is the tool of communication and content for the young generation. It has also become an essential attribute of social identity that lets them create daily life scenarios, affiliative strategies, and aspirational hierarchies. The Internet has changed their plans and time budgets, ways of education and spending their free time, and revolutionised the creation of so-called social identity. Smartphones and laptops have become the centre of the interaction with the world; most of the experience interactions, information, knowledge communication, entertainment are sometimes reduced and formatted to the abilities of the screen or data package.

The positive role of the Internet is undeniable, but at the same time, it is essential to remember that using the global web creates real threats. They relate to cybersecurity threats, content that occurs on the web, dangerous contacts, and more complex internet conduct. The typology (content-contact – conduct) created for the needs of a European research project concerning online dangers for kids is the best known – EU Kids Online [Livingstone et al. 2011]. Online safety and threats is a complex and inhomogeneous area. The list of threats to which a young internet user is exposed comprises an extensive catalogue of dangers. It is impossible to close it due to the incredible dynamics of web evolution. In general, the division involves the following categories of risks:

- contact with illegal and harmful content (presenting violence, physical injuries, cruelty towards humans and animals), encouraging self-destruction (self-injuries, suicides, taking harmful substances), inciting to intolerance, hostility or animosity as well as children pornography, including child sexual abuse material (CSAM),
- dangerous contacts, including child grooming,
- risky behaviour, including sexting,
- cyberbullying,
- internet addiction / problematic use of the Internet,
- risks connected with computer crime, cybercrime.

The above-presented classification does not include a growing spectrum of issues, and it may be assumed that it will be evolving in the following years. From the point of view of all threats connected with internet development, widely understood so-called anonymity and protection of internet users' privacy seem to be especially vital.

The scale of recorded threats and indicated social needs demand coordination of actions to provide safety in cyberspace. Reacting against threats in cyberspace ought to go in a few directions. One of them is initiating broad-based social activities in the scope of global education and prevention; the second one – difficult to complete because of the cross-border character of the Internet – applies to legislative actions. The necessity to guarantee the safety of the youngest internet users constitutes not only the execution of indicated in Art. 72 of the Polish Constitution the duty of children protection against violence, cruelty, abuse, and demoralisation. Regulations legitimised in criminal law which penalises various forms of online violence towards juveniles are mostly connected with crimes against freedom (e.g., persistent harassment, violation of sexual intimacy), sexual freedom and decency (e.g., sexual abuse of a minor, promotion of paedophilia). They also concern crimes against honour and physical integrity (e.g., defamation) and crimes against information (e.g., unauthorised access to information). It is related to compliance with regulations of international character, including recommendations of the European Strategy for a Better Internet for Children, the Comprehensive Strategy on the Rights of the Child, and the Convention on the Rights of the Child, to which Poland is the side. National and international safety policy cannot ignore any of the spaces of children and youth's activity, especially as important for personal human development, their social relations and the culture which makes cyberspace currently. In December 2020 European Committee presented long-awaited projects of horizontal regulation of actions and duties of internet services suppliers[6]. However, another step towards increasing safety on the Internet is protecting fundamental rights and establishing a solid and stable management structure in need of adequate supervision of intermediate services suppliers. Standardising European regulations should increase its effectiveness and simplify its implementation by service providers, who frequently operate internationally. When the safety of the youngest internet users is considered, it will be complementary for horizontal projects to present more precise Committee proposals dedicated to the children's rights protection.

NASK National Research Institute has conducted various actions dedicated to internet safety, including the safety of its youngest users. NASK experts organise social campaigns, accomplish educational programs, conduct studies on civilisational, economic, legal, and cultural phenomena in society and technology, prepare publications, and share their knowledge during local and international meetings. NASK is the coordinator of the Polish Safer Internet Centre (PCPSI), which was established in 2005 under the European Commission's Safer Internet Programme and now operates under the Connecting Europe Facility Programme[7]. Moreover, over 15 years ago, in response to the risk of producing and distributing sexual abuse materials, the team Dyżurnet. pl has been constituted. Since 2018 it has been accomplishing tasks of CSIRT Poland under the regulation of the National System of Cybersecurity. Dyżurnet.pl is a member of INHOPE[8], the association of reacting teams, which cooperates with Interpol and technological companies. The team of Dyżurnet.pl takes and analyses reports from internet users concerning illegal content, mainly including child's se-

6 <https://eur-lex.europa.eu/legal-content/en/TXT/?uri=COM:2020:825:FIN, https://eur-lex.europa.eu/legal-content/en/TXT/?uri=COM%3A2020%3A842%3AFIN> accessed 1 June 2021.

7 <https://www.saferinternet.pl> accessed 1 June 2021.

8 <https://www.inhope.org> accessed 1 June 2021.

xual abuse materials. The hotline has analysed over 133 000 incidents since 2005. Dyżurnet. pl develops tools that court experts use to identify illegal content and accomplish a project about developing automated technology to detect child sexual exploitation and abuse[9]. The team of Dyżurnet. pl analyses legal regulations which control aspects connected with fighting sexual abuse of children and prevention against the distribution of illegal content. NASK experts take actions in this scope to support government institutions with expert knowledge and experience.

The theoretical and empirical dimension of online threats and safety of the youngest Internet users in cyberspace refers to many theories and concepts related to children and adolescents' activity in the real world. An interdisciplinary approach is essential here. It is necessary to have appropriate competencies, tools, and solutions supporting protection and legislation to take advantage of the Internet's enormous potential while avoiding danger zones. The youngest Internet users require special care and support. Therefore social communication aimed at popularising and promoting the idea of taking care of their safety is a critical area of education, prevention, technology, and law.

3. *ICT threats and vulnerabilities*

The dynamically growing number and constantly appearing new types of threats on the Internet create many problems related to ensuring security for private network users, organisations and critical state institutions. Many types of malware attacks designed to perform undesirable operations on the victim's computer are identified. These include intercepting sensitive information and disrupting computers. When a software vulnerability is detected and maliciously exploited, the effects of the unwanted actions can affect multiple network users, e.g. by accessing an infected website. Furthermore, attackers are often responsible for automatically distributing malware from infected computers to other network users to increase the number of victims.

An exponentially growing number of cyber-attacks on Internet users occurs through malware applications installed by users from untrusted sources or even official resources provided by the operating system author (e.g. Google Play store for Android), and SMS or e-mail messages containing links to malicious applications or redirecting to fake websites. The

9 <https://dyzurnet.pl> accessed 1 June 2021.

most common threats currently targeting the digital society are phishing campaigns that target data. Check Point's research shows that the government and financial services are most vulnerable to attacks. Both areas offer attackers valuable caches, such as repositories of financial and personal information.

Cybersecurity teams from various countries confirm that a successive increase in incidents and notifications has been observed for many years. The CERT Polska team operating in the structure of CSIRT NASK handled 22 343 submissions in 2019 [CERT, 2019]. As a result of the analysis, it registered a total of 6 484 cybersecurity incidents. It is a record number and a record increase compared to the previous year (73 %). The most common type of attack was phishing, which accounted for about 54.2 % of all incidents. In second place were reports of malware - 14.9 %. Incidents in the "offensive and illegal content" category, including spam, accounted for approximately 12.1% of all recorded incidents. The use of false information is becoming increasingly common, whether for phishing sensitive data, criminal activities or propaganda campaigns. The year 2019 saw a significant increase in ransomware infections in the industrial, medical and government sectors. Ransomware is software that encrypts data to extract a ransom. An increasing number of incidents have been reports of illegal and offensive spam-like content. In Poland, the number of such reports increased by around 88 % compared to the previous year.

Distributed denial of service (DDoS)[10] attacks block the operation of important institutions for the state and citizens; their range of harmful influence is increasing. Mirkovic and Reiher provide a comprehensive taxonomy of DDoS attacks in [Mirkovic, 2004]. They classify DDoS attacks in terms of the type of exploited vulnerabilities, traffic source validity, the degree of automation required, attack rate dynamics, bots' persistence, victim type, and exerted impact. Modern DDoS attacks are complex, multidimensional attacks of time-varying dynamics, generating traffic from spoofed and highly distributed sources. Massive attacks often occur using a specific class of devices (e.g. WiFi routers, smartwatches, printers with wireless interfaces), usually from a single vendor, and exploiting a specific vulnerability. The intercepted devices are used to initiate DDoS attacks, distribute malicious software, or cryptocurrency mining depending on the attacker's intentions.

Nowadays, many industrial control systems are directly accessible from the Internet. A number of them provide remote control options. The US

---

10 <www.cloudflare.com/learning/ddos> accessed 1 June 2021.

Cybersecurity and Infrastructure Security Agency[11] (CISA) reports numerous incidents where attackers seek out such devices and use them as an attack vector against industrial networks.

The widespread use of Internet of Things (IoT) devices has significantly increased the interest of cybercriminals in IoT systems in recent years. The users of IoT are exposed to various new forms of attacks. Insecure IoT devices are already exploited and used in massive attacks and rapidly increase the number of victims [Zhuge, 2020], [Neshenko, 2019]. There are still many active botnets, with new ones taking advantage of increasingly common IoT devices. The most common threats listed in the Open-Web Application Security Project (OWASP) Top 10 Internet of Things list [OWASP, 2018] are weak guessable, or hardcoded passwords, insecure network services, ecosystem interfaces, data transfer and storage, lack of insecure update mechanism and device management, insufficient privacy protection. Unfortunately, removing even the well-known vulnerabilities is difficult and costly as it often requires modifications to the hardware and involves the manufacturer.

A famous example is the Mirai botnet performing large scale DDoS attacks [Antonakakis, 2017]. Attacks on IoT devices are becoming more advanced and specialised. They often target a single vulnerability in a specific model of a selected manufacturer. The purpose of using seized devices is also changing - in addition to DDoS attacks, attackers are increasingly interested in data theft, malware distribution or cryptocurrency mining. Moreover, more and more malicious applications are being developed for mobile devices.

To summarise, the topic of IoT security is still too little researched and developed. Cyber-attacks may become even larger and more frequent if no action is taken to secure the IoT systems. It is a reason while the security of IoT and mobile devices is such important for people and industry. At the same time, numerous manufacturers neglect security aspects. They often ignore vulnerabilities found in IoT devices and software. The report [IoTSF, 2018] of the research conducted by the IoT Security Foundation shows that in the 2018 year, only 10 % of 331 IoT vendors sampled have implemented any vulnerability disclosure policy. Moreover, even vulnerabilities are identified, disclosed to vendors, and mitigated by them, and they are rarely announced to the public by the vendors themselves. Therefore, there is a meagre amount of publicly known vulnerabilities, while the total amount of vulnerabilities is supposedly large. There is no universal

11 <https://www.cisa.gov> accessed 1 Juned 2021.

way to track and mitigate them. Solving these issues would greatly benefit from a publicly available source of structured information about known IoT vulnerabilities and exploits. Currently, none of the existing solutions is satisfactory. The available repositories are not focused on the IoT, highlighting the need for new projects in securing IoT. Recently, several research projects have been initiated to develop new techniques for detecting unknown vulnerabilities and exploits [Janiszewski, 2021]. The open-access databases of publicly known vulnerabilities and exploits affecting IoT devices are under development. An example is a system created within the Variot[12] project. The challenge is to detect vulnerabilities as fast as possible and immediately notify about new vulnerabilities.

4. *Cybersecurity protection methods and defence systems*

Malware and security incidents detection techniques

To meet today's security requirements and maintain the continuity of an organisation's operations, it is essential to ensure efficient and effective response activities to identify and quickly respond to cybersecurity incidents. Ensuring data transmission security is one of the most crucial problems faced by computer network administrators. Quick detection of threats, especially mass campaigns, allows protecting systems from the possibility of their damage or destruction. The fundamental problem is the high rate of spreading attacks and the vast amount of data necessary to process to identify them. Analysis and classification of network data collected from various sources and identification of security incidents effectively support software systems and services that significantly enhance the security of government, state administration, institutions and citizens. Strategies and mechanisms for effective and rapid detection of threats are the main elements of many defence systems. Many malware detection techniques can be listed. The most important of these are:

- anomaly detection, which involves the detection of abnormal behaviour, including deviations from typical network traffic loads,
- signature analysis, i.e. comparing the content of a tested file with a set of previously created threat patterns.

---

12 VARIoT (Vulnerability and Attack Repository for IoT) CEF project founded by the European Commission, <https://www.variot.eu> accessed 1 June 2021.

Intrusion Detection Systems (IDS) and Intrusion Prevention Systems (IPS) are parts of the network infrastructure used to protect networks from cyber-attacks. IDS systems continuously monitor the network for signs that indicate attackers that are using a known cyber threat to infiltrate or steal data from it. IDS systems compare the current network activity to a known threat database to detect such behaviours as malware, security policy violations, and port scanners to detect unusual situations. IPS systems operate at the interface between the internal network and the outside world. They proactively deny network traffic based on a security profile if that packet represents a known security threat. IDSs/IPSs implement various architectures and different approaches to the problem of detecting threats. They also offer different levels of security. The survey of intrusion detection systems is presented in [Gupta, 2021], [Khraisat, 2019].

Security Information and Event Management (SIEM) is a set of tools and services offering a holistic view of an organisation's information security. These tools provide real-time visibility across an organisation's information security systems. SIEM combines two technologies: (i) security information management, which collects data from log files for analysis and reports on security threats and incidents, (ii) security event management, which conducts real-time system monitoring and analysing, establishes correlations between security incidents, and notifies network administrators.

In general, IDS/IPS and SIEM are responsible for data collecting, analysing and correlating. They use similar techniques in their operation. The Endpoint Detection and Response (EDR) is a more advanced technology. It is an integrated endpoint security solution that combines real-time continuous monitoring and endpoint data with rules-based automated response and analysis capabilities. Therefore, EDR looks deep into the system, gathers and analyses all activity. It allows for data fusion and correlations and different detection techniques. Moreover, EDR uses forensics and analysis tools to research identified threats and search for suspicious activities.

Most institutions, especially the key ones, establish Security Operation Centers (SOCs) – the centralised units that deal with security issues on an organisational and technical level. SOC comprises professionals with expertise in information security, processes, and technology for monitoring, analysing and protecting an organisation from cyber-attacks. SOCs help organisations respond to intrusions quickly and constantly improve detection and prevention processes.

The ability to keep the networks and systems of an organisation secure is often dependent on the knowledge of the threat landscape, new attacks and trends, new vulnerabilities and changing best practices. It also requires specialised tools to monitor the global situation, detect security events, and provide data to network operators. The research and development teams in all countries conduct research and analyses regarding new technology applications and implementation. New services and innovative products make it possible to detect and counteract threats that significantly enhance government security, key institutions and citizens are developed. The example solutions presented in the following sections are designed to warn of cyber threats, detect DDoS attacks and prevent fraud in electronic transactions.

Early warnings of cyber threats

A crucial tool for observing attacks in the wild is a honeypot – a system deliberately exposed and seemingly vulnerable, designed to register and report connections and exploitation attempts. A significant non-technical advantage of using honeypots (apart from client-side honeypots) is that they are entirely passive endpoint systems. It is a very desirable trait in both ethical and legal contexts. By design, the honeypot is incapable of observing regular traffic. It only receives packets explicitly addressed to it – and since the honeypot offers no real services and is not advertised in any way, any traffic reaching it is suspicious. Most of this traffic will be either due to network scanning or an exploitation attempt, if deliberately addressed, or random, such as echos from DDoS attacks using source IP spoofing. The only non-malicious activity that may appear in a honeypot is either non-malicious scanning or a result of misconfiguration. In any case, the honeypot does not come in contact with any legitimate, sensitive user data.

Another technique of observing real-life attacks at scale involves using network telescopes, also known as darknets. Network telescopes are blocks of unused IP addresses. Like in the case of honeypots, any packets reaching them are by definition incorrect – apart from minor noise, such as misconfigured computers. However, unlike honeypots, network telescopes do not respond in any way to the incoming packets. It means that the information about the activity is limited, especially in the case of TCP. However, this also saves resources, enabling monitoring of ample address space. Also, while honeypots can often be identified and blacklisted by malicious actors due to imperfect emulation of real vulnerable services, network telescopes are indistinguishable from regular, unobserved unused IP space. The information in a network telescope is limited to single packets, which usually restricts them to a source of high-level statistics, such as top scanned ports, etc. However, more advanced analytical capabilities allow extracting far more actionable information from the available data. The significant size of the darknet allows observing less common events and getting more accurate statistics. Monitoring all ports and being aware of the standard "background noise level" is a suitable method of spotting new activity. A sudden increase in scanning activity on a specific port may indicate that a new vulnerability has been found by malicious actors looking for exploitable services – either as potential targets that could be made part of a botnet or potential reflectors for amplification attacks. Another cause of sudden increases in activity is ongoing UDP DDoS attacks with spoofed IP addresses – with a large enough darknet, it is possible to deduce from the observed reflection both the algorithm used for IP spoofing and the estimated size of the attack. Reflexions are generally easy to identify and group into one attack, as all the packets have the same source – the target of the initial attack.

Early warning systems are a constant focus of the research and development teams at NASK and CERT Polska. Many of those systems trace back to the SISSDEN[13] project, which developed many innovative tools and systems gathering, enriching and publishing actionable threat data. Together, they can be considered a global early warning system, capable of noticing new kinds of threats and informing interested users. SISSDEN built a global network of honeypots, deployed on over 250 nodes in 58 different countries, monitoring almost a thousand IP addresses using 12 different honeypots emulating various services. Reaching this global scale economically and technically scalable way required a new approach to building the network. Instead of deploying and maintaining honeypots remotely in all locations, SISSDEN standardised on a simple, low-resource Linux node that could be obtained cheaply from many providers and ran a minimal system, tunnelling the incoming traffic from honeypot IP addresses to the honeypots deployed in the central datacentre. Hence, NASK operates one of the largest network telescopes in the region, with hundreds of thousands of addresses.

The objective of another early warning system - ARAKIS[14] is to report threats in the IT and OT network. It has been developed to build a network security landscape overview and support the detection of new network threats. Events correlated by the system are received from various

13 Secure Information Sharing Sensor Delivery event Network (SISSDEN), European Commission project, Horizon 2020, 2015-2019.

14 <https://www.arakis.pl> accessed 1 June 2021.

sources, including honeypots, darknet probes, firewalls and antivirus systems. Advanced analyses are possible due to the unique system architecture of distributed sensor network. A distinctive feature is an innovative algorithm for automatic detection of recurring patterns threats and creating SNORT[15] signatures describing detected attacks based on machine learning and advanced network engineering methods. Unique algorithms correlating the data collected by sensors with the unique set of signatures for reactive systems generated by ARAKIS enable comprehensive threat analysis and quick reaction to detected threats, including zero-day.

Information on threats and malicious applications delivered through many channels and received from early warning systems is collected and available on the net. They are created by local CERTs, such as the n6[16] system developed at NASK, or databases created by user communities, such as Koodous[17]. Expert groups continuously monitor and analyse multiple sources of information about cyber threats that can affect the integrity and availability of IT systems of protected organisations and their customers. Multi-level threat analysis, both technical, behavioural, and contextual, is performed based on data sources such as darknet, honeypot, sinkhole, spampot, spamtrap, and other open and closed monitoring sources non-indexed Internet layers (Deep and Dark Web). Collective threat intelligence service (CTI) is the continuous acquisition and delivery of information from external sources regarding cyber threats. This service increases the protection of organisations against new and targeted attacks, supports internal security teams of SOC and protection systems: SIEM, IDS/IPS, EDR.

DDoS defence systems

Many cybersecurity systems protect network resources against distributed denial of service (DDoS) attacks. A comprehensive overview of defence systems is presented in [Zargar, 2013]. The defence mechanisms can be characterised by preventive and reactive activity levels, deployment location and degree of required cooperation with other network mechanisms and services. Most systems focus only on attack detection. More advanced provide mitigation services. Reactive mechanisms differ in attack response strategies, including source-based or flow-based packet dumping, routing

15 <https://www.snort.org> accessed 1 June 2021.
16 <https://n6.cert.pl> accessed 1 June 2021.
17 <https://docs.koodous.com> accessed 1 June 2021.

reconfiguration, and attack rate-limiting. However, in all cases, the efficiency of attack mitigation depends on packet filtering methods and their efficiency.

The design of DDoS detection and mitigation mechanisms is a subject of many surveys. Authors point to significant practical challenges, such as separating the attack from legitimate traffic and implementing response tools in the network environment. In particular, packet filtering and rate-limiting are primary mechanisms to respond against the DDoS attack traffic [Kalkan, 2016]. In general, the detection of attacks is based on pattern matching algorithms. The observed flows of packets are compared with known attack fingerprints. A flow consists of packets that match conditions describing packet attributes, i.e. IP source and destination addresses, source and destination port numbers, or protocol. Next, a malicious detected flow is redirected to a scrubbing centre to be cleaned from malicious components. The standard model of DDoS protection is based on managed security services delivered by ISPs or DDoS Protection Service (DPS) providers.

The FLDX[18] system is fast and highly effective in protecting the availability of network services in case of a volumetric DDoS attack or a sudden increase in user activity. Maintaining a fair distribution of network bandwidth is the primary goal of the system, achieved in an unrivalled time of even several seconds. The FLDX system uses machine learning algorithms to dynamically self-adjust filters to the current situation. This approach allows for a speedy response to observed changes in network load, as well as their forecast. FLDX is not only a protection tool - it is also a network knowledge discovery tool. The FLDX detection module offers high-resolution multidimensional monitoring of network activity, providing essential knowledge in near real-time. An extensive reporting system provides detailed descriptions of cybersecurity incidents, showing geolocation of sources, network connection structure and packet construction statistics. The speed and precision of the FLDX system is the result of years of research in the fields of control theory and adaptive signal processing.

18 <https://fldx.pl> accessed 1 June 2021.

Prevention of fraud in electronic transactions

The common threats currently targeting the digital society are phishing campaigns that target data, including personal information and users' financial resources. Theft of personal data occurs every 2 seconds[19]. Fraud can be committed in many different ways and many different settings. Fraud often affects banking, insurance, government, and healthcare sectors. The standard type of fraud in online banking is customer account takeover, through illegally gains access to a victim's bank account using bots. The current trend of threats consists of injecting malware (web injection) into web browsers allowing for modification of the bank's transaction site on the user's side (Man-in-the-Browser). The attack is depicted in Figure 1.

Fig. 1. Man-in-the-Browser attack.

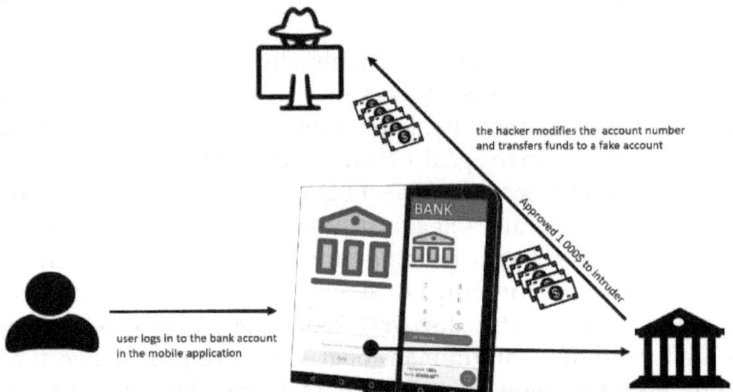

Web fraud attempts detection is a set of processes and analyses that identify and prevent unauthorised financial activity. The primary reason to use data analytics techniques is to tackle fraud since many internal control systems have serious weaknesses. The dedicated mechanisms for predicting conventional tactics and uncovering new, sophisticated schemes of fraud attacks have been developed. They apply predictive and adaptive analytics techniques, including data mining, statistics, clustering, machine learning

19 <https://mobilitynews.pl/raport-symantec-urzadzenia-mobilne-zagrozone-cyberatakiem> accessed 1 June 2021.

and deep learning [Babu, 2020], [Shirodkar, 2020]. The real-time monitoring is combined with big data gathered from multiple sources processing.

The BotSense[20] system enables real-time detection of all Web fraud attempts caused by a change of the transaction service content on the bank's customers' desktop or mobile device. The system's effectiveness is based on a signature management mechanism and dynamic analysis of the Document Object Model (DOM) structure for behaviours exceeding the regular operation of the electronic banking transaction system. It generates JavaScript code that detects web-injects on the bank customers computers based on the signatures of cyber-attacks. BotSense allows the banks to detect and monitor individual customers infected by malware and protect their customers against attempts to steal funds or sensitive data.

5. Global situational awareness

Protecting against a constantly growing number of increasingly sophisticated and complex cyber-attacks requires, as has been mentioned earlier, new functionalities enabling detection, assessing and preventing them. It also demands the achievement of a reliable cyber situational awareness picture, online delivering validated information on identified threats and risks and their impact on the behaviour of systems and related processes and services. It denotes particularly to those vital to the state security, public and economic order, functioning of public institutions, civil rights and freedoms, and human life and health. However, as presented in several works, for instance [Rinaldi, 2001], [Zimmerman, 2004], [Nieuwenhuijs, 2008], [Setola, 2016], the situation complicates the strong systems' dependencies and shared information and communications technology resources. The various infrastructures are complex in themselves, especially when factors such as markets, government regulations, policies, legal and other socio-technical aspects must be considered. However, infrastructures do not exist in isolation of one another – the malfunction of a single system can trigger a cascading effect leading to extensive failures, which can have significant economic consequences for a single entity or even an entire nation. For example, telecommunications networks require electricity; industrial systems use sophisticated computer control and information systems; electricity generation requires fuels, and so on. Such interrelations are of different and complex nature [Petit, 2016], which precise identification is

---

20 <https://botsense.pl> accessed 1 June 2021.

crucial for identifying threats in cyberspace and assessing their impact on the state's security.

Many authors like [Stergiopoulos, 2016] or [Han, 2019] confirm the need for analysing the network of interdependent infrastructures enabling identification of its security-critical components and better understanding the scale and scope of potential threats. Such an approach allows early identification of the threat propagation early and disseminates the warnings for pre-emptive actions to mitigate the related risk. However, effective threat response requires establishing procedures, a cooperation framework for reporting threat incidents and coordinating entities' activities, as presented by [Settanni, 2017], [Puuska, 2016] or [Turoff, 2016]. It enables a safe and reliable online collaboration of the IT security analysis and management teams from all interdependent entities. However, it should be noted that the scope and level of detail of threat information sharing are often limited in practice. It is most often due to fear of compromising the security or vital interests of the party providing the data, which it considers as sensitive information. Therefore it is also desirable to create mechanisms to encourage these entities to cooperate and ensure that their vital interests are protected. These activities should be supported by technical solutions that enable the efficient acquisition, processing, and dissemination of verified information about cybersecurity threats and their potential impacts.

Ensuring global protection against computer threats is possible not only by preventing unauthorised access to systems or protection against malicious software. In addition, new functions need to be built to detect cyber events early, assess potential threats and their propagation within interconnected infrastructure with an assessment of associated negative consequences, and implement appropriate preventive countermeasures. Thus, achieving a global and reliable situational awareness picture in the cyberspace of interconnected networks and systems is the basis for effective response to ongoing and potential threats.

Recently, many efforts and case studies have been undertaken internationally and nationally to achieve a global situational awareness to improve the reliability and continuity of systems and services essential to safety and broadly understood the state's economic interests. They are mainly stimulated by the NIS Directive [NIS, 2016] or national strategies for the security of networks and information systems. In addition, some stimulating approaches to improve an organisation's ongoing awareness of the risk posed to its business by cybersecurity attacks have been developed within

European Union research projects like CS-AWARE[21] or PROTECTIVE[22]. The first one focuses on creating solutions dedicated to the local public, providing tools for automatic detection, classification, and visualisation of computer incidents in near-real-time. The latter enables raising cyber situational awareness by enhancing security alert correlation and prioritisation, linking the relevance of an organisation's assets to its business.

In Poland, the National Cybersecurity System (NCS) [NCS, 2018] imposes, among others, on the cabinet minister the responsibility to develop and maintain the global cybersecurity awareness system supporting cooperation of all the national cybersecurity system entities. The prototype of such a system has been developed within the research project entitled "National Platform for Cybersecurity" (NPC) carried out within the framework of the CybeSecIdent Program on "Cybersecurity and e-Identity", supported by the National Centre for Research and Development. After extensive tests and several extensions, the system was entered to force in January 2021 under the S46 name. The system integrates components of the national cybersecurity system (Fig. 2), including three Cybersecurity Incidents Response Teams (CSIRT), essential and digital service providers, public entities and stakeholders exchanging information over the dedicated NPC secure network.

The S46 contains the mechanisms for integrating the security management systems used by various institutions and companies and aggregation of a distributed knowledge from numerous databases. In addition, it delivers procedural and technical mechanisms to ensure secure sharing and dissemination of information about events that could adversely affect cybersecurity. The exchange of data is carried out within the following basic functional processes, i.e., surveying the system's entities, handling incident reports, building global cybersecurity awareness and risk assessment at the national and company level, exchanging information on security events, warning on threats and risk, knowledge sharing, exchange of information on vulnerabilities and issuing recommendations.

---

21 <https://cs-aware.eu> accessed 1 June 2021.

22 <https://protective-h2020.eu> accessed 1 June 2021.

Fig. 2. S46 ecosystem

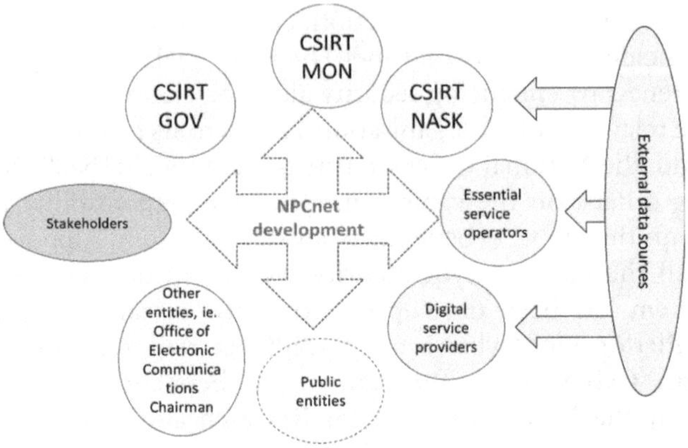

Achieving consistent and trustworthy cybersecurity awareness at the national level requires that all S46 users apply a uniform approach to cyber threat assessment. Therefore, the S46 applies a dedicated risk assessment methodology. It covers the users' dynamic risk assessment procedure and the static and dynamic risk analysis procedures carried out by the CSIRTs [Janiszewski, 2019]. The risk assessment results performed at CSIRTs (Fig. 3) are visualised on a network of interdependent services depicted in [Kamola, 2019]. The colours of the nodes correspond to the current risk values for the services. The width of the edges reflects the strength of the impact of a given service. By clicking on the selected node, one can get more detailed information. The panel to the right in Fig. 3 shows details of the selected service (indicated by the blue border), including the risk value and its trend.

Fig. 3. The visualisation of risk assessment

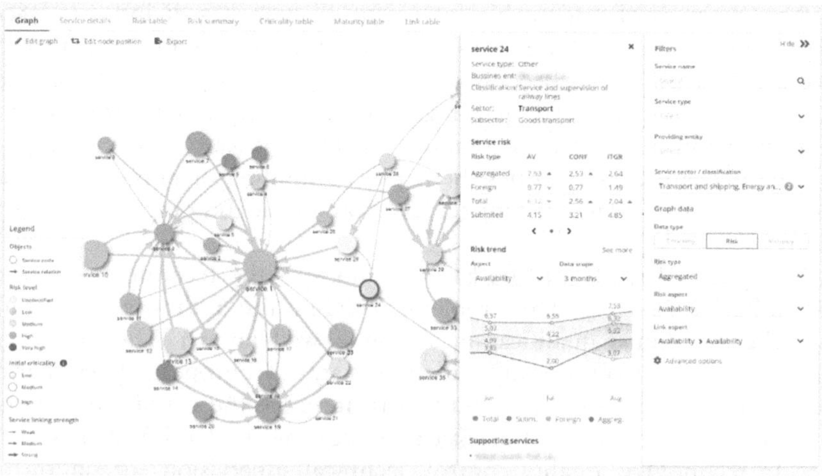

By correlating the results of analyses conducted by CSIRTs appropriately, it is possible to create a global picture of cybersecurity awareness. Elements of the global situational awareness picture are shared with S46 users, enabling them to obtain the necessary data to react promptly when threat symptoms appear in cyberspace and select appropriate measures to eliminate or reduce their impact.

Lessons learned from the implementation of S46 confirm that creating and understanding real cybersecurity awareness depends on the ability of all actors involved to effectively detect and effectively respond to cyber threats and their willingness to share cyber threat information. The presented solution offers effective mechanisms ensuring the expected level of trust of the system's users in external relations. It delivers tools for strengthening the users' collaboration, supports secure sharing of the threat data and building a shared cybersecurity awareness picture. All these lead to better understanding the threats and risks and increasing the protection against significant damage to the state's security, public order, and economic interests.

6. Conformity assessment and certification

Cybersecurity is of undeniable impact to all branches of industry, each public administration level and – as well – citizens. Combined with geopolitical interest, it has become an inherent part of legislative initiatives, formal and informal (status quo) regulations, industry-specific or sector-wise private and public standards and – last but not least – the vital aspect of supply chain characteristics. Be it private funding or public spending; no other security-related parameter has more impact on procurement decisions.

The pillar of trust and the basis of choice is the recommendation of an authority we trust. The problem to define the authority and set-up a well-programmed qualification system is well known. The recitals of Cybersecurity Act (European regulation) state: "A European cybersecurity certification framework is established to improve the conditions for the functioning of the internal market by increasing the level of cybersecurity." In technology, quality control, technical supervision, attestation or calibration mechanisms are widely used. We are not surprised that a weighing scale measures correctly and perfectly in line with another unit; to observe the attestation mark on facilities and devices such as fire extinguishers or elevators.

On the contrary, we intuitively and subconsciously know a systematic solution behind this predictable way of working. Rightly so, weighting scales are subject to calibration and elevators to inspection and periodic control. These are the elements of the "conformity assessment systems" as well as "market surveillance" that stand behind and ensure the quality (efficiency, performance, accuracy) of the equipment and services available on the market.

Preparing, setting, and introducing a similar systematic approach for cybersecurity has become a vital challenge to the market. Complaints about the below-expectations performance or unpredictable behaviour of IT equipment like computers or smartphones are common. Misbehaviour of such kind provokes the observation – it is possible that a device used hundred times daily (phone) and for most working hours of a week (computer) is not subjected to any systematic and regular control or tests. Furthermore, at the same time, we entrust these devices with personal data, sensitive information, financial transactions, professional and private secrets. On the contrary, devices responsible for the safety of the work and life environment (like fire extinguishers) are not likely to be used and are subject to check procedure at least once a year. What makes things even worse, a common approach has been developed to answer the persistent requests of antivirus software to run scheduled scans and operating system prompts for updates by choosing the "postpone" action. The above-described context of conformity assessment for cybersecurity is a combination of rules for development, acquisition, deployment and safe (secure) usage. Setting up a unified approach that would encompass and enforce all these rules is not an easy task.

Regulation (EU) 2019/881 of the European Parliament and of the Council of 17 April 2019 on ENISA (European Union Cyber-Security Agency) and on ICT cybersecurity certification, concerning the European Cybersecurity Certification Framework (The European Cybersecurity Act) provides for the creation of certification schemes at different levels of trust justification (national and European).

Currently, there is no functioning common certification scheme in cybersecurity evaluation in the European area. The European Commission developed the first draft program based on the ENISA document and the SOG-IS[23] input. It will be a certification scheme based on the Common Criteria standard. The subsequent schemes that can be expected to appear will be dedicated to cryptography, 5G technology, cloud solutions and the Internet-of-Things. The security of 5G networks is one of the most important issues being considered globally, in Europe and nationally (COMMISSION RECOMMENDATION (EU) 2019/534 of 26 March 2019, Cybersecurity of 5G networks)[24]. Furthermore, the European Commission encourages EU member states to give high priority to the issue of cooperation to certify 5G devices and networks (Press Release /19/4266, 19.07.2019).

[ECSO, 2020] "Certification scheme as defined in the EU Cybersecurity Act provides a framework within which a sound certification ecosystem can be organised. A European certification scheme is made of security requirements, a corresponding evaluation methodology and governance rules. The Cybersecurity Act suggests considering and referring to two main sources: (1) European, international and industry standards that define evaluation methodologies for a given vertical or context. (2) 'Security Profiles' that could be defined within a scheme or standard, and define precise requirements tailored for a given use case, product category, or vertical."

---

23 SOG-IS - Senior Officials Group Information Systems Security, <https://www.sogis.eu> accessed 1 June 2021.

24 <https://eur-lex.europa.eu/legal-content/EN/TXT/HTML/?uri=CELEX:32019H0534> accessed 1 June 2021.

A certificate confirms that the product, or sometimes only the product's design or its manufacturing process, is compliant with specific requirements. Verification of compliance with requirements established by standards is a common procedure. Note that neither in Poland nor Europe is normalisation obligatory. That means that both creating standards and applying them are voluntary [IK-GEOPOL, 2020]. Nevertheless, "standardisation translates directly and indirectly into the offered IT products as it may significantly influence the selection of technologies or manufacturing techniques. This influence is caused by the market pressure that treats compliance with standards as a quality indicator and a method of verification whether the product will be successfully launched and put into use. That is where the issue of conformity assessment appears" [IK-GEOPOL, 2020].

It should be remembered and understood that certification is one of the elements (stages) of a working conformity assessment system. Certainly an important one, often crucial for the manufacturer (when required for entering the domestic market or sale in a particular branch). Let us remember that issuing a certificate (attestation decision) without implementing control mechanisms that enforce continuant compliance with requirements will not guarantee the quality for the end-user (stability of features). That requires "mechanisms to demonstrate continued compliance with the specified cybersecurity requirements" – as required by Article 54 of [CSA, 2019]. In reality, the regular and systematic inspection regime applies to the most extent to industrial machinery and equipment. Operational quality (accuracy) is not given for an indefinite period. Due to the ageing of mechanical and electronic components, changes in the operating environment and ambient conditions, the performance and quality is constantly changing, usually for the worse. For this reason, the obligation of constant technical supervision, monitoring of parameters, quality control is being introduced.

On the European level, the above-mentioned systematic and unified approach that applies to the cybersecurity of devices intended for the general market (individual consumers) is at very early stages. At the same time, we observe a strong need to implement fail-safe mechanisms ("framework") that would lead the development of IT solutions towards building secure-by-design solutions. Several mature initiatives that support this line of thinking are worth mentioning:

- Microsoft's concept called Microsoft Security Development Lifecycle has been developed since 2004 as an integral part of the entire software development process. M-SDL is promoted among developers, partners, and customers of the company, who are encouraged to apply the principles of SDL in the development process and incorporate the best practices described in the Operational Security Assurance (OSA) approach. Microsoft's strategy of "embedding" the approach of the SDL software development strategy benefits with the significant share of certificate products in the portfolio, including core technologies like operating system and database engine[25]

- Safecode[26] initiative, which makes available several influential publications offering software security guidance, led by its flagship paper "Fundamentals of Secure Software Development",
- The white paper [NIST-SSDF, 2020] introduces a software development framework (SSDF), a mine of knowledge on mature practices on secure software development.

IT products are assessed and certified in Europe (and other countries) against requirements of Common Criteria standard (also ISO/IEC 15408). Thanks to the international agreements SOG-IS (Europe) and CCRA (world) signed by NASK, Poland joined the group that recognises certificates based on this standard. Poland is willing to elevate the certification potential; thus, a certifying authority (NASK[27]) was established to evaluate IT products for compliance with the Common Criteria standard.

7. *Future perspectives and open issues*

Cybersecurity is of strategic importance to countries' security and involves protecting critical sectors of the economy, citizens and businesses – this requires constant development and advancements. It is an ever-evolving industry, a permanent arms race. The malware developers attack, and the defence counters with better anti-attack technology. It is an often repeated pattern.

There is a consensus among network security experts that effective detection of network attacks requires collecting and processing as much data containing malware samples as possible. Due to the complexity and number of analysed data, developing advanced algorithms and building efficient computer systems to support the analysis process is necessary. Statistical methods, numerical analysis, data mining, machine learning, risk

25 <https://www.commoncriteriaportal.org/products> accessed 1 June 2021.
26 <https://safecode.org> accessed 1 June 2021.
27 <https://en.nask.pl/eng/activities/certification> accessed 1 June 2021.

analysis, signal processing, decision and control theory are widely used. Deep learning combined with big data processing and new computing paradigms (cloud, fog, edge, dust computing) can be expected to dominate in the near future. These techniques can be successfully used to correlate a broad range of security contexts and knowledge mining to create cyber threats intelligence in anticipation of cyberattacks.

Every year more and more devices are connected to the Internet, the number and complexity of cyber threats will also increase. The internet community is growing, the age of people connecting to the global web is decreasing. It raises enormous social risks. The global network, allowing knowledge and experience to be shared on an unprecedented scale, accelerates innovation and development, increases social inequalities, undermines economic stability, and poses severe threats to entire societies and individuals. Ensuring cybersecurity is and will be a huge challenge for governments, social organisations, education. The critical tasks to be tackled include:

- raising public awareness of online threats,
- adopting legislation to the changing reality,
- international cooperation of government representatives and commercial companies,
- investment in research and exchange of knowledge and experience.

It is not the aim to control the Internet - attempts to control such a dispersed system are somewhat doomed to failure. The objective is to limit the threats to which users of the global network will be exposed.

Conclusions and Recommendations for the UN Community

"Future of Internet" - does not look very optimistic. The development of technology, in particular the increasing complexity of algorithms, the growing use of Artificial Intelligence, new technological tools are a serious challenge for the UN community. Not only for scientists and lawyers, but also for politicians, NGOs, IT specialists and ordinary citizens. The United Nations, through the activities of the IGF, faces serious challenges in the regulation of the Internet, but as shown by the researchers participating in the research project, the results of which are presented in this monograph, above all in the regulation and control of algorithms, not only complex ones such as AI, but also others that increasingly affect human functioning. In fact, each chapter (expressing the views of its authors) points to the need for regulation of algorithms and a new approach to regulation. The monograph consists of four parts, covers various legal issues and problems: judiciary, consumers, new technologies for climate protection, consumer rights, AI, forensics, personal data, cyber security and others. This broad coverage of the research was intended to indicate the variety of problems we face. Our role was not to solve them, but to show the risks associated with the use of new technologies, but also the opportunities that technology offers for the future. The result of the work are recommendations for the UN community and a contribution to the international discussion on the future of new technologies.

Some authors have decided to make additional recommendations for future United Nations activities. Here we present these recommendations, indicating that the proposed recommendations represent the views of the individual authors:

Krzysztof Szubert:

Universal connectivity is the prerequisite for achieving social welfare headway. Yet, post-pandemic, the major concern is poverty that threatens to engulf many fragile communities across the world after COVID-19 had wiped out most of the progress made since 2000. That is why, first and foremost, the G20 statesmen and the Big Tech CEOs must come together to help the poorest countries carry on with digital investments, including affordable Internet connectivity and the Internet-enabled services. Next, the international community should promote open information resources for education purposes, as well as define the scope of responsibility of digital platforms to prevent misinformation/disinformation and the spread of violent content and hate speech. By extension, it should think of effective ways of protecting the freedom of expression from governments who pretext exercising their sovereign powers to censor the Internet and suppress human rights. Furthermore, it should address the Big Tech's monopoly in the digital sphere to ensure the level-playing field for smaller players, in addition to proposing fair taxation patterns to get the digital revolution winners to share their profits with society. Last but not least, it should sort out the issue of data ownership to promote the reuse of data and build liquid and trusted data markets that will drive economic growth.

Section One

Monika Jagielska, Monika Namysłowska, Aneta Wiewiórowska-Domagalska:

The decisive bodies and international organisations (like UN) should take into account while drafting the policies and protective measures that not only consumers but also users and other groups that may be described as vulnerable deserve special attention and protection as the development of AI may increase their exclusion and weaken their position against the "big business". Both the recognition of vulnerabilities in the digital reality and appropriate legal safeguards should now take priority.

Zofia Bednarz, Kayleen Manwaring:

Future regulation of emerging technologies, in particular AI and Big Data, in the area of financial services, presents important challenges for policy-makers and regulators. We argue that the most concerning problems may arise because of the opacity AI models potentially used by financial firms, and especially opacity resulting from complexity of machine learning models, as well as corporate secrecy. Therefore, regulation should focus on mandating transparency of corporate practices and explainability of models used. We have identified various consumer harms potentially arising out of the use of AI and Big Data tools by financial firms:

- algorithmic bias and resulting discrimination in provision of financial services;

- excessive collection of personal data from external sources to train the models;
- digital consumer manipulation, where that data is used to exploit consumer vulnerabilities, emotions and individual cognitive biases for commercial benefit;
- 'extreme' personalisation of financial services leading to exclusion of less valuable customers.

Although existing rules in the areas such as financial services law, consumer protection, privacy and data protection and anti-discrimination law should offer some level of consumer protection, the extent of this protection is uncertain. Therefore, policymakers and regulators need to carefully consider fitness for purpose of the current law and regulation, as in some instances it may turn out to be inadequate in this new socio-technical reality.

Heloísa Helena Silva Pancotti, Renato Bernardi:

There is no space to think about the implementation of distributive public policies outside the virtual environment of the internet. Paradoxically, the recipients of these policies are the ones who face the most difficulties accessing the internet. It is necessary to think of the right to connection as a fundamental right, under penalty of making the access of less favored citizens to welfare policies, unfeasible.

Ewa Rott Pietrzyk, Dariusz Szostek, Marek Świerczyński:

The development of artificial intelligence as well as the increasing implementation of law in algorithms makes it necessary to introduce regulations to control algorithms. It is suggested that the UN, together with the Council of Europe, prepare an international convention to regulate AI and the use of other algorithms, taking into account human rights as a basis for the operation of all algorithmic codes. It is necessary to supervise not only AI, but also other codes that have an increasing impact on human functioning. Human rights should form the basis when regulating algorithms.

Section Two

Fryderyk Zoll:

The need to prepare rules of professional ethics taking into account AI in legal work. Preparation of standard curricula for legal education taking into account AI work.

Gabriela Bar, Silvia A. Carretta, Shobana Iyer:

1) Introduce electronic communication with courts and public authorities in all countries.
2) The use of technology to conduct court hearings should become an inevitable requirement to keep access to justice open and to reduce the backlogs and delays created by adjournments.
3) Blockchain and distributed ledger technology (DLT) are technology that should be used by public services and courts (public registers) and by lawyers to improve their services. DLT can help the public and legal services become more accessible, transparent, automated and cost efficient. Usage of DLT to streamline and simplify transactional work, to be able to digitally sign documents and to store legal agreements in an immutable way. Practical examples of DLT uses in the legal industry include the recording of music works to protect copyright , safe storage of real estate deeds transforming documents into immutable tokenized assets, time stamp certification of agreements with verifiable digital signature, automation of payments (e.g., management of escrow accounts at a fraction of the cost of manual labour through smart contract).
4) Lawyers will be expected to embrace technology even further as technology develops in Legal Tech tools. Lawyers will be required to develop their know-how in the use of the underlying technology, and have more advanced digital and computational competences. In this respect, professional legal councils should set certain standards and educate their members.
5) Provision should be made for the possibilities, rules and requirements (standards) for the provision of legal services by lawyers. Legal teams consisting of people and AI could be a dynamic and very effective structure where humans have an important role to play thanks to their unique features and abilities: intellective judgment, empathy, creativity and adaptability.

6) In the context of compliance with the principles of professional ethics and professional responsibility, issues such as the need to use the so-called Explainable AI, carrying out audits of algorithms and the lawyer's responsibility for autonomous AI decisions. Perhaps the right solution to these problems would be to introduce a system of conformity assessment (digital certification) for lawyers.

Doug Surtees, Craig Zawada:

Lawyers have a professional and ethical duty to be technologically competent in areas they practice in. This creates an obligation on law schools and regulators to provide appropriate education and training. Such education and training can best be achieved by law schools and regulators working together to develop benchmarks and teach appropriate technological competence. We recommend that the UN facilitate law schools and regulators working together to explicitly state technological competence standards for lawyers, to share those standards, and to develop a rubric of international standards of lawyer technological competence.

Wilfried Bernhardt:

Artificial intelligence can provide improved and faster judicial legal protection by helping judges analyze incoming documents for specific facts and legal aspects to assign cases to the appropriate judges, attach documents to the correct files, filter out the factual issues and legal problems relevant to the decision within a dispute, help judges prepare their decisions. In a globalized world, artificial intelligence can help provide cross-border judicial protection and overcome language barriers through automatic translation tools. Artificial intelligence can help detect global cybercrimes - such as child pornography - and thus protect people. Artificial intelligence can help citizens seeking justice to be quickly informed about legal options (such as via chatbots) and also to explore the prospects for legal protection. Artificial intelligence can also empower people who do not have sufficient financial means to hire a lawyer to research the legal situation themselves.

However, artificial intelligence also poses risks, algorithms can infringe fundamental human rights and legal principles as human dignity, the principle of privacy and data confidentiality, the principle of non-discrimination, the principle of the natural and independent judge, the right to the legal judge, the right to an effective remedy, the fair trial, t the transparency principle, the principle of the right to be heard. It must be ensured that social and cultural stereotypes and gender discrimination are not replicated in AI programming and that the risks are transparent to the judges. Risks can also arise if the benefits of AI are only available to certain people in the judicial process and not to all participants of legal proceedings.

Therefore, the UN - as currently the European Union - should examine the Universal Declaration of Human Rights and the International Covenant on Civil and Political Rights for their content for the use in AI in the field of justice. The UN should work on globally valid standards and elaborate recommendations for possible additional norms which help to AI unfolding its rights-promoting effect, but at the same time help the risks remaining manageable and excluding unacceptable risks by prohibitions of certain forms of AI or the prohibition of the use of AI in certain justice scenarios. And the UN should define the cases in which a human judge may not be replaced by artificial intelligence.

Mariusz Załucki:

The future of the judiciary requires the use of new technologies. The UN should pilot solutions based on artificial intelligence and the Internet to be used in the judiciary of the future. Such solutions will solve the basic maladies of the justice system, including the problem of the length of proceedings. In this context, the legal acts concerning the functioning of the judiciary may need to be revised, in particular in relation to the existing standards for so-called fair trials.

Section Three

Charlie Northrup:

The digital world is transforming from the Web's client-server model, which ultimately centralized power and influence into a select group of corporations, to a new digital world of hyperconnected people, places and things. This new digital world will exists in digital form as a Multidimensional Graph of Things operating in accordance with the international laws set forth by the United Nations. Within the graph are a set of coordinates (nodes) representing the independently operating, yet hyperconnected, graphs of the host governments and then the individual citizens.

Each participant is represented in the digital world by a digital agent. In consideration of this transformation, we offer several recommendations. The first recommendation is for the United Nations to advocate that every individual, household, and organization has the right to be represented as a member of the digital world. Membership should provide for digital privacy rights. The second recommendation is to ensure every participant - citizen and/or legal guardian - has the sole right to manage their own graph within the rules and laws of their host government. The third recommendation is the formation of a United Nations digital agent consortium to standardize the exchange of value within and across the digital ecosystems. This will ensure every member country and its participants can be represented and participate equally in the hyperconnected world.

Alexandra R. Harrington, Magdalena Stryja:

The issues raised in this chapter are complex and demonstrate how the eco smart city has the ability to further the Sustainable Development Goals (SDGs) at the same time that it advances the goals of the UN Internet Governance Forum and the needs of individual States and municipalities. Based on the chapter's analysis and conclusions, several critical policy recommendations can be made to the UN IGF framework as well as the international and national systems more broadly.

1) Adopt and encourage the implementation of guidelines and oversight mechanisms to ensure that technology and associated infrastructures needed to support it are available and accessible to all. This is particularly important in crafting the eco smart city and enabling the creation of eco smart cities even when there are significant wealth disparities.
2) Overall, encourage national, regional and international Covid-19 pandemic recovery efforts that include steps toward achieving the eco smart city as essential elements and which encourage microfinance that can be critical in generating sustainable incomes.
3) Create and encourage mechanisms for technology transfer between developed and developing States as well as more advanced regions and municipalities within the same State to facilitate digital infrastructure. At the same time, ensure the promotion of digital infrastructure that is sustainable.
4) Encourage the entrenchment of the rule of law across all legal and regulatory systems, especially those relating to internet and digital infrastructure and governance. This will be of particular importance in

the post-pandemic world, where recovery is increasingly linked with access to information and technology.

5) Incorporate the lessons from the Covid-19 pandemic to design effective public health systems, provision of essential services during times of prolonged emergency, and design effective public information laws and rules to combat misinformation. These are essential in all contexts but particularly so in the urban contexts, where evidence has shown that access to essential services has been difficult, especially in lower and middle-income areas, and where public health infrastructure is not designed for mass illness response.
6) Encourage the mainstreaming of the eco smart city throughout IGF planning and policies, and encourage other UN-affiliated organizations and treaty bodies, particularly the United Nations Framework Convention on Climate Change, to do the same.
7) Increase focus on ways in which technology and internet innovation can be used to address zoonotic disease tracking and knowledge, especially in urban areas, where expansion and construction have often resulted in increased human and animal contact.
8) Encourage the discussion of mental health concerns in post-pandemic recovery planning, including through telemedicine and other forms of technological infrastructures which have been identified as serving critical roles in mental health treatment during the pandemic.
9) Facilitate discussion of educational access issues where online education has been used in the short-term, and where the potential for long-term use continues, in order to understand and address the infrastructural, technological and access disparities for students and their families.
10) Encourage the inclusion of sustainable energy sources and implementation in building and expansion – as seen in successful examples from eco smart cities – across a spectrum of developed and developing States and municipalities.
11) Promote the use of internet and other technological infrastructures and capacities to create opportunities for decent work that is sustainable and advances economic growth as well as the implementation of human rights, economic and environmental treaty obligations under international law.
12) Facilitate the development of partnerships between industries, actors and governments to ensure that the eco smart city concept continues to grow in a sustainable manner.
13) Ensure that debates and decisions taken by the IGF and Member States emphasize the need for flexibility and adaptability within the laws and

rules created for internet and technological governance in order to facilitate growth and up-to-date regulatory systems.

Wojciech Filipkowski, Rafał Rejmaniak:

The Internet plays a significant role in the implementation of the smart city concept, as it allows various intelligent subsystems (modules) to be combined into a synchronized system.
1. In terms of the proper functioning of such connected smart city components, the authors point to the need to develop minimum requirements for initial training and periodic verification of the competences of smart system operators, preventing the degradation of
their skills and ensuring real human control over such a system.
2. In addition, the authors recommend to conduct interdisciplinary research involving experts from various fields (i.e. IT, ethics, law) in the development of commonly accepted principles of liability for potential damage that may be caused as a result of the functioning of
fully autonomous intelligent systems.
3. Until then, efforts should be made to ensure real human supervision over fully autonomous systems. Implementation of fully autonomous solutions, in an ill-considered manner, may lead to unpredictable damage to legally protected goods, and it may be
impossible to identify and hold the perpetrator criminally responsible.
4. The UN should make efforts to harmonise legal standards in the above areas on a global scale in order to avoid regulatory asymmetries between countries or regions. The latter aspect may be exploited by persons or entities wishing to misuse technological solutions for their own purposes.

Section Four

Maddalena Castellani, Cesare Triberti, Roberto Giacobazzi:

While science and technology is progressing towards the new frontiers of privacy and encryption, still lots of issues are present in nowadays implementations of cloud services. In order to concretely rise the level of confidence in the use of these technologies, lawmakers and scientists have to work closely together to design best practices and rules making cloud services trustable. More work is required in the area of cloud technologies to make it acceptable by a wider set of cloud service consumers.

In particular this includes risk mitigation strategies, more strict policies for data storage and data transfer, inclusion of digital signatures in data and software artefacts, in such a way data and software can be traced, Proofs of Retrievability for data integrity, and last but not least, third party monitoring and assessment of quality of cloud services.

Matej Myška, Pavel Koukal, Zuzana Vlachová, Ondřej Woznica:

With regard to the principle of predictability of law and legal certainty, we recommend that the United Nations push for the negotiation of an international treaty that would harmonize the basic issues of limiting the liability of information society service providers.

Niewiadomska-Szynkiewicz, Amanowicz, Wrońska, Kostkiewicz:

The Internet community growing and decreasing the age of people connecting to the global web raises enormous social risks, thus ensuring cybersecurity maintains a huge challenge for international organisations, governments, social communities and education systems.

To function effectively in an intelligent networked society and seize digital transformation opportunities, the community needs new and constantly updated digital competencies. Activities that improve digital competence and prevent cyberspace threats should be interdisciplinary and addressed to many groups of recipients with different needs, abilities, and ages. Universal information and media education is a socially signalled need and has its legislative and economic justification. Education, as well as preventive and protective activities, bring more practical benefits. They are more effective and less costly than reducing or eliminating negative individual interactions, social neglect or the effects of crime.

The critical tasks include raising public awareness of online threats, adopting legislation to the changing reality, international cooperation of government representatives and commercial companies, and investment in research and exchange of knowledge and experience.

Effective detection of network attacks requires collecting and processing as much data containing malware samples and vulnerabilities as possible. It is necessary to develop advanced algorithms and build efficient computer systems to support this process.

Particular emphasis such be put on development, and successful implementation of deep learning techniques combined with big data processing and new computing paradigms (cloud, fog, edge, dust computing), enabling to correlate a broad range of security contexts and knowledge mining to create cyber threats intelligence in anticipation of cyberattacks.

Accepting the truth of information ruling the world as an empty truism allows us to lull one's vigilance to the most significant threat of modern times: the deprivation of truth over falsehood and the denial of the facts from reality. The losses that affect us are visible at every activity level, from value-creating through social activity to the advantage of technological development. It seems necessary to rebuild the influence of authority and factual-informational coherence. It is essential to recreate, or perhaps create, on a scale previously unknown, value chains in the flow of information. The problem we face is multilayered and multifaceted, and responding to a threat on a global range without international cooperation, is an optimization task beyond the scope of possible solutions. It is necessary for us to put factual information on the pedestal, laboriously knocking down misinformation and distorted information and technologically deficient ("indebted") information systems.

Let's consistently build high-quality supply chains to process the 'gold of modernity' - information - safely and reliably. Let's expand trust structures, introducing each layer control and assurance mechanisms such as the four-eyes principle, trusted third party services, peer-review, Fact-Checking Networks, conformity assessment and attestation.

* * *

The areas of future UN activity, as can be seen, could be many. Undoubtedly, the future of the UN is technological, but only the decision-makers of the UN will be able to decide what technology it will be and how far it will meet societal needs. We invite you to join the discussion, we are aware that the development of technology and law is inevitable.

Dariusz Szostek, Mariusz Załucki

About the Authors

Dariusz Szostek – he is a partner and founder of the Law Firm Szostek-Bar and Partners, of counsel in Maruta/Wachta, expert of the European Parliament Artificial Intelligence Observatory; Member of the European Law Institute in Vienna, member of the Programme Council of the IGF UN 2021, member of the Blockhaton EUiPO Brussels, chairman of the Scientific Council of the Virtual Chair of Ethics and Law (a consortium of Polish universities and NASK), professor at the Faculty of Law and Administration at the University of Silesia, lecturer, author of several dozen publications (including monographs and foreign publications, including bestsellers, e.g. Cyber Law - New York, Tokyo, Sydney, Amsterdam, London edition), author of several books. co-author of IT and data security in a law firm (also editor), author of a monograph "Blockchain a prawo" 2018 (Warsaw) - English edition "Blockchain and Law" (Nomos, Germany 2019), co-author of monograph Smart contarct and Insurance (London, in print).

Mariusz Załucki – full professor of law, head of the Institute of Private Law at the AFM Kraków University (Poland) A graduate of legal studies in Poland, he also learned about European economic and civil law at the University of Bielefeld in Germany and the University of Staffordshire in Stoke-on-Trent, England. He has worked as visiting professor at several foreign universities, e.g. University of Bristol (England), University of New South Wales in Sydney (Australia), Keele University (England), Staffordshire University (England), University of Las Palmas de Gran Canaria (Spain), University of Reggio Calabria Italy). He is the author of over 150 publications, scientific specialities: civil law, intellectual property law, private international law, protection and promotion of human rights. Since 2001, he is a member of the Bar Association in Rzeszów, he practises as an advocate. In 2021, he was recommended by the National Council of the Judiciary in Poland to become a judge in the Supreme Court of Poland.

Ricardo Pinha Alonso – Doctor in State Law (PUC-SP). Master in Law (UNIMAR-SP). Professor (UNIMAR-SP; UENP-PR and UNIFIO-SP). Public Lawyer in São Paulo-SP.

Marek Amanowicz – a graduate of the Military University of Technology. At the University, he held several positions, including dean of the faculty, vice-rector for R&D. He was vice-chairman of the Polish National Committee of the International Union of Radio Science. He served as the primary national representative in the Information Systems Technology Panel of the NATO Scientific and Technology Organization. He worked at TAC ONE, an international company in Paris, as the systems V&V manager. In 2017 he joined NASK - National Research Institute taking the position of professor. He is an elected member of the Committee on Electronics and Telecommunications of the Polish Academy of Sciences. He has led many national and international research projects in systems engineering, mobile communications, and modelling and simulation. He is the author or co-author of more than 200 papers presented in scientific journals or national and international scientific conferences. His current research interests focus on communication systems engineering and information security of complex technical systems.

Alexandre Cavalcanti Andrade de Araujo – Post-Doctorate from the University of Santiago de Compostela/Spain (USC, 2021). PhD from the Universidad del Museo Social Argentino (UMSA, 2015). Specialist in Constitutional Law from the Superior School of Law (ESA, 2007). Specialist in Criminal Law at the Superior School Foundation of the Public Ministry (FESMIP, 2008). Graduated in Law from Centro Universitário de João Pessoa (2003). Deputy General Controller of the Municipality of Cabedelo-PB. Member of the Academia Paraibana de Letras Jurídicas (APLJ, 2016). Professor at the João Pessoa-UNIPE University Center and Professor at FTM - Faculdade Três Marias, Guest Professor at the Federal University of Paraíba.

Gabriela Bar – Attorney at Law, doctor of law, managing partner at *Szostek_Bar and Partners*. Enthusiast of new technologies, with particular emphasis on Artificial Intelligence. Experienced expert in the field of electronic contracts, e-commerce, legal aspects of IT systems implementation and privacy protection. Member of the IEEE Legal Committee in the IEEE Global Initiative on Ethics of Autonomous and Intelligent Systems project; member of the New Technologies Law Association, Women in AI and AI4EU. Assistant profesor at the Opole University (SHOP4CF) and Silesia University (MAS4AI).

Zofia Bednarz – a post-doctoral Research Associate with the Centre for Law, Markets and Regulation, University of New South Wales, Sydney, Australia. She is a qualified lawyer in Spain and holds a graduate degree in law from the University of Warsaw, Poland and a postgraduate degree in commercial law from the University of Málaga, Spain. Her research focuses on commercial law and technology, company law and consumer contracts. She has published both in English and Spanish on information duties in electronic consumer contracts, consumers' right of withdrawal and unfair commercial practices, as well as blockchain technology and company law. She specialises in comparative and European Union Law. Currently, she is researching issues related to the use of Artificial Intelligence- and Big Data-powered analytics and provision of financial services to consumers. Prior to joining the Centre for Law, Markets and Regulation, she was a lecturer in commercial law at the Law Faculty of University of Málaga, where she taught commercial contracts, insolvency and company law in Spanish and in English at undergraduate and postgraduate levels.

Renato Bernardi - Postdoctoral internship at CESEG (Centro de Estudios de Seguridad) of the Universidad de Santiago de Compostela, Spain. Doctor in State Law (Tax Law sub-area) - PUC-SP. Master Degree in Constitutional Law - ITE-Bauru. Effective Professor of the Bachelor's, Master's and Doctorate programs, Member of the Executive Committee of the Undergraduate Course College and Member of the Coordination Committee of the Master's and Doctoral Program in Legal Science, all from the CCSA Law Course - UENP, Jacarezinho´s campus . Pedagogical Coordinator of PROJURIS Estudos Jurídicos Ltda. São Paulo´s State Attorney since 1994.

Wilfried Bernhardt – born in Lübeck (Germany), is a lawyer in Berlin, honorary professor for IT Law at the faculty of law of the University of Leipzig. He studied law in Augsburg and Kempten (Germany). CEO of the Bernhardt IT Management Consulting GmbH, Member of the board of the National eGovernment Competence Center and on the board of the German EDV-Gerichtstag. He is the author of numerous publications, in particular on issues relating to the use of information technology in administration and the judiciary.

Renata Soares Bonavides – Doctorate in Social Relations Law from the Pontifical Catholic University of São Paulo (2008). Currently Director of the Faculty of Law at Catholic University of Santos.

Silvia A. Carretta – an Italian qualified lawyer, founder of the IP and Tech Lab law firm, specialized in intellectual property rights and information technology law. She holds a quinquennial law degree, with a master of laws specialization in private international law and arbitration, from Università Cattolica of Milano, as well as a masters of laws in European intellectual property law from Stockholm University. Now also a doctoral researcher in AI & law at Uppsala University, Silvia is part of the postgraduate school at the Wallenberg foundation's AI, Autonomous Systems and

Software Program on Humanities and Society (WASP-HS). Her research project involves the study of artificial intelligence under the lens of private law and the impact of upcoming technology shifts on society. She regularly lectures in advanced courses both at universities and professional events, and she advises on topics such as IP rights, legal issues around blockchain and AI applications, data protection and legal design projects. Silvia is actively involved in various NGO and EU related projects. She is a member of the Global legal team at Women in AI, and the co-founder of the Foreign Lawyers Network-Sweden, a non-profit that unites the community of foreign professionals living in Sweden with the aim to broaden diversity and inclusion in the legal profession.

Maddalena Castellani – certified lawyer since 2007, specialized in Copyright ad IPR Law (copyright, trademarks, design, know how, patents, software) and in International Corporate and Commercial Law. She is partner of the Law Firm Triberti Castellani, established both in Milan and Verona. Since 2019 Member of the Anti-Counterfeiting Blockathon Forum set up by the European Commission and EUIPO. Professor of Law.

Zanda Davida – mg.iur.; senior lawyer of the Consumer Rights Protection Centre of Latvia; lecturer of University Turiba (Riga, Latvia); Ph.D. researcher and research assistant of the University of Latvia Faculty of Law. Her scientific results are published in scientific articles in peer-reviewed journals and conference proceedings including a publication indexed in Web of Science testifying that she is recognised expert in Latvia in the field of consumer protection law and data protection law. Furthermore, she has participated as an expert in court proceedings before the Constitutional Court of the Republic of Latvia including cases involving consumer protection law (such as the case on limitation of daily per cents in consumer credit contracts). Likewise, she has successful experience for participation as a national expert in working groups of the European Commission such as On accommodation platforms (including in the sharing economy); Car rental – Enterprise, Europcar, Hertz, Sixt, Avis; European Unfair Terms Strategy III and Citizen Energy Forum. She is qualified expert in the market surveillance at the consumer protection sector in the Latvia and European Union testifying that she have practical experience of application of the consumer protection and data protection law at the widespread infringement cases (such as Viagogo tickets selling practice case, Volkswagen Dieselgate case, Ryanair misleading practice).

Wojciech Filipkowski – Associate Professor, head of the Forensic Science Laboratory at the Department of Criminal Law and Criminology, Faculty of Law, University of Białystok (Poland). Author of over 150 publications on criminology, criminalistics, and criminal law. His scientific interests concentrate around issues of criminal intelligence analysis, predictive policing, and artificial intelligence. ORCID: 0000-0001-6248-0888.

Hongyu Fu – an associate professor at Beijing Foreign Studies University Law School.

Gabriela Soldano Garcez – Permanent Professor of the Post-Graduate Program Stricto Sensu (Doctorate and Master) in International Law at Catholic University of Santos. Post-Doctorate from the Santiago de Compostela University (Spain).

Roberto Giacobazzi – received the PhD in Computer Science in 1993 from the University of Pisa. From 1993 to 1995, he had a Post Doctoral Research position at Laboratoire d'Informatique (LIX), Ecole Polytechnique (Paris). From 1995 to 1998, he was Assistant Professor in Computer Science at the University of Pisa, and from 2000 until now, he is Full Professor in Computer Science at the University of Verona. During these two decades, he has been Provost for Education from 2001 to 2004, Provost for Research from 2004 to 2006, Dean of the College of Science & Technology of the University of Verona from 2006 to 2012, and Head of Department from 2019 to 2021. In 2012 he has been chair of the National Scientific Qualification Committee for Professorship in Computer Science in Italy. From 2016 he is also a senior scientist at the IMDEA Software Institute in Madrid (Spain) with a Cátedra de Excelencia of the Comunidad de Madrid awarded in 2017. The research interests of Roberto Giacobazzi include abstract interpretation, static program analysis, semantics of programming languages, program verification, abstract model-checking, program transformation and optimization, digital asset protection, code obfuscation, software watermarking and lattice theory. He was co-founder of JULIA s.r.l., a start-up company of the U. of Verona, now part of GrammaTech Inc., USA. And Cythereal.com USA. General Chair of ACM POPL2013 and of major conferences in program analysis and program verification, he received the Microsoft Research Software Engineering Innovation Foundation (SEIF) Award in 2013 and the Facebook Probability and Programming Research Award in 2020.

Jacek Gołaczyński – Professor with a postdoctoral degree in law, head of the Centre for Research in the Legal and Economic Problems of Electronic Communication at the Faculty of Law, Administration and Economics of Wrocław University, specialist and author of numerous publications on civil law and civil procedure, member of the Civil Law Codification

Committee of previous terms of office, judge at the Court of Appeal in Wrocław.

Alexandra R. Harrington – the founder and Executive Director of the Center for Global Governance and Emerging Law, Research Director of the Centre for International Sustainable Development Law, and Vice-Chair of the Board of Women in Ethics and Compliance Global. She has served as Fulbright Canada Special Foundation Fellow at the Balsillie School of International Affairs in Waterloo, Canada and was the 2018 – 2019 the Fulbright Canada Research Chair in Global Governance, based at the Balsillie School of International Affairs. She holds a doctoral degree in law from McGill University Faculty of Law. Prof. Harrington is the author of the book International Organizations and the Law (2018) and International Law and Global Governance: Treaty Regimes and Sustainable Development Goals Interpretation (2021). She serves as the Director of Studies for the International Law Association Colombian branch, a member of the International Law Association Committee on the Role of International Law in Sustainable Natural Resource Management for Development, a member of the Climate Law and Governance Initiative's Scientific Committee, and a member of the Green Economics Institute's Research Group. She also guest lectures globally on topics related to international law, environmental law, global governance and sustainable development, and is an international advisor to various faculties. Prof. Harrington has served as a consultant for entities such as the United Nations Framework Convention on Climate Change, Commission for Environmental Cooperation of the North American Agreement on Environmental Cooperation, UNEP and IDLO. Dr. Harrington's publications address a variety of fields relating to international law, including international organizations, governance issues, environmental law, legal issues relating to climate change, international child's rights, natural resources regulation, international human rights law, international trade law, corporate social responsibility, and criminal law.

Chong Liu I – a Juris Master candidate in the law school.

Shobana Iyer – a practicing commercial and corporate barrister and arbitrator (FCIArb) based in London. She has a full spectrum of expertise in the commercial and corporate law: corporate, finance, media and advertising, insurance, IP & IT aside from general contractual and regulatory issues. Shobana has extensive experience of working on challenging and technically complex cases, usually involving an international element and regularly deals with conflict of laws cases. She is well versed in both public and private international law. Shobana is commonly instructed as counsel on a wide range of commercial litigation and arbitration proceedings (both domestic & international) conducted under various institutional rules (including LCIA, ICC, SIAC, SCC, WIPO, CAS, AAA and UNCITRAL) and ad-hoc arrangements. She also sits as arbitrator in ad-hoc and institutional arbitrations. She is presently an elected Committee Member of the CIArb London Branch. In addition to dispute resolution, Shobana assist various corporates/institutions with specific compliance and regulatory issues, contract management (negotiating/drafting/reviewing contacts), M&A due diligence, data protection compliance, and with regard to climate change transition, disclosure, reporting and investment. She has experience in a variety of industry sectors including renewable energy, financial, retail, sports, creative and the 'technology, media and telecommunications' (TMT) sectors. She commonly teams up with international lawyers, law firms, in-house counsel and their teams to add high-impact, high-value additional capacity to their existing teams. Shobana is actively involved in several committees and boards on the implementation and use of emerging technologies including: (1) A Stakeholder Board Member of the SHEPA EU Project: an EU funded project which analyses how artificial intelligence and big data analytics impact ethics and human rights; (2) As Vice-Cochair of the Legal Services Committee and IT Panel Member for the Bar Council of England & Wales; (3) Society of Computer and Law Advisory Group Member; (3) Advisory Member of CyberArb raising awareness and practical guidance in mitigating cyber risks for the international arbitration community; (4) Member of 'Women in AI' Legal Team.

Monika Jagielska – Professor at the Institute of Legal Sciences, Faculty of Law, University of Silesia in Katowice. A former member of the working groups of the Codification Commission on Civil Law at the Polish Ministry of Justice. The author of several books and numerous articles on EU private law, sales law, consumer protection, product liability and private international law. Expert and reviewer in numerous EU and international projects. Chairwoman of the Ethics Committee and the Coordinator for Social Sciences in Doctoral School at the University of Silesia.

Paweł Kostkiewicz – head of the Standardisation and Certification Centre at NASK, manager of the Certification Unit, biocybernetics engineer. He is an IT practitioner - creator and manager of specialised IT teams, project manager and system architect - e.g. in projects related to creating governmental registers, monitoring the legislative process, and construction of ICT infrastructure. At NASK, he develops certification services for products and people in cybersecurity, acts as a member of national and international working groups related to cybersecurity certification, KT172 of the Polish Committee for Standardization, the presidium of the Sectoral Competence Council for Telecommunications and Cyber Security.

Pavel Koukal – an Associate professor within the Department of Civil law and also Institute of Law and Technology at the Faculty of Law of Masaryk University. He is focusing on the convergence of legal protection of design, copyright and trademarks as well as on the protection of intangible assets in terms of civil law's fundamental principles. In his habilitation thesis (2019), Pavel studied the public domain's topic, including its constitutional and human rights foundations formulated in Czech law.

Dominik Lubasz – doctor iuris, attorney-at-law, managing partner of Lubasz and Partners Law Firm. He specializes in new technology law, e-commerce, intellectual property, data protection and business law, including European business law. He is an author of numerous publications on personal data protection and e-commerce, including commentaries to the General Data Protection Regulation, Consumer Rights Act, Act on Provision of Electronic Services, Act on Protection of Certain Services Provided Electronically Based on or Consisting of Conditional Access, Act on Database Protection and Act on Personal Data Protection. Dr Dominik Lubasz has been awarded in the category "Data Protection" in Chambers and Partners rankings (2018-2021) and "TheLegal500" in 2020 and 2021 and as a Thought Leader in Data Privacy and Protection 2021 by Whoswholegal2021. His current activity is focused on issues related to AI and legal-tech - e.g. The Law of Artificial Intelligence, in which two chapters were developed by Dr. Lubasz and Prof. Namysłowska, who are also carrying out a project entitled "Consumer Protection and Artificial Intelligence. Between Law and Ethics", which is funded by the National Science Centre. Dr. Lubasz is a member of the Scientific Council of the Centre for Data Protection at the University of Łódź, SABI - Association of DPOs, Compliance Institute, and a member of the review committee of the Modern Technologies Law Association, as well as an expert of the Chamber of eCommerce and the Polish Ministry of Digital Affairs for the implementation of the GDPR in Poland.

Kayleen Manwaring – is a Senior Lecturer at the University of New South Wales, Sydney, Australia, in the Faculty of Law and Justice. She leads the research stream Challenges of a Cyber-Physical World as part of the Allens Hub for Technology, Law and Innovation, and is also a member of the UNSW Centre for Law, Markets and Regulation, Institute for Cyber Security, and Digital Grid Futures Institute. Her research concentrates on the intersection of sociotechnical change and private and commercial law. She has previously published work on the Internet of Things, ubiquitous/pervasive computing, cyber security, ambient intelligence, consumer protection, online contracting, directors' duties, network neutrality, copyright and digital technologies, privacy, spam and communications law. Her work has been cited by the Organisation for Economic Development, the World Economic Forum, the Australian Human Rights Commission, the NSW Law Reform Commission, the Australian Council of Learned Academies, the United States Department of Commerce National Telecommunications and Information Administration, the Austrian (EU) Ministry for Transport, Innovation and Technology, the Consumer Policy Research Centre and the Australian Communications Consumer Action Network (ACCAN). Prior to becoming an academic, she spent many years working as a technology-focussed commercial lawyer, as in-house counsel and in law firm knowledge management for several leading international law firms and a leading Australian financial services firm.

Rodrigo E. Galán Martínez – PhD by the Universidad Veracruzana. Senior Law Clerk at the Mexico City Electoral Court. rodrigo.galanmtz1@gmail.com.

Matěj Myška – a senior assistant professor at the Institute of Law and Technology, Faculty of Law, Masaryk University. Dr. Myška's professional focus is in ICT law and intellectual property, particularly digital copyright. Dr. Myška's is the editor-in-chief of the first Czech law journal specialized in ICT law, the Review of Law and Technology (Revue pro právo a technologie). He also assists the Technology Transfer Office of the Masaryk University as a lawyer. His habilitation thesis (2020) focused on exceptions and limitations in the digital networked environment.

Monika Namysłowska – is Professor of Law and Head of the Department of European Economic Law at the University of Lodz, Poland. Her main areas of research cover European, Polish and German Private Law, particularly IT law and consumer law. Visiting professor in Germany (Humboldt-University, Berlin; Georg-August-University, Göttingen; University of Regensburg; University of Münster), Italy (University of Naples Federico II), Spain (Universidad Publica de Navarra in Pamplona) and Hungary (University of Szeged). Principal investigator in the project "Consumer Protection and Artificial Intelligence. Between Law and Ethics" funded by the National Science Centre in Poland (DEC/2018/31/B/HS5/01169). Local coordinator of TechLawClinics – an international project [University of Nijmegen (NL), University of Lodz (PL), University of Krakow (PL),

University of Eastern Piedmont (IT)] on legal challenges and implications of digital technologies, supported by Erasmus+. Member of the Advisory Board of the President of the Office of Competition and Consumer Protection (UOKiK) in Poland (2014–2016). Expert in the Consumer Policy Advisory Group established by the European Commission.

Ewa Niewiadomska-Szynkiewicz – a deputy director - director for research at NASK - National Research Institute and head of the Center for Research and Technology Transfer. She took a Ph.D degree and D.Sc. degree in automatic control and robotics both from Warsaw University of Technology (WUT). In 2017 she received professor's nomination. Since 1988 with the Faculty of Electronics and Information Technology (WUT), currently a full professor and head of the Complex Systems Group. An elected member of the Committee on Automatic Control and Robotics of the Polish Academy of Sciences. She coordinated a number of the groups' activities participated in about 40 national and international research projects including EU projects and works carried out under the cooperation of research groups and commercial companies. She is involved in research on ICT systems, cybersecurity, modelling, simulation, control and optimization of complex systems, decision support systems and high performance computing. She is the author and co-author of books and about 200 journal and conference papers. Awarded many times for scientific works.

Charlie Northrup - serial inventor, author, and entrepreneur leading NeurSciences in an effort to hyperconnect the physical, bioloogical, and digital spheres of the world based on a reference implementation of his Universal Frameworkof Things. In Northrup's view every individual, household. And organization should be represented in the hyperconnected world and have a sense of agency - something the Web was never designed to enable.

Heloísa Helena Silva Pancotti - Social Security teacher, author, lawyer, master degree in UNIVEM, PhD student in UENP- Universidade Estadual do Norte do Paraná- Brazil. ID Lattes: 1948241510029657.

Przemysław Paul Polański – lawyer and programmer, for many years acting as an IT department director. associate professor at the Kozminski University in Warsaw (*Akademia Leona Koźmińskiego*) at the Department of Quantitative Methods & Information Technology. Legal counsel at OIRP in Warsaw. Author of more than 70 publications on IT Law, including two monographs. Director of two research grants from the National Science Centre.

Rafał Rejmaniak – Assistant Professor in the Department of Historical and Legal Sciences, Theory and Philosophy of Law, and Comparative Law, Faculty of Law, University of Białystok (Poland). ORCID: 0000-0003-1908-5844.

Mauro Artura Rivera – Professor of Law at the Universidad Iberoamericana (Mexico City) since 2016. He obtained his PhD at the Universidad Complutense de Madrid (Spain). He holds a Master in Parliamentary Law, Elections, and Legal Studies at the Universidad Complutense de Madrid. He obtained his Bachelor's degree in Law at the Universidad de Sonora (Hermosilllo). Mauro Arturo Rivera is a member of the Mexican National System of Researchers (SNI level I).

Ewa Rott-Pietrzyk – Doctor of Law, research associate at the Chair of Civil and Private International Law at the Faculty of Law and Administration of the University of Silesia in Katowice, legal adviser, arbitrator. She also participates in the work of the Civil Law Codification Commission on the preparation of a new Civil Law Code and is a member of the Acquis Group (European Group on Existing EC Private Law). She is the author of several dozen works on civil law and private international law.

Beata Stepien-Załucka – Professor at the University of Rzeszów (Poland), a specialist in constitutional law, human rights and issues related to the organisation of the judiciary. Author of several dozen scientific publications in this area. She completed scientific internships in Spain and Italy. Member of several international scientific societies (including IBEROJUR - Instituto Iberoamericano de Estudos Jurídicos), advocate, member of the local bar association in Rzeszów (Poland).

Magdalena Stryja – University of Silesia in Katowice Faculty of Law and Administration, District Bar Association in Katowice, Polish Bar Council. Legal Fellow Centre for International Sustainable and Development Law. Chair of the Science and Development Committee with the District Bar Association in Katowice. She acts as the Spokesperson for the Faculty of Law and Administration. University of Silesia in Katowice. She is a member of the interdisciplinary Polish Research Team Just Transition. She is a member of the University of Silesia-based bioethics research team dealing with legal and bioethical aspects of medicine and animal protection as well as environmental and climate protection. She is a member of a member of University of Silesia – based Labor law research team. She is a member of a research team within the project financed by the European Commission entitled "TRAIL - train in your language: multilingual transnational training in EU civil and commercial law". She was the manager of the research project on Social Dialogue as a constitutional principle of labour law at the University of Silesia. She has served as a member of the international research project Implementation and Enforcement of EU labour law in Visegrad Countries. Magdalena Stryja delivers lectures on labour law and social policy, teaches copyright law with a focus on employee-generated content and works, and also deals with legal aspects of climate change, including the social aspects of retraining employees. She regularly organises and participates in numerous national and international congresses, conferences in the scope of medical law, labour law and climate protection as well as legal aspects of new technology. She is also the initiator of numerous charity events. Over the past 10 years, she has organised 15 initiatives, events, and actions, all the proceeds from which went to charity. Additionally, She pursues broadscale artistic activity as an organiser or co-organiser of exhibitions, vernissages, concerts at the University of Silesia and in the Silesia region.

Doug Surtees – the Associate Dean Academic and an Associate Professor of Law at the College of Law, University of Saskatchewan in Canada. He has taught primarily in the areas of Wills, Contracts, Elder Law and Law and Disability. Doug has served as a board member for, and president of many community organizations including Easter Seals Canada, SaskAbilities, the Public Legal Education Association of Saskatchewan (PLEA), the Public Legal Education Association of Canada (PLEAC), his local Home and School Association and his local Community Organization.

Marek Świerczyński – advocate, consultant of the Council of Europe in the field of electronic evidence and digitization of judiciary. Chairman of the team for the law applicable to artificial intelligence at the Virtual Department of Law and Ethics (consortium of Polish universities). Of counsel at Kieszkowska Rutkowska Kolasiński Law Firm and associate professor at the Institute of Legal Sciences of the UKSW. Graduate of the Faculty of Law and Administration at the Jagiellonian University. He teaches new technologies law at INP PAN, the Jagiellonian University, University of Warsaw, University of Economics in Krakow and Kozminski University. He is a permanent arbitrator at the Arbitration Court for Internet Domains and a mediator at the UPRP/WIPO. Professor of Law at the Cardinal Stefan Wyszyński University of Warsaw.

Felipe Garcia Telò – Master of Laws (UNIMAR-SP). Lawyer in São Paulo-SP.

Cesare Triberti – lawyer in Milan, consultant of major companies in the field of information technology and telecommunications, expert in health law and law and bioethics, has collaborated since 1985 with the Chair of General Theory of Law at the University of Milan (Philosophy of Law course), since 1989 with the Chair of Theory and Applications of Computing Machines of the Department of Information Science, University of Milan, and since 1998 with the Chair of General Informatics at the Catholic University of Milan. He is visiting professor of Computer Law and Law and Bioethics at the "Faculdade de Direito de Itu in S. Paolo" (Brazil), and professor at the "Politecnico di Milano" (PhD Information Engineering) with the course of Computer Law, civil and criminal areas, protection of security and privacy, bioethics, genetic engineering and nanotechnology. Lecturer at the University of Curitiba (Brazil), for courses and masters in Neuroscience and Law (Stalking, bullying and violence against women).He is a member of the scientific committee of the Italian Association of EDP Auditors. He is a Councillor of AISPO and a member of the Ethics Committee of the San Raffaele Hospital in Milan, and a lecturer in the course of CME - Clinical Trials at the University Vita Salute / San Raffaele Hospital.

Zuzana Vlachová – currently pursues her doctoral studies in civil law at the Masaryk University in Brno. She focuses mainly on the field of intellectualproperty law. In her Master thesis, she dealt with legal succession in intellectual property law and related applicable law aspects. Within her doctoral studies, she analyses the relationship between intellectual property law and private international law, in particular, she focuses on the liability for damage in copyright law.

Aneta Wiewiórowska-Domagalska – a senior researcher at Osnabrück University, holds PhD from Utrecht University. Former researcher of the Study Group on a European Civil Code (co-author of Principles of European Law on Sales), she worked in Poland for the Ministry of Justice and the Civil Law Codification Commission. As a private and consumer law expert she was one of the persons responsible for transposition EU consumer law in Poland. Reporter of the ELI's Model Rules on Online Intermediary Platforms project; currently member of the ELI's Executive Committee.

Ondřej Woznica pursues his doctoral studies in intellectual property law at the Masaryk University in Brno. Ondřej studied abroad, particularly at the UIC John Marshall Law School in Chicago, before concluding his master's degree at the Masaryk University. His focus is mainly the Directive on copyright in the Digital Single Market, to which he also dedicated his Master thesis analyzing the video game streaming industry, and the economic analysis of law.

Agnieszka Wrońska – Advisor to the Director of the NASK National Research Institute, she was the creator of the department of the institute responsible for activities for the safety of children and young people on the Internet. Doctor of Humanities, university lecturer, licensed trainer and supervisor of the Polish Pedagogues and Animators Association Klanza. Specialist in the field of safe Internet use by the youngest users, member of expert working groups. Her research activity focuses on cyber threats to children and young people - their determinants and prevention methods. Author and co-author of books, scientific articles, school textbooks and educational materials. Initiator and coordinator of many educational, cultural and environmental animation projects for different age groups with diverse academic and social needs. In 2017 and 2019. included in the SPRUC List of "100 people who have contributed to developing digital skills in Poland".

Craig Zawada – Q.C. attended the University of Saskatchewan's College of Commerce (now Edwards School of Business) and obtained his LL.B. from Osgoode Hall in Toronto. In 1996 he helped found WMCZ Lawyers in Saskatoon, and was its CEO for 9 years. He is currently a Visiting Professor with the University of Saskatchewan's College of Law, helping to facilitate its collaborative projects with the Law Society of Saskatchewan. Craig has been active in local, provincial and national organizations. Some of his roles have included Chair of the Saskatchewan Research Council, University of Saskatchewan Senate, Trustee for Saskatoon's Mendel Art Gallery and the CanLII board of directors. Craig has been a sessional lecturer at the U of S College of Law for many years, teaching Intellectual Property as well as The Future of Law. He is a graduate of The Directors College Chartered Director program and continues to teach corporate governance. Craig has been a member of the Board of Directors of the Law Society of Saskatchewan since 2014, and served as its President in 2018.

Fryderyk Zoll – Professor of law, professor at the Chair of Civil Law at the Jagiellonian University and at the European Legal Studies Institute of Osnabrück University. Honorary Doctor of the Western Ukrainian National University in Ternopil. Author of nearly two hundred publications in the field of European private law, consumer law, law of new technologies, relationship of private and public law, independence of the judiciary. From 2019 to 2021 member of the Executive Committee of the European Law Institute. Since 2008, manager of 8 grant projects of the National Science Centre, Polish-German Science Foundation, European Commission.

Bibliography

-, 'Artificial intelligence summit focuses on fighting hunger, climate crisis and transition to 'smart sustainable cities'' UN News (28 May 2019) <https://news.un.org/en/story/2019/05/1039311> accessed on 14 April 2020;

-, 'Dronomat zamiast paczkomatu. Czy wkrótce niebo zaroi się od dronów?' (Rozmowy Instytutu Nowej Europy on Anchor.fm, 10 June 2020) <https://anchor.fm/instytutnowejeuropy/episodes/Dronomat-zamiast-paczkomatu--Czy-wkrtce-niebo-zaroi-si-od-dronw-ef77ru> accessed 27 February 2021;

-, 'ISO 3720:2018. Sustainable development of communities — Indicators for city services and quality of life' (International Organization for Standardization, July 2017) <https://www.iso.org/standard/68498.html> accessed 14 April 2020;

-, 'Secure, sustainable smart cities and the IoT' <https://www.gemalto.com/iot/inspired/smart-cities> accessed 27 February 2021;

-, 'Smart city. What is a smart city?' (Official website of the City of Vienna) <https://www.wien.gv.at/stadtentwicklung/studien/pdf/b008403j.pdf> accessed 14 April 2020;

-, 'Take Action for the Sustainable Development Goals' <https://www.un.org/sustainabledevelopment/sustainable-development-goals> accessed on 14 April 2020;

'GB/T39335-2020 Information Security Technology Personal Information Security Assessment Guidelines' (China Standard Press 2020);

'Privacy and Data Protection by Design – from policy to engineering' <https://www.enisa.europa.eu/publications/privacy-and-data-protection-by-design> accessed 23 March 2021;

Abbott R and Sarch A, 'Pushing Artificial Intelligence: Legal Fiction or Science Fiction' (2019) 53 University of California, Davis Law Review 323;

Act on the National Cybersecurity System. Journal of Laws of 2018, item 1560;

Adamski A, Prawo karne komputerowe (CH Beck 2000);

Advisory Board on Artificial Intelligence and Human Society, Report on Artificial Intelligence and Human Society, (2017) <https://www8.cao.go.jp/cstp/tyousakai/ai/summary/aisociety_en.pdf> accessed 22 June 2021;

Agencia Estado. Entenda melhor os ADRS. In: Estadão, 20 nov. 2000. Available in: <https://economia.estadao.com.br/noticias/geral,entenda-melhor-os-adrs,20001120p1082> Accessed: 12 November 2019;

Aletras N and others, 'Predicting Judicial Decisions of the European Court of Human Rights: A Natural Language Processing Perspective' (2016) 19 PeerJ Computer Science 93;

Aletras N, Tsarapatsanis D, Preoţiuc-Pietro D, Lampos V, 'Predicting judicial decisions of the European Court of Human Rights: a Natural Language Processing perspective' (PeerJ Computer Science 2016) <https://peerj.com/articles/cs-93/> accessed 20 May 2021;

Angelopoulos C, 'European Intermediary Liability in Copyright: A Tort-Based Analysis' <https://dare.uva.nl/search?identifier=a406e67d-b537-49ae-9f46-80e831b988d4> accessed 10 June 2021;

Angwin J, Larson J, Mattu S, Kirchner L, 'Machine Bias. There's software used across the country to predict future criminals. And it's biased against blacks', (ProPublica, 23 May 2016) <https://www.propublica.org/article/machine-bias-risk-assessments-in-criminal-sentencing> accessed 25 June 2021;

Anthopoulos LG, Understanding Smart Cities: A Tool for Smart Government or an Industrial Trick? (Springer 2018);

Apple, 'The App Store Turns 10' (Apple.com, 2018) <https://www.apple.com/newsroom/2018/07/app-store-turns-10/> accessed 7 July 2021;

Araszkiewicz M and Rodriguez-Doncel V (eds), Legal Konwledge and Information Systems (IOS Press 2019);

Araszkiewicz M, 'Algorithmization of legal thinking. Models, possibilities, limitations', in Dariusz Szostek (ed), Legal Tech (C.H. Beck 2021);

Arbeitsgruppe 'Modernisierung des Zivilprozesses' <https://www.justiz.bayern.de/media/images/behoerden-und-gerichte/oberlandesgerichte/nuernberg/thesenpapier_der_arbeitsgruppe.pdf> accessed 25 June 2021;

Arkin RC, Ulam P and Duncan B, 'An Ethical Governor for Constraining Lethal Action in an Autonomous System' (Technical Report GIT-GVU-09-02, Georgia Institute of Technology Atlanta Mobile Robot Lab, 2009);

Arkuszewska AM, Informatyzacja postępowania arbitrażowego (Wolters Kluwer 2019);

Armour J, Eidenmueller H, 'Self-Driving Corporations' (2019) 475 European Corporate Governance Institute - Law Working Paper;

Armour J, Parnham R, Sako M, 'Augmented Lawyering' (2020) 558 European Corporate Governance Institute - Law Working Paper;

Ashworth A and Holder J, Principles of Criminal Law (7th edn., Oxford University Press 2013);

Assembleia Geral da Organização das Nações Unidas, Transformar nuestro mundo: la Agenda 2030 para el Desarrollo Sostenible (A/70/L.1, 2015) (online at <https://unctad.org/meetings/es/SessionalDocuments/ares70d1_es.pdf> accessed 24 Nov 2020);

Azevedo R, Entenda o que é ADR: Criados há 70 anos, os American Depositary Receipts permitem que investidores dos EUA coloquem recursos em empresas estrangeiras. In: Revista Exame, 4 out. 2017. Available in: https://exame.abril.com.br/mercados/entenda-o-que-e-adr/. Acessed: 12 nov. 2019.

Bahia C, Carvalho E and Beninça A, Sociedade de Risco, mudanças climáticas e a função reguladora do Direito Ambiental (Instituto O Direito por um Planeta Verde, 2017);

Baig ZA and others, 'Future challenges for smart cities: Cyber-security and digital forensics' (2017) 22 Digital Investigation 3;

Bandara E, Keong W, Ranasinghe N, de Zoysa K, 'Smart contract Made Smart' in (ed) Zheng Z, Dai H, Tang M, Chen X, 'Blockchain and Trustworthy System' (Singapore 2020);

Bar G, 'Sztuczna inteligencja w kancelarii prawnej przyszłości' in Dariusz Szostek (ed), Legal Tech. Czyli jak bezpiecznie korzystać z narzędzi informatycznych w organizacji, w tym w kancelarii oraz dziale prawnym (C.H. Beck 2021);

Bar G, Explainability as a legal requirement for Artificial Intelligence, Medium.com, November 2020, <https://medium.com/womeninai/explainability-as-a-legal-requirement-for-artificial-intelligence-systems-66da5a0aa693> accessed 2 July 2021;

Barbieri J and Cajazeira J, Responsabilidade social e empresarial e empresa sustentável: da teoria à prática (Saraiva, 2010);

Barfield W, Pagallo U, Advanced Introduction to Law and Artificial Intelligence (Edward Elgar Publishing 2020);

Beck U, Sociedade de risco: rumo a uma outra modernidade (Editora 34, 2011);

Becker D, Ferrari I, Artificial Intelligence and the Supreme Court of Brazil –Beauty or a Beast? (22 June 2020) 2 <https://sifocc.org/app/uploads/2020/06/Victor-Beauty-or-the-Beast.pdf> accessed 31 May 2021;

Becker D, Ferrari Isabela F, The Brazilian Supreme Court's Artificial Intelligence: a beauty or a beast? (22 June 2020) <https://sifocc.org/app/uploads/2020/06/Victor-Beauty-or-the-Beast.pdf.> accessed 25 June 2021;

Bellaouar S, Guerroumi M, Derhan A and Moussaoui S, 'Towards Heterogeneous Architectures of Hybrid Vehicular Sensor Networks for Smart Cities' in Z Mahmood (ed.), Smart Cities, Development and Governance Frameworks (Springer 2018);

Bernhardt W, Leeb C, 'Elektronischer Rechtsverkehr' in Dirk Heckmann and Anne Paschke (ed) jurisPK-Internetrecht 7th edition, chapter 6 (status: 01 June2021);

Bertoncelli R de P, Compliance. In: Carvalaho AC, Bertoccelli R de P, Alvim TC, Venturini O, (Coordenadores). Manual de Compliance. Rio de Janeiro: Forense, 2019, Cap. 3, s. p.

BEUC, 'EU Consumer Protection 2.0 Structural Asymmetries in Digital Consumer Markets' (March 2021) <https://www.beuc.eu/publications/beuc-x-2021-018_eu_consumer_protection.0_0.pdf> accessed 13 May 2021;

Beyerlin U and Marauhn T, International Enviromental Governance (Hart Publishng, 2011);

BGH, 12 July 2012, I ZR 18/11

BGH, 22 April 2009, I ZR 216/06

BGH, 26 September 1985, I ZR 86/83

Biallaß I, 'Legal Tech und künstliche Intelligenz' in Ory and Weth (ed), jurisPK-ERV vol 1, 1st edition, chapter 8, status 28 August 2020;

Bienias M, 'Ochrona danych w fazie projektowania oraz domyślna ochrona danych (privacy by design oraz privacy by default) w ogólnym rozporządzeniu o ochronie danych' in Sibiga G (ed) Ogólne rozporządzenie o ochronie danych. Aktualne problemy prawnej ochrony danych osobowych (C. H. Beck 2016);

Billings ChE, 'Human-Centered Aviation Automation: Principles and Guidelines' (NASA Technical Memorandum 110381, Ames Research Center, February1996);

Bolton R, Hand D, Unsupervised profiling methods for fraud detection, Proceedings of credit scoring and credit control VII (2001);

Booth B, 'The Cloud: A Critical Smart City Asset' in S McCleallan, JA Jimenez and G Koutitas (eds.), Smart Cities, Applications, Technologies, Standards, and Driving Factors (Springer 2018);

Boyd JR, 'The Essence of Winning and Losing' (September 2012) <https://fasttransients.files.wordpress.com/2010/03/essence_of_winning_losing.pdf> accessed on 14 April 2020;

Bröhmer J, Transparenz als Verfassungsprinzip. Grundsatz und Europäische Union (Mohr Siebeck 2004);

Brunton F, Nissenbaum H, A User's Guide for Privacy and Protest (MIT Press 2015);

Bryce J, Flexible and Rigid Constitutions (1st edn Oxford University Press 1905);

C-236 to 238/08 Google France and Google [2010] ECR I–2417;

C-324/09, L'Oréal v eBay, ECR [2011] I-06011;

Campuzano A, Manual para entender el Juicio de Amparo (1st edn Thomson Reuters 2016);

Cannon JC, Bayers M, Compliance Descontructed. In: Queue Magazine, v. 4, 7 ed., setembro de 2006. Nova York, NY, USA. p. 30-37. Available in: <http://delivery.acm.org/10.1145/1170000/1160449/p30-cannon.pdf?ip=187.65.179.69&id=1160449&acc=OPEN&key=4D4702B0C3E38B35%2E4D4702B0C3E38B35%2E4D4702B0C3E38B35%2E6D218144511F3437&__acm__=1572443475_b950d9527f97833505d1901c3ce36234> Acessed: 30 October 2019;

Carioca KJF; De Luca M M M; Ponte VMR, Implementação da Lei Sarbanes-Oxley e seus Impactos nos controles internos e nas práticas de governança corporativa: um estudo na Companhia Energética do Ceará – Coelce, In: Revista Universo Contábil, v. 6, n. 4, p. 50-67, out./dez. 2010.

Carretta SA, Blockchain challenges to copyright : Revamping the online music industry, 2019. <http://urn.kb.se/resolve?urn=urn:nbn:se:su:diva-173248> accessed 2 July 2021;

Carvalho VM de; Rodrigues EF (org.). Guia Programas de Compliance: Orientações sobre estruturação e benefícios da adoção dos programas de compliance concorrencial. Brasília: Conselho Administrativo de Defesa Econômica (CADE), 2016. 43 p.

Case N, How To Become A Centaur, Journal of Design and Science MIT Media Lab, 02/02/2018, <https://jods.mitpress.mit.edu/pub/issue3-case/release/6> accessed 2 July 2021;

Castelnovo W, Misuraca G, Savoldelli A, 'Smart Cities Governance: The Need for a Holistic Approach to Assessing Urban Participatory Policy Making' (2015) Social Science Computer Review <https://doi.org/10.1177/0894439315611103> accessed 2 July 2021;

Castillo Y, "Las notificaciones" in Juan González and Fernando Sosa et al (eds), Teoría y Práctica del Juicio de Amparo (Tribunal Superior de Justicia de la Ciudad de México 2020);

Caton JL, Autonomous Weapon Systems: A Brief Survey of Developmental, Operational, Legal, and Ethical Issues (United States Army War College Press 2015);

Cavoukian A, 'Ethics by design' <www.ryerson.ca/pbdce> accessed 23 March 2021;

Cavoukian A, 'Private by Design. The 7 Foundational Principles. Originally' <https://www.ipc.on.ca/wp-content/uploads/resources/7foundationalprincip les.pdf> accessed on 25 April 2021;

Cholasta R and others, 'Safe Harbour: Režim Vyloučení Odpovědnosti Poskytovatelů Služeb Informační Společnosti v Kontextu Pasivní Role Poskytovatele' (2017) Právní rozhledy <www.beck-online.cz> accessed 10 June 2021;

Chomiczewski W, Lubasz D, 'Privacy by design a sztuczna inteligencja' (2020) 20 MoP 20 67 ff;

Choudhary M, 'Six technologies crucial for smart cities' (Geospatial world, 19 November 2019) <https://www.geospatialworld.net/blogs/six-technologies-cruci al-for-smart-cities> accessed 14 April 2020;

Christensen C, Disruptive Innovation (2020), http://www.claytonchristensen.com/ key-concepts accessed 14 April 2020;

Chui M, Manyika J, Miremadi M, Four fundamentals of workplace automation (McKinsey Digital, November 2015), <https://www.mckinsey.com/business-func tions/mckinsey-digital/our-insights/four-fundamentals-of-workplace-automation > accessed 14 April 2020;

Chunkun W, Security Fundamentals for Internet of Things (Science Press 2013);

Clooney A and Webb P, The Right to a Fair Trial in International Law (Oxford University Press 2021);

Collberg C, Davidson J, Giacobazzi R, Gu Y, Herzberg A, Wang F., 'Towards Digital Asset Protection' (2011) 26(6)IEEE Intelligent Systems;

Collins DAA: American Company. In: Encyplopaedia Britannica, 2018. Available in: https://www.britannica.com/topic/Arthur-Andersen. Acessed: 12 nov. 2019.

Comissão sobre Governança Global. Nossa comunidade global (Editora FGV, 1996);

Commission (EC) 'Guidance on Article 17 of Directive 2019/790 on Copyright in the Digital Single Market Guidelines' (Communication) COM (2021) 288 final 4

Commission to the European Parliament, the European Council, the Council, the European Economic and Social Committee and the Committee of the Regions, 'A coordinated plan for artificial intelligence' (Communication) COM (2018) 795 final;

Commission to the European Parliament, the European Council, the Council, the European Economic and Social Committee and the Committee of the Regions, 'Artificial Intelligence for Europe' (Communication) COM (2018) 237 final;

Commission, 'Communication from the Commission to the European Parliament, the Council, the European Economic and Social Committee and the Committee of the Regions - Building Trust in Human Centric Artificial Intelligence', COM (2019) 168 final;

Commission, 'Proposal for a Regulation of the European Parliament and of the Council Laying Down Harmonised Rules on Artificial Intelligence (Artificial Intelligence Act) and Amending Certain Union Legislative Acts' COM 2021 206 final;

Commission, 'White Paper on Artificial Intelligence – A European approach to excellence and trust' (Communication), COM (2020) 65 final;

Committee of Experts on Internet Intermediaries (MSI-NET), Study on the Human Rights Dimensions of Automated Data Processing Techniques (in Particular Algorithms) and Possible Regulatory Implications (6 October 2017) <https://rm.coe.int/study-hr-dimension-of-automated-data-processing-incl-algorithms/168075b94a> accessed 31 May 2021;

Contissa G, 'Automation and Liability: an Analysis in the Context of Socio-Technical Systems' (2017) 11 i-lex 17;

Council of Europe Commissioner for Human Rights, Recommendation Unboxing Artificial Intelligence: 10 steps to protect Human Rights (2019) <https://rm.coe.int/unboxing-artificial-intelligence-10-steps-to-protect-human-rights-reco/1680946e64> accessed 31 May 2021;

Coveware, 'Ransonware Costs Double in Q4 as Ryuk, Sodinokibi Proliferate' (Coveware.com, 2020) <https://www.coveware.com/blog/2020/1/22/ransomware-costs-double-in-q4-as-ryuk-sodinokibi-proliferate> accessed 7 July 2021;

Craig P and others, Rule of Law in Europe Perspectives From Practitioners and Academics (European Judicial Training Network 2020);

Croft J, More than 100,000 legal roles to become automated, Financial Times, 15 March 2016, https://www.ft.com/content/c8ef3f62-ea9c-11e5-888e-2eadd5fbc4a4;

Cui Y, Shanghai Intelligent Assistive Case-Handling System for Criminal Cases - System 206 (Springer 2020);

Cummings ML, 'Automation and Accountability in Decision Support System Interface Design' (2006) 32 The Journal of Technology Studies 23;

Data Protection and Privacy Commissioners, 'The Resolution on Privacy by Design' (32nd International Conference of Data Protection and Privacy Commissioners, Jerusalem, 27–29 October 2010. <http://www.giodo.gov.pl/pl/1520084/3830> accessed 13 May 2021;

De Almeida LCSS; Duarte Junior AMarcos, Desafios e soluções da Petrobras em seu projeto de atendimento à Lei Sarbanes-Oxley. In: RAUnP - Revista Eletrônica do Mestrado Profissional em Administração da Universidade Potiguar, Ano III, n. 1, out. 2010/mar. 2011. p. 27-40;

De Souza MMP, Figueiredo MD, A Lei Sarbanes-Oxley e Sua Importância para as Companhias Abertas Brasileiras a partir do Ano de 2004. In: Revista Pensar Contábil, Rio de Janeiro, v. 10, n. 42, p. 31-35, out./dez. 2008;

Decreto nº 9571 of 2018 <http://www.planalto.gov.br/ccivil_03/_ato2015-2018/2018/Decreto/D9571.htm> accessed 12 Dec 2020;

Der Standard (Internet edition), 'Estland will Richter durch künstliche Intelligenz ersetzen' (Der Standard, 3 April 2019) <https://www.derstandard.at/story/2000100613536/justiz-estland-will-richter-durch-kuenstliche-intelligenz-ersetzen> accessed 29 May 2021;

Directive (EU) 2016/1148 of the European Parliament and of the Council concerning measures for a high common level of security of network and information systems across the Union;

Directive (EU) 2019/790 of the European Parliament and of the Council of 17 April 2019 on Copyright and related rights in the Digital Single Market and amending Directives 96/9/EC and 2001/29/EC [2019] OJ L130/92;

Directive 2000/31/EC of the European Parliament and of the Council of 8 June 2000 on certain legal aspects of information society services, in particular electronic commerce, in the Internal Market [2002] OJ L178/1;

Donahue L, A Primer on Using Artificial Intelligence in the Legal Profession, JOLT Digest, 3 January 2018, https://jolt.law.harvard.edu/digest/a-primer-on-using-artificial-intelligence-in-the-legal-profession;

Drobek P, in Bielak-Jomaa E, Lubasz D (eds) RODO. Ogólne rozporządzenie o ochronie danych. Komentarz (C. H. Beck 2017);

Dysart J, AI Removes the Drudgery from Legal Due Diligence, Communications of the ACM, 8 January 2019, https://cacm.acm.org/news/233886-ai-removes-the-drudgery-from-legal-due-diligence/fulltext;

Ebers M and Navas S (eds), Algorithms and Law (Cambridge University Press 2020);

Ejaz W and Anpalagan A, Internet of Things for Smart Cities (Springer 2019);

Endsley MR, 'Automation and situation awareness' in R Parasuraman and M Mouloua (eds.), Automation and Human Performance. Theory and Applications (reprint, CRC Press 2009);

Engelman D, 'Kevin Kelly Holos Rising' (2014) <https://blog.longnow.org/02014/12/01/kevin-kellyseminar-media/> accessed 7 July 2021;

Engstrom DF and Gelbach JB, 'Legal Tech, Civil Procedure, and the Future of American Adversarialism' (2020) 169 University of Pennsylvania Law Review 1;

Engstrom DF, 'Post COVID Courts' (2020) 68 UCLA Law Review Discourse 246;

Escajeda HG, The Vitruvian Lawyer: How to Thrive in an Era of AI and Quantum Technologies, XXIX Kansas J. of Law & Pub. Pol'y 421-521 (2020), https://ssrn.com/abstract=3534683;

European Commission for the Efficiency of Justice (CEPEJ), European ethical Charter on the use of Artificial Intelligence in judicial systems and their environment (2018) <https://rm.coe.int/ethical-charter-en-for-publication-4-december-2018/16808f699c> accessed 31 May 2021;

European Commission for the Efficiency of Justice (CEPEJ), Report on the CEPEJ Conference "Artificial intelligence at the service of the Judiciary" (27 September 2018) <https://www.coe.int/en/web/cepej/justice-of-the-future-predictive-justice-and-artificial-intelligence> accessed 31 May 2021;

European Commission, 'Assessment list of trustworthy artificial intelligence' (Study, 1 March 2021) <https://digital-strategy.ec.europa.eu/en/library/assessment-list-trustworthy-artificial-intelligence-altai-self-assessment> accessed 27 April 2021;

European Commission, 'EU member states sign up to cooperate on artificial intelligence' (News, 8 March 2020) <https://ec.europa.eu/digital-single-market/en/news/eu-member-states-sign-cooperate-artificial-intelligence> accessed 6 March 2019;

European Commission, 'Member States and Commission to work together to boost artificial intelligence „made in Europe"' (Press release, 7 December 2018) <http://europa.eu/rapid/press-release_IP-18-6689_en.htm> access: 6 March 2019;

European Commission, Proposal for a Regulation of the European Parliament and of the Council laying down harmonized rules on artificial intelligence (Artificial Intelligence Act) and amending certain Union legislative acts, COM (2021) 206 final <https://digital-strategy.ec.europa.eu/en/library/proposal-regulation-laying-down-harmonised-rules-artificial-intelligence> accessed 30 May 2021;

European Commission's High-Level Expert Group on Artificial Intelligence (2018): Draft Ethics Guidelines for Trustworthy AI <https://ec.europa.eu/digital-single-market/en/news/draft-ethics-guidelines-trustworthy-ai>, accessed 30 Mai 2021;

European Data Protection Board, 'Guidelines 4/2019 on Article 25 Data Protection by Design and by Default' (20 October 2020) <https://edpb.europa.eu/sites/edpb/files/files/file1/edpb_guidelines_201904_dataprotection_by_design_and_by_default_v2.0_en.pdf> accessed 13 May 2021;

European Parliament, Regulation (EU) 2016/679 of the European Parliament and of the Council of 27 April 2016 on the protection of natural persons with regard to the processing of personal data and on the free movement of such data, and repealing Directive 95/46/EC [2016] OJ L199/1 (General Data Protection Regulation);

Farias F, Principais impactos da Sarbanes-Oxley Act. In: Revista ConTexto, Porto Alegre, v. 4, n. 6, 1º Semestre 2004. ISSN 1676-6016.

Federal Trade Commission, 'Consumer Privacy on the World Wide Web' (FTC,1998) <https://www.ftc.gov/sites/default/files/documents/public_statements/prepared-statement-federal-trade-commission-consumer-privacy-worldwide-web/privac98.pdf> accessed 7 July 2021;

Fereira F, 'Artificial Intelligence Makes its Mark in the Brazilian Judicial System' (Folha de S.Paulo, 10 March 2020) <https://www1.folha.uol.com.br/internacional/en/brazil/2020/03/artificial-intelligence-makes-its-mark-in-the-brazilian-judicial-system.shtml> accessed 31 May2021;

Fernandes P, Globalização, Sociedade de Risco e o futuro do Direito Penal (Livraria Almedina, 2001).

Fernández C, 'La sustitución directa de la actividad humana en la decisión judicial, al día de hoy, es puramente quimérica a corto y medio plazo' (Legal today, 11 September 2020) <https://www.legaltoday.com/legaltech/nuevas-tecnologias/la-realidad-y-el-deseo-inteligencia-artificial-y-decision-judicial-2020-09-11/> accessed 31 May 2021;

Filipkowski W, 'Prawo karne wobec sztucznej inteligencji' in L Lai and M Świerczyński (eds.), Prawo sztucznej inteligencji (C. H. Beck 2020);

Flavio Fereira, in Folha de S.Paulo" (Internet edn 10 March2020) „Artificial Intelligence Makes its Mark in the Brazilian Judicial System"<https://www1.folha.uol.com.br/internacional/en/brazil/2020/03/artificial-intelligence-makes-its-mark-in-the-brazilian-judicial-system.shtml> accessed 31 May2021;

Forester M, 'Catch Up on Privacy Around the World on Data Privacy Day 2021' (Morrison Foerster, 2021) <https://www.mofo.com/resources/insights/210127-data-privacy-day.html> accessed 7 July 2021;

Freitas GP, Ilícito Penal ambiental e reparação do dano (Revista dos Tribunais, 2005);

FTC, Protecting Consumer Privacy in an Era of Rapid Change, (FTC 2010);

Garlicki L, Polskie prawo konstytucyjne. Zarys wykładu (Wolters Kluwer Polska 2020);

Gentry C, 'Fully Homomorphic Encryption Using Ideal Lattices' (the 41st ACM Symposium on Theory of Computing (STOC) 2009);

Gerards J, General Principles of the European Convention on Human Rights (Cambridge University Press 2019);

Gesley J, 'Comparative Summary', Law Library of Congress (ed) Regulation of Artificial Intelligence in Selected Jurisdictions (January 2019) 1 <https://www.loc.gov/law/help/artificial-intelligence/regulation-artificial-intelligence.pdf> accessed 24 June 2021;

Gesley J, Comparative Summary, Law Library of Congress (ed), Regulation of Artificial Intelligence in Selected Jurisdictions (January 2019) 1 <https://www.loc.gov/law/help/artificial-intelligence/regulation-artificial-intelligence.pdf> accessed 24 June 2021;

Ghosal A and Halder S, 'Chapter 5. Building Intelligent Systems for Smart Cities: Issues, Challenges and Approaches' in Z Mahmood (ed.), Smart Cities, Development and Governance Frameworks (Springer 2018);

Gibney A (dir.), Enron: The Smartest Guys in the Room. Nova Iorque: Magnolia Pictures, 2015. Documentary.

Giezek J, 'Teorie związku przyczynowego oraz koncepcje obiektywnego przypisania' in R Dębski (ed.), System prawa karnego, tom 3: Nauka o przestępstwie. Zasady odpowiedzialności (C. H. Beck 2017);

Glavanits J and Bálint P (eds), Law 4 . 0 – Challenges of the Digital Age (Széchenyi István University 2019);

Gless S, Silverman E and Weigend T, 'If Robots Cause Harm, Who is to Blame? Self-Driving Cars and Criminal Liability' (2016) 19 New Criminal Law Review 412;

Global Pact, Sdg Action Manager (2020) <https://www.pactoglobal.org.br/pg/sdg-action-manager> accessed 14 December 2020;

Global Pandemic Network Ecological Rights Working Group, Position Paper: Environmental Protection and Human Rights in the Pandemic (2021);

Gonçalves A and Costa JJA, "Governança Ambiental Global: possibilidades e limites" in Granziera MLM and Rei FCF (eds), Direito Ambiental Internacional: Avanços e retrocessos (Atlas, 2015);

Gonçalves A, "Governança Global e o Direito Internacional Público" in JUBILUT LL (ed), Direito Internacional Atual (Elsevier, 2014);

González R, "Sobre la competencia" in Guadalupe Tafoya (ed), Elementos para el estudio del Juicio de Amparo (Suprema Corte de Justicia de la Nación 2017);

Goodenough O R, 'Legal Technology 3.0' (HuffPost, 6 April 2015) <https://www.huffpost.com/entry/legal-technology-30_b_6603658> accessed 29 May 2021;

Goodman C, AI/Esq: Impacts of Artificial Intelligence in Lawyer-Client Relationships, (2019) 72 Okla. L. Rev. 149;

Grześkowiak A, 'Komentarz do art. 2 k.k.' in A Grześkowiak, and K Wiak (eds.), Kodeks karny. Komentarz (6th edn, CH Beck 2018);

Guo Bing v. Hangzhou Wildlife Park Co., Ltd, Zhe0111MinChu No.6971(2019);

Gyuranecz FZ, Krausz B and Papp D, The AI Is Now in Session. The Impact of Digitalization on Courts (European Judicial Training Network 2019);

Hacker P, Krestel R, Grundmann S et al. Explainable AI under contract and tort law: legal incentives and technical challenges, Artificial Intelligence Law 28, 415–439 (2020). https://doi.org/10.1007/s10506-020-09260-6;

Hallevy G, 'The Criminal Liability of Artificial Intelligence Entities - from Science Fiction to Legal Social Control' (2016) 4 Akron Intellectual Property Journal 171;

Hallevy G, Liability for Crimes Involving Artificial Intelligence Systems (Springer 2015);

Hao K, 'When algorithms mess up, the nearest human gets the blame' (MIT Technology Review, 28 May 2019) <https://www.technologyreview.com/2019/05/28/65748/ai-algorithms-liability-human-blame> accessed on 26 April 2020;

Harašta J, 'Obecná Prevenční Povinnost Poskytovatele Služeb Informační Společnosti ve Vztahu k Informacím Ukládaným Uživatelem' (2014) Právní rozhledy 590 <www.beck-online.cz> accessed 10 June 2021;

Harrington A R, International Law and Global Governance: Treaty Regimes and Sustainable Development Goals Implementation (Routledge 2021);

Health Insurance Portability and Accountability Act of 1996, (1996) <https://www.congress.gov/104/plaws/publ191/PLAW-104publ191.pdf> accessed 7 July 2021;

Held D and McGrew A, Prós e Contras da Globalização (Zahar, 2001);

Hert P, Gutwirth S, 'Privacy, data protection and law enforcement: Opacity of the individual and transparency of power' in Claes E, Duff A, Gutwirth S (eds) Privacy and the Criminal Law (Intersentia, 2006);

High Court in Prague, 2 March 2011, file no. 3 Cmo 197/2010–82;

High Level Expert Group on Artificial Intelligence, 'The Assessment List on Trustworthy Artificial Intelligence' <https://futurium.ec.europa.eu/en/european-ai-alliance/pages/altai-assessment-list-trustworthy-artificial-intelligence> accessed 27 April 2021;

High-Level Expert Group on Artificial Intelligence, 'Ethics Guidelines for Trustworthy Artificial Intelligence' (2019);

Hosseini SB, Mahesh R, The lesson from Enron Case – Moral and Managerial Responsilities. In: International Journal of Current Research, vol. 8, Issue 8, pp. 37451-37460, August, 2016. ISSN 0975-833X. <http://www.openvotingconsortium.org/files/voting_good_bad_stupid.pdf> access by day 30.06. 2021;

Husovec M, 'Zodpovednosť na Internete: podľa českého a slovenského práva' (CZ.NIC 2014);

Husovec M, 'Zodpovednosť poskytovateľa za obsah diskusných príspevkov' (2011) 2 Revue pro právo a technologie 40, 41 <https://journals.muni.cz/revue/article/view/4015> accessed 10 June 2021;

Husovec M, Injunctions against Intermediaries in the European Union: Accountable but Not Liable? (Cambridge University Press 2017);

Hutson M, Artificial Intelligence Prevails at Predicting Supreme Court Decisions, Science, 2 May 2017, <https://www.sciencemag.org/news/2017/05/artificial-intelligence-prevails-predicting-supreme-court-decisions> accessed 10 June 2021;

Iaione C, The Right to the Co-City, 9 Italian J. Pub. L. 80;

ICO, Guidance on AI and data protection;

Inagaki T, 'Design of human-machine interactions in light of domain dependence of human centered automation' (2006) 8 Cognition, Technology & Work 161;

IPC, 'Privacy by Design. The 7 Foundational Principles' <https://www.ipc.on.ca/wp-content/uploads/Resources/7foundationalprinciples.pdf> accessed 23 March 2021;

Istoé, A constituição cidadã (2011) <https://istoe.com.br/161883_A+CONSTITUICAO+CIDADA/> accessed 09 December 2020;

Jabłonowska A, Kuziemski M, Nowak A M, Micklitz H, Pałka P, Sartor G, 'Consumer law and artificial intelligence. Challenges to the EU consumer law and policy stemming from the business' use of artificial intelligence' (EUI Working Papers, Florence 2018);

Jackson T, 'This Bug in Your PC is a Smart Cookie' (Financial Times, 02 December 1996);

Jimenez JA, 'Smart Transportation Systems' in S McCleallan, JA Jimenez and G Koutitas (eds.), Smart Cities, Applications, Technologies, Standards, and Driving Factors (Springer 2018);

Jiménez JML, 'Sistemas Judiciales Justos Y… Eficientes' (2013) 2013 eXtoikos 31;

Jobin A, Ienca M, 'Artificial Intelligence: the global landscape of ethics guidelines' (2019) AL/Digital ethics project <https://www.researchgate.net/publication/334082218_Artificial_Intelligence_the_global_landscape_of_ethics_guidelines> accessed 22 June 2021;

Johnston C, Artificial intelligence judge developed by UCL computer scientists, The Guardian (29 October 2016)<https://www.theguardian.com/technology/2016/oct/24/artificial-intelligence-judge-university-college-london-computer-scientists> accessed 25 June 2021;

Jones K, Jones M, Strategies supporting the development and deployment of high-quality legal software (221), Legal evolution blog, January 31, 2021 https://www.legalevolution.org/2021/01/tactics-supporting-the-development-and-deployment-of-high-quality-legal-software-221;

Junior PCN, Judiciário 5.0. Inovação, Governança, Usucentrismo, Sustentabilidade e Segurança Jurídica (Edgard Blücher 2020);

Kaminski M, Binary Governance: Lessons from the GDPR's approach to Algorithmic Accountability, (2019) 92 S. Cal. L. Rev. 1529;

Kasperska A, 'Problemy zastosowania sztucznych sieci neuronalnych w praktyce prawniczej' (2017) 11 Przegląd Prawa Publicznego 25;

Katz DM, Bommarito II MJ and Blackman J, 'A General Approach for Predicting the Behavior of the Supreme Court of the United States' (2017) 12 Plos One;

Kerikmäe T and Pärn-Lee E, 'Legal Dilemmas of Estonian Artificial Intelligence Strategy: In between of e-Society and Global Race' AI & Society 2020;

King T, 'The Future of Legal Education from the Profession's Viewpoint: A Brave New World?' in H Sommerlad et al. (eds), The Futures of Legal Education and the Legal Profession (Hart 2015);

Kirit N, Sarkar P, EscrowChain: Leveraging Ethereum Blockchain as Escrow in Real Estate, International Journal of Innovative Research in Computer and Communication Engineering, Vol. 5, Issue 10, October 2017, DOI: 10.15680/IJIRCCE.2017.0510022;

Kliś M, 'Źródła obowiązku gwaranta w polskim prawie karnym' (1999) 2 Czasopismo Prawa Karnego i Nauk Penalnych 169

Kluttz D, Mulligan D, 'Automated Decision Support Technologies and the Legal Profession' (2019) 34 Berkeley Technology Law Journal;

Kontargirys X., IT laws in the era of cloud computing, (Nomos, 2018);

Korbel F, Cholasta R and Molitorisová A, 'Safe Harbour: Vyloučení Odpovědnosti Poskytovatelů Hostingových Služeb Za Obsah Vložený Uživateli Internetu' [2016] Soudce 9;

Korenik A, Smart cities, Inteligentne miasta w Europie i Azji, (CeDeWu 2019)

Koulu R and Kontiainen L (eds), How Will AI Shape the Future of Law? (University of Helsinki Legal Tech Lab publications 2019);

Koutitas G, 'The Smart Grid: Anchor of the Smart City' in S McCleallan, JA Jimenez and G Koutitas (eds.), Smart Cities, Applications, Technologies, Standards, and Driving Factors (Springer 2018)

Kowalski Ł, 'Inteligentne miasta - przegląd rozwiązań' in M Soja and A Zborowski (eds.), Miasto w badaniach geografów (Wydawnictwo Uniwersytetu Jagiellońskiego 2015)

Kristol D, Montulli L, 'HTTP State Management Mechanism' (1997) IETF RFC 2109 <https://datatracker.ietf.org/doc/html/rfc2109> accessed 7 July 2021;

Krzysztofek M, 'Commentary to Article 10' in Ochrona danych osobowych w Unii Europejskiej po reformie. Komentarz do rozporządzenia Parlamentu Europejskiego i Rady (UE) 2016/679 (Legalis 2016);

Kulesza J, Problemy teorii kryminalizacji. Studium z zakresu prawa karnego i konstytucyjnego (Wydawnictwo Uniwersytetu Łódzkiego 2017)

Kurowska I, Szpyt K, 'Legal Tech w kancelariach prawnych oraz pracy prawników in-house' in Dariusz Szostek (ed), Legal Tech. Czyli jak bezpiecznie korzystać z narzędzi informatycznych w organizacji, w tym w kancelarii oraz dziale prawnym (C.H. Beck 2021);

Kurzweill R, The Singularity Is Near: When Humans Transcend Biology (Viking Press 2005);

Lawlor RC, What computers can do: analysis and prediction of judicial decisions, (1963) 49 American Bar Association Journal 337;

Lee JD and Seppelt BD, 'Human factors and ergonomics in automation design' in G Salvendy (ed.), Handbook of Human Factors and Ergonomics (John Wiley & Sons 2012)

Lee T B, 'Information Management: A Proposal' (w3.org,1989-1990) <https://www.w3.org/History/1989/proposal.html> accessed 7 July 2021;

Lei nº 12846 of 2013 (online at <http://www.planalto.gov.br/ccivil_03/_ato2011-2014/2013/lei/l12846.htm> accessed 10 Dec 2020);

Lei nº 130140 of 2015 (online at <http://www.planalto.gov.br/ccivil_03/_ato2015-2018/2015/lei/l13140.htm> accessed 10 Dec 2020);

Leistner M, 'Structural Aspects of Secondary (Provider) Liability in Europe' (2014) 9 Journal of Intellectual Property Law & Practice 75;

Leite JRM, "Sociedade de risco e estado" in Canotilho JJG and Leite JRM (eds), Direito constitucional ambiental brasileiro (Saraiva, 2015);

Leith P, Hoey A, The Computerised Lawyer (Springer 1998);

Lele A, 'Debating Lethal Autonomous Weapons Systems' (2019) 13 Journal of Defense Studies 51

Ling L, Shancang L, Shanshan Z, 'QoS-aware scheduling of service-oriented Internet of things' (2014) IEEE Trans on Industial Informatics;

Lubasz D (ed) Meritum Ochrona danych osobowych (Wolters Kluwer 2020);

Lubasz D, Witkowska K, 'Europejska reforma ochrony danych osobowych z perspektywy pełnomocnika przedsiębiorcy' in Flaga-Gieruszyńska K, Gołaczyński J, Szostek D (eds) Media elektroniczne. Współczesne problemy prawne (C. H. Beck 2016);

Lubasz D, Witkowska K, 'RODO. Ogólne rozporządzenie o ochronie danych. Komentarz' (LEX/el., comments on Art. 25 No 5);

Maddox T, 'Smart cities: 6 essential technologies' (TechRepublic, 1 August 2016) <https://www.techrepublic.com/article/smart-cities-6-essential-technologies> accessed 14 April 2020

Maisner M, 'Snaha o Zakázané Těžení Ze Zdánlivé Absence Výslovné Legislativní Úpravy a Nebezpečná Situace pro Poskytovatele Služeb Informační Společnosti' (Bulletin advokacie, 24 September 2015) <http://www.bulletin-advokacie.cz/snaha-o-zakazane-tezeni-ze-zdanlive-absence-vyslovne-legislativni-upravy> accessed 10 June 2021;

Maisner M, Zákon o Některých Službách Informační Společnosti: Komentář (C H Beck 2016);

Marra WC and McNeil SK, 'Understanding "The Loop": Regulating the Next Generation of War Machines' (2012) 36 Harvard Journal of Law & Public Policy 1139

Marrow PB, Karol M and Kuyan S, 'Artificial Intelligence and Arbitration: The Computer as an Arbitrator — Are We There Yet?' (2020) 74 Dispute Resolution Journal 35;

Matejka J, Krausová A, 'Odpovědnost poskytovatelů hostingových služeb se zřetelem k povaze a druhu přenášeného obsahu' (2017) 156 Právník;

McAfee A and Brynjolfsson E, Human Work in the Robotic Future: Policy for the Age of Automation, Foreign Affairs Vol. 95, No. 4 (JULY/AUGUST 2016), pp. 139-150, https://www.jstor.org/stable/43946940;

McGinnis JO, Pearce RG, The Great Disruption: How Machine Intelligence Will Transform the Role of Lawyers in the Delivery of Legal Services (2013) 82 Fordham L. Rev. 3041;

Mckamey M, 'Legal Technology: Artificial Intelligence and the Future of Law Practice' (2017) 22 Appeal: Review of Current Law and Law Reform 45;

Mclean B, Is Enron Overpriced? It's in a bunch of complex businesses. Its financial statements are nearly impenetrable. So why is Enron trading at such a huge multiple? In: Fortune Magazine, Nova Iorque, 5 mar. 2001. Available in: https://archive.fortune.com/magazines/fortune/fortune_archive/2001/03/05/297833/index.htm. Acessed: 12 nov. 2019.

Mednis A, 'Cechy zgody na przetwarzanie danych osobowych w opinii Grupy Roboczej Art. 29 dyrektywy 95/46 Nr 15/2011 (WP 187)' (2012) 7 MoP 26;

Medvedeva M, Vols M and Wieling M, 'Using Machine Learning to Predict Decisions of the European Court of Human Rights' (2020) 28 Artificial Intelligence and Law 237;

Melzer F in: Filip M and Petr T, Občanský Zákoník: Velký Komentář. Svazek IX: § 2894-3081 (Leges 2018);

México Evalúa, Guía de Buenas Prácticas en el uso de nuevas tecnologías para la impartición de justicia (1st edn Tinker Foundation 2020);

Milaré E, Direito do Ambiente (Editora Revista dos Tribunais, 2013);

Monreale A, Rinzivillo S, Pratesi F, Giannotti F, Pedreschi D, Privacy-by-design in big data analytics and social mining. (EPJ Data Science, 2014);

Mulligan D K, King J, 'Bridging the gap between privacy and design' (2012) 14 U. Pa. J. Const. L.;

Municipal Court in Prague, 12. 1. 2015, file no. 66 C 143/2013;

Municipal Court in Prague, 17 March 2010, file no. 10 Cm 47/2009;

N Helberger, B Zuiderveen, F and R Agustin, 'The Perfect Match? A Closer Look at the Relationship between EU Consumer Law and Data Protection Law' Common Market Law Review (October 6, 2017, vol. 54, No. 5), p. 11;

Nakamoto S, 'Bitcoin: A Peer-to-Peer Electronic Cash System' (Bitcoin.org, 2008) <https://bitcoin.org/bitcoin.pdf> accessed 7 July 2021;

Nauman J, Commentary to § 19 in Zbiór Zasad Etyki Adwokackiej i Godności Zawodu (Legalis 2020)

Nay J, Natural Language Processing and Machine Learning for Law and Policy Texts, April 7, 2018. http://dx.doi.org/10.2139/ssrn.3438276;

Nesterova I, 'Mass data gathering and surveillance: the fight against facial recognition technology in the globalized world' (SHS Web of Conferences 74, 03006, 2020);

Neumann T, 'Perspektywy wykorzystania pojazdów autonomicznych w transporcie drogowym w Polsce' (2018) 19 Autobusy 787

Newman P, 'Sustainable Cities of the Future: The Behavior Change Driver', (2010) 11, 7 Sustainable Dev. L & Pol'y;

Nordemann J B, 'Liability for Copyright Infringements on the Internet: Host Providers (Content Providers) - The Geman Approach', 2 JIPITEC 37 <https://nbn-resolving.org/urn:nbn:de:0009-29-29629> accessed 10 June 2021;

Norwegian data protection supervisory authority, 'Software development with Data Protection by Design and by Default' (Guidelines) <https://www.datatilsynet.no/en/about-privacy/virksomhetenes-plikter/innebygd-personvern/data-protection-by-design-and-by-default/?print=true> accessed 13 May 2021;

Oliviera MC, Linhares JS, A implantação de controle interno adequado às exigências da Lei Sarbanes-Oxley em empresas brasileiras – Um estudo de caso. In: BASE – Revista de Administração e Contabilidade da Unisinos, v. 4, n. 2, p. 160-170, maio/ago. 2007.

Opaliński B, Wolność wyborów parlamentarnych i jej gwarancje na gruncie Konstytucji Rzeczypospolitej Polskiej, „Przegląd Prawa Konstytucyjnego" 2012, no 2, p. 59 i n; http://www.marszalek.com.pl/przegladprawakonstytucyjnego/ppk10/03.pdf;

Organização das Nações Unidas, Agenda 2030 (2015) (online at <https://nacoesunidas.org/pos2015> accessed 10 Nov 2020);

Pantin L and Escamilla S, "La justicia digital en México: el saldo a un año del inicio de la Pandemia", <https://bit.ly/3sTibJi> accessed 27 April 2021;

Parasuraman R, Sheridan TB and Wickens ChD, 'A Model for Types and Levels of Human Interaction with Automation' (2000) 30 IEEE Transactions on Systems Man and Cybernetics - Part A Systems and Humans 286

Payandeh M, Judikative Rechtserzeugung: Theorie, Dogmatik und Methodik der Wirkungen von Präjudizien (Mohr Siebeck 2017);

Pérez F, "Artículo 17. Párrafo segundo" in José Ramón Cossío (ed), Constitución Política de los Estados Unidos Mexicanos Comentada" (Tirant lo Blanch 2017);

Polčák R, 'Information Society Between Orwell and Zapata: A Czech Perspective on Safe Harbours' in Graeme B Dinwoodie (ed), Secondary Liability of Internet Service Providers (Springer International Publishing 2017);

Polčák R, 'Odpovědnost ISP' in Radim Polčák and others, Právo Informačních Technologií (Wolters Kluwer ČR 2018);

Possible Introduction of a Mechanism for Certifying Artificial Intelligence Tools and Services in the Sphere of Justice and the Judiciary : Feasibility Study (European Comission 2020);

Put M van der, 'Kan artificiële intelligentie de rechtspraak betoveren' (2019) 2 Rechtstreeks 50;

Quintas JS, Introdução à gestão ambiental pública (IBAMA, 2006);

Radwan A, 'Edukacja prawnicza wobec wyzwań XXI wieku' in R Czarny et al. (eds), Państwo i prawo wobec wyzwań u progu trzeciej dekady XXI wieku. Księga jubileuszowa z okazji 70. urodzin Profesora Jerzego Jaskierni (Wydawnictwo Adam Marszałek 2020);

Ramos A and Márquez L, Observatorio: Avances de Justicia Abierta en línea en México 2020 (1st edn Escuela Libre de Derecho 2020);

Realing ADD, 'Courts and Artificial Intelligence' (2020) 11 International Journal for Court Administration 1;

Redo S, 'Chapter II. Priorytety Agendy na rzecz Zrównoważonego rozwoju 2030' in EW Pływaczewski, Redo S, Guzik-Makaruk EM, Laskowska K, Filipkowski W, Glińska E, Jurgielewicz-Delegacz E and Perkowska M, Kryminologia, Stan i perspektywy rozwoju, Z uwzględnieniem założeń Agendy ONZ na rzecz zrównoważonego rozwoju 2030 (Wolters Kluwer 2019)

Reeves J, BRIC Investing – ADR List for Brazil, Russia, India and China. In: Investor Place, 16 jun. 2010. Available in: https://investorplace.com/2010/06/bric-adr-list-brazil-china-india-russia-american-depositary-receipt-directory-listing/. Acessed: 12. nov. 2019.

Resolution no. 196 of the Council of Ministers of 28 December 2020 on establishing the 'Policy for the development of artificial intelligence in Poland until 2020' Monitor Polski 2021, item 23, Annex;

Rexha B, Neziri V, Dervishi R, Improving authentication and transparency of e-Voting system – Kosovo case, „International Journal Of Computers And Communications" 2012, Issue 1, Volume 6, s. 84; http://www.universitypress.org.uk/journals/cc/17-858.pdf [Access by day 30.06. 2021];

Ribas FS and Costa Junior A, 'A importância do compliance ambiental para as empresas: Interfaces entre governança corporativa e impactos socioambientais', Revista Jurídica Luso-Brasileira (2019) <http://www.cidp.pt/revistas/rjlb/2019/3/2019_03_0581_0610.pdf> accessed 12 Nov 2020;

Rivera M, "De Directores y Orquestas: Análisis comparado de la posición institucional del Consejo de la Judicatura Federal en México", (2020) 159 Boletín Mexicano de Derecho Comparado 1139;

Rivera M, "Understanding Constitutional Amendments in Mexico: Perpetuum Mobile Constitution" (2017) 2 Mexican Law Review 3;

Rodriguez JJF, ODS 16: paz, justicia e instituciones flertes (Universidade de Santiago de Compostela, 2018) <http://www.ieee.es/Galerias/fichero/docs_investig/2018/DIEEEINV18-2018ODS.pdf> accessed 24 Nov 2020;

Roseman A, State constitutional law—equal protection—the Indiana Supreme Court's less than rational basis review of equal protection claims resulted in the validation of the Indiana voter id law. League of Women Voters of Indiana, inc. v. Rokita, 929 n.e.2d 758 (ind. 2010), „Rutgers Law Journal" 2013, t. 43. No 3, p. 873 and n. http://lawjournal.rutgers.edu/sites/lawjournal.rutgers.edu/files/issues/16RosemanVol.43.4_v3.pdf;

Rożek S, Sprawność sądowego postępowania cywilnego na tle rozstrzygania spraw spadkowych (Krakowska Akademia 2020);

Salamon J, Polityczne konsekwencje wyboru metody dystrybucji mandatów na przykładzie elekcji do Sejmu RP z 21 października 2007 roku Studia Politicae Universitatis Silesiensis 4-5, p. 139 i n.

Santos L de AA, Lemes S, Desafios das empresas brasileiras na implantação da Lei Sarbanes-Oxley. In: BASE – Revista de Administração e Contabilidade da Unisinos, v. 4, jan./abr. 2007. p. 37-46.

Schabas WA, The European Convention on Human Rights: A Commentary (Oxford University Press 2015);

Schwab K, 'The Fourth Industrial Revolution: What it means and how to response' (weforum.org, 2014) <https://www.weforum.org/agenda/2016/01/the-fourth-industrial-revolution-what-it-means-and-how-to-respond/> accessed 7 July 2021;

Sharkey N, 'Saying 'No!' to Lethal Autonomous Targeting' (2010) 9 Journal of Military Ethics 369;

Sheppard B, Does Machine-Learning-Powered Software Make Good Research Decisions? Lawyers Can't Know for Sure, Legal Rebels, 22 November 2016, http://www.abajournal.com/legalrebels/article/does_machine-learning-powered_software_make_good_research_decisions_lawyers;

Sheppard B, Incomplete Innovation and the Premature Disruption of Legal Services, (2015) Mich. St. L. Rev. 1797 at 1842;

Sheridan TB and Parasuraman R, 'Human-Automation Interaction' (2006) 1 Reviews of Human Factors and Ergonomics 89;

Shi C, Sourdin T and Li B, 'The Smart Court – A New Pathway to Justice in China?' (2021) 12 International Journal for Court Administration 4;

Shimshaw D, 'Ethical Issues in Robo-Lawyering: The Need for Guidance on Developing and Using Artificial Intelligence in the Practice of Law' (2018) Hastings Law Journal;

Shneiderman B, 'Human Responsibility for Autonomous Agents' (2007) 22 IEEE Intelligent Systems 60;

Simmon E, 'Evaluation on cloud computing servicesbased on NIST 800-145' (National Institute of standards and Technology (NIST), February 2018) <https://doi.org/10.6028/NIST.SP.500-322> accessed 1 August 2021;

Simons B, Electronic Voting Systems: the Good, the Bad, and the Stupid, p. 3-11;

Singh IB and Pelton JN, 'The cyber city of the future' (2013) 47 The Futurist 22;

Skitka LJ, Mosier K and Burdick MD, 'Accountability and automation bias' (2000) 52 International Journal of Human-Computer Studies 701;

Skotnicki K, Kilka słów o i-votingu, http://repozytorium.uni.wroc.pl/Content/89856/35_K_Skotnicki_Kilka_slow_o_i-votingu.pdf.

Sobol A, 'INTELIGENTNE MIASTA VERSUS ZRÓWNOWAŻONE MIASTA' (2017) 320 Studia Ekonomiczne. Zeszyty Naukowe Uniwersytetu Ekonomicznego w Katowicach 76;

Sourdin T and Zariski A (eds), The Responsive Judge: International Perspectives (Springer);

Spamann H, Klöhn L, Justice is Less Blind, and Less Legalistic, Than We Thought: Evidence from an Experiment with Real Judges, (2017) 45 J.L.S. 255;

Staffler L, Jany O, 'Künstliche Intelligenz und Strafrechtspflege –eine Orientierung' (2020) 164 Zeitschrift für Internationale Strafrechtsdogmatik 170. < http://www.zis-online.com/dat/artikel/2020_4_1357.pdf> accessed 25 June 2021;

Staicu MAM, La réforme du système judiciaire roumain dans le processus d ' adhésion de la Roumanie à l ' Union européenne Mémoire présenté par (2006);

Staśkiewicz W, Stawecki T, 'Legal Databases and Their Functions in the Process of Interpreting and Applying the Law' (2012) 1 Archiwum Filozofii Prawa i Filozofii Społecznej;

Stephenson N, Snow Crash (Bantam Books (US) 1992);

Stępień-Załucka B, E-voting a Konstytucja RP [w:] Dwadzieścia lat obowiązywania Konstytucji RP. Polska myśl konstytucyjna a międzynarodowe standardy demokratyczne, red. Jaskiernia J, Spryszak K, Toruń 2017, s. 223-225;

Stępień-Załucka B, E-voting. Sukces czy porażka na przykładzie Estonii i Szwajcarii, [w:] Aktualne wyzwania demokracji partycypacyjnej w Polsce i na świecie, red. Kuczma P, Polkowice 2017, s. 244;

Study on the Use of Innovative Technologies in the Justice Field. Final Report (European Commission 2020);

Supreme Court of the Czech Republic, 31 July 2013, file no. 23 Cdo 2623/2011;

Susskind R, Online Courts and the Future of Justice (Oxford University Press 2019);

Susskind R, Susskind D, The Future of the Professions. How Technology Will Transform the Work of Human Experts (Oxford University Press 2015);

Susskind R, Tomorrow's Lawyers. An Introduction to Your Future (Oxford University Press 2017);

Szostek D (ed), LegalTech. Czyli jak bezpiecznie korzystać z narzędzi informatycznych w organizacji, w tym w kancelarii oraz dziale prawnym (C H Beck 2021);

Szostek D, Przechowywanie danych kancelarii w chmurze in D Szostek (ed), Bezpieczeństwo danych i IT w kancelarii prawnej. Czyli jak bezpiecznie przechowywać dane w kancelarii prawnej (C.H. Beck 2018);

Telec I, 'Zakázané těžení a nebezpečná situace na elektronických úložištích dat' 1–2 (2015) Bulletin advokacie;

Telec I, Tůma P, Autorský Zákon: Komentář (2nd edition, C H Beck 2019);

Thomas Hoeren and Silviya Yankova, 'The Liability of Internet Intermediaries – The German Perspective' (2012) International Review of Intellectual Property and Competition Law

Timana T, Manna Z (ed), Data Protection in The Era of Artificial Intelligence. Trends, existing solutions and recommendations for privacy-preserving technologies (GDVA, 2019);

Toka G, The impact of partial results on election, http://www.personal.ceu.hu/staff/Gabor_Toka/Papers/Toka04Chicago.pdf [Access by day 30.06. 2021];

Tokarczyk D, 'Obowiązek gwaranta w prawie karnym' (2014) 76 Ruch Prawniczy, Ekonomiczny i Socjologiczny 203;

Transparencia Mexicana, "¿Cómo será la justicia digital en la Nueva Era: Episodio 2" <https://bit.ly/3sl4UsG> accessed 10 April 2021;

Triberti C and Carrella G, Internet ,aspetti tecnici, tematiche sociali, incidenze giuridiche civili e penali, (Edizioni Maros Milano (ITA), 2000;

UNESCO, AI and the Rule of Law: Capacity Building for Judicial Systems <https://en.unesco.org/artificial-intelligence/mooc-judges> accessed 31 May 2021;

UNESCO, AI and the Rule of Law: Capacity Building for Judicial Systems <https://en.unesco.org/artificial-intelligence/mooc-judges> accessed 31 May 2021;

United Nations Conference on Trade Development, "UNCTAD Estimates of Global e-commerce 2018" (2020) <https://unctad.org/system/files/official-document/tn_unctad_ict4d15_en.pdf> accessed 7 July 2021;

United Nations General Assembly, Transforming our world: the 2030 Agenda for Sustainable Development, A/RES/70/1 (25 September 2015);

Urszczak W, Historia Państwa i Prawa Polskiego. Tom I (966-1795) (Wolters Kluwer 2013);

Valadés D, La Constitución reformada, (1st edn IIJ-UNAM 1987);

van Hooijdonk R, 'Top 10 smart cities that use tech to transform urban life' (Richard van Hooijdonk blog, 9 December 2019) <https://www.richardvanhooijdonk.com/blog/en/top-10-smart-cities-that-use-tech-to-transform-urban-life> accessed 14 April 2020;

Verizon, '2021 Data Breach Investigation' (Verizon.com, 2021) <https://www.verizon.com/business/resources/reports/dbir/> accessed 7 July 2021;

Wachter S, Mittelstandt B, 'A Right to Reasonable Interferences: R-thinking Data Protection Law in the Age of Big Data and Ai' (2019) Columbia Business Law Review;

Wagner B, 'Liable, but Not in Control? Ensuring Meaningful Human Agency in Automated Decision-Making Systems' (2019) 11 Policy & Internet 104;

Wagner J, Legal Tech und Legal Robots (Springer Gabler 2nd edn 2020);

Wahedi F, Verfassungsrechtliche Anforderungen an die Automatisierung der Justiz (Dr. Kovač 2021);

Walters E, 'The Model Rules of Autonomous Conduct: Ethical Responsibilities of Lawyers and Artificial Intelligence' (2019) 35.4 Georgia State University Law Review;

Watcher S, Mittelstadt B, Russel C, Counterfactual explanations without opening the black box: automated decisions and the GDPR, 2018 Harvard Journal of Law and Technology Vol 31.No2, https://jolt.law.harvard.edu/assets/articlePDFs/v31/Counterfactual-Explanations-without-Opening-the-Black-Box-Sandra-Wachter-et-al.pdf;

Wiewiórowski W R, 'Privacy by design jako paradygmat ochrony prywatności' in Szpor G, i Wiewiórowski W R (eds) Internet. Prawno-informatyczne problemy sieci, portali i e-usług (C. H. Beck 2012);

Wissenschaftliche Dienste Deutscher Bundestag „Künstliche Intelligenz in der Justiz - Internationaler Überblick" WD 7 -3000 -017/2<https://www.bundestag.de/resource/blob/832204/6813d064fab52e9b6d54cbbf5319cea3/WD-7-017-21-pdf-data.pdf> accessed 29 May 2021;

Wissenschaftliche Dienste Deutscher Bundestag „Künstliche Intelligenz in der Justiz - Internationaler Überblick" WD 7 -3000 -017/21,7 <https://www.bundestag.de/resource/blob/832204/6813d064fab52e9b6d54cbbf5319cea3/WD-7-017-21-pdf-data.pdf> accessed 29 May 2021;

World Commission on Environment and Development, 'Our Common Future. From one earth to one world' (Report, Annex A/RES/42/187, 11 December 1987);

Wortham L, 'The Future of the Legal Profession and Legal Services Delivery' in Wortham L et al. (eds), Learning from Practice. A Text for Experiential Legal Education (West Academic Publishing 2016);

WP29, 'Opinion 15/2011 on the definition of consent' (13 July 2011, WP 187), <http://www.giodo.gov.pl/pl/file/5341> accessed 13 May 2021;

Wu Feng S, The myth of the impartial machine, Parametric Press, 1 May 2019, <https://parametric.press/issue-01/the-myth-of-the-impartial-machine>;

Wu J, 'AI Goes to Court: The Growing Landscape of AI for Access to Justice' (Medium, 2019) <https://medium.com/legal-design-and-innovation/ai-goes-to-court-the-growing-landscape-of-ai-for-access-to-justice-3f58aca4306f> accessed 29 May 2021;

Wu J, AI Goes to Court: The Growing Landscape of AI for Access to Justice (2019) <https://medium.com/legal-design-and-innovation/ai-goes-to-court-the-growing-landscape-of-ai-for-access-to-justice-3f58aca4306f> accessed 29 May 2021;

Yanisky-Ravid S, Hallisey S K, 'Equality and Privacy by Design: Ensuring Artificial Intelligence (AI) is Properly Trained & Fed: A New Model of AI Data Transparency & Certification as Safe Harbor Procedures' <https://ssrn.com/abstract=3278490> accessed 13 May 2021;

Yong Y, Dumas-Menijvar M, Garcia-Banuelos L, Polyvyanyy A and Zhang L, 'Generalized aggregate Quality of Service computation for composite services' (2012) 85, 8 Journal of Systems and Software;

Zacharzewski K and Kłoda MT, Przegląd zastosowania technologii blockchain w wymiarze sprawiedliwości w wybranych państwach (Instytut Wymiaru Sprawiedliwości 2019);

Zaldívar A, Hacia una Nueva Ley de Amparo (1st ed IIJ-UNAM 2002);

Zalewski T, 'Definicja sztucznej inteligencji' in L Lai and M Świerczyński (eds.), Prawo sztucznej inteligencji (CH Beck 2020);

Zalewski T, Podstawowe zasady skutecznego wykorzystania narzędzi Legal Tech in Szostek D (ed), Legal Tech. Czyli jak bezpiecznie korzystać z narzędzi informatycznych w organizacji, w tym w kancelarii oraz dziale prawnym (C.H. Beck 2021);

Zalnieriute M, Moses B, Williams G, The Rule of Law and Automation of Government Decision-Making, (2019) 82 M.L.R. 425;

Załucki M, AI and dispute resolution (Javier García González, Álvaro Alzina Lozano and Gabriel Martín Rodríguez eds, Dykinson 2020);

Završnik A, 'Criminal justice, artificial intelligence systems and human rights' (Springer 2020) <https://link.springer.com/article/10.1007/s12027-020-00602-0> accessed 31 May 2021;

Završnik A, Criminal justice, artificial intelligence systems and human rights, <https://link.springer.com/article/10.1007/s12027-020-00602-0> accesssed 31 May 2021;

Zawłocki R, 'Pojęcie przestępstwa' in R Dębski (ed.), System prawa karnego, tom 3: Nauka o przestępstwie. Zasady odpowiedzialności (CH Beck 2017);

Zeleznikow J, Stranieri A, 'Split Up: An Intelligent Decision Support System Which Provides Advice Upon Property Division Following Divorce'(1998) 6, 2 International Journal of Law and Information Technology;

Zeleznikow J, Stranieri A, Split Up: An Intelligent Decision Support System Which Provides Advice Upon Property Division Following Divorce (1998), International Journal of Law and Information Technology, Vol 6. No. 2, 190–213;

Zhang Ch and others, 'Human-centered automation for resilient nuclear power plant outage control' (2017) 82 Automation in Construction 179;

Zhong H and others, 'Legal Judgment Prediction via Topological Learning' (2018) 1 Proceedings of the 2018 Conference on Empirical Methods in Natural Language Processing;

Zoll A, 'Komentarz do art. 1 k.k.' in W Wróbel and A Zoll (eds.), Kodeks karny. Część ogólna. Tom I. Komentarz do art. 1-52 (Wolters Kluwer 2016);

Zoll A, 'Komentarz do art. 2 k.k.' in W Wróbel and A Zoll (eds.), Kodeks karny. Część ogólna. Tom I. Komentarz do art. 1-52 (Wolters Kluwer 2016); 31 May 2021;

Zoll F, 'Przyszłość kształcenia prawników w Polsce' (2010) 6 Państwo i Prawo 25.